THE ENCYCLOPEDIA OF
WILD FLOWERS

This is a Dempsey Parr Book
Dempsey Parr is an imprint of Parragon

PARRAGON
Queen Street House,
4 Queen Street,
Bath BA1 1HE

ISBN 1-84084-503-1

Produced for Parragon by
Foundry Design & Production, part of
The Foundry Creative Media Company Ltd,
Crabtree Hall, Crabtree Lane,
Fulham, London SW6 6TY

Special thanks to Polly Willis.

A copy of the CIP data for this book is available in the British Library.

Printed and bound in Italy

THE ENCYCLOPEDIA OF
WILD FLOWERS

JOHN AKEROYD

DP
DEMPSEY
PARR

Contents

How to Use this Book

This book contains a number of important features:

- **Introductory notes** Covering flowers, fruits, leaves, growth and life history, how to find wild flowers and conservation.
- **Descriptions of over 350 flower species** Each page covers an individual wild flower, illustrated with two or more colour photographs. In many cases, a closely related, similar plant is described as well for comparison, perhaps with notes on other related species. This is followed by notes on particular features of interest, including botanical details, folklore and medicinal use.
- **Icons provide additional information** A simple outline key to flower type, leaf identification, habitat, population and distribution.
- **Species information box** Each entry has a summary table of basic information, a section that outlines the plant's main distinguishing features, habitat and distribution, and flowering time.
- **Reference section** Comprises a reading list, useful addresses, a glossary of useful terms and an extensive index.

KEY TO SYMBOLS

FLOWER TYPE

- 4 REGULAR PETALS
- 5 REGULAR PETALS
- 6 REGULAR PETALS
- NUMEROUS REGULAR PETALS
- 4 IRREGULAR PETALS
- 4 IRREGULAR PETALS PLUS SPUR
- CONE-SHAPED
- TUBULAR
- LOOSE CLUSTER
- DENSE CLUSTER
- DENSE HEAD
- MINUTE SCATTERED
- LOOSE HEAD WITH EQUAL STALKS
- DUCKWEED
- ARUM

IDENTIFICATION

- VERY NARROW
- NARROW
- OVAL OR ELLIPTICAL
- BROADLY OVAL
- HEART SHAPED
- SPEAR OR ARROW SHAPED
- DEEPLY LOBED
- CLOVER-LIKE
- NUMEROUS SIMPLE LEAFLETS
- FERN-LIKE
- FLESHY AND JOINTED
- UMBRELLA SHAPED
- IVY-LIKE
- SCALE-LIKE, USUALLY VERY SMALL
- CHESNUT-LIKE
- IRIS-LIKE
- SIMPLE FRILLY LEAFLETS
- TOOTHED CHESNUT-LIKE

HABITAT

- WASTELAND
- CLIFFS
- CONIFEROUS WOODLAND
- DECIDUOUS WOODLAND
- ESTUARY AND SALTMARSH
- FIELDS
- GARDENS
- GRASSLAND
- HEATH
- HEDGES
- LAKES
- MARSHES
- MOORLAND WITH MOUNTAINS
- MOUNTAINS
- REEDS AND EMERGENT VEGETATION
- RIVERS
- ROCKS
- SAND
- SCRUB
- SHINGLE
- WALLS

POPULATION

- RARE, BUT OCCASIONALLY PRESENT IN QUANTITY.
- SCARCE, BUT LOCALLY COMMON.
- LOCAL, AND ABSENT FROM MANY AREAS.
- WIDESPREAD, BUT NOT FOUND EVERYWHERE.
- WIDESPREAD AND COMMON

MAP

THE PINK SHADING ON THE MAP SHOWS THE TOTAL DISTRIBUTION IN BRITAIN AND IRELAND (WITHOUT AN INDICATION OF RARITY).

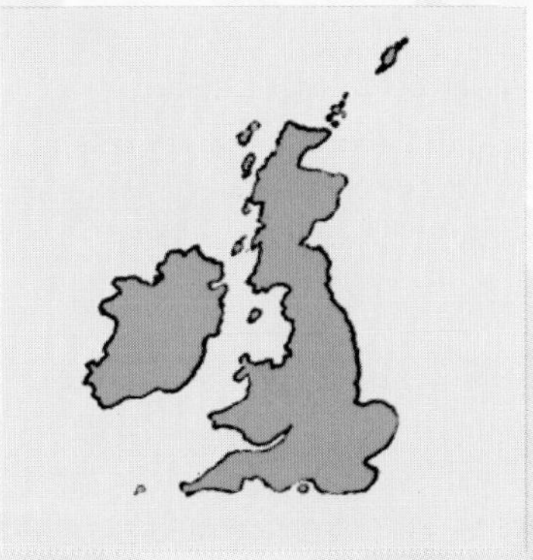

Introduction

WILD FLOWERS are a national treasure. They add pleasure and interest to a car journey, a ramble or a picnic. They brighten the countryside and colour or lend atmosphere, even a sense of place, to landscapes. Think of a Bluebell wood, Foxgloves on a Welsh hillside, a northern streamside golden with Monkey-flower, or suburban lawns and road-verges shimmering blue with Slender Speedwell. Yet it can be frustrating not to know what they are called – or where to find out more about them.

This book is an introduction to what is known about the most widespread or common wild flowers of Britain and Ireland. It also includes some scarcer flowers that are of particular interest. The book describes in full 365 of the estimated 1500 or so wild flowers that are native or established introductions in these islands. In addition, a further 200 species that are closely related to these selected examples are briefly described and compared.

Wild plants vary in size and form, from the tiny, simple floating fonds of Great Duckweed, Common Duckweed and Rootless Duckweed (top), to the large complex flower of Lords-and-Ladies (middle). The different types of flower – as shown oposite, Hottentot Fig (top), Yellow Horned Poppy (middle) and Giant Hog Weed (bottom) – help to tell the families and species apart.

It is never easy to select species for a book of this sort. Botanists especially will worry that there are not, for example, enough of the numerous Forget-me-nots or Fumitories; and all of us have our personal favourites that may have been omitted or sidelined. The general rule has been to include all those wild flowers that one is likely to encounter out on a walk or a drive in the lowlands, whether in countryside, suburb or town. At the same time, we have selected a number of upland and mountain species, especially those that are locally frequent or impart character to the landscape.

We have also included a selection of the most attractive of the less-common wild flowers. Not only are some of them, like Spring Gentian or Fritillary, abundant in a few choice areas, but also they are too visually striking and fascinating to omit from a book of flowers aimed at a general readership. It would be a pity if the reader were to be left unaware of our wealth of native lilies, orchids and saxifrages.

In some cases, we have selected one or a few species from a group of closely related plants. We have where possible indicated when other related species exist. To distinguish, say, all the numerous species of speedwell or thistle, would be beyond the scope of a book of this sort. Field guides, Floras and other specialised works of identification are available for the further study that we hope this book will encourage.

This book does not include grasses, sedges and rushes (except the common Field Woodrush of damp lawns!). These plants have flowers with inconspicuous, green, flower-parts and their identification requires some botanical experience. Nor does it include the ferns, horsetails and their allies, which lack flowers – although they do possess other complex reproductive structures.

Text arrangement The text is arranged by plant family, following a conventional botanical order that many European botanists believe to reflect natural relationships. The order roughly moves from the most 'primitive' families towards the more specialised, 'advanced' families such as the daisies and dandelions and the orchids. This grouping by family allows comparisons to made between closely related plants – those most likely to be confused with one another. It also gives the reader an idea of

which plants are related. It is, for example, odd but true that Common Duckweed (p.356) is related to Lords-and-Ladies (p.355). Many botanists today use molecular techniques to distinguish plants and assess their relationships. However, for practical purposes, nothing will ever replace assessing characters by eye.

Each of these plants is a species, a well-defined unit of variation that mostly cross-breeds among its own kind. The second half of the scientific or Latin name labels the species precisely. The name often reflects attributes of the plant, or it may commemorate a person or a geographical region. Botanists group related species into a genus (plural genera), indicated by the first half of the scientific name. The genus is often a clear-cut, natural grouping, whereas boundaries between species can be subject to scientific opinion. Buttercups (the genus Ranunculus) have yellow, cup-shaped flowers with numerous free parts; the precise limits between one buttercup species and another may, in some cases, be less easy to decide.

Variants We sometimes mention that variants of a particular species exist, either in the wild or in cultivation, particularly subspecies. A subspecies is a race of a species that occurs in a particular geographical region or habitat, for example coastal sand-dunes. We have avoided giving these names to avoid confusion. We have, however, included a few garden cultivar names.

Native or introduced We have tried to strike a balance in the book between true native plants and those that have been introduced. Our flora is dynamic and changes continuously over time. The 20th century has seen great changes in the countryside, especially since 1945, as a result of expanding agricultural production, large-scale drainage of wetlands and the building of new suburbs, industrial estates and motorways.

Plants that are in decline Some plants that were once widespread have declined, but others have responded well to the changed conditions. These include the weeds, which certainly are more than just 'plants out of place', as many people call them. On the contrary, they are highly specialised, opportunist plants that colonise habitats disturbed and modified by human activity. Many prosper in today's disturbed landscape; and we thus include many of them here in their rightful place as wild flowers.

Alongside the weeds, another group, the introduced plants or aliens, has thrived in the modern world. The Earth is now a small place for plants, which have never recognised national boundaries. Plants and people interact constantly, and plants have long followed us along our trade and migration routes. Many of our most interesting or attractive wild flowers were introduced by people, often decades, centuries or millenia ago. Each of these plants has a fascinating tale to tell. Some of these stories are outlined in this book.

Invasive plants Invasive plants can be a problem. They may take over natural habitats and displace native species, like Hottentot Fig (p.33) from South Africa does on cliffs and sand-dunes in the West Country. They may become established, pestilential weeds, like Common Field-speedwell (p.260). They may also be injurious to human health, like Giant Hogweed (see under Hogweed, p.179), which has poisonous sap that sensitises the skin to sunlight. In other words they may be a nuisance and become rightly detested for it. Nevertheless, we cannot ignore them, for they are now part of our flora.

Conversely, numerous introduced plants do little or no harm, whilst adding beauty, character and ecological diversity to the countryside. They are now well-loved wild flowers, and we would be much the poorer without them. The last Ice Age, which ended just 10,000 years ago, scraped away most of our vegetation. Plants slowly returned, but the opening of the English Channel prevented many from recolonising. The numerous aliens that have come in since make up for this natural poverty of flora (c.1500 species compared with c.5000 in Greece or Spain).

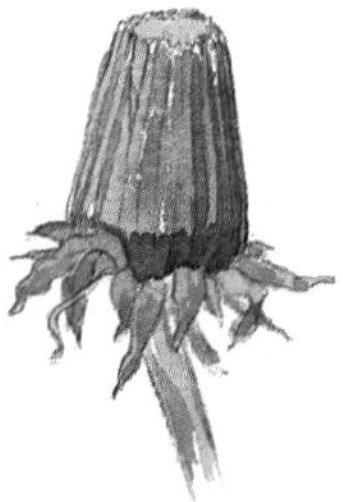

PARTS OF THE FLOWER AND PLANT

THE FLOWER IS the plant's main reproductive structure and categorises a family or group of species. At a glance, Yellow Water-lily (p.49) and Fringed Water-lily (p.208) are superficially similar, with round, floating leaves and yellow flowers. Yet a look at the flowers reveals them to be in quite different families.

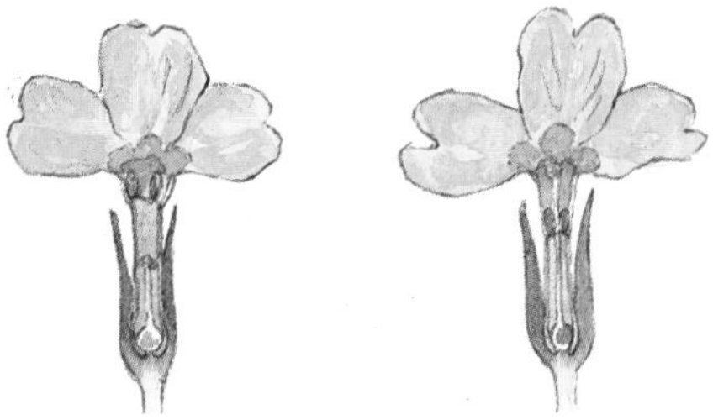

Structure All flowers have a similar structure. This has been modified by the reduction, fusion or modification of the parts over millions of years of evolution. In Britain and Ireland, flowers are mostly insect-pollinated. (Many tropical flowers are pollinated by birds, bats or other animals.) The flower is an elaborate structure that attracts insects in order that they should transfer male pollen to a female ovule (analogous to the egg of an animal). The pollen fertilizes the ovule, giving rise to a seed. Seeds are specialised reproductive units, each with a hard coat and usually a food store, and often able to survive dormant in the soil for some time.

Flowers are complex structures designed for pollination. One of the most advanced families is the daidy and dandelion (top left); Primrose flowers (top right), with stamens held either high or low, ensure that insects brush off and transfer pollen; White Dead-nettle (bottom left) attracts bees by plentiful nectar in a curved tube.

The basic structure of the flower is a condensed shoot with whorls of parts derived from modified leaves. Sometimes it is surrounded by whorls of leaf-like, green or coloured *bracts*. The outermost whorl of true floral parts is the *sepals* (collectively the *calyx*), which enclose and protect the young flower in bud. They are usually green, but in some flowers such as those of Pasque Flower (p.60) or Common Milkwort (p.146) they are coloured and petal-like. Within lies a whorl of often brightly coloured *petals*. Some plants, such as Stinging Nettle (p.13), have wind-pollinated flowers. These are small and green, often massed in long clusters, with the petals absent or much reduced.

Enclosed by the sepals and petals is a whorl of stalked *stamens*, the male reproductive organs. These produce the coloured, dust-like pollen. The central structure of the flower is the female *ovary*, containing one or more minute *ovules*. The ovary, made up of 1-seeded or fused units, is topped by a pointed, knobbed or feathery, often stalked, *stigma*, which traps the pollen. Pollen germinates to push a tube down into the ovary to fertilize the ovule or ovules. These result is *seeds*, contained within a *fruit*.

Different types of flower The first flowers, contemporary with the dinosaurs, were probably solitary, simple, cup-shaped, and with numerous unfused parts, rather like a buttercup. Flowers later became more specialised, with complex pollination mechanisms to attract different insects. Flower parts became reduced or fused, and flowers often became massed in spikes or clusters. More advanced families usually have fused petals, and the numbers of stamens and ovules may also be reduced. In the figwort and foxglove family, for example, the stamens are often reduced to two (as in the speedwells, pp. 258–261). In the advanced daisy and dandelion family (*Compositae*, pp.286–331), the flowers are small, 1-seeded florets, the calyx reduced to scales or hairs, massed in a head as in Greater Knapweed (centre).

THE FRUIT

A FRUIT CONTAINS one or more fertilized seeds. Fruits come in a range of form, 1-seeded or many-seeded, dry or fleshy, splitting or non-splitting, and have their own elaborate classification. Principal types include the *capsule* (a dry fruit, splitting to release the seeds), the *berry* (a many-seeded, fleshy fruit), the *drupe* (a 1-seeded, fleshy fruit) and the *nut* or *nutlet* (a 1-seeded dry fruit).

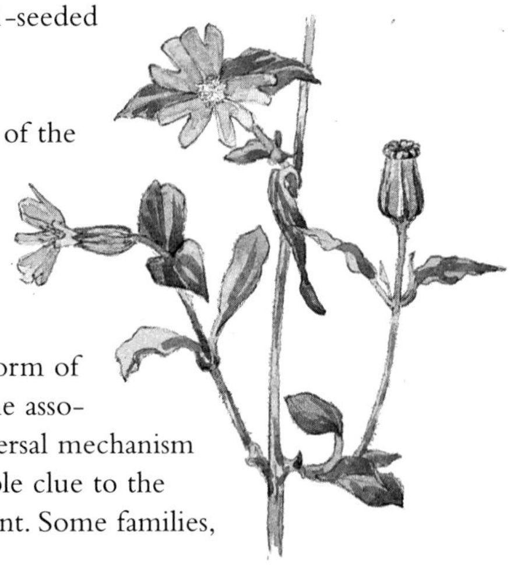

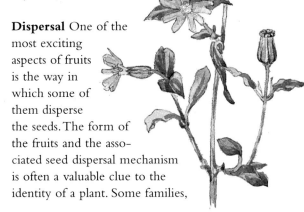

Dispersal One of the most exciting aspects of fruits is the way in which some of them disperse the seeds. The form of the fruits and the associated seed dispersal mechanism is often a valuable clue to the identity of a plant. Some families, like the rose family (*Rosaceae*, pp.98–112), have a range of fleshy fruits, like those of the Wild Strawberry (p.111), that are eaten by animals, and hooked or bristly fruits that are caught up on the fur of animals. Perhaps the most perfect dispersal mechanism of all is the dandelion 'clock', a head of tiny fruits, each with a parachute of hairs derived from the reduced and modified sepals. When the parachute finally comes to earth, hooks on the fruit-wall hold it to the soil.

Some fruits split, sometimes explosively, like the dry pods of Gorse (p.113) or the fleshy capsules of Indian Balsam (p.147). Others, like those of Common Poppy (p.64) or Red Campion (p.42), act like salt-cellars, scattering seeds from pores as they wave in the wind. Some fruits, especially those of seashore plants such as Sea Beet (p.27) or Sea Kale (p.80), have corky walls and float on water. The corky warts or tubercles on the persistent flower-parts of docks (pp.16–26) allow them to disperse in this way. At the same time spines enable them to be carried on the fur of animals.

Distinguishing features Fruits provide useful features for distinguishing the different families of plants. Some families, like the nightshade family (*Solanaceae*, pp.246–249), usually have shiny berries. Others always have dry fruits, perhaps a characteristic number, like the cluster of four hard nutlets of the mint family (*Labiatae*, pp.228–245).

Some families or groups of plants have heads of numerous 1-seeded fruits, notably the buttercup family (*Ranunculaceae*, p.50–63). In the daisy and dandelion family, each 1-seeded fruit derives from a single small flower or floret.

THE LEAF

PLANT LEAVES VARY considerably between species. They may be simple and undivided, lobed or dissected; or compound, divided once, twice or sometimes three or four times into a series of leaflets that share a common stalk. The margins of leaves and leaflets may be entire or variously toothed. Sometimes the teeth are extended into a prickle or spine. Leaves of different species also vary considerably in their degree and type of hairiness. They may vary in thickness, texture (fleshy, leathery, wrinkled, etc.) and colour.

Same leaf, different flower The same type of leaf can turn up in different plant families. This means that one should always look at flowers when identifying a plant. However, certain families can to some extent be identified by a particular type of leaf. For example, the leaves of the carrot family (*Umbelliferae*, pp.170–185), and the daisy and dandelion family (*Compositae*, pp.286–312), are frequently finely cut into fern-like segments. Those of the orchids (*Orchidaceae*, pp.364–377) are strap-shaped and hairless.

The large clover and pea family (*Leguminosae*, pp.113–133) is partly characterised by compound leaves in which pairs of leaflets are arranged in opposite rows or in the classic 3-leaf or trefoil pattern of the clovers. Members of the related rose family (*Rosaceae*, pp.98–112) have similar compound leaves with paired leaflets (known to botanists as pinnate leaves), but these tend to be more irregular in form. Both of these families have paired flanges or stipules at the base of the leaves.

Fruits: Red Campion (opposite page, bottom right) has dry seed-capsules that open to scatter the seeds; Blackberry (top left) and Dog Rose (centre) have fleshy fruits eaten by birds. Leaves may be simple – Stinging Nettle (bottom right) – or compound – Ground Elder (top right).

Special leaves Sometimes the form of the leaves directly reflects ecological adaptation. The carnivorous Round-leaved Sundew (p.86) has leaves armed with sticky hairs that trap and digest small insects. These provides a very distinctive feature for identification. Water plants often possess very finely dissected or floating leaves. In their case the flower is generally essential for even tentative identification. Leaves of coastal plants tend to be fleshy in order to conserve water against salt and drought.

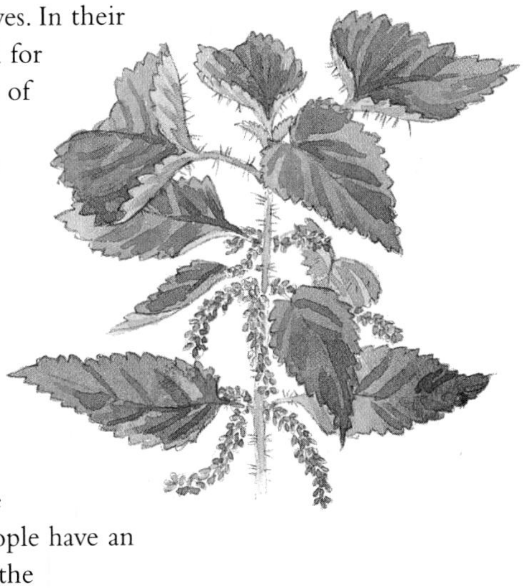

In Britain and Ireland, only Stinging Nettle and Annual Nettle (p.13) have stinging hairs. Always remember that some plants have poisonous leaves and that it is best not to handle them. The leaves of the carrot family, and perhaps other plants, may make the skin sensitive to sunlight. Some people have an allergy to particular plants, such as the Wild Daffodil (p.349).

Shepherd's Purse (bottom) is a typical annual plant. Arising from a small taproot, within a few weeks of growing from seed it has leaves, flowers and fruits. Foxgloves at Dungeness Power Station (top). Wild flowers grow everywhere, even on scruffy waste ground or industrial sites.

GROWTH AND LIFE HISTORY

A PLANT CONSISTS of an underground root and one or more aerial green shoots. The root is the structure that anchors the plant to the ground and absorbs water and mineral nutrients from the soil. It varies greatly in form between species.

The above-ground shoot The above-ground shoot consists of stems and leaves. The stems, which may be prostrate, sprawling, semi-erect or erect, provide mechanical support for other plant structures. Special plumbing tissue within them distributes water and plant foods. They can often give useful clues as the identity of a plant. For instance, some plant families, notably the mint family (*Labiatae*, pp.228–245), have square stems. The quantity and type of hairs on the stem is often a useful way to separate related species.

Structure of the plant The leaf is the power-house of the plant, where carbon dioxide is fixed by combinbation with water to make the sugars that are the plant's basic food. This takes place via the agency of the green molecule chlorophyll – which gives plants their colour – in the presence of sunlight. This process releases the oxygen that we breathe.

The plant bears its flowers mostly on the upper part of the stem. These may be solitary or in spikes or clusters. After pollination and fertilization the flowers are replaced by fruits, each containing one or more seeds. The plant then either dies down for the year or in some cases completely.

The plants described in this book may be annual, biennial or perennial, familiar terms to gardeners. We have also included a few small shrubs, like heathers and gorses, which are woody plants, but without trunks.

An *annual* grows, flowers, sets seed and dies within one season or year. It survives winter cold or summer drought as a dormant seed.

A *biennial* forms an overwintering rosette of leaves, flowering and dying in its second year.

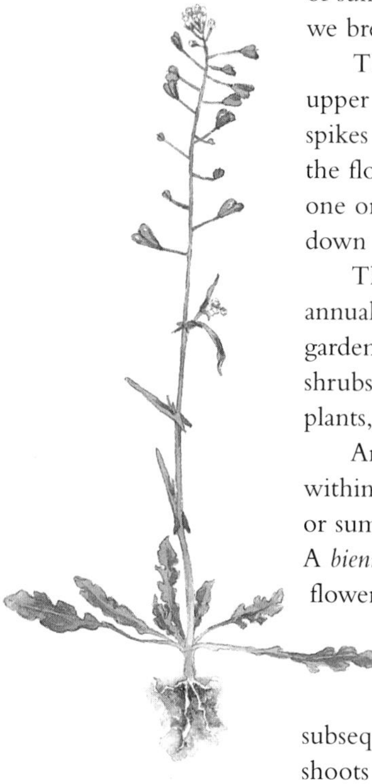

A *perennial* grows and flowers over several years. The roots are often modified to store food over the winter or summer, subsequently providing energy to produce new shoots in spring or autumn. These structures vary: a *bulb* is a fleshy underground shoot; a *corm* is a swollen stem-base; a *rhizome* is a fleshy, creeping root, which may fragment to produce new plants.

LOOKING FOR WILD FLOWERS

YOU NEED NOT go far to see wild flowers. The weeds in your garden (indeed some of the cultivated flowers), the numerous plants on waste ground or in churchyards, even those that emerge from cracks in a city pavement, are all wild flowers. Nevertheless, to see many species one needs to explore the wider countryside or the less built-over or tidied parts of the suburbs, like the tow-paths and banks of canals and rivers. As a general rule, anywhere in the countryside outside cultivated fiedls should yield some flowers. Alas, they are no longer present in the numbers that they were 50 years ago. For the best flowers one may have to go further afield.

Many of the most interesting and beautiful wild flowers occur in fragments of natural or semi-natural vegetation, sometimes surrounded by species-poor agricultural land. Modern agricultural landscapes are probably poorer in wild flowers than most suburbs. Flowers survive best on commons or heaths, in traditionally managed meadows and pastures, in woodlands and hedgerows, in and beside rivers, streams, ponds and lakes, anywhere with rock outcrops or dry, sunny banks, and by the sea, especially on saltmarshes, sand-dunes, shingle beaches and cliffs. Some plants may indeed have persisted in these sort of habitats since earliest times.

Many of the best shows of wild flowers are in habitats on lime-rich soils, such as chalk grassland or limestone pavement. Lime-poor heaths and moors also support their own special plants. A few regions are notably rich: like the sandy heaths of the Breckland in East Anglia, the coastal heaths of the West Country, notably those on the Lizard peninsula, the limestone Dales of Derbyshire and the West Riding of Yorkshire, mountainous areas like Snowdonia in North Wales and Ben Lawers in Scotland, and of course the famous low limestone mountains of the Burren, on the coast of County Clare in western Ireland.

One of the best ways to find flowers is to seek advice from others. County Naturalists' Trusts often organise lectures on wild flowers, as do local Natural History Societies and museums, who may also organise excursions to see them. Botanists are great networkers and are mostly pleased to direct others to good places for plants. They may, however, be unwilling to reveal the sites of some rarer species. Some universities organise extra-mural courses on botany that involve looking at local habitats. Alas, most university botany research and teaching today is concerned with molecular biology rather than 'real' plants.

CONSERVATION

WE HAVE IN BRITAIN one of the most crowded, modified landscapes in the world. Pressure on land continues to damage and fragment the habitats of wild flowers. For it is habitat destruction that is their principal enemy, certainly not the casual picking of flowers by individuals.

Modern agriculture has created 'wildlife deserts', and new roads, suburbs and industrial estates devour great tracts of land. Wetland plants especially have retreated over the last century, and since the Second World War many agricultural weeds such as Cornflower have all but disappeared. Climate change may also threaten some plants at the edge of their range, although other species may benefit. It is the combination of such factors that may push particular species towards extinction, locally or nationally. The picture is not completely grim. Many plants continue to thrive in the mosaic of habitats that remain in the countryside, while others favour the open, disturbed sites created by human activities. Most of all, an active conservation movement has grown up since 1945, spearheaded by the work of County Naturalists' Trusts and non-governmental organisations such as the Royal Society for the Protection of Birds (who own many plant-rich nature reserves) and Plantlife, a relatively young but active and rapidly expanding group dedicated to protecting our wild plants and their habitats.

The Wildlife and Countryside Act (1981), together with subsequent reviews, confers some degree of protection upon wild plants. It makes it illegal to uproot any wild plant without the permission of the owner of the land on which it grows. The Act also fully protects a group of our rarest plants from picking or uprooting. In the Republic of Ireland, the Flora Protection Order (1987), and in Northern Ireland the Wildlife (NI) Order (1985), protect the habitat of the most threatened species. (Note that some of these may be common or widespread in Britain.) Another important step forward has been the European Union's Directive on the Conservation of Habitats of Wild Fauna and Flora, which obliges the UK and other EU governments to protect the most important habitats and wild plants. Other international laws and agreements cover international trade in rare or threatened plants.

It is not yet illegal to pick flowers, and one hopes that children might not be forbidden from so doing, but the best advice must always be to 'leave wild flowers for others to enjoy'. Remember too that plant nurseries now stock almost all our native wild flowers, propagated in cultivation without the need to pillage natural populations.

Sea Campion (bottom) in quantity at the seaside. Coasts are always good places for wild flowers. Wild flowers are fragile and precious. Although grown as a garden plant many agricultural weeds, such as the Cornflower (top), have all but disappeared in the wild in Britain.

Hop

HOP AND CANNABIS FAMILY (Cannabaceae)

SPECIES INFORMATION	
COMMON NAME	Hop
SCIENTIFIC NAME	Humulus lupulus
RELATED SPECIES	Hemp
HEIGHT/SPREAD	Stems 3–6 m long
FLOWERING TIME	June–September
HABITAT	Hedges, scrub or on fences

Note: Our only climber with cone-like, papery fruits.

FLOWER TYPE

IDENTIFICATION

HABITAT

POPULATION

MAP

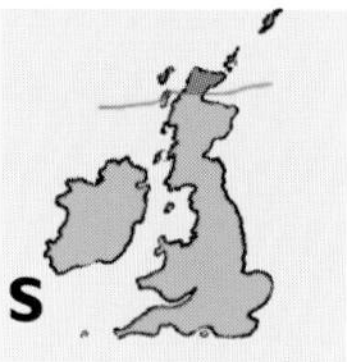

Size and appearance: A rough-hairy perennial, with tough, scrambling, twining or trailing stems 3–6 m (9–18 ft) long.
Leaves: In opposite pairs, up to 10 cm (4 in) long, more or less heart-shaped, 3- to 5-lobed, coarsely toothed.
Flowers: Either male or female on separate plants, in greenish, hanging clusters; male clusters branched, the female cone-like with pale green scales.
Fruits: Cone-like, hanging, about 30 mm (1⅕ in) long.
Related or similar plants: The unrelated White Bryony, another climber with greenish flowers, has corkscrew tendrils; Hemp, though related, looks quite different.
Habitat and distribution: Climbing over hedges, shrubs, trees or wire-netting fences as a widespread escape from cultivation. It is probably native in damp woods in southern England and East Anglia; in Scotland and Ireland rare and always introduced.
Flowering time: June to September, but most conspicuous in fruit from August until late autumn.

HOPS BEGAN TO be used in Britain during the late Middle Ages as a preservative and flavouring for beer, to which they impart a characteristic bitter, fruity taste. Previously, other herbs such as Ground-ivy had been used for this purpose. Hop pillows are said to aid sleep, and the young spring shoots can be cooked as a green vegetable.

Hops are largely imported today, but so-called 'real ales' demand native fruits, and the plant is still grown as a crop in south-east England from Surrey to Kent, and in the Vale of Evesham.

The closely related Hemp is another useful plant, and one that sometimes turns up in quantity on rubbish tips and waste land, especially around large towns. An ancient source of fibre, it was formerly widely grown in Britain to make ropes for the navy, and is now making a small comeback as a crop. The seeds yield an oil and the plant has medicinal properties, apparently alleviating symptoms of multiple sclerosis and other ailments. The notorious narcotic races (marijuana, hashish or ganja) grow in warmer climates.

Top *Hop* (Humulus lupulus) *is a rough-hairy climber with twining stems which scrambles over hedges and shrubs. Male and female flowers are on separate plants and the female flowers produce cone-like fruits.*

Bottom *Hemp* (Cannabis sativa), *a vigorous, branched annual 1–3 m (120–360 in) tall, that has dark green, toothed leaves with 6-9 narrow segments, is a denizen of waste ground and rubbish tips, and is sometimes grown as a crop.*

SPECIES INFORMATION	
COMMON NAME	Stinging Nettle
SCIENTIFIC NAME	Urtica dioica
RELATED SPECIES	Annual and Small Nettle
HEIGHT/SPREAD	50–150 cm tall
FLOWERING TIME	June–September
HABITAT	Rich waste land

Note: The stinging hairs distinguish stinging-nettles.

Stinging Nettle

NETTLE FAMILY
(Urticaceae)

Size and appearance: An erect, mostly unbranched perennial, with tough, yellow roots and creeping underground stems, often forming large patches; stems 50–150 cm (20–60 in) tall, sometimes up to 250 cm (100 in), square in section, armed with long stinging hairs.
Leaves: In opposite pairs, up to 10 cm (4 in) long, heart- or spear-shaped, pointed, regularly and sharply toothed, densely or sometimes sparsely covered with stinging hairs.
Flowers: Male or female on separate plants, in tiny, greenish, tassel-like hanging clusters.
Fruits: In small, arched clusters, each 1–2 mm ($\frac{1}{25}$–$\frac{1}{13}$ in) across and enclosing a single seed.
Related or similar plants: Small Nettle is an annual plant, not more than 60 cm (24 in) tall, of cultivated ground.
Habitat and distribution: Abundant on waysides and waste ground, around buildings and ruins, especially on farm land where the soil is enriched by animal manure or fertiliser, and in untended gardens, ditches, marshes and damp woods,
Flowering time: June to September.

FLOWER TYPE

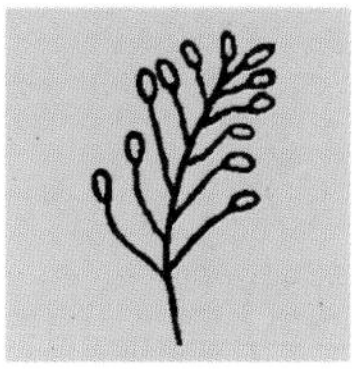

IDENTIFICATION

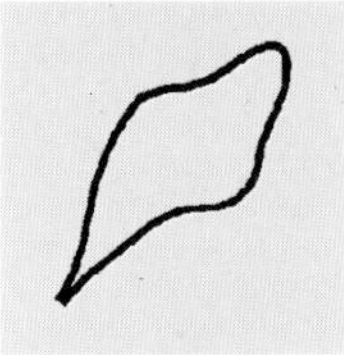

HABITAT

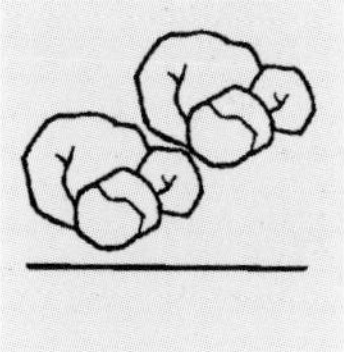

POPULATION

MAP

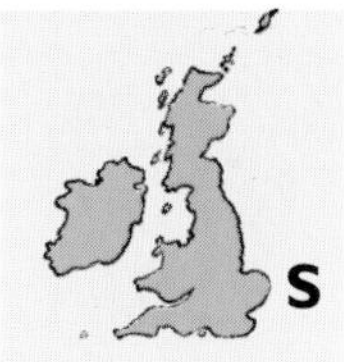

NETTLES GROW ON rich soils, especially those manured by animals and rich in nitrogen and phosphorus. They often persist around old ruins and their presence in large clumps away from buildings in woods or in fields may indicate former human habitation.

Distinctive plants, which some botanists regard as a different species or at least a variety, occur here and there in wet woodland and fens, where nettles are probably ancient natives. They are taller, up to 250 cm (100 in) or more, with broadly spear-shaped leaves and few stinging hairs on the stems and leaves.

Nettle stems are an ancient source of fibre for fabric and clothes, and some people still cook the shoots as a spring green vegetable. Caterpillars of several butterflies feed on the leaves. Dead-nettles are unrelated members of the mint family.

Top *Stinging Nettle* (Urtica dioica) *has male and female flowers on separate plants in tiny, greenish, tassel-like hanging clusters arising along the stem at the base of the leaf stalks.*

Bottom *Stinging Nettle* (Urtica dioica) *is an erect, mostly unbranched perennial, 50-150 cm (20-60 in) tall with heart-shaped toothed leaves covered in stinging hairs.*

Pellitory-of-the-Wall

NETTLE FAMILY

(Urticaceae)

SPECIES INFORMATION	
COMMON NAME	Pellitory-of-the-Wall
SCIENTIFIC NAME	Parietaria judaica
RELATED SPECIES	Mind-your-own-Business (see below)
HEIGHT/SPREAD	15–40 cm tall
FLOWERING TIME	June–October
HABITAT	Walls and rocky hedge-banks

Note: A distinctive plant of walls (Latin paries: wall).

FLOWER TYPE

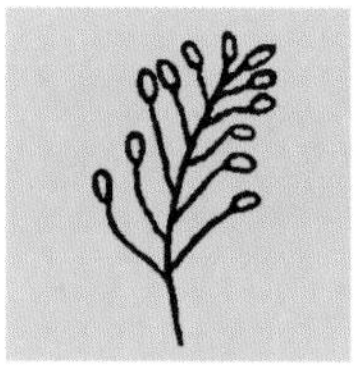

IDENTIFICATION

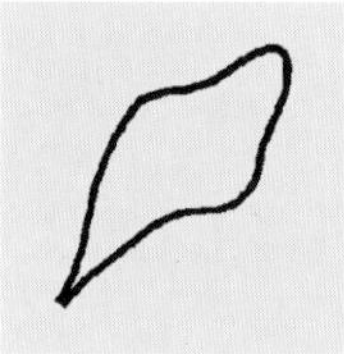

HABITAT

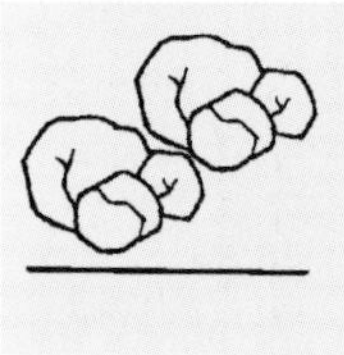

POPULATION

MAP

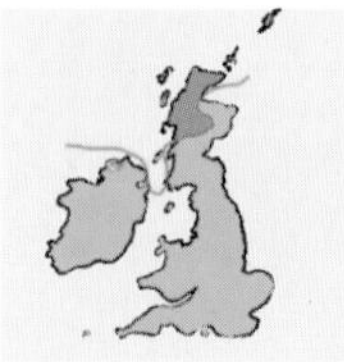

Size and appearance: A downy perennial with erect or spreading, reddish stems 15–40 cm (6–16 in) tall, without stinging hairs, forming loose clumps.
Leaves: Alternate along the stem, up to 5 cm (2 in) long but often smaller, spear-shaped, rather glossy.
Flowers: Male or female, 2–2.5 mm ($\frac{1}{12}$–$\frac{1}{10}$ in) across, greenish or brownish with pale yellow stamens, in small clusters along the stems.
Fruits: Nutlets (each enclosing a single seed), shiny black.
Related or similar plants: Nettles (p.13) are armed with stinging hairs; Mind-your-own-Business, often growing at the base of walls, is much smaller.
Habitat and distribution: Widespread and sometimes common on walls, around buildings and ruins, and on rocky hedge-banks; rare in Scotland.
Flowering time: June to October.

***Top** Pellitory-of-the-Wall* (Parietaria judaica) *is a downy perennial with erect or spreading reddish stems which are 15-40 cm (6-16 in) tall and have small clusters of male or female flowers on them. As its name suggests it is found on walls or at their bases, and it is frequent in churchyards.*

PELLITORY-OF-THE WALL is an ancient medicinal plant. Since, like the saxifrages, it grows on or among stones, many ancient herbalists imagined it would remove stones from the bladder. It is nevertheless a healing plant that has been a useful remedy for inflammation, burns and coughs. Its long use in medicine probably accounts for its frequency about ruined castles, churches and monasteries.

***Bottom** Mind-your-own-Business or Mother-of-Thousands* (Soleirolia soleirolii) *is a diminutive member of the nettle family, also without stinging hairs, that has tiny, rounded, evergreen, shiny leaves and minute pinkish flowers. A weed of greenhouses and mild gardens, especially in south-west England and parts of Ireland.*

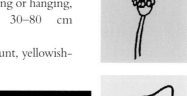

SPECIES INFORMATION	
COMMON NAME	Mistletoe
SCIENTIFIC NAME	Viscum album
RELATED SPECIES	None
HEIGHT/SPREAD	Stems 30–80 cm long
FLOWERING TIME	March–May
HABITAT	Parasitic on branches of trees

Note: Especially in winter, easily visible from a distance.

Mistletoe

MISTLETOE FAMILY

(Loranthaceae)

Top *Mistletoe* (Viscum album) *has white berries, which are a traditional Christmas decoration and also provide food for birds, who help transfer the seeds to new trees.*

Size and appearance: A hairless, evergreen perennial with a mass of drooping or hanging, repeatedly-branched stems 30–80 cm (12–32 in) long.

Leaves: In distinctive pairs, blunt, yellowish-green, leathery, persistent.

Flowers: Tiny, greenish-yellow, male or female in stalkless clusters.

Fruits: Spherical, whitish, translucent berries (drupes) 6–10 mm (¼–⅜ in) across, each with a single seed.

Related or similar plants: None in Britain or Ireland – the family is mainly tropical.

Habitat and distribution: Widespread but local in England and Wales on various trees, mainly apple, pear and hawthorn in the rose family, especially on apple trees in old orchards; very rare north of the River Humber and almost absent from Ireland.

Flowering time: March to May, but the fruits, which are ripe in autumn and winter, are more prominent than the flowers.

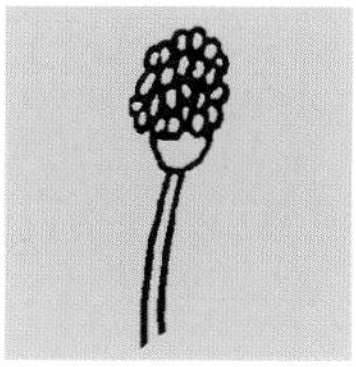

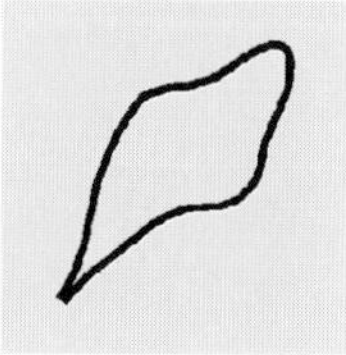

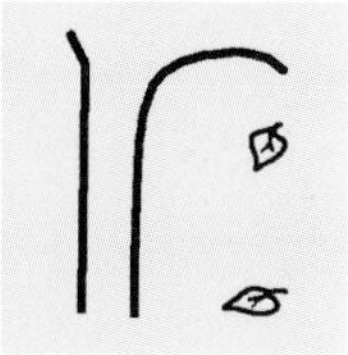

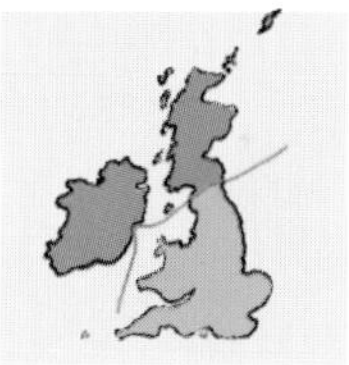

MISTLETOE IS A PARASITE, although the green chlorophyll pigment in its leaves enables it to make its own sugars and other foods by fixing carbon dioxide in the presence of sunlight (photosynthesis). The plant pushes root-like structures deep inside the branch of the tree, from which it extracts water and minerals.

The sticky seeds adhere to the beaks of birds that eat the fruits. While wiping its beak in a bark crevice, a bird may transfer seeds to a place where they can germinate and grow successfully.

Mistletoe is an ancient sacred plant associated with the Winter Solstice. The green shoots, sprouting from the apparently lifeless winter branches of trees, imbued the plant with mystery and inspired awe. Its present-day role in Christmas decorations, especially the ritual of kissing under the mistletoe, keeps alive a vestige of an ancient midwinter fertility rite.

Bottom *Mistletoe is a parasite which attaches itself to the branch of a tree. Favoured trees are apples, but it can also be found on limes, willows and poplars.*

Common Knotgrass

DOCK AND KNOTWEED FAMILY
(Polygonaceae)

SPECIES INFORMATION	
COMMON NAME	Common Knotgrass
SCIENTIFIC NAME	Polygonum aviculare
RELATED SPECIES	Equal-leaved Knotgrass
HEIGHT/SPREAD	Stems 10–100 cm long
FLOWERING TIME	June–October
HABITAT	Cultivated and waste land, pathsides

Note: Like a large buttercup with several seeded fruits.

FLOWER TYPE

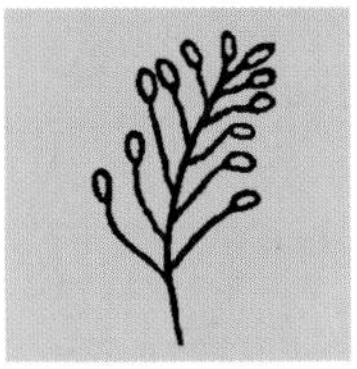

IDENTIFICATION

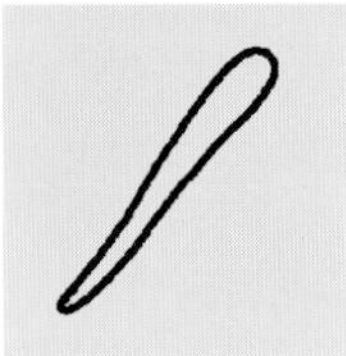

HABITAT

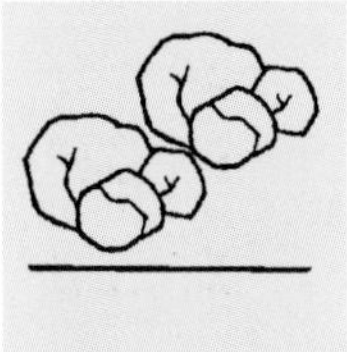

POPULATION

MAP

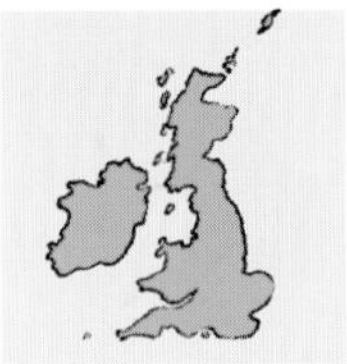

Size and appearance: More or less hairless annual, with prostrate, sprawling or sometimes erect, leafy stems 10–100 cm (4–40 in) long, occasionally up to 200 cm (80 in).
Leaves: Narrow, spear-shaped, blunt or pointed; those on the main stems larger than those on the branches, 25–50 mm (1–2 in) long.
Flowers: Tiny, pale or bright pink, solitary or in clusters of 2–6 scattered along the stems in the angles of the leaves.
Fruits: 2–3.5 mm (1/12–1/8in) long, triangular, dark brown, dull.
Related or similar plants: Three other very similar species occur, the commonest of which, Equal-leaved Knotgrass (see below), has blunt leaves 10–20 mm (2/5–4/5in) long and forms mats on trampled ground.
Habitat and distribution: A common plant of cultivated, disturbed and waste ground, road-verges and seashores. It will tolerate some trampling and often occurs on pathsides.
Flowering time: June to October, sometimes into November.

THIS UNDISTINGUISHED PLANT is one of the commonest but most overlooked weeds of waste and cultivated land, where it can be a pest in potato fields, the long stems clogging machinery. It is sometimes abundant in stubble just before ploughing in late summer. The English and scientific names of this plant and its family reflect the swollen knot-like joints or 'knees' along the stems, where the leaves emerge from the stem. *Polygonum* comes from the ancient Greek, literally 'many-kneed'. Common Knotgrass hass a sheath around each joint like a miniature knee bandage.

Common Knotgrass (Polygonum aviculare) *is a sprawling plant 10-100 cm (4-40 in) long with narrow, spear-shaped leaves, which can be blunt or pointed and are often of different sizes. It is common on cultivated and disturbed soils.*

SPECIES INFORMATION	
COMMON NAME	Persicaria, Redshank
SCIENTIFIC NAME	Persicaria maculosa
RELATED SPECIES	Pale Persicaria
HEIGHT/SPREAD	10–80 cm tall
FLOWERING TIME	July–October
HABITAT	Cultivated and waste land

Note: The tiny massed, bright pink flowers are a feature.

Persicaria

DOCK AND KNOTWEED FAMILY

(Polygonaceae)

Size and appearance: More or less hairless, erect or sometimes sprawling annual 10–80 cm (4–32 in) tall.

Leaves: Narrow, spear-shaped, pointed.

Flowers: Pale or bright pink, small but massed in dense, cylindrical spikes.

Fruits: 2–3 mm ($\frac{1}{12}$–$\frac{1}{8}$in) long, triangular or lens-shaped, black, shiny.

Related or similar plants: Pale Persicaria has greenish-white or dull pink flowers and rough, yellowish flower-stalks.

Habitat and distribution: An abundant weed of cultivated land, including gardens. It is also a colonist of bare mud and gravel beside streams, rivers and lakes.

Flowering time: July to October.

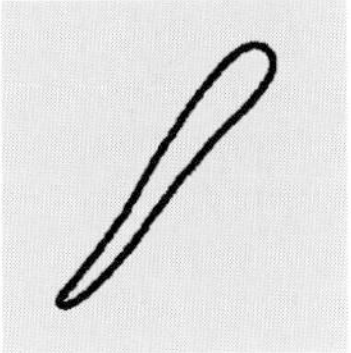

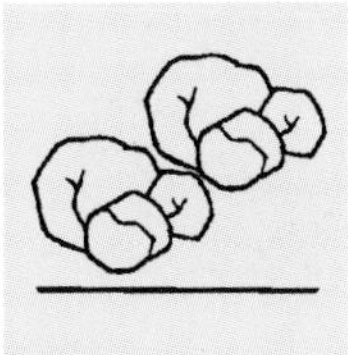

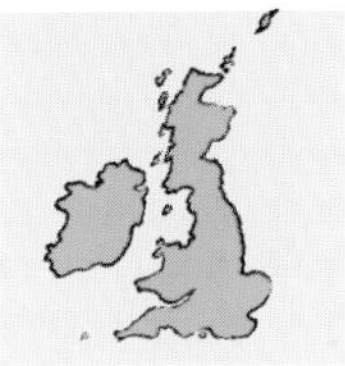

ONE OF THE MOST widespread and persistent weeds of arable land, sometimes colouring crops pink where the farmer's weedkiller spray has missed, and a common plant of gardens and disturbed, waste places, especially on rich soils. Plants from waterside mud or gravel are often smaller and less branched.

The starch-rich fruits were formerly gathered and used as a grain. They are one of the main foods found in the stomachs of Tollund Man and other preserved bodies excavated from Iron Age bog burials in Denmark. Persicaria also had some former medicinal use in the treatment of inflammation and urinary infections.

Top *Water Pepper* (Persicaria hydropiper) *is a plant of damp woodland rides, stream sides or marshy areas. It takes it name from the peppery taste of its leaves.*

Bottom *Persicaria* (Persicaria maculosa) *is an abundant weed of cultivation, where its pale or bright pink spikes of flowers can make a splash of colour amongst the crop.*

Amphibious Bistort

DOCK AND KNOTWEED FAMILY
(Polygonaceae)

SPECIES INFORMATION	
COMMON NAME	Amphibious Bistort
SCIENTIFIC NAME	Persicaria amphibia
RELATED SPECIES	Persicaria
HEIGHT/SPREAD	Stems 10–100 cm long
FLOWERING TIME	June–September
HABITAT	Lakes, ponds and flooded ditches

Note: The only aquatic species in this family in Britain.

FLOWER TYPE

IDENTIFICATION

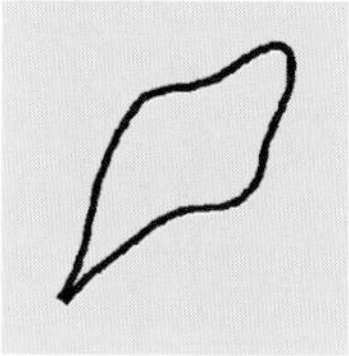

HABITAT

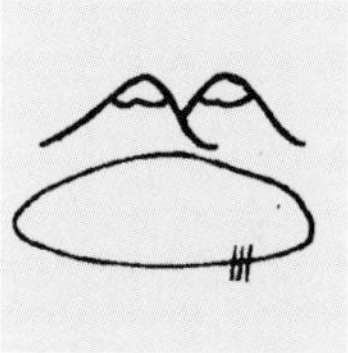

POPULATION

MAP

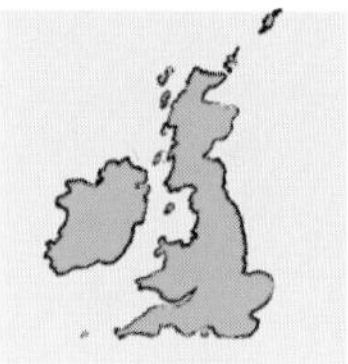

Size and appearance: Usually an aquatic, little-branched perennial with creeping roots, floating stems 10–100 cm (4–40 in) long and floating leaves.
Leaves: Floating leaves spear-shaped, blunt, hairless; leaves of plants growing on land pointed, minutely hairy.
Flowers: Deep pink, small but massed in dense, stout, cylindrical spikes atop long stems.
Fruits: Lens-shaped, 2–3 mm ($\frac{1}{12}$–$\frac{1}{8}$in) long, brown, shiny.
Related or similar plants: Plants growing on land can be confused with Persicaria, but are taller, leafier and hairier.
Habitat and distribution: A widespread plant of lakes, ponds, canals and flooded ditches; also a weed of damp cultivated ground.
Flowering time: June to September.

IN SUMMER THIS plant sometimes forms large patches in a conspicuous pink band around the margins of still or slow-moving bodies of water. It can also grow on land, on road-verges, margins of reed-beds, wet hollows or sometimes as a weed of cultivation, when the plants are erect, have narrow, rather hairy leaves and produce fewer, scruffier heads of flowers.

***Top** Amphibious Bistort* (Persicaria amphibia) *has the ability to form large patches in a conspicuous pink band around the margin of a lake.*

***Bottom** Amphibious Bistort is an aquatic perennial with floating stems 10-100cm (4-40 in) long and deep pink, cylindrical spikes of flowers. It is widespread at the edges of lakes and in ponds, canals and flooded ditches.*

SPECIES INFORMATION	
COMMON NAME	Bistort
SCIENTIFIC NAME	Persicaria bistorta
RELATED SPECIES	Alpine Bistort, Persicaria
HEIGHT/SPREAD	20–50 cm tall
FLOWERING TIME	June–August
HABITAT	Damp grassland

Note: The basal leaves have winged stalks.

Bistort

DOCK AND KNOTWEED FAMILY (Polygonaceae)

Top *Bistort* (Persicaria bistorta) *is common in northern England where it is found in damp grassland. Its massed, dense, cylindrical, pink spikes of flowers means that it is often introduced around farms and villages.*

BISTORT IS PARTICULARLY common in northern England, in Cumbria and the Pennines. In this region, notably in Calderdale in the West Riding of Yorkshire, under the name of Easter-giants or Easter-ledges the young leaves are an ingredient of traditional herb puddings served at Easter. Bistort often grows around villages and farmhouses, and is undoubtedly introduced or spread by people over much of its range.

It is a popular plant in cultivation, particularly suitable for the traditional cottage garden or herbaceous border, especially the cultivar 'Superbum', with its dense spikes of pink flowers.

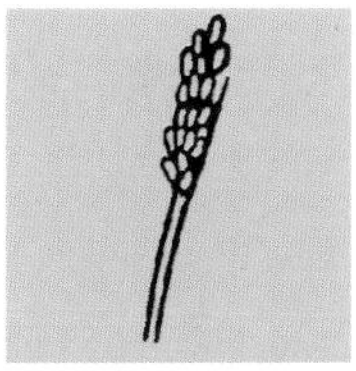

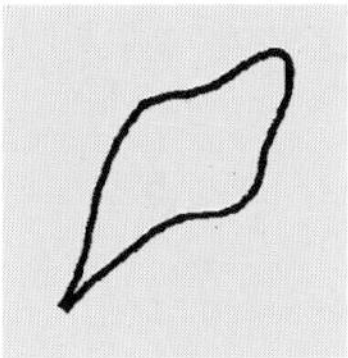

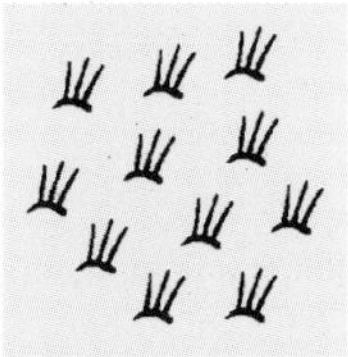

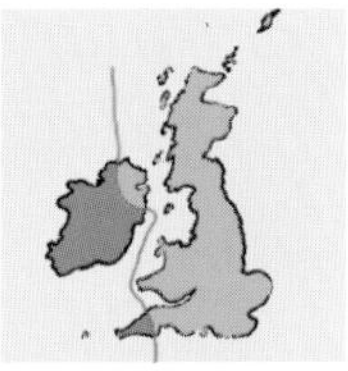

Size and appearance: A leafy perennial, rising from a stout, contorted rhizome, forming clumps of little-branched stems 20–50 cm (8–20 in) tall.

Leaves: Basal leaves with winged stalks, the blade oval to almost triangular, rather blunt, minutely hairy beneath; stem leaves narrowly triangular.

Flowers: Pink, 4–5 mm (⅙–⅕ in) long, massed in dense, stout, cylindrical spikes 2–5 cm (⅘–2 in) long.

Fruits: Triangular, brown, shiny.

Related or similar plants: Alpine Bistort is a much smaller plant with purplish bulbils; Persicaria and Pale Persicaria (p.17) are annuals of cultivated land.

Habitat and distribution: A plant of damp grassland on rather lime-poor soils, especially in northern and upland Britain, but sometimes in old meadows in the south; rare and introduced in Ireland.

Flowering time: June to August.

Bottom *Alpine Bistort* (Persicaria vivpara) *is a smaller, hairless perennial 10–30 cm (4–12 in) tall, with narrowly spear-shaped leaves and slender spikes of pink or whitish flowers. Purplish bulbils or detachable buds replace the lower flowers in the spike. It is widespread in mountainous areas.*

Black Bindweed

DOCK AND KNOTWEED FAMILY (Polygonaceae)

SPECIES INFORMATION	
COMMON NAME	Black Bindweed
SCIENTIFIC NAME	Fallopia convolvulus
RELATED SPECIES	Copse Bindweed
HEIGHT/SPREAD	Stems 10–120 cm long
FLOWERING TIME	June–October
HABITAT	Cultivated ground

Note: The unrelated Field Bindweed is a perennial.

FLOWER TYPE

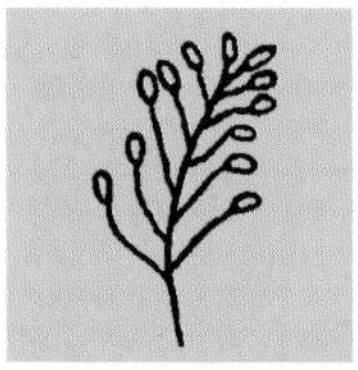

IDENTIFICATION

HABITAT

POPULATION

MAP

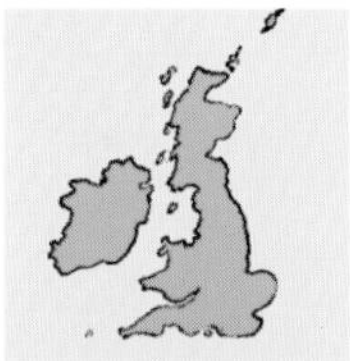

Size and appearance: Prostrate or scrambling and clockwise-twining, hairless annual with stems 10–120 cm (4–48 in) long.
Leaves: Heart- or arrow-shaped, with long-pointed tips.
Flowers: Inconspicuous, on slender stalks, greenish-white or greenish-pink in small clusters or loose spikes.
Fruits: Matt black, triangular nuts 4–5 mm (⅙–⅕ in) long, each enclosed in persistent, papery flower-parts.

Related or similar plants: Copse Bindweed is a much more robust plant of woodland margins and hedges.

Habitat and distribution: A widespread weed of disturbed ground, especially arable fields, gardens and allotments, but also in waste places and on coastal shingle beaches.

Flowering time: June to October

ONE OF OUR commonest and most distinctive weeds of cultivation. Archeological evidence suggests that Black Bindweed has long been a major weed of cultivation in Britain and Ireland. Its fruits were until recently a principal contaminant of agricultural seed, and still comprise a significant proportion of the soil seed-bank of cultivated land.

Plants, especially those growing on richer soils, sometimes have winged flower-parts when in fruit, and thus resemble Copse Bindweed, with which they may be confused. The larger, matt black nuts of Copse Bindweed are diagnostic.

Top *Black Bindweed* (Fallopia convolvulus) *is a scrambling and twining annual of disturbed ground, with arrow-shaped leaves and greenish-white clusters of flowers.*

Bottom *The very similar Copse Bindweed* (Fallopia dumetorum) *is more robust, with climbing stems up to 3 m (9 ft) or more lolong, enclosed by persistent, enlarged, winged flower-parts. It is a rare plant of hedges and woodland ng, and shiny black nuts no more than 3 mm (⅛ in) long, enclosed by persistent, enlarged, winged flower-parts. It is a rare plant of hedges and woodland margins in southern England from Dorset to Kent.*

SPECIES INFORMATION	
COMMON NAME	Japanese Knotweed
SCIENTIFIC NAME	Fallopia japonica
RELATED SPECIES	Giant Knotweed
HEIGHT/SPREAD	1–3 m tall
FLOWERING TIME	August–October
HABITAT	Waste ground

Note: Forming thickets of giant red stems and large leaves.

Japanese Knotweed

DOCK AND KNOTWEED FAMILY

(Polygonaceae)

Top left and right
Japanese Knotweed (Fallopia japonica) *is a native of Japan. First introduced in 1825, it has run rampant throughout Britain ever since and, as a result of this, it is now illegal to introduce it in to the wild.*

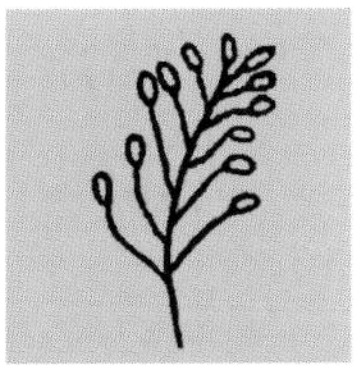
FLOWER TYPE

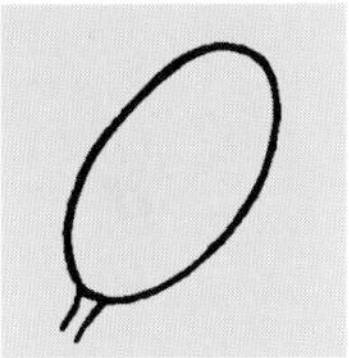
IDENTIFICATION

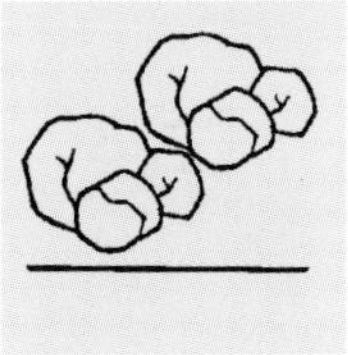
HABITAT

POPULATION

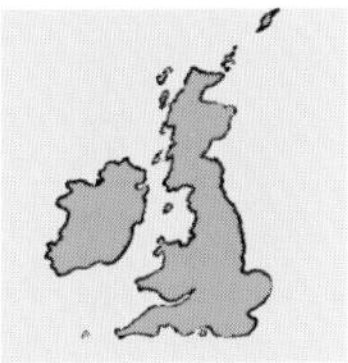
MAP

Size and appearance: Robust, hairless perennial with vigorous, far-creeping rhizomes and stout, hollow, reddish stems 1–3 m (3–9 ft) tall, arching and branched above.
Leaves: Heart-shaped, abruptly cut off at the base, pointed, rather stiff.
Flowers: Greenish-white, sometimes pink, in branched clusters.
Fruits: Rarely formed in Britain and Ireland.
Related or similar plants: Giant Knotweed is an even more robust plant of similar habitats.
Habitat and distribution: A frequently abundant weed of waste ground, railway land, road-verges and streamsides. It has now spread to most parts of Britain and Ireland, but is particularly common in some areas such as London and South Wales.
Flowering time: Late August to October.

THIS CONSPICUOUS AND most aggressive plant is an alien from Japan, introduced in 1825 and widely grown in 19th-century gardens. It now forms dense thickets almost everywhere, invading waste ground, derelict land, railway embankments and cuttings, road-verges, and the banks of rivers and streams. It is perhaps the worst weed ever to have reached these islands, where it continues its rapid spread. The Wildlife and Countryside Act 1981 forbids its introduction into the wild in Britain.

Bottom
Giant Knotweed (Fallopia sachalinensis) *is even larger, up to 4 m (12 ft) tall, with broadly oblong leaves that are heart-shaped at the base. It is less common but generally widespread.*

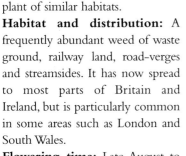

Sorrel

DOCK AND KNOTWEED FAMILY
(Polygonaceae)

SPECIES INFORMATION	
COMMON NAME	Sorrel
SCIENTIFIC NAME	Rumex acetosa
RELATED SPECIES	Sheep's Sorrel
HEIGHT/SPREAD	10–80 cm tall
FLOWERING TIME	May–July
HABITAT	Cultivated ground

Note: The leaves taste of acid.

FLOWER TYPE

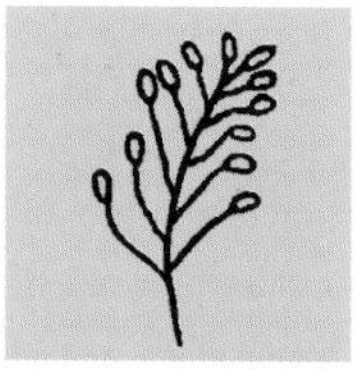

IDENTIFICATION

HABITAT

POPULATION

MAP

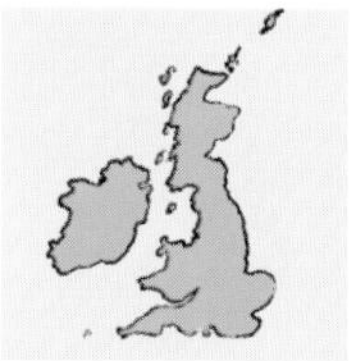

Size and appearance: Erect perennial with little-branched stems 10–80 cm (4–32 in) tall, sometimes up to 130 cm (52 in).
Leaves: Slightly fleshy, those at the base and on the lower stem stalked, spear- to arrow-shaped, blunt, with a pair of downward-pointing basal lobes; upper leaves clasping the stem, often pointed.
Flowers: Male and female on separate plants, minute, reddish or greenish in branched spikes.
Fruits: Small, triangular, shiny brown nuts, each enclosed in the brown, papery remains of the flower.
Related or similar plants: Sheep's Sorrel is smaller, and the leaves have basal lobes that spread outwards rather than downwards.
Habitat and distribution: Widespread in grassland and woodland rides, and on road-verges, sand-dunes and rocky ground.
Flowering time: Late May to July.

THIS PLANT often gives a reddish tint to meadows in mid-summer. The flowers are pollinated by the wind. The whole plant tastes of acid and the leaves can be used in salads or to flavour sauces and soups - although the true Garden Sorrel, with broad, rounded leaves, is a different species.

Plants from sand-dune grassland or machair in western and northern Scotland and in western Ireland are shorter and less branched, and have shorter white hairs on the stems and leaves. Botanists regard them as a distinct subspecies.

Top *Sorrel* (Rumex acetosa) *is an erect perennial, 10-80 cm (4-32 in) tall with the leaves on the lower part of the stem showing a pair of downward-pointing basal lobes.*

Bottom
Sorrel with its reddish and greenish flowers, is widespread in meadows and woodland rides but it can also occur on sand-dunes and rocky ground.

SPECIES INFORMATION	
COMMON NAME	Sheep's Sorrel
SCIENTIFIC NAME	Rumex acetosella
RELATED SPECIES	Sorrel
HEIGHT/SPREAD	5–30 cm tall
FLOWERING TIME	May–September
HABITAT	Cultivated ground

Note: The smallest dock-like plant, forming patches on heathland.

Sheep's Sorrel

DOCK AND KNOTWEED FAMILY

(Polygonaceae)

Size and appearance: Erect perennial with stems 5-30 cm (2–12 in) tall, sometimes up to 50 cm (20 in), branched above; roots far-creeping, forming patches.

Leaves: Slightly fleshy, often reddish, narrow, spear-shaped, with a pair of outward-spreading basal lobes.

Flowers: Male and female on separate plants, minute, reddish in branched spikes.

Fruits: Tiny, triangular, shiny brown nuts, each enclosed in the brown, papery remains of the flower.

Related or similar plants: Sorrel (p.22) is larger and the basal lobes of the leaves spread downwards rather than outwards.

Habitat and distribution: Common on heathland, in dry grassland, on rock outcrops, wall-tops, shingle beaches and sand-dunes on soils poor in lime and other nutrients.

Flowering time: May to September.

THIS PLANT COLOURS heathy grassland with patches of red in summer. On sandy or peaty soils this plant can be a persistent garden and agricultural weed. The whole plant tastes of acid. The flowers are pollinated by the wind. A very variable species. Particularly distinctive are plants from dry heathland with very narrow, strap-like leaves.

Top *Sheep's Sorrel* (Rumex acetosella)*, with its small size and long slender leaves with basal lobes that point outwards, make for easy distinction from Sorrel.*

Bottom *Sheep's Sorrel can dominate patches of heathland, with its flower spikes turning the area red. It also occurs on well-drained substrate such as shingle beaches, sand-dunes and bare areas of sea walls.*

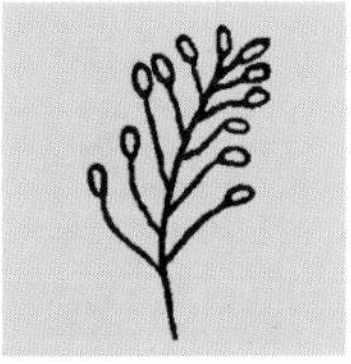

FLOWER TYPE

IDENTIFICATION

HABITAT

POPULATION

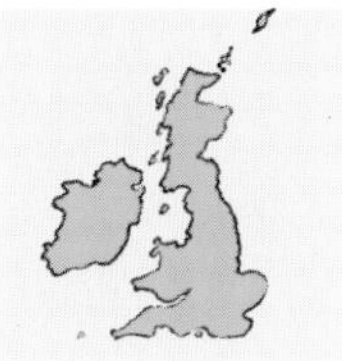

MAP

Broad-leaved Dock

DOCK AND KNOTWEED FAMILY
(Polygonaceae)

SPECIES INFORMATION	
COMMON NAME	Broad-leaved Dock
SCIENTIFIC NAME	Rumex obtusifolius
RELATED SPECIES	Curled Dock
HEIGHT/SPREAD	50–150 cm tall
FLOWERING TIME	May–October
HABITAT	Cultivated and waste ground

Note: The commonest dock.

FLOWER TYPE

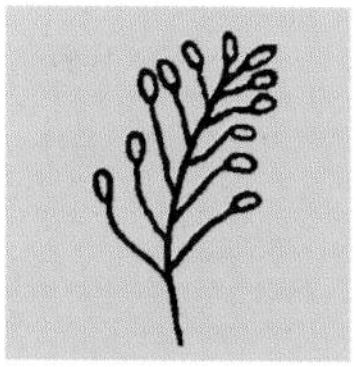

IDENTIFICATION

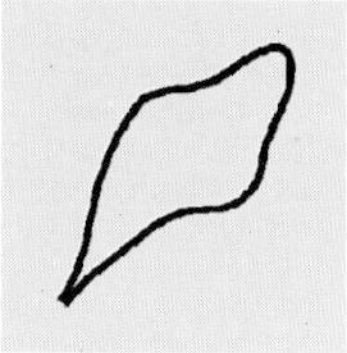

HABITAT

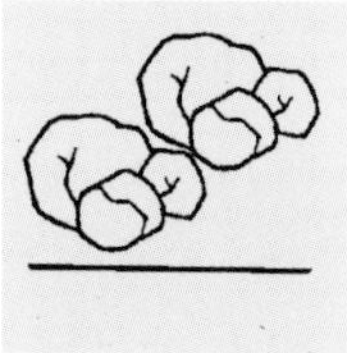

POPULATION

MAP

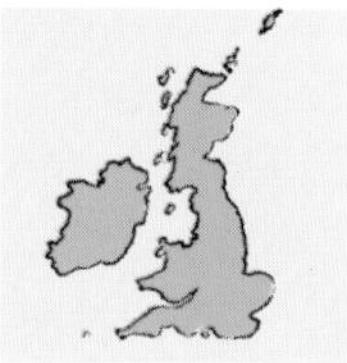

Size and appearance: Robust, leafy perennial, rising from a stout tap-root, the much-branched stems 50–150 cm (20–60 in) tall.

Leaves: Broad, oblong, heart-shaped at base, blunt.

Flowers: Tiny, green or reddish, in large, loose, leafy spikes.

Fruits: Triangular nuts, each enclosed in the brown, papery remains of the flower, with soft-spiny margins and a single (rarely 3) corky wart.

Related or similar plants: Curled Dock (p.25) has spear-shaped, pointed leaves with curly margins and spineless persistent flower-parts in fruit.

Habitat and distribution: Common on cultivated land, in waste places and along river-banks.

Flowering time: May to October.

Below *Water Dock* (Rumex hydrolapathum) *is similar but is a huge aquatic plant, with clumps of leaves up to 120 cm (48 in), stems up to 200 cm (80 in) long, spineless persistent flower-parts in fruit. Flowering in watersides north to the Moray Firth, but rare in the west and in Ireland.*

VERY COMMON AND sometimes in great crowds, forming conspicuous leafy clumps on waste land and in overgrazed pastures. It was, before modern weed-killers, a major weed of cultivation and is listed under the Weeds Act 1959. It often crosses with Curled Dock (p.25) when the two grow together. The large leaves were once used to wrap butter and are still a popular remedy for relieving nettle stings. The flowers are pollinated by the wind, but sometimes by bumble-bees.

Above *Broad-leaved Dock* (Rumex obtusifolius) *is a robust plant with broad, oblong leaves, heart-shaped at their base. It is a very common plant of disturbed soils.*

SPECIES INFORMATION	
COMMON NAME	Curled Dock
SCIENTIFIC NAME	Rumex crispus
RELATED SPECIES	Broad-leaved Dock
HEIGHT/SPREAD	50–120 cm tall
FLOWERING TIME	June–August
HABITAT	Cultivated and waste ground.

Note: The dock of seashores, but also common inland.

Curled Dock

DOCK AND KNOTWEED FAMILY

(Polygonaceae)

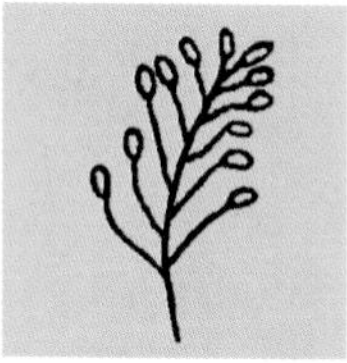

FLOWER TYPE

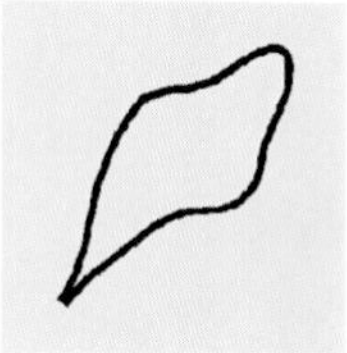

IDENTIFICATION

HABITAT

POPULATION

MAP

Size and appearance: An erect annual, biennial or perennial, rising from a long taproot; stems 50–120 cm (20–48 in) tall, rarely up to 250 cm (100 in).

Leaves: Slightly fleshy (especially when growing on the coast), spear-shaped, pointed, with wavy margins.

Flowers: Tiny, green or somewhat reddish, massed in large, branched spikes.

Fruits: Small triangular nuts, each enclosed in brown, papery remains of the flower, with spineless margins and 1-3 corky warts.

Related or similar plants: Broad-leaved Dock (p.24) has broader, blunt leaves without wavy margins, and persistent flower-parts with soft spines in fruit.

Habitat and distribution: Common on cultivated and waste ground, shingle beaches, sand-dunes and along the tidal reaches of rivers.

Flowering time: Mostly mid-June to August, but from late May in some habitats and a few plants in flower until October.

THE SEEDS are produced in huge numbers and can survive for more than 50 years in soil. Curled Dock was, before modern weed-killers, a major weed of cultivation and is listed under the Weeds Act 1959. Late 19th-century countryside writer Richard Jefferies described farm labourers removing great bundles of them from crops. The flowers are pollinated by the wind, but sometimes by bumble-bees.

A very variable species, with particularly distinct variants that live on seashores, especially shingle beaches, and steep banks of tidal mud in rivers. In these 'semi-natural' habitats plants can occur in considerable numbers. Curled Dock growing along the tidal reaches of the Wye, Shannon and other large rivers looks most unusual. The plants have almost uncrisped, upright, spear-like leaves, stems up to 2 m (6 ft) or more tall, and great, loose, branched spikes of flowers and fruits from late May and June. Conversely, plants from shingle beaches are short and compact, and have slightly fleshy leaves. These attributes are retained when plants are grown from seed in garden soil.

Curled Dock (Rumex crispus) *is a tall, erect plant with spear-shaped leaves, which are pointed and have wavy margins. It is generally a plant of disturbed soils but also occurs on sand-dunes and shingle beaches.*

Fiddle Dock

DOCK AND KNOTWEED FAMILY
(Polygonaceae)

SPECIES INFORMATION	
COMMON NAME	Fiddle Dock
SCIENTIFIC NAME	Rumex pulcher
RELATED SPECIES	Golden Dock
HEIGHT/SPREAD	20–50 cm tall
FLOWERING TIME	June–August
HABITAT	Roadsides and dry grassland

Note: A dock with tangled branches and fiddle-shaped leaves.

FLOWER TYPE

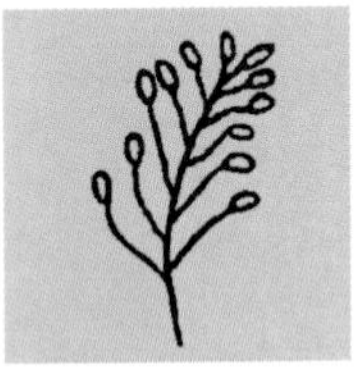

IDENTIFICATION

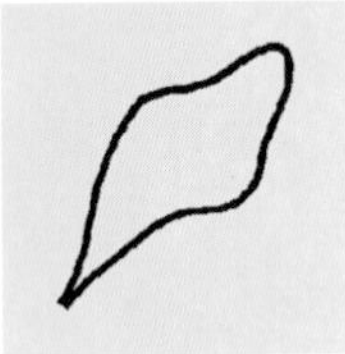

HABITAT

POPULATION

MAP

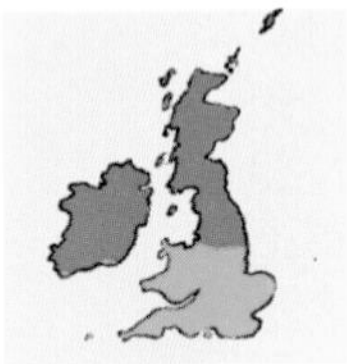

Fiddle dock (Rumex pulcher) *is an untidy dock with wide-spreading branches, whose basal leaves have the distinctive shape of a violin; they are narrower in the middle than at either end.*

Size and appearance: An untidy, hairless biennial or short-lived perennial, with a tough rootstock and stems 20–50 cm (8–20 in) tall, with wide-spreading branches.
Leaves: Mostly in basal rosette, fiddle-shaped, blunt.
Flowers: Tiny, green, in loose, leafy spikes.
Fruits: Triangular nuts, each enclosed in the brown, papery remains of the flower, with spiny margins and 3 knobbly, corky warts.
Related or similar plants: Golden Dock has spear-shaped leaves; the whole plant is yellowish in fruit.
Habitat and distribution: Widespread but local in dry grassland, village greens, churchyards and waste places, on roadsides and sometimes on cliffs and in pastures by the sea, on well-drained soils; mainly in southern England, especially near coasts, but locally extending as far north as Anglesey; in Ireland only near the sea in County Wexford and West Cork.
Flowering time: June to August.

THIS IS ONE of the most distinctive docks, and a frequent colonist of village greens, especially where the ground is scuffed by football and other activities. The rosettes of waisted, fiddle-like leaves are held close to the ground, but the tangled stems, brown and almost like a tumbleweed when mature, are more conspicuous. Fiddle Dock, a mainly Mediterranean plant, is probably native by and near the sea. However, it is also a classic plant of unmanicured greens and waysides across southern England, to where it may have spread by human activity.

It is a weed in southern Europe and frequently turns up around ports and docklands.

Golden Dock (*Rumex maritimus*), much our handsomest dock, is more erect, with narrow, pointed, spear-shaped leaves and dense, yellowish masses of fruits, the persistent flower-parts with long, bristle-like spine. Growing beside ponds and in other wet places, it is scattered north to Yorkshire and here and there in Ireland.

SPECIES INFORMATION	
COMMON NAME	Sea Beet, Wild Beet
SCIENTIFIC NAME	Beta vulgaris
RELATED SPECIES	Fat Hen
HEIGHT/SPREAD	Stems 30–100 cm long
FLOWERING TIME	July–September
HABITAT	Coastal habitats, especially shingle

Note: The dark green, fleshy, glossy leaves are conspicuous.

Sea Beet

GOOSEFOOT FAMILY (Chenopodiaceae)

THE CLUMPS and hummocks of this plant are a prominent feature of the coastal scene, especially on shingle beaches. The stout taproot is rich in sugar. Indeed, the cultivated sugar-beet and fodder-beet are variants of this species, as are beetroot, spinach beet and Swiss chard of gardens. The corky fruiting structure allows the seeds to float and so be dispersed by the tide.

Sugar Beet and Fodder Beet, similar to Sea Beet but more robust and erect plants, sometimes persist as weeds on or around arable fields.

Left *Sea Beet* (Beta vulgaris ssp maritima) *is widespread around the coasts of Britain and Ireland, occurring on many substrates from the soft muds of saltmarshes to coastal rocks.*

Size and appearance: An erect or sprawling, untidy, fleshy perennial with stems 30–100 cm (12–40 in) long, forming large clumps.
Leaves: Triangular, leathery, fleshy, dark green, glossy, with wavy margins.
Flowers: Green, 3–4 mm ($\frac{1}{8}$–$\frac{1}{6}$) in diameter, in dense, leafy spikes.
Fruits: Enclosed in a corky structure derived from the flower-parts.
Related or similar plants: Fat Hen (p28) is an erect annual of cultivated and waste land, with paler, often floury leaves.
Habitat and distribution: Widespread on shingle beaches, the edges of salt-marshes, along sea-walls and on coastal rocks and cliffs, all around the coast of Britain and Ireland; scarcer in Scotland and absent from the north.
Flowering time: July to September.

Bottom left *Sea Beet is an erect plant 30-100 cm (12-40 in) tall, with fleshy, dark green, glossy leaves and green flowers in dense leafy spikes.*

Bottom right *Sea Beet is often found growing out of a concrete faced sea wall.*

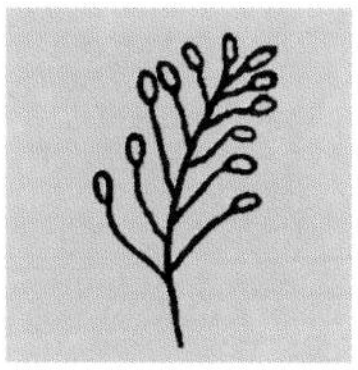

FLOWER TYPE

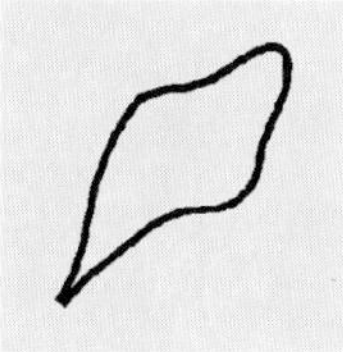

IDENTIFICATION

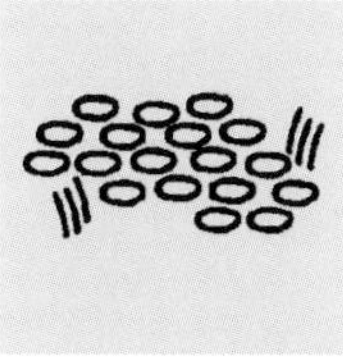

HABITAT

POPULATION

MAP

Fat Hen

GOOSEFOOT FAMILY
(Chenopodiaceae)

SPECIES INFORMATION	
COMMON NAME	Fat Hen, Common Goosefoot
SCIENTIFIC NAME	Chenopodium album
RELATED SPECIES	Sea Beet, Oraches, other Goosefoots
HEIGHT/SPREAD	20–150 cm tall
FLOWERING TIME	June–October
HABITAT	Cultivated ground

Note: A tall, greyish-green, leafy weed of gardens.

FLOWER TYPE

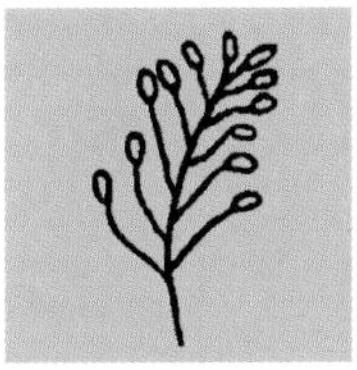

IDENTIFICATION

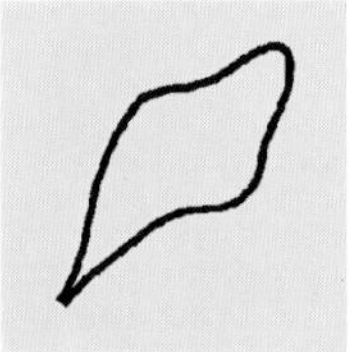

HABITAT

POPULATION

MAP

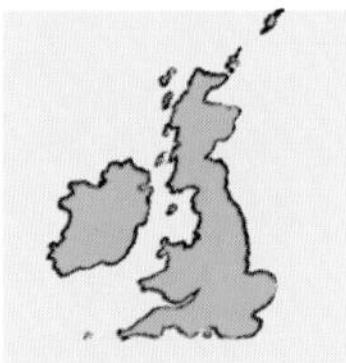

Top *Fat Hen* (Chenopodium album) *is an abundant weed of cultivated soils with greyish-green leaves which can range through oval, diamond- or paddle-shaped and can be slightly toothed.*

Size and appearance: Erect, often mealy and therefore slightly greyish-green, branched annual 20–50 cm (8–60 in) tall.
Leaves: Slightly fleshy, oval, diamond- or paddle-shaped, almost untoothed or coarsely and bluntly toothed.
Flowers: Tiny, green, massed in many dense, branched clusters.
Fruits: Tiny, papery, each enclosing a black or brown, flattened, glossy seed.
Related or similar plants: Sea Beet (p.27) is perennial and has dark green, glossy leaves; Red Goosefoot has shiny, jagged-toothed leaves.
Habitat and distribution: An abundant weed of waste ground and cultivated land, especially on richer soils.
Flowering time: June to October.

THIS IS THE commonest of the dozen or so native and introduced goosefoots, all plants of disturbed or open ground or coastal habitats. The other species are mostly very difficult to distinguish from one another. Fat Hen was once a valued substitute for spinach and the seeds were eaten as a grain. It is a plant that apparently has no natural habitat and probably evolved, like the dog, alongside human habitation. A very variable species.

Bottom *Red Goosefoot* (Chenopodium rubrum) *is an often very robust plant with reddish stems and shiny, diamond-shaped leaves that are irregularly and jaggedly toothed. It favours rich farm soils, especially around buildings and dung-heaps; also on the edges of salt-marshes.*

SPECIES INFORMATION	
COMMON NAME	Halberd-leaved Orache
SCIENTIFIC NAME	Atriplex prostrata
RELATED SPECIES	Common Orache
HEIGHT/SPREAD	20–100 cm tall
FLOWERING TIME	June–October
HABITAT	Cultivated ground, coastal regions

Note: Sometimes in masses on seashores.

Halberd-leaved Orache

GOOSEFOOT FAMILY

(Chenopodiaceae)

FLOWER TYPE

IDENTIFICATION

HABITAT

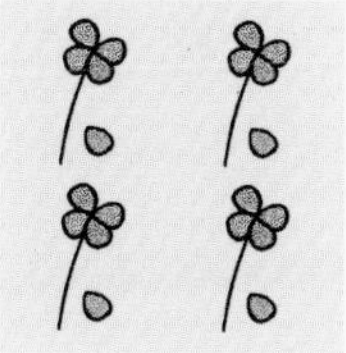

POPULATION

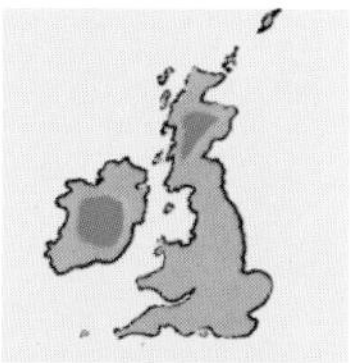

MAP

Size and appearance: Erect or sprawling, often mealy, branched, leafy annual 20–100 cm (8–40 in) tall.

Leaves: Slightly fleshy, triangular or spear-shaped, variably toothed, with a pair of prominent basal teeth spreading at a right angle from the cut-off base.

Flowers: Tiny, green, in slender but dense clusters.

Fruits: Numerous, 1-seeded nutlets, between a pair of triangular, fleshy, leaf-like flaps or bracts.

Related or similar plants: Common Orache has leaves with a pair of forward-pointing teeth near the wedge-shaped base.

Habitat and distribution: An abundant weed of waste ground and cultivated land, especially on richer soils, and also on seashores and in salt-marshes.

Flowering time: July to October.

THIS SCRUFFY AND undistinguished plant is perhaps the commonest of the half dozen or so oraches native to Britain and Ireland, all plants of seashores, salt-marshes or open and disturbed ground. It is a plant that, like Fat Hen, apparently has no natural habitat and probably evolved alongside human settlements. It too can be cooked and eaten like spinach, although in quantity it is a mild laxative.

Bottom right *Common Orache* (Atriplex patula) *is a common weed of waysides, arable fields, allotments and other cultivated land, but not seashores.*

Sea Purslane

GOOSEFOOT FAMILY
(Chenopodiaceae)

SPECIES INFORMATION	
COMMON NAME	Sea Purslane
SCIENTIFIC NAME	Halimione portulacoides
RELATED SPECIES	Halberd-leaved Orache
HEIGHT/SPREAD	20–80 cm tall
FLOWERING TIME	July–October
HABITAT	Salt-marshes and rocks

Note: A prominent feature of English salt-marshes.

FLOWER TYPE

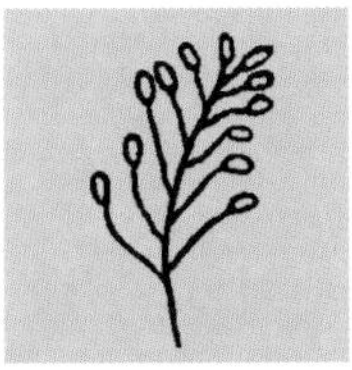

IDENTIFICATION

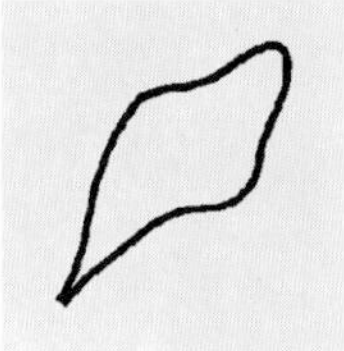

HABITAT

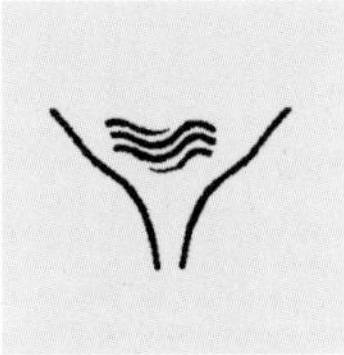

POPULATION

MAP

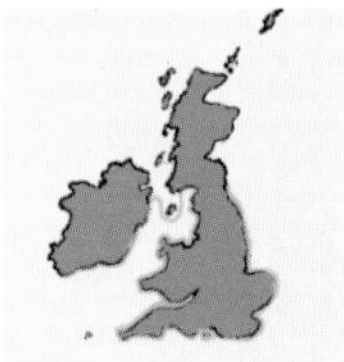

Size and appearance: An evergreen, sprawling, grey-mealy, branched shrublet 20–80 cm (8–32 in) tall.

Leaves: Elliptical, fleshy, leathery, untoothed, with obscure veins.

Flowers: Tiny, yellowish, in dense, branched clusters.

Fruits: Numerous, stalkless, 1-seeded nutlets, between a pair of tiny 3-lobed, leaf-like flaps or bracts.

Related or similar plants: Halberd-leaved Orache and Common Orache (p29) are annuals, and the ripe seeds are surrounded by a pair of swollen, leaf-like bracts.

Habitat and distribution: Forming dense grey stands in salt-marshes, mainly along the sides of tidal creeks and in well-drained areas of the upper marsh, also at the base of sea-walls, on muddy shingle and on rocks and cliffs, especially in the west; north to Galloway and Northumbria, and along the east and south coasts of Ireland.

Flowering time: July to October.

SEA PURSLANE is a conspicuous feature of salt-marshes in England and Wales, fringing creeks and sometimes covering great areas. It is not a pretty plant, but its massed grey hummocks add to the sombre charm of the salt-marsh landscape on a sunny day. It is commoner in the east, although its distribution in the west has probably been limited by a history of heavy grazing on salt-marshes. In the damper climate of western Britain and Ireland, Sea Purslane occurs on cliffs and rocks, as do other salt-marsh plants such as Sea Aster (p.289).

Another fleshy shrub, Shrubby Sea-blite (*Suaeda vera*), sometimes dominates the salt-marsh-shingle boundary, locally from The Wash to Dorset. It is more erect and has narrow, cylindrical, dark green leaves.

Top *Sea Purslane* (Atriplex portulacoides) *has tiny, yellowish flowers in dense, branched clusters, contrasting with the grey foliage of its elliptical, leathery leaves.*

Bottom *A major component of the plant communities on saltmarshes, the hummocky bushes of Sea Purslane form dense swards along creeks and in well-drained areas of the upper marsh.*

SPECIES INFORMATION	
COMMON NAME	Marsh Samphire, Glasswort
SCIENTIFIC NAME	Salicornia europaea
RELATED SPECIES	Annual Sea-blite
HEIGHT/SPREAD	5–30 cm tall
FLOWERING TIME	July–October
HABITAT	Salt marshes

Note: Like a miniature, fleshy Christmas tree.

Marsh Samphire

GOOSEFOOT FAMILY

(Chenopodiaceae)

Size and appearance: An erect, hairless annual 5–30 cm (2–12 in) tall, green or yellowish-green in summer, red or purplish in autumn, with cylindrical, jointed fleshy stems and paired branches.

Leaves: Paired, fleshy sheaths that are indistinct from the stems.

Flowers: Minute, in 3s at the margin of the stem joints, green, marked by 1-2 tiny yellow stamens.

Fruits: Tiny, hairy, embedded in the stems.

Related or similar plants: Annual Sea-blite is a fleshy seashore annual, but has well-developed leaves.

Habitat and distribution: In sometimes vast stands in muddy or sandy salt-marshes all around the coasts of Britain and Ireland, but especially in East Anglia and on the south coast.

Flowering time: August to September.

Bottom left *Annual Sea-blite* (Suaeda maritima) *is fleshy and has distinct, pointed, bluish-green to reddish or purplish leaves, with clusters of greenish flowers approximately 2.5 mm (1/10 in) across.*

THIS IS THE commonest of a half-dozen native annual glassworts (and a similar perennial species), each adapted to live at a particular level of the marsh. To identify the various glassworts precisely involves the use of a microscope or powerful hand-lens, patience and more than a modicum of expertise. They comprise an important little community that helps to bind and consolidate sediment.

Glasswort is still gathered on the salt-marshes of East Anglia and elsewhere, and sold by fishmongers and delicatessen shops as samphire. Boiled and served with butter or (cold) vinaigrette, this is just as delicious as asparagus, although it goes a bit gritty in autumn as the tiny seeds mature. The samphire famously mentioned in William Shakespeare's King Lear is Rock Samphire (p.177), a member of the carrot family.

Top and bottom right *Marsh Samphire* (Salicornia europaea) *can occur in vast stands on muddy or sandy salt-marshes. In East Anglia it is commonly gathered and sold as a delicacy.*

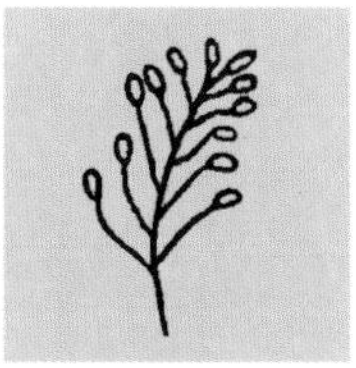

FLOWER TYPE

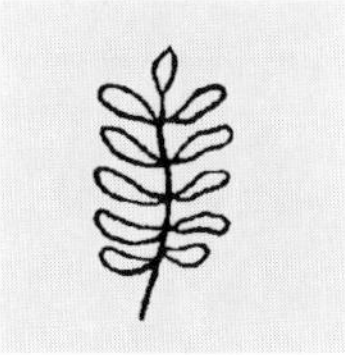

IDENTIFICATION

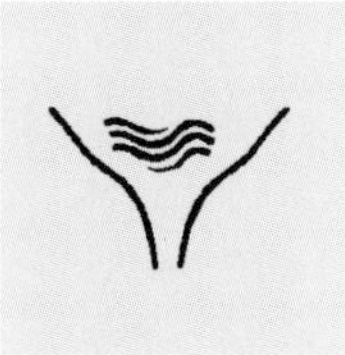

HABITAT

POPULATION

MAP

Spring Beauty

PURSLANE FAMILY
(Portulacaceae)

SPECIES INFORMATION	
COMMON NAME	Spring Beauty
SCIENTIFIC NAME	Claytonia perfoliata
RELATED SPECIES	Pink Purslane
HEIGHT/SPREAD	5–30 cm tall
FLOWERING TIME	March–July
HABITAT	Disturbed ground on light soils

Note: Unlikely to be confused with any other plant.

FLOWER TYPE

IDENTIFICATION

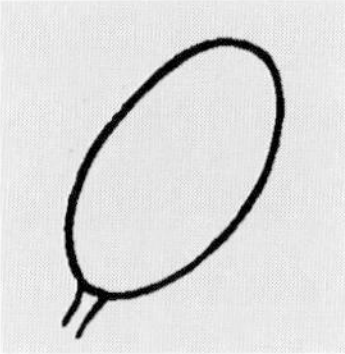

HABITAT

POPULATION

MAP

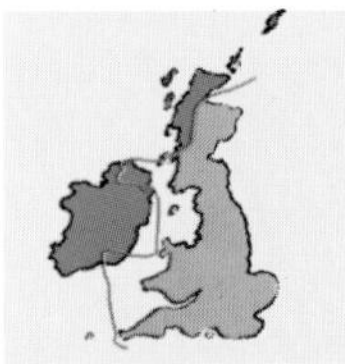

Size and appearance: A slender, tufted, slightly fleshy, pale green annual 5–30 cm (2–12 in) tall.

Leaves: Mostly in a basal rosette, long-stalked, broadly oval; stem leaves fused into a collar beneath the flowers.

Flowers: White, 5–8 mm (1/5–1/3 in) across, in small clusters framed by a leaf-collar.

Fruits: Small, spherical capsules.

Related or similar plants: Pink Purslane has unfused stem leaves and pink, notched petals.

Habitat and distribution: Sometimes present in great numbers on light soils, on cultivated land, dry banks, woodland margins and bare, sandy ground, throughout Britain except northern Scotland, but much rarer in the west; occasional in Ireland.

Flowering time: March to July.

SPRING BEAUTY, INTRODUCED from western North America in 1852, is as familiar to some people as it is unfamiliar to others. It does not grow everywhere, for it requires light, usually lime-poor soils on which to thrive. However, where it does occur, the plants are often remarkably abundant. It is, for example, one of many interesting and exotic bulbfield weeds in the Isles of Scilly. The plant can be cooked like spinach and goes well in salads, where it is decorative as well as edible.

Bottom left *Pink Purslane* (Claytonia sibirica) *is a similar but slightly taller, more perennial plant with narrower basal leaves, unfused stem leaves and pink flowers 10-15 mm (2/5-3/5 in) across, with veined, notched petals. It is locally common in damp, shady places, mainly in northern Britain and the West Country.*

Top *The flowers of Spring Beauty* (Claytonia perfoliata) *are unusual in that they arise from the centre of the leaves, appearing to be framed by an Elizabethan ruff.*

SPECIES INFORMATION	
COMMON NAME	Hottentot Fig
SCIENTIFIC NAME	Carpobrotus edulis
RELATED SPECIES	Other 'mesems'
HEIGHT/SPREAD	Stems 1–4 m long
FLOWERING TIME	April–August
HABITAT	Cliffs, rocks, sand-dunes

Note: Prominant mats of fleshy leaves and huge flowers.

Hottentot Fig

MESEMBRYANTHEMUM FAMILY
(Aizoaceae)

Top *Hottentot Fig* (Carpobrotus edulis) *flowers can be pale yellow or a rich pinkish-purple with yellow centres, and are 5-10 cm (2-4 in) across.*

Bottom *Hottentot Fig forms dense swathes with its far-creeping stems over the coastal cliffs of the south-west.*

FLOWER TYPE

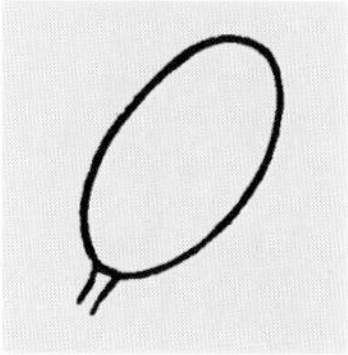
IDENTIFICATION

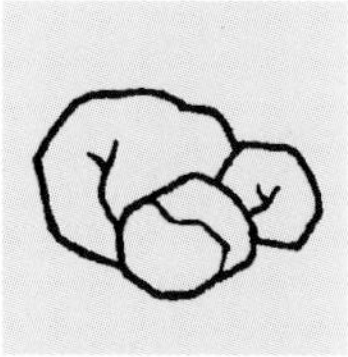
HABITAT

POPULATION

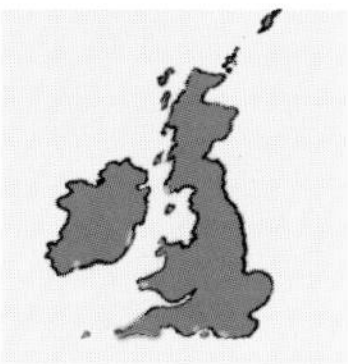
MAP

Size and appearance: A far-creeping, hairless perennial, with tough, often woody, prostrate or trailing stems 1–4 m long (3–12 ft) long.
Leaves: Up to 10 cm (4 in) long, fleshy, 3-angled, slightly curved, pointed, dark green, often becoming reddish.
Flowers: Pale yellow or rich pinkish-purple 5–10 cm (2–4 in) across, with numerous petals and yellow stamens.
Fruits: Fleshy knobs, decaying to release the numerous small seeds.
Related or similar plants: Other related mesems sometimes escape on to rocks and banks.
Habitat and distribution: An established garden escape that drapes cliffs, rocks, seaside banks and sand-dunes along the coasts of the West Country and here and there elsewhere in Britain and Ireland.
Flowering time: April to August.

THIS HUGE, EXTREMELY conspicuous plant has come to be a feature of the seaside landscape in several coastal areas, especially Cornwall and the Isles of Scilly. It is a magnificent sight in flower in late spring and early summer, but conservationists are concerned that it is invading fragile and important native vegetation, especially on sand-dunes and on some cliffs in the Lizard peninsula. The plant is salt- and drought-tolerant, and will root readily from fragments. Seagulls are thought to spread it to remote cliffs and islets by taking lengths of stem for nesting material.

Hottentot Fig is one of several members of its family (known to succulent-enthusiasts as mesems), all natives of South Africa, that are grown in gardens in the mild climate of Cornwall and the west. Other species, also with brightly coloured flowers, sometimes escape or are planted into the wild.

Greater Stitchwort

CARNATION AND CAMPION FAMILY
(Caryophyllaceae)

SPECIES INFORMATION	
COMMON NAME	Greater Stitchwort
SCIENTIFIC NAME	Stellaria holostea
RELATED SPECIES	Chickweed, Lesser Stitchwort
HEIGHT/SPREAD	Stems 20–60 cm tall
FLOWERING TIME	March–July
HABITAT	Woods and hedge-banks

Note: The large, white flowers on their slim stalks are distinctive.

FLOWER TYPE

IDENTIFICATION

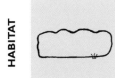

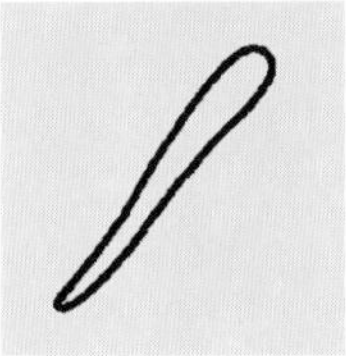

HABITAT

POPULATION

MAP

Size and appearance: A slender perennial with weak, 4-angled, semi-erect or straggling stems 20–60 cm (12–24 in) long.
Leaves: In opposite pairs, narrow, tapered to a point, with rough margins, slightly greyish-green.
Flowers: White, 15–25 mm (3/5–1 in) across, with 5 petals divided to half-way and 10 pale yellow stamens, in loose clusters.
Fruits: Spherical nodding capsules, splitting by 6 teeth.
Related or similar plants: Lesser Stitchwort is a more slender, straggling plant, with smaller petals divided almost to the base.
Habitat and distribution: Common and often forming extensive patches in hedgerows, woodland rides and margins, and grassy waysides, avoiding the most lime-poor soils; throughout, but scarcer in northern Scotland and western Ireland.
Flowering time: March to July.

Bottom right and top left *Greater Stitchwort* (Stellaria holostea) *has white flowers 15-25 mm (3.5-1 in) across with five petals divided to half-way. Leaves are narrow, tapering to a point and in opposite pairs.*

Bottom left *Greater Stitchwort commonly forms extensive patches on hedgerow banks, woodland rides and margins.*

GREATER STITCHWORT IS one of the earliest and most atmospheric of spring flowers, brightening woods and hedgerows with bold splashes of white. It makes a wonderful natural colour combination with Red Campion (p.42) and Bluebell (p.338). The individual flowers are delicate, on slender stalks that reflect the English name. It was also a supposed remedy for a stitch or sudden pain in the side or stomach. Like several wild flowers, Stitchwort was once regarded by the superstitious as a thunder plant, one which would induce thunder if picked. Other untoward events after picking might be an adder bite or the gatherer being led astray by elves or fairies.

SPECIES INFORMATION	
COMMON NAME	Chickweed
SCIENTIFIC NAME	Stellaria media
RELATED SPECIES	Sandworts
HEIGHT/SPREAD	Stems 5–40 cm long
FLOWERING TIME	February–November
HABITAT	Cultivated ground and waste places

Note: A familiar garden weed.

Chickweed

CARNATION AND CAMPION FAMILY

(Caryophyllaceae)

Size and appearance: A prostrate or sprawling annual, with weak, straggling stems 5–40 cm (2–16 in) long, marked on opposite sides by a line of whitish hairs.

Leaves: In opposite pairs, only the lower stalked, oval or spear-shaped, 1-veined, pointed.

Flowers: White, 4–10 mm (1/6–2/5 in) across, with 5 deeply notched petals and 3–8 reddish stamens, in branched clusters.

Fruits: Egg-shaped capsules, splitting by 6 teeth, nodding when ripe.

Related or similar plants: Thyme-leaved Sandwort has greyish-downy leaves and unnotched petals.

Habitat and distribution: A ubiquitous and abundant weed of cultivated land and waste ground, especially on light but rich soils, and also on river shingle and coastal cliffs and islets where seabirds nest.

Flowering time: February to November, but all through mild winters.

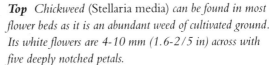

Top *Chickweed* (Stellaria media) *can be found in most flower beds as it is an abundant weed of cultivated ground. Its white flowers are 4-10 mm (1.6-2/5 in) across with five deeply notched petals.*

CHICKWEED IS A familiar garden weed, but nevertheless its early flowers are a welcome sight as spring emerges from winter. It is one of the very first flowers of the year, alongside Shepherd's Purse (p.72), Red Dead-nettle (p.234) and Groundsel (p.307). It can be a serious weed of vegetable crops, since it requires and tolerates high nutrient levels, growing even on the periphery of manure heaps. One of its ancestral habitats may well have been seabird nest-sites, but it is now very much one of our camp-followers.

Several members of this family have small, white flowers. As well as Thyme-leaved Sandwort, one may come across Three-veined Sandwort (*Moehringia trinervia*). This delicate, straggling annual of woodland has 3–5 veins on each leaf, and unnotched petals.

FLOWER TYPE

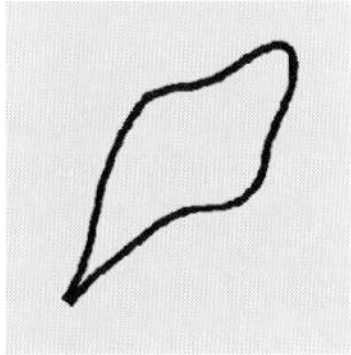

IDENTIFICATION

HABITAT

POPULATION

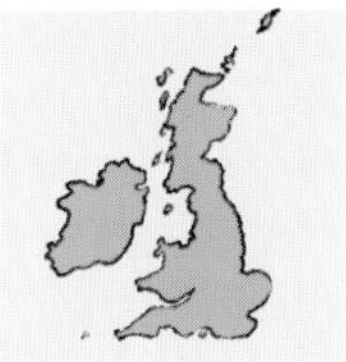

MAP

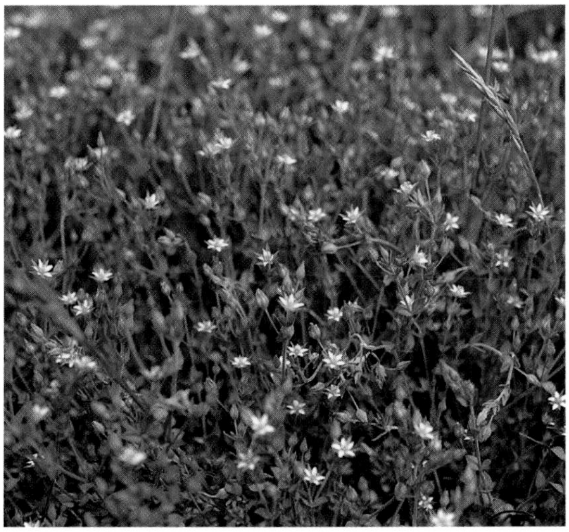

Bottom *Thyme-leaved Sandwort* (Arenaria serpyllifolia) *is similar but has tiny, stalkless, greyish-downy leaves, unnotched petals and erect, flask-shaped capsules. Flowering April–September, it grows on dry, open or cultivated ground; throughout, but less common in the north and west.*

Common Mouse-ear Chickweed

CARNATION AND CAMPION FAMILY
(Caryophyllaceae)

SPECIES INFORMATION	
COMMON NAME	Common Mouse-ear Chickweed
SCIENTIFIC NAME	Cerastium fontanum
RELATED SPECIES	Chickweed
HEIGHT/SPREAD	Stems 10–60 cm long
FLOWERING TIME	April–November
HABITAT	Cultivated ground and grassland

Note: Like a hairy, stiffer and more erect Chickweed.

FLOWER TYPE

IDENTIFICATION

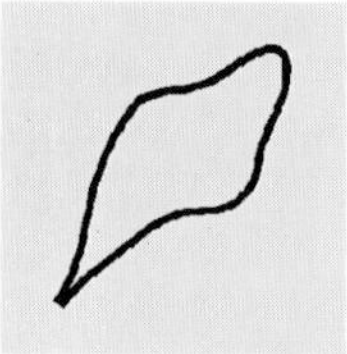

HABITAT

POPULATION

MAP

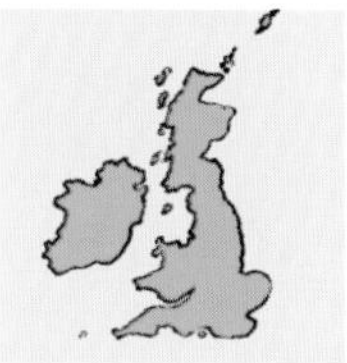

COMMON MOUSE-EAR CHICKWEED is the commonest of a small group of native annual and perennial species. It is ubiquitous in grassy places, especially where scuffing or other mechanical disturbance has created small gaps. It is extremely variable, divided up into a series of poorly-defined subspecies of different habitats and geographical regions across Europe. On mountains the flowers are often large and conspicuous; on river-banks plants are larger and more sprawling, the stems up to 90 cm (36 in) long and the leaves up to 35 mm (1⅜ in) long.

Size and appearance: A sprawling or erect, hairy short-lived perennial, with flowering stems 10–60 cm (4–24 in) long and shorter, leafy, non-flowering shoots.
Leaves: Stalkless, up to 25 mm (1 in) long, narrowly oval, blunt, densely hairy.
Flowers: White, 6–10 mm (¼–⅜ in) across, with 5 deeply notched petals scarcely longer than the sepals, in branched clusters.
Fruits: Erect, slightly curved, cylindrical capsules.
Related or similar plants: Chickweed (p.35) is more prostrate, with thinner, paler, hairless leaves; Field Mouse-ear Chickweed has flowers up to 20 mm (⅘ in) across.
Habitat and distribution: Common throughout in disturbed grassland and waste ground, and by the sea, on cliffs, mountains and riversides.
Flowering time: April to November.

Top and bottom right *Common Mouse-ear* (Cerastium fontanum) *has stalkless opposite leaves which are densely hairy. Its flowers have five deeply notched white petals.*

Bottom left *Field Mouse-ear Chickweed* (Cerastium arvense) *is similar but more prostrate and with showy flowers 12–20 mm (½–⅘ in) across, more like those of Greater Stitchwort. Flowering April–August, it is widespread but local on light or lime-rich soils, especially in eastern Britain.*

SPECIES INFORMATION	
COMMON NAME	Sand Spurrey
SCIENTIFIC NAME	Spergularia rubra
RELATED SPECIES	Corn Spurrey
HEIGHT/SPREAD	Stems 5–25 cm long
FLOWERING TIME	May–October
HABITAT	Open, stony or sandy places

Note: Superficially like a sticky-hairy, pink-flowered Chickweed.

Sand Spurrey

CARNATION AND CAMPION FAMILY

(Caryophyllaceae)

FLOWER TYPE

IDENTIFICATION

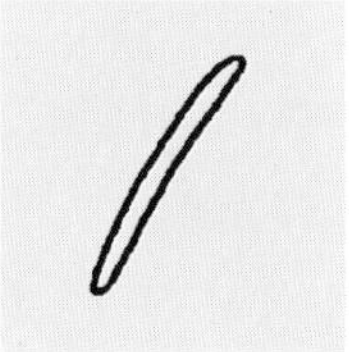

HABITAT

POPULATION

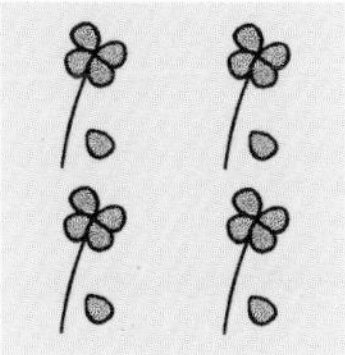

MAP

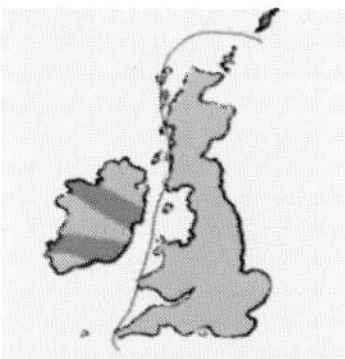

Size and appearance: A sticky-hairy annual, biennial or short-lived perennial, with spreading, leafy stems 5–25 cm (2–10 in) long.
Leaves: In whorls, small, greyish-green, very narrow, with bristle-pointed tips; each with a pair of minute, silvery scales or stipules at the base.
Flowers: Pale pink, 3–5 mm (⅛–⅕ in) across, in small clusters, with 5 un-notched petals slightly shorter than the sepals.
Fruits: Egg-shaped capsules containing numerous unwinged seeds.
Related or similar plants: Other spurreys.
Habitat and distribution: Widespread and often locally frequent in open ground on sandy and gravelly soils of heaths, dry, lime-poor grassland and rocky ground; throughout, but rarer in the north and west, and very scattered in Ireland.
Flowering time: May to October.

SAND SPURREY IS especially a plant of pathsides and car-parks, sometimes forming thick mats. It belongs within a group of slightly scruffy, low-growing plants, related but different from Chickweed (p.35) and Stitchwort (p.34). Most grow in bare ground; several are rare and at the northern edge of their range.

Other species in this group grow by the sea and have thick, fleshy leaves. These include Rock Sea-spurrey (*Spergularia rupicola*), similar to Sand Spurrey but a more robust perennial, with pink flowers 8–12 mm (⅓–½ in) across, of coastal cliffs, rocks and walls in western Britain and Ireland. Another species, Greater Sea-spurrey grows in salt-marshes.

Bottom *Greater Sea-spurrey* (Spergularia media) *is similar to Sand Spurrey but is a hairless perennial, with pink or whitish flowers 8–12 mm (⅓–½ in) across, the petals longer than the sepals, and mostly winged seeds. It is widespread around Britain in salt-marshes where it occurs on the drier parts.*

Corn Spurrey

CARNATION AND CAMPION FAMILY
(Caryophyllaceae)

SPECIES INFORMATION	
COMMON NAME	Corn Spurrey
SCIENTIFIC NAME	Spergula arvensis
RELATED SPECIES	Sand Spurrey
HEIGHT/SPREAD	5–30 cm tall
FLOWERING TIME	May–October
HABITAT	Cultivated Ground

Note: A distinctive weed of cultivated land on lime-poor soils.

FLOWER TYPE

IDENTIFICATION

HABITAT

POPULATION

MAP

Size and appearance: A hairless, downy or sticky-hairy, straggling or erect annual 5–30 cm (2–12 in) tall.
Leaves: In whorls of 8, small, narrow, blunt, furrowed beneath; each with a pair of minute, papery scales or stipules at the base.
Flowers: White, 3–5 mm (1/8–1/5 in) across, in branched clusters, with 5 un-notched petals slightly longer than the sepals.
Fruits: Egg-shaped capsules containing numerous very narrowly winged seeds.
Related or similar plants: Sand Spurrey (p.37) is more prostrate and has pink flowers.
Habitat and distribution: A widespread weed of cereal fields and other cultivated land on lime-poor, usually light soils, and on disturbed waysides, more rarely in sandy ground by the sea; decreasing, like many weeds of cultivation.
Flowering time: May to October.

CORN SPURREY IS an attractive little weed that still sometimes appears in great crowds. It was once as much a fodder crop and food plant as a weed. Like those of Persicaria (p.17), the seeds formed part of the last meal of the unfortunate Tollund Man and other ancient bog burials in Denmark. A robust, larger-seeded variant turns up from time to time, suggesting that farmers used to select high-yielding plants from the wild populations. Fossil finds from all over Europe indicate that the seeds of Corn Spurrey were mixed with those of other wild plants that we no longer eat.

The flowers of Corn Spurrey (Spergularia arvensis) *consist of five unnotched white petals, which occur in branched clusters above the leaves, in whorls of eight up the stem. Although an attractive weed, it can appear as a straggling mass when in quantity. It is usually found on light soils disturbed by cultivation although it is often now more plentiful in places such as allotments than cereal fields.*

SPECIES INFORMATION	
COMMON NAME	Sea Sandwort
SCIENTIFIC NAME	Honckenya peploides
RELATED SPECIES	Chickweed
HEIGHT/SPREAD	5–15 cm tall
FLOWERING TIME	May–July
HABITAT	Sandy and gravelly seashores

Note: Patches of fleshy leaves in 4 ranks.

Sea Sandwort

CARNATION AND CAMPION FAMILY
(Caryophyllaceae)

Size and appearance: A creeping, prostrate, hairless, fleshy perennial, with mats of semi-erect stems 5–15 cm (2–4 in) long, pushing through sand or fine shingle.
Leaves: In 4 ranks like a miniature houseplant, stout, fleshy, stalkless, pointed, yellowish-green.
Flowers: Either male or female, greenish-white or white, 6–10 mm (¼–⅔ in) across, in clusters of up to 6, the 5 spoon-shaped petals slightly shorter than the sepals.
Fruits: Spherical, yellowish-green capsules up to 10 mm (⅔ in) across, splitting by 6 teeth.
Related or similar plants: Chickweed (p.35) and other members of the family are somewhat similar but lack the 4-ranked, fleshy leaves.
Habitat and distribution: Locally common all around the coast on sandy seashores or shingle beaches, especially where the shingle is fine, sometimes near the front of sand-dunes but never far away from the shore.
Flowering time: May to July.

***Top** The fruit of Sea Sandwort* (Honckenya peploides) *is very conspicuous amongst the four yellowish-green ranked fleshy leaves. The spherical capsules can be up to 10 mm (⅔ in) across.*

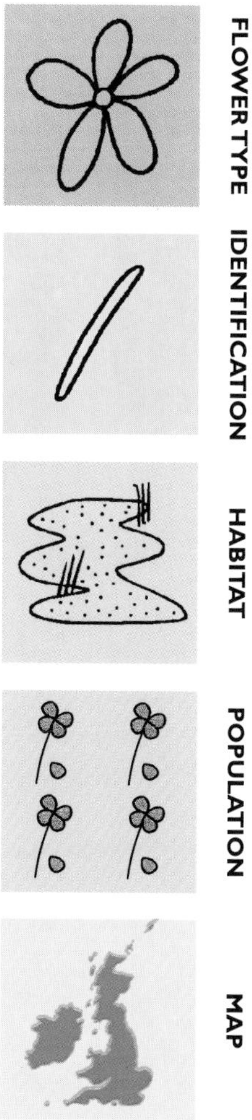

A STRIKING PLANT of sandy seashores, just occasionally among rocks, its geometrical, fleshy spires of leaves seemingly cry out for attention from the passer-by. The leaves used to be pickled and eaten, especially in northern England. The rather odd first half of the scientific name commemorates an obscure 18th century German botanist, G. H. Honkeny.

Although still common, this and other plants of sandy seashores are vulnerable to the excessive trampling of beaches by summer visitors. Sand Purslane is able to grow up through accreting sand and sometimes small embryonic sand-dunes develop around its colonies. Other plants will subsequently colonise these hummocks and bind the sand further, helping to stabilise the shore.

***Bottom left and right** Common on shingly shores, Sea Sandwort forms carpets of green across the beach. Flowers appear from May to July, and are white or greenish-white and 6-10 mm (¼ – ⅔ in) across in clusters.*

Mossy Pearlwort

CARNATION AND CAMPION FAMILY
(Caryophyllaceae)

SPECIES INFORMATION	
COMMON NAME	Mossy Pearlwort
SCIENTIFIC NAME	Sagina procumbens
RELATED SPECIES	Other pearlworts
HEIGHT/SPREAD	Stems 5–20 cm long
FLOWERING TIME	May–October
HABITAT	Open, stony or grassy places

Note: A small green weed of paths and paved areas.

FLOWER TYPE

IDENTIFICATION

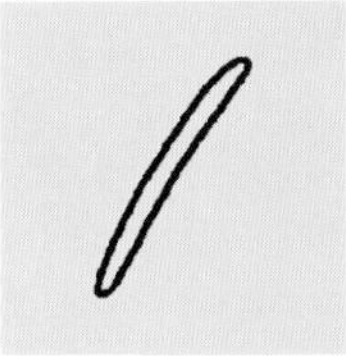

HABITAT

POPULATION

MAP

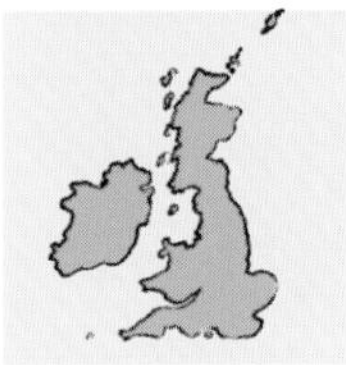

Size and appearance: A moss-like, more or less hairless, prostrate or trailing perennial, with a central leaf-rosette and spreading, leafy stems 5–20 cm (2–8 in) long.

Leaves: In opposite pairs, small, very narrow, pointed.

Flowers: Solitary on slender, erect stalks, white, 4–6 mm ($\frac{1}{6}$–$\frac{1}{4}$ in) across, with 4 (rarely 5) petals, often minute or absent.

Fruits: Egg-shaped capsules on long stalks, drooping before they ripen; the 4 sepals spreading in fruit.

Related or similar plants: Other pearlworts.

Habitat and distribution: A very common but overlooked little plant of damp, open, stony or grassy places, walls, paths, pavements and terraces, also in the mountains and on shingle beaches.

Flowering time: May to October.

MOSSY PEARLWORT IS the sort of plant that one passes by every day and fails to notice, except when weeding. It is a persistent weed of damp, paved areas and paths. It is one of a group of related species that are difficult to tell apart. The other common species of this group, Annual Pearlwort (*Sagina apetala*), is a sparser-looking, more erect plant without a central leaf-rosette. It has a more scattered and more southern distribution. Neither quite merits the appellation 'wild flower', but both are important colonist species of bare ground.

Top *With a central rosette of leaves, the Pearlwort produces procumbent lateral stems which root and then ascend at their tips. It can form quite dense patches in lawns, on walls and pavements and in flower beds.*

Bottom *Mossy Pearlwort* (Sagina procumbens) *has solitary flowers, which are 4–6 mm ($\frac{1}{6}$–$\frac{1}{4}$ in) in size. The four sepals are conspicuous as the petals are often minute or absent.*

SPECIES INFORMATION	
COMMON NAME	Ragged Robin
SCIENTIFIC NAME	Lychnis flos-cuculi
RELATED SPECIES	Red Campion
HEIGHT/SPREAD	25–100 cm tall
FLOWERING TIME	May–July
HABITAT	Marshes and damp meadows

Note: The deeply lobed pink petals are unusual.

Ragged Robin

CARNATION AND CAMPION FAMILY

(Caryophyllaceae)

Size and appearance: An almost hairless, often reddish, branched perennial, with erect stems 25–100 cm (10–40 in) tall.

Leaves: In opposite pairs, the lower oblong or spoon-shaped, the upper narrow, spear-shaped, pointed.

Flowers: Deep pink, 20–25 mm (⅘–1 in) across, the 5 petals each deeply 4-lobed, in loose, branched clusters; calyx 10-veined.

Fruits: Cylindrical capsules opening by 5 short teeth, enclosed within the persistent, prominently red-veined calyx.

Related or similar plants: Red Campion (p.42) has shallowly 2-lobed petals and capsules with 10 back-curved teeth.

Habitat and distribution: A widespread but locally decreasing plant of marshes, damp meadows, and wet woodland clearings and rides; throughout, but commoner in the north and west.

Flowering time: May to July.

RAGGED ROBIN, WITH its apparently ragged, deeply-lobed pink petals, is one of the most attractive and typical wild flowers of wet meadows. Like so many once-common plants, it is a good deal less frequent in much of lowland Britain than of old, because of the destruction of the traditionally managed meadows by modern agriculture. Ragged Robin does at least have a great future in gardens, and there one sees both the meadow plant and choice dwarf and white-flowered variants. Four centuries ago, John Gerard observed charitably of this species that: 'These are not used either in medicine or in nourishment: but they serve for garlands or crowns, and to decke up gardens.' How right he was.

Top *Ragged Robin* (Lychnis flos-cuculi) *is widespread in damp woodland rides and marshy areas, but its colourful display is less frequent than in the past due to changes in agricultural practice.*

Bottom *The bright pink flowers are 20-25 mm (4/5-1 in) across and each of the five petals is deeply four-lobed. At first they have a very elegant appearance but wind and rain soon make them look ragged.*

FLOWER TYPE

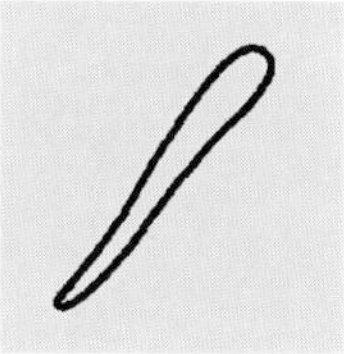
IDENTIFICATION

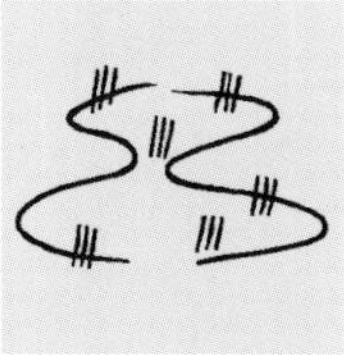
HABITAT

POPULATION

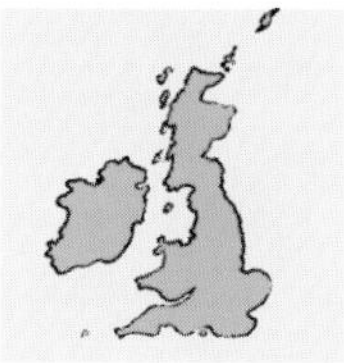
MAP

Red Campion

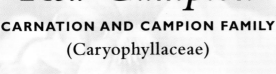

CARNATION AND CAMPION FAMILY (Caryophyllaceae)

SPECIES INFORMATION	
COMMON NAME	Red Campion
SCIENTIFIC NAME	Silene dioica
RELATED SPECIES	Ragged Robin
HEIGHT/SPREAD	20–80cm tall
FLOWERING TIME	April to November
HABITAT	Woods and hedgerows

Note: The deeply pink flower of woods in spring.

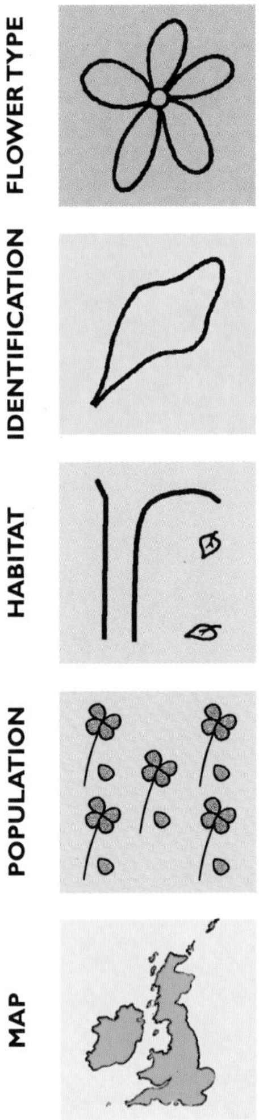

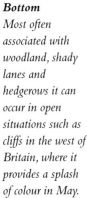

Size and appearance: A hairy, sometimes reddish, branched biennial or perennial, with erect stems 20–80 cm (12–32 in) tall.
Leaves: In opposite pairs, broadly spear-shaped, pointed, persisting in winter.
Flowers: Male and female on separate plants, deep pink, 15–25 mm (⅗–1 in) across, unscented, the 5 petals each deeply notched, in loose clusters; calyx (male) 10- or (female) 20-veined.
Fruits: Cylindrical capsules opening by 10 curved-back teeth.
Related or similar plants: Ragged Robin (p.41) has deeply 4-lobed petals and seed-capsules with 5 teeth.
Habitat and distribution: For the most part widespread and abundant in woodland, shady lanes, hedgerows, and on mountain ledges and coastal cliffs, but scarce and scattered in Ireland, mainly in the north and east, and local in parts of East Anglia.
Flowering time: April to November, but all through mild winters.

Top *The deep pink flowers of Red Campion* (Silene dioica) *have five deeply notched petals 15–25mm (3.5–1 in) across and grow in branched clusters above opposite pairs of leaves on the stem.*

Bottom
Most often associated with woodland, shady lanes and hedgerows it can occur in open situations such as cliffs in the west of Britain, where it provides a splash of colour in May.

RED CAMPION and White Campion (p.43) often cross where they meet, especially where the habitat has been disturbed, perhaps by the grubbing out of a hedge. The hybrids are somewhat similar to Red Campion but taller, with pale pink flowers. Red Campion is a native woodland plant that appears to have expanded its range, owing to adaptation to more open habitats introduced into its hereditary material by generations of this crossing and backcrossing. Gardeners grow a handsome double-flowered variant, and a compact coastal variant occurs naturally in Shetland and elsewhere.

SPECIES INFORMATION	
COMMON NAME	White Campion
SCIENTIFIC NAME	Silene latifolia
RELATED SPECIES	Bladder Campion
HEIGHT/SPREAD	30–100 cm tall
FLOWERING TIME	May–October
HABITAT	Waysides and cultivated land

Note: A robust, hairy campion with white flowers.

White Campion

CARNATION AND CAMPION FAMILY
(Caryophyllaceae)

Size and appearance: A softly and densely hairy biennial or short-lived perennial, with erect, branched stems 30–100 cm (12–40 in) tall.

Leaves: In opposite pairs, broadly spear-shaped, pointed.

Flowers: Male and female on separate plants, white, 20–30 mm ($\frac{4}{5}$–$1\frac{1}{5}$ in) across, clove-scented, the 5 petals each deeply notched, in broad, loose clusters; calyx (male) 10- or (female) 20-veined.

Fruits: Egg-shaped capsules opening by 10 erect teeth.

Related or similar plants: Bladder Campion (p.44) has greyish, hairless leaves and a more inflated, bladder-like calyx.

Habitat and distribution: Locally common on waysides, hedge-banks, field margins and cultivated ground.

Flowering time: May to October.

THE LARGE WHITE FLOWERS are at their most conspicuous and richly scented at dusk, in order to attract the moths that pollinate them. As noted under Red Campion (p.42), White and Red Campions cross where they meet, especially where the habitat has been disturbed. This produces mixed populations, the flowers exhibiting a range of shades of pink. The subsequent backcrosses tend to move in the direction of Red Campion, and most populations of White Campion, isolated in open and disturbed ground, are fairly 'pure'-looking.

White Campion has a wide distribution from north-west Africa to Central Asia, and probably arrived in Britain with migrating peoples during the Stone Age.

Top The flowers of the White Campion are similar to those of its relative the Red Campion but, as its name suggests, they are white, except in the proximity to Red Campion where they can be various shades of pink due to hybridisation between the two species. It is a plant of waysides, field margins and cultivated ground.

FLOWER TYPE

IDENTIFICATION

HABITAT

POPULATION

MAP

Bottom
White Campion (Silene latifolia) *is a softly and densely haired plant with erect, branched stems 30-100 cm (12-40 in) tall. Its leaves are in opposite pairs as is typical of the Campions.*

Bladder Campion

CARNATION AND CAMPION FAMILY

(Caryophyllaceae)

SPECIES INFORMATION	
COMMON NAME	Bladder Campion
SCIENTIFIC NAME	Silene vulgaris
RELATED SPECIES	Sea Campion
HEIGHT/SPREAD	20–60 cm tall
FLOWERING TIME	May–September
HABITAT	Open grassland
Note: The bladder-like calyx is unusual.	

FLOWER TYPE

IDENTIFICATION

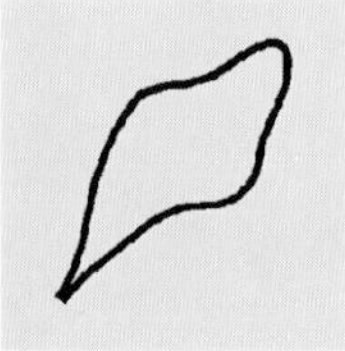

HABITAT

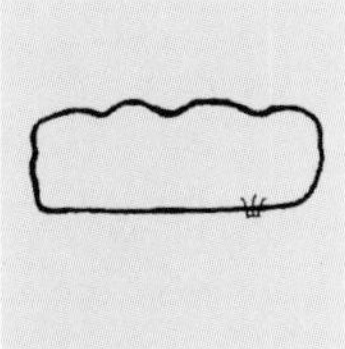

POPULATION

MAP

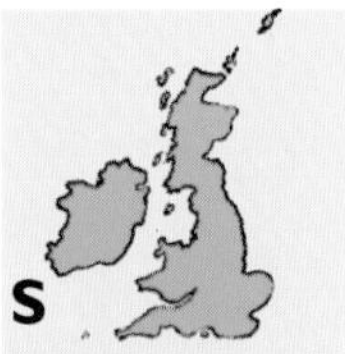

Top The white flowers, 10-18 mm (⅖-¾ in) across, have five deeply notched petals and an inflated 'bladdery' calyx which narrows at its mouth.

Size and appearance: A more or less hairless, greyish perennial, with semi-erect, branched stems 20–60 cm (12–36 in) tall.

Leaves: In opposite pairs, oval, rather stiff, pointed, waxy, greyish.

Flowers: White, 10–18 mm (⅖–¾ in) across, scented, the 5 petals each deeply notched, in loose clusters; calyx egg-shaped, bladder-like, yellowish or purplish.

Fruits: Cylindrical capsules, opening by 5 teeth, enclosed within the persistent papery calyx.

Related or similar plants: Sea Campion (p.45) has more prostrate, unbranched stems and flowers up to 25 mm (1 in) across.

Habitat and distribution: Generally widespread, if rather local, in open grassland, on dry banks and cultivated ground, especially on stony field margins; throughout, but scarce in western Scotland and northern Ireland.

Flowering time: May to September

BLADDER CAMPION IS a very variable species that many botanists do not separate from the larger-flowered Sea Campion (p.45). The flowers, like those of the showier White Campion (p.43), are most conspicuous and scented at dusk and are pollinated by night-flying moths.

A variant of Bladder Campion with pinkish petals and large seeds has long been established on Plymouth Hoe, from where it was even described as a new subspecies. We now know this plant to be identical to the common lowland subspecies of the Mediterranean region, where Bladder Campion is a weed of cultivated land. It is presumably an introduction, along with other interesting plants, reflecting Plymouth's long maritime history.

Bottom right and left *Bladder Campion* (Silene vulgaris) *is an almost hairless, greyish perennial with semi-erect, branched stems 20-60 cm (12-36 in) tall. It is generally widespread particularly where there is a chalky influence to the soil on dry banks and open grassland. The variant with pinkish petals is shown to the left.*

SPECIES INFORMATION	
COMMON NAME	Sea Campion
SCIENTIFIC NAME	Silene uniflora
RELATED SPECIES	Bladder Campion
HEIGHT/SPREAD	20–30 cm
FLOWERING TIME	May–August
HABITAT	Cliffs and shingle beaches

Note: Grey seaside mats, with plentiful white flowers in summer.

Sea Campion

CARNATION AND CAMPION FAMILY

(Caryophyllaceae)

Size and appearance: A hairless or slightly downy perennial, forming patches and loose cushions, with prostrate or sprawling, unbranched stems 10–30 cm (4–12 in) tall.

Leaves: In opposite pairs, spear-shaped, stiff, pointed, fleshy, grey.

Flowers: 2–3 together, white, 20–25 mm (⅘–1 in) across, the 5 petals each deeply notched, in loose clusters; bladder-like calyx cylindrical, greenish, yellowish or purplish.

Fruits: Cylindrical capsules, opening by 5 teeth, enclosed within the persistent, papery calyx.

Related or similar plants: Bladder Campion (p.44) has more erect, branched stems and smaller flowers, and is usually found inland.

Habitat and distribution: A feature of shingle beaches, cliffs, rocks and walls near the sea, all around the coasts of Britain and Ireland, although absent from parts of the east and south-east coasts of England; also inland in few places in the mountains and hilly districts, especially on lead-rich rocks and the spoil-heaps of old lead mines.

Flowering time: May to August, with a few flowers until October.

FLOWER TYPE

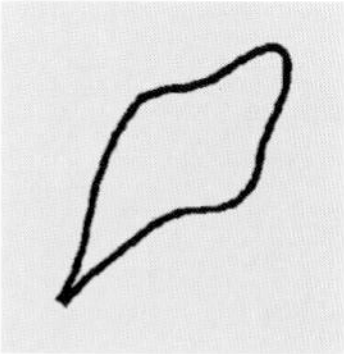

IDENTIFICATION

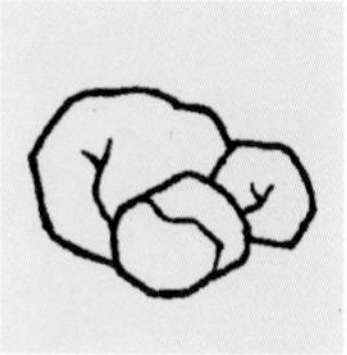

HABITAT

POPULATION

MAP

LIKE THE CLOSELY related Bladder Campion , this is a very variable species; many botanists do not separate the two, which sometimes grade together in appearance. The greatest variation occurs in the mountains of west and central Europe, and there several subspecies are recognised within both of these species. The flowers, like those of Bladder Campion and the showier White Campion (p.43), are most conspicuous and scented at dusk and are pollinated by night-flying moths.

The isolated inland sites of this lead- and copper-tolerant plant are most interesting, for example the ancient lead-mining district in the Mendips of Somerset, and lake-shores near old mine workings near Killarney in County Kerry. A particularly unusual habitat for Sea Campion is churchyards in west Wales, where it grows on lead-rich rock chippings used to cover graves.

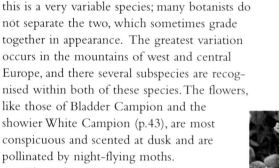

Sea Campion (Silene uniflora) *is a greyish perennial 10-30 cm (4-12 in) tall, which forms patches and loose cushions on coastal cliffs, rocks and shingle beaches. It can occur inland in specific situations.*

Moss Campion

CARNATION AND CAMPION FAMILY

(Caryophyllaceae)

SPECIES INFORMATION	
COMMON NAME	Moss Campion
SCIENTIFIC NAME	Silene acaulis
RELATED SPECIES	Campions
HEIGHT/SPREAD	2.5–5 cm tall
FLOWERING TIME	June–August
HABITAT	Mountain rocks and ledges

Note: Mountain cushions dotted with small, pink flowers.

FLOWER TYPE

IDENTIFICATION

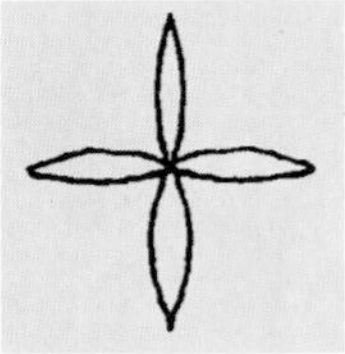

HABITAT

POPULATION

MAP

Size and appearance: A densely tufted perennial, forming compact, moss-like cushions 2.5–5 cm (1–2 in) tall.
Leaves: Tiny, in opposite pairs, narrow, stiff, pointed, hairy along the margin.
Flowers: Solitary, pale or deep pink, 8–12 mm (⅓–½ in) across, the 5 petals each notched; calyx bell-shaped.
Fruits: Cylindrical capsules twice as long as the calyx.
Related or similar plants: An unusual and distinctive campion.
Habitat and distribution: One of our commoner native alpine plants, of cliffs, rocks, screes and short grassland in the Highlands of Scotland, where it descends to near sea-level in the north, as it does extensively in Shetland; extending locally to the mountains of the Lake District and Snowdonia, and a few mountains and sea-cliffs in north-western Ireland.
Flowering time: June to August.

THIS DELIGHTFUL LITTLE PLANT is just as one imagines a true alpine to look in its natural habitat. The cushions are neat, tight and spongy, and in midsummer often covered with almost stalkless pink flowers. It is locally common at higher levels in parts of the Scottish Highlands, and the remote Irish populations are also said to be healthy. Elsewhere it occurs in the Arctic and on the higher mountain ranges of Europe south to northern Spain and the Balkans.

Top *Moss Campion* (Silene acaulis) *is an alpine occurring at the high levels in the Scottish mountains, but further north it can occur at sea level, as it does in the Shetlands.*

Bottom *Moss Campion is a densely tufted plant which forms dome-like mounds which are covered in bright pink flowers in summer.*

SPECIES INFORMATION	
COMMON NAME	Soapwort, Bouncing Bett
SCIENTIFIC NAME	Saponaria officinalis
RELATED SPECIES	Campions
HEIGHT/SPREAD	30–100 cm tall
FLOWERING TIME	May–September
HABITAT	Waysides and hedges

Note: Our largest campion-like plant, with very showy flowers.

Soapwort

CARNATION AND CAMPION FAMILY (Caryophyllaceae)

SOAPWORT IS AN OLD cottage garden plant that has become a fully naturalised member of our flora. It was used as a primitive soap for linen and wool cloth, by crushing the stems in hot water. All over Europe it occurs around villages and small rural communities, perhaps as a relic of its former use for soap. The plant's native range is probably southern and central Europe. It also had medicinal value as an expectorant for congested chests.

Variants with white and pink flowers, either single or double, are grown in gardens, but most plants established in the wild have pink flowers.

FLOWER TYPE

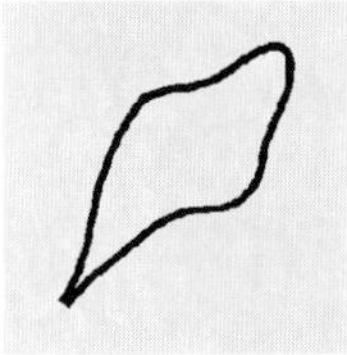

IDENTIFICATION

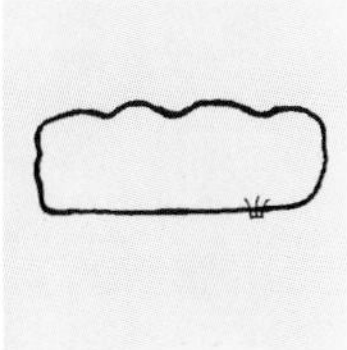

HABITAT

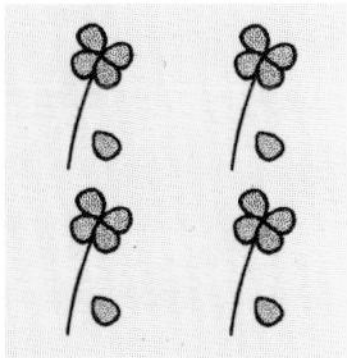

POPULATION

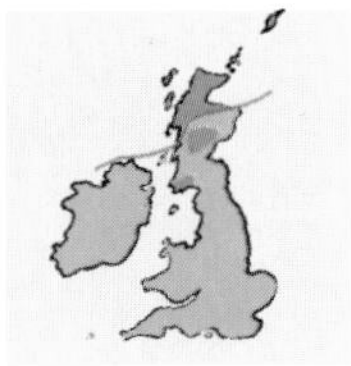

MAP

Size and appearance: A hairless, semi-erect or straggling perennial, with a mass of underground runners giving rise to large patches, and stout, brittle stems 30–100 cm (12–40 in) tall.
Leaves: In opposite pairs, up to 10 cm long, oval, pale green, prominently 3-veined, pointed.
Flowers: Pale pink, often double, or sometimes white, 25–35 mm (1–1 2/5 in) across, scented, the 5 petals un-notched, in loose, branched clusters; calyx cylindrical, reddish.
Fruits: Cylindrical capsules, opening by 4 teeth, enclosed within the persistent calyx.
Related or similar plants: Red Campion (p.42) and White Campion (p.43) are hairy and have notched petals.
Habitat and distribution: A garden escape widely established along hedgerows and woodland margins, on roadsides, waste ground, riverbanks and around villages, although rare in Scotland and much of northern England.
Flowering time: May to September.

Soapwort (Saponaria officinalis) *is a garden escape and thus a variety of shades of pink occur as well as both single- and double-flowered forms.*

White Water-lily

WATER-LILY FAMILY
(Nymphaeaceae)

SPECIES INFORMATION	
COMMON NAME	White Water-lily
SCIENTIFIC NAME	Nymphaea alba
RELATED SPECIES	Yellow Water-lily
HEIGHT/SPREAD	Stems 1–3 m long
FLOWERING TIME	June–September
HABITAT	Lakes and ponds

Note: The large white water-lily of still waters.

FLOWER TYPE

IDENTIFICATION
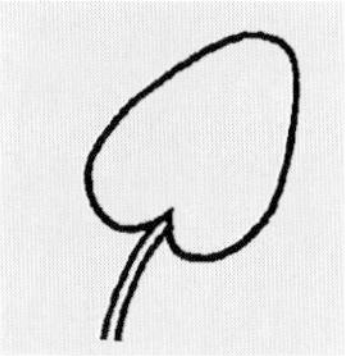

HABITAT

POPULATION

MAP
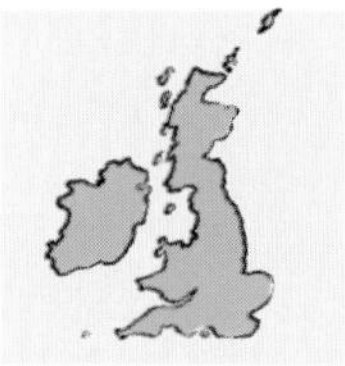

Size and appearance: A robust, aquatic perennial, with a massive, corky rhizome, forming patches of floating leaves and submerged hollow stems 1–3m (3–9 ft) long.
Leaves: Very long-stalked, 10–30 cm (4–12 in) across, almost circular with a narrow cleft, leathery, waxy and water-repellent on the upper surface, reddish beneath.
Flowers: Solitary, deeply cup-shaped, white, 10–20 cm (4–8 in) across, scented; 4 sepals, green beneath; stamens numerous, yellow.
Fruits: Almost spherical, green, spongy, warty capsules, sinking below the water surface as they ripen.
Related or similar plants: Yellow Water-lily (p.49) has smaller, yellow flowers, and submerged as well as floating leaves.
Habitat and distribution: Widespread but rather scattered in still or slow-flowing, open waters of lakes, ponds, disused canals and slow-moving rivers, especially where the bottom is muddy and the water nutrient-rich; especially common in western Scotland and north-western England, and western Ireland.
Flowering time: June to September.

THIS IS OUR largest wild flower and one of the most instantly recognisable. In some areas, as in south-east England, some populations have been replaced by garden water-lilies, and it has also suffered from over-collection for the lucrative aquatic nursery trade. It is still common in the west of Scotland and Ireland, where it is a feature of quiet upland loughans, a wonderful sight on a sunny day.

White Water-lily recolonised these islands shortly after the end of the Ice Age. Pollen deposits in lake muds show that in western Ireland and elsewhere the forebears of the water-lilies that still bloom in the lakes there were present 10,000 years ago.

Top *White Water-lily* (Nymphaea alba) *is Britain's largest wild flower, measuring 10-20 cm (4-8 in) across. These float on the surface of the water among the almost circular, leathery leaves.*

Bottom *Still common in the remoter parts of England, Scotland and Ireland, it is no longer found in many of the lakes and ponds in the nutrient-enriched waters of the south.*

SPECIES INFORMATION	
COMMON NAME	Yellow Water-lily, Brandy Bottle
SCIENTIFIC NAME	Nuphar lutea
RELATED SPECIES	White Water-lily
HEIGHT/SPREAD	Stems 1–5 m long
FLOWERING TIME	June–September
HABITAT	Rivers and slow-moving water

Note: The water plant with the largest yellow flowers.

Yellow Water-lily

WATER-LILY FAMILY (Nymphaeaceae)

Size and appearance: A robust, aquatic perennial, with a massive rhizome, forming patches of floating leaves and slightly emergent hollow stems 1–5 m (3–15 ft) long.
Leaves: Very long-stalked, 10–40 cm (4–16 in) across, almost circular with a narrow cleft, waxy and water-repellent on the upper surface, or submerged and rather cabbage-like.
Flowers: Slightly above the water, solitary, cup-shaped, with 4–6 yellow petal-like sepals, 4–6 cm (1⅗–2⅖ in) across, smelling faintly of brandy; petals small, inconspicuous, stamens numerous, both yellow.
Fruits: Carafe- or flask-shaped.
Related or similar plants: White Water-lily (p.48) has larger, white flowers and only floating leaves.
Habitat and distribution: Often common in slow-flowing rivers, canals and muddy streams, where the water is nutrient-rich, especially in lowland rivers of central and southern England; throughout, but absent from Cornwall and much of northern and eastern Scotland.
Flowering time: June to September.

Top *The flowers of the Yellow Water-lily* (Nuphar lutea) *are raised on stalks above the water and are 4-6 cm (1 ⅗-2 ⅖ in) across. The surface leaves are similar to those of the White Water-lily but larger.*

Bottom *The Yellow Water-lily is locally common in the nutrient-enriched waters of slow-flowing rivers and canals.*

FLOWER TYPE

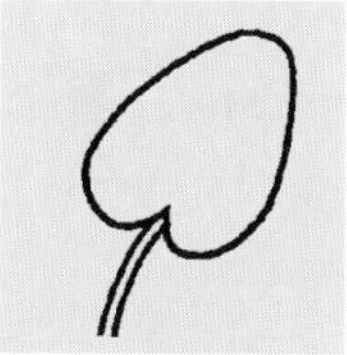
IDENTIFICATION

HABITAT

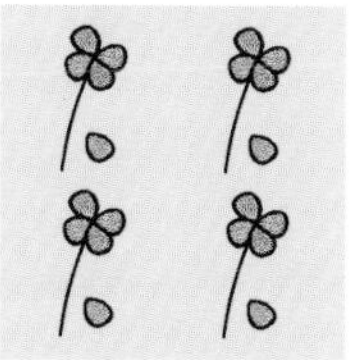
POPULATION

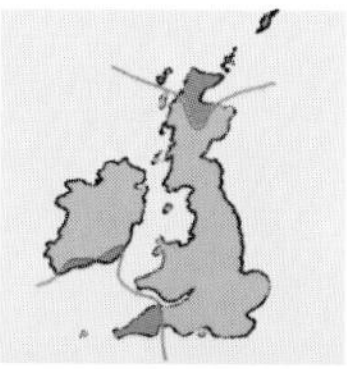
MAP

THIS CONSPICUOUS AND attractive plant en masse provides one of the most evocative images of the English countryside, the very essence of hot summer days on the river. The quaint English name of Brandy Bottle comes both from the winy smell of the flowers and the carafe-like fruits.

Yellow Water-Lily is rare in the Scottish Highlands, where it is replaced by Least Yellow Water-lily (*Nuphar pumila*), a miniature version of it with small leaves and flowers 15–35 mm (3/5–1 2/5 in) and gaps between the sepals. This other also grows in the Shropshire meres, perhaps an ancient relic from post-Glacial times.

Globeflower

BUTTERCUP FAMILY
(Ranunculaceae)

SPECIES INFORMATION	
COMMON NAME	Globeflower
SCIENTIFIC NAME	Trollius europaeus
RELATED SPECIES	Buttercups, Marsh Marigold
HEIGHT/SPREAD	25–60 cm tall
FLOWERING TIME	May–August
HABITAT	Mountain meadows and streamsides

Note: The ball of yellow sepals distinguishes it from buttercups.

FLOWER TYPE

IDENTIFICATION

HABITAT

POPULATION

MAP

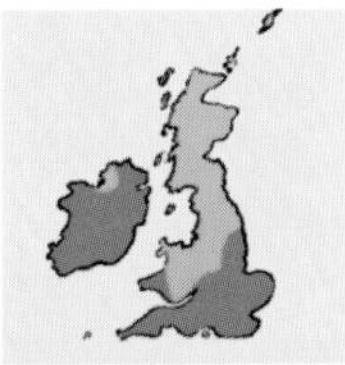

Size and appearance: A hairless perennial with stems 25–60 cm (10–24 in) tall.
Leaves: Mostly basal, long-stalked, 5-lobed, the lobes divided, and deeply and sharply toothed.
Flowers: 25–40 mm (1–1⅜ in) across, lemon-yellow; sepals 8–15, petal-like, curved to enclose the inconspicuous, strap-shaped petals.
Fruits: Dense cluster of several-seeded, shortly beaked, wrinkled fruits; seeds black.
Related or similar plants: The buttercups have 5 yellow petals and 5 green sepals.
Habitat and distribution: A local plant of damp meadows, streamsides and open woods in the mountains of northern Britain, Wales and a few places in northern Ireland, occasionally descending to the lowlands.
Flowering time: May to August.

A PLANT OF northern and central Europe, widespread in the Alps, that extends to the Auvergne and the Pyrenees. Globeflower is a good example of how, in the flowers of the buttercup family, coloured sepals sometimes replace or complement the petals.

The yellow flowers of the Globeflower (Trollius europaeus) *form colourful patches which are 25-60 cm (10-24 in) tall. The species is found in damp meadows and along streamsides in Wales and northern Britain.*

SPECIES INFORMATION	
COMMON NAME	Marsh Marigold, Kingcup
SCIENTIFIC NAME	Caltha palustris
RELATED SPECIES	Buttercups, Lesser Celandine
HEIGHT/SPREAD	10–45 cm tall, forming patches
FLOWERING TIME	March to June
HABITAT	Marshes and wet meadows

Note: Like a large buttercup but with several-seeded fruits.

Marsh Marigold

BUTTERCUP FAMILY (Ranunculaceae)

Size and appearance: A robust, leafy perennial, forming clumps and patches, 10–45 cm (18 in) tall, with hollow branched stems.

Flowers: 2–5 cm (⅘–2 in) across, golden-yellow, shiny, with numerous yellow stamens.

Leaves: Kidney- or heart-shaped, up to 10 cm (4in) across, dark green, with regular, rounded teeth.

Fruits: A head of 5–15 several-seeded, beaked pods 10–18 mm (⅖–¾ in) long.

Related or similar plants: The buttercups and Lesser Celandine (p.55), which also have yellow petals and green sepals, have mostly smaller flowers and 1-seeded fruits.

Habitat and distribution: Widespread in marshes, damp fields, ditches and wet woods, but less common now in the lowlands due to the draining and resowing of damp meadows.

Flowering time: March to June, but often later in the mountains.

Top *The fruits are a head of five-15 beaked pods which split to release the seeds as can be seen above.*

Bottom *Marsh Marigold is locally very abundant, but many of its habitats in the lowlands have been lost to modern intensive farming. In areas of Europe (such as Poland) it still carpets seasonally flooded river-valleys.*

FLOWER TYPE

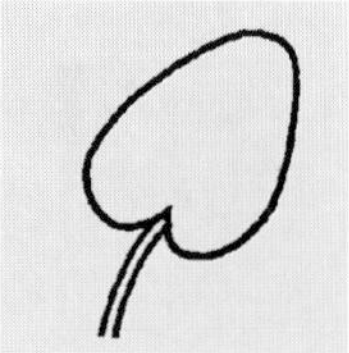

IDENTIFICATION

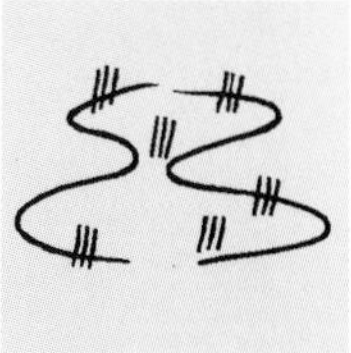

HABITAT

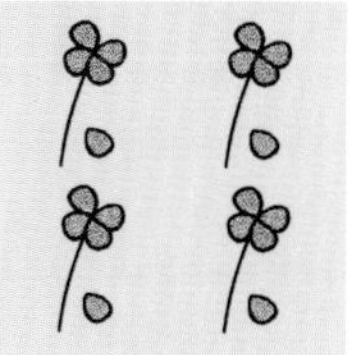

POPULATION

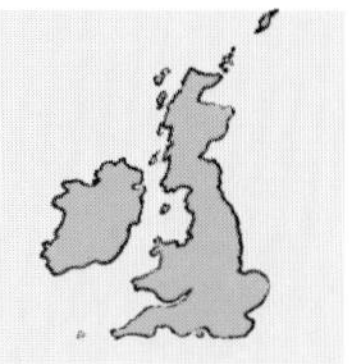

MAP

MARSH MARIGOLDS BRIGHTEN wet fields and marshes in early spring, in one of the awakening year's first really bold displays of floral colour. The five conspicuous yellow 'petals' are in fact sepals, and true petals are absent. The similar buttercups have yellow petals and an outerwhorl of green sepals. The several-seeded fruits are another feature that separates this species from the buttercups.

Plants growing in the mountains are often smaller, with stems that creep and root at the nodes. Similar sprawling and rooting plants have been described from tidal river-banks in the Netherlands and probably occur in the British Isles.

In Ireland, where it is known as Lus buí Bealtaine or May-flower, it formerly featured in May Day ritual, being supposed to keep away evil spirits. A yellow dye was extracted from the flower. The whole plant is poisonous and grazing animals avoid eating it.

Wood Anemone

BUTTERCUP FAMILY

(Ranunculaceae)

SPECIES INFORMATION	
COMMON NAME	Wood Anemone, Windflower
SCIENTIFIC NAME	Anemone nemorosa
RELATED SPECIES	Buttercups, Pasque Flower
HEIGHT/SPREAD	8–25 cm tall, forming loose clumps
FLOWERING TIME	February–May
HABITAT	Woodland, hedgerows, old pastures

Note: The pink nodding buds are protected by the leaves.

FLOWER TYPE

IDENTIFICATION

HABITAT

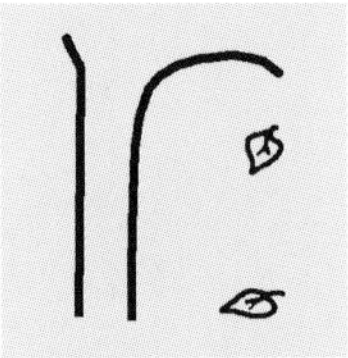

POPULATION

MAP

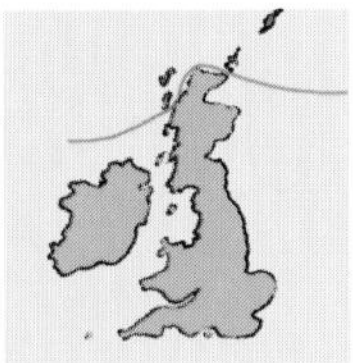

Size and appearance: Elegant, erect perennial 8–25 cm (3–10 in) tall, with solitary flowers; rhizome creeping, forming loose clumps.

Leaves: Divided into 3 main lobes, these subdivided and toothed; stem leaves all in a protective whorl below the flower.

Flowers: 2–4 cm (⅘–1½ in) across, white tinged with pink or purple beneath, rarely lilac or blue, with many pale yellow stamens.

Fruits: A round head of 1-seeded, minutely hairy fruits.

Related or similar plants: Escaped spring-flowering cultivated anemones usually have blue or yellow flowers.

Habitat and distribution: Locally common, but rare or absent over much of northern Scotland and central and southern Ireland. A plant of well-drained soils in open woodland, coppices and hedgerows, also old pastures and mountain ledges.

Flowering time: February to May, until July in the mountains.

WOOD ANEMONE IS a welcome sight in early spring, often flowering with primroses. It sometimes grows in great crowds, the dainty flowers seeming to dance in the breeze (hence 'Windflower'). The white 'petals' are in fact sepals; true petals are absent and the leaf-whorl protects the young flower, which nods in bud.

This is a characteristic plant of ancient woodland, and its presence in hedge-banks and pastures may indicate the former presence of woodland.

The whole plant is poisonous.

Wood Anemones can be very abundant in woods, especially in coppices where the trees have recently been cut, letting more light on to the woodland floor. The flowers can be pure white or tinged with pink or purple beneath.

SPECIES INFORMATION	
COMMON NAME	Meadow Buttercup
SCIENTIFIC NAME	Ranunculus acris
RELATED SPECIES	Bulbous and Creeping Buttercups
HEIGHT/SPREAD	30–100 cm tall
FLOWERING TIME	May–October
HABITAT	Grassland, woodland clearings

Note: The tallest of the common buttercups.

Meadow Buttercup

BUTTERCUP FAMILY

(Ranunculaceae)

FLOWER TYPE

IDENTIFICATION

HABITAT

POPULATION

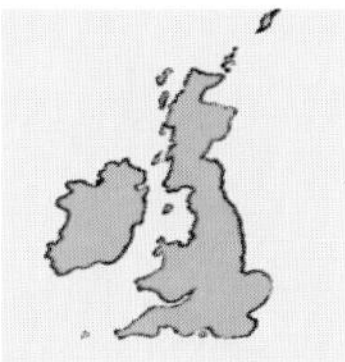

MAP

Size and appearance: A rather hairy perennial, with erect stems 30–100 cm (12–40 in) tall, sometimes more.

Leaves: Circular in general outline, deeply divided into 3, 5 or 7 lobes, each one itself deeply divided.

Flowers: In loose, branched clusters, bright yellow, shiny, 15–25 mm (⅝–1 in) across, with 5 petals and spreading sepals; flower-stalk not furrowed.

Fruits: 1-seeded, with a hooked beak, in a round head.

Related or similar plants: Bulbous Buttercup (p.54) has flowers with down-curved sepals; Creeping Buttercup (p.54) has vigorous, rooting runners.

Habitat and distribution: Common in damp grassland, woodland rides and marshes, and on mountain ledges.

Flowering time: May to October

THE COMMONEST BUTTERCUP, sometimes colouring fields yellow, although less so than formerly, owing to the destruction of old grassland by modern agriculture. The whole plant is poisonous, with acrid sap that can blister the skin. It is therefore avoided by grazing animals and is sometimes abundant in pastures.

The burnished appearance of buttercup flowers derives from light reflecting from starch grains within the structure of the petals.

Top *A field of Meadow Buttercup: although still common, the plant is no longer seen in the huge masses that once coloured the countryside in early summer.*

Bottom *The Goldilocks Buttercup* (Ranunculus auricomus) *is a local woodland herb which is about 10-40 cm tall.*

Bulbous Buttercup

BUTTERCUP FAMILY
(Ranunculaceae)

SPECIES INFORMATION	
COMMON NAME	Bulbous Buttercup
SCIENTIFIC NAME	Ranunculus bulbosus
RELATED SPECIES	Meadow and Creeping Buttercups
HEIGHT/SPREAD	10–50 cm tall
FLOWERING TIME	April–June
HABITAT	Well-drained grassland

Note: The down-curved sepals are diagnostic.

FLOWER TYPE

IDENTIFICATION

HABITAT

POPULATION

MAP
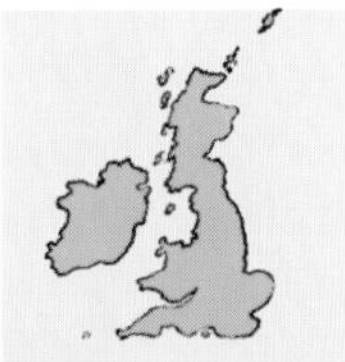

Size and appearance: A hairy perennial with a distinctly swollen stem-base or corm, and erect stems 10–50 cm (4–20 in) tall.
Flowers: Bright yellow, shiny, 20–30 mm (4/5–1 1/5 in) across, with 5 petals, solitary or in small, branched clusters; sepals down-turned; flower-stalk furrowed.
Leaves: Deeply divided into 3 lobes, each divided and toothed, the middle one usually distinctly stalked.
Fruits: 1-seeded, with a curved beak, in a round head.
Related or similar plants: Meadow Buttercup (p.53) is taller, with more deeply dissected leaves and spreading sepals; Creeping Buttercup (see below) has rooting runners.
Habitat and distribution: Widespread on well-drained soils, especially those rich in lime, in dry, mostly lime-rich grassland and on sand-dunes. In northern Scotland and Ireland it is local and generally found only on the coast.
Flowering time: April to June.

Bottom left *The down-turned sepals of Bulbous Buttercup which separate it from both the Meadow and Creeping Buttercups.*

THE EARLIEST of the three common large-flowered, buttercups to flower, this species has a short flowering season and its green shoots die down from midsummer to autumn. Unlike Creeping and Meadow Buttercup, it always grows on well-drained soils and does not tolerate flooding. The whole plant is poisonous, with acrid sap that can blister the skin.

Top *The Bulbous Buttercup* (Ranunculus bulbosus) *is an early buttercup to flower and can often be found among the turf in April. Where semi-natural grassland is no longer common, it may occur in the churchyard.*

Bottom right *Creeping Buttercup* (Ranunculus repens) *is similar but has vigorous, rooting runners and leaves with a stalked central leaflet. It is common in damp grassland, roadsides, waste ground and neglected gardens, especially on clay soils.*

SPECIES INFORMATION	
COMMON NAME	Lesser Celandine
SCIENTIFIC NAME	Ranunculus ficaria
RELATED SPECIES	Buttercups, Crowfoots
HEIGHT/SPREAD	5–30 cm tall, forming patches
FLOWERING TIME	February–May
HABITAT	Woodland and hedge-banks

Note: Early flowering and with starry flowers.

Lesser Celandine

BUTTERCUP FAMILY

(Ranunculaceae)

FLOWER TYPE

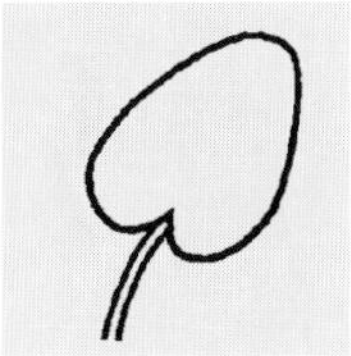

IDENTIFICATION

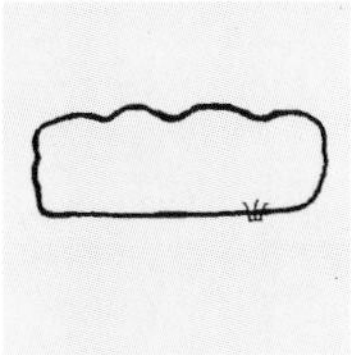

HABITAT

POPULATION

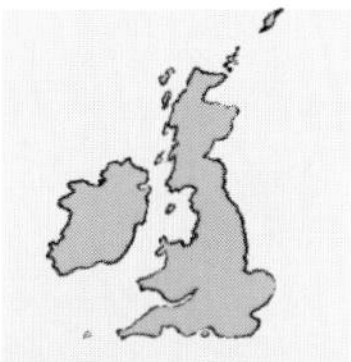

MAP

Size and appearance: Low-growing, hairless perennial, 5–30 cm tall, forming extensive patches.

Leaves: Heart-shaped, rounded or blunt, deeply notched at the base, shallowly toothed, generally mottled with purplish or pale blotches.

Flowers: Solitary, bright yellow, shiny, 15–30 mm ($\frac{3}{5}$–$1\frac{1}{5}$ in) across, with 8–12 rather narrow petals, opening only in bright sun; 3 sepals only.

Fruits: 1-seeded, without a beak, in a round head, but often not developing at all.

Related or similar plants: The buttercups and crowfoots have 5 sepals and divided leaves, and they mostly flower later.

Habitat and distribution: Damp places in woods, in hedgerows, churchyards, gardens, along the banks of rivers and streams, and sometimes in grassland.

Flowering time: February to May, but in mild winters in flower from January.

The Lesser Celandine is like the Marsh Marigold in appearance, and is one of the first woodland flowers of the year. The eight-12 shiny, narrow petals make a carpet of yellow stars across the woodland floor although they can also be found along stream and ditchsides.

ONE OF THE very first flowers to appear at winter's end, often in huge crowds, and a welcome sign of the advancing spring. On sunny days it colours lanes and hedge-banks. The roots develop swollen tubers, which serve as a means of reproduction, and later in the season, tuber-like bulbils often develop in the angles between the leaf-stalks and stems. The plant dies down by the end of June.

Robust plants with flowers 25–40 mm (1–$1\frac{3}{5}$ in) across are grown in gardens and sometimes escape on to lane-sides and elsewhere. Other variants selected by gardeners, mostly from chance wild 'sports', have purple leaves or double, whitish or copper-coloured flowers.

Lesser Spearwort

BUTTERCUP FAMILY

(Ranunculaceae)

SPECIES INFORMATION	
COMMON NAME	Lesser Spearwort
SCIENTIFIC NAME	Ranunculus flammula
RELATED SPECIES	Buttercups, Crowfoots
HEIGHT/SPREAD	10–50 cm tall
FLOWERING TIME	May–September
HABITAT	Marshes, beside streams and lakes

Note: The undivided leaves separate it from the buttercups.

FLOWER TYPE

IDENTIFICATION

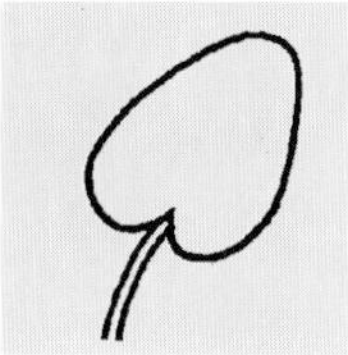

HABITAT

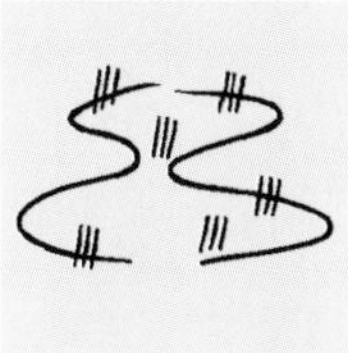

POPULATION

MAP

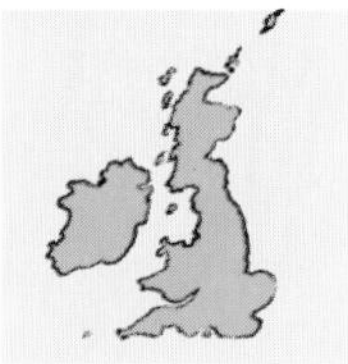

Size and appearance: Hairless, erect, ascending, sprawling or creeping perennial, 10–50 cm (4–20 in) tall, the lower stems often reddish and hollow, rooting in the lower part.
Leaves: Spear-shaped or narrowly oval, with untoothed or shallowly-toothed margins.
Flowers: Pale yellow, shiny, 8–20 mm (⅓–1in) across, with 5 petals.
Fruits: 1-seeded, with a small beak, in a round head.
Related or similar plants: The buttercups and crowfoots have divided leaves.
Habitat and distribution: A common plant of marshes, bogs, damp grassland and the margins of ponds and lakes, especially in the north and west.
Flowering time: May to September.

IT IS POISONOUS, with acrid sap that can blister the skin, and in Scotland and Ireland was formerly used medicinally. The crushed roots would be applied as a poultice to ulcers and sores; and more drastically to try to 'draw out' illnesses like bubonic plague.

Lesser Spearwort is a very variable plant, especially in leaf-shape. Two interesting variants, one erect with narrow leaves, the other prostrate with rounded leaves, occur only in Scotland and western Ireland.

Top *Greater Spearwort* (Ranuncolus lingua), *is much more local in distribution. It is larger and very robust, with hollow stems 50–120 cm (20–48 in) tall and flowers 30–50 mm (1⅕–2 in) across.*

Bottom *Lesser Spearwort* (Ranunculus flammula) *has spear-shaped or narrowly oval leaves, which are not like the divided leaves of the other yellow buttercups.*

SPECIES INFORMATION	
COMMON NAME	Celery-leaved Buttercup
SCIENTIFIC NAME	Ranunculus sceleratus
RELATED SPECIES	Lesser Spearwort, Other buttercups
HEIGHT/SPREAD	15–50 cm tall
FLOWERING TIME	May–September
HABITAT	Marshes and the margins of ponds

Note: The clusters of fruits are like tiny green fir-cones.

Celery-leaved Buttercup

BUTTERCUP FAMILY

(Ranunculaceae)

Size and appearance: Erect, often much-branched, mostly hairless annual, with stout, hollow stems 15–50 cm (6–20 in) tall.

Leaves: The basal deeply 3-lobed, the lobes subdivided; stem leaves less divided; all pale green, shiny.

Flowers: Pale yellow, shiny, 5–10 mm (⅕–⅜ in) across, with 5 petals, in branched clusters.

Fruits: 1-seeded, hairless, in a short, cylindrical head.

Related or similar plants: The commonest of several buttercups with small, pale yellow flowers.

Habitat and distribution: A common but not very well-known plant of muddy, trampled and open places in marshes, damp grassland and the margins of ponds, lakes and rivers.

Flowering time: May to September.

IT IS POISONOUS, especially at flowering time, with acrid sap that has a bitter, burning taste and readily blisters the mouth and skin. This plant is the main cause of buttercup poisoning amongst farm animals. It is, nevertheless, safe to feed them with hay containing dried buttercups.

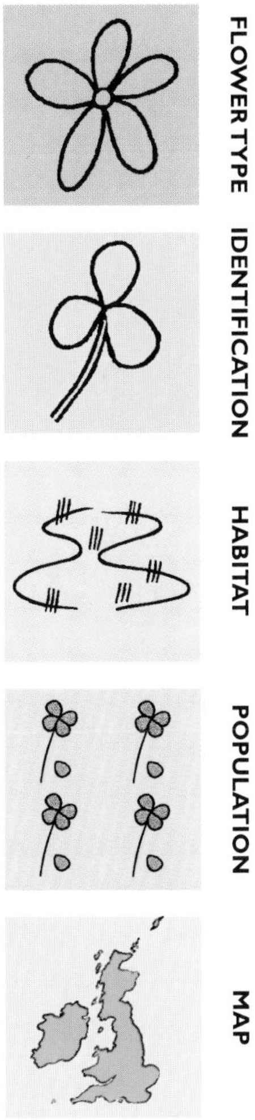

Top *The fruits of the Celery-leaved Buttercup* (Ranunculus sceleratus) *occur in a short cylindrical head which could look like a type of microphone.*

Bottom *The leaves are pale green and shiny; those at the base are deeply three-lobed with the lobes subdivided. Those up the stem are toothed and narrower.*

Pond Water-crowfoot

BUTTERCUP FAMILY

(Ranunculaceae)

SPECIES INFORMATION	
COMMON NAME	Pond Water-crowfoot
SCIENTIFIC NAME	Ranunculus peltatus
RELATED SPECIES	Other Water-crowfoots
HEIGHT/SPREAD	10–50 cm long
FLOWERING TIME	April–June
HABITAT	Ponds, lakes and slow streams

Note: It has both floating and submerged leaves.

FLOWER TYPE

IDENTIFICATION

HABITAT

POPULATION

MAP

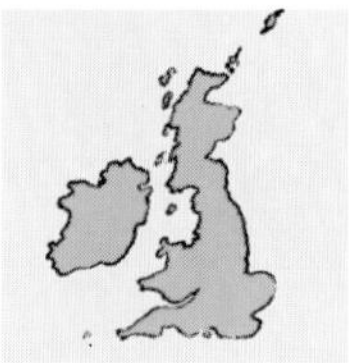

THIS TRAILING, AQUATIC PERENNIAL can form large populations in still, unpolluted waters of slow streams, lakes and ponds. The flowers, emerging on long, erect stalks above the surface of the water, can be an impressive sight on a sunny spring day.

It is one of a group of 10 or so Water-crowfoots in Britain and Ireland, some in still or slowly-flowing water, with both floating and submerged leaves; some in fast-flowing water, with submerged leaves only; others on mud, without submerged leaves.

Size and appearance: Trailing, aquatic perennial with flexible stems 10–50 cm (4–20 in) long.

Leaves: Floating leaves kidney-shaped or almost round, 5-lobed (sometimes 3- or 7-lobed), glossy; submerged leaves divided into thread-like segments.

Flowers: Solitary, on stalks 5 cm (2 in) or more long, white, shiny, 15–30 mm (3/5–2 1/5 in) across, with 5 petals, each yellow-spotted at the base.

Fruits: 1-seeded, with a small beak, hairy, in a round head.

Related or similar plants: Water-crowfoots differ from buttercups in having white, not yellow flowers. Common Water-crowfoot (*Ranunculus aquatilis*) has more toothed leaf-lobes and smaller flowers.

Habitat and distribution: Widespread and sometimes abundant in still waters of slow streams, lakes and ponds.

Flowering time: April to June.

Top *Many species of Water-crowfoot occur but all have white buttercup flowers which protrude above floating leaves.*

Bottom *Large populations occur on suitable stretches of rivers and streams, lakes and ponds. The type of river and the substrate can determine the species of Water Crowfoot.*

SPECIES INFORMATION	
COMMON NAME	Common Meadow-rue
SCIENTIFIC NAME	Thalictrum flavum
RELATED SPECIES	Lesser Meadow-rue
HEIGHT/SPREAD	60–120 cm tall
FLOWERING TIME	June–August
HABITAT	Marshes and wet meadows

Note: Similar to the anemones but has tiny petals.

Common Meadow-rue

BUTTERCUP FAMILY

(Ranunculaceae)

Size and appearance: Perennial with erect, angled stems 60–120 cm tall.
Leaves: Compound, deeply divided 2–3 times into numerous wedge-shaped or oblong leaflets.
Flowers: Dense clusters of yellowish flowers with erect, feathery stamens; petals tiny, whitish.
Fruits: A head of small, several-seeded, beaked pods.
Related or similar plants: Meadowsweet (p.98) is superficially similar but has leaves divided once and flowers with cream petals; Lesser Meadow-rue has leaflets as wide as long and hanging stamens.
Habitat and distribution: Widespread in fens, marshes and wet meadows, and beside rivers, especially on lime-rich soils, north to southern Scotland; in Ireland mainly in the Midlands and around Lough Neagh.
Flowering time: June to August

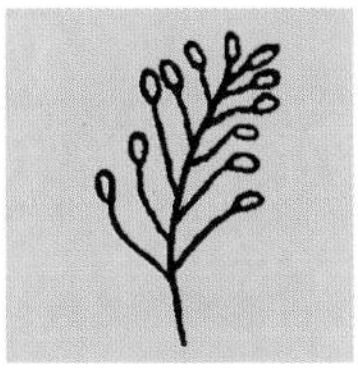

FLOWER TYPE

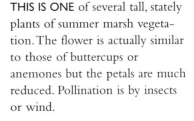

IDENTIFICATION

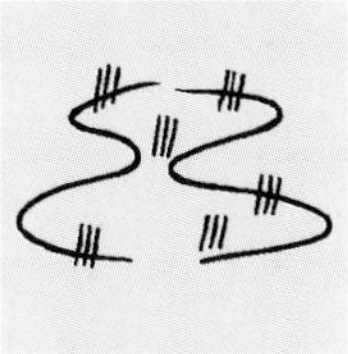

HABITAT

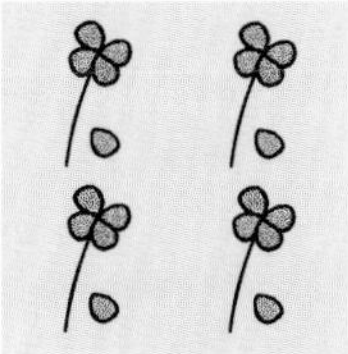

POPULATION

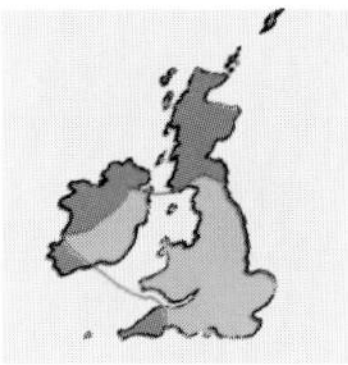

MAP

THIS IS ONE of several tall, stately plants of summer marsh vegetation. The flower is actually similar to those of buttercups or anemones but the petals are much reduced. Pollination is by insects or wind.

Top *Although a member of the same family, the Common Meadow-rue* (Thalictrum flavum) *flowers do not have buttercup-shaped flowers; instead they have dense clusters of creamy-yellow heads.*

Bottom *An erect plant 60-120 cm (24-47 in) tall with deeply-divided compound leaves, this is widespread in fens, marshes and wet meadows.*

Pasque Flower

BUTTERCUP FAMILY

(Ranunculaceae)

SPECIES INFORMATION	
COMMON NAME	Pasque Flower
SCIENTIFIC NAME	Pulsatilla vulgaris
RELATED SPECIES	Wood Anemone
HEIGHT/SPREAD	8–20 cm tall
FLOWERING TIME	April–May
HABITAT	Grassland on chalk and limestone

Note: A distinctive flower of spring, but rare.

FLOWER TYPE

IDENTIFICATION

HABITAT

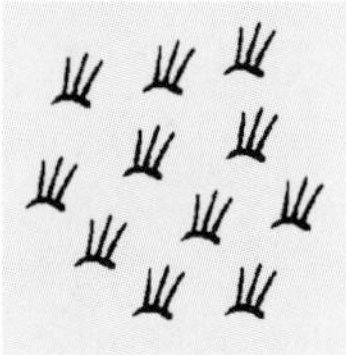

POPULATION

MAP

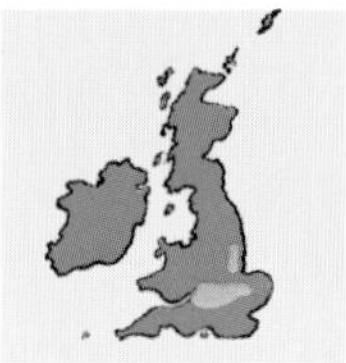

Size and appearance: A handsome, silky-hairy perennial, with erect stems 8–20 cm (4–8 in) tall, sometimes more.
Leaves: Mostly basal, compound, deeply divided, fern-like; a ruff of stalkless, undivided leaves sits beneath the flower.
Flowers: Solitary, 5–10 cm (1–2 in) across, purplish-violet, silky-hairy on the backs of the 6 petal-like sepals; stamens many, yellow.
Fruits: 1-seeded, with a long, silky plume derived from the stigma, in a head that persists after flowering.
Related or similar plants: Wood Anemone (p.52) and other anemones that sometimes escape from gardens have more than 5 'petals'.
Habitat and distribution: Rare, but locally in some quantity in short, undisturbed and unploughed grassland over chalk and limestone, from the Cotswolds to Cambridgeshire and north to the Lincolnshire Wolds.
Flowering time: April to May, sometimes in two flushes, early and late.

The now-rare Pasque Flower (Pulsatilla vulgaris) *is still found in quantity on undisturbed chalk downland, where it makes a glorious sight with its large purple flowers.*

THIS RARE AND BEAUTIFUL plant is one of the most striking native species of our flora. It lives only in grassland that has been undisturbed for centuries – and does not come back after a site has been ploughed. For this reason it has decreased all across northern Europe.

Pasque Flower is fully protected under the provisions of the Wildlife And Countryside Act 1981, and it is an offence to damage the wild plants in any way. Plants for garden cultivation are readily available from nurseries or good garden centres.

SPECIES INFORMATION	
COMMON NAME	Green Hellebore
SCIENTIFIC NAME	Helleborus viridis
RELATED SPECIES	Stinking Hellebore
HEIGHT/SPREAD	15–40 cm tall
FLOWERING TIME	March–May
HABITAT	Woodland on chalk and limestone

Note: Our only wild plant with such large green flowers.

Green Hellebore

BUTTERCUP FAMILY

(Ranunculaceae)

Size and appearance: An erect, bushy perennial with stems 15–40 cm (6–16 in) tall.
Leaves: Compound, rather leathery when mature, divided into a fan of finger-like, toothed segments.
Flowers: In loose clusters of 2–5, cup-shaped, green, 3–5 cm (1⅕–2 in) across, the petals persisting in fruit.
Fruits: A head of several-seeded, beaked pods.
Related or similar plants: Stinking Hellebore has numerous, smaller flowers.
Habitat and distribution: Generally scarce, but sometimes in good-sized colonies, on humus-rich soils in woods over chalk and limestone north to Yorkshire; absent from Ireland.
Flowering time: March to May, but from February onwards in mild winters.

Bottom left A bushy perennial 15-40 cm (6-16 in) tall, Green Hellebore (Helleborus viridis) *has large, divided, fan-shaped leaves. It grows in woods on chalk and limestone soils as far north as Yorkshire but is rather scarce.*

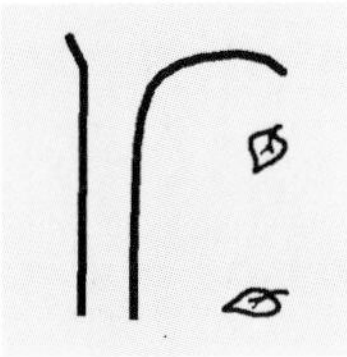

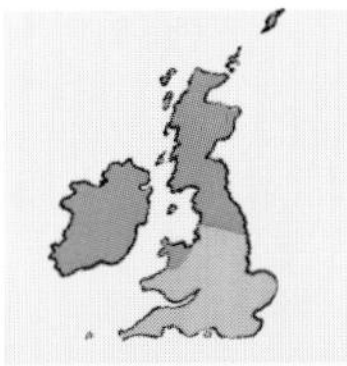

OUR TWO NATIVE hellebores are among the most exciting wild flowers of late winter and early spring. Both look exotic, and are certainly denizens of the cottage garden, but many plants have hopped back and forth from field to garden. In woodlands over chalk in the Chilterns and elsewhere both seem convincingly native. Green Hellebore is the more fragile-looking of the two, the leafy shoots and attractive, fresh green flowers emerging mysteriously from the ground at winter's end.

Note that both Green Hellebore and Stinking Hellebore are highly poisonous.

Top *The cup-shaped green flowers, which are 3-5 cm (1 1/5-2 in) across, occur in loose clusters of two-five in late winter to early spring.*

Bottom right *Stinking Hellebore* (Helleborus foetidus) *is taller, to 80 cm (32 in) or more, with evergreen, dark green leaves and clusters of numerous yellowish bell-shaped flowers 1–3 cm (2⁄5–1 1⁄5 in) across from Christmas in mild winters. It is scarce in woods and scrub on chalk and limestone north to Cumbria; in Ireland it is only a rare escape.*

Columbine

BUTTERCUP FAMILY

(Ranunculaceae)

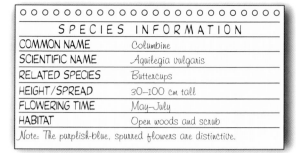

SPECIES INFORMATION	
COMMON NAME	Columbine
SCIENTIFIC NAME	*Aquilegia vulgaris*
RELATED SPECIES	Buttercups
HEIGHT/SPREAD	30–100 cm tall
FLOWERING TIME	May–July
HABITAT	Open woods and scrub

Note: The purplish-blue, spurred flowers are distinctive.

FLOWER TYPE

IDENTIFICATION

HABITAT

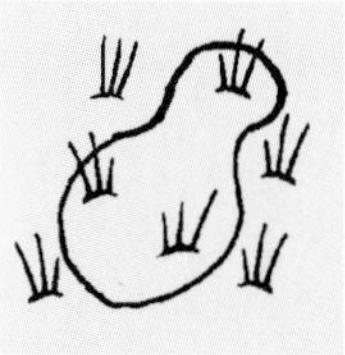

POPULATION

MAP

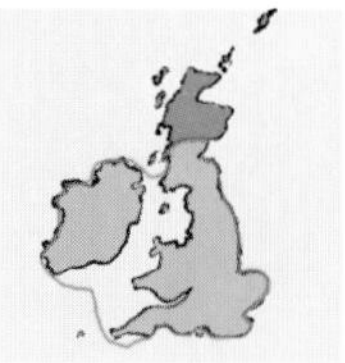

Size and appearance: Elegant, downy perennial, with stems 30–100 cm (12–40 in) tall, branched above.

Flowers: 30–50 mm (1⅕–2 in) long, nodding, violet-blue; petals 5, each with a long, hooked spur; sepals 5, petal-like.

Leaves: Mostly basal, compound, the lobed segments in groups of 3, bluntly and irregularly toothed.

Fruits: A cluster of many-seeded fruits; seeds greenish-brown.

Related or similar plants: A distinctive plant that is unlikely to be confused with any other.

Habitat and distribution: Local but sometimes common in open woods, scrub and other shady places, and in marshes and damp habitats.

Flowering time: May to July.

THIS IS A POPULAR subject for cottage gardens, and crosses between this species and others have given rise to the wide range of columbines found in cultivation. The plant, like many other members of the buttercup family, is poisonous.

Columbine (Aquilegia vulgaris) *is a distinctive plant with its spurred, violet-blue, nodding flowers. It can attain a height of 100 cm (40 in) but is generally less. As with other plants popular in gardens, many of the Columbines that occur near habitations are garden escapées and these can be of many different colours.*

SPECIES INFORMATION	
COMMON NAME	Traveller's Joy, Old Man's Beard
SCIENTIFIC NAME	Clematis vitalba
RELATED SPECIES	Garden Clematis
HEIGHT/SPREAD	Stems 1–10 m long
FLOWERING TIME	July–September
HABITAT	Woodland and hedge-banks
Note: The most robust of our native climbing plants (except ivy).	

Traveller's Joy

BUTTERCUP FAMILY

(Ranunculaceae)

Top right and left *The fluffy seed-heads ('Old Man's Beard') are locally a conspicuous and attractive feature of the autumn and winter landscape.*

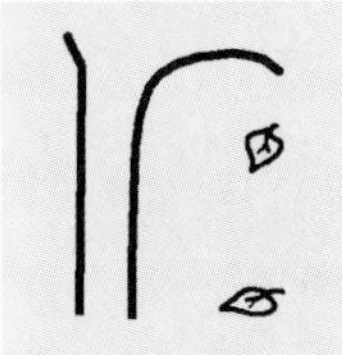

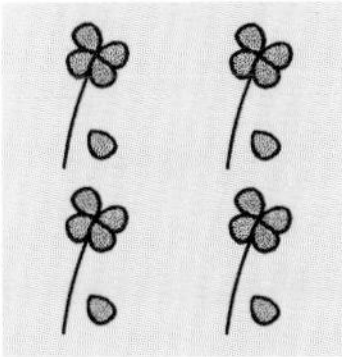

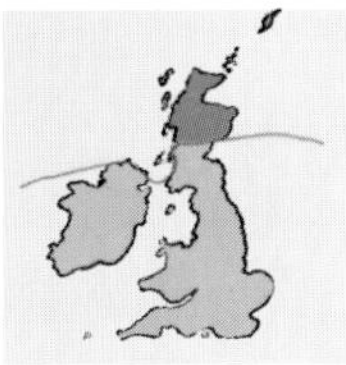

THIS IS ONE of the most characteristic plants, indeed landscape features, of the chalk and limestone of southern and central England. The older stems often form great looping lianes in woods, the bark peeling off in strings.

Bottom
A characteristic plant of chalk and limestone soils, where it is common in the hedgerows and roadside banks, Traveller's Joy is distinctive enough to recognise from a passing car.

Size and appearance: Climbing shrub, with woody stems up to 10 m (30 ft) long, scrambling untidily over hedges, scrub and banks, and high into the branches of trees.
Flowers: In small loose clusters, without petals but with 4 greenish-cream sepals and numerous cream stamens.
Leaves: In opposite pairs, compound, each with usually 5 leaflets; leaf-stalks twining around twigs and other supports.
Fruits: 1-seeded, with a plume derived from the stigma, in a fluffy, round head.
Related or similar plants: Garden clematis species and hybrids, with larger coloured flowers, sometimes escape and become established in the wild.
Habitat and distribution: Common in woods, scrub, roadside banks and railway cuttings on chalk and limestone in southern Britain, extending to north Wales and much of the Midlands, but introduced further north and in Ireland.
Flowering time: July to September, but most conspicuous in fruit from October onwards.

Common Poppy

POPPY FAMILY

(Papaveraceae)

SPECIES INFORMATION	
COMMON NAME	Common Poppy, Field Poppy
SCIENTIFIC NAME	Papaver rhoeas
RELATED SPECIES	Long-headed Poppy
HEIGHT/SPREAD	20–80 cm tall
FLOWERING TIME	May–September
HABITAT	Cultivated and disturbed ground
Note: The smooth, almost spherical fruits are diagnostic.	

FLOWER TYPE

IDENTIFICATION

HABITAT

POPULATION

MAP

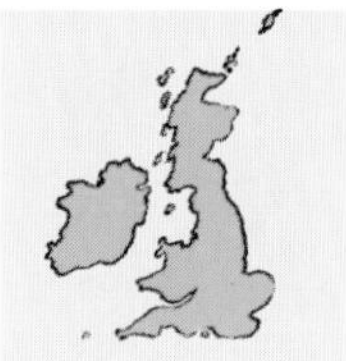

Top *Long-headed Poppy* (Papaver dubium) *is similar to Common Poppy but has paler, scarlet flowers not more than 5 cm (2 in) across and club-shaped fruits up to 25 mm (1 in) long. It occurs throughout Britain and Ireland, but is less common, although the commoner poppy of the north and west.*

Size and appearance: An erect or semi-erect, hairy annual, 20–80 cm (8–32 in) tall, with bristly stems, exuding white sap when cut.
Leaves: Compound, deeply and coarsely cut into toothed lobes.
Flowers: Solitary on a long, bristly stalk, scarlet, flimsy, 5–9 cm (2–3½ in) across, the petals often with a dark spot at the base, with numerous blackish stamens; the 2 sepals soon falling off.
Fruits: Hairless, almost spherical capsules 1–2 cm (⅖–⅘ in) long, releasing ripe seed from an upper ring of pores.
Related or similar plants: Long-headed Poppy has paler scarlet flowers and club-shaped fruits.
Habitat and distribution: The common poppy of cereal crops and other arable fields, allotments, waste land and the disturbed ground of newer road-verges, sand-dunes and shingle beaches, especially on lighter or lime-rich soils in southern and eastern England; more or less throughout, but rare over much of Wales, Scotland, and western and northern Ireland.
Flowering time: May to September.

POPPIES ARE PERHAPS the most famous weeds of cultivation, and still regularly appear in huge crowds where the soil has been disturbed by farming or building. This is because the seeds can survive in soil for decades, until conditions of light and moisture allow them to germinate.

A classic instance of this dormancy was demonstrated on the shell-churned chalk soil of the Somme battlefield, sometime farmland, as wild flowers recolonised the land fought over in 1916. Later the flower of this humble arable weed was adopted by the British Legion, and the nation, as a poignant symbol to commemorate the dead of the First World War. The association with death, and resurrection, goes back a long way: the Romans regarded poppies in the corn as sacred to Ceres, goddess of crops.

Bottom *Once abundant in corn fields, agricultural sprays now keep the Common Poppy* (Papaver rhoeas) *in check. If a part of the field is missed by the herbicide the dormant seeds will germinate.*

SPECIES INFORMATION	
COMMON NAME	Opium Poppy
SCIENTIFIC NAME	Papaver somniferum
RELATED SPECIES	Common Poppy
HEIGHT/SPREAD	20–150 cm tall
FLOWERING TIME	June–September
HABITAT	Cultivated and disturbed ground

Note: The bluish-green, waxy leaves are unlike other poppies.

Opium Poppy

POPPY FAMILY

(Papaveraceae)

Size and appearance: A robust, erect, bluish-green, sparsely bristly annual, 20–150 cm (8–60 in) tall, exuding white sap when cut.

Leaves: Oblong, shallowly lobed, toothed, almost hairless.

Flowers: Solitary on a usually hairless stalk, mauve, lilac or scarlet, flimsy, 5–10 cm (2–4 in) across, the petals with a purplish spot at the base, with numerous blackish stamens; the 2 sepals soon falling off.

Fruits: Smooth, almost spherical, flat-topped capsules 2.5–5 cm (1–2 in) long, releasing ripe seed from an upper ring of pores.

Related or similar plants: Corn Poppy always has scarlet flowers and much smaller fruits.

Habitat and distribution: A sporadic and sometimes abundant colonist of waste and disturbed ground, new road verges and cultivated land, including cereal crops, especially as a garden weed; throughout, but commoner in southern and central England.

Flowering time: June to September.

Top *Opium Poppy* (Papaver somniferum) *often has lilac flowers with a purplish spot at the base of the four petals. Other colours also occur, including mauve, pink and scarlet.*

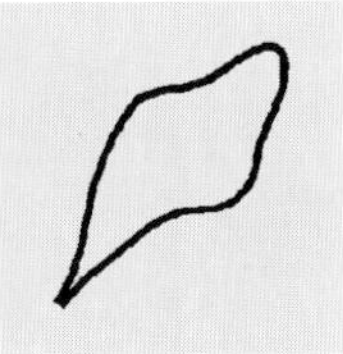

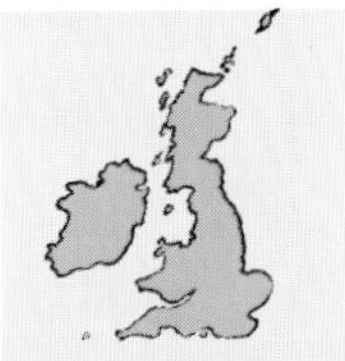

OPIUM, A POWERFUL ANESTHETIC and narcotic, the basis of morphine and codeine, is one of the oldest and most valued of medicinal drugs. The seeds are used for cooking and are the source of a useful edible oil. Opium Poppy probably originated in the western Mediterranean region, and traces of this species are known from the remains of Stone Age lake villages. Today, it survives as a crop in small fields in the Balkans and elsewhere.

Once it grew in Britain too, especially in East Anglia, and it persists here and there as a weed of cereal fields and roadsides. However, it is mainly now a spontaneous garden annual, thriving as an up-market weed and often escaping on to waste ground and waysides.

Bottom right *The seeds are released from the pores situated around the top of the capsule as it is blown around in the breeze.*

Bottom left *Poppies are now cultivated for the pharmaceutical industry. When ripe, they are processed to provide the drugs necessary for the medical research.*

Horned Poppy

POPPY FAMILY

(Papaveraceae)

SPECIES INFORMATION	
COMMON NAME	Horned Poppy
SCIENTIFIC NAME	Glaucium flavum
RELATED SPECIES	Welsh Poppy
HEIGHT/SPREAD	30–100 cm tall
FLOWERING TIME	June–October
HABITAT	Shingle beaches

Note: Silvery-grey, bristly leaves, and long pods.

FLOWER TYPE

IDENTIFICATION

HABITAT

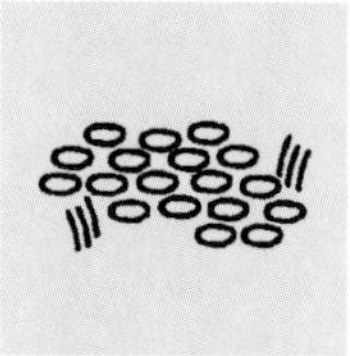

POPULATION

MAP

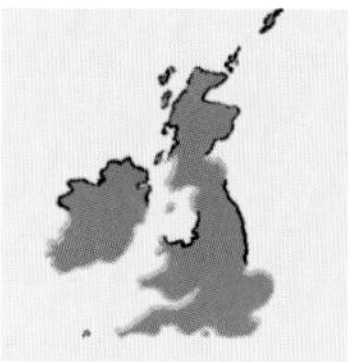

Size and appearance: A semi-erect or sprawling, branched, greyish-green biennial or perennial, 30–100cm (12–40 in) tall, exuding yellow sap when cut.

Leaves: Silvery-grey, deeply lobed, toothed, bristly, almost hairless; upper leaves clasping the stems.

Flowers: Solitary, yellow, flimsy, 5–9 cm (2–3½ in) across, with 4 petals and numerous yellow stamens; the 2 sepals soon falling off.

Fruits: Smooth, slender, curved, cylindrical capsules 10–30 cm (4–12 in) long, splitting lengthwise to release the ripe seeds.

Related or similar plants: Welsh Poppy (p.68) also has yellow flowers but has green leaves and much smaller fruits, and grows in shady places.

Habitat and distribution: A rather local but conspicuous plant of coastal shingle beaches and open waste places by the sea, less often on sandy beaches, north to the Firths of Clyde and Forth; in Ireland mostly on south-western and eastern coasts.

Flowering time: June to September, often into October.

Top *The flowers of the Yellow Horned Poppy* (Glaucium flavum) *soon give way to a curved, cylindrical, slender fruit 10-30 cm (4-12 in) long.*

HORNED POPPY IS a significant feature of coastal shingle beaches, colouring the pebbles and sparse vegetation with its yellow flowers through the summer and well into autumn. Shingle is a particularly British formation, including some of Europe's most extensive shingle beaches on the south and east coasts of England.

Horned Poppy is widely distributed around the Mediterranean, extending up the Atlantic coasts of Europe to Norway. In the Mediterranean region it extends well inland as a weed, although in Britain and Ireland it is almost wholly coastal. However, it certainly thrives among the scruffy vegetation of weeds and garden escapes that establishes about seaside waste ground, beach huts and car-parks.

Bottom *A plant of shingle beaches and other pebbly, sandy areas by the sea, it is a conspicuous plant with large yellow flowers, long pods and silvery-grey foliage.*

SPECIES INFORMATION	
COMMON NAME	Greater Celandine
SCIENTIFIC NAME	Chelidonium majus
RELATED SPECIES	Welsh Poppy
HEIGHT/SPREAD	20–60 cm tall
FLOWERING TIME	May–September
HABITAT	Shady places and hedges

Note: The orange sap is unusual.

Greater Celandine

POPPY FAMILY

(Papaveraceae)

Size and appearance: A slender, branched perennial 20–60 cm (8–24 in) tall, exuding orange sap when cut.

Leaves: Compound, slightly hairy, with pairs of large, irregular, coarsely toothed lobes.

Flowers: 2–8 in loose clusters, yellow, flimsy, 20–25 mm (⅘–1 in) across, with 4 petals, 2 sepals and numerous yellow stamens.

Fruits: Hairless, slender, cylindrical capsules 3–5 cm (1⅕–2 in) long, splitting to release the ripe seeds.

Related or similar plants: Welsh Poppy (p.68) also has yellow flowers but they are much larger.

Habitat and distribution: Fairly common in rather damp or shady places such as hedges, banks and along the base of walls throughout England and Wales, but rare in Scotland and western Ireland; usually around houses or former settlements.

Flowering time: May to September.

THIS IS ONE of those plants that never look quite native, even when growing on rocky banks in woods. Mostly it is associated with human activity and clearly it has been widely introduced. It is now best known as a persistent weed of gardens and waysides, but the acrid, orange sap was once prized as a remedy for the removal of warts. Since at least Anglo-Saxon times, it was also used to treat sore eyes. Neither remedy would appear to work, and may well have done more damage to the patient.

Note that Lesser Celandine (p.55) is an unrelated plant in the buttercup family, similar only in having acrid sap.

Top The four petals, set cross-wise, indicate the Greater Celandine's (Chelidonium majus) membership of the Poppy family. The yellow flowers are set in loose clusters on this slender, branched perennial.

Bottom Greater Celandine is common along wayside hedges and banks, and at the base of walls. It has been grown extensively in cottage gardens and is therefore usually near habitation.

FLOWER TYPE

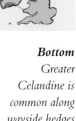

IDENTIFICATION

HABITAT

POPULATION

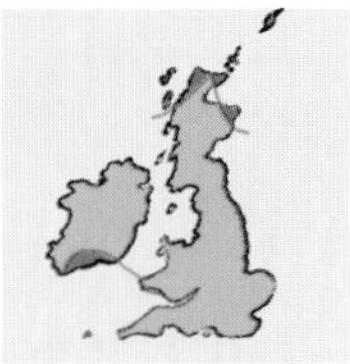
MAP

Welsh Poppy

POPPY FAMILY

(Papaveraceae)

SPECIES INFORMATION	
COMMON NAME	Welsh Poppy
SCIENTIFIC NAME	Meconopsis cambrica
RELATED SPECIES	Horned Poppy
HEIGHT/SPREAD	20–60 cm tall
FLOWERING TIME	June–September
HABITAT	Damp, shady places and rocks

Note: The yellow poppy of damp, rocky place.

FLOWER TYPE

IDENTIFICATION

HABITAT

POPULATION

MAP

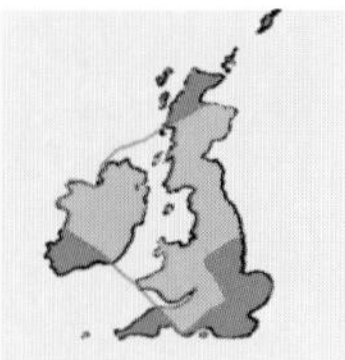

Size and appearance: A semi-erect or erect, green perennial, 20–60 cm (8–24 in) tall, exuding yellow sap when cut.
Leaves: Compound, deeply lobed, coarsely toothed, slightly hairy.
Flowers: Colitary, yellow, flimsy, 3–5 cm (1⅕–2 in) across, with 4 petals and numerous yellow stamens; the 2 sepals soon falling off.
Fruits: Hairless, slender, narrowly club-shaped capsules 2–4 cm (⅘–1⅗ in) long, splitting to release the ripe seeds.
Related or similar plants: Horned Poppy (p.66) also has yellow flowers but has greyish-green leaves and much longer fruits, and grows on shingle beaches.
Habitat and distribution: Damp, rocky places on lime-poor soils in upland areas of Wales, south-west England and Ireland, mainly in the east and north; widely established elsewhere as a garden escape, especially in the mountainous belt from Cumbria to central Scotland, both around houses and in the wild.
Flowering time: June to September.

WELSH POPPY IS a plant of cottage gardens, untended rockeries, damp pathsides and shady corners around old houses. It is also a true native, but generally a scarce one, although with a wider distribution through the far west of Europe. However, it has escaped widely from gardens to establish or re-establish in the wild.

The genus Meconopsis, to which Welsh Poppy belongs, is more familiar to gardeners. It includes the fabled blue poppies of the Himalayas and China, which also grow best on lime-poor and peaty mountain soils.

Although called the Welsh Poppy (Meconopsis cambrica)*, this flower does occur naturally in other parts of Britain and has also been widely grown in cottage gardens.*

SPECIES INFORMATION	
COMMON NAME	Common Fumitory
SCIENTIFIC NAME	Fumaria officinalis
RELATED SPECIES	Yellow Corydalis
HEIGHT/SPREAD	20–100 cm long
FLOWERING TIME	March–November
HABITAT	Shady places and hedges

Note: One of the commonest fumitories.

Common Fumitory

POPPY FAMILY

(Papaveraceae)

Size and appearance: A slender, hairless, semi-erect or sprawling, branched perennial with stems 20–100 cm (8–40 in) long; sap colourless.
Leaves: Compound, feathery, slightly greyish, deeply cut into small oblong or spear-shaped lobes.
Flowers: Pinkish-purple tipped with dark purplish-red, c. 10 mm (3/8 in) long, with 2 tiny, shield-shaped, toothed sepals, in rather dense spikes of 10–50 up to 8 cm (3 1/5 in) long.
Fruits: Spherical, 1-seeded nutlet, c. 2.5 mm (1/10 in) across.
Related or similar plants: Yellow Corydalis has dense heads of yellow flowers and grows on walls.
Habitat and distribution: Widespread and sometimes common, but sporadic in appearance, on arable land and allotments, in gardens, and on waysides and new road-verges; throughout, but less frequent in western Britain and western Ireland.
Flowering time: March to November, but all through mild winters, especially in the south-west.

Top Common Fumitory (Fumaria officinalis) *has pinkish-purple spikes of 10-50 flowers, which are held erect above the sprawling, feathery, greyish leaves. It is widespread in such places as allotments, waysides and other disturbed ground.*

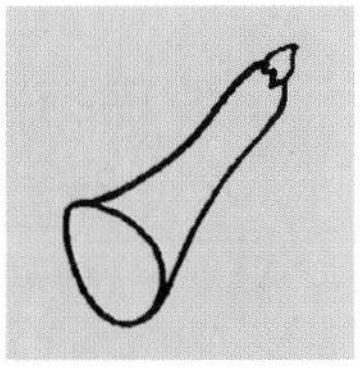
FLOWER TYPE

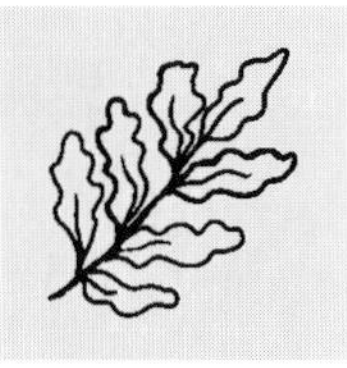
IDENTIFICATION

HABITAT

POPULATION

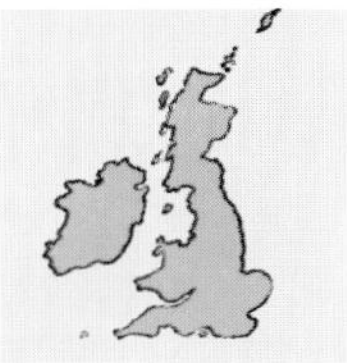
MAP

FUMITORIES COMPRISE A group of a dozen or so native species related to the poppies, but with bilaterally rather than radially symmetrical flowers. They are difficult to tell apart. The usually pinkish or purplish flowers are in spikes and the leaves are compound and feathery, said to look from a distance like smoke, hence the scientific and English names (Latin fumus terrae, smoke of the earth).

These plants are all more or less restricted to disturbed or cultivated ground. North-west Europe is a centre of distribution for fumitories, and several other species and varieties of fumitory occur only in Britain and Ireland.

Bottom
Yellow Corydalis (Pseudofumaria lutea) *is a tufted perennial up to 30 cm (12 in) tall, with compact clusters of yellow, fumitory-like flowers 15–20 mm (3/5–4/5 in) long and a hanging, several-seeded capsule. A native of the Alps.*

Pale Ramping-fumitory

POPPY FAMILY

(Papaveraceae)

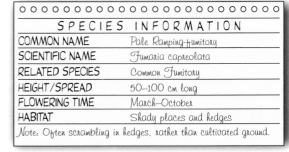

SPECIES INFORMATION	
COMMON NAME	Pale Ramping-fumitory
SCIENTIFIC NAME	Fumaria capreolata
RELATED SPECIES	Common Fumitory
HEIGHT/SPREAD	50–100 cm long
FLOWERING TIME	March–October
HABITAT	Shady places and hedges

Note: Often scrambling in hedges, rather than cultivated ground.

FLOWER TYPE

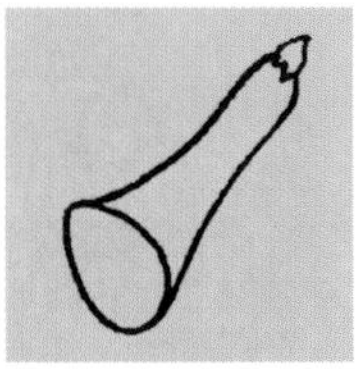

IDENTIFICATION

HABITAT

POPULATION

MAP

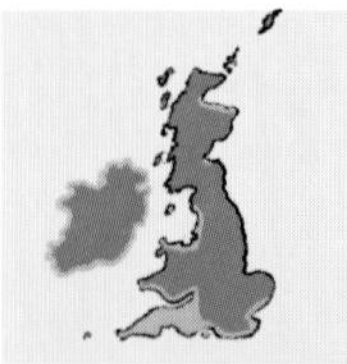

Size and appearance: A slender, hairless, branched perennial with stems 50–100 cm (20–40 in) long, sprawling or climbing by twisting leaf-stalks.

Leaves: Compound, feathery, slightly greyish, deeply cut into small oblong or spear-shaped lobes.

Flowers: Cream, often lightly tinged pinkish-purple, tipped with blackish-red, 10–15 mm ($\frac{2}{5}$–$\frac{3}{5}$ in) long, with 2 shield-shaped, toothed sepals, in rather loose spikes of 10–20 up to 5 cm (2 in) long.

Fruits: Spherical, 1-seeded nutlet, c.2.5 mm ($\frac{1}{10}$ in) across, smooth, on thick, down-turned stalks.

Related or similar plants: Common Fumitory (p.69) is more erect and has pinkish-purple flowers; and other fumitories.

Habitat and distribution: Locally common near the sea, and occasionally inland, in hedges and earthy walls, on arable land and in gardens north to the Moray Firth, but absent from the Scottish Islands and much of eastern Britain.

Flowering time: March to October, but all through mild winters in the south-west.

THIS HANDSOME FUMITORY of West Country hedge-banks and walls, is a very special plant: botanists regard the British and Irish plants of this species as a distinct, endemic subspecies — found nowhere else in the world. Another endemic fumitory, the rarer, closely related Purple Ramping-fumitory (*Fumaria purpurea*), differs in the more purplish flowers and less downturned fruit-stalks and other small features. It is also mostly coastal.

***Top** The flowers of the Pale Ramping-fumitory* (Fumaria capreolata) *are mostly cream, tipped with contrasting blackish-red in spikes of 10-20 flowers up to 5 cm (2 in) long.*

***Bottom** Common Ramping-fumitory* (Fumaria muralis) *has pink flowers in spikes that are much longer than the flower stalk. This plant of arable and waste ground and hedgebanks is scattered over most of Britain but is commonest in the west of England, Wales and Ireland.*

SPECIES INFORMATION	
COMMON NAME	Hedge Mustard
SCIENTIFIC NAME	Sisymbrium officinale
RELATED SPECIES	Other yellow 'crucifers'
HEIGHT/SPREAD	20–100 cm tall
FLOWERING TIME	May–September
HABITAT	Waysides and hedge-banks

Note: The flowers are paler yellow than in other 'cresses'.

Hedge Mustard

CABBAGE AND CRESS FAMILY

(Cruciferae or Brassicaceae)

Size and appearance: An erect, rough-downy annual or sometimes biennial, 20–100 cm (8–40 in) tall, with stiff, tough, wide-spreading branches.

Leaves: Deeply cut into spear-shaped lobes, the end lobe larger and more or less triangular.

Flowers: With 4 sulphur-yellow petals arranged in a cross, 2–4 mm ($\frac{1}{12}$–$\frac{1}{6}$ in) across, in narrow, flat-topped spikes that elongate considerably as the fruits mature.

Fruits: Short, tapering, cylindrical pods up to 20 mm ($\frac{4}{5}$ in) long, held close against the branch.

Related or similar plants: the combination of wide-spreading branches and pale yellow flowers distinguish Hedge Mustard from other common yellow-flowered 'crucifers' (although see Hairy Cabbage, under Black Mustard, p.77).

Habitat and distribution: A common plant of waste ground, pathsides, hedge-banks, field margins, untended gardens, and sometimes as a weed of cultivated ground; throughout, except the most mountainous areas and far northern Scotland.

Flowering time: May to September.

Top *As the season progresses the branches of the Hedge Mustard* (Sisymbrium officinale) *become stiffer, tougher and widely-spread, often at right-angles.*

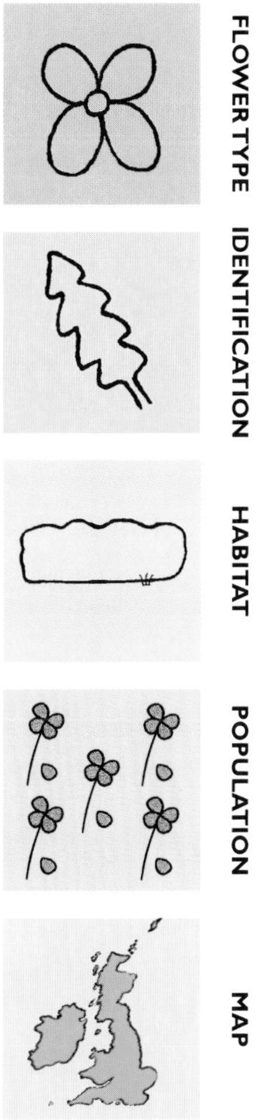

NOT THE HANDSOMEST of wild flowers, but a familiar, scruffy plant that is a feature of waysides and hedge-banks in summer. Hedge Mustard illustrates the principal features of the cabbage and cress family, one of the most easily recognised plant families. The petals, always four only, are arranged in the form of an equal-armed or Greek cross. The many-seeded fruit, with an internal papery partition up the middle, splits into two when ripe. The presence of special mustard oils gives the whole plant a smell of mustard when bruised, together with an acrid taste. These oils evolved to protect the plants against insects and other predators. They are the basis of the pungent flavours of cabbage, cress and other vegetables that make them popular foods.

Bottom *Hedge Mustard is common on waste ground, pathsides and any area of untended disturbed ground, where it is usually trampled giving it a scruffy appearance.*

Shepherd's Purse

CABBAGE AND CRESS FAMILY

(Cruciferae or Brassicaceae)

SPECIES INFORMATION	
COMMON NAME	Shepherd's Purse
SCIENTIFIC NAME	Capsella bursa-pastoris
RELATED SPECIES	Other Penny-cresses
HEIGHT/SPREAD	5–60 cm tall
FLOWERING TIME	February–November
HABITAT	Cultivated ground

Note: The heart-shaped pods are characteristic.

FLOWER TYPE

IDENTIFICATION

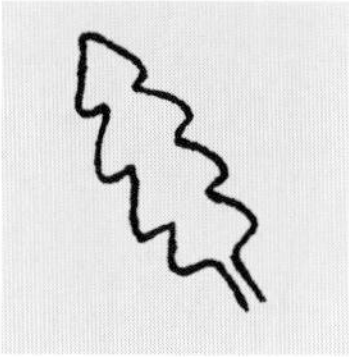

HABITAT

POPULATION

MAP

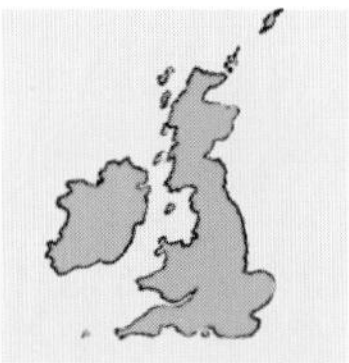

Size and appearance: An erect, shortly rough-hairy, often branched annual 5–60 cm (2–24 in) tall.

Leaves: Mostly in a neat basal rosette, spear-shaped or oblong, deeply cut into pointed lobes, the end lobe larger and more or less triangular; upper stem leaves few, arrow-shaped, clasping the stem.

Flowers: With 4 white petals arranged in a cross, 2–4 mm ($\frac{1}{12}$–$\frac{1}{6}$ in) across, in flat-topped spikes that elongate considerably as the fruits mature; sepals often reddish.

Fruits: Small, flattened, triangular or heart-shaped pods, held at a wide angle on slender stalks.

Related or similar plants: Field Penny-cress (p.73) has more conspicuous flowers and larger, almost circular fruits; Thale cress (see under Hairy Bitter-cress, p.82) has long, thin fruits.

Habitat and distribution: An abundant weed of gardens, allotments, arable crops, pathsides and waste ground throughout Britain and Ireland.

Flowering time: February to November, but all through mild winters.

ONE OF THE COMMONEST weeds, well known for its neat fruits, like old-fashioned purses or pouches, which have inspired both the English and scientific names. It had some herbal use for digestive and blood disorders, and was probably widely eaten as winter greens, as it is today in the Himalayas and elsewhere.

Shepherd's Purse regularly grows and flowers throughout the winter months, when it is frequently infected by two species of white parasitic fungus that cover and distort the stems and seed-pods. Younger, healthier plants grow up rapidly in late winter and early spring, producing healthy flowers and fruits. Shepherd's Purse is one of the first flowers at winter's end, alongside Chickweed (p.35), Common Field-speedwell (p.26), Red Dead-nettle (p.234) and Groundsel (p.307).

The species shows considerable variation in the shape of the leaves and pods, the amount of reddish coloration of the sepals, and the size of the flowers.

Top *The plant acquired both its English and scientific name from the shape of its fruits, which are like old-fashioned purses.*

Middle *Shepherd's Purse* (Capsella bursa-pastoris) *has white flowers 2-4 mm ($\frac{1}{12}$-$\frac{1}{6}$ in) across in flat-topped spikes which elongate as the fruit matures.*

Bottom *This is an abundant weed of gardens, allotments, arable crops and disturbed ground throughout the British Isles.*

SPECIES INFORMATION	
COMMON NAME	Field Penny-cress
SCIENTIFIC NAME	Thlaspi arvens
RELATED SPECIES	Other Penny-cresses
HEIGHT/SPREAD	10–60 cm tall
FLOWERING TIME	April–October
HABITAT	Cultivated grounds

Note: The almost circular, winged pods are diagnostic.

Field Penny-cress

CABBAGE AND CRESS FAMILY

(Cruciferae or Brassicaceae)

Size and appearance: An erect, hairless, little-branched annual 10–60 cm (4–24 in) tall, foetid when bruised.
Leaves: In a basal rosette, oblong or spear-shaped, toothed, or along the stem, arrow-shaped and clasping at the base.
Flowers: With 4 white petals arranged in a cross, 4–6 mm ($\frac{1}{6}$–$\frac{1}{4}$ in) across, in flattish clusters that elongate as the fruits mature.
Fruits: Flattened, almost circular, 10–15 mm ($\frac{2}{5}$–$\frac{3}{5}$ in) long, broadly winged with a deep notch at the tip, on curving, slender stalks.
Related or similar plants: Shepherd's Purse (p.72) has less leafy stems and smaller, heart-shaped fruits.
Habitat and distribution: A widespread weed of cultivated ground, especially fields of vegetable crops, waste ground and waysides in southern and eastern England; scarcer and usually on or near coasts in northern Britain and Wales; rare and mostly eastern in Ireland.
Flowering time: April to October.

SUPERFICIALLY LIKE A ROBUST Shepherd's Purse, Field Penny-cress is much more local in distribution. It is still a serious weed in parts of North America, where it is known as Jim Hill Weed. James Jerome Hill (1838–1916) built many of the railways along which it spread after its introduction. The whole plant, especially the distinctive fruits, has a fetid, mustard and garlic smell when bruised.

Two other penny-cresses are native to Britain and another two dozen to Europe, most of them plants of mountain rocks and screes. Alpine Penny-cress (*Thlaspi alpestre*) is similar to Field Penny-cress but is a variable perennial plant with untoothed leaves of limestone rocks, screes and mine spoil-heaps on soils rich in lead and zinc. Flowering April to August, it is found mostly in the northern Pennines, with scattered localities from the Scottish Highlands to the Mendip Hills in Somerset.

FLOWER TYPE

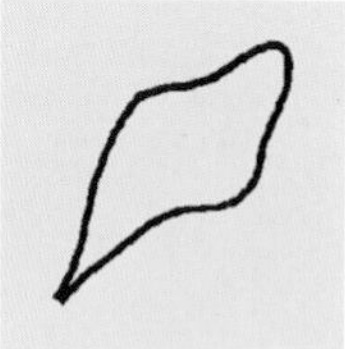

IDENTIFICATION

HABITAT

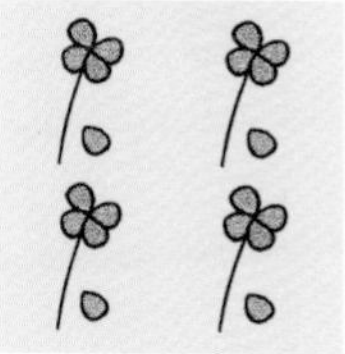

POPULATION

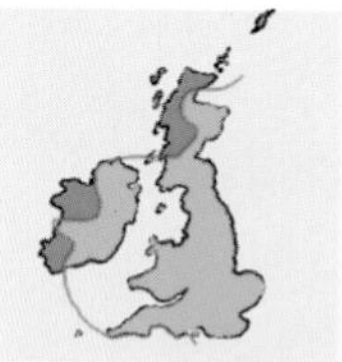

MAP

Field Penny-cress (Thlaspi arvense) *is very distinctive once it is fruiting with its flattened, circular, broadly-winged seeds. It has a notch at the top and are held erect on the end of slender, curving stalks.*

Garlic Mustard

CABBAGE AND CRESS FAMILY
(Cruciferae or Brassicaceae)

SPECIES INFORMATION	
COMMON NAME	Jack-by-the-Hedge
SCIENTIFIC NAME	Alliaria petiolata
RELATED SPECIES	Field Penny-cress
HEIGHT/SPREAD	30–120 cm tall
FLOWERING TIME	April–June
HABITAT	Hedgerows and woodland margins

Note: The heart-shaped leaves and garlic smell are unique.

FLOWER TYPE

IDENTIFICATION

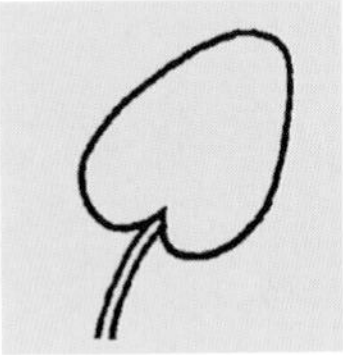

HABITAT

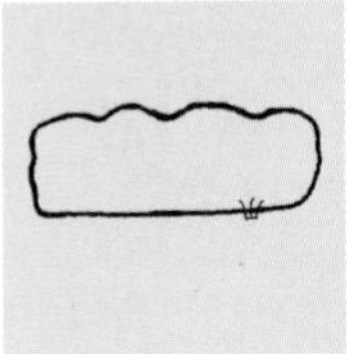

POPULATION

MAP

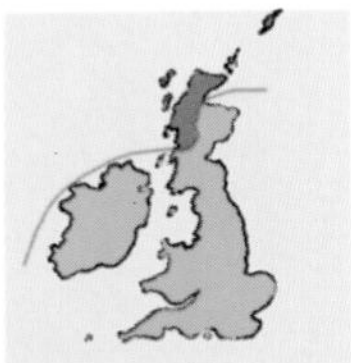

IN MAY ESPECIALLY, the rosettes of rounded, fresh green leaves, the upright stems and the white flowers of Garlic Mustard, which often appears in crowds, are a feature of lanes and hedge-banks. The garlic smell, rare outside the penny-cresses and more especially the onions and garlics, is also a distinctive character. Garlic Mustard is an important food plant of the caterpillars of the Green-veined White and Orange Tip butterflies, which can be seen seeking out the plants on which to lay their eggs. Butterflies home in on the scent of mustard oils in the leaves. In the past people too have eaten the leaves in salads and sauces.

Garlic Mustard (Alliaria petiolata) *is a plant commonly found in hedgerows and woodland margins, where it brings a fresh look to the spring vegetation with its bright green foliage topped with white flowers.*

Size and appearance: A robust, almost hairless, erect perennial 30–120 cm (12–48 in) tall, smelling strongly of garlic when bruised.
Leaves: Long-stalked, oval or triangular, with a heart-shaped base, coarsely toothed, wrinkled, bright green.
Flowers: With 4 white petals arranged in a cross, 4–6 mm (⅙–¼ in) across, in domed clusters that elongate as the fruits mature.

Fruits: Cylindrical, slightly 4-angled, 2–7 cm (⅘–5¾ in) long, on short, stiff, spreading stalks.
Related or similar plants: Field Penny-cress (p.73), smelling somewhat of garlic, is a smaller annual with almost circular fruits.
Habitat and distribution: Common in hedgerows, woodland margins, shady lanes, churchyards and untended gardens; throughout, northwards to the Moray Firth, but more scattered in western Scotland and much of Ireland.
Flowering time: April to June.

SPECIES INFORMATION	
COMMON NAME	Wallflower
SCIENTIFIC NAME	Erysimum cheiri
RELATED SPECIES	Hoary Stock
HEIGHT/SPREAD	20–60 cm tall
FLOWERING TIME	March–June
HABITAT	Hedgerows and woodland margins

Note: The yellow-flowered shrubby flower of walls and cliffs.

Wallflower

CABBAGE AND CRESS FAMILY

(Cruciferae or Brassicaceae)

Size and appearance: A branched, bushy biennial or perennial, becoming shrubby with age, 20–60 cm (8–24 in) tall.

Leaves: Almost stalkless, narrow, spear-shaped, with a short dense pile of minute, branched hairs.

Flowers: With 4 golden-yellow (sometimes streaked orange or red) petals arranged in a cross, 4–6 mm (1/6–1/4 in) across, richly scented, in domed clusters that elongate as the fruits mature.

Fruits: Cylindrical, slightly 4-angled and flattened, 2–8 cm (4/5–5 3/5 in) long, on short, stiff, semi-erect stalks.

Related or similar plants: Hoary Stock (*Matthiola incana*), also scented and growing on cliffs and open ground near the sea, either as a rare native or a garden escape, has purple or white flowers and greyish leaves.

Habitat and distribution: A long-time garden escape that is locally a feature of old ruins, walls, natural cliffs and quarries, and road and railway cuttings; throughout, but rarer and scattered in Scotland and Ireland.

Flowering time: March to June.

THIS IS ONE of the most cheering of early spring flowers, adding a dash of brilliant colour to grey cliffs and walls. These naturalised wild plants are shrubbier than they are in gardens, where they are too often treated as biennials to be discarded after flowering in their second year. Wallflower is of garden origin, and probably originated as an old cross between two closely related species from Greece and the Aegean region. There, several wallflowers grow wild on coastal cliffs and the sides of gorges. Plants in the wild, both the putative ancestors and naturalised plants, mostly have yellow flowers, but when found in gardens the colour is often orange, red or purplish, with complex streaking and mottling.

FLOWER TYPE

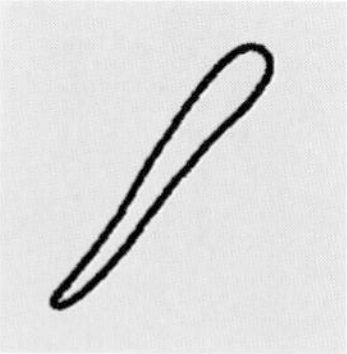
IDENTIFICATION

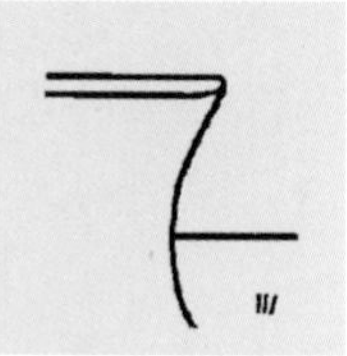
HABITAT

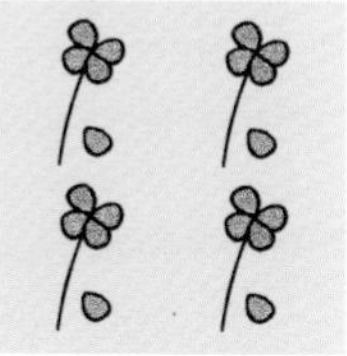
POPULATION

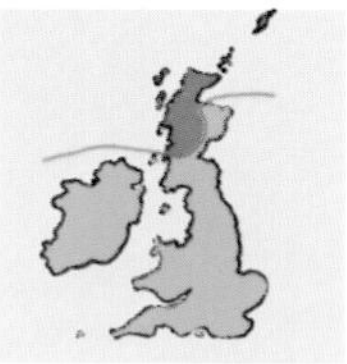
MAP

***Top** Wallflower* (Erysimum cheiri) *is a garden plant that escaped so long ago that it has found its own niche, bringing colour to old walls and ruins as well as natural cliffs and quarries.*

***Bottom** Hoary Stock* (Matthiola incana) *with purple flowers. It occurs on sea cliffs in a few places in southern England and south Wales.*

Charlock

CABBAGE AND CRESS FAMILY
(Cruciferae or Brassicaceae)

SPECIES INFORMATION	
COMMON NAME	Charlock, Wild Mustard
SCIENTIFIC NAME	Sinapis arvensis
RELATED SPECIES	White Mustard
HEIGHT/SPREAD	20–150 cm tall
FLOWERING TIME	March–June
HABITAT	Cultivated ground

Note: The common yellow-flowered cabbage or mustard.

FLOWER TYPE

IDENTIFICATION

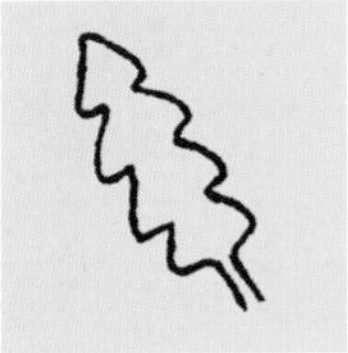

HABITAT

POPULATION

MAP

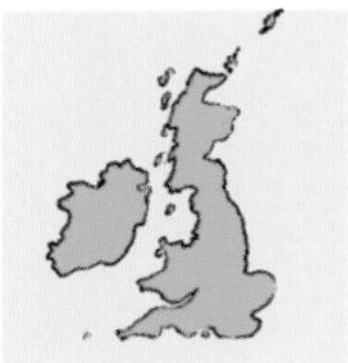

Size and appearance: Rather scruffy, rough-hairy, branched annual 20–150 cm (8–60 in) or more tall.
Leaves: Stalked, lyre-shaped, with irregular and coarsely toothed lobes; upper leaves unlobed, narrow.
Flowers: With 4 yellow petals arranged in a cross, 12–18 mm (½–¾ in) across, in ragged, domed clusters that will later elongate as the fruits mature.
Fruits: Cylindrical, hairless or sometimes hairy, waisted between the seeds, up to 5 cm (2 in) long, including a conical beak; seeds are reddish-brown.

Related or similar plants: White Mustard (see below) has pods with flattened beaks.
Habitat and distribution: A widespread and abundant weed of arable land, new road-verges and waste ground, especially on lighter soils.
Flowering time: March to June.

CHARLOCK IS A frequent sight in sandy or chalky cultivated fields, sometimes appearing in huge numbers. The seeds can survive in the soil in a state of dormancy for decades, until conditions of light and moisture enable them to germinate. Charlock was one of many arable weeds, like Common Poppy (p.64), that sprang up from buried seed on the former battlefields of the First World War. Modern weedkillers have controlled this plant in field crops, but it remains common enough. The leaves were formerly cooked and eaten like spinach during late winter and early spring.

Bottom right
White Mustard (Sinapis alba)*, another field weed and a former crop, has deeply lobed upper leaves and pods covered with stiff white hairs and topped by flattened beaks. It is widespread, but commonest on the chalk of southern and eastern England, although it can turn up as a bird seed alien.*

SPECIES INFORMATION	
COMMON NAME	Black Mustard
SCIENTIFIC NAME	Brassica nigra
RELATED SPECIES	Hoary Mustard
HEIGHT/SPREAD	40–200 cm tall
FLOWERING TIME	May–September
HABITAT	Waysides, waste places and cliffs

Note: Tall plant of West Country roadsides.

Black Mustard

CABBAGE AND CRESS FAMILY

(Cruciferae or Brassicaceae)

FLOWER TYPE

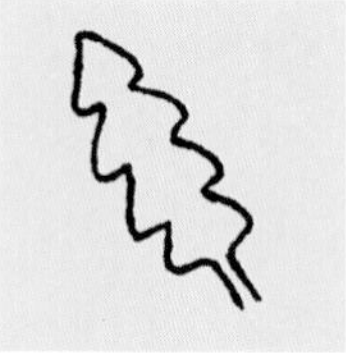

IDENTIFICATION

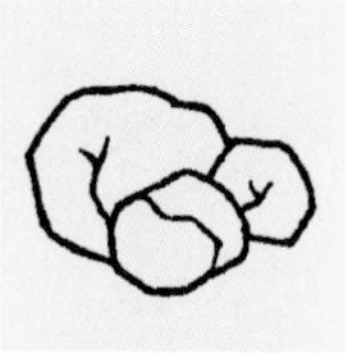

HABITAT

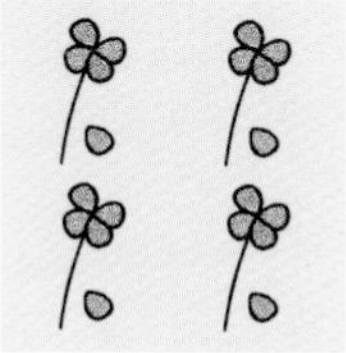

POPULATION

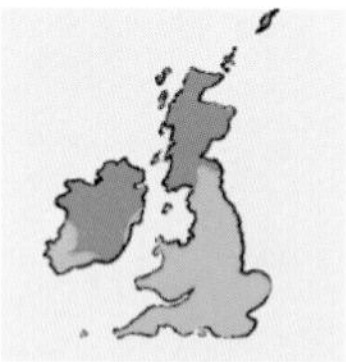

MAP

Size and appearance: Tall, branched annual 40–200 cm (16–80 in) tall, the stems hairy below.

Leaves: Lower leaves bristly-hairy, with 1–3 pairs of lobes plus a much larger end lobe; upper leaves stalked, spear-shaped, unlobed, hairless.

Flowers: With 4 bright yellow petals arranged in a cross, 8–10 mm (⅓–⅖ in) across, in long clusters that elongate further as the fruits mature.

Fruits: Cylindrical, 1–3 cm (⅖–1⅕ in) long, including a slender seedless beak, on upright stalks held close against the branches.

Related or similar plants: Hoary Mustard has smaller, paler yellow flowers and pods with stout beaks that contain a seed.

Habitat and distribution: A widespread and sometimes common plant of waste and disturbed ground, especially new road-verges, and on coastal cliffs, slopes and banks, north to the Firth of Forth; rare and mostly coastal in Ireland. It was formerly cultivated as mustard seed.

Flowering time: May to September.

THIS IS THE TALL, bright yellow-flowered wild mustard of roadsides and seaside banks in the West Country and elsewhere, sometimes in great swaying crowds. These bring to mind the masses of related 'crucifers' on the roadsides of the Mediterranean region, where the family is a dominant component of the flora. The native habitat is probably open or broken ground and cliffs on the coast and along rivers. The paler-flowered Hoary Mustard (see below), with which Black Mustard has been confused, is beginning to occupy similar roadside habitats, especially in urban areas.

***Bottom right** Hoary Mustard* (Hirschfeldia incana) *is similar but often whitish-hairy below, with paler yellow flowers 5–8 mm (¼–⅓ in) across; seed-pods, pressed close to the stem, have stout beaks, usually containing a seed. Originally from southern Europe, it has spread rapidly in recent years, especially on waste ground in cities such as London.*

Rape

CABBAGE AND CRESS FAMILY
(Cruciferae or Brassicaceae)

SPECIES INFORMATION	
COMMON NAME	Rape
SCIENTIFIC NAME	Brassica napus
RELATED SPECIES	Black Mustard
HEIGHT/SPREAD	30–150 cm tall
FLOWERING TIME	April–September
HABITAT	Cultivated ground

Note: The greyish-green leaves separate this species from others.

FLOWER TYPE

IDENTIFICATION

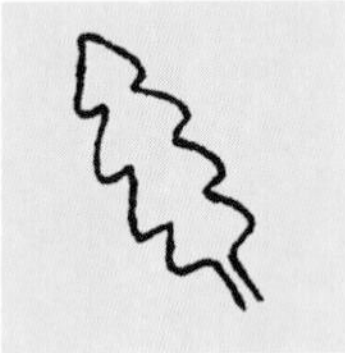

HABITAT

POPULATION

MAP

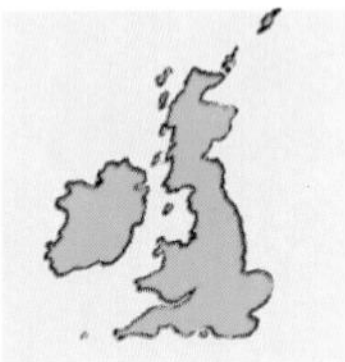

Size and appearance: Greyish-green, almost hairless annual or biennial 30–150 cm (12–60 in) tall,
Leaves: Stalked, regularly lobed, the end lobe larger, with a few bristles on the veins beneath; upper leaves unlobed but for a pair of clasping, rounded basal flanges.
Flowers: With 4 yellow petals arranged in a cross, 10–18 mm (⅖–¾ in) across, in domed clusters that elongate as the fruits mature.
Fruits: Cylindrical, 5–10 cm (2–5 in) long, including a slender beak; seeds grey or blackish.
Related or similar plants: Black Mustard (p.77), another former crop and field weed, has shorter pods.
Habitat and distribution: An increasingly common weed of arable land, new road-verges and embankments, and waste ground. The species is not known in the wild but has been cultivated in Europe for centuries.
Flowering time: April to September.

Top *Wild Cabbage* (Brassica oleracea) *often grows on a sea-cliff, although it can very occasionally be found growing as a casual on tips.*

RAPE IS FAST becoming a frequent weed of field edges and newer road-verges, especially in southern and eastern England. This has resulted from the large-scale cultivation of this plant for oil-seed, a crop that colours huge areas of countryside a sickly yellow in late spring. Now fingers of yellow are spreading along field margins and roads, and we may be seeing a new weed problem. Weed Rape could become a real menace should plants genetically modified for weedkiller resistance escape into the wild – or transfer this attribute to wild plants by cross-pollination. Weedkiller resistance is already known to have evolved independently in some weeds.

Wild Cabbage (*Brassica oleracea*), also has greyish-green leaves but is a perennial with a thick woody stem and larger, pale yellow flowers; it grows on a few coastal cliffs, perhaps as an ancient escape from cultivation.

Bottom *Rape* (Brassica napus) *turns much of the countryside yellow in April each year. Some people find its scent pleasant whilst others consider it to be over-poweringly sickly.*

SPECIES INFORMATION	
COMMON NAME	Common Scurvy-grass
SCIENTIFIC NAME	Cochlearia officinalis
RELATED SPECIES	Early Scurvy-grass
HEIGHT/SPREAD	Up to 50 cm tall, forming patches
FLOWERING TIME	March–July
HABITAT	Cliffs, rocks and seaside banks

Note: The rounded fleshy leaves are unusual.

Common Scurvy-grass

CABBAGE AND CRESS FAMILY

(Cruciferae or Brassicaceae)

Related or similar plants: Early Scurvy-grass is an annual with stalked stem leaves and egg-shaped pods.
Habitat and distribution: Locally common around most of our coasts, on cliffs, rocks, salt-marshes, seaside banks and walls, and on road-verges by and near the sea; also on open or boggy ground in the mountains of northern Britain, and a few sites in Wales and Ireland.
Flowering time: March to May on the coast, to July in the mountains.

Size and appearance: A rather stout, hairless biennial or short-lived perennial, with erect, sprawling or prostrate stems 10–50 cm (4–20 in) tall.
Leaves: Stalked, fleshy, dark green, kidney-shaped to almost circular; stem leaves stalkless, clasping, oval, toothed.
Flowers: With 4 white or sometimes pale lilac petals arranged in a cross, 6–10 mm (¼–⅜ in) across, scented, in loose low-domed clusters that elongate as the fruits mature.
Fruits: Numerous small, almost spherical pods that become corky when ripe.

SCURVY-GRASS CAN be very conspicuous in spring, flowering in great crowds that splash some coastal landscapes with white. The English name derives from the former use of the leaves as a winter greenstuff or infusion that would stave off scurvy, both at sea and on land. Scurvy-grass was, for instance, collected from Thames-side creeks and salt-marshes to be sold in London.

The species is variable in growth form, leaf-shape and flower size. Plants on mountains are particularly variable, and botanists continue to disagree as to how they should classify them. (Some favour splitting off more than one other species.) In muddy salt-marshes and estuaries, English Scurvy-grass (*Cochlearia anglica*), with larger flowers, more elongate pods and basal leaves tapered at the base, replaces Common Scurvy-grass.

Early Scurvy-grass (Cochlearia danica) *is similar but is a smaller, more compact annual with stalked stem leaves, usually lilac flowers 4–6 mm (⅙–¼ in) across and egg-shaped pods. Flowering February–June, it is widespread around the coast on open ground and shingle, and in recent years has spread inland beside railway tracks and road-verges, particularly dual-carriageways, forming white swathe in April.*

FLOWER TYPE

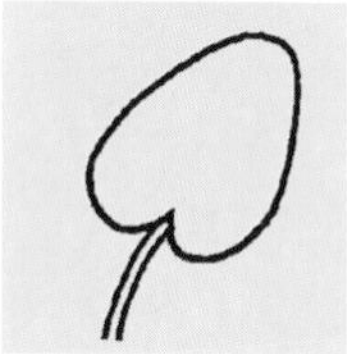

IDENTIFICATION

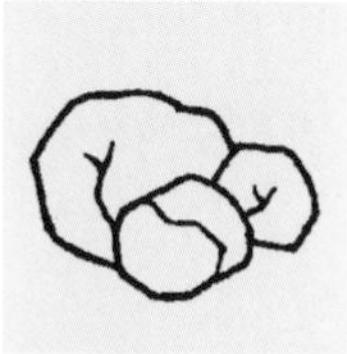

HABITAT

POPULATION

MAP

Sea Kale

CABBAGE AND CRESS FAMILY
(Cruciferae or Brassicaceae)

SPECIES INFORMATION	
COMMON NAME	Sea Kale
SCIENTIFIC NAME	Crambe maritima
RELATED SPECIES	Wild Radish
HEIGHT/SPREAD	30–75 cm tall
FLOWERING TIME	May–August
HABITAT	Coastal shingle beaches

Note: A robust, grey-leaved, cabbage-like, seaside plant.

FLOWER TYPE

IDENTIFICATION

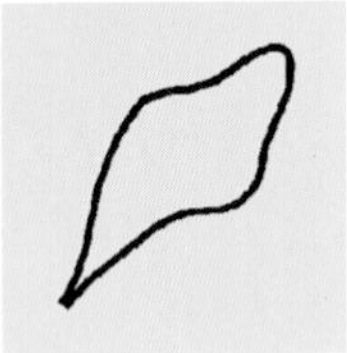

HABITAT

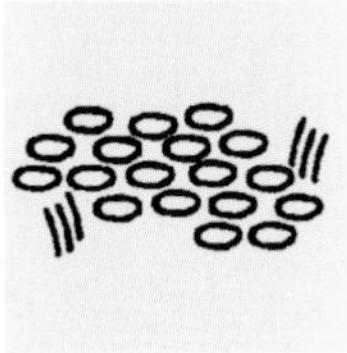

POPULATION

MAP

Size and appearance: A stout, grey, hairless perennial, with a huge, woody rootstock and erect or sprawling stems 30–75 cm (12–30 in) tall, branched above.

Leaves: Large, stalked, fleshy, leathery, grey or purplish with crinkly lobes and teeth; upper stem narrow, unlobed.

Flowers: With 4 white petals arranged in a cross, 12–18 mm (½–¾ in) across, in dense, branched, flat-topped clusters that elongate and bush out as the fruits mature.

Fruits: Numerous small pods, corky when ripe, each with a stalk-like, seedless lower segment and an almost spherical, 1- to 2-seeded upper segment.

Related or similar plants: Wild Radish is an annual or perennial with compound leaves and jointed, long-beaked pods.

Habitat and distribution: Locally common but very scattered around the coast, characteristically on shingle beaches but also on sand and low cliffs; its headquarters is the belt of extensive shingle formations along the south coast of England; rare in Ireland.

Flowering time: May to August.

Sea Kale (Crambe maritima) *is a plant of shingle beaches, readily identifiable with its large, grey, purple-tinged leaves and dense clusters of white flowers, which produce small corky pods with almost spherical tops.*

SEA KALE IS one of our most impressive native wild plants and a major feature of open coastal landscapes. In some places, notably the great shingle beaches that extend from Chesil Beach to Dungeness, it occurs in very large numbers. It was formerly gathered by local people and sold as a spring vegetable, after they had blanched new shoots by piling up shingle on top of the plants. From there it moved into market gardens and more sustainable trade. Sea Kale is a nice example of a native wild plant that we ourselves have brought into cultivation rather than, like cabbage and lettuce, it being introduced from the Mediterranean. It remains an unfashionable but peculiarly English vegetable.

The ripe corky pods float in sea-water and so disperse the seeds. Colonies tend to survive for a long time, although the plants are susceptible to damage from excessive trampling and bulldozing for coastal defences.

SPECIES INFORMATION	
COMMON NAME	Lady's Smock, Cuckooflower
SCIENTIFIC NAME	Cardamine pratensis
RELATED SPECIES	Hairy Bitter-cress, Sea Rocket
HEIGHT/SPREAD	15–50 cm tall
FLOWERING TIME	April–June
HABITAT	Damp grassy places

Note: The pink-flowered 'cress' of damp grassland in spring.

Lady's Smock

CABBAGE AND CRESS FAMILY
(Cruciferae or Brassicaceae)

Size and appearance: An elegant, hairless perennial, with erect stems 15–50 cm (6–20 in) tall.
Leaves: Basal leaves stalked, compound, with 1–7 pairs of broadly elliptical, slightly toothed leaflets, the end leaflet larger; stem leaves smaller, with narrower leaflets.
Flowers: With 4 pale lilac or whitish petals arranged in a cross, 12–20 mm (½–⅘ in) across, in loose clusters that elongate slightly as the fruits mature.
Fruits: Narrow, cylindrical pods 2.5–4 cm (1–1⅗ in) long, splitting explosively to disperse the seeds.
Related or similar plants: Another lilac-flowered crucifer, Sea Rocket is a fleshy annual of seashores; Hairy Bitter-cress is like a miniature Lady's Smock with white flowers.
Habitat and distribution: Common in marshes, wet grassland, woodland rides and other damp and grassy places such as unmanicured lawns throughout Britain and Ireland, although locally scarce in areas of intensive agriculture.
Flowering time: April to June.

FLOWER TYPE

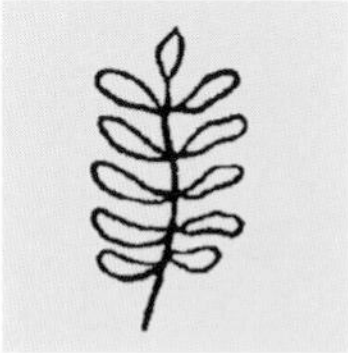
IDENTIFICATION

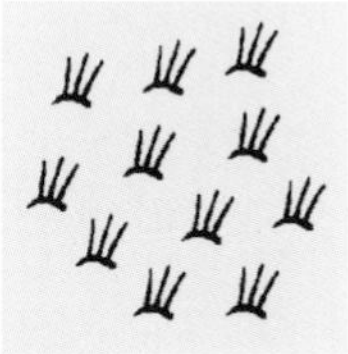
HABITAT

POPULATION

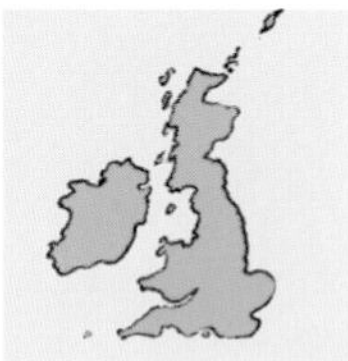
MAP

LADY'S SMOCK, one of our prettiest and best-loved wild flowers, has long been a symbol of emerging spring to poets and country people alike. John Gerard evoked beautifully in his 1597 *Herball* the season at which this plant flowers: 'for the most part in April and May, when the Cuckoo begins to sing her pleasant note'. One has an immediate image of a green meadow, birdsong and the smells of springtime. Gerard also noted that it had no medicinal properties, for this seems to be a plant that has always been appreciated for its looks and charm alone. Nevertheless, the cress-like leaves have probably been eaten at some time.

It is a variable species, with botanists describing several subspecies. An attractive variant with double flowers turns up occasionally in the wild, but is specially prized by gardeners. Unable to produce seed, it buds off new plants (like a begonia or African violet) from the leaves.

Top and middle *Lady's smock* (Cardamine pratensis) *is an elegant plant of damp meadows and marshes, where its lilac clusters of flowers make a delicate show in April and May.*

Bottom *Sea Rocket* (Cakile maritima) *also has lilac or whitish flowers but is a sprawling, fleshy annual plant of seashores, with short, stout fruits. Flowering June–September, it grows all round the coasts of Britain and Ireland.*

Hairy Bitter-cress

CABBAGE AND CRESS FAMILY
(Cruciferae or Brassicaceae)

SPECIES INFORMATION	
COMMON NAME	Hairy Bitter-cress
SCIENTIFIC NAME	Cardamine hirsuta
RELATED SPECIES	Lady's Smock, Thale Cress
HEIGHT/SPREAD	5–25 cm tall
FLOWERING TIME	February–November
HABITAT	Cultivated and open ground

Note: The explosive seed-pods are a notable feature.

FLOWER TYPE

IDENTIFICATION

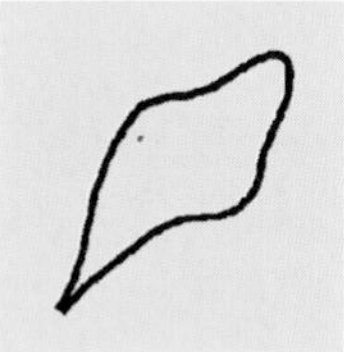

HABITAT

POPULATION

MAP

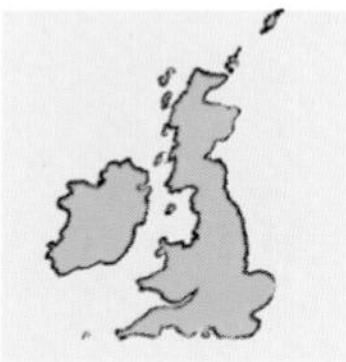

Size and appearance: A neat, rather compact, hairy perennial, with erect stems 5–25 cm (4–10 in) tall.

Leaves: Mostly basal, stalked, dark green, compound, with 1–5 pairs of oval or elliptical leaflets, the end leaflet slightly larger; stem leaves smaller.

Flowers: With 4 white petals arranged in a cross, 2–3 mm (1/12–1/8 in) across, in loose, branched clusters that elongate as the fruits mature.

Fruits: Narrow, cylindrical pods 1.5–2.5 cm (3/5–1 in) long, splitting explosively to disperse the seeds.

Related or similar plants: Thale Cress is a more slender plant with undivided leaves and very slender pods; Lady's Smock (p.81) is a larger perennial plant with lilac flowers.

Habitat and distribution: A ubiquitous weed of gardens, allotments, nurseries, open waste ground, paths and wall-tops, also on cliffs, rocks and sand-dunes away from human activity and disturbance, throughout Britain and Ireland.

Flowering time: February to November, but all through cold winters and with peaks in spring and autumn.

THIS IS THE little weed that so infuriates gardeners with its capacity to spread its tight rosettes of leaves over cultivated soil and paths and among the cold-frames. Its secret weapon is one of the fastest life cycles in the flora, flowering in a few weeks from germination, the explosive seed-pods projecting the seeds across the garden – and into the gardener's eye! Its redeeming feature is that it is a pungent, cress-like addition to salads.

Hairy Bittercress (Cardamine hirsuta) *is common on any disturbed soil but is most familiar as a garden weed. It has a neat rosette of compound basal leaves from which arises a flower stalk 5-25 cm (4-10 in) tall, it only takes a few weeks for its seeds to reach maturity. The fruits split explosively thus sending the seeds flying across the flower bed to start another generation, much to the chagrin of the gardener.*

SPECIES INFORMATION	
COMMON NAME	Watercress
SCIENTIFIC NAME	Rorippa nasturtium-aquaticum
RELATED SPECIES	Common Scurvy-Grass
HEIGHT/SPREAD	10–50 cm tall
FLOWERING TIME	May–October
HABITAT	Streams and wet ditches

Note: The vigorous 'watercress' of running water.

Watercress

CABBAGE AND CRESS FAMILY

(Cruciferae or Brassicaceae)

Size and appearance: An evergreen, creeping or floating, hairless, leafy, aquatic perennial, with erect or rather sprawling, branched stems 10–50 cm (4–20 in) tall that root readily below.
Leaves: Stalked, dark green, compound, with 1–4 pairs of oval or broadly spear-shaped, blunt, slightly toothed leaflets, the end leaflet larger, lobed.
Flowers: With 4 white petals arranged in a cross, 4–5 mm ($\frac{1}{6}$–$\frac{1}{5}$ in) across, in loose, branched clusters that elongate as the fruits mature.
Fruits: Straight or slightly curved, cylindrical pods 1–1.8 cm ($\frac{2}{5}$–$\frac{3}{4}$ in) long; seeds numerous, in 2 rows on each side of the pod.
Related or similar plants: The white-flowered Common Scurvy-grass (p.79) has kidney-shaped, unlobed leaves and almost spherical fruits.
Habitat and distribution: A familiar and often abundant plant, forming dense stands in the running water of springs, streams, small rivers and wet ditches, also on open mud, throughout Britain and Ireland except on higher mountains.
Flowering time: May to October.

FLOWER TYPE

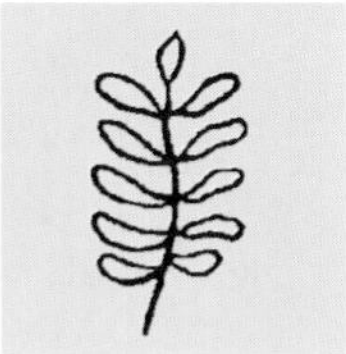
IDENTIFICATION

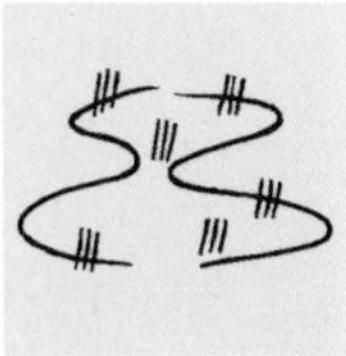
HABITAT

POPULATION

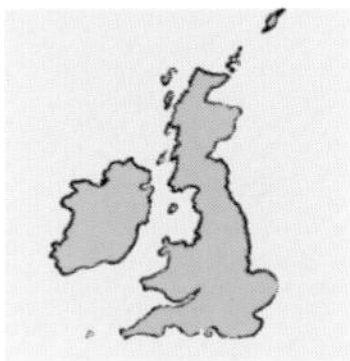
MAP

WATERCRESS HAS BEEN cultivated in England for almost two centuries in clear, unpolluted spring water. Like Common Scurvy-grass (p.79) but much more palatable, Watercress was always a useful winter green, rich in vitamin C, that could stave off scurvy. Note that we have two species in Britain: the other, One-rowed Watercress (*Nasturtium microphyllum*) has slightly longer pods, with the seeds in two single rows. The leaves turn brown in the winter. It is less widespread, but more common in the north.

Watercress, like Sea Kale, is a native British vegetable, and we seem to eat more of it than anybody else except another Atlantic people, the Portuguese. The 19th-century painter Edward Lear described the amusement of the Albanians at seeing him gather and eat watercress from a stream. However, the plant has a bad reputation in upland areas here for being infested with the larvae of the liver fluke of sheep.

Top *The flower head of Watercress* (Rorippa nasturtium-aquaticum) *gradually elongates, with the four white-petalled flowers at the top, behind which are the cylindrical pods of the ripening fruit.*

Bottom *Its dark green compound leaves often form patches at the edge of springs, streams and small rivers, but the plant we eat comes from commercial watercress beds which have a supply of pure water.*

Weld

MIGNONETTE FAMILY (Resedaceae)

SPECIES INFORMATION	
COMMON NAME	Weld, Dyer's Greenweed
SCIENTIFIC NAME	Reseda luteola
RELATED SPECIES	Wild Mignonette
HEIGHT/SPREAD	30–100 cm tall
FLOWERING TIME	June–September
HABITAT	Dry, open or waste ground

Note: Tall, yellow spikes on road-verges, with strap-shaped

FLOWER TYPE

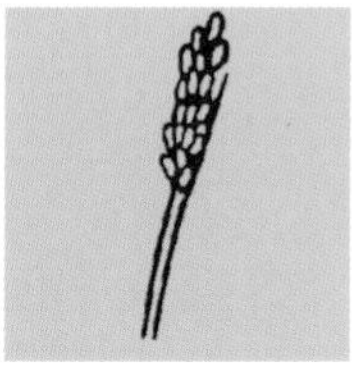

IDENTIFICATION

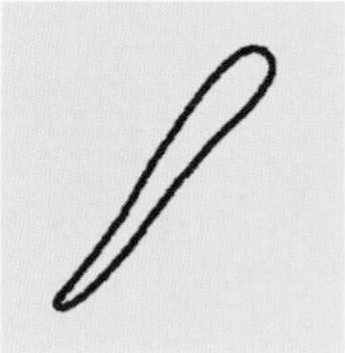

HABITAT

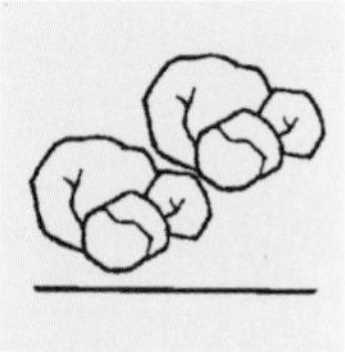

POPULATION

MAP

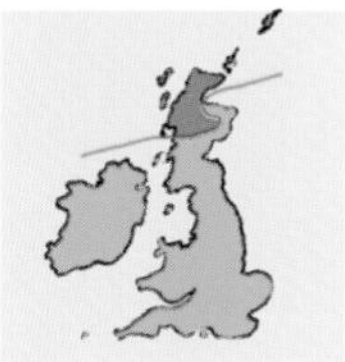

Size and appearance: An erect, leafy biennial 30–100 cm (12–40 in) tall, sometimes taller, with hollow stems branched in the upper part.

Leaves: Narrow, strap-shaped, dark green, glossy, with wavy margins.

Flowers: Numerous, 4–5 mm (⅙–⅕ in) across, pale greenish-yellow, with 4 petals and 20–30 stamens, in long, narrow spikes 20–30 cm (8–12 in) long.

Fruits: Almost spherical capsules with 3 teeth, open at the top; seeds numerous, black and shiny.

Related or similar plants: Wild Mignonette (p.85) has deeply divided leaves and club-shaped capsules.

Habitat and distribution: Widespread and often common in the open, dry, stony or sandy ground of dry banks, waste places, fallow fields, roadsides and abandoned railway land, mostly where the soil is lime-rich; more local in the north and west, rare over much of Scotland and rather local in Ireland.

Flowering time: June to September, but still conspicuous in fruit in the autumn.

Weld (Reseda luteola) *is an erect, leafy plant with narrow, dark green, glossy leaves with wavy margins. It is widespread in field margins and on roadsides.*

WELD IS A PLANT that one is likely to see on stony waste ground that is being recolonised by vegetation. It can form great crowds on the verges, embankments and cuttings of new or recently-constructed roads. It appears to be spreading in some areas with contractors' machinery and through the transport of topsoil.

It is an ancient source of bright yellow and green, fast dyes. At one time it was grown as a crop for this purpose in eastern England. It remains a good plant for the wild garden. The fruits, like those of Wild Mignonette (p.85) are unusual in that they are not completely closed up, even before they are ripe.

SPECIES INFORMATION	
COMMON NAME	Wild Mignonette
SCIENTIFIC NAME	Reseda lutea
RELATED SPECIES	Weld
HEIGHT/SPREAD	20–80 cm tall
FLOWERING TIME	June–October
HABITAT	Dry, open ground, field margins

Note: Sprawling plant with pale yellow spikes, of dry places.

Wild Mignonette

MIGNONETTE FAMILY

(Resedaceae)

THE ENGLISH NAME reflects that of the related Mignonette (*Reseda odorata*), an old-fashioned cottage garden plant with richly scented flowers. Wild Mignonette too is a good, hardy garden flower, especially for the wild garden. The unusual, partly open fruits are a feature of this group of plants (see Weld, p.84).

Wild Mignonette (Reseda lutea) *is an erect or sprawling perennial with numerous long narrow spikes of pale yellow flowers. The black and shiny seeds can be seen in the club-shaped capsules of the partly open fruits. It is found on chalk or lime-rich soils growing around field margins and along dry banks but also occurs on stony ground and can be found in quarries.*

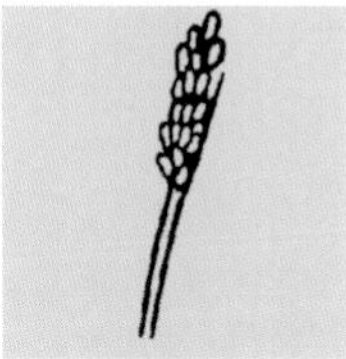

FLOWER TYPE

IDENTIFICATION

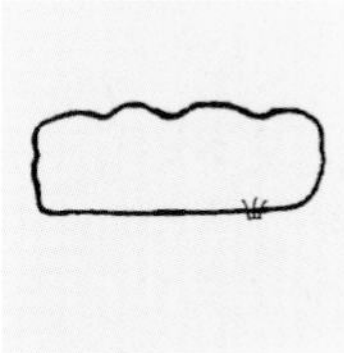

HABITAT

POPULATION

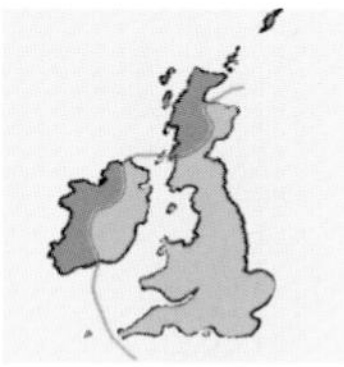

MAP

Size and appearance: An erect or sprawling, branched, leafy biennial or short-lived perennial 20–80 cm (8–32 in) tall, with solid stems.

Leaves: Divided into 1–3 pairs of long, narrow, blunt lobes, pale green, with slightly wavy margins.

Flowers: Numerous, c. 6 mm (¼ in) across, pale yellow, with 6 petals and 12–20 stamens, in long, narrow spikes 10–20 cm (4–8 in) long.

Fruits: Club-shaped capsules with 3 short teeth, open at the top; seeds numerous, black and shiny.

Related or similar plants: Weld (p.84) has undivided, strap-shaped leaves and almost spherical capsules.

Habitat and distribution: Common in open, disturbed or stony ground on lime-rich soils, field margins, quarries and dry banks, especially on chalk; most frequent in the south and east, almost absent from western and northern Scotland, and from Ireland except near the east coast.

Flowering time: June to October.

Round-leaved Sundew

SUNDEW FAMILY

(Droseraceae)

SPECIES INFORMATION	
COMMON NAME	Round-leaved Sundew
SCIENTIFIC NAME	Drosera rotundifolia
RELATED SPECIES	Other sundews
HEIGHT/SPREAD	5–15 cm tall
FLOWERING TIME	June–August
HABITAT	Wet peat and peat bogs

Note: A specialised plant of bogs, with red, sticky-hairy leaves.

FLOWER TYPE

IDENTIFICATION

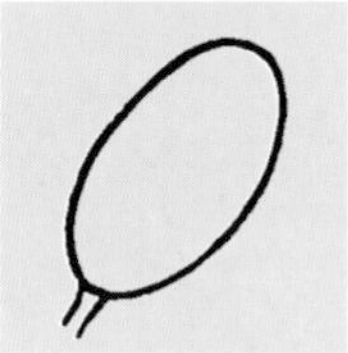

HABITAT

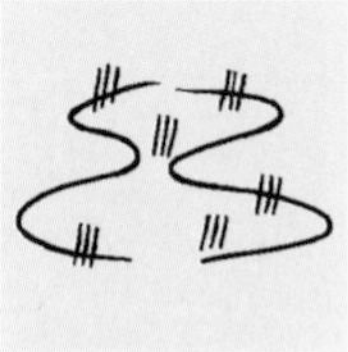

POPULATION

MAP

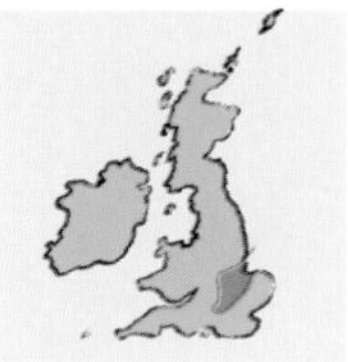

Size and appearance: Small, compact, tufted perennial 5–15 cm (2–6 in) tall.
Leaves: All in a spreading, basal rosette, long-stalked, almost circular, green beneath, reddish on the upper surface and covered with long sticky-tipped hairs; these trap and digest insects.
Flowers: Numerous, c. 5 mm (⅕ in) across, with 6 white petals, in small, elongate clusters.
Fruits: Small, smooth capsules.
Related or similar plants: The two other native sundews have oval leaves.
Habitat and distribution: A plant of wet peat and the sopping bog-moss carpets of peat-bogs throughout Britain and Ireland, but most frequent in upland areas towards western coasts; almost absent from lowland central England and parts of the south and east.
Flowering time: June to August, opening only on sunny days.

Top *Two other species of sundew occur in Britain. Oblong-leaved Sundew* (Drosera intermedia) *with narrowly oval leaves that taper into the stalk, and short flower-stalks, grows on wet peaty ground, mostly in western Britain and western Ireland; Great Sundew* (Drosera anglica) *with similar leaves up to 3 cm (1 ⅕in) long, grows in the wettest parts of peat-bogs, mainly in Scotland and western Ireland. The sticky-tipped hairs can be clearly seen in the picture.*

ROUND-LEAVED SUNDEW, the commonest of our three native sundews, is a classic example of an insectivorous plant (see also Common Butterwort, p.269). These plants trap insects to supplement their nutrition in the mineral-poor environment of the peat-bog. When a small insect like a midge lands on a sundew leaf it is trapped by the sticky drops. The hairs bend over on to the insect, further trapping it and holding it fast. Digestive substances exuded in the drops slowly break down the body, and the plant absorbs the nutrients released.

Round-leaved Sundew is naturally scarce in the drier lowlands, and continues to decrease because of drainage and the commercial extraction of peat for horticulture. In the uplands it remains common, often occurring in vast crowds.

SPECIES INFORMATION	
COMMON NAME	Wall Pennywort, Navelwort
SCIENTIFIC NAME	Umbilicus rupestris
RELATED SPECIES	Orpine
HEIGHT/SPREAD	10–80 cm tall
FLOWERING TIME	May–August
HABITAT	Rocks, walls and hedge-banks

Note: The button-like fleshy leaves are instantly recognisable.

Wall Pennywort

STONECROP FAMILY
(Crassulaceae)

Size and appearance: A fleshy, hairless, tufted perennial 10–80 cm (4–32 in) tall, often woody at the base.
Leaves: Mostly in a basal rosette, stalked, circular with a central depression, 3–8 cm (2⅕–3⅕ in) across, very fleshy, rubbery, with slightly wavy margins; stem leaves spoon- or wedge-shaped.
Flowers: 5–10 mm (⅕–⅖ in) long, tubular, greenish-yellow or reddish, numerous in long, slender spikes.
Fruits: Fused clusters of 5 pods, enclosed by the persistent flower.
Related or similar plants: Orpine has toothed, fleshy leaves and domed heads of flowers.
Habitat and distribution: Locally common in open, disturbed or stony ground on cliffs, rock outcrops, field and churchyard walls, hedge-banks and the branches and crooks of trees in western Britain and Ireland, north to Mull; locally extending eastwards to Kent.
Flowering time: May to August.

THIS IS ONE of the most characteristic wild plants of western districts and is sometimes extremely abundant, a conspicuous feature of walls and the sides of lanes, often tinged purplish. The western distribution reflects its frost-sensitive nature; it also avoids lime-rich soils and rocks. Its European distribution extends down western Europe into the Mediterranean region, so summer drought is less of a limiting factor.

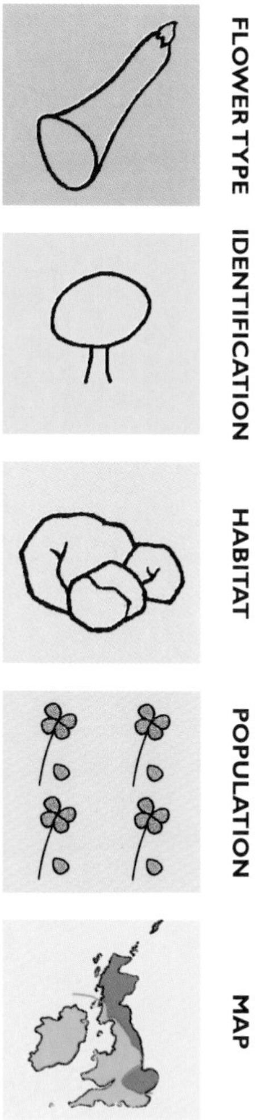

***Top** Wall Pennywort* (Umbilicus rupestris) *is a charming plant of rocky outcrops, walls and hedgebanks in western Britain. Its basal leaves are circular with a central depression and wavy margins. From between these arises the flower spike which carries numerous tubular creamy or greenish-yellow flowers.*

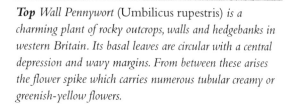

***Bottom** Orpine* (Sedum telephium)*, another fleshy plant of hedge-banks, also woodland and scrub, has oval, toothed leaves and domed heads of purplish or lilac flowers.*

Biting Stonecrop

STONECROP FAMILY

(Crassulaceae)

SPECIES INFORMATION	
COMMON NAME	Biting Stonecrop, Wall-pepper
SCIENTIFIC NAME	Sedum acre
RELATED SPECIES	Other Stonecrops
HEIGHT/SPREAD	5–10 cm tall, in patches
FLOWERING TIME	May–August
HABITAT	Walls, railway ballast, sand-dunes

Note: The acrid taste of the leaves distinguishes this plant.

FLOWER TYPE

IDENTIFICATION

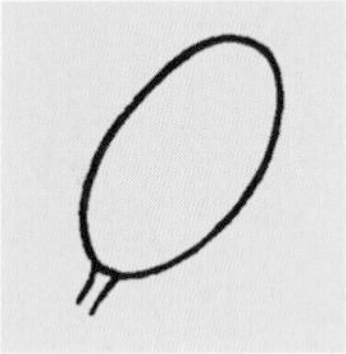

HABITAT

POPULATION

MAP

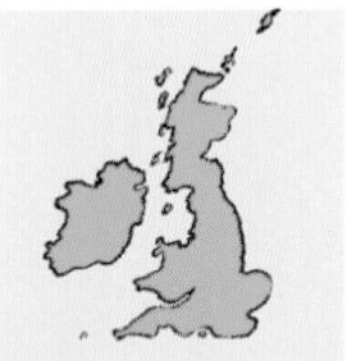

Size and appearance: A fleshy, hairless perennial, forming low cushions, with erect flowering stems 5–10cm (2–4 in) tall.

Leaves: Tiny, very fleshy, narrowly egg-shaped, overlapping, green or reddish, with a sharp, peppery taste.

Flowers: Starry, bright yellow, up to 10 mm (⅜ in) across, in small, terminal clusters.

Fruits: Fused clusters of 5 pods, enclosed by the persistent flower.

Related or similar plants: Other stonecrops, mostly escaped from gardens.

Habitat and distribution: Forming large patches on rocks, walls, dry waysides, railway ballast, sand-dunes and shingle beaches throughout Britain and Ireland, but scarce in the uplands; often associated with former human building activity.

Flowering time: May to August.

FOR MOST OF THE YEAR this plant is inconspicuous, often red- or purplish-tinged due to mineral deficiency on poor, shallow soils and dry or stony ground. However, in July, Biting Stonecrop is one of the most showy of wild flowers, its gold masses colouring great stretches of railway ballast, old airfields and concrete tracks.

Biting Stonecrop is a popular garden plant, and grows well on walls and roofs made of natural materials. A long association with people has enabled it to gather a jolly assemblage of vernacular names, but who knows where it picked up one elongated epithet: Welcome-home-husband-however-drunk-you-be. Perhaps it was a yellow beacon on a cottage roof on the way home from the pub in the summer dusk.

Biting Stonecrop (Sedum acre) *flowers in midsummer on a tiled roof, adapting from its natural habitat of rocks, sand-dunes and shingle beaches. The bright yellow star-like flowers make an eye-catching splash of colour wherever they occur. The fleshy leaves help the plant to maintain a supply of water for, where it grows, there is either a surplus when it rains or none available between showers. The plant, therefore, grabs what it can when it can and stores the water until required.*

SPECIES INFORMATION	
COMMON NAME	Opposite-leaved Golden-saxifrage
SCIENTIFIC NAME	Chrysosplenium oppositifolium
RELATED SPECIES	Alternate-leaved Golden-saxifrage
HEIGHT/SPREAD	5–20 cm tall, forming patches
FLOWERING TIME	April–July
HABITAT	Wet woods and streamsides

Note: Leafy clusters of small yellow flowers in spring.

Opposite leaved Golden-saxifrage

SAXIFRAGE FAMILY

(Saxifragaceae)

Habitat and distribution: Common in wet woods, on shady streamsides, wet rocks and mountain ledges, especially on lime-poor soils.

Flowering time: April to July; from mid-March after mild winters.

THIS IS A COMMON wild flower of early spring, but is frequently overlooked. Mats of this plant are a characteristic feature of wet woodland rides and the banks of streams that flow through woods. It is worth looking for the rarer Alternate-leaved Golden-saxifrage, sometimes growing with it in small numbers in the wettest places.

Bottom *Alternate-leaved Golden-saxifrage* (Chrysosplenium alternifolium) *is similar to Opposite-leaved Golden-saxifrage but the leaves, which are arranged alternately along the stem are heart-shaped at the base and slightly paler; and the flowers are 5–6 mm (c.⅕ in) across. It is found in similar habitats, but is rarer (and absent from Ireland) and favours wetter, more lime-rich sites.*

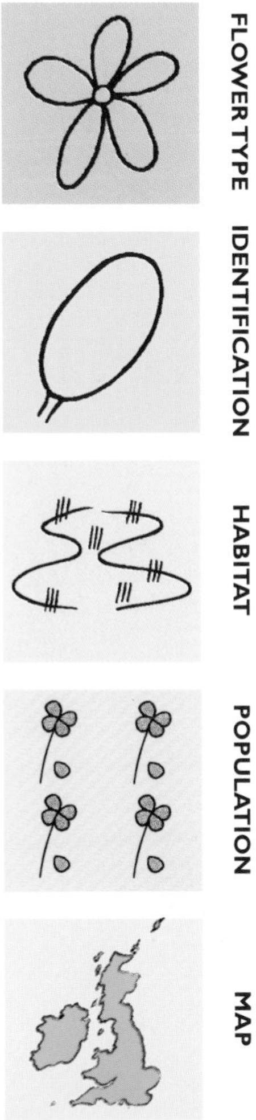

Size and appearance: Low-growing, creeping perennial with numerous, leafy stems, 5–20 cm (2–8 in) tall.

Flowers: Inconspicuous in a flat, leafy cluster, 4–5 mm (c.⅕ in) across, with yellow sepals (petals absent).

Leaves: Almost circular, wedge-shaped at the base, shallowly and bluntly toothed.

Fruits: Small, inconspicuous capsules.

Related or similar plants: Alternate-leaved Golden-saxifrage has leaves that are heart-shaped at the base and arranged alternately along the stem, and flowers 5–6 mm (c.⅕ in) across.

Starry Saxifrage

SAXIFRAGE FAMILY

(Saxifragaceae)

SPECIES INFORMATION	
COMMON NAME	Starry Saxifrage
SCIENTIFIC NAME	Saxifraga stellaris
RELATED SPECIES	Alpine Saxifrages
HEIGHT/SPREAD	5–30 cm tall
FLOWERING TIME	June–August
HABITAT	Wet mountain rocks, streamsides

Note: The only common white-flowered mountain saxifrage.

FLOWER TYPE

IDENTIFICATION

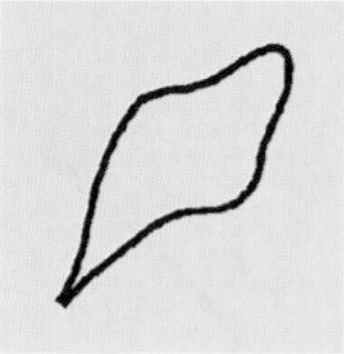

HABITAT

POPULATION

MAP

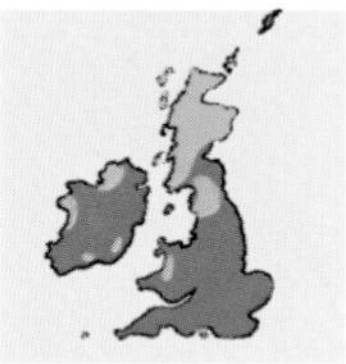

Size and appearance: A densely tufted and sparsely hairy perennial, with leafless flowering stems 5–30 cm (2-12 in) tall.
Leaves: Unstalked, wedge- to spoon-shaped, toothed.
Flowers: In loose clusters, 10–15 mm (⅜-⅝ in) across, white with 2 yellow spots at base of each petal; sepals turned back.
Fruits: 2-horned, many-seeded capsules.
Related or similar plants: The rarer Alpine Saxifrage has stalked leaves and flowers in a tight head.
Habitat and distribution: Widespread on wet rocks and screes, by streams and springs in the mountains of Scotland, northern England, Snowdonia and western Wales and Ireland.
Flowering time: June to August.

STARRY SAXIFRAGE IS one of the commoner native alpine wild flowers. It rarely occurs away from the dampest rocks.

Bottom *Alpine Saxifrage* (Saxifraga nivalis) *is similar but has leaves that are stalked and purplish underneath, flowers in tight clusters, petals without yellow spots, and erect or spreading sepals. It is scarcer but fairly widespread on damp, usually lime-rich rocks in the mountains of Scotland; it also occurs in the Lake District and Snowdonia, and on Ben Bulbin, County Sligo.*

SPECIES INFORMATION	
COMMON NAME	St Patrick's Cabbage
SCIENTIFIC NAME	Saxifraga spathularis
RELATED SPECIES	Kidney Saxifrage
HEIGHT/SPREAD	10–30 cm tall
FLOWERING TIME	June–August
HABITAT	Wet mountain rocks in Ireland

Note: A feature of damp rocks in SW Ireland.

St Patrick's Cabbage

SAXIFRAGE FAMILY

(Saxifragaceae)

Size and appearance: A tufted perennial, with leafless reddish stems 10–30 cm (3–12 in) tall.
Leaves: In a compact basal rosette, rounded or spoon-shaped, coarsely and sharply toothed, rather leathery, hairless on the upper surface.
Flowers: Numerous in loose, branched clusters, the petals white with yellow spots at the base and many red spots.
Fruits: 2-horned, many-seeded capsules.
Related or similar plants: Kidney Saxifrage (see below) has kidney-shaped leaves that are hairy on both surfaces.
Habitat and distribution: Widespread in gullies and on cliffs, on wet rocks and by streams in the mountains of western Ireland, especially Kerry and Connemara; locally extending to the mountains to the east.
Flowering time: June to August.

FLOWER TYPE

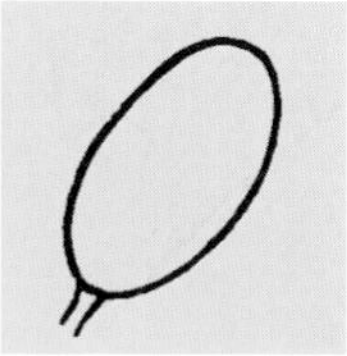

IDENTIFICATION

HABITAT

POPULATION

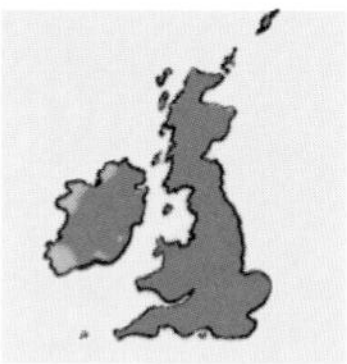

MAP

ST PATRICK'S CABBAGE and the closely related Kidney Saxifrage have the distinction of being among a select group of 15 Irish native plants that do not occur in Britain. The two often grow together and they hybridise freely in western Ireland, giving rise to a bewildering array of intermediate variation. Sometimes these intermediate plants occur where one or other of the parents is now absent.

Pyrenean Saxifrage is similar to St Patrick's Cabbage but has leaves with blunt, rounded teeth and flowers in June and July. A native of the Pyrenees, it has been naturalised at Haseldon Gill in Yorkshire for some 200 years. The well-known garden plant London pride (*Saxifraga x urbium*) is a cross between this species and St Patrick's Cabbage. It sometimes escapes on to rocks and old walls in western Britain and Ireland.

***Bottom** Kidney Saxifrage* (Saxifraga hirsuta) *is similar to St Patrick's Cabbage but the leaves are kidney-shaped and hairy on both sides, and the flowers have fewer red spots. It occurs in similar habitats in the mountains of Kerry and and adjacent west Cork in south-west Ireland, flowering in summer.*

Meadow Saxifrage

SAXIFRAGE FAMILY
(Saxifragaceae)

SPECIES INFORMATION	
COMMON NAME	Meadow Saxifrage
SCIENTIFIC NAME	Saxifraga granulata
RELATED SPECIES	Rue-leaved Saxifrage
HEIGHT/SPREAD	10–40 cm tall
FLOWERING TIME	April–June
HABITAT	Pastures, banks and churchyards

Note: The only large-flowered saxifrage of the lowlands.

FLOWER TYPE

IDENTIFICATION

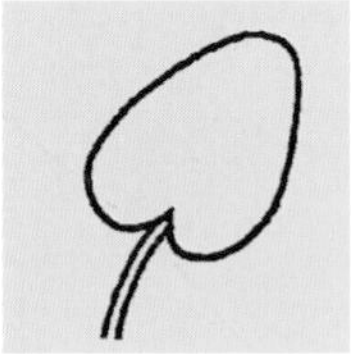

HABITAT

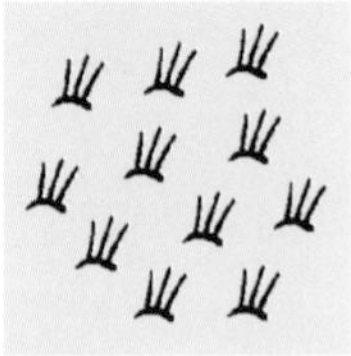

POPULATION

MAP

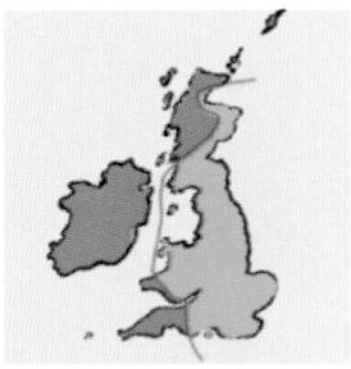

Size and appearance: Tufted, hairy, short-lived perennial, 10–40 cm (4–16 in) tall, with bulbils or detachable buds at the base of the flowering stems.
Leaves: Mostly basal, long-stalked, kidney-shaped, bluntly toothed.
Flowers: 10–18 mm (⅖–¾ in) across, white, in loose, branched clusters.
Fruits: 2-horned, many-seeded capsules.
Related or similar plants: Rue-leaved Saxifrage (p.93) is much smaller and has deeply lobed leaves.
Habitat and distribution: Local but sometimes abundant in old, unploughed pastures, on dry roadside banks and in churchyards, especially in the east; absent from most of Cornwall, Devon and Scotland, and in Ireland only in a few places on the east coast.
Flowering time: April to June.

THIS ATTRACTIVE LOWLAND saxifrage has decreased markedly in recent decades as old meadows and pastures have been fertilised or reseeded. It is still locally abundant, especially in churchyards and on dry, roadside banks, where it sometimes dusts the grass with white in May. The plants reproduce both by seed and by the small bulbils at the base of the basal leaf rosette. It is an example, like the Red Campion (p.42) of a plant that is widespread in Britain but very rare in Ireland.

Top *Meadow Saxifrage* (Saxifraga granulata) *is a tufted, hairy plant with white flowers in loose, branched clusters.*

Bottom *Once far more frequent across the country, the loss of old meadows and pastures has resulted in a decline in numbers of the flower. However, where the ancient grassland has survived it can be quite plentiful.*

SPECIES INFORMATION	
COMMON NAME	Rue-leaved Saxifrage
SCIENTIFIC NAME	Saxifraga tridactylites
RELATED SPECIES	Meadow Saxifrage
HEIGHT/SPREAD	2.5–15 cm tall
FLOWERING TIME	April–June
HABITAT	Rocks, sand-dunes and walls

Note: Our only annual saxifrage.

Rue-leaved Saxifrage

SAXIFRAGE FAMILY
(Saxifragaceae)

Size and appearance: Small, sticky-hairy, often reddish annual, 2.5–15 cm (1–6 in) tall.
Leaves: Unlobed or 3- to 5-lobed.
Flowers: In branched clusters, 2–5 mm ($\frac{1}{12}$–$\frac{1}{5}$ in) across, white.
Fruits: 2-horned, many-seeded capsules.
Related or similar plants: Meadow Saxifrage is larger and has kidney-shaped, bluntly toothed leaves.
Habitat and distribution: Widespread but local on dry heaths, sand-dunes, wall-tops and limestone rocks, but very rare in Scotland.
Flowering time: April to June.

A CHARACTERISTIC PLANT of walls, where its populations may be very isolated from its native heathland or other dry open semi-natural habitats. The plants are often small and reddish, as a result of low levels of vital plant nutrients found in the soil, especially potassium.

Rue-leaved Saxifrage (Saxifraga tridactylites) *is a small, sticky-hairy, often reddish annual which flowers in early spring and can be found on seemingly diverse habitats from sand-dunes to wall-tops.*

FLOWER TYPE

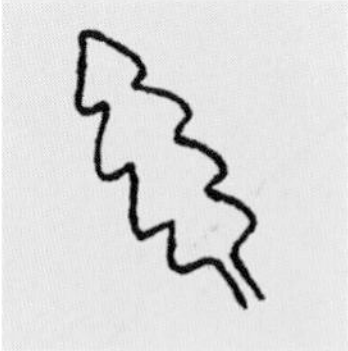

IDENTIFICATION

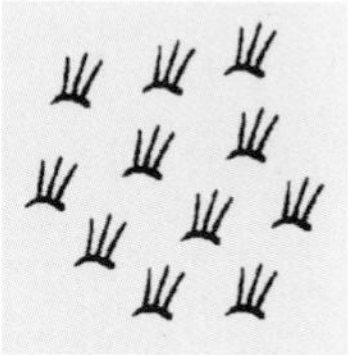

HABITAT

POPULATION

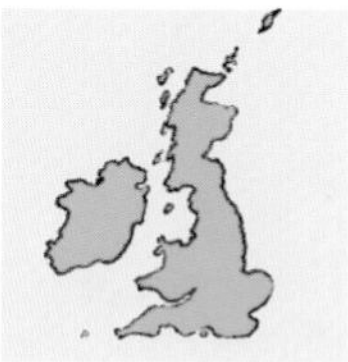

MAP

Mossy Saxifrage

SAXIFRAGE FAMILY

(Saxifragaceae)

SPECIES INFORMATION	
COMMON NAME	Mossy Saxifrage.
SCIENTIFIC NAME	Saxifraga hypnoides
RELATED SPECIES	Irish Saxifrage
HEIGHT/SPREAD	5–20 cm tall, forming patches
FLOWERING TIME	May to July
HABITAT	Limestone rocks, stony grassland

Note: The deeply cut leaves are distinctive.

FLOWER TYPE

IDENTIFICATION

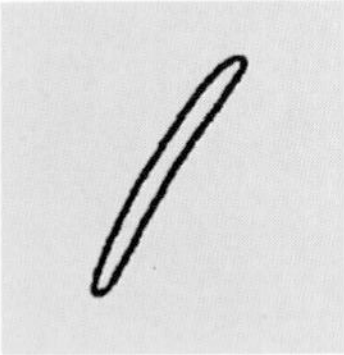

HABITAT

POPULATION

MAP

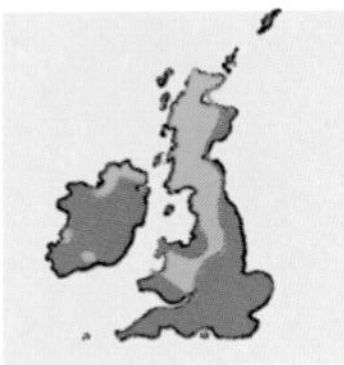

Size and appearance: A perennial 5–20 cm (2–8 in) tall, with a mat of prostrate non-flowering shoots, often with bulbils or detachable buds in the leaf-angles.
Leaves: Long-stalked, divided into 3–5 narrow, pointed lobes not more than 1 mm wide.
Flowers: Solitary or in groups of 2–5, 10–12 mm (⅖–½ in) across, white.
Fruits: 2-horned, many-seeded capsules.
Related or similar plants: Irish Saxifrage.
Habitat and distribution: Limestone rocks and stony grassland in northern England, Scotland and Wales, mainly in the mountains, also in the Cheddar Gorge, Somerset. In Ireland it occurs mainly in the Burren, where it is common.
Flowering time: May to July.

THIS PLANT, TOGETHER with crosses with other saxifrage species, is one of the commonest rock garden saxifrages. These garden plants sometimes escape on to walls.

Irish Saxifrage (*Saxifraga rosacea*) is similar but has a more tufted appearance, leaves usually with 5 often blunt lobes, pink stems, erect flower-buds, and pure white flowers 10–15 mm (⅖–⅗ in) across. It occurs on wet rocks and screes, and in damp grassland and streamsides in the mountains of western Ireland from Mayo to Kerry and County Tipperary, flowering from June to August. It formerly occurred in Snowdonia but is now extinct. Hart's Saxifrage (*Saxifraga rosacea subsp. hartii*), which has sticky-hairy leaves, occurs on the sea-cliffs of Arranmore Island, County Donegal, and nowhere else.

Top *Mossy Saxifrage* (Saxifraga hypnoides) *forms a mat of prostrate non-flowering shoots from which the white flowers arise, either solitary or in small groups.*

Bottom *Flowering from May to July, it grows by the sides of mountain streams, on cliffs and in rocky pastures as in the photograph below. However, as a popular rock garden component, it also escapes and can be found on walls in urban areas.*

SPECIES INFORMATION	
COMMON NAME	Yellow Mountain-saxifrage
SCIENTIFIC NAME	Saxifraga aizoides
RELATED SPECIES	Yellow Marsh-saxifrages
HEIGHT/SPREAD	5–30 cm tall
FLOWERING TIME	June–September
HABITAT	Wet mountain rocks, streamsides
Note: Our only common yellow-flowered saxifrage.	

Yellow Mountain-saxifrage

SAXIFRAGE FAMILY
(Saxifragaceae)

Size and appearance: Loosely tufted, 5–30 cm (2–12 in) tall, with numerous leafy non-flowering and flowering shoots.
Leaves: Narrow, rarely toothed.
Flowers: In clusters, 10–12 mm (⅖–½ in) across, yellow to orange, spotted with red.
Fruits: 2-horned, many-seeded capsules.
Related or similar plants: The much rarer Yellow Marsh-saxifrage has mostly solitary flowers 20–30 mm across.
Habitat and distribution: Locally common on lime-rich wet rocks and boulders, stony ground and streamsides in the mountains of northern Britain; scattered and rare in the mountains of northern Ireland.
Flowering time: June to September.

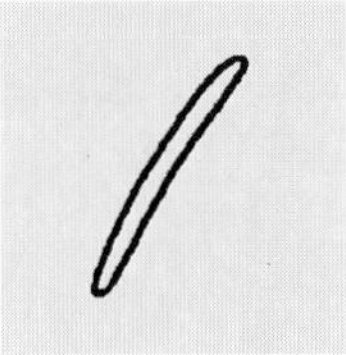

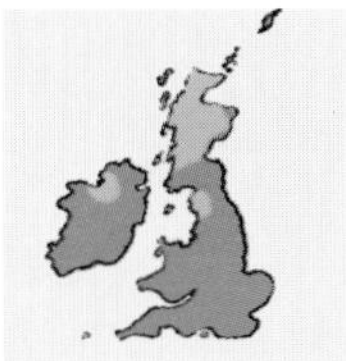

YELLOW MOUNTAIN-SAXIFRAGE is one of the commonest and most attractive of our native alpine wild flowers.

Yellow Marsh-saxifrage (*Saxifraga hirculus*) is similar but the buttercup-like flowers 20–30 mm (⅘–1⅕ in) across are usually solitary and produced (shyly) in July–August. It occurs in a few mineral-rich bogs of northern Britain, and West Mayo and Co. Antrim in northern Ireland.

***Top** The bright yellow flowers are spotted with red and occur in clusters 5-30 cm (2-12 in) tall above numerous leafy non-flowering shoots.*

***Bottom** Yellow Mountain-saxifrage* (Saxifraga aizoides) *can be found from June to September on wet rocks and boulders, streamsides and flushes in the mountains of northern Britain.*

Purple Saxifrage

SAXIFRAGE FAMILY

(Saxifragaceae)

SPECIES INFORMATION	
COMMON NAME	Purple Saxifrage
SCIENTIFIC NAME	Saxifraga oppositifolia
RELATED SPECIES	Other saxifrages
HEIGHT/SPREAD	2–5 cm tall
FLOWERING TIME	March–June
HABITAT	Mountain rocks

Note: Our only purple-flowered saxifrage.

FLOWER TYPE

IDENTIFICATION

HABITAT

POPULATION

MAP

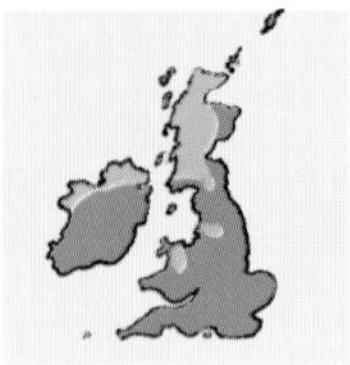

Size and appearance: Attractive and conspicuous perennial, forming a mat of prostrate or trailing shoots in cushions or patches, growing 2–5 cm (⅘–2 in) tall.
Leaves: Compact, very small, in 4 rows and opposite pairs, encrusted with lime.
Flowers: On short stalks, 8–12 mm (⅓–½ in) across, purple or pinkish-purple.
Fruits: 2-horned, many-seeded capsules.
Related or similar plants: The other alpine saxifrages mostly have white flowers, between June and August.
Habitat and distribution: Widespread on lime-rich cliffs, rocks and screes in the mountains of northern Britain, Wales (Snowdonia and Brecon Beacons) and northern and western Ireland, especially Connemara.
Flowering time: March to June, but sometimes as early as February; a few flowers may be produced in late summer.

THE EARLIEST OF our select band of native alpine wild flowers to bloom, often coming out in March, even February, and a magnificent sight in the Scottish Highlands during April and May, especially when growing near melting snow. By mid-June, when other alpines are coming into flower, it is over or almost so.

In northern Scotland and County Donegal it grows down to sea-level. On Clare Island off the coast of West Mayo it grows in plenty on towering coastal cliffs.

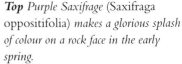

Top *Purple Saxifrage* (Saxifraga oppositifolia) *makes a glorious splash of colour on a rock face in the early spring.*

Bottom *The purple flowers bloom just above the cushion, forming leaves in order to withstand the rigours of the mountain winds and weather, and huddling low in the crevices for shelter.*

SPECIES INFORMATION	
COMMON NAME	Grass-of-Parnassus
SCIENTIFIC NAME	Parnassia palustris
RELATED SPECIES	Saxifrages
HEIGHT/SPREAD	10–40 cm tall
FLOWERING TIME	July–October
HABITAT	Marshes and wet moorland

Note: Rather like a large saxifrage.

Grass-of-Parnassus

GRASS-OF-PARNASSUS FAMILY
(Parnassiaceae)

GRASS-OF-PARNASSUS is one of out handsomest wild flowers, and feature of damp places in the north and west in late summer. Plants growing in the marshy slacks of sand-dunes are often dwarf and compact in growth. The ring of sterile feathery stamens serves to attract polinating insects, mainly flies. These structures secrete nectar from their bases and give the flower its sweet scent.

Top *Grass-of-Parnassus* (Parnassia palustris) *has five white petals with green veins on flowering stems 10-40 cm (4-16 in) tall arising from a basal rosette of heart-shaped leaves. It flowers later in the summer from July to October.*

FLOWER TYPE

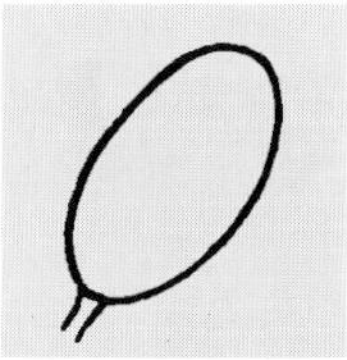

IDENTIFICATION

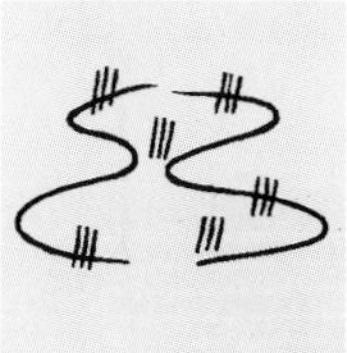

HABITAT

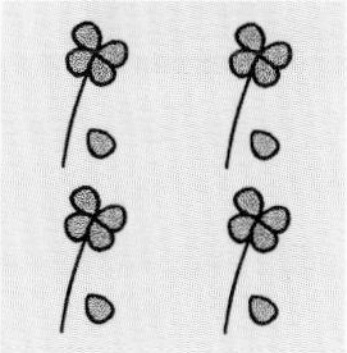

POPULATION

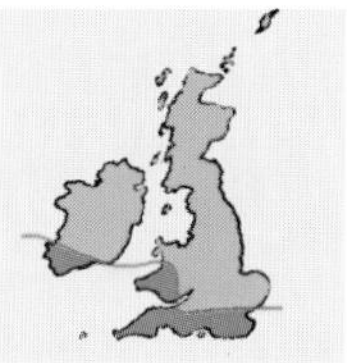

MAP

Size and appearance: Handsome perennial with several, almost leafless flowering stems 10–40 cm (4–16 in) tall.
Leaves: Basal leaves heart-shaped, long-stalked; usually a single heart-shaped stem leaf only.
Flowers: 15–30 mm (⅗–1⅕ in) across, petals white with green veins; stamens 5, plus a conspicuous ring of sterile feathery stamens.
Fruits: Almost spherical, many-seeded capsules.
Related or similar plants: The white-flowered saxifrages have similar but smaller flowers, rarely more than 15 mm (⅗ in) across.
Habitat and distribution: Marshes, fens, damp moorland and wet slacks in sand-dunes; common in northern Britain but local elsewhere and quite absent from most of Wales, southern England and south-western Ireland.
Flowering time: July to October.

Bottom *It is a plant of marshes, fens, damp moorland and dune-slacks, and is more likely to be found in northern Britain.*

Meadowsweet

ROSE FAMILY

(Rosaceae)

SPECIES INFORMATION	
COMMON NAME	Meadowsweet
SCIENTIFIC NAME	Filipendula ulmaria
RELATED SPECIES	Dropwort
HEIGHT/SPREAD	50–120 cm tall
FLOWERING TIME	June–September
HABITAT	Marshes and wet grassland

Note: A large, leafy plant of marshy places.

FLOWER TYPE

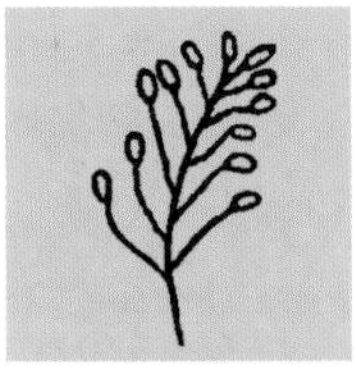

IDENTIFICATION

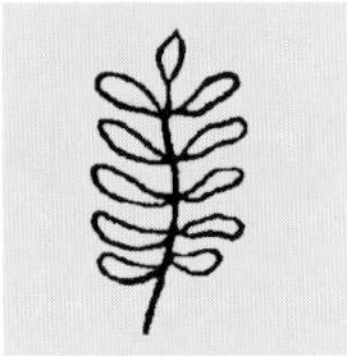

HABITAT

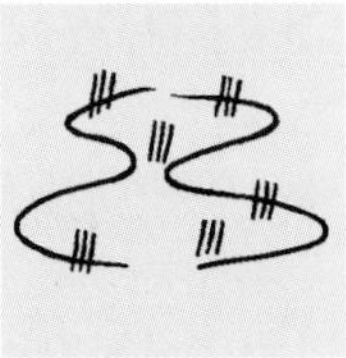

POPULATION

MAP

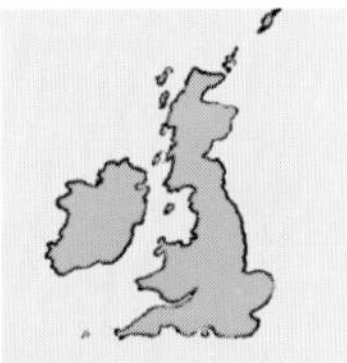

Size and appearance: A hairy perennial, with creeping rhizomes and erect, leafy stems 50–120 cm (20–48 in) tall, sometimes up to 200 cm (80 in).

Leaves: Compound, white-hairy beneath, up to 5 pairs of large, sharply toothed leaflets alternating with pairs of smaller leaflets, the end leaflet larger and 3- to 5-lobed.

Flowers: Creamy-white. 4–8 mm (⅙–⅓ in) across, sweetly and sickly scented, in dense, branched, frothy masses.

Fruits: 6–10 small pods in twisted clusters.

Related or similar plants: Dropwort, a plant of dry grassland, has leaves with 8–20 pairs of leaflets and larger flowers.

Habitat and distribution: A prominent plant of wet and marshy places, damp grassland, streamsides and swampy, open woods; throughout, but especially abundant in the west.

Flowering time: June to September.

Top *Meadowsweet* (Filipendula ulmaria) *produces creamy-white frothy masses of flowers. These give off a sweet and sickly scent which is heady on a balmy summer's evening.*

Bottom *In damp, wet and marshy places, Meadowsweet can form extensive stands or is found bordering a stream or small river.*

THE FROTHY CLUSTERS of Meadowsweet flowers are an evocative image of the summer countryside. Hence perhaps the popular name Queen-of-the-Meadow, which is the same in French. The flowers in quantity have a decidedly sickly scent, but the complex of smells in the dried foliage is more pleasant. Thus Meadowsweet was one of the plants that were formerly strewn on the floors of churches and other buildings to sweeten the air. The plant was used to flavour mead, and medicinally in the treatment of arthritis and rheumatism. The roots were a source of a black dye.

SPECIES INFORMATION	
COMMON NAME	Dog Rose
SCIENTIFIC NAME	Rosa canina
RELATED SPECIES	Burnet Rose
HEIGHT/SPREAD	3 m tall
FLOWERING TIME	June–July
HABITAT	Hedges and woodland margins

Note: The common wild rose of hedges.

Dog Rose

ROSE FAMILY

(Rosaceae)

PERHAPS THE BEST-LOVED of all wild flowers, the 'unofficial English Rose', splashing hedges pink in midsummer. A dozen or so closely related species occur in Britain and Ireland, all loosely known as dog roses. They are often difficult to separate, and the picture is complicated because the various species cross with one another, and with escaped garden roses.

Dog Rose was formerly used as grafting stock for garden roses, but other species are now preferred. The fruits (rose-hips) are rich in vitamin C and volunteers, mainly children, gathered hundreds of tons for this purpose during the Second World War. Children too have long used the scratchy seeds from inside the fruit-cup as a natural itching powder.

FLOWER TYPE

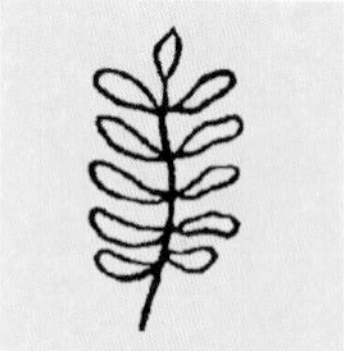

IDENTIFICATION

HABITAT

POPULATION

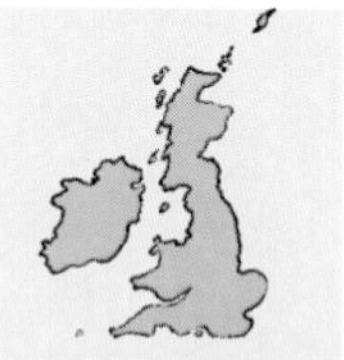

MAP

Size and appearance: A shrub with stout, arched stems 1–3 m (3–9 ft) tall, armed with ferocious, curved prickles.
Leaves: Compound, downy beneath, with 3–5 oval, toothed, green leaflets.
Flowers: Pale pink, 2–6 cm ($\frac{4}{5}$–$2\frac{2}{5}$ in) across, with 5 petals and numerous stamens, slightly scented.
Fruits: Fleshy, flask-shaped or nearly spherical, scarlet or pale orange, topped by the withered flower-parts.
Related or similar plants: Burnet Rose is smaller and bushier, with white flowers.
Habitat and distribution: Common in hedges and scrub, and along woodland margins throughout Britain and Ireland, but scarcer in areas of intensive agriculture where hedges have been removed.
Flowering time: June to July.

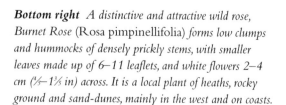

Bottom right *A distinctive and attractive wild rose, Burnet Rose* (Rosa pimpinellifolia) *forms low clumps and hummocks of densely prickly stems, with smaller leaves made up of 6–11 leaflets, and white flowers 2–4 cm ($\frac{4}{5}$–$1\frac{3}{5}$ in) across. It is a local plant of heaths, rocky ground and sand-dunes, mainly in the west and on coasts.*

Bramble

ROSE FAMILY

(Rosaceae)

SPECIES INFORMATION	
COMMON NAME	Bramble, Blackberry
SCIENTIFIC NAME	Rubus fruticosus
RELATED SPECIES	Raspberry
HEIGHT/SPREAD	1–4 m long
FLOWERING TIME	June–September
HABITAT	Hedges and woods

Note: The common bramble.

FLOWER TYPE

IDENTIFICATION

HABITAT

POPULATION

MAP

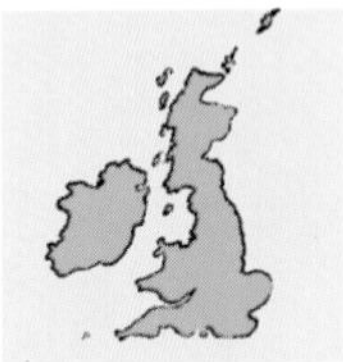

Size and appearance: A shrub with a tangle of stems 1–4 m (3–12 ft) long, armed with ferocious, curved prickles, climbing or trailing on or near the ground.
Leaves: Compound, with 3–5 stalked, oval, coarsely toothed leaflets.
Flowers: White, pink or purplish-pink, 20–30 mm ($\frac{4}{5}$–$1\frac{1}{5}$ in) across, with 5 petals and numerous stamens, in branched clusters.
Fruits: Numerous black, fleshy, 1-seeded fruitlets in an almost spherical head 10–20 mm ($\frac{2}{5}$–$\frac{4}{5}$ in) across.
Related or similar plants: Raspberry is an erect plant with leaves whitish beneath, and red fruits.
Habitat and distribution: Common in hedges and scrub, and along woodland margins throughout Britain and Ireland, but scarcer in areas of intensive agriculture where hedges have been removed.
Flowering time: June to September.

Bottom *Raspberry* (Rubus idaeus) *is similar but has erect stems to 2 m (6 ft) tall, tiny soft prickles, leaves white-hairy beneath, white flowers and softer, red fruits that detach more easily. The narrow white petals are erect and surrounded by the pointed sepals, flowering and fruiting in June – August, and forming thickets in ditches and woods.*

BRAMBLE IS ONE of the most abundant of all wild plants, providing cover and food for many animals. It remains a popular wild food for people, although in our affluent times perhaps not so widely as previously. It has other uses too: the roots are the source of an orange dye, the fruits a purple dye, and the leaves have been used to treat wounds and are still an ingredient of herbal teas. Nevertheless, Bramble can be a serious weed of woods, gardens and waste ground, especially where the soil has been enriched.

Botanists divide Blackberry up into more than 400 similar 'microspecies', many of them very local in distribution. They vary in the taste and texture of the fruits as well as the more mundane attributes such as the size and number of the prickles. The views of keen blackberry pickers as to the relative merits of their favourite patches may well have a sound scientific basis.

SPECIES INFORMATION	
COMMON NAME	Agrimony
SCIENTIFIC NAME	Agrimonia eupatoria
RELATED SPECIES	Fragrant Agrimony
HEIGHT/SPREAD	30–150 cm tall
FLOWERING TIME	June–September
HABITAT	Grassland and woodland margins

Note: The curious hooked fruits are unusual.

Agrimony

ROSE FAMILY

(Rosaceae)

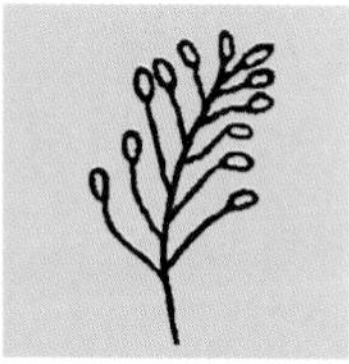

FLOWER TYPE

IDENTIFICATION

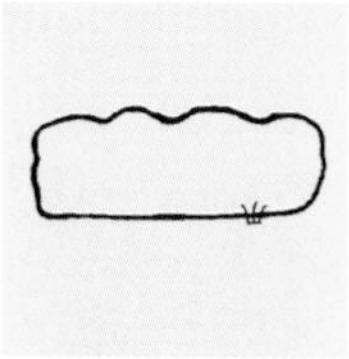

HABITAT

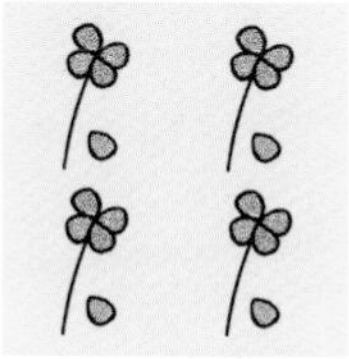

POPULATION

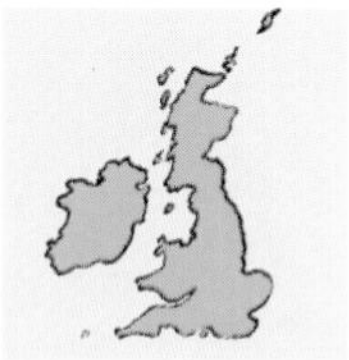

MAP

Size and appearance: A softly-hairy perennial, with erect, leafy stems 50–150 cm (20–48 in) tall.

Leaves: Compound, the basal in a rosette, greyish-hairy beneath, the 6–8 pairs of large leaflets alternating with 2– pairs of smaller.

Flowers: Yellow, 6–8 mm across, with 5 petals and 10–20 stamens, massed in a long, slender spike.

Fruits: In shape of inverted cone (like an old-fashioned top), grooved, half enclosed by the cup-like calyx-tube, covered with hooked bristles.

Related or similar plants: Fragrant Agrimony, has all-green leaves that are fragrant when bruised, and bell-shaped fruits.

Habitat and distribution: Widespread in hedgerows, scrub, woodland margins and tall grassland, most conspicuous in late summer; throughout, but scarce over much of Scotland, especially the north.

Flowering time: June to September.

Top *Agrimony* (Agrimonia eupatoria) *produces bright, yellow five-petalled flowers on long slender spikes. The fruits are shaped like tiny bells, with a fringe of hooked hairs around their base.*

Bottom *Widespread in rough grassland, it is often overlooked until later in the year when it is in flower or fruit as the leaves nestle down among the grasses.*

THE FRUITS READILY attach themselves to fur or clothing by the hooked spines of the calyx that surrounds the ripe fruit. This enables the fruits to disperse far from the parent plant. Agrimony yields a yellow dye and has been used medicinally as an antiseptic and general tonic. It is also a purgative. A very similar but more robust species, Fragrant Agrimony (*Agrimonia procera*), has all-green leaves, fragrant when bruised, slightly paler yellow flowers and bell-shaped, ungrooved fruits. It is widespread but very scattered in distribution.

Salad Burnet

ROSE FAMILY

(Rosaceae)

SPECIES INFORMATION	
COMMON NAME	Salad Burnet
SCIENTIFIC NAME	Sanguisorba minor
RELATED SPECIES	Great Burnet
HEIGHT/SPREAD	20–90 cm tall
FLOWERING TIME	May–September
HABITAT	Dry grassland

Note: The leaves are typical for the rose family; the flowers not.

FLOWER TYPE

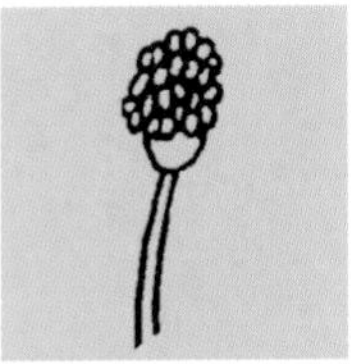

IDENTIFICATION

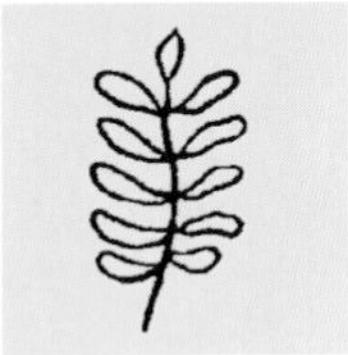

HABITAT

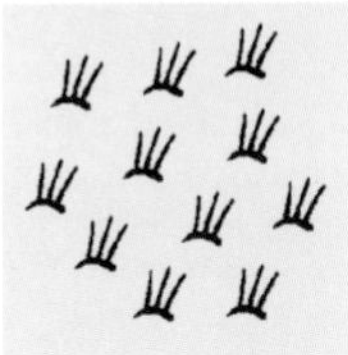

POPULATION

MAP

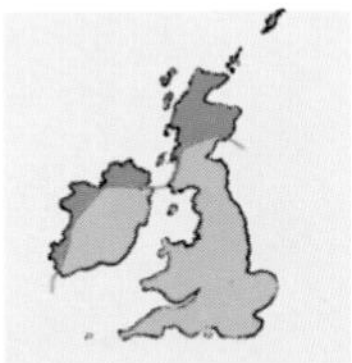

Size and appearance: A hairless or slightly downy perennial, with erect, leafy stems 20–90 cm (8–36 in) tall.

Leaves: Basal leaves in a rosette; compound, greyish-green, with 3–12 pairs of neat, more or less equal, oval, sharply toothed leaflets.

Flowers: Small, with a 4-lobed, petal-like calyx, in green, reddish or purplish, globular heads up to 1 cm across.

Fruits: 1-seeded, within the persistent, 4-angled, wrinkled calyx, forming small round clusters.

Related or similar plants: Great Burnet is a larger plant with oblong heads of red flowers.

Habitat and distribution: Widespread in dry grassland, on rocky slopes and cliffs on lime-rich soils north to central Scotland; scarce and mostly coastal in Scotland, and local in Ireland.

Flowering time: May to September.

SALAD BURNET IS ONE of the grassland plants that best indicates lime-rich soils. Unusually for the rose family, the flowers are pollinated by wind rather than insects, so the stamens are long, with flexible stalks. The leaves smell and taste of cucumber when bruised, giving this plant its place in the herb garden. A much more robust, leafier plant, with larger, much-wrinkled fruits, often occurs on road verges and embankments, and in recently sown grassland. This is Fodder Burnet, a subspecies of Salad Burnet from southern Europe that used to be grown as a fodder crop. Now it is a frequent component of wild flower seed mixtures.

Top *Salad Burnet* (Sanguisorba minor) *is a plant of chalk and limestone grassland, where its globose heads appear above the short turf. The bright purple-red of the brush-like female stigmas often attract attention.*

Bottom *Great Burnet* (Sanguisorba officinalis) *is a larger, more robust plant with leaflets larger towards the apex of the leaf, and red flowers in oblong heads 1–3 cm (⅖–1⅕ in) long. It is local in damp meadows, mostly from Wales and central England to southern Scotland.*

SPECIES INFORMATION	
COMMON NAME	Wood Avens, Herb Bennet
SCIENTIFIC NAME	Geum urbanum
RELATED SPECIES	Water Avens
HEIGHT/SPREAD	20–60 cm tall
FLOWERING TIME	May–September
HABITAT	Woods and hedgerows

Note: Plants may grade into Water Avens (p.108).

Wood Avens

ROSE FAMILY

(Rosaceae)

Size and appearance: A hairless or slightly downy perennial, with a short rhizome and semi-erect, branched, leafy stems 20–60 cm (8–36 in) tall.

Leaves: Basal leaves in a rosette; compound, with 1–5 pairs of unequal leaflets and much larger end leaflet.

Flowers: Yellow, shallowly cup-shaped, 10–15 mm (⅜–⅝ in) across, the calyx green, in small, very loose clusters; stamens numerous.

Fruits: Hairy, 1-seeded fruits, with persistent, hooked stigmas, in a spherical cluster c. 12 mm (½ in) across.

Related or similar plants: Water Avens (p.104), with larger, bell-shaped, pink flowers, grows in damp places.

Habitat and distribution: A common and distinctive plant of open woodland, woodland margins and rides, hedgerows, beside paths and as a persistent weed of shady gardens; throughout, but scarcer in north-west Scotland, parts of western Ireland and areas of extensive agriculture.

Flowering time: May to September.

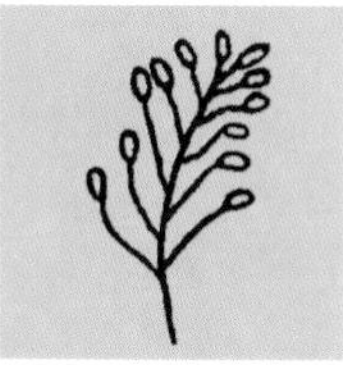

FLOWER TYPE

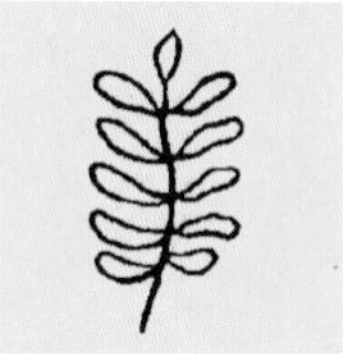

IDENTIFICATION

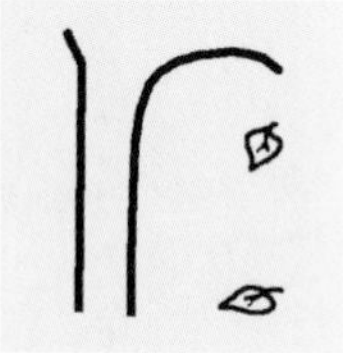

HABITAT

POPULATION

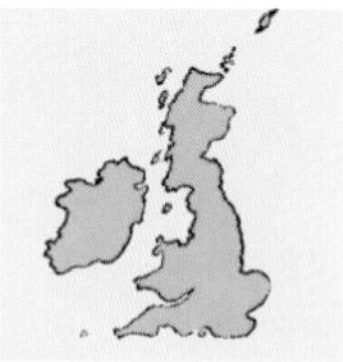

MAP

THE CLUSTERS OF fruits soon break apart — do not be tempted to use them for flower arranging! The long hook on each fruit attaches itself to fur or clothing and is so dispersed far from the parent plant. The hairy, hooked structures are difficult to remove from socks. It is widespread, but is local in northern Scotland.

The flowers are mostly pollinated by flies, but this does not prevent crossing with Water Avens, pollinated largely by bumble-bees, in western and northern Britain. Some populations, especially where there has been some recent habitat disturbance, contain a bewildering array of crosses and backcrosses that intermix attributes of both parents.

Wood Avens (Geum urbanum) *is a common and distinctive woodland flower with its loose clusters of yellow, cup-shaped flowers. The photograph above is of a hybrid between the Wood Avens and Water Avens.*

Water Avens

ROSE FAMILY

(Rosaceae)

SPECIES INFORMATION	
COMMON NAME	Water Avens
SCIENTIFIC NAME	Geum rivale
RELATED SPECIES	Wood Avens
HEIGHT/SPREAD	20–40 cm tall
FLOWERING TIME	May–September
HABITAT	Woods and hedgerows
Note: Plants may grade into Wood Avens (p.107).	

FLOWER TYPE

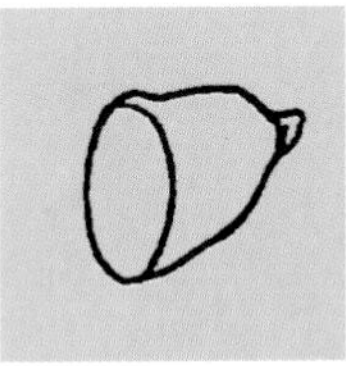

IDENTIFICATION

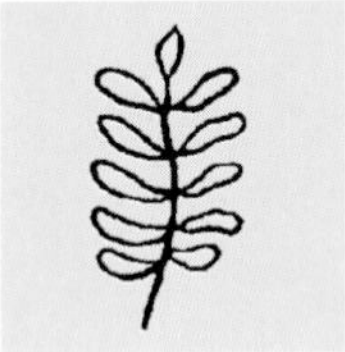

HABITAT

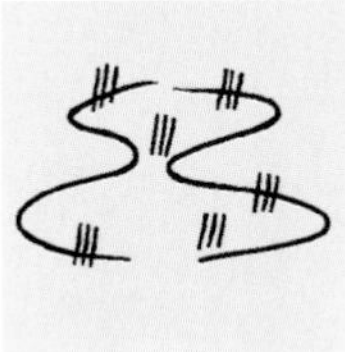

POPULATION

MAP

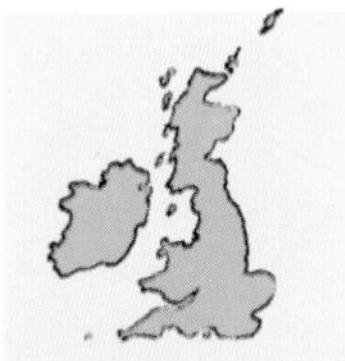

Size and appearance: A hairless or slightly downy perennial, with a short rhizome and semi-erect, branched, leafy stems 20–40 cm (8–16 in) tall.

Leaves: Basal leaves in a rosette; leaves compound, with 3–6 pairs of unequal leaflets and much larger end leaflet.

Flowers: Purplish-pink, bell-shaped, nodding, 10–15 mm ($\frac{2}{5}$–$\frac{3}{5}$ in) long, the calyx brownish-purple, in small, very loose clusters; stamens numerous.

Fruits: Hairy, 1-seeded fruits, with persistent, hooked stigmas, in a spherical cluster c. 12 mm ($\frac{1}{2}$ in) across.

Related or similar plants: Wood Avens (p.103), with cup-shaped, yellow flowers, grows in dry, shady places.

Habitat and distribution: Widespread in woods, hedgerows and damp, shady places, but much commoner in northern and western Britain (and almost absent from the south-east); scattered and mainly in Ireland.

Flowering time: May to September.

THE FLOWERS ARE pollinated by bumble-bees. The long hooks on the fruits attach themselves to fur or clothing in the same way as in Wood Avens (p.103). These two species often cross in western and northern Britain, the crosses and backcrosses displaying features of both parents. Since the two species occur in different habitats, these 'hybrid swarms' often follow habitat disturbance, which brings these two different but related species together. The new, mixed or intermediate habitat also gives the progeny somewhere to colonise and survive away from competition with either parent.

Top left Water Avens (Geum rivale) has pinkish, bell-shaped, nodding flower heads which produce the same hooked stigmas as Wood Avens.

Right and left More common in the wetter north and west of Britain, Water Avens can be found by streamsides and is widespread in damp, shady places, including woodlands.

SPECIES INFORMATION	
COMMON NAME	Mountain Avens
SCIENTIFIC NAME	Dryas octopetala
RELATED SPECIES	Wood Avens, Water Avens
HEIGHT/SPREAD	Stems 10–50 cm long
FLOWERING TIME	May–September
HABITAT	Limestone rocks

Note: A handsome plant like no other in these islands.

Mountain Avens

ROSE FAMILY

(Rosaceae)

MOUNTAIN AVENS is a plant of the Arctic regions and the high mountains of Eurasia. As the ice sheets retreated at the end of the Ice Age, it was present in quantity in Britain and Ireland, as a principal component of a special community of dwarf Arctic plants that botanists have named Dryas-heath after this plant. What we see today in the Burren and parts of north-western Scotland is a relic of this once-abundant vegetation (which still occurs in Arctic regions). The most remarkable feature of the Burren flora is the combination of this Arctic plant with the alpine Spring Gentian (p.205) and even Mediterranean plants.

Size and appearance: A rather hairy, creeping shrublet, forming a semi-prostrate, leafy mat, with stems 10–50 cm (4–20 in) long.

Leaves: Like tiny, oblong oak leaves, dark green on the upper surface, densely white-woolly beneath, with small, rounded teeth.

Flowers: Solitary, white, cup-shaped, 25–35 mm (⅖–⅗ in) long, with 8 or more petals; numerous golden-yellow stamens.

Fruits: A feathery cluster of small 1-seeded fruits, with persistent, plumed stigmas 20–30 mm (⅘–1⅕ in).

Related or similar plants: Wood Avens (p.103) has cup-shaped, yellow flowers; Water Avens (p.104) has bell-shaped, purplish-pink flowers.

Habitat and distribution: A rare but occasionally locally abundant plant of limestone rocks, pavements and screes, cliff-ledges and rocky grassland in the mountains, but descending to sea-level in western Ireland and northern Scotland. Locally frequent in the western Highlands of Scotland and in western Ireland, in the Burren region of County Clare and about adjacent Galway Bay; here and there elsewhere in the mountains.

Flowering time: May to September, but at its best in May to June; conspicuous in fruit in summer and autumn.

***Top** Mountain Avens* (Dryas octopetala) *has solitary white 8-petalled flowers with numerous golden-yellow stamens. Once the flowers are over the plant keeps its charming presence with the feathery plumed stigmas.*

***Bottom** Rocky mountain pastures, cliff-ledges and screes on limestone rocks are places where Mountain Avens can be found as well as limestone pavements as shown in the photograph below.*

FLOWER TYPE

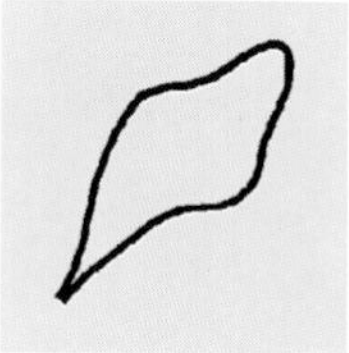

IDENTIFICATION

HABITAT

POPULATION

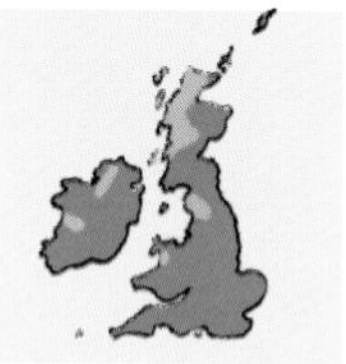

MAP

Silverweed

ROSE FAMILY

(Rosaceae)

SPECIES INFORMATION	
COMMON NAME	Silverweed
SCIENTIFIC NAME	Potentilla anserina
RELATED SPECIES	Creeping Cinquefoil
HEIGHT/SPREAD	10–30 cm tall, forming patches
FLOWERING TIME	May–September
HABITAT	Damp, grassy place

Note: The slender, red runners are distinctive.

FLOWER TYPE

IDENTIFICATION

HABITAT

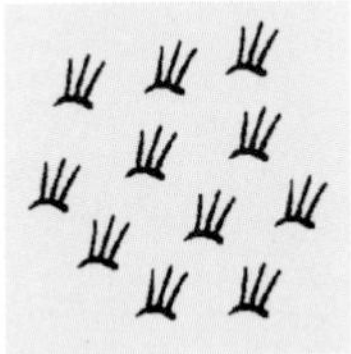

POPULATION

MAP

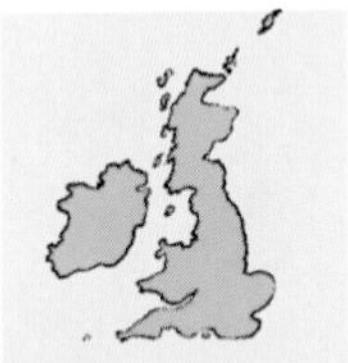

Size and appearance: Prostrate, silver-hairy perennial, with numerous red, rooting runners up to 100 cm (40 in) long, forming extensive patches; leaves and flowering stems 10–30 cm (4–12 in) tall.

Leaves: All in a basal rosette, densely silver-hairy beneath, compound, with 3–12 pairs of coarsely and sharply toothed, oblong or oval leaflets and a similar end leaflet.

Flowers: Solitary on long stems, golden-yellow, 15–20 mm (3/5–4/5 in) across, with 5 petals and numerous stamens.

Fruits: Numerous small, 1-seeded fruits in a spherical head.

Related or similar plants: Creeping Cinquefoil (p.108), also with creeping runners, has all-green leaflets in 5s.

Habitat and distribution: Sometimes abundant in damp, grassy places, on roadsides and waste ground, trampled places like farm gates, and on low, rocky seashores and raised beaches near the point reached by the highest tides; throughout, except on the highest mountains.

Flowering time: May to September.

THE FLESHY ROOTS were formerly extensively eaten, either boiled or roasted or ground into a meal for bread or porridge. They were a staple during times of famine, especially in northern and western Britain and in Ireland. In some upland and western parts, Silverweed may even have been a truly cultivated plant, a meagre equivalent to the parsnip of the lowlands.

The old herbalists prized the leaves of this plant as an anti-inflammatory and healing herb for external and internal use. Stuffed in the shoes, they were said to be a remedy to ease the sore or tired feet of the traveller.

Top *Silverweed (Potentilla anserina) is a prostrate plant which has rooting runners allowing it to spread and form large patches in damp, grassy places.*

Left *The golden-yellow flowers are solitary their long stems raising them above the distinctive silvery leaves.*

SPECIES INFORMATION	
COMMON NAME	Tormentil
SCIENTIFIC NAME	Potentilla erecta
RELATED SPECIES	Cinquefoil
HEIGHT/SPREAD	10–40 cm tall
FLOWERING TIME	June–September
HABITAT	Heaths and lime-poor grassland

Note: Superficially like a tiny 4-petalled buttercup.

Tormentil

ROSE FAMILY

(Rosaceae)

Size and appearance: A dainty, tufted perennial with slender, sprawling or weakly erect stems 10–40 cm (4–16 in) tall.

Leaves: In a basal rosette that often withers by flowering, and all along the stems, with 3–5 wedge-shaped, deeply toothed leaflets.

Flowers: Yellow, 8–18 mm (⅓–¾ in) across, with 4 (rarely 5) petals and sepals and numerous stamens, in loose, leafy clusters.

Fruits: Numerous small, hairless, 1-seeded fruits in a spherical head.

Related or similar plants: Creeping Cinquefoil (p.108) and Silverweed have creeping runners, and leaves with 5 or more leaflets.

Habitat and distribution: Common on the lime-poor soils of bogs, damp grassland, open birch woods, commons, heaths and moors, especially in hilly and western districts and in the mountains, throughout Britain and Ireland.

Flowering time: June to September.

TORMENTIL IS A CHARMING plant of heathy grassland, adding little dots of yellow to the predominant greens and browns of the sward. It is a good indicator plant for the presence of lime-poor soils. The rather woody roots are the source of a red dye, and in Scotland and elsewhere they were formerly of use in tanning, as a substitute for oak bark. The roots also had medicinal use in the treatment of pain and looseness of the bowel.

Tormentil sometimes crosses with Creeping Cinquefoil (p.108) to form plants that are intermediate in form. Occasional backcrossing probably accounts for the odd Tormentil flower with five petals.

Right *Tormentil* (Potentilla erecta) *has flowers with 4 yellow petals and sepals with numerous stamens.*

Bottom *A plant of acid grassland, heaths and moors, Tormentil will reach 1-40 cm (4-16 in) tall if allowed but is more often found growing flat on the ground due to the grazing pressure of sheep.*

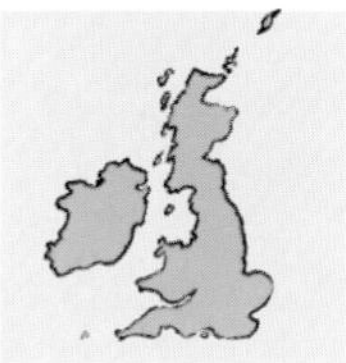

Creeping Cinquefoil

ROSE FAMILY

(Rosaceae)

SPECIES INFORMATION	
COMMON NAME	Creeping Cinquefoil
SCIENTIFIC NAME	Potentilla reptans
RELATED SPECIES	Silverweed, Tormentil
HEIGHT/SPREAD	5–10 cm tall, forming loose patches
FLOWERING TIME	June–September
HABITAT	Dry grassland and banks

Note: Leaves with 5 leaflets combined with slender runners.

FLOWER TYPE

IDENTIFICATION

HABITAT

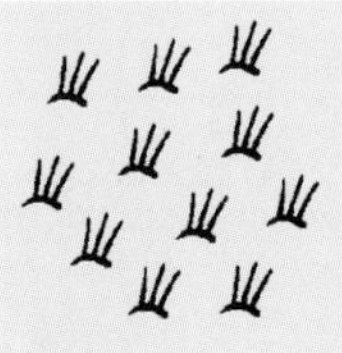

POPULATION

MAP

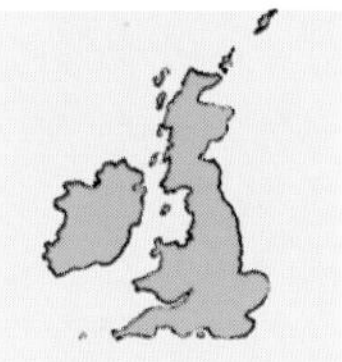

THE NAME CINQUEFOIL is a corruption of the French cinq feuilles (five leaves). In Ireland it becomes cúig mhear Mhuire or Five-Fingers-of-Mary. In France especially, Creeping Cinquefoil has a long history of association with magic and healing, dating back to the civilization of ancient Greece and even ancient Egypt. Its use as a healing plant is not unexpected, as it is so closely related to two other ancient remedies, Silverweed (p.106) and Tormentil (p.107).

The half-dozen native cinquefoils and their allies (a group that includes Silverweed and Tormentil) are not always easy to tell apart.

Size and appearance: Prostrate perennial, with numerous red, rooting runners up to 100 cm (40 in) long, forming loose patches; leaves and flowering stems 5–10 cm (2–4 in) tall.

Leaves: Compound, long-stalked, with usually 5 oblong or wedge-shaped, blunt, toothed leaflets.

Flowers: Solitary, yellow, 15–20 mm ($\frac{3}{5}$–$\frac{4}{5}$ in) across, with 5 petals and sepals and numerous stamens.

Fruits: Numerous small, hairless, 1-seeded fruits in a spherical head.

Related or similar plants: Silverweed (p.106) also has creeping runners, but has leaves with 3–12 pairs of leaflets.

Habitat and distribution: Generally common on dry banks, stony waste ground and old walls, and as a weed of gardens; throughout Britain and Ireland, although rare in Scotland north of the Firths of Clyde and Forth.

Flowering time: June to September.

Bottom *Hoary Cinquefoil* (Potentilla argentea) *has leaflets in 5s, a tufted sprawling habit, leaves densely silver-hairy beneath, and clusters of flowers 8–12 mm ($\frac{1}{3}$–$\frac{1}{2}$ in). It is local in dry or sandy ground from Devon and Kent to central Scotland, but mainly in the east.*

SPECIES INFORMATION	
COMMON NAME	Marsh Cinquefoil
SCIENTIFIC NAME	Potentilla palustris
RELATED SPECIES	Water Avens
HEIGHT/SPREAD	20–60 cm tall
FLOWERING TIME	May–June
HABITAT	Pools and marshes

Note: The greyish leaves and reddish-purple flowers are unusual.

Marsh Cinquefoil

ROSE FAMILY

(Rosaceae)

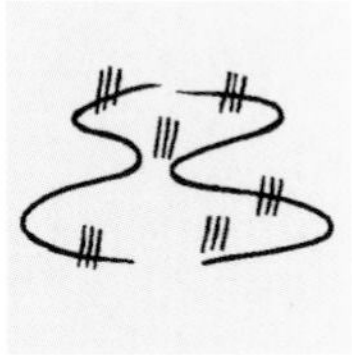

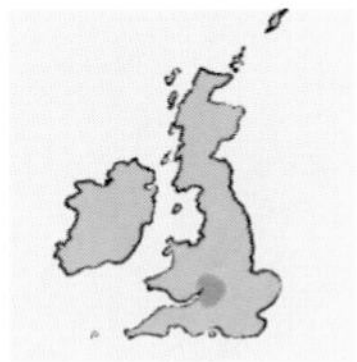

Size and appearance: Hairless, rather robust perennial, with erect, leafy stems 20–60 cm (8–24 in) tall.

Leaves: Compound, greyish-green, paler beneath, long-stalked, with 3–7 oblong, toothed leaflets up to 5 cm (2 in) long.

Flowers: Dull reddish-purple, 20–30 mm (⅘–1⅕ in) across (including sepals), with 5 petals and numerous stamens, in a loose cluster; sepals purple, more conspicuous than the petals.

Fruits: Numerous small, hairless, 1-seeded fruits in a spherical head.

Related or similar plants: Water Avens (p.104) has paler, nodding flowers and hairy, green leaves.

Habitat and distribution: Locally plentiful in marshes, ditches, along the margins of lakes and in boggy pools in north Britain, south to central Wales and Norfolk, and in Ireland; occasionally elsewhere, such as the New Forest.

Flowering time: May to June.

THIS UNUSUAL-LOOKING plant is botanically one of the cinquefoils (see Creeping Cinquefoil, p.108), but is very different in appearance and ecology. Not small and seemingly fragile like the others, it is rather impressive in flower, with its large, greyish leaves and clusters of flowers the colour of red wine. It always grows in lime-poor waters.

Marsh Cinquefoil (Potentilla palustris) *has reddish-purple flowers where the sepals are more conspicuous than the petals. It is a plant of marshes, ditches, lake margins and boggy pools more common in the north of Britain but coming as far south as central Wales and Norfolk.*

Barren Strawberry

ROSE FAMILY

(Rosaceae)

SPECIES INFORMATION	
COMMON NAME	Barren Strawberry
SCIENTIFIC NAME	Potentilla sterilis
RELATED SPECIES	Tormentil, Creeping Cinquefoil
HEIGHT/SPREAD	5–15 cm tall
FLOWERING TIME	February–May
HABITAT	Hedgerows and open woods

Note: Like a wild strawberry plant and flower in early spring.

FLOWER TYPE

IDENTIFICATION

HABITAT

POPULATION

MAP

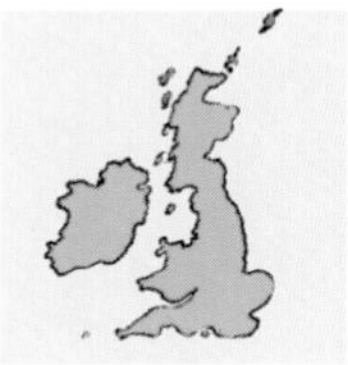

Size and appearance: A tufted perennial with sprawling, hairy stems 5–15 cm (4–16 in) tall, and a few short runners.
Leaves: Mostly in basal rosettes, compound, greyish-green, hairy beneath, with 3 oval, coarsely toothed leaflets.
Flowers: White, 10–15 mm (⅖–⅗ in) across, with 5 petals and sepals, many stamens and a ring of tiny orange nectaries.
Fruits: Minute, 1-seeded fruits in a spherical head.
Related or similar plants: Wild Strawberry has bright green leaves, far-creeping runners and scarlet, fleshy fruits; it flowers in early summer.
Habitat and distribution: Inconspicuous but widespread on hedge-banks and lanesides, in dry grassland, churchyards and open woods; throughout except for a few areas without suitable habitats, such as parts of northern Scotland and Ireland, and the Fens.
Flowering time: February to May.

THIS DELIGHTFUL LITTLE flower is one of the first signs of life in late winter to early spring in a dry woodland ride or country churchyard. It is too often overlooked, or merely often confused with the true Wild Strawberry, also in the rose family. It is not a strawberry at all, but sits closer to the yellow-flowered species like Tormentil. That said, the little hard knob of tiny fruits comes as a shock if one is unfamiliar with the plant. John Gerard's 1597 Herball described these deeply disappointing fruits most effectively: 'a barren or chaffie head, in shape like a Strawberrie, but of no worth or value'.

Barren Strawberry (Potentilla sterilis) *can be found in flower as early as February in grassland, hedgebanks and woodland rides. The leaves are greyish-green with three oval, coarse-toothed leaflets.*

SPECIES INFORMATION	
COMMON NAME	Wild Strawberry
SCIENTIFIC NAME	Fragaria vesca
RELATED SPECIES	Tormentil, Creeping Cinquefoil
HEIGHT/SPREAD	5–30 cm tall
FLOWERING TIME	May–July
HABITAT	Hedgerows and open woods

Note: A perfect miniature strawberry plant.

Wild Strawberry

ROSE FAMILY

(Rosaceae)

Size and appearance: A softly hairy perennial with slender, far-creeping, reddish runners and erect stems 5–30 cm (2–12 in) tall.
Leaves: Mostly in basal rosettes, with 3 oval, coarsely toothed, bright green leaflets.
Flowers: White, 10–18 mm (⅖–¾ in) across, with 5 petals and sepals and numerous stamens, in small, loose clusters.
Fruits: Fleshy, almost spherical or somewhat pointed, scarlet head 10–20 mm (⅖–⅘ in) across, studded with minute 1-seeded fruits.
Related or similar plants: Barren Strawberry has greyish-green leaves, shorter runners and minute, dry fruits; it flowers in early spring.
Habitat and distribution: A familiar and often abundant plant of open woods and rides, scrub, sunny banks, waste ground and open, stony ground, especially on railway ballast, throughout Britain and Ireland.
Flowering time: May to July.

WILD STRAWBERRY SOMETIMES appears in great crowds, for example on chalk, on partly vegetated roadside banks and where ground vegetation is regenerating after the felling of beech woodland. Colonisation is rapid, both by the vigorous runners and from buried seed suddenly exposed to light. The sweet fruits are, like blackberries, a popular free product of the countryside. They used to be gathered for sale, but few people now bother to take more than a few at a time. In Poland and other European countries they remain an important wild-collected product.

The much larger garden strawberries (*F. ananassa*) do not derive from this species, but from a cross between two cultivated species originally from the Americas. Barren Strawberry is related to the cinquefoils.

Wild Strawberry (Fragaria vesca) *can be found in open woods and rides and is often abundant on sunny banks. The leaves, whilst superficially similar to those of the Barren Strawberry, are a bright green and the miniature strawberries confirm identification.*

FLOWER TYPE

IDENTIFICATION

HABITAT

POPULATION

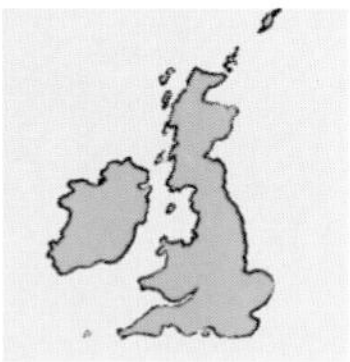

MAP

Common Lady's Mantle

ROSE FAMILY

(Rosaceae)

SPECIES INFORMATION	
COMMON NAME	Common Lady's Mantle
SCIENTIFIC NAME	Alchemilla xanthochlora
RELATED SPECIES	Alpine Lady's Mantle
HEIGHT/SPREAD	20–50 cm tall
FLOWERING TIME	May–July
HABITAT	Damp grassland, mainly in the north

Note: The leaf-lobes spread like the fingers of an open hand.

FLOWER TYPE

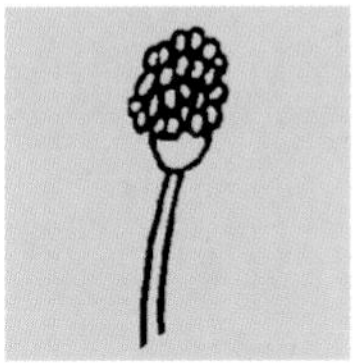

IDENTIFICATION

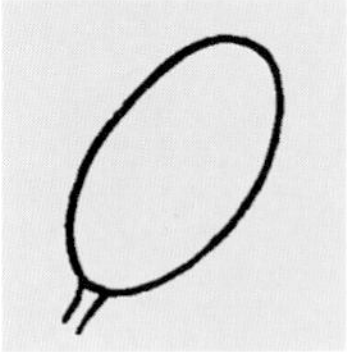

HABITAT

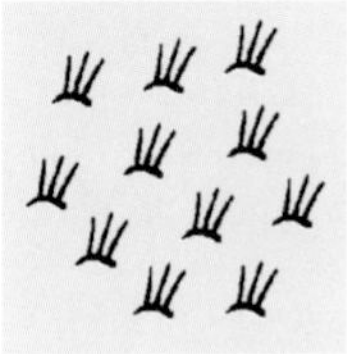

POPULATION

MAP

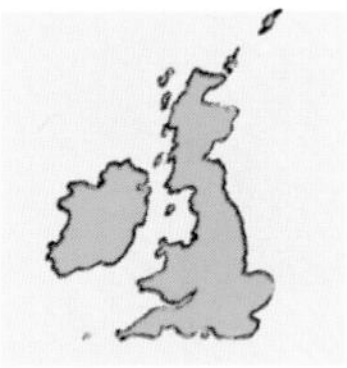

Size and appearance: A rather robust, tufted perennial with erect or semi-erect stems 20–50 cm (8–20 in) tall.

Leaves: Almost circular but with 7–9 shallow, rounded, finely toothed lobes in the form of an open hand, pale or yellowish-green, hairless on the upper surface, hairy beneath and on the stalk.

Flowers: Tiny, the 4 yellowish-green sepals replacing petals, in spreading, rather flat-topped clusters.

Fruits: 1-seeded fruitlets enclosed within the persistent flower-parts.

Related or similar plants: A complex group of several species, of which Alpine Lady's Mantle, which has divided leaves with silver-silky hairs beneath, is the most distinct.

Habitat and distribution: Damp grassland, from old meadows to roadsides, rocky ground and streamsides, especially in upland districts, throughout Britain but much more common north of a line between the Rivers Severn and Humber, and in northern Ireland.

Flowering time: May to July.

COMMON LADY'S MANTLE is the most widespread and common of a complex group of closely related species, mainly of mountainous regions in Britain and Europe. These plants have evolved an unusual method of reproduction, whereby seeds develop without the need for fertilisation by pollen, which in Lady's Mantles is mostly defective. As a result, different populations of these plants, unable to cross normally with each other, have over time evolved into distinct species.

The mountains of northern Britain are rich in Lady's Mantles, the mountains of Ireland much less so. The commonest species in highland districts is Smooth Lady's Mantle (*Alchemilla glabra*), similar to Common Lady's Mantle, but the darker green leaves have 9–11 lobes; also Alpine Lady's Mantle.

Bottom *Alpine Lady's Mantle* (Alchemilla alpina) *is a small plant not more than 25 cm (10 in) tall, that has leaves divided to the base into 5–7 leaflet-like lobes densely covered beneath with silver-silky hairs, and small, dense flower clusters. It is locally common in the mountains of Scotland and north-western England, and at a very few sites in southern Ireland.*

SPECIES INFORMATION	
COMMON NAME	Gorse, Furze, Whin
SCIENTIFIC NAME	Ulex europaeu
RELATED SPECIES	Western Gorse
HEIGHT/SPREAD	1–3 m tall
FLOWERING TIME	March–October
HABITAT	Heaths, scrub and cliffs

Note: Spiny, yellow-flowered shrub.

Gorse

CLOVER AND PEA FAMILY

(Leguminosae or Fabaceae)

Size and appearance: A dense, spiny shrub 1–3 m (3–9ft) tall, with rigid, furrowed spines up to 2.5 cm (1 in) long.
Leaves: 3-foliate on young shoots, but reduced to scales or dark green spines on mature plants.
Flowers: Golden-yellow, 15–20 mm (⅗–⅘ in) long, richly scented, in spiny clusters at the ends of branches.
Fruits: Flattened, black, hairy pods 10–25 mm (⅖–1 in) long, splitting explosively when ripe.
Related or similar plants: Western Gorse is more compact, with smaller, deeper yellow flowers in late summer; Broom (p.114) is spineless.
Habitat and distribution: Forming impenetrable thickets on moors, heaths, cliffs, open woods, hedgerows, derelict industrial or railway land, and road-verges and embankments on lime-poor soils, especially in heathland districts in the south and in the north and west.
Flowering time: March to July, but often continuing until October, and with a few flowers through the autumn and winter.

GORSE IS ONE of the great floral displays of these islands. On warm days the flowers scent the air with their vanilla and coconut fragrance. It is generally possible to find a few Gorse flowers open at any time of year, even Christmas, hence the old proverb: 'When gorse is out of bloom, kissing's out of season'. It was reported that the great 18th century botanist Carl Linnaeus fell on his knees and wept at the sight of English gorse in its full glory. It is rare in his native Sweden. On hot summer days the ripe seed-pods split with an audible crack to release the seeds.

Gorse regenerates well after burning. It was formerly a mainstay of the rural economy: cut for kindling and fuel, thatch, bedding and (chopped up) fodder for farm animals. A gorse bush hauled up and down a chimney on a rope swept away soot, and the farmer would tow a bush across ploughed land as a primitive harrow.

Top *Gorse* (Ulex europaeus) *here in full flower on a cliff-top.*

Bottom *Western Gorse* (Ulex gallii) *is similar but not more than 2 m (6 ft) tall, with deeper yellow flowers 10–12 mm (⅖–½ in) long and pods c. 10 mm (⅖ in) long. Flowering July–September, it occurs in western Britain north to southern Scotland, but also in a few places in the east, and across much of Ireland. It is particularly characteristic of coastal heathland and here grows on a clifftop.*

Broom

CLOVER AND PEA FAMILY
(Leguminosae or Fabaceae)

SPECIES INFORMATION	
COMMON NAME	Broom
SCIENTIFIC NAME	Cytisus scoparius
RELATED SPECIES	Gorse
HEIGHT/SPREAD	1–3 m tall
FLOWERING TIME	April–July
HABITAT	Heaths, cliffs and waste ground

Note: Upright, twiggy, leafless yellow-flowered shrub.

FLOWER TYPE

IDENTIFICATION

HABITAT

POPULATION

MAP

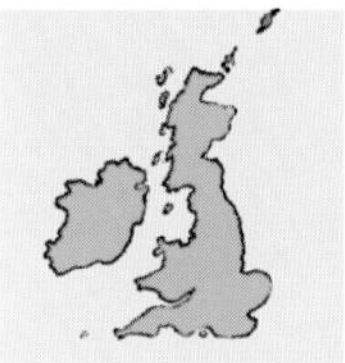

Size and appearance: An upright (rarely prostrate), much-branched, mostly leafless shrub 1–3 m (3–9 ft) tall, with green, 5-angled stems.
Leaves: 3-foliate and silky-hairy on young shoots, but absent from mature plants.
Flowers: Golden-yellow, 15–25 mm (⅗–1 in) long, richly scented, solitary or in pairs in loose clusters at the ends of branches.
Fruits: Flattened, black pods 25–40 mm (1–1⅗ in) long, hairy on the margins, splitting when ripe.

Top and bottom left *Broom* (Cytisus scoparius) *can form large stands which make a blaze of colour when in flower. Later in the year it is possible to hear the ripe pods splitting on a sunny day.*

Related or similar plants: Gorse (p.113) and Western Gorse are spiny, with shorter seed-pods.
Habitat and distribution: Locally abundant and sometimes forming thickets on heaths, cliffs, open woods, dry banks, disused railway lines, shingle beaches and road-verges on lime-poor soils, although often absent in areas with chalk and limestone exposures.
Flowering time: April to July.

LIKE GORSE, MASSED Broom can be a magnificent sight in flower in early summer. And like Gorse, it was once a mainstay of the rural economy, especially on heathland. The twigs were used for animal fodder and bedding, as well as being gathered and bundled up to make brooms. An infusion of the twigs and flowers made a diuretic tonic said to have been drunk by the dropsical Henry VIII.

The flowers also made a country wine. The plant features in legend and folklore, as in the ballads of Tam Lin and Broomfield Hill, powerful stories of love and magic set on medieval heaths. Broom has given its name to many towns and villages, including Bromley and Brompton.

A striking, prostrate variant of Broom occurs here and there on coastal cliffs in Cornwall, Wales and western Ireland, also on the great Dungeness shingle beach in Kent. It can also occasionally be seen in gardens.

Bottom right *Spanish Broom* (Spartium junceum) *is similar to Broom but has cylindrical stems, flowers in long, loose clusters and silky-hairy pods. An escape from gardens, flowering in Summer, it spreads along railway embankments in urban areas.*

SPECIES INFORMATION	
COMMON NAME	Tufted Vetch
SCIENTIFIC NAME	Vicia cracca
RELATED SPECIES	Bush Vetch
HEIGHT/SPREAD	Stems 50–200 cm long
FLOWERING TIME	June–September
HABITAT	Hedges and grassy places

Note: Other vetches have fewer flowers per cluster.

Tufted Vetch

CLOVER AND PEA FAMILY

(Leguminosae or Fabaceae)

Size and appearance: A more or less hairy, scrambling perennial, with a creeping rootstock and stems 50–200cm (20–80 in) long, climbing by tendrils.
Leaves: Compound, with 6–15 pairs of oval to oblong, often narrow leaflets, the end leaflet replaced by a branched, convoluted tendril.
Flowers: Bluish-purple, 8–15 mm (1/5–3/5 in) long, 10–40, in long-stalked, dense, 1-sided clusters.
Fruits: Flattened, brown, hairless pods 10–25 mm (2/5–1 in) long, splitting when ripe.
Related or similar plants: Bush Vetch (p.116) has flowers in clusters of 2–6; in Common Vetch (p.117) they are solitary or paired.
Habitat and distribution: Common in bushy and grassy places such as hedgerows, scrub, woodland margins and old meadows throughout Britain and Ireland.
Flowering time: June to September.

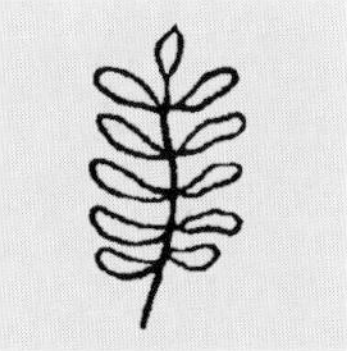

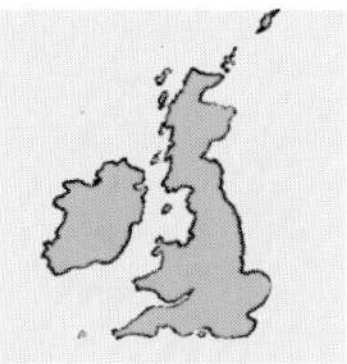

TUFTED VETCH IS a feature of the summer hedgerow, its flower-laden stems festooning the bushes and the long grasses of the wayside. It remains common, but has more or less disappeared from meadowland, one of its former habitats that has been diminished so severely by modern agriculture. It still survives in a few meadows, and in the *machair* or grassland over blown sand in the Hebrides.

It is variable, particularly in the shape and hairiness of the leaflets, and five very similar vetch species occur elsewhere in Europe. The vetches in the genus *Vicia* are a large group, complex to classify and identify, and about a dozen of them are native to Britain.

Tufted Vetch (Vicia cracca) *has compound leaves with many small pairs of leaflets, the ends are a tendril which wraps around other vegetation to aid its scramble through the hedgerows.*

Bush Vetch

CLOVER AND PEA FAMILY

(Leguminosae or Fabaceae)

SPECIES INFORMATION	
COMMON NAME	Bush Vetch
SCIENTIFIC NAME	Vicia sepium
RELATED SPECIES	Tufted Vetch, Common Vetch
HEIGHT/SPREAD	20–100 cm tall
FLOWERING TIME	April–November
HABITAT	Hedges and woodland margin

Note: The rather dowdy clusters of 2–6 flowers are distinctive.

FLOWER TYPE

IDENTIFICATION

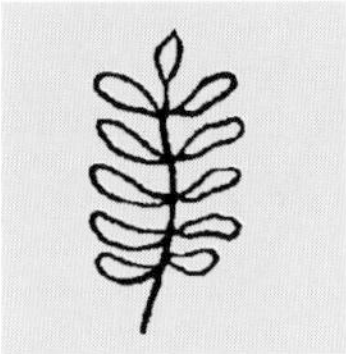

HABITAT

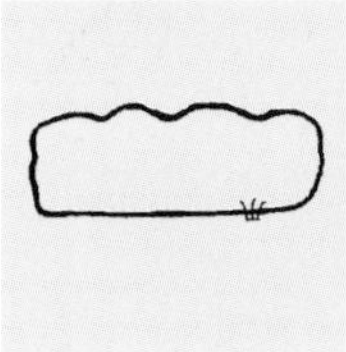

POPULATION

MAP

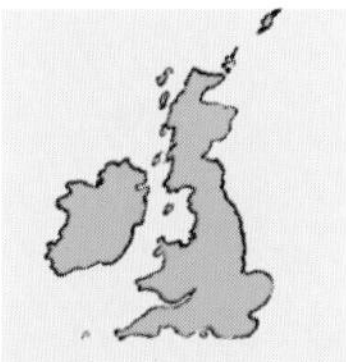

Size and appearance: A downy, scrambling or trailing perennial 20–100 cm (8–40 in) tall, with far-creeping slender rhizomes, forming patches.

Leaves: Compound, with 3–9 pairs of oval or broadly oblong leaflets, the end leaflet replaced by a branched tendril.

Flowers: Pale bluish-purple, rarely lilac or cream, 10–15 mm (⅖–⅗ in) long, 2–6, in short-stalked clusters.

Fruits: Flattened, black, hairless pods 20–35 mm (⅘–1⅖ in) long, splitting when ripe.

Related or similar plants: Tufted Vetch (p.115) has flowers in dense clusters of 10–40; in Common Vetch (p.117) they are solitary or paired.

Bottom *Wood Vetch* (Vicia sylvatica) *has trailing stems up to 2 m (6 ft) long, leaves with 5–12 pairs of leaflets and clusters of 5–20, larger flowers, whitish with purple veins, in June–July. It is a widespread but local plant of woods, rocky places and occasionally coastal shingle.*

Habitat and distribution: A common and often abundant plant of hedgerows, sunken lanes, open woods and woodland margins, scrub and roadsides, occasionally on sand-dunes, throughout Britain and Ireland.

Flowering time: April to November.

BUSH VETCH IS a characteristic plant of hedgerows and lanes, sometimes forming quite extensive, leafy patches. The plants climb only weakly by their tendrils. The flowers seen in close-up are quite attractive and neatly marked with darker veins, but from a distance they appear faded and dowdy by comparison with those of vetches. Attractive cream and lilac-flowered variants turn up from time to time.

A curious variant of Bush Vetch grows on sand-dunes on coasts of northern and western Scotland and north-western Ireland. The plants, which are compact, prostrate and almost without tendrils, grow in sparse vegetation and bare sand.

SPECIES INFORMATION	
COMMON NAME	Common Vetch, Tare
SCIENTIFIC NAME	Vicia sativa
RELATED SPECIES	Bush Vetch, Tufted Vetch
HEIGHT/SPREAD	Stems 20–120 cm long
FLOWERING TIME	May–August
HABITAT	Grassy places, hedge-banks

Note: The combination of solitary or paired flowers.

Common Vetch

CLOVER AND PEA FAMILY
(Leguminosae or Fabaceae)

COMMON VETCH IS a very variable species, with a complex history of cultivation. The native plant of old grasslands and coastal habitats tends to have narrow leaflets, rather bright pink flowers and black seed-pods. Plants that have some history of cultivation have larger and 2-tone, purplish and pink flowers. The largest and most robust plants, with rounded leaflets, showy flowers and yellowish-brown seed-pods often more than 5 cm (2 in) long, are true fodder plants, usually sown on roadsides or amenity grassland as part of wild flower seed mixtures. Farmers on the continent still grow large numbers of vetches for animal fodder and green manure.

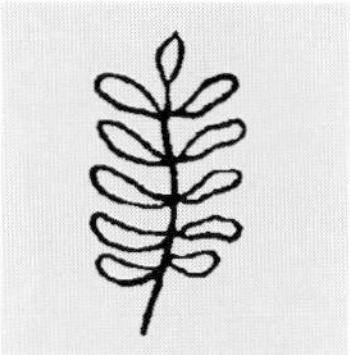

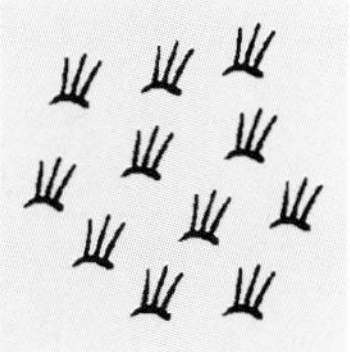

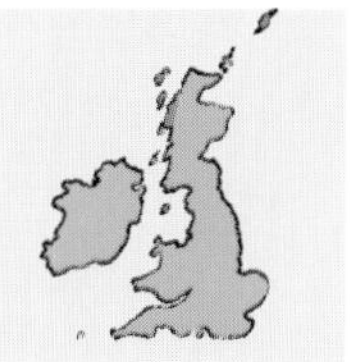

Size and appearance: A downy, climbing or trailing perennial, with stems 20–120 cm (8–48 in) long, forming small patches.
Leaves: Compound, with 3–8 pairs of oblong, oval or narrowly heart-shaped leaflets, the end leaflet replaced by a branched tendril.
Flowers: stalkless, solitary or in pairs, bright pink, purplish-pink or purple, 10–25 mm (⅖–1 in) long.
Fruits: Flattened, black or yellowish-brown, hairless or downy pods 2.5–5 cm (1–2 in) long, sometimes longer, splitting when ripe.
Related or similar plants: Bush Vetch (p.116) has clusters of 2–6 flowers, Tufted Vetch (p.115) clusters of 10–40.
Habitat and distribution: Widespread and generally common in grassy and shrubby places, along the margins of fields, on waysides and hedge-banks, either native or in some areas as a relic of cultivation for fodder; throughout, but more local, in Ireland.
Flowering time: May to August.

Common Vetch is a member of the pea family and is often found in grassy places, waysides and hedgebanks. Its pink and purple flowers are set singly or in pairs directly on the plant stem and often have a dark spot at their base.

Meadow Vetchling

CLOVER AND PEA FAMILY

(Leguminosae or Fabaceae)

SPECIES INFORMATION	
COMMON NAME	Meadow Vetchling, Yellow Vetchling
SCIENTIFIC NAME	Lathyrus pratensis
RELATED SPECIES	Bird's Foot Trefoil
HEIGHT/SPREAD	Stems 30–120 cm long
FLOWERING TIME	May–August
HABITAT	Hedge-banks and grassy places

Note: Our only yellow peaflower with winged stems.

FLOWER TYPE

IDENTIFICATION

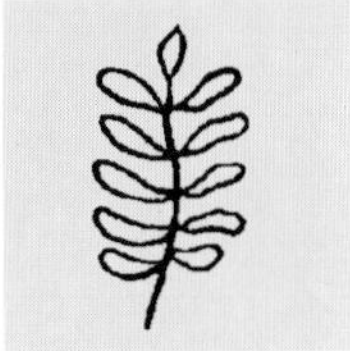

HABITAT

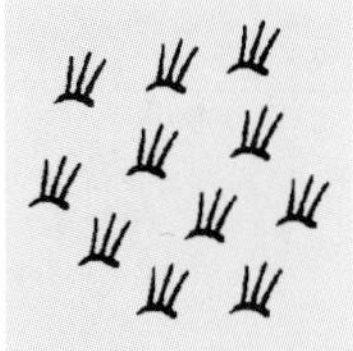

POPULATION

MAP

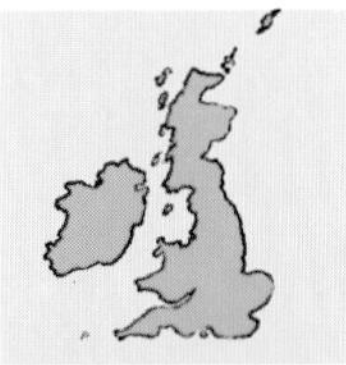

Size and appearance: A hairless, scrambling perennial, with a slender rhizome and 4-angled stems 30–120 cm (12–48 in) long, climbing by tendrils.

Leaves: With a single pair of spear-shaped leaflets up to 5 cm (2 in) long, the end leaflet replaced by a branched tendril; each leaf with a pair of arrow-shaped, leaflet-like flanges or stipules at the base.

Flowers: Yellow, 12–20 mm (½–¾ in) long, 5–12 in long-stalked, compact clusters.

Fruits: Flattened, black, hairless pods 20–40 mm (⅘–1⅗ in) long, splitting when ripe.

Related or similar plants: Bird's-foot Trefoil (p.130) has leaflets in 5s, no tendrils and smaller flowers.

Habitat and distribution: Widespread and common in grassy places, marshes, scrub, woodland margins and hedge-banks throughout Britain and Ireland.

Flowering time: May to August.

Meadow Vetchling (Lathyris pratensis) *produces a cluster of yellow flowers which are held erect above the foliage. The leaves are spear-shaped with a branched tendril at the end and a pair of large arrow-shaped stipules at their base.*

MEADOW VETCHLING IS one of the most showy of our grassland wild flowers, and is still reasonably abundant, despite the destruction of so much old grassland by modern intensive farming. It is the main food plant for the caterpillars of the attractive and local Wood White Butterfly. Meadow Vetchling has been used as a herbal remedy for the treatment of coughs and bronchitis.

This plant illustrates the main features of the vetchlings and the wild peas (*Lathyrus*). These are similar to the vetches (*Vicia*), but generally have more winged or angled stems, leaves with a pair of large flanges or stipules at the base, fewer leaflets and larger flowers. Both groups possess tendrils, but these are sometimes absent or replaced by a leaflet. Botanists themselves admit that there are few consistent differences between these two groups.

SPECIES INFORMATION	
COMMON NAME	Sea Pea
SCIENTIFIC NAME	Lathyrus japonicus
RELATED SPECIES	Bitter Vetch
HEIGHT/SPREAD	Stems 20–100 cm long
FLOWERING TIME	May–September
HABITAT	Shingle beaches

Note: The large purple peaflower of shingle beaches.

Sea Pea

CLOVER AND PEA FAMILY

(Leguminosae or Fabaceae)

Top *Sea Pea* (Lathyrus japonicus) *makes a charming display on shingle beaches, with purple flowers set off by the bluish-green foliage that creeps across the pebbles.*

FLOWER TYPE

IDENTIFICATION

HABITAT

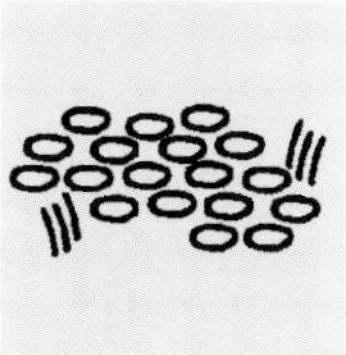

POPULATION

MAP

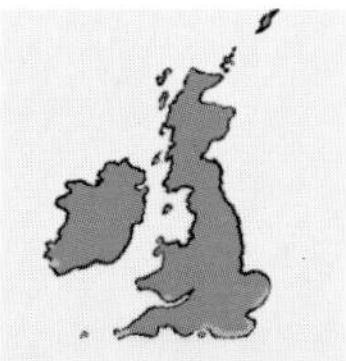

Size and appearance: A robust perennial, with woody rhizomes, forming extensive patches, and 4-angled, prostrate stems 20–100 cm (8–40 in) long.

Leaves: Slightly fleshy, bluish-green, compound, with 2–5 pairs of oval leaflets, the end leaflet replaced by a tendril; each leaf with a pair of arrow-shaped, leaflet-like flanges or stipules at the base.

Flowers: Purple, becoming blue, 15–20 mm (⅗–⅘ in) long, 2–15, in long-stalked clusters.

Fruits: Like a small pea-pod, dark brown, hairless, 3–5 cm (1⅕–2 in) long, splitting when ripe.

Related or similar plants: Bitter Vetch is a smaller plant of lime-poor soils inland, with winged stems, no tendrils and reddish-purple flowers.

Habitat and distribution: Rare and sometimes sporadic, but locally in quantity on the shingle beaches of southern and eastern England, and also occurring at isolated sites from Cornwall to Shetland; very rare in western Ireland, where it usually grows on sand, as it does in Scotland.

Flowering time: May to September.

SEA PEA IS a handsome and conspicuous plant of shingle beaches that sometimes forms great stands. It grows with a few other colonist species on the barest shingle banks, subject to wave erosion. However, the principal threat to the plant is human disturbance of beaches. Sea Pea has declined considerably over the last 50 years outside its south-eastern headquarters. In Ireland it is extremely sporadic, and it has been suggested that at least some plants derive from seed that was washed ashore after being transported from North America via the Gulf Stream.

In Suffolk, where it is still abundant, the people of Aldeburgh used to harvest the pea-pods. The protein-rich but bitter peas are said to have staved off famine on at least one occasion. Plants on the Chesil Beach in Dorset formerly provided summer grazing for sheep.

Bottom *Bitter Vetch (*Lathyrus montanus*), superficially similar, has smaller, reddish-purple flowers, fading to bluish, winged stems and leaves without tendrils. Flowering April–July, it is widespread in heathy grassland and scrub on lime-poor soils; absent from East Anglia.*

Broad-leaved Everlasting-pea

CLOVER AND PEA FAMILY
(Leguminosae or Fabaceae)

SPECIES INFORMATION	
COMMON NAME	Broad-leaved Everlasting-pea
SCIENTIFIC NAME	Lathyrus latifolius
RELATED SPECIES	Narrow-leaved Everlasting Pea
HEIGHT/SPREAD	Stems 1–3 m long
FLOWERING TIME	June–September
HABITAT	Scrub and grassy places

Note: Like a perennial garden sweet-pea.

FLOWER TYPE

IDENTIFICATION

HABITAT

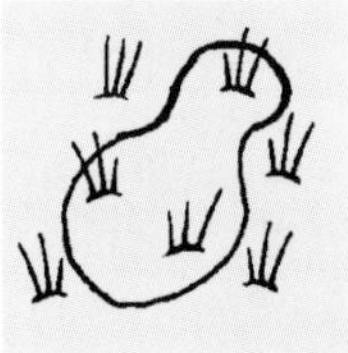

POPULATION

MAP

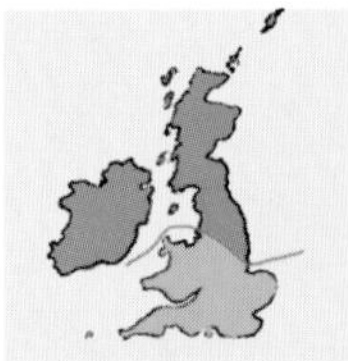

Size and appearance: A robust, downy, climbing perennial with broadly winged stems 1–3 m (3–9 ft) long.
Leaves: A single pair of oval or broadly spear-shaped, rather blunt leaflets, the end leaflet replaced by a branched, convoluted tendril; each leaf with a pair of spear-shaped, leaflet-like flanges or stipules at the base.
Flowers: Bright purplish-crimson, 20–30 mm (⅘–1⅕ in) long, 5–15, in long-stalked, compact clusters; teeth of the calyx shorter than the tube.
Fruits: Like a small pea-pod, brown, hairless, 5–10 cm (2–4 in) long, splitting when ripe.

Broad-leaved Everlasting Pea (Lathyrus latifolius) *is an escape from the cottage garden and it can now be found adorning many hedgerows and waysides. Through June to September, its erect spikes of bright purple-crimson flowers make a splash of colour against the backdrop of greenery.*

Related or similar plants: Narrow-leaved Everlasting-pea is a native plant of hedges and woods that has narrower leaves and smaller, greenish-pink flowers.
Habitat and distribution: An increasing garden escape, well established in hedges, on bushy commons, waste land, roadsides and railway embankments, even on sand-dunes, north to Lancashire, and in parts of Ireland.
Flowering time: June to September.

THIS MAGNIFICENT INCOMER provides welcome splashes of colour to sometimes drab or workaday landscapes, such as alongside suburban railway lines in and about London. It is as much at home festooning scrub in rural Wiltshire or brightening a Norfolk hedgerow, or on a mature sand-dune in Ireland. Although alien plants are often a problem, displacing native plant communities here and worldwide, plants like the Broad-leaved Everlasting-pea embellish our flora and should be welcomed to the countryside.

This is another old friend from the cottage garden, where white- and pink-flowered variants are also grown.

SPECIES INFORMATION	
COMMON NAME	Grass Vetchling
SCIENTIFIC NAME	Lathyrus nissolia
RELATED SPECIES	Vetches, Vetchlings and Peas
HEIGHT/SPREAD	20–80 cm tall
FLOWERING TIME	May–July
HABITAT	Grassy places and dry banks

Note: Like a grass, but with crimson peaflowers.

Grass Vetchling

CLOVER AND PEA FAMILY

(Leguminosae or Fabaceae)

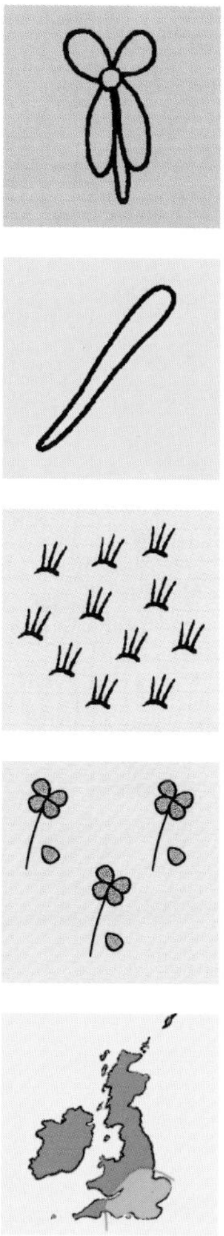

Size and appearance: A slender, almost hairless annual 20–80 cm (8–32 in) tall, with erect, angled stems.

Leaves: Very narrow, grasslike, with a pair of tiny, narrow flanges or stipules at the base, but without a tendril.

Flowers: Solitary or in pairs, on long, slender stalks, crimson, 10–18 mm (⅖–¾ in) long.

Fruits: Narrow, brown, hairless, 3–6 cm (1⅕–2⅖ in) long, splitting when ripe.

Related or similar plants: All other vetches, vetchlings and peas have paired leaflets.

Habitat and distribution: A local but also much-overlooked plant of grassy places, dry banks and track-sides, on clayey or lime-rich soils, often near the sea, mostly in south-eastern England, but locally extending west and north to Devon and Lincolnshire.

Flowering time: May to July.

GRASS VETCHLING IS one of the most elusive and attractive of all our wild flowers. It is effectively disguised as a grass except when in full flower. Also, being an annual, a precarious life history for a grassland plant, its numbers can fluctuate from year to year. In a good year in early summer, an apparently flowerless grassy bank suddenly becomes splashed with crimson. Close up, the flowers are elegant and, because of their slender stalks, fragile-looking. Seductive as they are, they soon wither if picked.

The 'leaves' are of great botanical interest because they lack true leaf-blades. They are in fact flattened leaf-stalks, known technically as phyllodes. The pair of tiny flanges or stipules at the base of each reveals that here we have a peaflower rather than a grass. (Grasses have conventional leaves, but they are always very narrow.) One sees a parallel modification of plant organs in Butcher's Broom (p.342), where the true leaves are replaced by flattened stems.

Grass Vetchling (Lathyrus nissolia) *is a plant that will go unnoticed among the grasses until it comes into bloom, when the solitary crimson flower seems to hang in the grass as though by magic, its long slender stalk camouflaged by the grass stems. Once the pods develop they too allow this vetchling to be spotted in the vegetation.*

Tall Melilot

CLOVER AND PEA FAMILY

(Leguminosae or Fabaceae)

SPECIES INFORMATION	
COMMON NAME	Tall Melilot, Golden Melilot
SCIENTIFIC NAME	Melilotus altissima
RELATED SPECIES	Common Melilot
HEIGHT/SPREAD	40–150 cm tall
FLOWERING TIME	May–September
HABITAT	Waste ground and field borders

Note: The tallest non-shrubby yellow peaflower.

FLOWER TYPE

IDENTIFICATION

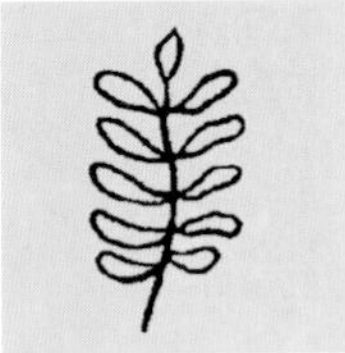

HABITAT

POPULATION

MAP

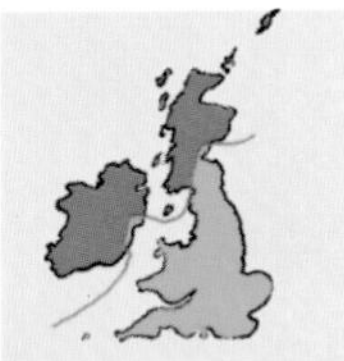

Size and appearance: An erect, rather robust, branched annual, biennial or short-lived perennial 40–150 cm (16–60 in) tall.
Leaves: 3-foliate on a stalk, the leaflets wedge-shaped, oblong or oval, toothed.
Flowers: Numerous in rather dense, 1-sided clusters up to 5 cm (2 in) long; yellow, 5–7 mm (⅕–⅓ in) long, the petals all the same length.
Fruits: Flattened egg-shaped, black, downy, 5–6 mm (⅕–¼ in) long, slightly wrinkled, splitting when ripe.
Related or similar plants: Common Melilot differs in having the lowest pair of petals shorter than the others, and brown, hairless pods.
Habitat and distribution: Widespread, sometimes in quantity, on waste ground, field borders and tracksides, sometimes in open woods, often on clayey soils, mostly south-east of a line from the Humber to the Severn, but locally extending north to central Scotland; in Ireland mostly on the coast of Co. Dublin.
Flowering time: May to September.

TALL MELILOT IS perhaps an introduction to Britain, brought in by 16th-century herbalists and physicians, who valued this plant for use in healing poultices. These help scar tissue to form; an infusion also aids digestion. The circumstantial evidence suggests that one of these herbalists, William Turner (1508–68), the so-called Father of English Botany, may have introduced Tall Melilot from the Netherlands to the garden at Syon House, Middlesex, now a well-known garden centre.

Melilots contain coumarin, the chemical that imparts the sweet scent to new-mown hay and to Sweet Woodruff (p.211). Both Tall Melilot and Common Melilot are useful plants to grow for green manure, although the very high coumarin content makes them toxic to animals. They are tolerant of poor and saline soils, and are a good source of nectar for bees.

Bottom right *Common Melilot* (Melilotus officinalis) *is very similar to Tall Melilot but up to 250 cm (10 ft) tall and less compact, with the pods brown, hairless and wrinkled. It is widespread in England and Ireland.*

Bottom left *White Melilot* (Melilotus albus) *is naturalised in fields and wasteland, mainly in the south.*

SPECIES INFORMATION	
COMMON NAME	Common Restharrow
SCIENTIFIC NAME	Ononis repens
RELATED SPECIES	Spiny Restharrow
HEIGHT/SPREAD	Stems 10–70 cm long
FLOWERING TIME	June–September
HABITAT	Dry grassland and sand-dunes

Note: The sticky-hairy leaves are unusual.

Common Restharrow

CLOVER AND PEA FAMILY (Leguminosae or Fabaceae)

Spiny Restharrow (Ononis spinosa) *is similar but often erect, with spiny stems that are hairy on 2 opposite sides, narrower leaflets, and seed-pods longer than the surrounding calyx. It is a local and decreasing plant of clayey, mostly lime-rich soils, in southern and central England but extending to Somerset and southern Scotland; not in Ireland.*

FLOWER TYPE

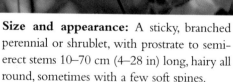

IDENTIFICATION

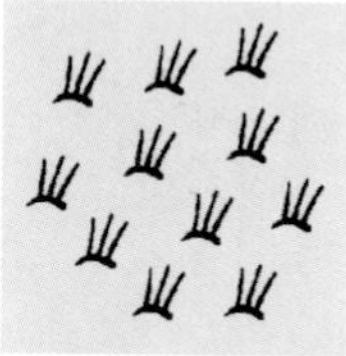
HABITAT

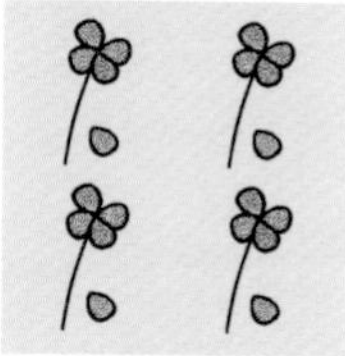
POPULATION

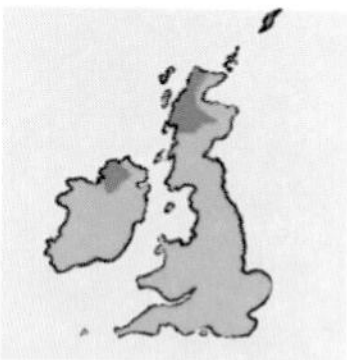
MAP

Size and appearance: A sticky, branched perennial or shrublet, with prostrate to semi-erect stems 10–70 cm (4–28 in) long, hairy all round, sometimes with a few soft spines.

Leaves: Densely sticky-hairy, simple or 3-foliate, the leaflets wedge-shaped, oval, sharply toothed.

Flowers: Pink or purplish-pink, 15–20 mm (⅗–⅘ in) long, in loose, leafy clusters; calyx densely hairy.

Fruits: Flattened, 5–7 mm (⅕–¼ in) long, enclosed within the persistent calyx.

Related or similar plants: The more erect Spiny Restharrow has spiny stems that are hairy on 2 opposite sides.

Habitat and distribution: Typical of grassland on dry and lime-rich soils, and on sand-dunes and shingle beaches; almost throughout, but scarce in western and much of northern Scotland and in western Ireland.

Flowering time: June to September.

THE TOUGH ROOTS and stems of this low-growing plant give it the evocative English name, which has also been spelled Wrestharrow. In the days before tractors, this and Spiny Restharrow impeded cultivation with old-fashioned implements, and these plants were regarded as indicative of poor or neglected land. Both readily invaded fallow fields, where the foliage is said to have tainted the milk of grazing cattle. However, children in northern England apparently chewed the roots as a natural liquorice (liquorice is obtained from another member of this family, of warm climates).

Lucerne

CLOVER AND PEA FAMILY
(Leguminosae or Fabaceae)

SPECIES INFORMATION	
COMMON NAME	Lucerne, Alfalfa
SCIENTIFIC NAME	Medicago sativa
RELATED SPECIES	Sickle Medick
HEIGHT/SPREAD	30–80 cm tall
FLOWERING TIME	June–October
HABITAT	Grassy places and roadsides

Note: Upright violet-flowered peaflower of roadsides.

FLOWER TYPE

IDENTIFICATION

HABITAT

POPULATION

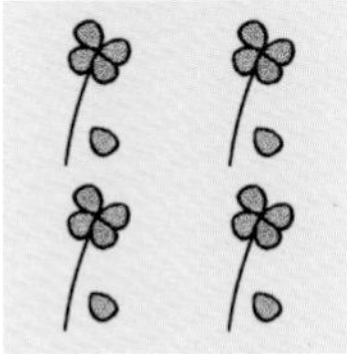

MAP

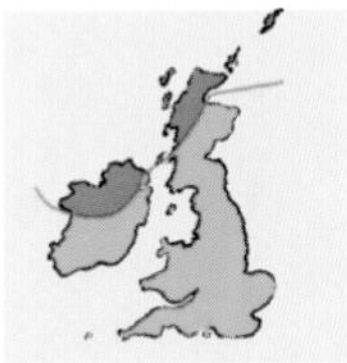

Size and appearance: A hairless short-lived perennial 30–80 cm (12–32 in) tall.
Leaves: 3-foliate, the leaflets oval or oblong, toothed near the tip.
Flowers: Bluish- or purplish-violet or lilac, 6–12 mm (¼–½in) long, up to 40 in loose, cylindrical clusters.
Fruits: Spiralled 1½–3½ times, hairless, with 10–20 seeds.
Related or similar plants: Sickle Medick has yellow flowers and sickle-shaped pods.
Habitat and distribution: Field margins, roadsides and waste places, also as a field crop; mainly in eastern and central England, but widely distributed north to the Moray Firth and here and there in Ireland.
Flowering time: June to October.

LUCERNE, ORIGINALLY FROM south-west Asia, is one of the world's great fodder and green manure plants. It persists after cultivation, and is often seen on roadsides and waste ground, even in towns. In the dry, sandy Breckland of East Anglia it encounters the native Sickle Medick in fallow fields and on sandy roadsides. The two cross and backcross to form a range of natural hybrids, which combine the characters of the two species. Many botanists regard them as just two subspecies of a single species. Sickle Medick and the hybrid have also been grown as fodder crops.

Bottom
Sickle Medick (Medicago falcata) *is more sprawling or prostrate in habit, with yellow flowers and curved or sickle-shaped seed-pods containing 2–5 seeds. A native of Breckland, it persists elsewhere as a relic of cultivation.*

SPECIES INFORMATION	
COMMON NAME	Black Medick
SCIENTIFIC NAME	Medicago lupulina
RELATED SPECIES	Lesser Trefoil
HEIGHT/SPREAD	Stems 10–60 cm long
FLOWERING TIME	May–October
HABITAT	Grassland, cliffs and beaches

Note: Like a little yellow clover, but with larger, black fruits.

Black Medick

CLOVER AND PEA FAMILY

(Leguminosae or Fabaceae)

FLOWER TYPE

IDENTIFICATION

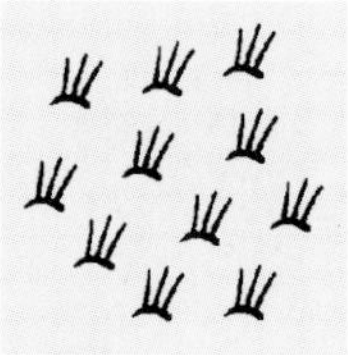
HABITAT

POPULATION

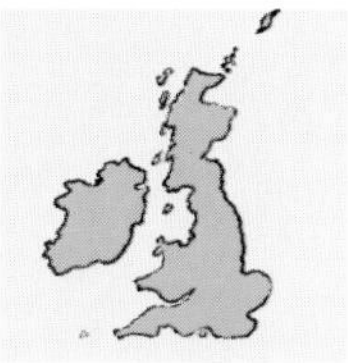
MAP

Size and appearance: A variably hairy (sometimes slightly sticky-hairy), prostrate or untidily semi-erect annual, biennial or short-lived perennial, with stems 10–60 cm (4–24 in) long.

Leaves: 3-foliate, the leaflets oval or almost circular, the middle one shortly stalked, blunt, notched, with a tiny point in the notch.

Flowers: Tiny, golden-yellow, up to 50 in long-stalked spherical heads 3–10 mm (1/8–3/8 in) across.

Fruits: Kidney-shaped, 1-seeded, black, hairless pods 2–3 mm (1/12–1/8 in) long.

Related or similar plants: Lesser Trefoil (p.126) is a very similar clover; the seed-pods are smaller, brown and enclosed within the persistent flower-parts.

Habitat and distribution: Common in dry grassland, on sunny slopes and banks, pathsides, wall-tops, cliffs, sand-dunes and shingle beaches throughout Britain and Ireland, but scarcer in northern Scotland and north-western Ireland.

Flowering time: May to October.

THIS IS A CHARACTERISTIC plant of sunny banks and open grassy places, where it is certainly native. Plants in chalk grassland are often small, compact and slightly sticky-hairy. Black Medick is probably native in these sorts of habitats, but increasingly we are seeing more vigorous, robust, erect plants, with large rounded leaflets, on roadsides and in amenity grassland. Some of these may derive from former fields of Black Medick grown for fodder and green manure, but many have come in with commercial wild flower seed mixtures. These mixtures frequently contain agricultural seed of foreign origin.

Black Medick is often confused with Lesser Trefoil (p.126) and other small- and yellow-flowered clovers which occur in similar habitats. These clovers have smaller, yellow heads of flowers that turn brown in seed. The seed-pods are enclosed within the persistent flower-parts and are brownish in colour.

Black Medick (Medicago lupulina) *can be either prostate or semi-erect. It is a common plant, occurring in many habitats but they all tend to be open and sunny.*

Lesser Trefoil

CLOVER AND PEA FAMILY

(Leguminosae or Fabaceae)

SPECIES INFORMATION	
COMMON NAME	Lesser Trefoil, Suckling Clover
SCIENTIFIC NAME	Trifolium dubium
RELATED SPECIES	Black Medick, Hop Trefoil
HEIGHT/SPREAD	Stems 10–30 cm long
FLOWERING TIME	May–August
HABITAT	Dry grassland and sunny banks

Note: The common, small-flowered yellow clover of dry banks.

FLOWER TYPE

IDENTIFICATION

HABITAT

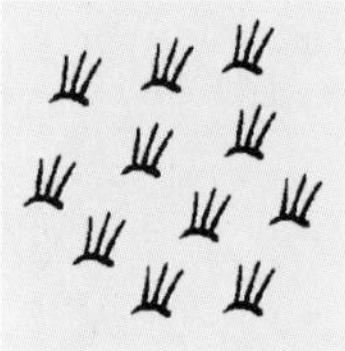

POPULATION

MAP

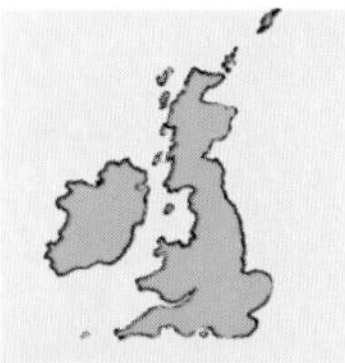

Size and appearance: An almost hairless, prostrate or more or less semi-erect annual 10–30 cm (4–12 in) long, sometimes up to 50 cm (20 in).

Leaves: 3-foliate, the leaflets oval, toothed, the middle one shortly stalked, blunt.

Flowers: Tiny, yellow, 10–20 in long-stalked spherical heads 6–8 mm (¼–⅓ in) across.

Fruits: Brownish heads of tiny, inconspicuous, 1-seeded, brown pods enclosed within the persistent flower-parts.

Related or similar plants: Black Medick (p.125), which is not a clover, is a hairier plant with conspicuous black fruits.

Habitat and distribution: Common in dry grassy places, on sunny slopes and banks, cliffs, rocky ground and wall-tops, pathsides, shabby lawns and sometimes cultivated ground, throughout Britain and Ireland.

Flowering time: May to August.

LIKE THE SUPERFICIALLY similar Black Medick, this is a plant of sunny banks and open grassy places. Where the grass is lusher it survives on the looser, well-drained soil of large anthills. Lesser Trefoil was once a fodder crop, known to farmers as Suckling Clover. One sometimes comes upon large plants with stems up to 50 cm (20 in) long and flower-heads c. 1 cm (⅜ in) across, which may be relics of cultivation. They may also derive from some wild flower seed mixtures (see note under Black Medick, p.125).

Lesser Trefoil is the clover most often sold in Ireland and elsewhere as *Seamróg* or Shamrock in the run-up to St Patrick's Day on 17 March. It has the strongest case among native clovers to be regarded as the true plant of legend, but Wood-Sorrel (p.134) may well be a better candidate.

Top left and right *Lesser Trefoil* (Trifolium dubium)
Has small yellow flowers and long-stalked spherical heads.

Bottom *Hop Trefoil* (Trifolium campestre)
Also has small yellow flowers which resemble hops, and turn brown with age.

SPECIES INFORMATION	
COMMON NAME	Red Clover
SCIENTIFIC NAME	Trifolium pratense
RELATED SPECIES	White Clover
HEIGHT/SPREAD	20–60 cm tall
FLOWERING TIME	May–October
HABITAT	Grassland and waysides
Note: The familiar red-flowered clover.	

Red Clover

CLOVER AND PEA FAMILY
(Leguminosae or Fabaceae)

Size and appearance: A rather hairy, tufted, short-lived perennial, with sprawling, semi-erect or erect stems 20–60 cm (8–24 in) tall, sometimes up to 100 cm (40 in).

Leaves: 3-foliate, the leaflets narrowly oval to almost circular, blunt, hairy beneath, often marked with a whitish crescent.

Flowers: Reddish-purple, pale or dark pink, sometimes white, 12–15 mm (½–⅗ in) long, massed in stalkless, solitary or paired, almost spherical heads 2–4 cm (⅘–⅘ in) across, with 2 leaves immediately below.

Fruits: Brown heads of 1-seeded pods enclosed within the persistent flower-parts.

Related or similar plants: White Clover (p.128) has prostrate, rooting stems and leafless flowering stems.

Habitat and distribution: Common in grassy places, from mountain ledges to sand-dunes and even pockets of grassland like unmanicured lawns, on waysides and waste ground, including those in towns, throughout Britain and Ireland.

Flowering time: May to October.

A VARIABLE SPECIES, probably present in many areas more as a relic of cultivation than as a native plant. The true native plant tends to be prostrate or sprawling in habit with smaller heads of deep reddish-purple flowers. Red Clover is still grown as a crop for animal fodder and green manure. Fodder plants are tall, erect and have large heads of often pale pink flowers. The flowers are pollinated by bumble-bees that find them a valuable source of nectar.

One of Charles Darwin's classic natural history observations was the relationship between numbers of farm cats, which control the mice that raid bumble-bee nests – thus reducing the pollination of clover seed-crops. Irish humorous writer Flann O'Brien added the corollary that the countryside needed more spinsters, in other words ladies who have a cat for company, to keep the cycle going.

Red Clover (Trifolium pratense) *is a familiar clover with its large reddish-purple flowers subtended by two leaves. Grown as a crop for animal fodder, there are many different strains which has resulted in the variation of flower colour and size of plant. The majority of plants along the waysides and footpaths are relics of cultivation and tend to be larger, more erect plants.*

FLOWER TYPE

IDENTIFICATION

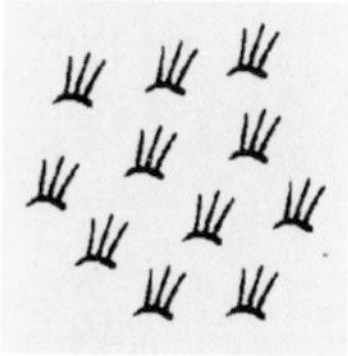
HABITAT

POPULATION

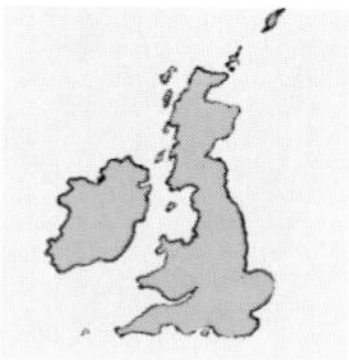
MAP

White Clover

CLOVER AND PEA FAMILY

(Leguminosae or Fabaceae)

SPECIES INFORMATION	
COMMON NAME	White Clover
SCIENTIFIC NAME	Trifolium repens
RELATED SPECIES	Red Clover
HEIGHT/SPREAD	20–50 cm tall
FLOWERING TIME	May–October
HABITAT	Grassland and waysides

Note: The familiar, abundant white-flowered clover.

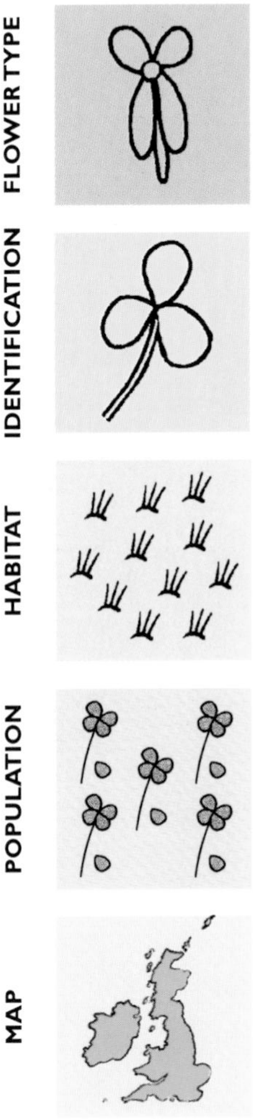

Size and appearance: An almost hairless perennial, with prostrate, far-creeping, rooting vegetative stems forming often extensive patches, and erect, leafless flowering stems 20–50 cm (8–20 in) tall.

Leaves: Long-stalked, 3-foliate, leaflets oval or circular, rounded, usually marked with a whitish crescent or other, darker markings.

Flowers: White, often tinged palest pink, 8–15 mm ($\frac{1}{3}$–$\frac{3}{5}$ in) long, scented, massed in long-stalked, solitary, spherical heads 1–3 cm ($\frac{4}{5}$–1$\frac{1}{5}$ in) across.

Fruits: Brown heads of 1- to 4-seeded pods enclosed within the persistent flower-parts.

Related or similar plants: Red Clover (p.127) is tufted in habit and has leafy flowering stems.

Habitat and distribution: Ubiquitous in grassy places, from mountain ledges to sand-dunes and forgotten pockets of grassland like unmanicured lawns, on waysides and waste ground, even in towns, throughout Britain and Ireland.

Flowering time: May to October.

White Clover (Trifolium repens) *with its far-creeping, rooting stems is the bane of any gardener who wishes for a perfect unblemished lawn. However, it is a valuable source of nectar for bees and a valuable fodder crop, making its nitrogen requirement from the bacteria in its root nodules.*

LIKE RED CLOVER (p.127) a very variable species, and one that undoubtedly derives in most areas from cultivated rather than native plants. Indeed it is hard to imagine what the true native plant might look like, as even remote upland areas have been reseeded at some time. Probably the very prostrate, small-flowered plants of coastal cliffs and sand-dunes are the most representative 'native' stocks.

White Clover, an easy plant to grow, remains a valuable fodder crop and nectar plant for bees. Like those of all clovers, the roots have small nodules packed with symbiotic or mutually co-existing bacteria that convert nitrogen in the air into plant nutrients. These nodules are tinted pink with haemoglobin, the same substance that we have in our own blood to transfer oxygen.

SPECIES INFORMATION	
COMMON NAME	Hare's-foot Clover
SCIENTIFIC NAME	Trifolium arvense
RELATED SPECIES	Other clovers
HEIGHT/SPREAD	10–40 cm tall
FLOWERING TIME	June–August
HABITAT	Dry grassland and sand-dunes

Note: A softly-hairy, reddish, annual clover with silky heads.

Hare's-foot Clover

CLOVER AND PEA FAMILY

(Leguminosae or Fabaceae)

Size and appearance: A soft-hairy, erect or semi-erect, branched annual or biennial 10–40 cm (4–16 in) tall.
Leaves: 3-foliate, the leaflets narrow, oblong, scarcely toothed, often reddish, the upper ones stalkless.
Flowers: White or pale pink, c. 4 mm (⅙ in) long, shorter than the calyx, in stalked, dense, cylindrical flower-heads 15–25 mm (⅗–1 in) long.
Fruits: Silky-hairy heads (calyx-teeth softly bristle-like in fruit) of pods enclosed within the persistent flower-parts.
Related or similar plants: Other small, annual clovers.
Habitat and distribution: Sometimes common in dry grassy places, especially near the sea, on sandy or gravelly banks, rocky heathland, sand-dunes, shingle beaches and wall-tops; throughout, but commoner in the east north to the Moray Firth, and mostly coastal in the West Country, Scotland and Ireland.
Flowering time: June to August, but tending to come into flower later than any of the other clovers.

THIS IS ONE OF the more widespread clovers in a group of several often inconspicuous, native annual and biennial clovers of open, heathy or sandy ground. The others are for the most part restricted to coastal districts in the south and south-west of England and the east coast of Ireland. Most are very local or rare.

Hare's-foot Clover (Trifolium arvense) *is a delightful clover with silky-hairy heads. It can be plentiful but requires a well-drained sandy substrate and is often found on sand-dunes and shingle beaches.*

FLOWER TYPE

IDENTIFICATION

HABITAT

POPULATION

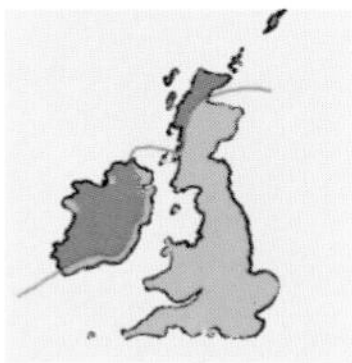
MAP

Bird's-foot Trefoil

CLOVER AND PEA FAMILY

(Leguminosae or Fabaceae)

SPECIES INFORMATION	
COMMON NAME	Bird's-foot Trefoil, Eggs-and-Bacon
SCIENTIFIC NAME	Lotus corniculatus
RELATED SPECIES	Greater Bird's-foot Trefoil
HEIGHT/SPREAD	5–60 cm tall, forming patches
FLOWERING TIME	May–September
HABITAT	Grassland, rocks and sand-dunes

Note: The common yellow peaflower of short grassland.

FLOWER TYPE

IDENTIFICATION

HABITAT

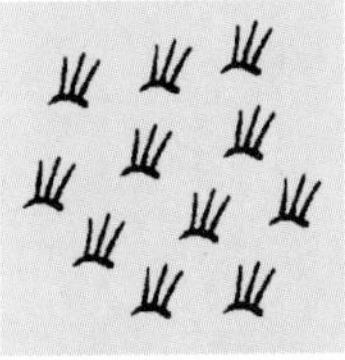

POPULATION

MAP

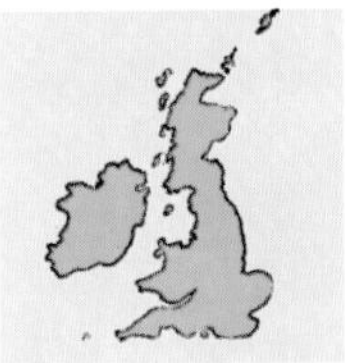

Size and appearance: A variably hairy, prostrate, sprawling or weakly erect perennial 5–60 cm (2–24 in) tall, sometimes rather woody at the base.

Leaves: Compound, 5-foliate, the leaflets spear-shaped, oval or almost circular, sometimes rather fleshy.

Flowers: Yellow, streaked or flushed red or orange, 10–18 mm (⅖–¾ in) long, slightly scented, 3–8 in long-stalked clusters, leafless but for 3 small leaf-like bracts.

Fruits: Clusters of cylindrical pods 10–15 mm (⅖–⅗ in) long, arranged almost like a bird's foot.

Related or similar plants: Greater Bird's-foot Trefoil is taller and more robust, the buds with spreading calyx-teeth; Horseshoe Vetch (p.132) has 4–8 pairs of leaflets and slightly smaller, pure yellow flowers; Meadow Vetchling (p.118) has tendrils.

Habitat and distribution: A common and characteristic plant of dry, grassy places, sunny banks, cliffs, mountain ledges, rocky ground, sand-dunes and shingle beaches, disused railway tracks and unmanicured lawns, wherever the grass is fairly short and the soil is well drained or lime-rich, throughout Britain and Ireland.

Flowering time: May to September, but mostly in June–July.

ANOTHER VERY VARIABLE peaflower species of grassland, but with more of a claim to native status in most areas.

Nevertheless, along road-verges and embankments and in other recently landscaped areas, plants are often robust and erect, with pointed leaflets and rather pure yellow flowers. This variant of Bird's-foot Trefoil, a native of the mountains of southern and central Europe, is grown on the Continent for fodder. In Britain, and now to a lesser extent in Ireland, it is a widely included component of wild flower seed mixtures. In some areas of intensive agriculture, the native plant has all but disappeared, sometimes to be replaced by the alien fodder plant.

Bird's-foot Trefoil has more than 70 recorded local names, some of which refer to eggs and bacon (the flower colour), while several others take up the theme of shoes and slippers (the flower shape). It is clearly a well-loved and long-familiar flower of the countryside.

Bird's-foot Trefoil (Lotus corniculatus) *is a common plant of grassy places occurring throughout Britain. It carpets a rocky seashore but it is just at home on mountain ledges, sand-dunes and the local horse's paddock. The fruits are clusters of cylindrical pods which are arranged like a bird's foot.*

SPECIES INFORMATION	
COMMON NAME	Kidney Vetch
SCIENTIFIC NAME	Anthyllis vulneraria
RELATED SPECIES	Bird's-foot Trefoil
HEIGHT/SPREAD	10–60 cm tall
FLOWERING TIME	May–September
HABITAT	Grassland, rocks and sand-dunes

Note: The crowded head or paired heads are distinctive.

Kidney Vetch

CLOVER AND PEA FAMILY

(Leguminosae or Fabaceae)

FLOWER TYPE

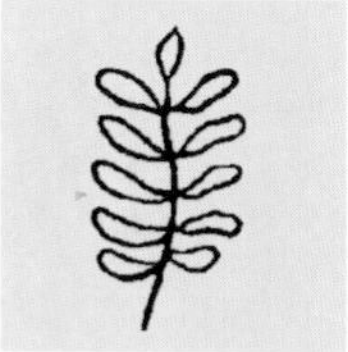
IDENTIFICATION

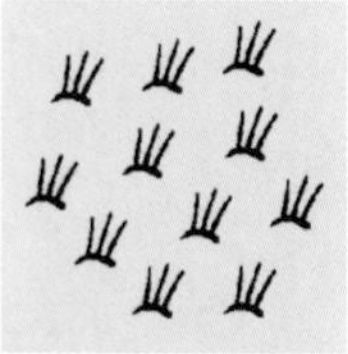
HABITAT

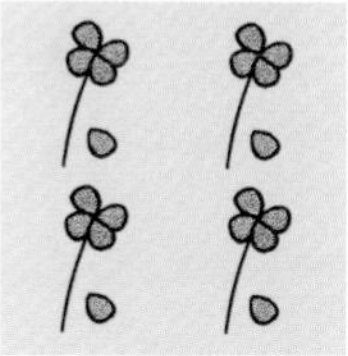
POPULATION

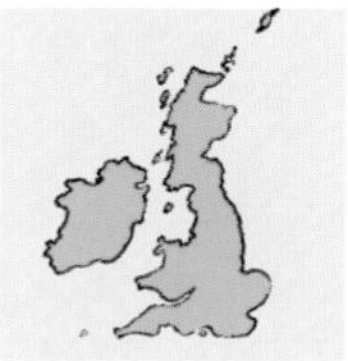
MAP

A VARIABLE SPECIES of grassland, with botanists recognising at least five distinct subspecies in these islands. On western coasts the flowers vary considerably in colour, from pale yellow and golden-yellow through orange and cream to pink, red and purple. This floral variation is particularly pronounced in some areas, such as Cornwall, west Wales and County Cork, with a tendency to various shades of pink.

Inland, tall and erect variants on road-verges derive from wild flower seed mixtures. Most of these plants seem to originate from seed imported from central and eastern Europe. Sadly, as with Bird's-foot Trefoil (p.130), the native plant has all but disappeared in some inland areas as a result of habitat destruction, to be replaced with these alien plants.

Size and appearance: A shortly silky-hairy, prostrate, sprawling or erect biennial or perennial 10–60 cm (4–24 in) tall, sometimes rather woody at the base.

Leaves: Compound, the leaflets 3–9, oval or oblong, silky-hairy beneath, sometimes rather fleshy, the end leaflet larger, especially that of the lower leaves.

Flowers: Usually yellow, 12–15 mm (½–⅝ in) long, in dense, mostly paired heads, with a pair of deeply divided, leaf-like bracts immediately below; calyx inflated, hairy, usually red-tipped.

Fruits: Flattened egg-shaped, 1-seeded pods enclosed within the persistent flower-parts.

Related or similar plants: No other peaflower has the paired flower-heads and 2 deeply divided bracts.

Habitat and distribution: A local but sometimes abundant plant of dry, lime-rich or rocky grassland, especially over chalk, limestone or serpentine, and on mountain ledges, coastal cliffs and sand-dunes throughout Britain and Ireland. The species is particularly common on dry, eroding slopes on chalk or by the sea.

Flowering time: May to September, but mostly in June–July.

Kidney Vetch (Anthyllis vulneraria) *has hairy, rather globular heads, with typical pea family flowers arising from this. With several sub-species, the flower colour can vary from a deep pink to a lemon yellow. It can be abundant on coastal cliffs or mountain ledges with chalk or limestone soils.*

Horseshoe Vetch

CLOVER AND PEA FAMILY

(Leguminosae or Fabaceae)

SPECIES INFORMATION	
COMMON NAME	Horseshoe Vetch
SCIENTIFIC NAME	Hippocrepis comosa
RELATED SPECIES	Bird's-foot Trefoil
HEIGHT/SPREAD	5–40 cm tall
FLOWERING TIME	May–July
HABITAT	Chalk grassland

Note: The neat heads of yellow flowers are distinctive.

FLOWER TYPE

IDENTIFICATION

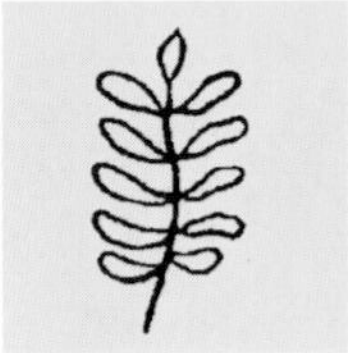

HABITAT

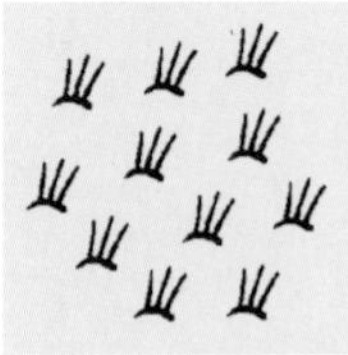

POPULATION

MAP

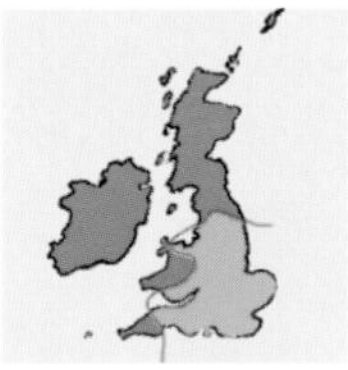

HORSESHOE VETCH, superficially similar to Bird's-foot Trefoil, is a plant of pastures and other short grassland. Where it is abundant it makes attractive splashes of yellow in midsummer.

Horseshoe Vetch is the food plant of the caterpillars of the Chalkhill Blue and the much rarer Adonis Blue butterflies.

Size and appearance: A hairless or slightly hairy perennial, with sprawling or erect stems 5–40 cm (2–16 in) tall, often woody at the base.

Leaves: Basal and on the stem, compound, with 3–8 pairs of narrowly oval or oblong leaflets and a similar end leaflet.

Flowers: Yellow, often finely veined red, 5–10 mm (⅕–⅖ in) long, 5–12, in long-stalked, loose heads; calyx blackish-green.

Fruits: Clusters of slender, wavy pods up to 30 mm (1⅕ in) long, arranged almost like a bird's foot, the 1-seeded horseshoe-shaped segments ornamented with small, reddish-brown warts.

Related or similar plants: Bird's-foot Trefoil (p.130) has 5 leaflets and larger flowers, often flushed red or orange.

Habitat and distribution: A rather local plant of dry, lime-rich grassland on chalk and limestone north to Cumbria; mostly on the chalk downs of southern England, and rare and only coastal in Wales and the West Country; absent from Ireland.

Flowering time: May to July.

Horseshoe Vetch (Hippocrepis comosa) *occurs on chalk or lime-rich grassland where it can make large splashes of yellow across the turf. The fruits are clusters of slender pods arranged in the shape of a bird's foot, but each pod is a series of individual horseshoe-shaped segments which contain one seed each.*

SPECIES INFORMATION	
COMMON NAME	Sainfoin
SCIENTIFIC NAME	Onobrychis viciifolia
RELATED SPECIES	Bird's-foot Trefoil
HEIGHT/SPREAD	20–100 cm tall
FLOWERING TIME	May–July
HABITAT	Chalk grassland

Note: The handsome spikes of pink flowers are very striking.

Sainfoin

CLOVER AND PEA FAMILY

(Leguminosae or Fabaceae)

FLOWER TYPE

IDENTIFICATION

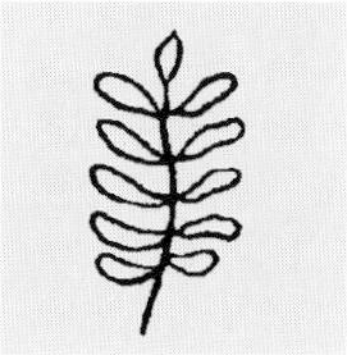

HABITAT

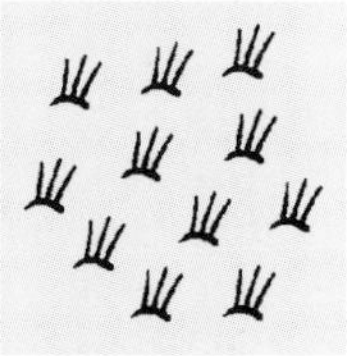

POPULATION

MAP

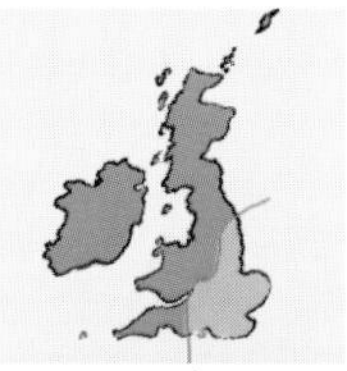

Size and appearance: A tufted perennial, with sprawling or erect stems 20–100 cm (8–40 in) tall, forming bushy clumps.

Leaves: Compound, with 6–14 pairs of oval or oblong leaflets and a similar end leaflet.

Flowers: Rich pink, veined purple, 10–14 mm (1/5–2/5 in) long, numerous in dense pyramidal spikes up to 9 cm long.

Fruits: 1-seeded, flattened egg-shaped, strongly veined and toothed pods.

Related or similar plants: Bird's-foot Trefoil (p.130) has 5 leaflets and larger flowers, often flushed red or orange.

Habitat and distribution: A local plant of grassland, banks, disturbed ground and road-verges on chalk and limestone, also sown on to recently constructed road embankments; mainly on the chalk of south and south-east England, but extending locally to Yorkshire and West Gloucestershire.

Flowering time: May to July.

Sainfoin (Onobrychis viciifolia) *is a striking member of the pea family of chalk grassland; it is a tufted perennial 20-100 cm (8-40 in) tall with dense pyramidal spikes of rich pink flowers veined with purple.*

SAINFOIN IS ONE of our most handsome wild plants and clumps of its pink flowers are locally a striking feature of chalk grassland and roadsides. It is certainly a native, if an exotic-looking one. John Gerard knew it when he wrote his 1597 *Herball*, and on the chalk one can see prostrate plants, with flowers of a deeper pink, similar to plants growing wild on limestone in adjacent Europe.

In the late 17th century, antiquary John Aubrey mentioned a taller variant of Sainfoin as a valuable new crop. It may be that at least some populations of Sainfoin derive from this period and subsequent introductions. Larger plants, sometimes known as Giant Sainfoin, have since been introduced as a fodder crop, and latterly in wild flower seed mixtures.

Wood-sorrel

WOOD-SORREL FAMILY
(Oxalidaceae)

SPECIES INFORMATION	
COMMON NAME	Wood-sorrel
SCIENTIFIC NAME	Oxalis acetosella
RELATED SPECIES	Other-sorrels
HEIGHT/SPREAD	10–20 cm tall
FLOWERING TIME	March–May
HABITAT	Shady woodland
Note: A delicate woodland plant with clover-like leaves.	

FLOWER TYPE

IDENTIFICATION

HABITAT
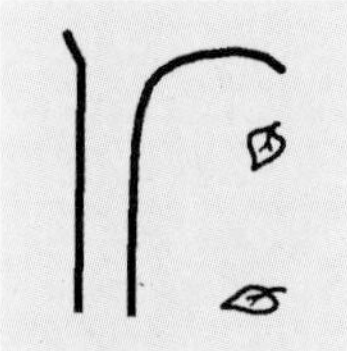

POPULATION

MAP
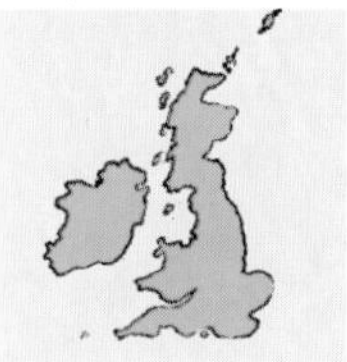

Size and appearance: A delicate, slender, hairless perennial, with creeping rhizomes, forming patches, and slender, erect stems 10–20 cm (4–8 in) tall; rhizome clothed in the swollen, scale-like remains of leaf-bases.
Leaves: Long-stalked, 3-foliate, the leaflets heart-shaped, notched, pale green but often purplish beneath.
Flowers: Solitary on almost leafless stems, bell-shaped, white with lilac veins or lilac, 8–15 mm long, nodding.
Fruits: Egg-shaped, 5-angled capsules, exploding when ripe to disperse the seeds.
Related or similar plants: The unrelated clovers (pp.127–129) have thicker, usually hairy leaves and rarely grow in woodland.
Habitat and distribution: Widespread on humus-rich soils, in moist, shady woods, especially of oak, hazel and beech, on old hedge-banks and mountain-ledges, throughout Britain and Ireland, but local in parts of East Anglia and areas with little woodland.
Flowering time: March to May.

THIS FRAGILE PLANT is common but rather shy-flowering and sometimes overlooked. Wood-sorrel is one of many spring flowers that appear before the woodland trees come fully into leaf. The clover-like leaves are usually much more numerous than the flowers. The leaves have a sharp acid taste and were formerly used to flavour food, in the same way as Sorrel (p.22).

Wood-sorrel has a good claim to be the *seamróg* or shamrock, with which St Patrick is said to have illustrated the concept of the Holy Trinity to the then pagan Irish. Or he may have used Lesser Trefoil (p.126). Another religious connection is that one of the plant's many old English names is Alleluia, in celebration of Christ's resurrection at Easter. Wood-sorrel is still known by this name in France.

Wood-sorrel (Oxalis acetosella) *is a plant of shady woodland banks, often found by streamsides, where the white flowers with delicate lilac veins can be found peeping out from amongst the three-foliate clover-like leaves in early spring.*

SPECIES INFORMATION	
COMMON NAME	Procumbent Yellow-sorrel
SCIENTIFIC NAME	Oxalis corniculata
RELATED SPECIES	Pink-sorrel, Upright Yellow-sorrell
HEIGHT/SPREAD	Stems 10–50 cm long
FLOWERING TIME	May–October
HABITAT	Weed of gardens

Note: The yellow-flowered clover-like weed of paths and borders.

Procumbent Yellow-sorrel

WOOD-SORREL FAMILY (Oxalidaceae)

Size and appearance: A low-growing downy perennial, with slender, fleshy runners and prostrate to semi-erect stems 10–50 cm (4–20 in) long, rooting to form patches.
Leaves: Long-stalked, 3-foliate, the leaflets heart-shaped, notched, purplish or green.
Flowers: Solitary or in pairs on slender, leafless stalks, yellow, bell-shaped, 4–8 mm (⅙–⅓ in) long, nodding.

Fruits: Cylindrical, densely downy, 5-angled capsules up to 25 mm (1 in) long, on downturned stalks, exploding when ripe to disperse the seeds.
Related or similar plants: Pink-sorrel has bright pink flowers; Upright Yellow-sorrel has erect stems.
Habitat and distribution: An invasive and prolific weed of gardens and plant nurseries, growing on cultivated ground, paths and between the slabs and cobbles of pavements and terraces, and sometimes on roadside banks and waste places; commonest in southern Britain but probably throughout, but more scattered in Ireland.
Flowering time: May to October.

THIS SEEMINGLY DELICATE plant is one of the most invasive of all small weeds. If it can be contained within a small area of path or terrace, it is an attractive little garden flower. Unfortunately it is a classically successful weed: it combines rapid growth from seed to flowering with vigorous vegetative spread and copious seed production. The seeds disperse up to 100 cm (3 ft) from the parent plant as the fruits explode.

Procumbent Yellow-sorrel, more romantically also known as Sleeping Beauty, is one of those weeds that has travelled the world with the migrations and trade of people. It was once thought to have originated in southern Europe, but the available evidence suggests that it is more likely to be a native of the mountains of Central Asia. Upright Yellow-sorrel (*Oxalis europaea*) is similar but erect, with flowers in flat-topped clusters of one to seven. It is an occasional weed of gardens, mainly in south-eastern England.

FLOWER TYPE
IDENTIFICATION
HABITAT
POPULATION
MAP

Top and middle *There are several yellow-sorrels which have been brought to these islands from around the world and which have subsequently escaped over the garden fence; they tend to be found in and around habitation.*

Bottom *The Least Yellow-sorrel* (Oxalis exilis) *is a diminutive representative with solitary flowers.*

Meadow Cranesbill

GERANIUM FAMILY
(Geraniaceae)

SPECIES INFORMATION	
COMMON NAME	Meadow Cranesbill
SCIENTIFIC NAME	Geranium pratense
RELATED SPECIES	Bloody Cranesbill
HEIGHT/SPREAD	30–80 cm tall
FLOWERING TIME	June–August
HABITAT	Grassland and road-verges

Note: The blue-flowered wild geranium of roadsides.

FLOWER TYPE

IDENTIFICATION

HABITAT

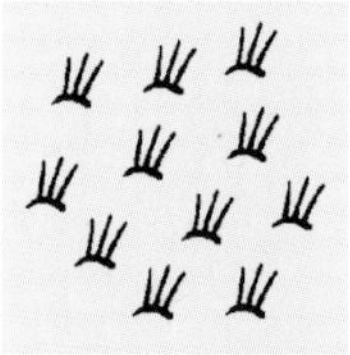

POPULATION

MAP

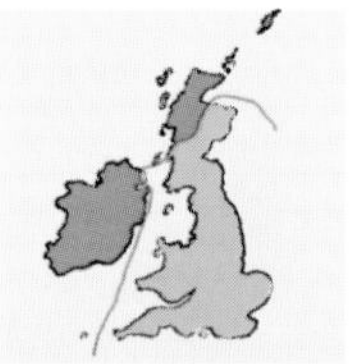

Size and appearance: A robust, hairy perennial, with a woody rootstock, forming conspicuous clumps, and erect stems 30–80 cm (12–32 in), somewhat sticky in the upper part.
Leaves: Long-stalked, deeply divided into 5–7 oblong lobes that are further dissected and toothed.
Flowers: Bluish-violet, cup-shaped, 25–40 mm (1–1⅗ in) across, on long stalks in compact clusters; the 5 petals are not notched.
Fruits: Hairy, beak-like, with 5 segments that curl upwards explosively when ripe to disperse the seeds; the flower-stalks curve down after flowering but are erect in ripe fruit.
Related or similar plants: Bloody Cranesbill (p.137) has solitary, reddish-purple flowers with notched petals.
Habitat and distribution: Widespread and in some areas conspicuously abundant in scrub, woodland margins, grassy places, hedge-banks and roadsides, often on lime-rich soils, north to the Moray Firth but rarer in East Anglia and introduced in Cornwall; in Ireland native on and near the coast of County Antrim, rarely naturalised elsewhere.
Flowering time: June to August.

THIS IS THE MOST stately of several native cranesbills, and one that is widely grown in gardens. Indeed, its native range has probably been obscured by a history of garden escapes. These wild species of *Geranium* are related to the showy, red garden geraniums, which are more correctly pelargoniums, introduced from South Africa.

Wood Cranesbill (*Geranium sylvaticum*) is similar but has broader, less dissected leaf-lobes, reddish-purple flowers up to 25 mm (1 in) across, and fruit-stalks remaining erect. It replaces Meadow Cranesbill in open woods and grassland in northern England and Scotland, extending high into the mountains; locally in County Antrim and the Welsh marches.

Bottom *Wood Cranesbill* (Geranium sylvaticum) *is similar but has broader, less dissected leaf-lobes, reddish-puprle flowers up to 25mm (1 in) across, and fruit-stalks remaining erect. It replaces Meadow Cranesbill in open woods and grassland in northern England and Scotland, extending high into the mountains; locally in County Antrim and the Welsh marches.*

SPECIES INFORMATION	
COMMON NAME	Bloody Cranesbill
SCIENTIFIC NAME	Geranium sanguineum
RELATED SPECIES	Meadow Cranesbill
HEIGHT/SPREAD	20–100 cm tall
FLOWERING TIME	June–August
HABITAT	Grassland and rocky ground

Note: The reddish-purple flowers are distinctive.

Bloody Cranesbill

GERANIUM FAMILY

(Geraniaceae)

Bloody Cranesbill (Geranium sanguineum) *is a stunning plant when in flower, the purple-red flowers 20-30 mm (4/5-1 1/5 in) across, set against the backdrop of the dark green divided leaves. Although best-known from its coastal locations on cliffs or sand-dunes, it occurs inland where there is chalk or limestone, such as on the pavements in northern England.*

FLOWER TYPE

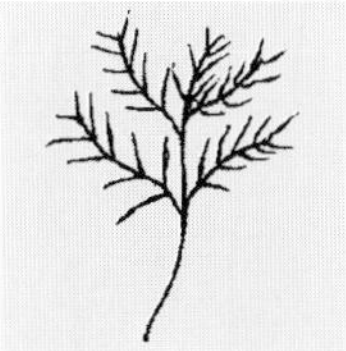

IDENTIFICATION

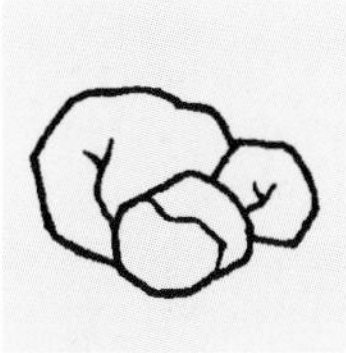

HABITAT

POPULATION

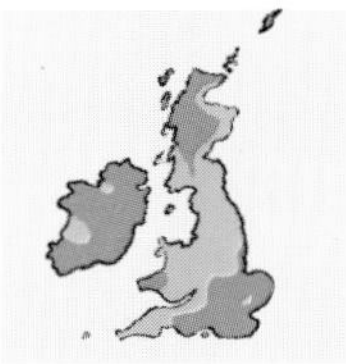

MAP

Size and appearance: A hairy perennial, with a woody rootstock, forming patches, and semi-erect, leafy stems 20–100 cm (8–40 in) tall.

Leaves: Long-stalked, deeply divided into 5–7 narrow, oblong, toothed lobes.

Flowers: Solitary on long stalks, bright reddish-purple, cup-shaped, 20–30 mm (4/5–1 1/5 in) across; the 5 petals are notched.

Fruits: Hairy, beak-like, with 5 segments that curl upwards explosively when ripe to disperse the seeds.

Related or similar plants: Meadow Cranesbill has small clusters of bluish-violet flowers with unnotched petals.

Habitat and distribution: Mainly coastal and on lime-rich soils, on cliffs, rocks, seaside slopes and sand-dunes, but also inland, as on the limestone rocks and pavements of northern England or, as in eastern England, in chalk grassland; in Ireland mainly in the Burren of County Clare and other limestone around Galway Bay.

Flowering time: June to August.

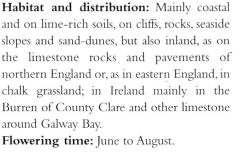

BLOODY CRANESBILL IS a magnificent sight in full flower in summer. It is especially a feature of the Burren of County Clare, but it puts on a good show in plenty of other places: Great Orme Head in North Wales, the Derbyshire Dales, the Ingleborough area of the West Riding of Yorkshire, and basalt cliffs on the coast of Fife spring to mind. Bloody Cranesbill is widely grown in gardens, both the wild-type plant and a white-flowered variant; also a prostrate variant with pink flowers discovered originally in the 18th century grows on the coast of Lancashire.

Cut-leaved Cranesbill

GERANIUM FAMILY

(Geraniaceae)

SPECIES INFORMATION	
COMMON NAME	Cut-leaved Cranesbill
SCIENTIFIC NAME	Geranium dissectum
RELATED SPECIES	Dove's-foot Cranesbill
HEIGHT/SPREAD	20–60 cm tall
FLOWERING TIME	May–September
HABITAT	Grassland and rocky ground

Note: Like a miniature garden geranium.

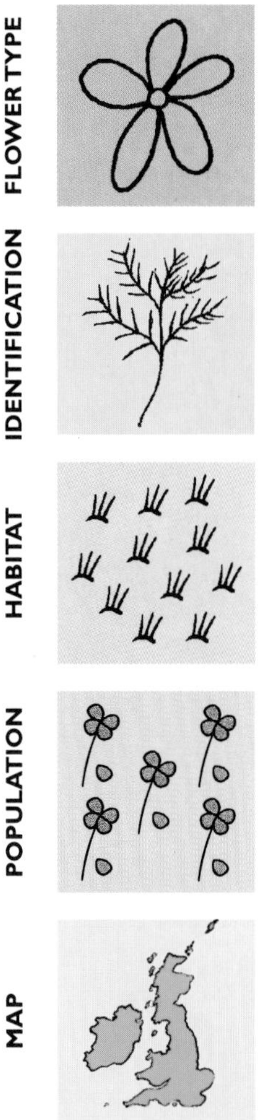

Size and appearance: A hairy, semi-erect or sprawling, branched annual 20–60 cm (8–24 in) tall.

Leaves: The lower long-stalked, all divided almost to the base into 7 narrow, toothed lobes.

Flowers: Pinkish or purple, cup-shaped, 5–10 mm ($\frac{1}{5}$–$\frac{2}{5}$ in) across, on short stalks; the 5 petals are notched.

Fruits: Downy, beak-like, with 5 segments that curl upwards explosively when ripe to disperse the seeds.

Related or similar plants: Dove's-foot Cranesbill and other annual cranesbills usually have less finely dissected leaves

Habitat and distribution: Common in open, bare and disturbed ground, grassy places, waysides and cultivated land, usually on well-drained soils, throughout Britain and Ireland, although locally rare in Scotland.

Flowering time: May to September.

THERE ARE HALF A DOZEN native annual cranesbills, all with small pinkish or purplish flowers, variously dissected leaves and slender beak- or bill-like fruits. They are plants of open, disturbed and cultivated ground, where they sometimes appear in large numbers. Cut-leaved Cranesbill and Dove's-foot Cranesbill are the two species that are likely to turn up almost anywhere.

***Bottom** Dove's-foot Cranesbill* (Geranium molle) *is more densely hairy, often only 10 cm (4 in) tall, the leaves divided to c. $\frac{2}{3}$ in to 5–7 lobes, and hairless fruits. Flowering April–September, it is common in grassy places.*

SPECIES INFORMATION	
COMMON NAME	Herb Robert
SCIENTIFIC NAME	Geranium robertianum
RELATED SPECIES	Annual cranesbills
HEIGHT/SPREAD	20–50 cm tall
FLOWERING TIME	May–October
HABITAT	Damp rocks and shady places

Note: A cranesbill with fern-like leaves.

Herb Robert

GERANIUM FAMILY (Geraniaceae)

Size and appearance: An aromatic, rather delicate-looking, hairy, annual, biennial or short-lived perennial, with sprawling, fleshy, reddish, brittle stems 20–50 cm (8–20 in) long.
Leaves: Fern-like, divided almost to the base into 3–5 deeply lobed segments.
Flowers: Purplish-pink, dish-shaped, 15–30 mm (⅗–1⅕ in) across, in very loose clusters; the 5 petals unnotched; stamens orange.
Fruits: Slightly wrinkled, beak-like, with 5 segments that curl upwards explosively when ripe to disperse the seeds.
Related or similar plants: Most likely to be confused initially with the members of the carrot family (pp.170—185) that have fern-like leaves.

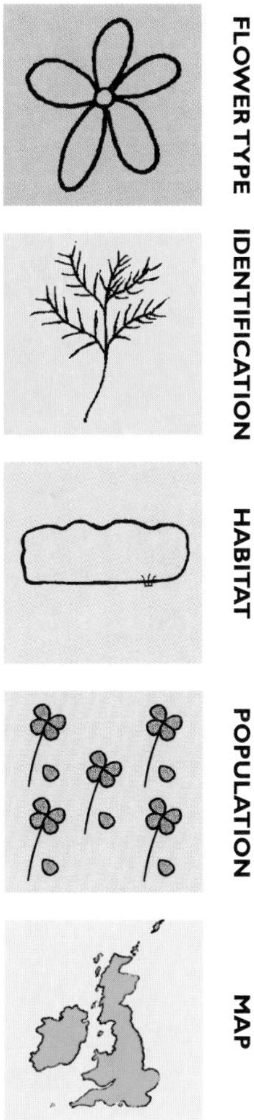

Habitat and distribution: Common on shady cliffs, rocks, walls, lanesides, fallen logs and coastal shingle beaches, also as a weed of shady gardens and old glasshouses, throughout Britain and Ireland.
Flowering time: May to October.

AS WELL AS the characteristic, ubiquitous pink-flowered plant of shady and damp places, there is a white-flowered variant found mostly in Wales and in Ireland. Plants on coastal shingle beaches are compact, with rather fleshy leaves. Herb Robert is an example of a plant with large numbers of local names, although apparently it had no medicinal or other use.

A small-flowered subspecies of Herb Robert, often more erect, with yellow stamens and more wrinkled fruits, is distinctive enough to have picked up the English name Little Robin. A common plant in the Mediterranean region it grows on walls and coastal shingle, mainly in southern England and a few places in County Cork, Ireland.

Shining Cranesbill (*Geranium lucidum*) is quite different from Herb Robert, with kidney-shaped, 5- to 7-lobed, shiny leaves, but grows in the same sort of habitats. It is more local and often on limestone.

Herb Robert (Geranium robertianum) *has fern-like leaves divided almost to the base into three to five deeply lobed segments. In shady woodland and hedgerow situations, these leaves are quite green but the plants that occur on shingle beaches in full sunlight are much redder.*

Common Storksbill

GERANIUM FAMILY
(Geraniaceae)

SPECIES INFORMATION	
COMMON NAME	Common Storksbill
SCIENTIFIC NAME	Erodium cicutarium
RELATED SPECIES	Cranesbills
HEIGHT/SPREAD	Stems 5–60 cm long
FLOWERING TIME	April–September
HABITAT	Open sandy or stony ground

Note: Like a cranesbill, but prostrate with like leaves.

FLOWER TYPE

IDENTIFICATION

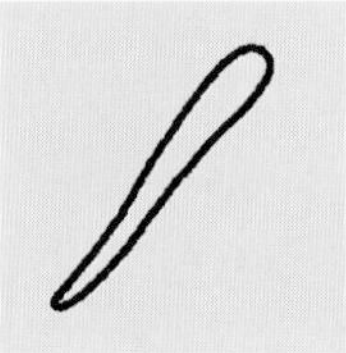

HABITAT

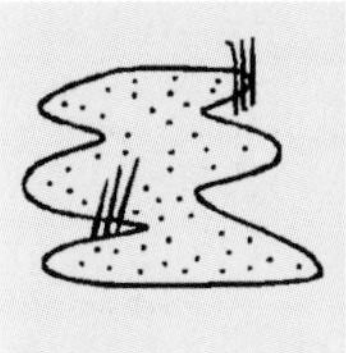

POPULATION

MAP

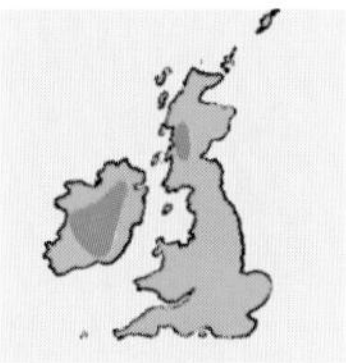

Common Storksbill is a low-growing plant with divided leaves and fragile pink flowers, that is sometimes common on sand-dunes, dry heaths and tracksides.

Size and appearance: A hairy annual, biennial or short-lived perennial, with prostrate or sprawling, fleshy, often reddish, stems 5–60 cm (2–24 in) long.

Leaves: Almost fern-like, twice-divided into deeply lobed segments, softly-hairy or sometimes (by the sea) sticky-hairy.

Flowers: Purplish-pink, lilac or sometimes white, dish-shaped, 8–20 mm (1/3–4/5 in) across, 2–12, in loose clusters.

Fruits: Slightly wrinkled, beak-like, with 5 segments that curl upwards explosively when ripe to disperse the seeds.

Related or similar plants: The fruit-segments of the closely related cranesbills (pp.136–138) do not twist spirally when they split.

Habitat and distribution: Common on open sandy and stony ground and thin grassland, sometimes in sandy fields, especially by the sea, and recently on suburban road-verges; a very common plant on sand-dunes, throughout Britain, but mainly coastal in Ireland.

Flowering time: April to September.

THE EXPLOSIVE RELEASE of the seeds disperses them most effectively. Each is attached to a spiral, auger- or corkscrew-like strip of the fruit wall, which serves to screw the seed into loose sand or soil. There it can germinate safely.

Common Storksbill is a variable species, especially in some coastal areas, where plants may be densely sticky-hairy. Plants also vary in the colour and size of their petals. Two other storksbills occur in Britain, both scarce and mostly on coasts.

SPECIES INFORMATION	
COMMON NAME	Flax
SCIENTIFIC NAME	Linum usitatissimum
RELATED SPECIES	Fairy Flax
HEIGHT/SPREAD	30–100 cm tall
FLOWERING TIME	June–August
HABITAT	Roadsides and field margins

Note: A very slender plant with blue flowers.

Flax

FLAX FAMILY
(Linaceae)

Size and appearance: A slender, erect, little-branched annual 30–100 cm (12–40 in) tall.
Leaves: Greyish-green, narrow, spear-shaped, up to 5 cm (2 in) long, pointed, with entire margins.
Flowers: Solitary, flimsy, pale blue with darker veins, dish-shaped, 20–25 mm (⅘–1 in) across.
Fruits: Almost spherical capsules 6–8 mm (¼–⅓ in) across, with a short pointed beak.
Related or similar plants: Fairy Flax (p.142) is a much smaller plant of grassland, with white flowers.
Habitat and distribution: Commonly cultivated as an oilseed crop, and escaping on to field margins, tracksides and road-verges, river-banks and waste ground northwards to central Scotland; much rarer and scattered in Ireland.
Flowering time: June to August; the petals fall early in the afternoon.

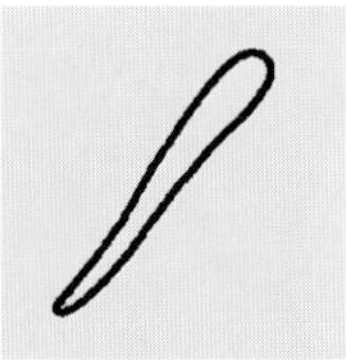

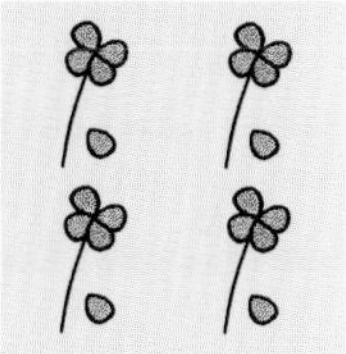

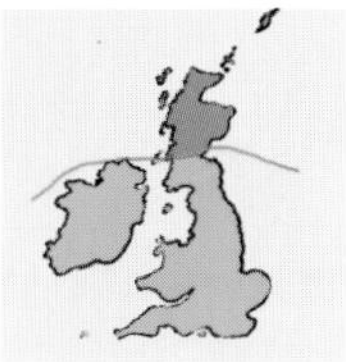

FLAX AS A CROP in Britain has made a come-back during the last decade or so, at least the variant known as Linseed. Traditionally, Flax had been grown for fibre, used to make linen, especially in northern Ireland. The dainty, sky-blue flowers are a wonderful sight in fields, and the plant is escaping more and more on to waysides.

Flax has been cultivated for at least 7,000 years, both for fibre and for linseed oil, extracted from the seeds. This most valuable oil is used in food for people and animals, in the manufacture of linoleum, paints, varnishes and other products, oil for preserving cricket bats, furniture and antiquarian books, and in surgical dressings for inflamed skin or wounds.

Flax is a distinctive plant with pale blue flowers that fall in the afternoon. It is increasingly common on waysides and field borders as a relic of cultivation.

Fairy Flax

FLAX FAMILY
(Linaceae)

SPECIES INFORMATION	
COMMON NAME	Fairy Flax, Purging Flax
SCIENTIFIC NAME	Linum catharticum
RELATED SPECIES	Species Flax
HEIGHT/SPREAD	5–15 cm tall
FLOWERING TIME	June–September
HABITAT	Grassland
Note: A miniature, white-flowered flax of grassland.	

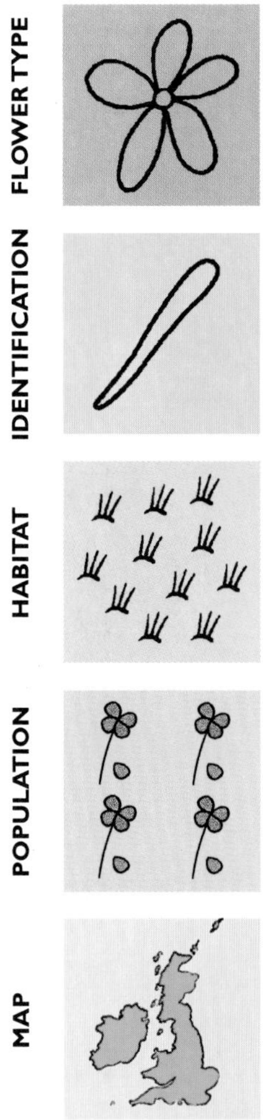

FAIRY FLAX IS a delightful, tiny flower of short turf, on a variety of soils but usually those that are mineral-rich. It had a great and justified reputation as a mild purgative, hence the alternative (and widely used) English name. Country people, especially in Scotland and Ireland, associated this plant with fairies, perhaps because of its small size and being recognisable as a wild flax that the little people might well use. Linum is the Latin word for flax, hence lint (a linen-like cloth) and linseed.

The flowers look superficially like those of the quite unrelated Greater Stitchwort (p.34) and similar plants, but the petals of Fairy Flax are fused into a tube and un-notched.

Size and appearance: A diminiutive, slender, erect annual 5–15 cm (2–6 in) tall.
Leaves: Greyish-green, narrow, oval or spear-shaped, 1-veined, blunt.
Flowers: white with darker veins, dish-shaped, 4–6 mm (⅙–¼ in) across, in loose clusters, on thread-like stalks that nod in bud.
Fruits: Small spherical capsules, with a short pointed beak.
Related or similar plants: Flax (p.141) is a much more robust plant of waysides and fields, with blue flowers.
Habitat and distribution: Widespread, if sometimes overlooked, in short, dry or damp grassland and damp open ground, especially on lime-rich soils but only avoiding the most lime-poor sites, throughout Britain and Ireland.
Flowering time: June to September.

Fairy flax (Linum catharticum) *is a low, graceful, slender annual with greyish-green leaves. The thread-like flower stalks often rise, then drop down and rise again like a miniature roller-coaster with the white flowers held outwards at the end.*

SPECIES INFORMATION	
COMMON NAME	Dog's Mercury
SCIENTIFIC NAME	Mercurialis perennis
RELATED SPECIES	Annual Mercury
HEIGHT/SPREAD	20-50 cm tall
FLOWERING TIME	February–May
HABITAT	Woodland and hedges
Note: Forming dense, dark green stands in woods.	

Dog's Mercury

SPURGE FAMILY (Euphorbiaceae)

Size and appearance: A hairy perennial with a far-creeping, branched rhizome that gives rise to extensive patches, and erect, unbranched stems 20–50 cm (12–20 in) tall.

Leaves: In opposite pairs, elliptical, pointed, the margins neatly toothed.

Flowers: Male and female on separate plants, green, 4–5 mm across, with 3 sepals instead of petals; the male numerous in erect tassel-like spikes, the female 2–3.

Fruits: 2-lobed, hairy capsules 6–8 mm (¼–⅓ in) long.

Related or similar plants: Annual Mercury is an annual of cultivated and waste ground.

Habitat and distribution: Common and frequently forming dense carpets in woodland and shady hedge-banks, and in northern England in the cracks or grykes of limestone pavement, throughout Britain, except the Fens and parts of northern Scotland; rare and scattered in Ireland.

Flowering time: February to May.

DOG'S MERCURY IS an indicator plant of ancient woodland, but often spreads out from woodland into hedges. It is an example of a species that is common in Britain but rare in Ireland, where, apart from possibly native plants on limestone in County Clare, it has been introduced into a few wooded demesnes. The whole plant is poisonous, as is Annual Mercury – hence the scientific and English names. Dog's Mercury is one of the first wild flowers of late winter and early spring. The catkin-like flower clusters are pollinated by wind in early spring while woods are open and leafless.

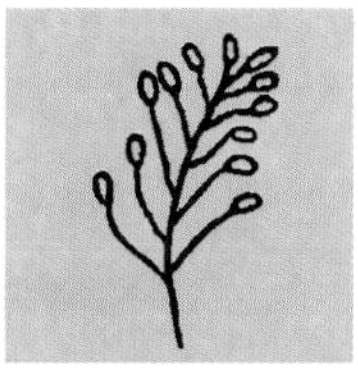

FLOWER TYPE

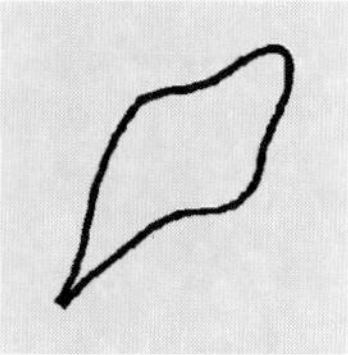

IDENTIFICATION

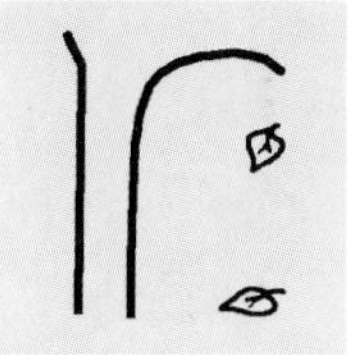

HABITAT

POPULATION

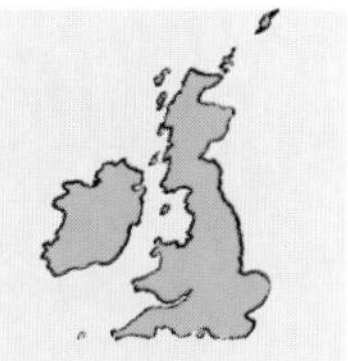

MAP

Dog's Mercury (Mercurialis perennis) *forms dense carpets in woodlands where it flowers in early spring, the catkin-like clusters being wind-pollinated as male and female flowers are on separate plants.*

Wood Spurge

SPURGE FAMILY
(Euphorbiaceae)

SPECIES INFORMATION	
COMMON NAME	Wood Spurge
SCIENTIFIC NAME	Euphorbia amygdaloides
RELATED SPECIES	Sun Spurge
HEIGHT/SPREAD	20–60 cm tall
FLOWERING TIME	April–June
HABITAT	Open woods

Note: A conspicuous and distinctive woodland plant.

FLOWER TYPE

IDENTIFICATION

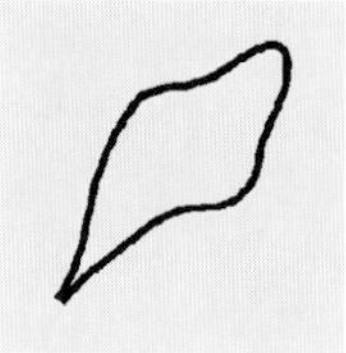

HABITAT

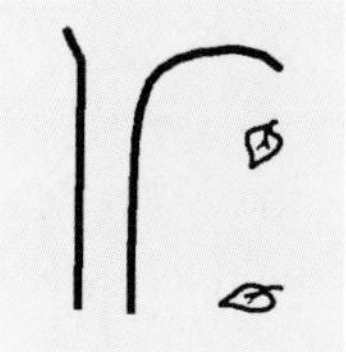

POPULATION

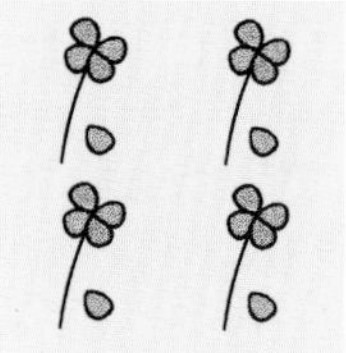

MAP

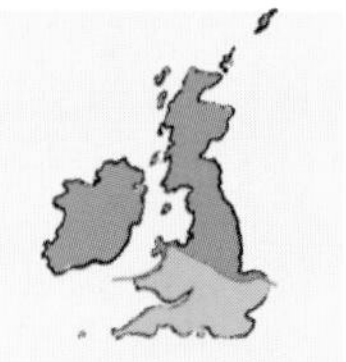

Size and appearance: A hairy, often deep reddish or purplish-tinged perennial, with clumps of erect, leafy stems 20–50 cm (12–20 in) tall, sometimes up to 80 cm (32 in).

Leaves: Numerous, spear-shaped, oblong or somewhat spoon-shaped; a ruff of yellowish, leaf-like bracts surrounds the flower clusters.

Flowers: Yellowish, with the complex structure of spurge flowers; each cluster of tiny male and female flowers surrounded by a cup or involucre and crescent-shaped nectaries ('glands').

Fruits: 2-celled, pitted and grooved capsules, hanging sideways on a short stalk.

Related or similar plants: Sun Spurge (p.145) and other spurges are either annual or smaller with narrower leaves.

Habitat and distribution: Common in oak, hazel and beech woods, coppices and sometimes on hedge-banks in southern England and much of Wales; in Ireland only in County Cork.

Flowering time: April to June.

WOOD SPURGE CAN BE a feature of woods in early spring, forming striking clumps of purplish leaves topped by the yellowish-green flowers. It is a distinctive plant of wooded parts of southern England. In the Isles of Scilly, where trees are few, it is widespread on open heaths near the sea. A similar spurge of gardens, *Euphorbia robbii*, originally collected in northern Turkey, is regarded by many botanists as a subspecies of Wood Spurge.

Some 15 different spurges occur in Britain and Ireland, several of them rare. They all share the narrow, undivided leaves and unusual flower structure, and exude an irritant milky sap when cut.

Bottom left and right *The parts of the flower: the green disc is the involucre; the yellow crescent-shaped nectaries have in their centre what would have been the flowers but which has now been replaced by the fruit on a elongated stalk.*

Top *The species Wood Spurge* (Euphorbia amygdaloides) *is a common spring spurge of southern woodlands with numerous, narrow leaves which are often tinged red.*

SPECIES INFORMATION	
COMMON NAME	Sun Spurge
SCIENTIFIC NAME	Euphorbia helioscopia
RELATED SPECIES	Petty Spurge
HEIGHT/SPREAD	10–50 cm tall
FLOWERING TIME	April–November
HABITAT	Cultivated land

Note: A yellowish weed of cultivated land.

Sun Spurge

SPURGE FAMILY (Euphorbiaceae)

Size and appearance: An erect, yellowish-green, hairless annual 10–50 cm tall (6–20 in) tall.

Leaves: Numerous, oval or spoon-shaped, toothed near the tip, up to 50 mm (2 in); a ruff of usually 5 yellowish, leaf-like bracts surrounds the flower clusters.

Flowers: In yellowish, flat-topped groups, with the complex structure of spurge flowers; each cluster of tiny male and female flowers surrounded by a cup or involucre and oval nectaries ('glands').

Fruits: Smooth capsules 2–4 mm ($\frac{1}{12}$–$\frac{1}{6}$ in) across, hanging sideways on a short stalk.

Related or similar plants: Petty Spurge is a branched, leafy annual plant with untoothed leaves; it is more a weed of gardens.

Habitat and distribution: A common but rarely abundant weed of disturbed and cultivated ground, especially good arable land, throughout Britain and Ireland; rarer in upland areas, especially western Scotland.

Flowering time: April to November.

THIS PLANT GROWS best on rich soils and is an accumulator of the important plant trace nutrient boron. The milky sap of several species of spurge has been used to remove warts, and was said to alleviate other skin conditions. Spurges were also employed as a somewhat drastic purgative. Note that the sap is too acrid to be taken safely as a medicine, especially internally.

Top *Petty Spurge* (Euphorbia peplus)*, another widespread annual of cultivated ground, has untoothed leaves up to 25 mm (1 in) long, and flowers with crescent-shaped glands. It is especially a weed of gardens*

Middle and bottom *Sun Spurge* (Euphorbia helioscopia) *is an erect, yellowish-green annual and our only common spurge with toothed leaves. It is a weed of disturbed and cultivated ground.*

FLOWER TYPE

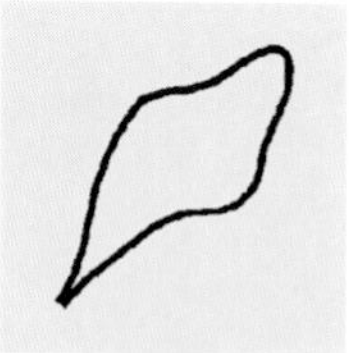

IDENTIFICATION

HABITAT

POPULATION

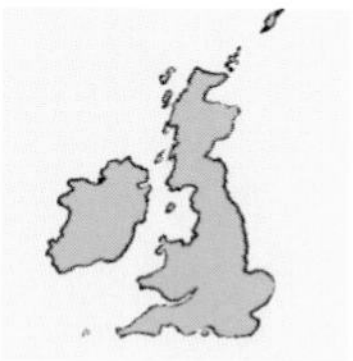

MAP

Common Milkwort

MILKWORT FAMILY
(Polygalaceae)

SPECIES INFORMATION	
COMMON NAME	Common Milkwort
SCIENTIFIC NAME	Polygala vulgaris
RELATED SPECIES	Heath Milkwort
HEIGHT/SPREAD	Stems 5–35 cm long
FLOWERING TIME	May–September
HABITAT	Grassland and sand-dunes
Note: A blue-flowered plant of short grassland.	

FLOWER TYPE

IDENTIFICATION
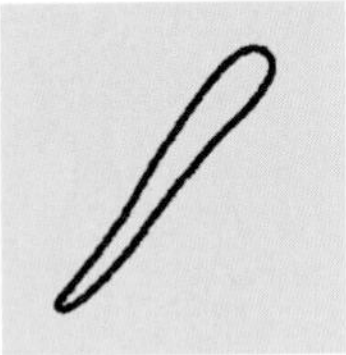

HABITAT
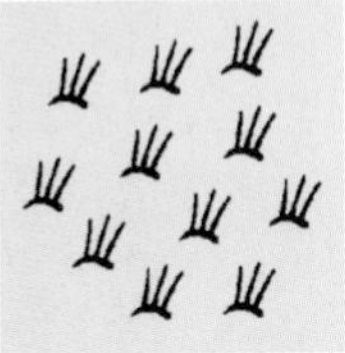

POPULATION

MAP

Size and appearance: A slender perennial with numerous weakly erect, sprawling or prostrate stems 5–35 cm long (4–14 in) tall.
Leaves: Alternate along the stem, narrowly elliptical, the lower smaller than the upper, not in a basal rosette.
Flowers: Usually blue, or magenta, lilac, pink, white or white flushed with blue, 4–8 mm (⅙–¼.in) long, with 5 petal-like sepals and tiny petals, 10–40 in loose, erect clusters.
Fruits: Flattened, egg-shaped capsules c. 5 mm (⅕ in) long, each enclosed by green, persistent sepals.
Related or similar plants: Heath Milkwort has at least some lower leaves in opposite pairs, and grows on lime-poor soils.
Habitat and distribution: Widespread in short, dry grassland, on coastal cliffs, rocky ground and banks, and on sand-dunes, especially on lime-rich soils, throughout Britain and Ireland.
Flowering time: May to September.

Bottom left and right Common Milkwort (Polygala vulgaris) *flowers come in various colours from pink and purple through blue to white.*

Top and bottom left Heath milkwort (Polygala serpyllifolia) *is similar to Common Milwort, but with at least the lower leaves opposite and more crowded. It is widespread on heaths and in dry acid grassland.*

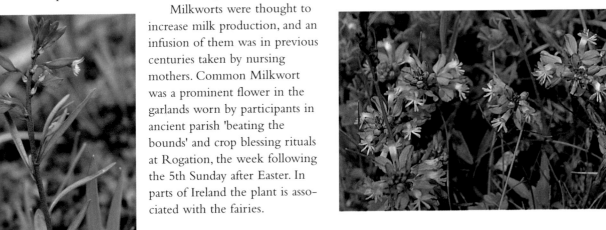

FIVE SPECIES OF MILKWORT occur in Britain, two of them very rare. By far the commonest of these other species is Heath Milkwort (*Polygala serpyllifolia*), this is a somewhat more slender plant with fewer flowers that has at least the lowest leaves in opposite pairs. It is mainly a common plant of heaths and lime-poor grassland.

Milkworts were thought to increase milk production, and an infusion of them was in previous centuries taken by nursing mothers. Common Milkwort was a prominent flower in the garlands worn by participants in ancient parish 'beating the bounds' and crop blessing rituals at Rogation, the week following the 5th Sunday after Easter. In parts of Ireland the plant is associated with the fairies.

SPECIES INFORMATION	
COMMON NAME	Indian Balsam, Policeman's Helmet
SCIENTIFIC NAME	Impatiens glandulifera
RELATED SPECIES	Touch-me-not Balsam
HEIGHT/SPREAD	100–200 cm tall
FLOWERING TIME	July–October
HABITAT	Watersides and shady places
Note: A large and conspicuous plant of watersides.	

Indian Balsam

BALSAM FAMILY

(Balsaminaceae)

Size and appearance: A stout, hairless, often reddish annual, with hollow, brittle, juicy, erect stems 100–200 cm (40–80 in) tall, sometimes up to 300 cm (9 ft), with knobbly joints.

Leaves: In opposite pairs or 3s, spear-shaped or elliptical, pointed, the margins with red teeth.

Flowers: Purplish-pink, pink or white, 25–40 mm (1–1½ in) long, with 5 fused petals and 3 sepals, the largest of which is sac-like and inflated, with a short, curved spur.

Fruits: Fleshy, cylindrical to club-shaped capsules that explode violently, scattering the black seeds.

Related or similar plants: Other (rarer) balsams have yellow or orange flowers.

Habitat and distribution: Locally abundant, often in dense crowds, on river-banks, streamsides and in woodland rides or damp and shady waste places; throughout, but more scattered in Scotland and Ireland.

Flowering time: July–October.

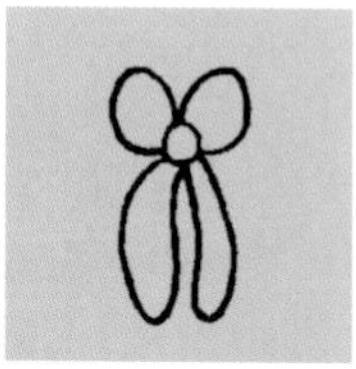

FLOWER TYPE

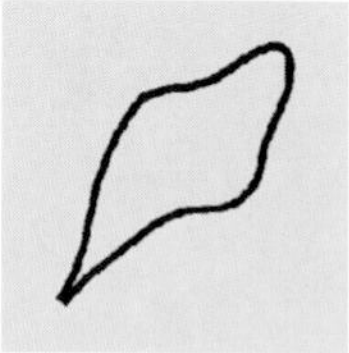

IDENTIFICATION

HABITAT

POPULATION

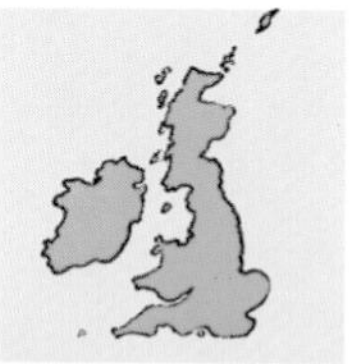

MAP

INDIAN BALSAM IS increasingly a conspicuous and impressive feature along rivers and streams, especially in parts of western and northern England. A native of the Himalayas, it has spread rapidly in Britain since its introduction as a showy garden plant in 1839. It colonises new sites with ease, having such an efficient seed dispersal mechanism. The capsules explode at the slightest touch. Indian Balsam has no problem with pollination in its adopted country, because the flowers are very attractive to bumble-bees. The juicy stems snap easily, and the whole plant emits a sickly-sweet aromatic smell when cut or bruised.

Bottom right *Touch-me-not Balsam* (Impatiens noli-tangere)*, our only native balsam, the name alluding to the explosive fruits, is a smaller plant with more branched stems, oval leaves alternate along the stem, and yellow, long-spurred flowers. It is a native of watersides in north-western England and north Wales, two other balsams are established introductions in Britain.*

Common Mallow

MALLOW FAMILY
(Malvaceae)

SPECIES INFORMATION	
COMMON NAME	Common Mallow
SCIENTIFIC NAME	Malva sylvestris
RELATED SPECIES	Musk Mallow
HEIGHT/SPREAD	20–100 cm tall
FLOWERING TIME	June–October
HABITAT	Waysides and waste land

Note: A conspicuous, pink-flowered plant of waysides.

FLOWER TYPE

IDENTIFICATION

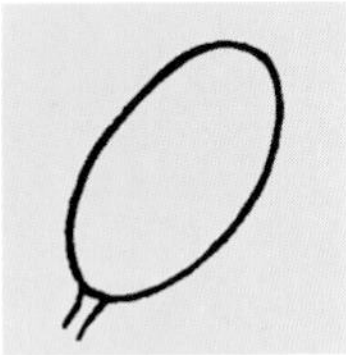

HABITAT

POPULATION

MAP

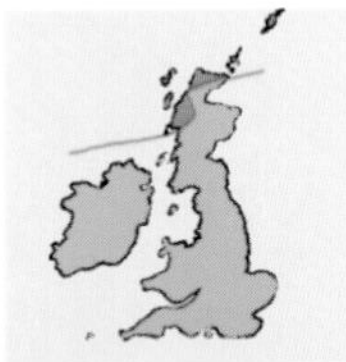

Size and appearance: A softly-hairy biennial or short-lived perennial, with prostrate, sprawling or erect stems 20–100 cm (8–40 in) tall, sometimes up to 150 cm (60 in).

Leaves: Long-stalked, kidney-shaped or almost circular, often with a dark blotch, with 3–7 toothed lobes.

Flowers: Pinkish-purple or lilac with darker veins, 20–40 mm (⅘–1⅗) across, with 5 rather flimsy, deeply notched petals; stamens joined in a tube.

Fruits: A neat, disc-shaped whorl of 1-seeded nutlets.

Related or similar plants: Musk Mallow (p.150) has deeply cut leaves and pale pink or white flowers.

Habitat and distribution: Widespread and common in dry and disturbed grassland, hedge-banks and waste places, especially on roadsides and by paths, often in quantity; almost throughout, except parts of northern Scotland.

Flowering time: June to October.

Bottom left *Dwarf Mallow* (Malva neglecta) *is similar to Common Mallow but as its name suggests it is smaller, generally prostrate with rounded, crinkled and lobed leaves. The flowers are a pale lilac, often with purple markings. It is widespread in gateways and around farmyards.*

COMMON MALLOW IS a plant of scruffy waysides and waste places, which it brightens with a bold show of flowers in late summer. The leaves of Common Mallow and other members of this family are very mucilaginous, which is the basis of their use in medicine and food. They have been valued as medicine since ancient times for their soothing and healing properties, especially when employed in poultices and ointments. In Mediterranean countries the leaves are an essential ingredient of some winter soups. The edible fruits are a free summer snack, long known by country children as Cheeses or, in France, Fromages – now largely superseded by potato crisps.

SPECIES INFORMATION	
COMMON NAME	Tree Mallow
SCIENTIFIC NAME	Lavatera arborea
RELATED SPECIES	Common Mallow
HEIGHT/SPREAD	1–3m tall
FLOWERING TIME	July–September
HABITAT	Cliffs, rocks and hedge-banks

Note: A large softly-downy mallow of the seaside.

Tree Mallow

MALLOW FAMILY

(Malvaceae)

Size and appearance: A stout, almost tree-like biennial to short-lived perennial with erect, often massive and woody stems 1–3 m (3–9 ft) tall.

Leaves: Long-stalked, up to 20 cm (8 in) across, ivy-like, shallowly 5- to 7-lobed, soft and downy.

Flowers: Purplish-pink or lilac, with purple veins, 25–50 mm (1-2 in) across, with 5 flimsy notched petals, in a loose spike of long clusters of 2–7; stamens joined in a tube.

Fruits: A downy, disc-shaped whorl of 1-seeded nutlets, covered by the persistent and expanded calyx.

Related or similar plants: Common Mallow (p.148) is much less robust and often prostrate or sprawling in habit, with more shallowly lobed leaves.

Habitat and distribution: Locally common on coastal cliffs and rocks, and in hedge-banks and on waste ground and waysides near the sea, sometimes escaping from gardens; mainly in south-western England, Wales, south-western Ireland and County Dublin, but a few sites elsewhere north to southern Scotland.

Flowering time: July to September.

FLOWER TYPE

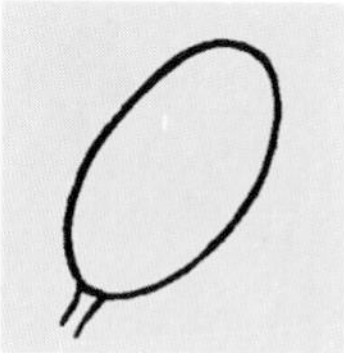

IDENTIFICATION

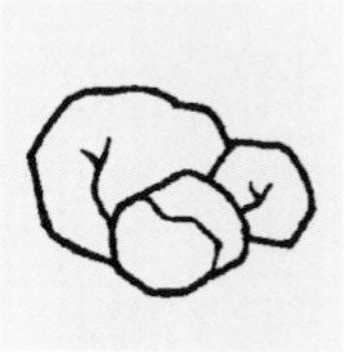

HABITAT

POPULATION

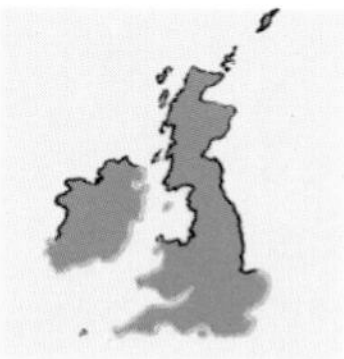

MAP

THIS ROBUST PLANT, like a great, soft-leaved hollyhock, seems hardly to be a native, yet it is a plant of bird-cliffs and islets as well as cottage gardens. It is very much a wayside plant of the seaside, thriving on the edges of villages and around car-parks or fishermen's boats.

Like the other mallows it would have been grown for medicine as well as ornament. It sometimes crops up a little way inland but seems not to tolerate frost. However, it will readily tolerate fierce Atlantic gales and salt spray. It is native all along Europe's Atlantic seaboard, extending round into the Mediterranean.

Tree Mallow (Lavatera arborea) *is a substantial well-branched species with ivy-shaped crinkled leaves. The flowers are purplish-pink, often darker at the base, and set in a loose spike. It is common on coastal cliffs in the south-west but can also be found around other parts of the coast.*

Musk Mallow

MALLOW FAMILY
(Malvaceae)

SPECIES INFORMATION	
COMMON NAME	Musk Mallow
SCIENTIFIC NAME	Malva moschata
RELATED SPECIES	Common Mallow
HEIGHT/SPREAD	30–80 cm tall
FLOWERING TIME	July–September
HABITAT	Grassland and hedge-banks

Note: The only mallow with deeply cut leaves.

FLOWER TYPE

IDENTIFICATION
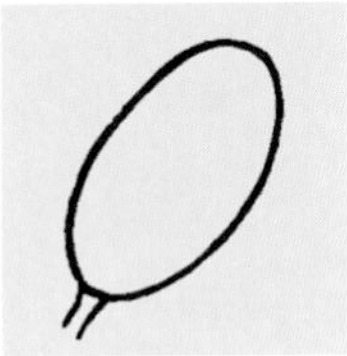
HABITAT
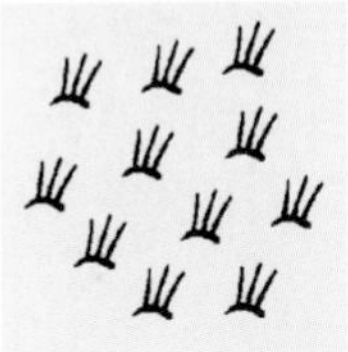
POPULATION

MAP

Size and appearance: An elegant perennial with erect, little-branched, hairy stems 30–80 cm (12–32 in) tall.
Leaves: Long-stalked, the lower leaves rounded, the rest cut deeply into narrow, strap-shaped lobes.
Flowers: Pale pink or white, 25–50 mm (1–2 in) across, musk-scented, with 5 flimsy notched petals; stamens joined in a tube.
Fruits: A hairy, disc-shaped whorl of 1-seeded nutlets.
Related or similar plants: Common Mallow (p.148) is often prostrate or sprawling, with shallowly lobed leaves.
Habitat and distribution: A widespread plant of grassland, scrub and hedge-banks, especially on lighter soils; throughout, but less frequent further north, becoming very local in northern Scotland; in Ireland, mostly in the south-east.
Flowering time: July to September.

Musk Mallow (Malva moschata) *is an enchanting plant with its handsome rose-pink flowers appearing in loose spikes from July to September. Its upper leaves are deeply and narrowly cut, with the lower leaves being rounded but rarely completely undivided. It is widespread in grassland and hedge-banks on the lighter soils.*

LIKE OTHER MALLOWS, Musk Mallow has been included in cough medicines for the soothing properties of the mucilaginous leaves. Greek and Roman writers praised mallows for their healthy virtues, and they are probably among our most ancient medicines. Today, Musk Mallow is seen as more of an ornamental plant, being popular for inclusion in old-fashioned cottage gardens and wild flower seed mixtures. This is one of our many wild flowers that has probably spread through cultivation, and has repeatedly jumped back and forth between gardens and the wild. The faint musky smell of the flowers is enhanced when placed in a vase indoors.

SPECIES INFORMATION	
COMMON NAME	Spurge Laurel
SCIENTIFIC NAME	Daphne laureola
RELATED SPECIES	Mezereon
HEIGHT/SPREAD	30–80 cm tall
FLOWERING TIME	February–April
HABITAT	Woods on lime-rich soil
Note: Like a miniature, little-branched laurel bush.	

Spurge Laurel

DAPHNE FAMILY
(Thymelaeaceae)

Size and appearance: A small, hairless, evergreen shrub with semi-erect, woody stems 30–80 cm (12–32 in) tall.
Leaves: Broadly spear-shaped, pointed, dark green, leathery, shiny, rather like those of a small laurel.
Flowers: Yellowish-green, tubular with 4 spreading lobes, 5–10 mm (⅕–⅖ in) long, scented, with orange stamens, in tight clusters just below the top of the stems.
Fruits: A cluster of black, shiny, egg-shaped berries.
Related or similar plants: Mezereon, mainly a garden plant, is similar but has purplish-pink flowers and red berries.
Habitat and distribution: Sometimes common in woods, often of beech, in scrub and on hedge-banks on chalk and limestone in southern England, but extending north almost to the Solway Firth; a rare introduction in Scotland and Ireland.
Flowering time: February to April.

SOME COMPARE SPURGE LAUREL, neither spurge nor laurel, unfavourably with its showy garden cousin Mezereon and other cultivated daphnes. Nevertheless, it is a cheering sight in full flower on a cold February day, often amid lying snow.

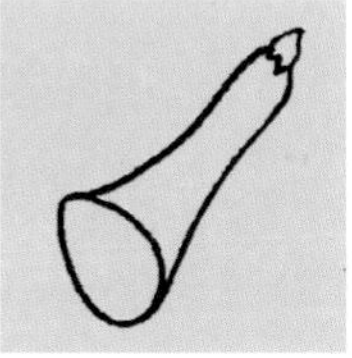

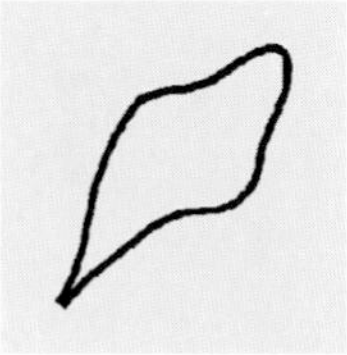

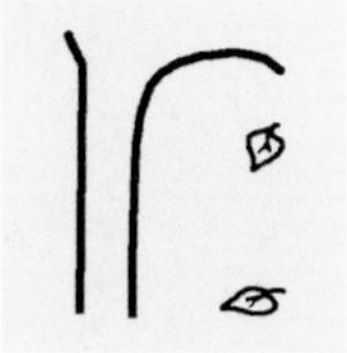

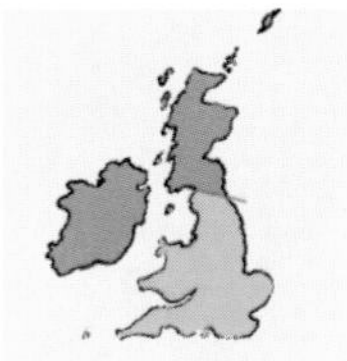

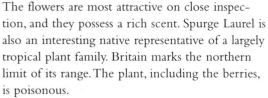

The flowers are most attractive on close inspection, and they possess a rich scent. Spurge Laurel is also an interesting native representative of a largely tropical plant family. Britain marks the northern limit of its range. The plant, including the berries, is poisonous.

Mezereon (*Daphne mezereon*) is a slightly taller shrub, flowering January–March, with deciduous, pale green leaves, purplish-pink flowers and red berries. It is a classic plant of cottage gardens, and also a handful of native sites in southern England, on chalk and limestone. It is one of several daphnes, mostly plants of temperate mountain regions.

Spurge Laurel (Daphne laureola) *has yellowish-green flowers clustered around the top of the stem, appearing as early as February. These contrast with the shiny evergreen leaves which blend into the background of shady hedgerows and copses.*

Common St John's Wort

ST JOHN'S WORT FAMILY
(Guttiferae)

SPECIES INFORMATION	
COMMON NAME	Common St John's Wort, Perforate St John's Wort
SCIENTIFIC NAME	Hypericum perforatum
RELATED SPECIES	Slender St John's Wort
HEIGHT/SPREAD	30–100 cm tall
FLOWERING TIME	June–September
HABITAT	Grassland and waste places

Note: The translucent dots on the leaves are very characteristic.

FLOWER TYPE

IDENTIFICATION

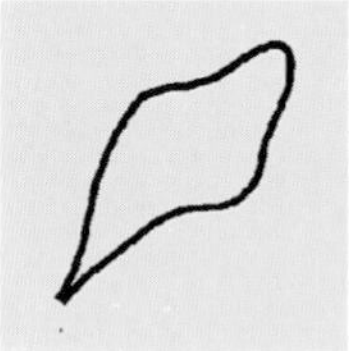

HABITAT

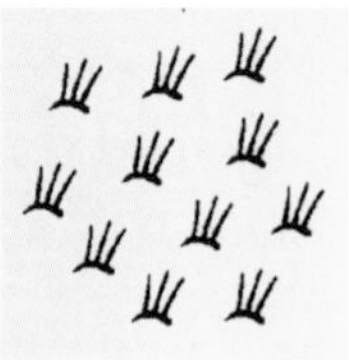

POPULATION

MAP

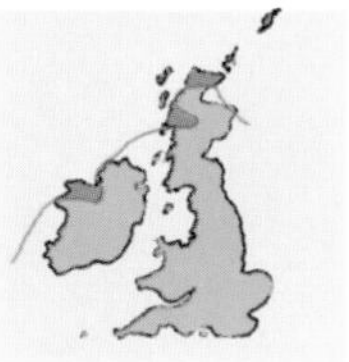

Size and appearance: A hairless perennial with erect stems 30–100 cm (12–40 in) tall, rounded, with 2 raised lines.

Leaves: In opposite pairs, stalkless, oblong or oval, with numerous translucent dots.

Flowers: In branched, spreading clusters, deep yellow, 15–20 mm (3/5–4/5 in) across, with 5 petals twisted and reddish in bud, and numerous yellow stamens, the 5 sepals usually with a few black dots.

Fruits: Pear-shaped capsules splitting into 3 segments.

Related or similar plants: Slender St John's Wort (p.153) has narrow clusters of smaller orange-yellow flowers, with orange stamens and more numerous black dots on the sepals.

Habitat and distribution: Common in dry grassland, scrub, open woods and stony waysides and waste ground, especially on lime-rich, light or sandy soils; throughout, but rare over much of northern Scotland and western Ireland.

Flowering time: June to September.

Bottom Right *Hairy St John's Wort* (Hypericum hirsutum)*, is similar but downy, with round stems, denser clusters of pale yellow flowers c. 15 mm (3/5 in) across), and sepals with stalked black dots. Flowering July–August, it is widespread in grassland and scrub on lime-rich or clay soils; rare in Scotland and Ireland.*

THIS IS THE COMMONEST of our dozen or so native St John's Worts, although Slender St John's Wort (p.153) replaces it on lime-poor soils. Common St John's-wort and other species were traditionally supposed to ward off witchcraft and magic. They thus became associated with Christian and pagan festivals, especially in Scotland and Ireland, to celebrate the Summer Solstice around St John the Baptist's Day on 24 June.

Introduced into North America, Common St John's Wort seriously infests grazing land, especially in western states, where it is known as Klamath Weed (named after a Californian river). It is poisonous to livestock, sensitising their skin to sunlight. On the plus side, the plant has healing properties, and in recent years an extract from it has proved a valuable herbal remedy to alleviate depression.

SPECIES INFORMATION	
COMMON NAME	Slender St John's Wort
SCIENTIFIC NAME	Hypericum pulchrum
RELATED SPECIES	Common St John's Wort
HEIGHT/SPREAD	20–80 cm tall
FLOWERING TIME	July–August
HABITAT	Heathland and open woods

Note: The most orange-flowered of the St John's Worts.

Slender St John's Wort

ST JOHN'S WORT FAMILY (Guttiferae)

Size and appearance: A hairless perennial with stiffly erect stems 20–80 cm (8–32 in) tall, rounded, without raised lines.

Leaves: In opposite pairs, stalkless, narrowly heart-shaped to oval, clasping the stem, with numerous translucent dots.

Flowers: In narrow, very loose clusters, orange-yellow with red dots, c.15 mm (⅗ in) across, with 5 petals twisted and red in bud, and numerous yellow stamens, the 5 sepals with numerous black dots.

Fruits: Pear-shaped capsules, splitting into 3 segments.

Related or similar plants: Common St John's Wort (p.152) has stems with 2 raised lines, denser, spreading clusters of larger, yellow flowers, and yellow stamens.

Habitat and distribution: Common in dry grassland, open woods and heathland, always on lime-poor, often peaty but well-drained soils, throughout Britain and Ireland, but commoner in the west and north.

Flowering time: July to August.

FLOWER TYPE

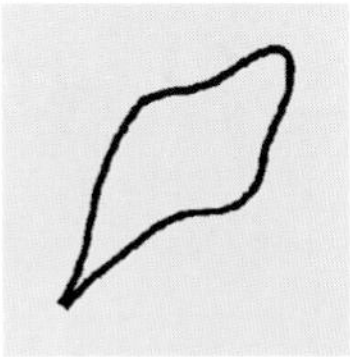
IDENTIFICATION

HABITAT

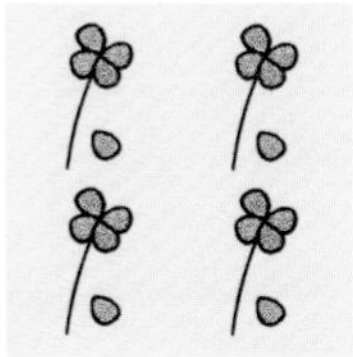
POPULATION

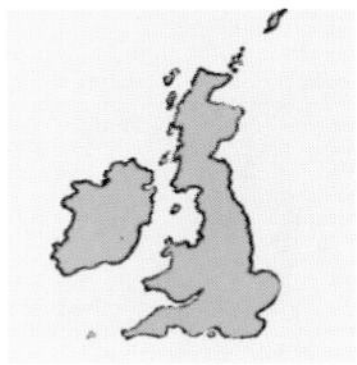
MAP

SLENDER ST JOHN'S WORT is by far the most elegant and attractive of this group of plants. It would be a famous garden plant if it was more tolerant of a wider range of habitats. A semi-prostrate, few-flowered variant occurs in exposed places near the sea in northern Scotland and elsewhere.

Trailing St John's Wort (Hypericum humifusum) is another neat and slender plant of heaths and waysides on lime-poor soils. It has numerous creeping and trailing stems, and pale yellow flowers c. 10 mm (⅖ in) across. It is widespread, although mainly western.

***Bottom** Trailing St John's Wort* (Hypericum humifusum) *is a prostrate perennial with small, pale green elliptical leaves, usually with translucent glands. The flowers are set along the stem and their yellow petals are scarcely longer than the unequal sepals, sometimes black-dotted.*

Marsh St John's Wort

ST JOHN'S WORT FAMILY
(Guttiferae)

SPECIES INFORMATION	
COMMON NAME	Marsh St John's Wort
SCIENTIFIC NAME	Hypericum elodes
RELATED SPECIES	Hairy St John's Wort
HEIGHT/SPREAD	20–30 cm tall
FLOWERING TIME	June–September
HABITAT	Lime-poor, wet places

Note: The St John's Wort of wet places with pale yellow flowers.

FLOWER TYPE

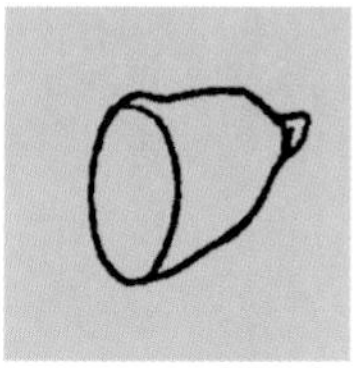

IDENTIFICATION

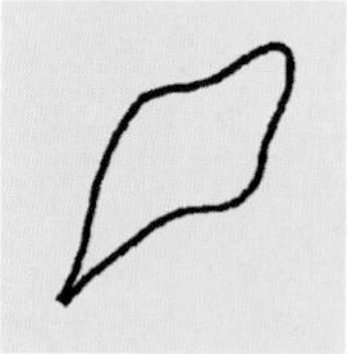

HABITAT

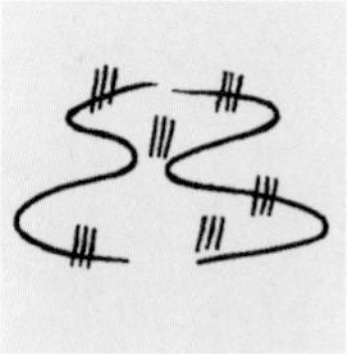

POPULATION

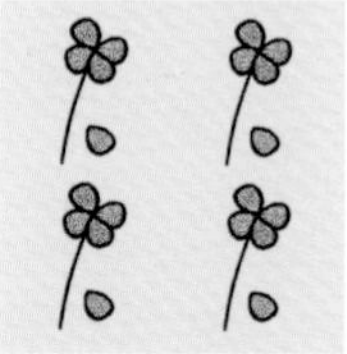

MAP

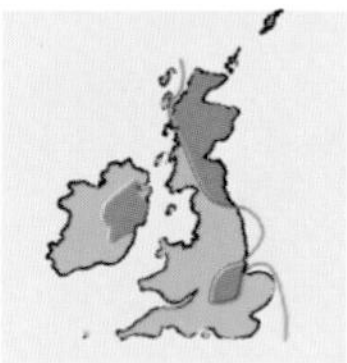

Size and appearance: A greyish-hairy perennial with creeping, rooting stems and semi-erect flowering stems 20–30 cm (8–12 in) tall.

Leaves: In opposite pairs, oval to almost circular, slightly clasping the stem.

Flowers: In loose clusters, pale yellow, funnel-shaped, 10–15 mm (⅜–⅝ in) across, with 5 petals and numerous yellow stamens, the 5 sepals with red hairs.

Fruits: Pear-shaped capsules, splitting into 3 segments.

Related or similar plants: Hairy St John's Wort (see under Common St John's Wort, p.152) is a taller plant of dry places, with denser clusters of wide-open flowers.

Habitat and distribution: Local but rather widespread in lime-poor, wet, peaty and sandy places, on mud in shallow water and in hollows on damp heaths, mainly in southern and western Britain and in southern and western Ireland, extending north to the Outer Hebrides.

Flowering time: June to September.

MARSH ST JOHN'S WORT is an unusual member of this group, with its very hairy, rounded leaves and funnel-shaped flowers. Indeed, botanists regard it as a distinct subgroup all on its own within *Hypericum*. It is a rather characteristic plant of peaty pools and wet ground on sandy or lime-poor soils, for example in the New Forest or in parts of south-western Ireland. It sometimes forms a broad, conspicuous fringe around a pool or along a flooded ditch. Marsh St John's Wort is restricted to within western Europe, and its Scottish sites mark the northern extent of its world distribution.

Marsh St John's Wort (Hypericum elodes) *is a greyish-hairy mat-forming perennial with loose clusters of pale yellow, funnel-shaped flowers which occurs in wet, peaty places, acid bog pools and shallow water in hollows in damp heaths.*

SPECIES INFORMATION	
COMMON NAME	Sweet Violet
SCIENTIFIC NAME	Viola odorata
RELATED SPECIES	Hairy and Dog-violet
HEIGHT/SPREAD	5–10 cm tall, forming patches
FLOWERING TIME	February–May
HABITAT	Woodland and hedge-banks

Note: The only violet with richly scented flowers.

Sweet Violet

VIOLET AND PANSY FAMILY

(Violaceae)

Size and appearance: A perennial with numerous rosettes of leaves, far-creeping runners and solitary flowers on slender leafless stalks 5–10 cm (2–4 in) tall.

Flowers: 8–15 mm (¼–½ in) long, fragrant, usually white but also violet, purplish-violet, pink, lilac, or apricot.

Leaves: Long-stalked, heart-shaped, slightly pointed, neatly scalloped, downy.

Fruits: Pointed capsules, splitting into 3 boat-shaped segments.

Related or similar plants: Hairy Violet; Commom Dog violet (p.156) has hairless leaves and scentless, bluish-violet flowers on leafy stems.

Habitat and distribution: Widespread on woodland margins and hedge-banks, in scrub, churchyards and in or near gardens, especially on richer soils with plenty of leaf-mould. Probably a true native only in southern England, it is locally common in England and Wales, but much scarcer in Scotland and Ireland.

Flowering time: February to May, and sometimes again in September to October and through the winter in milder western districts.

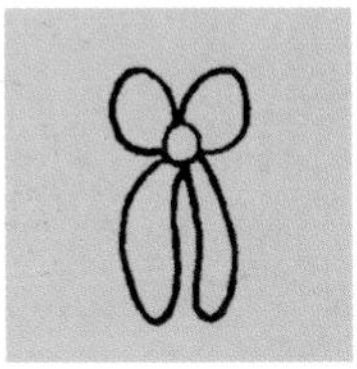

FLOWER TYPE

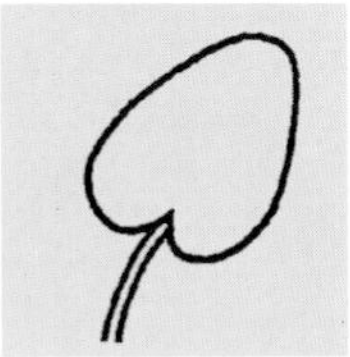

IDENTIFICATION

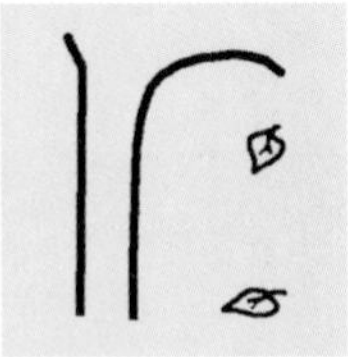

HABITAT

POPULATION

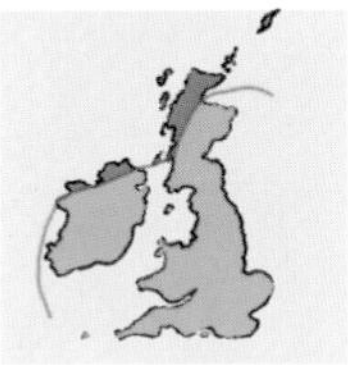

MAP

THERE ARE SEVERAL WILD violets, but Sweet Violet is for most people the true violet of spring. Other violets have only faintly scented or scentless flowers. Ironically, white is the commonest flower colour among wild plants of Sweet Violet, although the violet variant is also widespread. Sometimes a range of colour can be seen within a single wood. Apricot is the rarest flower colour, and prized by gardeners. The flowers of violets actually hang upside-down, as the flower-stalk bends sharply just below the insertion of the flower. The seeds are attractive to, and dispersed by, foraging ants.

Long grown in gardens and often found near houses, the popularity of Sweet Violet among gardeners has long obscured its natural distribution. As a garden plant it was particularly treasured by the Victorians, both as a love-token and for funeral tributes, and it remains a favourite in cottage-style gardens.

Bottom *Hairy Violet* (Viola hirta) *also flowers in early spring, but has scentless, pale violet flowers and hairier leaves, and lacks runners. It grows in grassland and scrub, usually on chalk or limestone or by the sea, and is sometimes abundant in chalk grassland.*

Common Dog-violet

VIOLET AND PANSY FAMILY
(Violaceae)

SPECIES INFORMATION	
COMMON NAME	Common Dog-violet
SCIENTIFIC NAME	Viola riviniana
RELATED SPECIES	Wood Dog-violet
HEIGHT/SPREAD	5–10 cm tall
FLOWERING TIME	March–May
HABITAT	Woodland, hedges and coastal heaths

Note: The common woodland violet of spring.

FLOWER TYPE

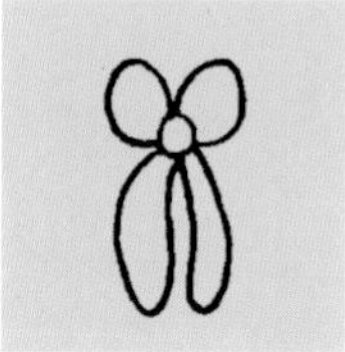

IDENTIFICATION

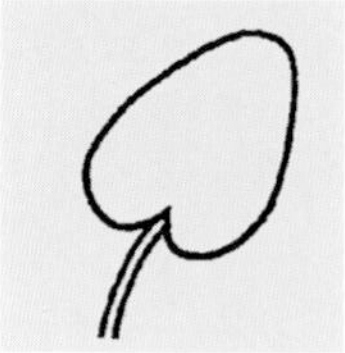

HABITAT

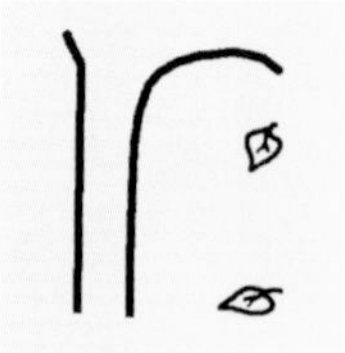

POPULATION

MAP

Size and appearance: A perennial with rosettes of leaves and leafy flowering stems, creeping runners and solitary flowers on slender stalks 5–10 cm (2–4 in) tall.

Flowers: 15–25 mm (⅝–1 in) long, bluish-violet, with a cream or pale violet spur.

Leaves: Heart-shaped, slightly scalloped, long-stalked, hairless.

Fruits: Pointed capsules, splitting into 3 boat-shaped segments.

Related or similar plants: Sweet Violet (p.155) has downy leaves and scented, white or violet flowers.

Habitat and distribution: Widespread in woodland and on hedge-banks, in scrub, grassland and coastal heathland, throughout Britain and Ireland.

Flowering time: March to May, well into June in the mountains, and sometimes again in September to October.

COMMON DOG-VIOLET is also widely grown in gardens, where it can become a weed. Plants growing on coastal heathland that have a compact growth form and small leaves and flowers are regarded by some botanists as a distinct subspecies.

Bottom right *Wood Dog-violet* (Viola reichenbachiana) *has smaller flowers, 12–18 mm long, which are all-violet, including the spur. The leaves are slightly more pointed. It tends to grow in shadier places on richer soils than Common Dog-violet. Flowering March–April, it is less common, except in southern and central England; rare in Scotland and Ireland.*

SPECIES INFORMATION	
COMMON NAME	Marsh Violet
SCIENTIFIC NAME	Viola palustris
RELATED SPECIES	Common Dog-violet
HEIGHT/SPREAD	5–50 cm tall
FLOWERING TIME	April—July
HABITAT	Lime-poor bogs and marshes
Note: The violet of peat-bogs and moorland.	

Marsh Violet

VIOLET AND PANSY FAMILY

(Violaceae)

MARSH VIOLET IS a common plant of wet places on lime-poor soils. It is a very distinctive plant, easily identified by the rounded leaves sticking out of mossy, wet ground. As well as the plant described above, a widespread subspecies has more pointed leaves with slightly hairy stalks. Violets in general have had a long use in herbal medicine, especially for the relief of chest congestion, rheumatic pains and urinary disorders.

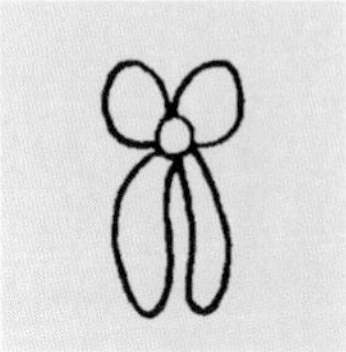
FLOWER TYPE

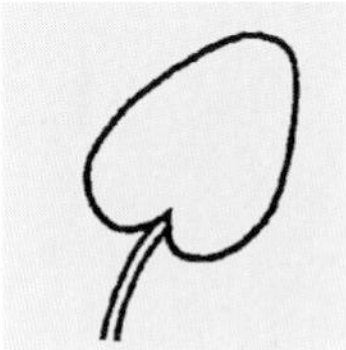
IDENTIFICATION

HABITAT

POPULATION

MAP

Size and appearance: A perennial with creeping underground stems and solitary flowers on slender stalks 5–15 cm (2–6 in) tall.

Flowers: 10–15 mm (⅖–⅗ in) long, lilac with purplish veins.

Leaves: Heart- to kidney-shaped, rounded at the tip, shallowly toothed, long-stalked, mostly hairless.

Fruits: Pointed capsules, splitting into 3 boat-shaped segments.

Related or similar plants: Dog-violets (p.156) are generally plants of well-drained soils and have violet flowers and more pointed leaves.

Habitat and distribution: Widespread in woodland and on hedge-banks, in scrub, grassland and coastal heathland, throughout Britain and Ireland, but much commoner in the north and west.

Flowering time: April to July.

Marsh Violet (Viola palustris) *is widespread in the north of Britain in boggy marshes and woods. It has conspicuously kidney-shaped leaves arising direct from the stem base. The flower stalk holds the pale lilac flowers, which are veined dark purple.*

Field Pansy

VIOLET AND PANSY FAMILY
(Violaceae)

SPECIES INFORMATION	
COMMON NAME	Field Pansy
SCIENTIFIC NAME	Viola arvensis
RELATED SPECIES	Heartsease
HEIGHT/SPREAD	5–30 cm tall
FLOWERING TIME	April–October
HABITAT	Arable land, as a weed

Note: A small, often pale-flowered, pansy of cultivated land.

FLOWER TYPE

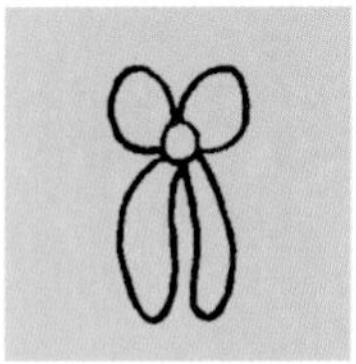

IDENTIFICATION

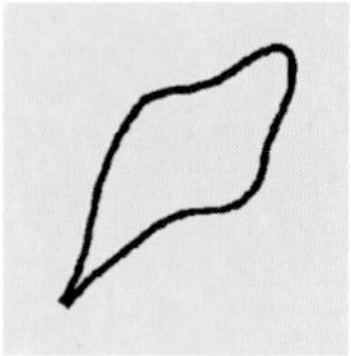

HABITAT

POPULATION

MAP

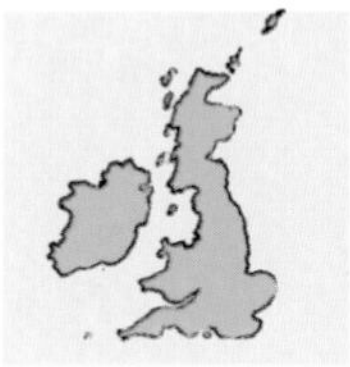

Size and appearance: Annual with rather weak, semi-erect or erect, leafy stems 5–30 cm tall.
Flowers: Solitary, 10–18 mm (⅖–¾ in) long, cream, variably flushed with orange-yellow and violet, with a violet spur; petals shorter than sepals.
Leaves: Oblong or spoon-shaped, lobed or toothed; each with a pair of deeply divided, leaf-like flanges or stipules at the base.
Fruits: Pointed capsules, splitting into 3 boat-shaped segments.
Related or similar plants: Sweet Violet has downy leaves and scented, white or violet flowers.
Habitat and distribution: Widespread in arable land, open and sandy field borders and grassland, and waste places throughout Britain and Ireland, but much commoner in the east.
Flowering time: April to October.

Bottom *Heartsease* (Viola tricolor) *is similar but either annual or (mainly on coasts) perennial, with larger flowers, 15–25 mm (3/5–1 in) long, violet or yellow, the petals distinctly longer than the sepals. It is less common, a plant of open grassland on heaths and sand-dunes.*

FIELD PANSY IS one of the most resilient of our common weeds, and appears to be expanding and more common than ever before. It is an opportunist that grows rapidly in a range of open habitats and it may be somewhat resistant to weedkillers. This variable species crosses with other pansies, including Heartsease and also the hybrid, purple- and yellow-flowered dwarf garden pansies. Certainly its genes already lurk in many other popular garden hybrids.

Pansies are very similar to violets. They differ to some extent in having petals of unequal size and different colours, but most of all in having pairs of large, leaf-like flanges or stipules at the base of the leaves. The stipules of the violets are mostly small and, even if lobed and divided, rather scale-like.

SPECIES INFORMATION	
COMMON NAME	Rock-rose
SCIENTIFIC NAME	Helianthemum nummularium
RELATED SPECIES	Hoary Rock-rose
HEIGHT/SPREAD	Stems 10–40 cm long
FLOWERING TIME	May–September
HABITAT	Grassland and rocky ground

Note: A dwarf shrub with flimsy yellow flowers.

Rock-rose

ROCK-ROSE AND SUN-ROSE FAMILY

(Cistaceae)

Size and appearance: A sprawling, branched shrublet, woody at the base, with straggly stems 10–40 cm (4–16 in) long.

Leaves: Narrow, oblong, 1-veined, white-hairy beneath.

Flowers: In few-flowered clusters, yellow, 18–25 mm (¾–1 in) across, flimsy, with 5 dark-veined sepals, 5 petals and numerous stamens; buds nodding.

Fruits: Egg-shaped capsules, splitting into 3 segments.

Related or similar plants: Hoary Rock-rose, with narrower leaves and smaller flowers, occasionally replaces Rock-rose, especially in the Burren of County Clare, Ireland.

Habitat and distribution: Widespread in grassland and broken, rocky ground on chalk, limestone and basalt across most of Britain, except Cornwall and western and far-northern Scotland; in Ireland only at one site on the County Donegal coast.

Flowering time: May to September.

THIS AND TWO rare species are our only native fragment of an important family of Mediterranean shrubs that includes the sun-roses (*Cistus*). All the members of the family are shrubby and have flimsy petals. The second half of the scientific name refers to the circular, vaguely coin-like flowers (Latin: *nummularius*, coin-like).

In a few places on limestone in northern England and on the Welsh coast, and in the Burren of County Clare, this species is replaced by Hoary Rock-rose (*Helianthemum canum*), with narrower, silver-hairy leaves and flowers 10–15 mm (⅖–⅗ in) across.

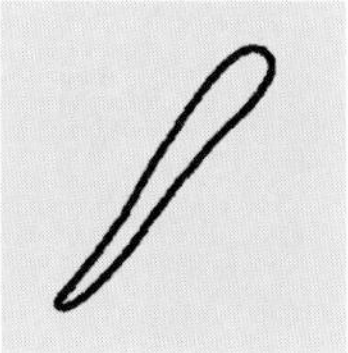

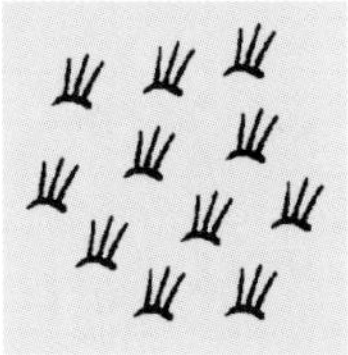

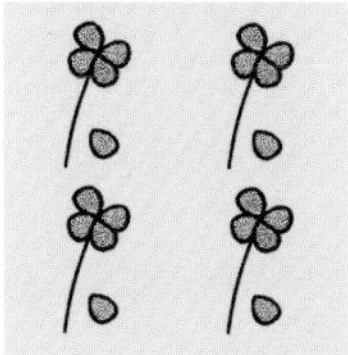

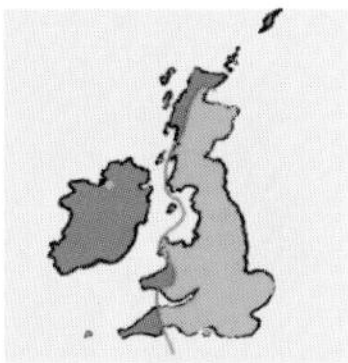

***Top** The Hoary Rock-rose is restricted to outcrops of limestone.*

***Bottom** Rock-rose* (Helianthemum nummularium) *is widespread on chalk and limestone soils across most of Britain. More common on broken and rocky pastures, it can occur on road-verges.*

White Bryony

CUCUMBER AND MARROW FAMILY
(Cucurbitaceae)

SPECIES INFORMATION	
COMMON NAME	White Bryony
SCIENTIFIC NAME	Bryonia dioica
RELATED SPECIES	None
HEIGHT/SPREAD	Stems 1–4 m long
FLOWERING TIME	June–September
HABITAT	Hedges

Note: An ivy-like climber with coiled tendrils.

FLOWER TYPE

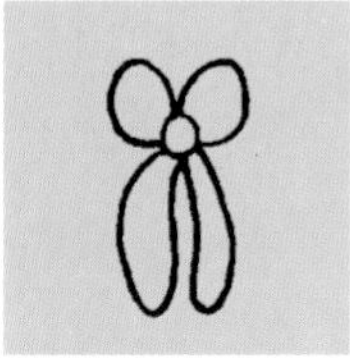

IDENTIFICATION

HABITAT

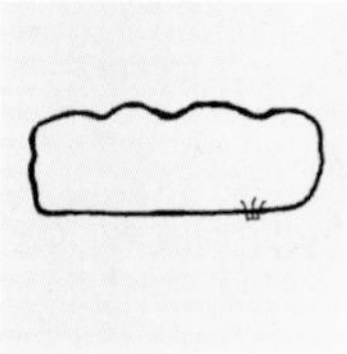

POPULATION

MAP

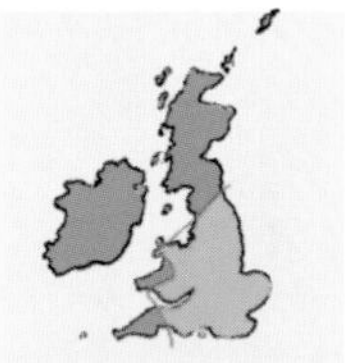

Size and appearance: A rough-hairy perennial, with a stout tuber and ridged, climbing or trailing stems 1–4 m (3–12 ft) long.

Leaves: Ivy-like, pale green, 5- or 7-lobed, with a long, coiled spring-like tendril opposite each leaf-stalk.

Flowers: The male and female on different plants, greenish-white with darker veins, up to 18 mm (¾ in) across, with 5 spreading lobes, in stalked clusters.

Fruits: Loose clusters of spherical red berries 6–10 mm (¼–⅜ in) across.

Related or similar plants: The unrelated Black Bryony (p.351), which also climbs hedges and has red berries, has hairless, shiny, heart-shaped leaves.

Habitat and distribution: Widespread in hedges and scrub and on woodland margins, mostly in the south and east, and absent from Scotland and most of the south-west peninsula and west Wales; introduced in Ireland, near Dublin.

Flowering time: June to September.

WHITE BRYONY IS the only native member of the largely tropical cucumber family. The rough leaves and the tendrils are indeed similar to those of the garden cucumber. However, it is a perennial. The great, lobed, white tuber, thought fancifully to resemble a human body, was once thought to be the legendary Mandrake. The true Mandrake (*Mandragora officinalis*) grows only in the Mediterranean region and flowers in winter. It was an important medicinal plant in ancient times, an early anaesthetic. Those who sold Bryony tubers under this name in England were probably disreputable, but may have been in genuine ignorance of a plant known here only as a much-copied illustration in *Herball*. The whole plant, especially the tuber and the berries, is very poisonous.

White Bryony (Bryonia dioica) *has ivy-shaped, pale green, hairy leaves with a coiled spring-like tendril opposite each leaf stalk. This twines round what it comes into contact with whether it be a hedgerow shrub, a wire fence or another branch.*

SPECIES INFORMATION	
COMMON NAME	Purple Loosestrife
SCIENTIFIC NAME	Lythrum salicaria
RELATED SPECIES	None
HEIGHT/SPREAD	50–180 cm tall
FLOWERING TIME	June–September
HABITAT	Watersides and marshes
Note: A waterside plant with showy spikes of purplish flowers.	

Purple Loosestrife

PURPLE LOOSESTRIFE FAMILY (Lythraceae)

Habitat and distribution: Common on the banks of rivers and streams, in marshes, on damp waste ground and, in the west, damp pastures and abandoned fields, throughout Britain and Ireland, except much of northern and eastern Scotland.
Flowering time: June to September.

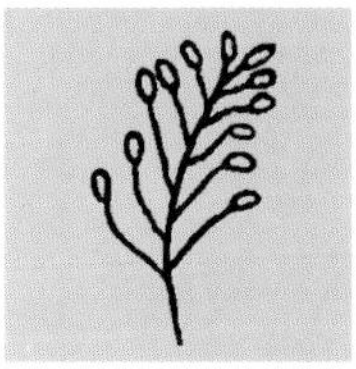
FLOWER TYPE

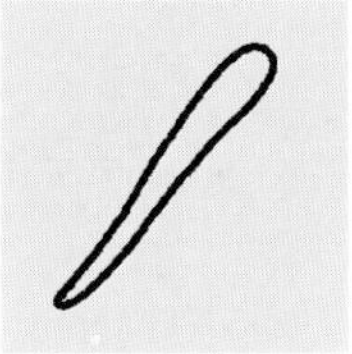
IDENTIFICATION

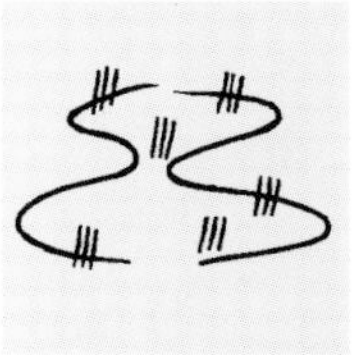
HABITAT

POPULATION

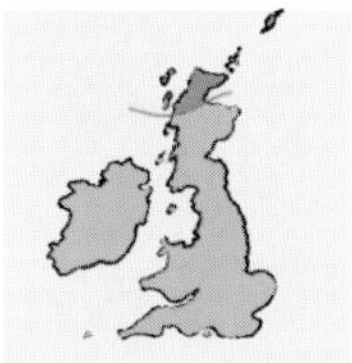
MAP

THIS STRIKING FLOWER colours watersides in late summer, and in some western districts, like West Cork, whole landscapes. Different plants produce three separate types of flower, each with stigmas of differing length. This modification enhances cross-pollination by insects, like the two forms of primrose flower (p.190). Purple Loosestrife makes a handsome garden plant and gardeners have selected cultivars with different shades of pink and purple flowers. Introduced to North America, it is there a serious weed of wetlands, displacing native plants. Plants can reproduce rapidly by fragmentation of the roots and stems, and birds disperse the sticky seeds on their feet and feathers.

Size and appearance: A short-hairy perennial, with creeping rhizomes, forming clumps, and erect, 4-angled stems 50–180 cm (20–72 in) tall.
Leaves: In opposite pairs or in 3s, stalkless and slightly clasping the stem, spear-shaped or oval, pointed.
Flowers: Reddish-purple, c. 10 mm (⅜ in) long, with 6 (rarely 4) petals, in whorls massed in long, dense spikes.
Fruits: Egg-shaped capsules 3–4 mm long (⅛–⅙ in), with many tiny seeds.
Related or similar plants: The unrelated Rosebay Willow-herb (p.164), always in dry places, has larger flowers with 4 petals; the other loosestrifes are in the Primrose family (pp.190—199).

Purple Loosestrife (Lythrum salicaria) *is a striking waterside flower, with long spikes of narrow-petalled, bright reddish-purple flowers arranged in whorls up the four-angled stem 50-180 cm (20-72 in) tall. The unstalked lanceolate leaves are set in opposite pairs up the stem and gradually get smaller towards the top of the plant.*

Mare's-tail

MARE'S-TAIL FAMILY
(Hippuridaceae)

SPECIES INFORMATION	
COMMON NAME	Mare's-tail
SCIENTIFIC NAME	Hippuris vulgaris
RELATED SPECIES	None
HEIGHT/SPREAD	30–80 cm tall
FLOWERING TIME	June–August
HABITAT	Shallow waters

Note: A stiff, horsetail-like plant of still or slow-moving waters.

FLOWER TYPE

IDENTIFICATION

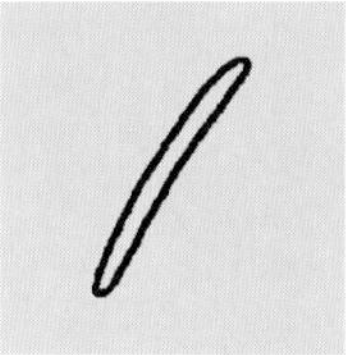

HABITAT

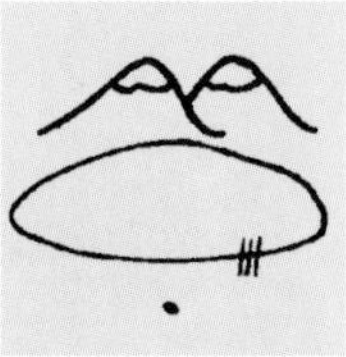

POPULATION

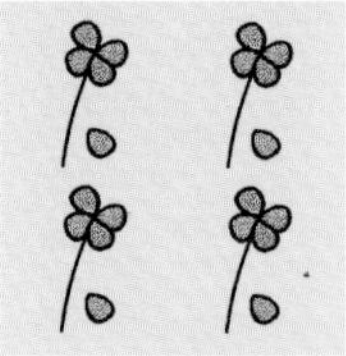

MAP

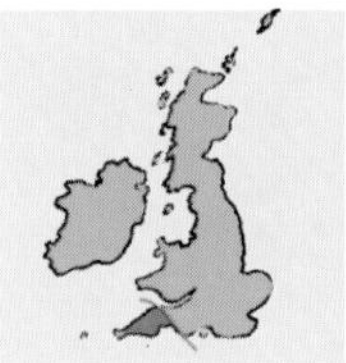

Size and appearance: A hairless, aquatic perennial, with creeping rhizomes and erect, leafy, unbranched stems 30–80 cm (12–32 in) tall.
Leaves: In whorls of 6–12, stalkless, strap-shaped, rigid, pointed; underwater leaves longer, limp, paler green.
Flowers: Tiny, green or pinkish, in whorls in tapering spikes; a single stamen.
Fruits: Nuts 2–3 mm (1/12–1/8 in) long.
Related or similar plants: In a family of its own, but superficially similar to the horsetails, which are flowerless fern allies.
Habitat and distribution: Widespread along slow-moving rivers and streams, in ponds and lakes, scattered all through Britain and Ireland, except much of south-western England and Wales.
Flowering time: June to August.

MARE'S-TAIL IS A strange-looking plant that is easily confused with the horsetails (*Equisetum*). They are fern allies that produce cone-like masses of spores, rather than flowers, mostly in the spring. The old herbalists considered the two to be the same, although they regarded Mare's-tail as being the more feminine, hence the name. Mare's-tail lacks the silica-impregnated stems of the horsetails (they themselves lack leaves), which earned them a useful role as pot-scourers in both Europe and North America. The flowers of Mare's-tail are diminutive and have much-reduced floral parts, but they are true flowers and produce tiny nuts in late summer.

Mare's-tail (Hippuris vulgaris) *is an aquatic plant of slow-moving rivers, shallow lake margins and ponds. The creeping rhizomes spread in the muddy bottom, from where they send forth erect leafy unbranched stems which look like a forest of slender Christmas trees.*

SPECIES INFORMATION	
COMMON NAME	Spiked Water-milfoil
SCIENTIFIC NAME	Myriophyllum spicatum
RELATED SPECIES	Other water-milfoils
HEIGHT/SPREAD	Stems 1–3 m long
FLOWERING TIME	July–September
HABITAT	Lakes and ponds

Note: Aquatic plant with whorls of feathery leaves and spikes.

Spiked Water-milfoil

WATER-MILFOIL FAMILY

(Haloragaceae)

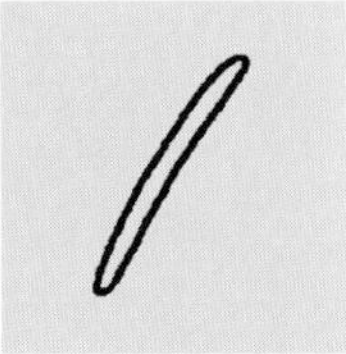

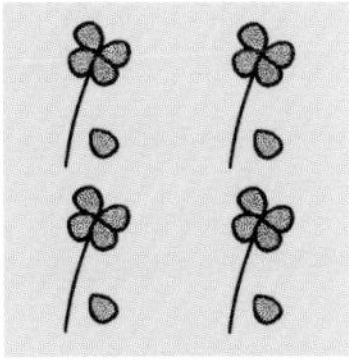

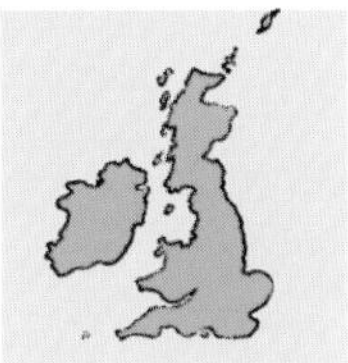

Size and appearance: A submerged aquatic perennial, with long, branched stems 1–3 m (3–9 ft) long.

Leaves: In whorls of 4 (sometimes 5), feathery, cut into thread-like segments, mostly submerged.

Flowers: Small, greenish-yellow or reddish, in whorls in almost leafless spikes emerging from the water.

Fruits: 4 1-seeded nutlets, covered with small warts.

Related or similar plants: Two other water-milfoils occur in Britain; Water Violet (p.193) has similar leaves but larger, violet flowers.

Habitat and distribution: Widespread in slow-moving rivers and streams, in ponds and lakes, especially in more lime-rich waters, throughout Britain and Ireland, but commonest in eastern England.

Flowering time: July to September.

THE TWO OTHER native, and one introduced, water-milfoils are not as common and widespread as Spiked Water-milfoil. It can sometimes be very abundant, literally choking a pond or small lake, being especially evident in summer when it is in flower. Aquatic plants like this are highly specialised, with long, rather weak stems that reach up to the light, and submerged stems and leaves without any waxy or hairy covering, allowing gas and nutrient take-up and excretion over the whole surface of the plant. The feathery leaves do not impede the flow of water, and they present a large surface area for photosynthesis and other life functions. However, most aquatic plants emerge above the water surface in order to flower, facilitating pollination and seed dispersal.

Spiked Water-milfoil (Myriophyllum spicatum) *is a submerged aquatic with long, branched stems that have whorls of feathery leaves. The flowers are also in whorls which rise out of the water on almost leafless spikes.*

Rosebay Willow-herb

WILLOW-HERB FAMILY

(Onagraceae)

SPECIES INFORMATION	
COMMON NAME	Rosebay Willow-herb, Fireweed
SCIENTIFIC NAME	Chamerion angustifolium
RELATED SPECIES	Great Willow-herb
HEIGHT/SPREAD	80–250 cm tall
FLOWERING TIME	June–September
HABITAT	Woodland clearings and waste ground
Note: Forming dense stands on waste ground.	

FLOWER TYPE

IDENTIFICATION

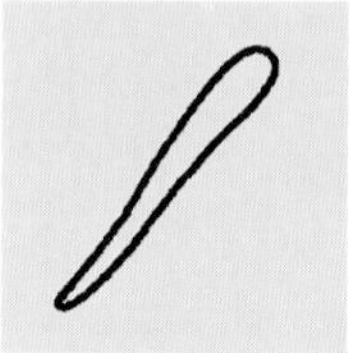

HABITAT

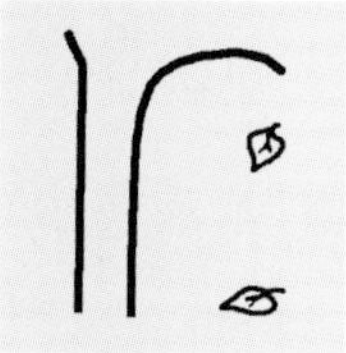

POPULATION

MAP

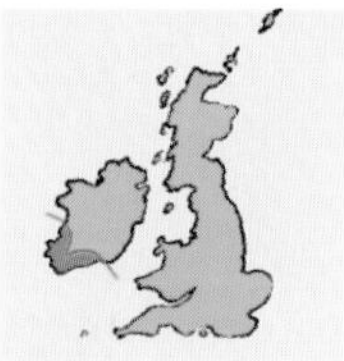

Size and appearance: An almost hairless perennial with creeping rhizomes, forming extensive patches, and tough, erect stems 80–250 cm (32–100 in) tall.

Leaves: Numerous, short-stalked, narrow, spear-shaped.

Flowers: Purplish-pink, 20–30 mm (⅘–1⅕ in) across, with 4 petals, in long, loose, pyramidal spikes.

Fruits: Slender capsules 3–6 cm (1⅕–2⅖ in) long, splitting to release the numerous silky-hairy seeds.

Related or similar plants: The unrelated Purple Loosestrife (p.161), mostly a plant of watersides, has denser spikes of flowers with 6 petals.

Habitat and distribution: A common and conspicuous plant of woodland clearings, scrub, heaths, waste ground and derelict industrial land, railway embankments and sand-dunes, throughout Britain; local and mostly north-eastern in Ireland.

Flowering time: June to September.

IN LATE SUMMER, Rosebay Willow-herb often produces spectacular displays of flowers in forestry clearings or on waste land. It grows best in any dry, open ground, especially after fires. The wind-dispersed seeds greatly aid its colonising ability. This species has expanded its range enormously during the present century, especially since the Second World War, when it famously grew in abundance in bombed parts of London. Either more habitats are available now, or perhaps a more vigorous variant has been introduced from North America. Native Americans used to eat the young shoots, and wove the tough stems into fishing nets and baskets. The flowers yield copious nectar for bees.

Rosebay Willow-herb can produce stunning displays when en masse with its loose, tapering spikes of large bright pinkish-purple flowers, the upper petals of which are broader than the lower. Once in fruit the slender capsules split to release plumed seeds which disperse freely on the wind.

SPECIES INFORMATION	
COMMON NAME	Great Willow-herb
SCIENTIFIC NAME	Epilobium hirsutum
RELATED SPECIES	Rosebay Willow-herb
HEIGHT/SPREAD	100–200 cm tall
FLOWERING TIME	June–September
HABITAT	Open ground and damp places
Note: A very large, hairy waterside plant.	

Great Willow-herb

WILLOW-HERB FAMILY (Onagraceae)

Top *Great Willowherb* (Epilobium hirsutum) *is an erect, softly-downy plant widespread along stream and riversides, pond edges, marshes and ditches.*

GREAT WILLOW-HERB is one of the most conspicuous and handsome plants of late summer, and can dominate wet places. It is our largest willow-herb and forms great thickets that more or less block small streams. One of its widespread traditional names is the evocative Codlins-and-Cream – codlin is an old word for cooking apple – which refers to the combination of rosy petals and cream-coloured stigma and stamens. At the end of the summer the fruits split to release clouds of seeds, each dispersed on the wind by its plume of silky hairs. This seed rain demonstrates just how this and other willow-herbs are such successful colonists of open ground and damp places.

FLOWER TYPE

IDENTIFICATION

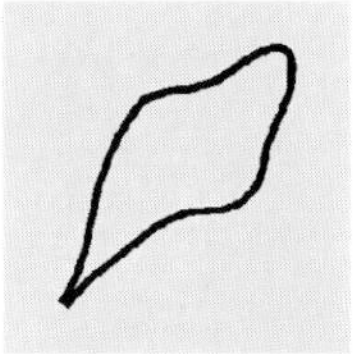

HABITAT

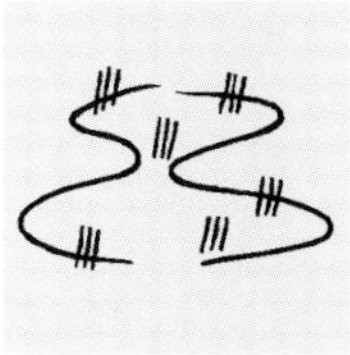

POPULATION

MAP

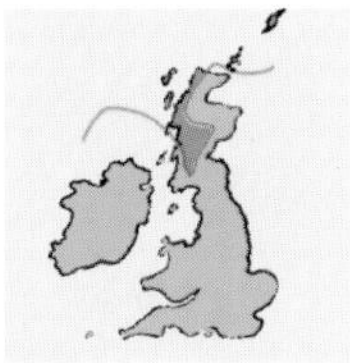

Size and appearance: An erect, softly-downy perennial with vigorous, pink, creeping runners and erect stems 100–200 cm (40–80 in) tall, forming large patches.

Leaves: In opposite pairs, half-clasping the stem, oblong or spear-shaped, slightly pointed, shallowly toothed.

Flowers: Purplish-pink or occasionally white, 20–25 mm (⅘–1 in) across, with 4 shallowly notched petals and a prominent, 4-lobed stigma, numerous in broad, loose clusters.

Fruits: Slender, downy capsules 40–80 mm (1⅗–3⅕ in long, splitting to release the numerous silky-hairy seeds.

Related or similar plants: Rosebay Willow-herb (p.164) has hairless leaves and flowers in long, narrowly pyramidal spikes, and grows in dry sites.

Habitat and distribution: A widespread and sometimes abundant plant of marshes, streamsides and river-banks, also in drier sites on waste ground, coastal shingle or as a garden weed; throughout Britain and Ireland, although absent from much of Scotland.

Flowering time: June to September.

Bottom *The purplish-pink four notched petals contrast with the prominent four-lobed cream stigma in broad, loose clusters of heads.*

Broad-leaved Willow-herb

WILLOW-HERB FAMILY

(Onagraceae)

SPECIES INFORMATION	
COMMON NAME	Broad-leaved Willow-herb
SCIENTIFIC NAME	Epilobium montanum
RELATED SPECIES	Great Willow-herb
HEIGHT/SPREAD	20–80 cm tall
FLOWERING TIME	June–September
HABITAT	Waste ground and gardens

Note: The common willow-herb of damp soil and shady places.

FLOWER TYPE

IDENTIFICATION

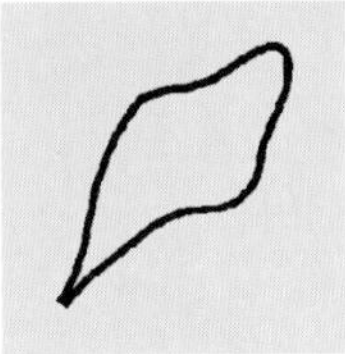

HABITAT

POPULATION

MAP

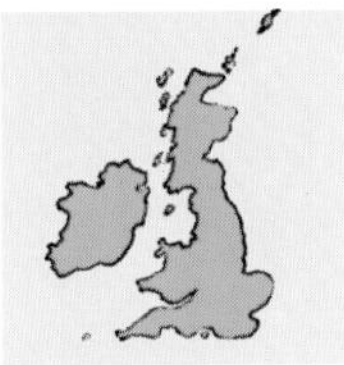

APART FROM ROSEBAY Willow-herb (p.164) and Great Willow-herb (p.165), this is the commonest of our dozen or so native or introduced willow-herbs, mostly plants of similar appearance and habitat preference. The numerous wind-dispersed seeds make them natural invaders. As well as seed, Broad-leaved Willow-herb spreads by sturdy runners from the base. Two rarer willow-herbs are plants of mountain rocks in northern Britain.

Top left *Broad-leaved Willow-herb (Epilobium montanum) has broad, short-stalked, mostly opposite leaves, rounded at the base.*

Right *Pale Willow-herb (Epilobium roseum) has deeply notched petals, white at first and then becoming a characteristic pale rose. The leaves have a longish stalk 3-20 mm (⅕-⅘ in) long.*

Size and appearance: An almost hairless perennial, with erect stems 20–80 cm (8–32 in); clusters of leaf-rosettes grow from the base of the stems.

Leaves: Mostly in opposite pairs, short-stalked, narrow, oval, pointed, shallowly toothed.

Flowers: Purplish-pink, 6–10 mm (¼–⅖ in) across, with 4 notched petals and a 4-lobed stigma, numerous in loose clusters.

Fruits: Slender, downy capsules 50–75 mm (2–3 in) long, splitting to release the numerous silky-hairy seeds.

Related or similar plants: The other willow-herbs differ in hairiness, leaf shape, flower size and other characters.

Habitat and distribution: Widespread and common in damp, shady places, woodland, waste ground and gardens, particularly abundant on damp, disturbed or cultivated ground.

Flowering time: June to September.

SPECIES INFORMATION	
COMMON NAME	Enchanter's Nightshade
SCIENTIFIC NAME	Circaea lutetiana
RELATED SPECIES	Willow-herbs
HEIGHT/SPREAD	10–50 cm tall
FLOWERING TIME	June–September
HABITAT	Woods lanes and gardens

Note: A Striking flower of shady places.

Enchanter's Nightshade

WILLOW-HERB FAMILY

(Onagraceae)

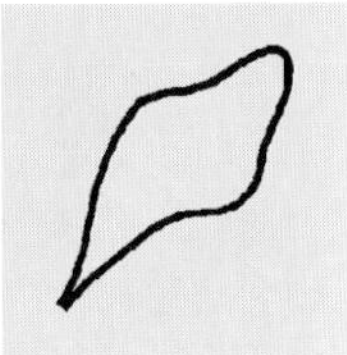

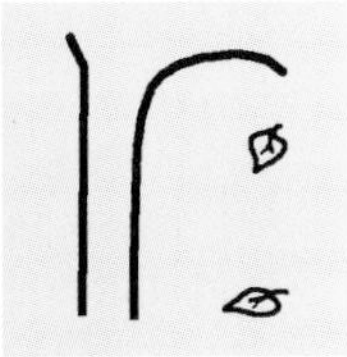

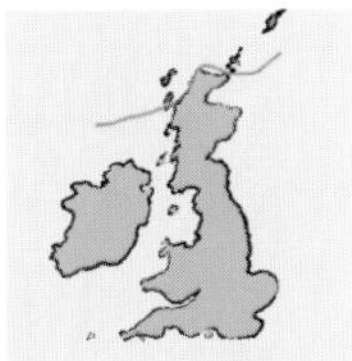

ENCHANTER'S NIGHTSHADE is not very conspicuous but can occur in large numbers. Like Broad-leaved Willow-herb (p.166), it spreads both by runners and by seed. It is less invasive, but infests some shady gardens. The bristles on the fruits adhere readily to animal fur and human clothes, and disperse the seeds efficiently. This species is replaced in parts of Scotland by the rarer Alpine Enchanter's Nightshade (*Circaea alpina*). Many plants in upland Wales, northern Britain and northern Ireland are intermediate between the two species and appear to be crosses, not setting seed. Alpine Enchanter's Nightshade is smaller and has more toothed leaves with winged stalks; the flowers are pink and the flower-spikes elongate after flowering.

Size and appearance: A small, erect, sparsely-downy perennial 10–50 cm (4–20 in) tall.
Leaves: In opposite pairs, with short, unwinged stalks, heart-shaped or broadly oval, sparsely toothed.
Flowers: White or pinkish, 5–8 mm (⅕–⅓ in) across, with 4 petals, 2 of them deeply notched; in loose, leafless spikes that elongate as the flowers open.
Fruits: Small, pear-shaped, 2-seeded, covered with minute, hooked bristles.
Related or similar plants: The very similar Alpine Enchanter's Nightshade, and a cross with that species, replaces it in northern Britain.
Habitat and distribution: Widespread in damp, shady places in woods, lanes and gardens, where it can be a troublesome weed; throughout, but largely absent north from central Scotland.
Flowering time: June to September.

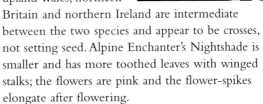

Enchanter's Nightshade (Circaea lutetiana) *is widespread in damp shady places where it can carpet the ground; it only becomes really noticeable in flower, when it sends forth leafless spikes of white flowers.mm (⅗—1 in) long, violet or yellow, the petals distinctly longer than the sepals. It is less common, a plant of open grassland on heaths and sand-dunes.*

Evening Primrose

WILLOW-HERB FAMILY

(Onagraceae)

SPECIES INFORMATION	
COMMON NAME	Evening Primrose
SCIENTIFIC NAME	Oenothera biennis
RELATED SPECIES	Willow-herbs
HEIGHT/SPREAD	80–150 cm tall
FLOWERING TIME	June–September
HABITAT	Open and waste ground

Note: The clusters of yellow, poppy-like flowers are distinctive.

FLOWER TYPE

IDENTIFICATION

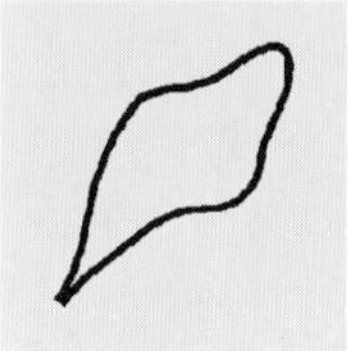

HABITAT

POPULATION

MAP

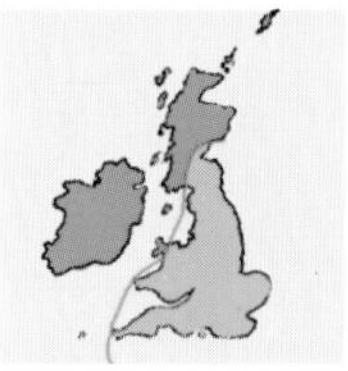

Size and appearance: An erect, little-branched, downy annual or biennial 80–150 cm (32–60 in) tall.
Leaves: Short-stalked, broadly spear-shaped, shallowly toothed.
Flowers: Pale yellow, 40–60 mm (1⅗–2⅖ in) across, with 4 rather flimsy petals and green, hairy sepals, in a long, erect cluster.
Fruits: Slender, cylindrical, downy capsules c. 3 cm (1⅕ in) long.
Related or similar plants: Large-flowered Evening Primrose has hairs with red, swollen bases and larger flowers.

Habitat: Sometimes occurring in great crowds on roadsides and in other open, sandy ground, waste places and neglected gardens, mainly in the south and east, rarer further north and in Wales; very rare in Ireland.
Flowering time: June to September.

EVENING PRIMROSE is a 17th-century introduction to Europe from North America that has become both a popular cottage garden plant and a familiar roadside weed. It is a most useful plant, having roots and (young) leaves that are edible raw or cooked, as well as attractive flowers. The plant is increasingly being grown for its oil, which is a valuable ingredient of numerous cosmetic, health food and medical products. The flowers are at their best by night, opening in the evening, snapping open suddenly as you watch. They are pollinated by night-flying moths.

Bottom *Large-flowered Evening Primrose* (Oenothera erythrosepala) *is similar but has hairs with red, swollen bases and flowers 50–80 mm (2–3⅕ in) across, with reddish sepals. It is more scattered, north to Yorkshire, and occasionally in Ireland.*

SPECIES INFORMATION	
COMMON NAME	Ivy
SCIENTIFIC NAME	Hedera helix
RELATED SPECIES	None
HEIGHT/SPREAD	1–5 m long
FLOWERING TIME	September–November
HABITAT	Woods, hedges and walls

Note: A familiar and unmistakable plant.

Ivy

IVY FAMILY
(Araliaceae)

Size and appearance: A woody climber, trailing on the ground or in trees, climbing by dense, sucker-like roots or with shrubby flowering branches; stems 1–5 m (3–15 ft) long, often longer.

Leaves: Dark green, often patterned, 3- or 5-lobed, of characteristic 'ivy shape'; leaves on the flowering branches elliptical, unlobed, pointed.

Flowers: Yellowish-green, with parts in 5s and yellow stamens, in erect, stalked, domed clusters.

Fruits: Erect clusters of spherical, flat-topped, black berries 6–8 mm (¼–⅓ in) across.

Related or similar plants: An unmistakable plant, although the leaves vary greatly in colour and shape.

Habitat and distribution: Ubiquitous, especially in shady places, carpeting the ground in woods or festooning trees, hedges and rocks, old buildings and walls; on coastal cliffs in the west.

Flowering time: September to November.

FLOWER TYPE

IDENTIFICATION

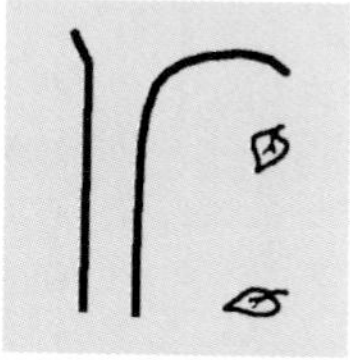
HABITAT

POPULATION

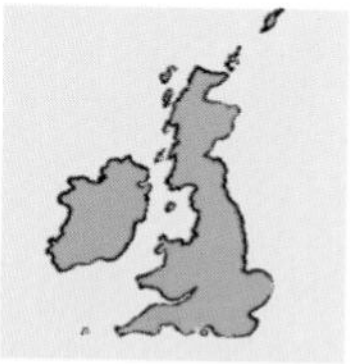
MAP

IVY IS A DISTINCTIVE landscape feature in many districts. It is less common in ancient woodland, and is more a plant of disturbed woodland, certainly thriving where people live and have created new habitats for it to invade. Ivy's greatest virtue is that it is the final plant of the floral year, attracting late-flying, often shabby-looking butterflies and other insects on quiet autumn days. Ivy is the foodplant of midsummer broods of caterpillars of the Holly Blue butterfly. It is our only representative of a mostly tropical, western Pacific family. The garden plant *Fatsia japanica*, which can be crossed with Ivy, comes from the same family.

Ivy is a plant with many mystical associations, from the Greek god Bacchus and drinking, through to the rituals of midwinter and Christmas.

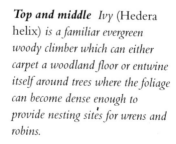

Top and middle *Ivy* (Hedera helix) *is a familiar evergreen woody climber which can either carpet a woodland floor or entwine itself around trees where the foliage can become dense enough to provide nesting sites for wrens and robins.*

Bottom *Flowering in autumn, it is an invaluable nectar source for late-flying butterflies and moths.*

Marsh Pennywort

CARROT AND HOGWEED FAMILY (Umbelliferae)

SPECIES INFORMATION	
COMMON NAME	Marsh Pennywort
SCIENTIFIC NAME	Hydrocotyle vulgaris
RELATED SPECIES	None
HEIGHT/SPREAD	5–25 cm tall
FLOWERING TIME	June–July
HABITAT	Wet, grassy places

Note: A distinctive little plant of wet places.

FLOWER TYPE

IDENTIFICATION

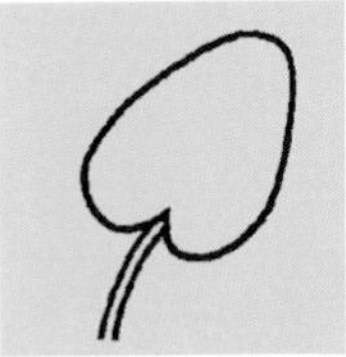

HABITAT

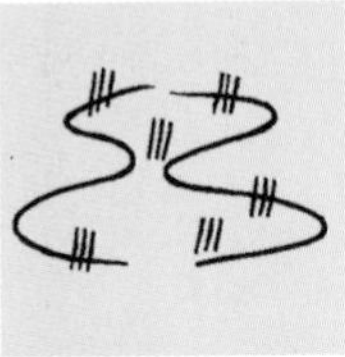

POPULATION

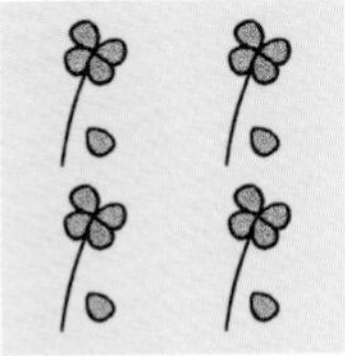

MAP

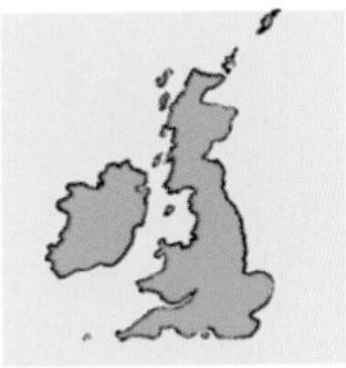

MARSH PENNYWORT is a rather inconspicuous plant that generally turns up in damp, grassy places after a search on hands and knees. It is hard to believe that it is related to carrot, hogweed and parsnip, but some botanists do put it into its own family (with some 75 related plants worldwide). Like Lousewort (p.266) and Bog Asphodel (p.335), this plant was believed to be detrimental to the health of sheep, but more likely it was its often mineral-poor, liver fluke-infested habitat that was to blame for any ill-health of livestock.

Size and appearance: An almost hairless perennial, with slender, creeping, rooting stems, and leaf-stalks 5–25 cm (2–10 in) tall; flowering stems shorter.
Leaves: On long, erect stalks, almost circular, with rounded teeth, up to 25 mm (1 in), sometimes more, across.
Flowers: Tiny, greenish-white, tinged pink, usually 3–6, in a small, whorled cluster c. 3 mm ($\frac{1}{8}$ in) across.
Fruits: Almost circular, flattened, rounded, c. 2 mm ($\frac{1}{12}$ in) long, ridged.
Related or similar plants: Distinct from other members of the family, and sometimes placed in one of its own.
Habitat and distribution: Widespread and often common in marshes, the margins of bogs and damp grassland, and beside streams, throughout Britain and Ireland, although more frequent in the west and north.
Flowering time: June to July.

Marsh Pennywort (Hydrocotyle vulgaris) *is a prostrate, creeping perennial with round, shallowly lobed leaves. The flowers have to be searched for as they are inconspicuous heads at the base of the leaves; they are easier to find when in fruit.*

SPECIES INFORMATION	
COMMON NAME	Sanicle
SCIENTIFIC NAME	Sanicula europaea
RELATED SPECIES	None
HEIGHT/SPREAD	20–60 cm tall
FLOWERING TIME	June–August
HABITAT	Woods

Note: Leaves like a crane's-bill, but with carrot-like flowers.

Sanicle

CARROT AND HOGWEED FAMILY (Umbelliferae)

SANICLE WAS A famous healing herb all over Europe, and native Americans prized a closely related North American species as a medicinal plant. The English name and the first half of the scientific name derive from the Latin (*sanus*: whole or healed). In parts of France, Sanicle is called Herbe de St.Laurent, after St. Lawrence, a Christian martyr whose tormentors literally grilled him to death; in other words it was frequently used as a treatment for burns.

Sanicle has a very wide distribution in the Old World, extending across Eurasia and south into mountainous, tropical regions. Far from the beechwoods of southern England and western Europe, it occurs, for example, on Mt Olympus in Greece and Mt Kinabalu in Borneo, two of the most famous plant-rich mountains in the world.

Size and appearance: A hairless, tufted perennial, with a short, tough rootstock and almost leafless flowering stems 20–60 cm (8–24 in) tall.

Leaves: Long-stalked, almost circular in outline, deeply 5-lobed, each lobe itself 3-lobed, sharply toothed.

Flowers: White or pinkish, c. 3 mm ($\frac{1}{8}$ in) across, in a group of small, rounded clusters.

Fruits: Almost spherical, c. 4 mm ($\frac{1}{6}$ in) long, densely covered with hooked bristles.

Related or similar plants: Rather different from the other members of this family, especially in leaf-shape.

Habitat and distribution: Widespread and often common in shady places and woods, especially of beech, but also ash and oak; throughout, but more local in eastern Scotland and in Ireland.

Flowering time: June to August.

Sanicle (Sanicula europaea) *can usually be found in shady places and woods which are situated on chalk soils. It has long-stalked shiny, deeply lobed leaves out of which arise the white or pinkish flowers in bobbly umbels.*

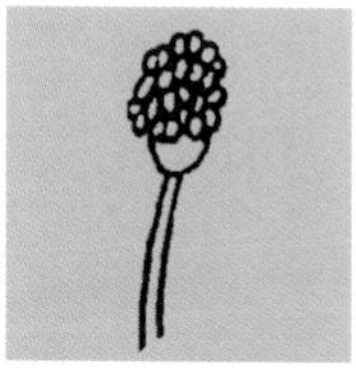

FLOWER TYPE

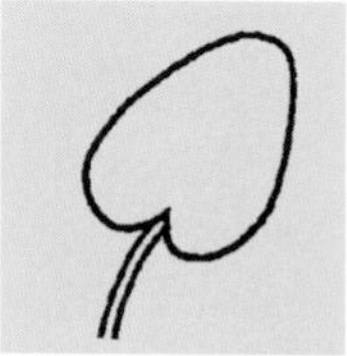

IDENTIFICATION

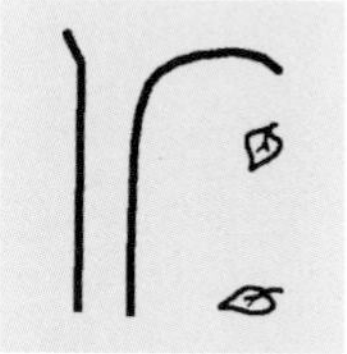

HABITAT

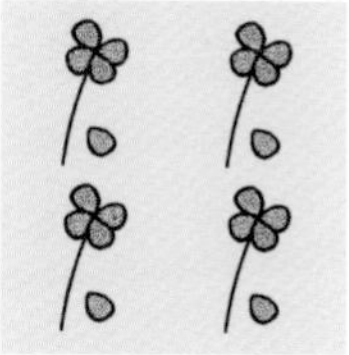

POPULATION

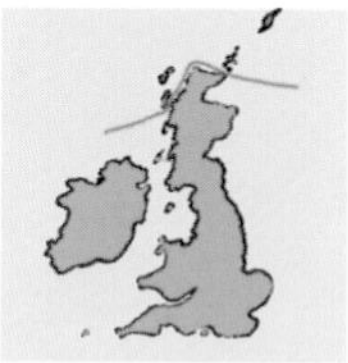

MAP

Sea Holly

CARROT AND HOGWEED FAMILY (Umbelliferae)

SPECIES INFORMATION	
COMMON NAME	Sea Holly
SCIENTIFIC NAME	Eryngium maritimum
RELATED SPECIES	Garden eryngos
HEIGHT/SPREAD	Up to 60 cm tall, forming patches
FLOWERING TIME	July–August
HABITAT	Coastal beaches and sand-dunes

Note: The holly-like leaves and blue flowers are unique.

FLOWER TYPE

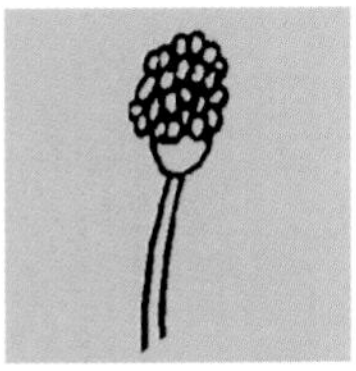

IDENTIFICATION

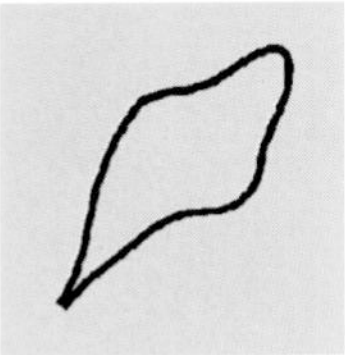

HABITAT

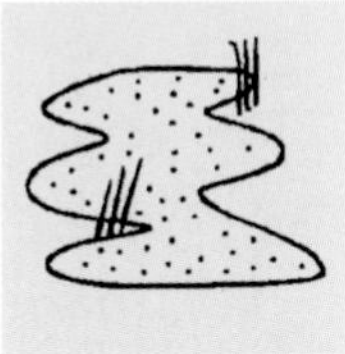

POPULATION

MAP

Size and appearance: A hairless, spiny, bluish-green perennial, forming patches, with stiff, branched stems 20–60 cm (8–24 in) tall.
Leaves: Almost circular, 3-lobed, wavy, with large, spine-tipped teeth, the upper clasping the stem.
Flowers: Blue, numerous in tight, almost spherical heads 2–3 cm (4/5–1⅕ in) across, with a ruff of leaf-like, spiny bracts.
Fruits: A head of paired, elliptical, spiny, 1-seeded fruits.
Related or similar plants: Several similar plants (*eryngos*) are grown in gardens.
Habitat and distribution: Locally common on sandy seashores and the front edges of sand-dunes, less frequently on shingle beaches, sometimes persisting in dune grassland, north to the Outer Hebrides but extinct in eastern Scotland.
Flowering time: July to August, but the unusual leaves identify the plant throughout the year.

THIS STRIKING AND decorative plant looks much more like a thistle than a relative of the carrot. It is a prominent feature of many seashores, and is well adapted to a dry, difficult habitat. It has very deep roots up to 2 m (6 ft) long that enable it to reach fresh water, and the tough, waxy leaf surface cuts back on excessive water loss and spray damage in the dry, salty conditions. The roots were formerly candied and sold as a sweet snack, popular from Elizabethan times onwards. They were believed by some to be a cure for impotence. The fresh, young shoots were eaten as a salad, and those of related species are still eaten by Arabs and other Mediterranean peoples.

Sea Holly (Eryngium maritimum) *is an unmistakable plant of sandy beaches, with spiny bluish-green leaves with white edges and veins, and globular flowers. Heads are striking powder-blue and mauve, with broad spiny bracts.*

SPECIES INFORMATION	
COMMON NAME	Cow Parsley, Queen Anne's Lace
SCIENTIFIC NAME	Anthriscus sylvestris
RELATED SPECIES	Sweet Cicely
HEIGHT/SPREAD	40–150 cm tall
FLOWERING TIME	April–June
HABITAT	Roadsides and shady places

Note: The white wild 'carrot' of May roadsides.

Cow Parsley

CARROT AND HOGWEED FAMILY
(Umbelliferae)

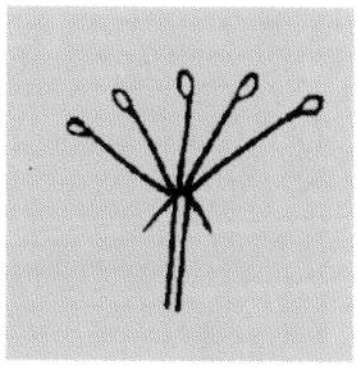

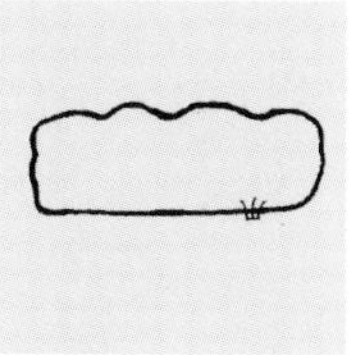

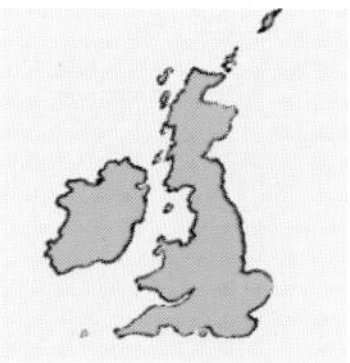

Size and appearance: A rather robust perennial with erect, branched stems 40–150 cm (16–60 in) tall.

Leaves: Compound, up to 30 cm (12 in) or more long, 3-times divided into toothed, feathery, fern-like segments.

Flowers: White, in dense, flat-topped heads or umbels 3–8 cm (1⅕–3⅕ in) across.

Fruits: Paired, egg-shaped, flattened, smooth, dark brown or black, 1-seeded fruits c. 10 mm (⅖ in) long.

Related or similar plants: Hemlock (p.180) is taller, with more feathery leaves and purple-blotched stems; in the north it may be confused with Sweet Cicely.

Habitat and distribution: Abundant along roads, often in great crowds, on waysides and wood margins, and in neglected, often shady corners of parks, gardens and churchyards, throughout Britain and Ireland.

Flowering time: April to June, but a few plants flower throughout the year, especially in mild winters.

COW PARSLEY IS by far the most common and best-known wild member of the carrot family, colouring whole landscapes, especially along roads and lanes, in May and early June. It is an enduring image of rural England, like bluebells, hawthorn or gorse. The leaves grow all through mild winters, and plants will even put up an occasional head of flowers in wintertime. Many plants, the actual number varying between populations, have purplish stems and sometimes purplish leaves. Young leaves have sometimes been used in salads but it is best to regard the plant as poisonous. For one thing, it is just too easily confused with Hemlock (p.180) and several other very poisonous members of the same family.

In northern England, Scotland and northern Ireland, the very similar Sweet Cicely (*Myrrhis odorata*) is widely naturalised in hedges and other semi-shady places. Flowering May to June, it is readily distinguished by the leaves, which smell of aniseed when bruised, and angled fruits up to 25 mm (1 in) long.

Cow Parsley (Anthriscus sylvestris) *is generally the commonest white umbellifer of road verges and hedgerows, often creating a long white ribbon along waysides in May. Later in the season similar species take its place in the hedges.*

Ground Elder

CARROT AND HOGWEED FAMILY (Umbelliferae)

SPECIES INFORMATION	
COMMON NAME	Ground Elder, Goutweed
SCIENTIFIC NAME	Aegopodium podagraria
RELATED SPECIES	None
HEIGHT/SPREAD	30–100 cm tall
FLOWERING TIME	June–August
HABITAT	Gardens and shady road-verges

Note: The long, white, fleshy rhizomes are distinctive.

IDENTIFICATION

FLOWER TYPE

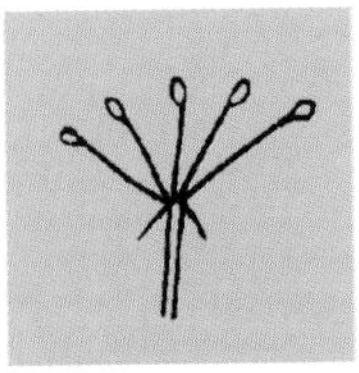

HABITAT

POPULATION

MAP

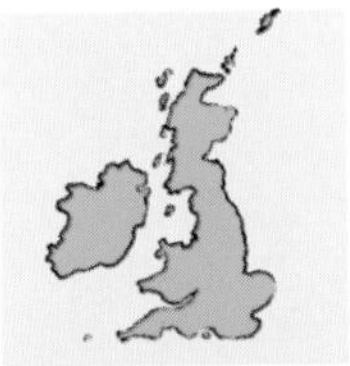

Size and appearance: A hairless, rather aromatic perennial, with far-creeping, white, fleshy rhizomes, forming patches, and erect stems 30–100 cm (12–40 in) tall.

Leaves: Compound, long-stalked, divided 1–2 times into 3 oval or broadly spear-shaped, toothed leaflets.

Flowers: White, small, numerous in dense, flat-topped heads or umbels up to 6 cm (2⅜ in) across.

Fruits: Paired, narrowly egg-shaped, flattened, smooth, 1-seeded fruits up to 10 mm (⅜ in) long, with 5 ridges.

Related or similar plants: Unlikely to be confused with any other plant because of the rhizomes.

Habitat and distribution: Widespread and common in damp, rather shady places, especially gardens, where it is an aggressive and persistent weed, also at the edge of woods, in hedgerows and on roadsides, usually where it has been introduced, throughout Britain and Ireland.

Flowering time: June to August.

THE BANE OF SO many gardeners, Ground Elder spreads rapidly and effectively through its extensive network of shallowly rooted rhizomes. These are fleshy and brittle, and regenerate readily and quickly to produce new plants. Ground Elder is widespread in woods in Europe, especially in the east, but in these islands rarely occurs far from human habitation, and is almost certainly introduced. It frequently forms patches in woodland and on shady roadsides, often spreading from tipped garden rubbish. It is not wholly undesirable. The leaves can be cooked and eaten like spinach and the plant was formerly regarded as a remedy for gout. Real enthusiasts may purchase a white-variegated variant of Ground Elder from nurseries; it is less aggressive.

Ground Elder (Aegopodium podagraria) *is generally found in close proximity to habitation having been grown in centuries past for its food and medicinal properties. Now, however, its aggressive nature no longer kept in check, it has spread on to many road verges and woodland margins.*

SPECIES INFORMATION	
COMMON NAME	Wild Parsnip
SCIENTIFIC NAME	Pastinaca sativa
RELATED SPECIES	Fennel
HEIGHT/SPREAD	30–150 cm tall
FLOWERING TIME	July–September
HABITAT	Dry grassland and roadsides

Note: The commonest yellow-flowered carrot-like plant.

Wild Parsnip

CARROT AND HOGWEED FAMILY

(Umbelliferae)

FLOWER TYPE

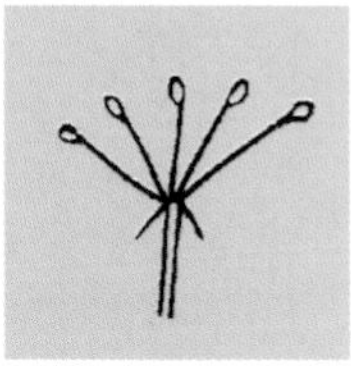

IDENTIFICATION

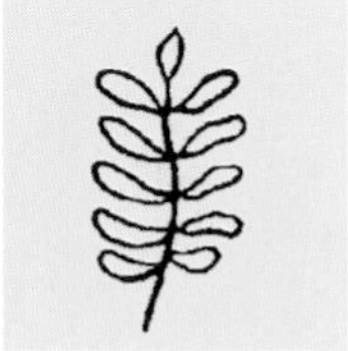

HABITAT

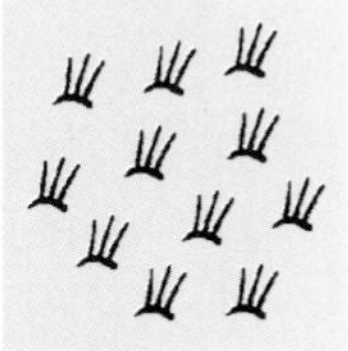

POPULATION

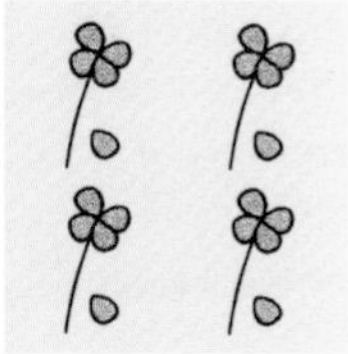

MAP

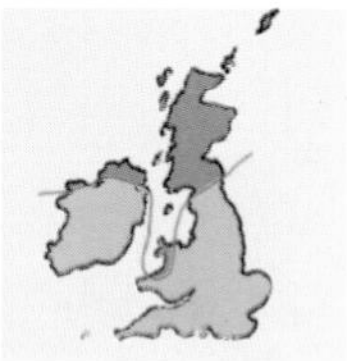

Size and appearance: A rough-hairy, often robust, biennial 30–150 cm (12–60 in) tall.

Leaves: Compound, divided into 5–11 oblong to oval, coarsely toothed leaflets, smelling strongly of parsnip when bruised.

Flowers: Yellow, numerous in dense, flat-topped heads or umbels up to 10 cm (4 in) across.

Fruits: Paired, elliptical, flattened, narrowly winged, brown, 1-seeded fruits 5–8 mm (1/5–1/3 in) long.

Related or similar plants: Fennel is hairless and has feathery leaves.

Habitat and distribution: Local in dry grassland, on roadsides and waste ground, usually wild, although sometimes a relic of cultivation, generally on lime-rich soils, north to north Yorkshire, but only widespread south and east of a line between the estuaries of the Rivers Severn and Humber; introduced and very local in Ireland.

Flowering time: July to September.

WILD PARSNIP SOMETIMES occurs in great numbers on chalky or disturbed ground, and can be a feature of road-verges in some districts in the south and east. The wild plant is a subspecies of garden Parsnip, which is generally taller, but less hairy and with larger seeds, and escapes on to road-verges and the edges of fields.

The first half of the scientific name is the Latin word that the Romans used for the carrot. Parsnips did not come into cultivation until medieval times. They then became a major root vegetable in England before potatoes came in from the Americas. The wild plant has a long taproot, but this is hard and woody.

Bottom *Fennel* (Foeniculum vulgare) *also has yellow flowers but is hairless and has 3–4 times-divided, feathery leaves that smell of aniseed on bruising. A widespread escape from gardens on dry banks and waste ground, particularly near the sea, flowering July-October.*

Scots Lovage

CARROT AND HOGWEED FAMILY (Umbelliferae)

SPECIES INFORMATION	
COMMON NAME	Scots Lovage
SCIENTIFIC NAME	Ligusticum scoticum
RELATED SPECIES	None
HEIGHT/SPREAD	30–80 cm tall
FLOWERING TIME	June–August
HABITAT	Rocky coasts

Note: A plant of northern coastal rocks.

FLOWER TYPE

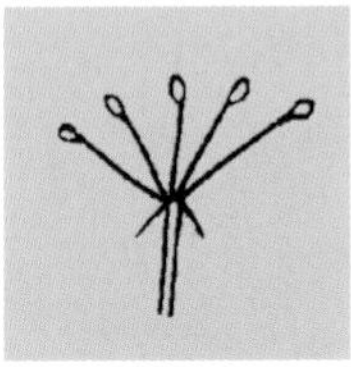

IDENTIFICATION

HABITAT

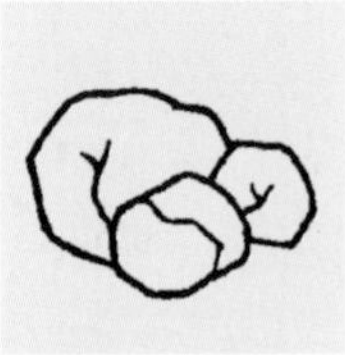

POPULATION

MAP

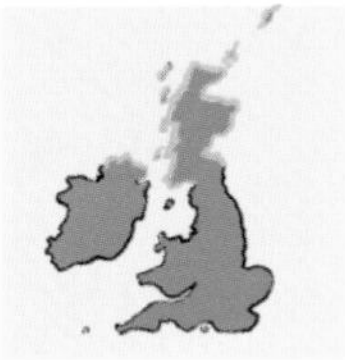

Size and appearance: A hairless perennial, with a rather woody base and semi-erect, hollow stems 30–80 cm (12–32 in) tall, rarely up to 100 cm (40 in).

Leaves: Compound, twice divided into oval or wedge-shaped, toothed or shallowly lobed leaflets, leathery, dark green, shiny; base of stalk inflated, sheathing.

Flowers: White, numerous in dense, flat-topped heads or umbels.

Fruits: Paired, egg-shaped, flattened, 1-seeded fruits 4–8 mm (⅙–⅓ in) long, with prominent, winged ridges.

Related or similar plants: A distinctive plant with a specialised ecological niche, unlikely to be confused with any other.

Habitat and distribution: Locally common on rocky shores, cliffs and shingle beaches, rarely on sand-dunes, around the coasts of Scotland, from Kirkcudbrightshire to Berwickshire, extending south just to Northumberland and into northern Ireland.

Flowering time: June to August.

SCOTS LOVAGE IS a characteristic plant of seashores in Scotland, and is tolerant of both salt spray and frost. The fruits are able to float and disperse in seawater. The leaves, known locally in Scotland as Sea Parsley, were formerly cooked and eaten, both as a winter green and as a herb that would prevent scurvy. The plant is adapted and restricted to regions with cool summers, occurring no further south than Denmark in Europe and Hudson Bay in Canada. Rock Samphire (p.177), replaces it to the south, occupying a very similar ecological niche of open, rock and cliff vegetation. The two occur together only in a small area of Galloway. Both are plants of open sites; neither survives well in grassland at the top of cliffs.

Garden Lovage (*Levisticum officinale*), originally from south-west Asia, is a more robust plant that grows much taller, up to 200 cm (6 ft) tall, and has yellowish flowers. The aromatic roots were a medicinal herb, used to treat coughs and bad chests.

Scots Lovage (Ligusticum scoticum) *is locally common on rocky shores, cliffs and shingle beaches around the Scottish coast. Its compound twice-divided leaves have a dark green, shiny, leathery look which smell of celery or parsley when crushed.*

SPECIES INFORMATION	
COMMON NAME	Rock Samphire
SCIENTIFIC NAME	Crithmum maritimum
RELATED SPECIES	None
HEIGHT/SPREAD	10–50 cm tall
FLOWERING TIME	June–August
HABITAT	Rocky coasts

Note: A plant of coastal rocks, with divided, fleshy leaves.

Rock Samphire

CARROT AND HOGWEED FAMILY
(Umbelliferae)

Size and appearance: A hairless perennial, with a woody base and sprawling or semi-erect, branched stems 10–50 cm (4–20 in) tall.
Leaves: compound, twice divided into narrow, untoothed, rather pale green, fleshy segments.
Flowers: yellowish, numerous in dense, flat-topped heads or umbels.
Fruits: paired, narrowly egg-shaped, flattened, 1-seeded fruits 5–6 mm (⅕–¼ in) long, with prominent, winged ridges.
Related or similar plants: A distinctive plant with a specialised ecological niche, unlikely to be confused with any other.
Habitat and distribution: Locally common on rocky shores, cliffs, shingle beaches and sea-walls, rarely on sand-dunes or in cliff-top turf, around the coasts of Britain and Ireland north to County Donegal and Galloway, with a few sites further north; on the east coast, no further north than East Anglia.
Flowering time: June to August

ROCK SAMPHIRE, which has an aromatic, unusual taste, was formerly much eaten, either cooked or pickled. The collection of this wholly wild crop was from at least the 16th to the 19th century a significant coastal industry, for example on the Isle of Man and along the chalk cliffs from Kent to the Isle of Wight, immortalised by William Shakespeare in King Lear: 'Half-way down [the cliff] hangs one that gathers samphire, dreadful trade!' The main harvest was in May, before the plants had flowered. Rock Samphire was both vegetable and herbal tonic, a valued source of minerals and vitamins.

Marsh Samphire (p.31), sometimes confused with Rock Samphire, is a very different, annual plant of salt-marshes, still gathered as a wild food crop.

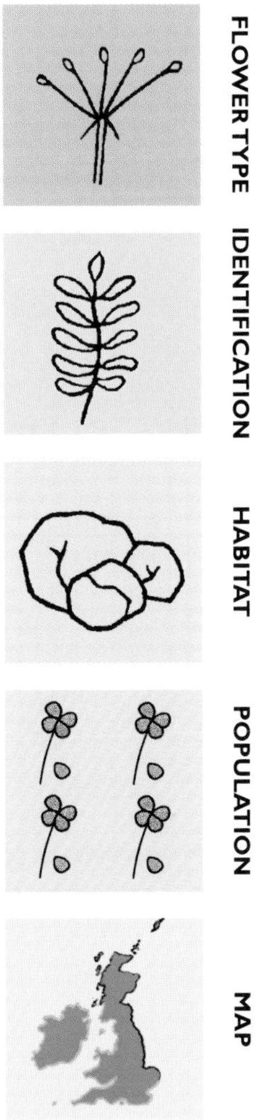

Rock Samphire (Crithmum maritimum) *grows in similar habitats to the previous species but around the English, Welsh and Irish coasts. Its leaves are divided into narrow untoothed, pale green, fleshy segments and smell like shoe polish when crushed.*

Wild Carrot

CARROT AND HOGWEED FAMILY
(Umbelliferae)

SPECIES INFORMATION	
COMMON NAME	Wild Carrot
SCIENTIFIC NAME	Daucus carota
RELATED SPECIES	Wild Parsnip
HEIGHT/SPREAD	20–100 cm tall
FLOWERING TIME	June–September
HABITAT	Dry grassland and roadsides

Note: The ruff beneath the flowers is characteristic.

FLOWER TYPE

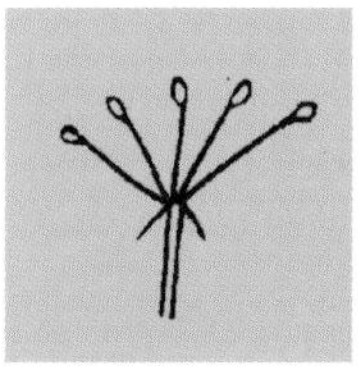

IDENTIFICATION

HABITAT

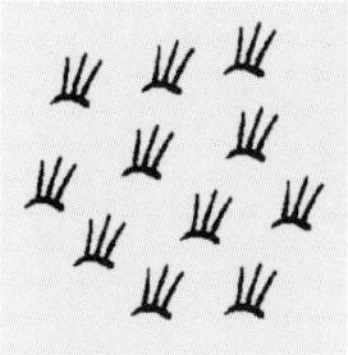

POPULATION

MAP

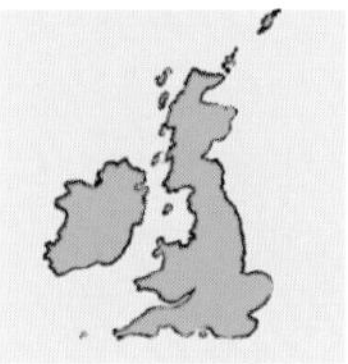

Carrot (Daucus carota) *is the only common umbellifer with conspicuous three-forked or pinnate lower bracts bordering the flat dense umbels of white flowers, the centre flower of which is sometimes a deep red. When flowering is over, the outer spokes close upwards constricting and packing the inner flowers.*

WILD CARROT IS a subspecies of the garden Carrot, but has a thin, pale taproot rather than a swollen, orange one. The concave heads of fruits waving in the wind are a distinctive feature of roadsides and grassland in many districts in summer. It is a very variable species and similar to garden carrot, with which it crosses, especially in North America, where the introduced Wild Carrot is regarded as a weed. On the coast, many plants are shorter and have fleshy, shiny leaves and flat, rather than concave, heads of fruits.

In North America, this plant is known as Queen Anne's Lace, a name that we tend to bestow upon Cow Parsley (p.173). In fact, Queen Anne's Lace is really only a general name for several members of the carrot family that whiten waysides in summer. Various stories try to explain the name. The red floret in the centre could be a drop of blood from the lacemaker's needle! It is also said to commemorate the many children of Queen Anne who died in infancy (giving us a German dynasty of monarchs). Clearly, however, all these white flowers are lacy, and St Anne, mother of the Virgin Mary, is patron saint of lacemakers.

Size and appearance: A rough-hairy annual, biennial or short-lived perennial with erect stems 20–100 cm (8–40 in) tall.

Leaves: Compound, 2–3 times divided into toothed, fern-like segments, smelling of carrot when bruised.

Flowers: White or lilac, numerous in dense, flat-topped, concave or domed heads or umbels 2–6 cm (4/5–2 2/5 in) across, usually with a red or purple, sterile flower in the centre; many deeply divided bracts forming a ruff.

Fruits: Paired, oval, flattened, densely spiny, 1-seeded fruits 2–3 mm (1/12–1/8 in) long.

Related or similar plants: Readily distinguished from other members of the family by the feathery ruff of deeply divided leaf-like bracts below the flowers.

Habitat and distribution: Widespread and common in dry grassland and on sunny banks, especially on chalk and limestone or by the sea, on roadsides and waste ground; throughout, but rare in the uplands and only coastal in the north.

Flowering time: June to September.

SPECIES INFORMATION	
COMMON NAME	Hogweed
SCIENTIFIC NAME	Heracleum sphondylium
RELATED SPECIES	Giant Hogweed
HEIGHT/SPREAD	1–3 m tall
FLOWERING TIME	June–October
HABITAT	Grassland and roadsides

Note: The robust common carrot-like plant of late summer.

Hogweed

CARROT AND HOGWEED FAMILY (Umbelliferae)

Size and appearance: A robust, hairy perennial, with erect, stout, ridged, hollow stems 1–3 m (3–9 ft) tall.

Leaves: Compound, divided into 5 or more lobed and coarsely toothed segments, rough-hairy, smelling strongly when bruised; base of stalk inflated, sheathing.

Flowers: White, sometimes purplish-pink or greenish, numerous in dense, flat-topped heads or umbels up to 25 cm (10 in) across.

Fruits: Paired, broadly oval, flattened, broadly winged, 1-seeded fruits 6–8 mm (¼–⅓ in) long.

Related or similar plants: This is the largest of several carrot-like plants with white flowers (but see Giant Hogweed, below).

Habitat and distribution: A widespread and common plant of rank or rough grassland, roadsides, hedge-banks, woodland margins, streamsides and untended gardens, throughout Britain and Ireland.

Flowering time: June to October.

Top *Seedheads of Hogweed* (Heracleum sphondylium) *covered in hoar frost.*

Bottom *Giant Hogweed* (Heracleum mantegazzianum) *is a similar but titanic plant 2–5 m (6–15 ft) tall, with huge stems, leaves up to 250 cm (6½ ft) long, and flower-heads 20 –50 cm (8–20 in) across. Flowering June–July, this mid-19th century introduction from the Caucasus is a widespread escape from gardens on roadsides and by rivers and streams.*

HOGWEED IS OFTEN DESPISED as a coarse, unsightly weed, but it has a certain grandeur in flower. A few flower-heads sometimes appear during mild winters. The flowers are very attractive to numerous foraging beetles and other insects. It is traditional food for the family pig which was once an essential part of the rural economy; hence the English name. The young shoots can be eaten as a late winter green. In County Kerry, and perhaps elsewhere, the plant is called 'the singer', after the whistling of the winter winds through the dead stems. Hogweed is not poisonous as such, but the sap can induce severe and unpleasant blistering and soreness to the skin in the presence of sunlight. Giant Hogweed, and occasional crosses between it and Hogweed, cause particularly bad burns. Note that several members of the carrot family (perhaps the majority) can cause the same painful condition, which may take some time to heal.

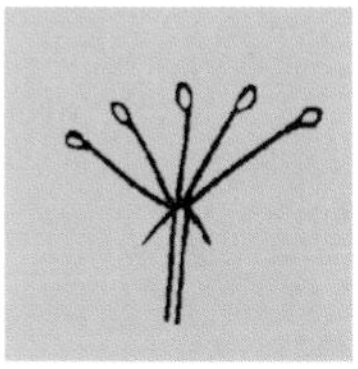

FLOWER TYPE

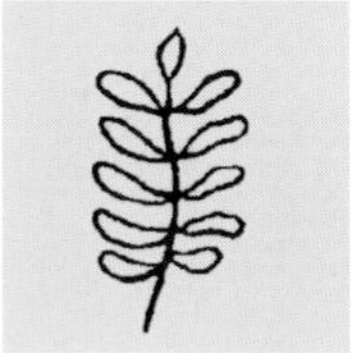

IDENTIFICATION

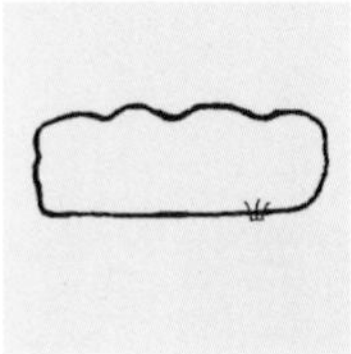

HABITAT

POPULATION

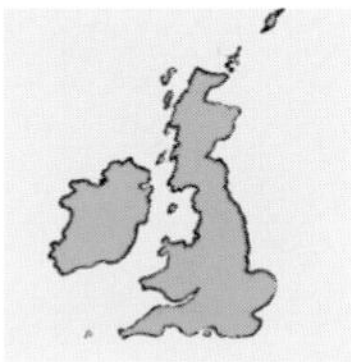

MAP

Hemlock

CARROT AND HOGWEED FAMILY (Umbelliferae)

SPECIES INFORMATION	
COMMON NAME	Hemlock
SCIENTIFIC NAME	Conium maculatum
RELATED SPECIES	Fool's Parsley
HEIGHT/SPREAD	100–250 cm tall
FLOWERING TIME	June–August
HABITAT	Damp waste gound

Note: The tall roadside carrot-like plant with feathery leaves.

FLOWER TYPE

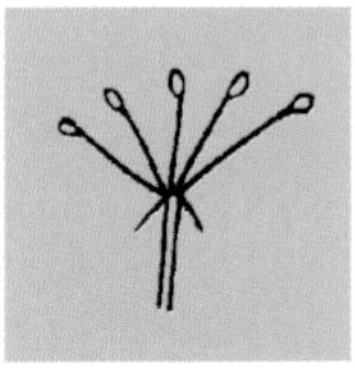

IDENTIFICATION

HABITAT

POPULATION

MAP

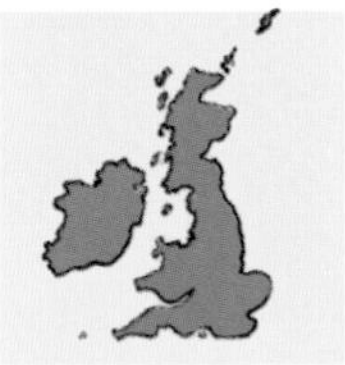

Size and appearance: A rather elegant, hairless annual or biennial, with erect, hollow, purple-spotted stems 100–250 cm (40–100 in) tall.

Leaves: Compound, divided 2–4 times into toothed, fern-like segments, smelling mousy when bruised.

Flowers: White, numerous in dense, flat-topped heads or umbels 3–6 cm ($1\frac{1}{5}$–$2\frac{2}{5}$ in) across.

Fruits: Paired, almost spherical, 1-seeded fruits 6–8 mm ($\frac{1}{4}$–$\frac{1}{3}$ in) long, with wavy ridges.

Related or similar plants: Readily distinguished from other members of the family by the tall, purple-spotted stems; Hemlock Water-dropwort (p.181), of wet places, is quite different, and has cylindrical fruits.

Habitat and distribution: Locally common by streams, on damp waste ground, rubbish-tips and road-verges, often around buildings or ruins and very abundant along new roads; throughout, but rare and mainly coastal in Scotland, and local in Ireland.

Flowering time: June to August.

HEMLOCK IS VERY POISONOUS, but fortunately the plant has a sinister, if not unattractive, look about it – and is difficult to confuse with other species in the family. The Greek philosopher Socrates is reputed to have been executed by drinking a fatal infusion of this plant in 399 BC. However, as Plato recorded that his end was peaceful, it is likely the fatal draught also contained opium and other drugs. Death from poisoning by this plant would be decidedly unpleasant and lingering. *Coneion*, corrupted to *Conium* in the Latin of the scientific name, was the Ancient Greek name for this plant.

Top right *Hemlock* (Conium maculatum) – *dead stems in winter*

Bottom Right *Fool's Parsley* (Aethusa cynapium) *is another poisonous plant with much-divided, feathery leaves and white flowers, its ridged, egg-shaped fruits 2–4 mm ($\frac{1}{12}$–$\frac{1}{6}$ in) long. Flowering June–September, it has similar distribution on cultivated land.*

SPECIES INFORMATION	
COMMON NAME	Hemlock Water-dropwort
SCIENTIFIC NAME	Oenanthe crocata
RELATED SPECIES	Other water-dropworts
HEIGHT/SPREAD	50–150 cm tall
FLOWERING TIME	June–September
HABITAT	Damp waste grounds and marshes

Note: A large carrot-like plant that forms dense stands by rivers.

Hemlock Water-dropwort

CARROT AND HOGWEED FAMILY (Umbelliferae)

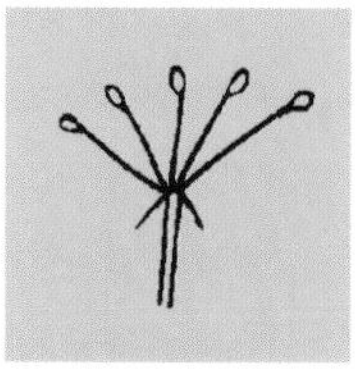

FLOWER TYPE

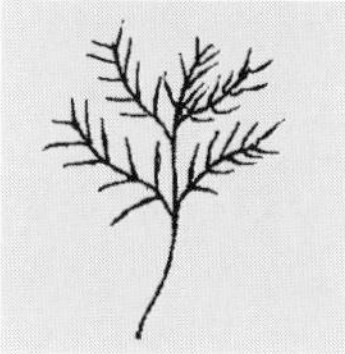

IDENTIFICATION

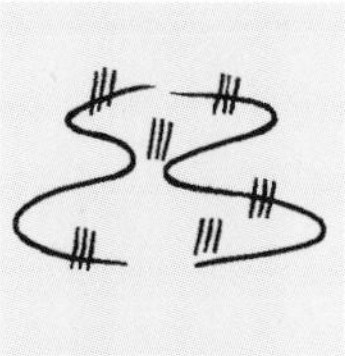

HABITAT

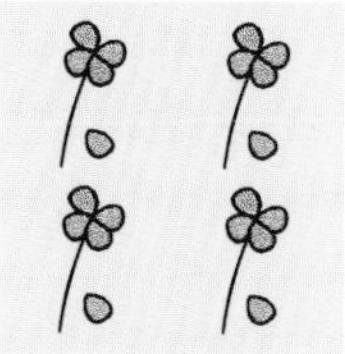

POPULATION

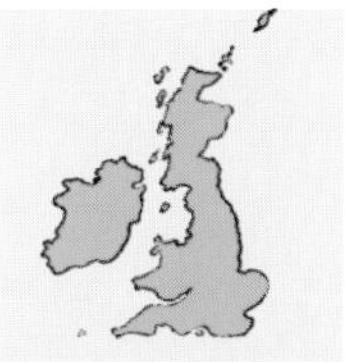

MAP

Size and appearance: A leafy, hairless perennial, with clusters of yellowish tap-root-like tubers and stout, erect, much-branched stems 50–150 cm (20–60 in) tall.

Leaves: Compound, divided 2–4 times into flat parsley-like segments.

Flowers: White, numerous in dense, domed heads or umbels 5–15 cm (2–6 in) across.

Fruits: Paired, cylindrical, 1-seeded fruits 4–6 mm (1/6–1/4 in) long.

Related or similar plants: Other Water-dropworts also occur in wet places.

Habitat and distribution: Widespread and locally common by streams and rivers, and in marshes and on damp waste ground, mostly on lime-poor soils; throughout, but absent from large parts of eastern England, northern Scotland and central Ireland.

Flowering time: June to September.

HEMLOCK WATER-DROPWORT sometimes forms large, dense stands on wet ground beside rivers, or along the banks of streams. It is one of seven native water-dropworts, all plants of wet places, either on land or partly submerged.

The others are more local or likely to be overlooked, although Parsley Water-dropwort (*Oenanthe lachenalii*), with white flowers and leaves twice-divided into narrow segments, is sometimes conspicuous in brackish, seaside marshes. All are poisonous.

Note that Hemlock Water-dropwort is a very poisonous plant, especially the tubers. Over the years several people have been severely poisoned as a result of mistaking the leaves for celery or the roots for parsnips. More than half the cases have proved to be fatal. It is probably best to avoid eating all wild members of the carrot family, many of which, like the fungi, can be difficult to tell apart. Animals sometimes eat the roots after ditch clearing has exposed them, again often with fatal consequences.

Hemlock Water-dropwort (Oenanthe crocata) *is a stout hairless perennial that is widespread by streams and rivers and in marshy areas. It has hollow stems and its glossy compound leaves are divided two to four times into leaflets with wedge-shaped bases.*

Angelica

CARROT AND HOGWEED FAMILY (Umbelliferae)

SPECIES INFORMATION	
COMMON NAME	Angelica
SCIENTIFIC NAME	Angelica sylvestris
RELATED SPECIES	Garden Angelica
HEIGHT/SPREAD	50–200 cm tall
FLOWERING TIME	June–September
HABITAT	Damp, grassy places and woods

Note: The whole plant is often tinged purple.

FLOWER TYPE

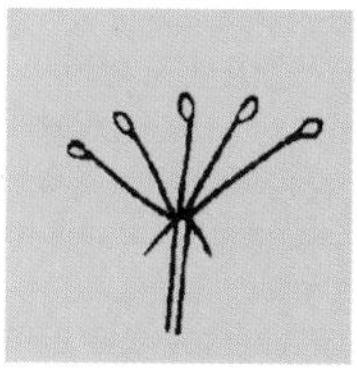

IDENTIFICATION

HABITAT

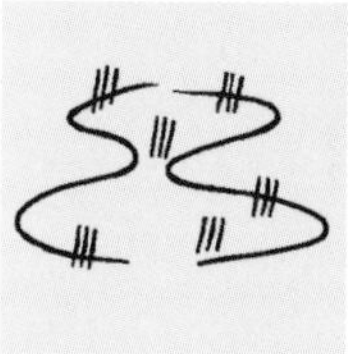

POPULATION

MAP

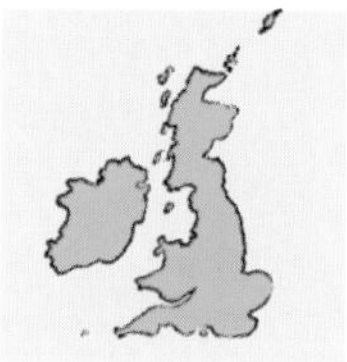

ANGELICA IS A FINE, stately plant that stands out from among marsh vegetation in high summer. It is a variable species, which is hardly surprising since it is so widespread, occurring even on the remotest and smallest islands. Dwarf, compact plants not more than 30 cm (12 in) tall occur on western and north-western sea-cliffs, and even smaller, more slender, ones in summer-dry lakes or turloughs in western Ireland.

The old-fashioned, green cake decoration known as angelica is made from the candied stems of another species, Garden Angelica (*Angelica archangelica*). A native of northern Eurasia, it is a robust plant with more steeply domed flower-heads, and is locally naturalised, especially along the Thames in and around London, and by the Manchester Ship Canal.

Size and appearance: A robust, almost hairless, often purple-tinged perennial, with stout, erect, hollow, purplish stems 50–200 cm (20–80 in) tall.

Leaves: Compound, stalked, up to 60 cm (24 in) long, divided 2–3 times into oval, toothed segments; base of stalks sheathing.

Flowers: White or pinkish, numerous in dense, domed heads or umbels 5–15 cm (2–6 in) across.

Fruits: Paired, egg-shaped, flattened, 1-seeded fruits 4–5 mm (1/6–1/5 in) long, with 4 broad wings.

Related or similar plants: Hogweed (p.179) is also very robust with somewhat similar compound leaves, but is hairy, coarser and much less a plant of damp places.

Habitat and distribution: Widespread and common in marshy ground, in damp, open woods, scrub and grassland, by streams and ditches, and on damp or coastal cliffs, throughout Britain and Ireland.

Flowering time: June to September.

Angelica (Angelica sylvestris) *is a robust plant, often suffused with purple and with the inflated sheaths at the base of the leaf and flower stalks. It is widespread and common in wet woods, fens and damp grassy places as well as on coastal cliffs.*

SPECIES INFORMATION	
COMMON NAME	Alexanders
SCIENTIFIC NAME	Smyrnium olusatrum
RELATED SPECIES	None
HEIGHT/SPREAD	50–150 cm tall
FLOWERING TIME	April–June
HABITAT	Coastal regions and waste ground
Note: The large carrot-like yellow flower of coastal hedgerows.	

Alexanders

CARROT AND HOGWEED FAMILY (Umbelliferae)

Size and appearance: A leafy, hairless perennial, with stout, erect, much-branched stems 50–150 cm (20–60 in) tall.
Leaves: Compound, divided 2–3 times into elliptical, irregularly toothed or sometimes lobed segments, dark green, shiny, with an aromatic smell when bruised.
Flowers: Yellow, numerous in dense, slightly domed heads or umbels 5–15 cm (2–6 in) across.
Fruits: Paired, egg-shaped, black, 1-seeded fruits 6–8 mm (¼–⅓ in) long, with 3 ridges.
Related or similar plants: A distinctive plant unlikely to be confused with any other.
Habitat and distribution: Widespread near the sea in hedges and grassy roadsides, on cliffs and banks, by streams and on waste ground and around villages, around most of the coast north to north Yorkshire, with a few scattered sites in Scotland, and around much of the Irish coast; sometimes inland, especially in East Anglia.
Flowering time: April to June.

ALEXANDERS IS A CURIOUS and distinctive landscape feature of many coastal areas. In North Norfolk, for example, it begins to appear abundantly in the hedges as you approach the sea, a belt of shiny green leaves in late winter and yellow flowers in April to May. It is much less a coastal plant than a sub-coastal one, although it does occur in sand-dunes and seaside waste ground. In East Anglia especially, it sometimes turns up on roadsides far inland. The plant is not native, but was introduced from southern Europe, perhaps by returning Crusaders. It can often be found around the ruins of castles and abbeys. Alexanders was a valued late-winter green, cooked like spinach with other vegetables and herbs. The young shoots can be eaten like celery, and the flower-buds added to salads.

This intriguing plant has a fine pair of names. The English name may be a descendant of an older Parsley of Macedon, reflecting the plant's exotic origin. Alexander the Great, Macedonia's most famous son, has long been a figure in popular legend. The first half of the scientific name comes from the Greek word for the celebrated spice myrrh (*smyrna*), because of the plant's aromatic smell.

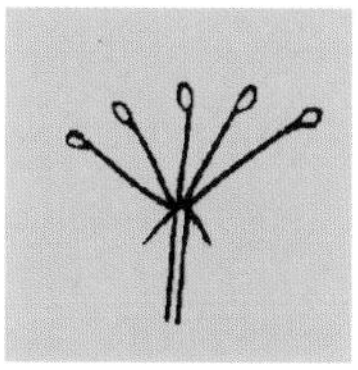
FLOWER TYPE

IDENTIFICATION

HABITAT

POPULATION

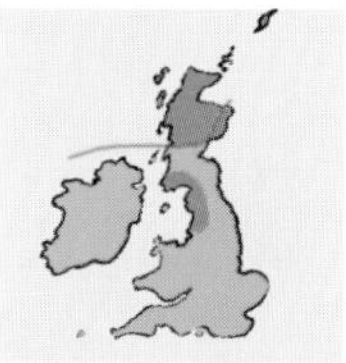
MAP

Alexanders (Smyrnium olusatrum) *is a stout bushy plant with large, glossy, dark green leaves divided into broad leaflets. Widespread and locally common in hedge banks and waste places near the sea, it has yellow domed umbels that appear early in the year.*

Fool's Watercress

CARROT AND HOGWEED FAMILY
(Umbelliferae)

SPECIES INFORMATION	
COMMON NAME	Fool's Watercress
SCIENTIFIC NAME	Apium nodiflorum
RELATED SPECIES	Celery
HEIGHT/SPREAD	Stems 20–100 cm long
FLOWERING TIME	July–August
HABITAT	Ditches, pools and streams
Note: A watercress-like plant with carrot-like flowers.	

FLOWER TYPE

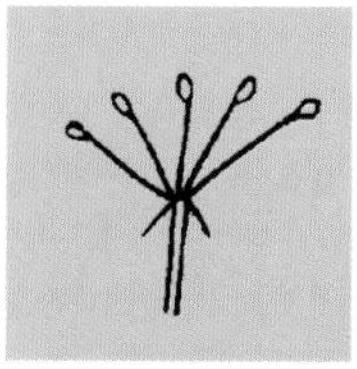

IDENTIFICATION

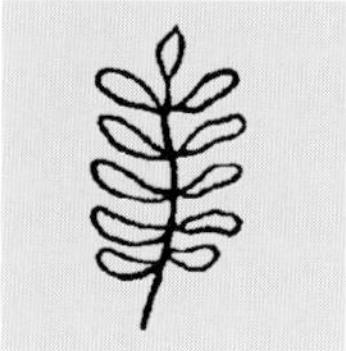

HABITAT

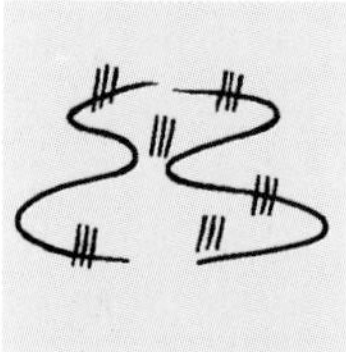

POPULATION

MAP

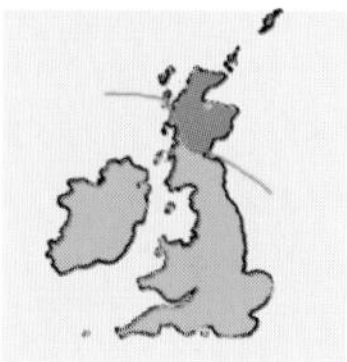

FOOL'S WATERCRESS is often abundant, looking like Watercress (p.83) and choking small streams in the same way. One can tell the two apart with a little care, and Fool's Watercress is happily not poisonous, Indeed, people in the West Country used to add it to pies and pasties. Nevertheless, it is best as a rule to avoid eating wild members of the carrot family: for example, the poisonous water-dropworts grow in similar wet habitats.

The plant resembles the closely related Celery (*Apium graveolens*), a garden biennial that is also a wild native of brackish marshes. Too tough to be worth eating, the plant has erect stems, is more slender than garden Celery, and smells strongly of that vegetable. It is local around the coasts of England, Wales and Ireland.

Size and appearance: A hairless perennial, with numerous, prostrate or sprawling, branched, hollow stems 20–100 cm (8–40 in) long.

Leaves: Compound, divided into 2–6 pairs of oval or spear-shaped, regularly toothed leaflets.

Flowers: Yellow, numerous in dense, slightly domed heads or umbels 5–15 cm (2–6 in) across.

Fruits: Paired, egg-shaped, 1-seeded fruits 2–3 mm ($\frac{1}{12}$–$\frac{1}{8}$ in) long.

Related or similar plants: In leaf, very similar to the unrelated Watercress (p.83), but with hollow stems, and regularly toothed leaflets, and without the strong mustard taste of Watercress.

Habitat and distribution: Widespread and common in wet ditches, shallow pools and streams, throughout Britain and Ireland.

Flowering time: July–August.

Fool's Watercress (Apium nodiflorum) *has sometimes been mistaken for watercress because of the compound divided leaves; however, the rayed umbel of flowers soon shows this to be a member of the carrot family.*

SPECIES INFORMATION	
COMMON NAME	Pignut, Earthnut
SCIENTIFIC NAME	Conopodium majus
RELATED SPECIES	None
HEIGHT/SPREAD	20–80 cm tall
FLOWERING TIME	May–June
HABITAT	Woods and grassland

Note: A distinctive plant with upright, solitary stems.

Pignut

CARROT AND HOGWEED FAMILY (Umbelliferae)

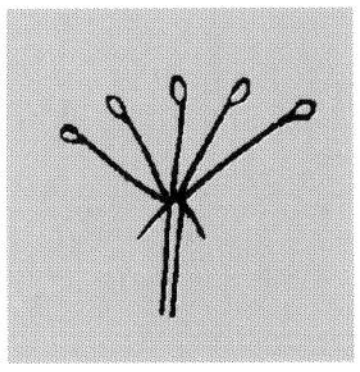

FLOWER TYPE

IDENTIFICATION

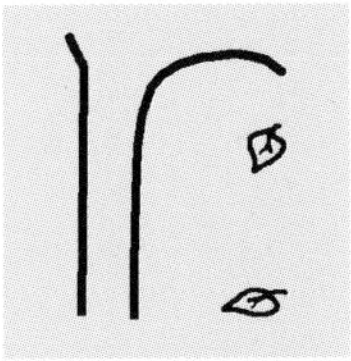

HABITAT

POPULATION

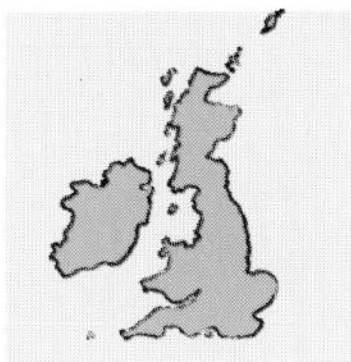

MAP

Size and appearance: A slender perennial, with an almost spherical, dark brown tuber and a single, erect, branched stem 20–80 cm (8–32 in) tall.
Leaves: Mostly basal and soon withering, compound, long-stalked, divided 2–3 times into very narrow, feathery segments.
Flowers: White, numerous in dense, flat-topped heads or umbels, 2.5-7.5 cm (1–3 in) across.
Fruits: Paired, egg-shaped, 1-seeded fruits 3–4 mm (⅛–⅙ in) long, each with a beak.
Related or similar plants: The very narrow, much-divided leaf-segments distinguish this from most members of the family; Fennel (see under Wild Parsnip, p.175) has similar leaves that smell of aniseed.
Habitat and distribution: Widespread and common in hedge-banks, open woods and heathy grassland on well-drained, usually more lime-poor soils; throughout, but it is much more local over much of East Anglia, and the midlands and south of Ireland.
Flowering time: May–June.

THIS PLANT IS a frequent sight in woods and hedgerows in late spring, soon withering once the fruits are ripe in high summer. Its life-history is more like that of Bluebell (p.338) or other bulbous lilies than that of a typical carrot-like plant. Both Pignut and Earthnut refer to the edible, starch-rich tubers, some 15 cm (6 in) or more down, which were once both forage for pigs and a free snack for industrious country children, before the discovery of potato crisps. Nobody has ever tried to grow this plant as a field crop, and it is more a plant of wooded places.

Villagers in Turkey and elsewhere eat similar tubers belonging to other members of this family that are found in cultivated land.

Pignut (Conopodium majus) *is a delicate umbellifer found in open woods and heathy grassland on well-drained, usually acid, soils. It appears in May, its white flowers contrasting with the bluebells and red campion.*

Ling

HEATHER FAMILY
(Ericaceae)

SPECIES INFORMATION	
COMMON NAME	Ling, Heather
SCIENTIFIC NAME	Calluna vulgaris
RELATED SPECIES	Bell Heather, Cross-leaved Heath
HEIGHT/SPREAD	20–60 cm tall
FLOWERING TIME	July–September
HABITAT	Lime-poor heaths and moors

Note: The commonest heather.

FLOWER TYPE

IDENTIFICATION

HABITAT

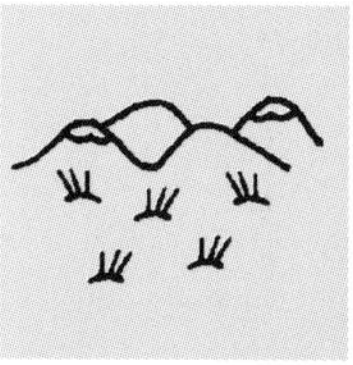

POPULATION

MAP

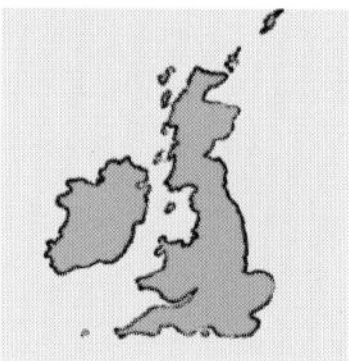

Habitat and distribution: Common on heaths, moors and mountains, the drier parts of bogs, open woods on sandy soils and lime-poor sand-dunes; throughout, but absent from large lowland areas of central England.
Flowering time: Late July to September.

Size and appearance: Erect, evergreen, variably downy shrublet, woody below and much-branched above, 20–60 cm (8–24 in) tall, sometimes up to 100 cm (35 in).
Leaves: Small, stiff, overlapping in 2 opposite rows, clasping the stem, narrowly oblong.
Flowers: Tiny, bell-shaped, pinkish-purple, sometimes lilac or white, in leafy spikes; corolla and the slightly longer petal-like calyx 4-lobed.
Fruits: Small, spherical capsules enclosed by the dry, persistent flower.
Related or similar plants: Other heathers (p.187) have larger flowers and leaves that do not overlap.

LING IS ONE OF THE most welcome flowers of late summer, colouring moorland and heaths with its massed pinkish-purple spikes. It was formerly an important economic resource in the Highlands of Scotland and other upland regions, being used for thatch, bedding material for people and animals, kindling for fires, and for making brooms and ropes. It provided an orange dye for cloth and was the basis of heather beer, the original recipe for which is said to be lost. The flowers are still an important source of nectar for bees, which produce from it a flavoursome dark honey.

Regular burning and grazing keeps Ling plants from becoming too woody and overgrown, especially for the management of grouse, which feed on the young shoots. As well as fire and grazing, Ling tolerates trampling and salt spray. Thus it covers such huge areas of marginal land. It is also a popular and much seen garden plant, including double- and white-flowered cultivars and those with yellowish leaves.

Ling (Calluna vulgaris) *is the heather that turns huge areas of moorland purple in late summer. It can vary in flower colour from pinkish-purple to almost white. The bottom photograph shows a paler coloured ling on the right and the closely related Bell Heather* (Erica cinerea) *on the left.*

SPECIES INFORMATION	
COMMON NAME	Bell Heather
SCIENTIFIC NAME	Erica cinerea
RELATED SPECIES	Cross-leaved Heath, Ling
HEIGHT/SPREAD	10–75 cm tall
FLOWERING TIME	July–September
HABITAT	Lime-poor heaths and moors

Note: The common purple bell heather.

Bell Heather

HEATHER FAMILY
(Ericaceae)

Size and appearance: Erect, evergreen, hairless shrublet, rather woody below and branched above, 10–75 cm (4–30 in) tall.
Leaves: In 3s, small, very narrow, with inrolled margins.
Flowers: Egg-shaped, sac-like, 4–8 mm (⅙–⅓ in) long, reddish-purple, sometimes white, scented, in compact or elongate clusters.
Fruits: Small, spherical capsules enclosed by the dry, persistent flower.
Related or similar plants: Cross-leaved Heath has pink flowers and greyish leaves in 4s; Ling (p.186) has smaller flowers and overlapping leaves in 2 ranks.

Habitat and distribution: Common on drier heaths and moors, rocky ground and open woods on sandy soils; throughout, especially in the north and west, but absent from large lowland areas of central England, East Anglia and much of the Irish midlands.
Flowering time: July to September, slightly earlier to come into flower than Ling.

THIS PLANT PROVIDES a fine floral display in late summer, especially when it grows with Ling (p.186) and the late-flowering Western Gorse (see under Gorse, p.113) in western and south-western Britain and Ireland. The flowers are an important source of nectar for bees.

Whereas Ling (p.186) has a wide distribution in Europe, and extends to Anatolia and north-west Africa, Bell Heather is restricted to Atlantic Europe. Its range is centred on the British Isles and France, extending south to central Spain and northern Italy and north-east to southern Norway. It is therefore, like the Bluebell (p.338), one of our more special wild plants.

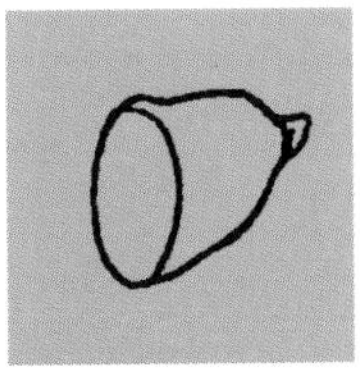

FLOWER TYPE

IDENTIFICATION

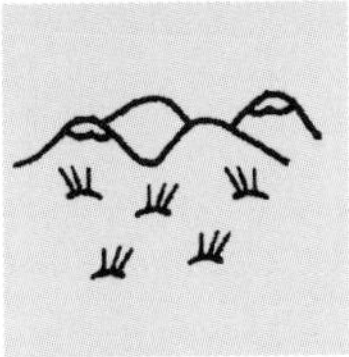

HABITAT

POPULATION

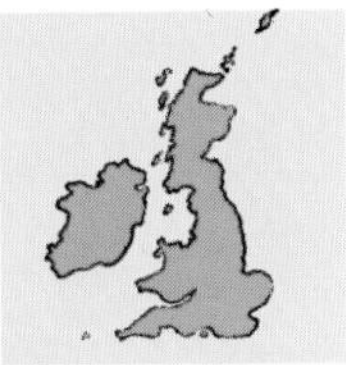

MAP

Bottom *Cross-leaved Heath* (Erica tetralix) *is similar to Bell Heather but has greyish leaves which are paler beneath, fringed with hairs with downward-rolling margins. It has compact heads of rose-pink flowers.*

Bilberry

HEATHER FAMILY
(Ericaceae)

SPECIES INFORMATION	
COMMON NAME	Bilberry, Blaeberry, Whortleberry
SCIENTIFIC NAME	Vaccinium myrtillus
RELATED SPECIES	Heathers
HEIGHT/SPREAD	20–40 cm tall
FLOWERING TIME	April–July
HABITAT	Lime-poor heaths and moors

Note: The common wild berry of moors and heaths.

FLOWER TYPE

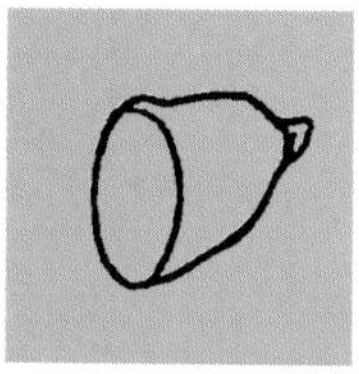

IDENTIFICATION

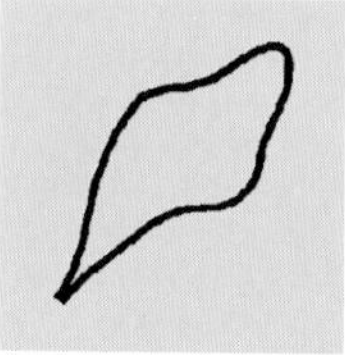

HABITAT

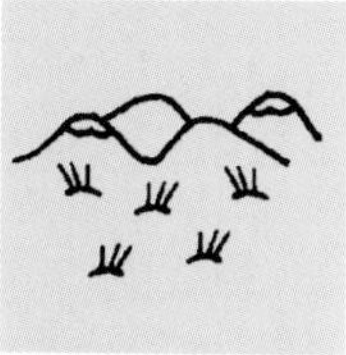

POPULATION

MAP

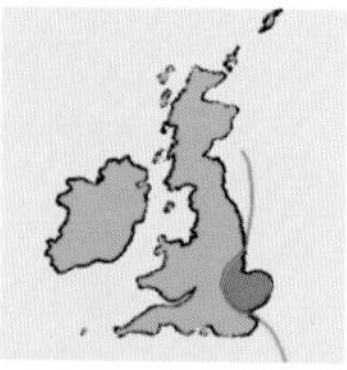

Size and appearance: Erect, hairless shrublet, rather woody below, the stems 20–40 cm (8–16 in) tall, angled and little-branched.

Leaves: 10–20 mm (⅖–⅘ in) long, oval, pointed, neatly toothed, bright green, turning red and falling in autumn.

Flowers: Solitary or in pairs, almost spherical, sac-like, 4–6 mm (⅙–¼ in) long, pale green tinged pink.

Fruits: Spherical berries 5–8 mm (⅕–⅓ in) across, black with bluish bloom.

Related or similar plants: Bilberry is the commonest of several berry-bearing shrublets in the heather family, such as Cowberry.

Habitat and distribution: Common and sometimes abundant on mountains, moors, dry heaths, rocky ground and open woods of pine, oak and birch on well-drained, lime-poor soils; throughout but uncommon over much of central England and East Anglia, and rather scattered in the Irish midlands.

Flowering time: April to July, but also conspicuous in fruit July to August.

THE EDIBLE, SWEET FRUITS used to be gathered widely, but are today found in just a few specialised shops and restaurants. They are good raw or made into tarts, jellies and jams, and such dishes remain popular on the Continent – like the French *tarte aux myrtes*. The fruits also yield a purple dye.

The Irish name for Bilberry is fraochán. In some country districts of Ireland people still celebrate the last Sunday in July, a traditional time to pick bilberries, as Fraoghán Sunday, a survival of the ancient pagan festival of Lúnasa. In Shropshire and elsewhere the bilberry harvest (as much for dye as for food) was a major event in the summer, making a considerable contribution to the local economy.

Top and middle *Bilberry is one of several related shrublets in the heather family with black or red berries, often inedible; all grow on lime-por soils of bog, moor or mountain.*

Bottom *The next most widespread, Cowberry* (Vaccinium vitis-idaea) *has leathery, untoothed leaves, small, drooping clusters of flowers and red, acid berries. It is common on moors in Scotland, but more local in northern England, Wales and Ireland.*

SPECIES INFORMATION	
COMMON NAME	Common Wintergreen
SCIENTIFIC NAME	Pyrola minor
RELATED SPECIES	Other wintergreens
HEIGHT/SPREAD	10–25 cm tall
FLOWERING TIME	June–August
HABITAT	Woods, moors and sand-dunes

Note: The loose spike of hanging flowers on a leafless stem.

Common Wintergreen

WINTERGREEN FAMILY (Pyrolaceae)

Size and appearance: Evergreen, hairless perennial with a creeping rhizome and erect stems 10–25 cm (4–10 in) tall.
Leaves: All in a loose basal rosette, up to 4 cm (1⅗ in) across, stalked, elliptical, rounded, shortly and bluntly toothed.
Flowers: White or pinkish, bulbously bowl-shaped, 5–7 mm (⅕–⅓ in) across, hanging, in a loose spike; petals 5.
Fruits: Small rounded capsules.
Related or similar plants: Superficially similar to Lily-of-the-Valley (p.346), which has 2–3 large basal leaves.
Habitat and distribution: Widespread but local in damp, humus-rich soil in woods, on moors and rocky ground, and sometimes in damp slacks of sand-dunes; mainly in northern Britain, but also in central southern England; rare in Ireland, mainly in Ulster.
Flowering time: June to August.

IN THE NORTH, Common Wintergreen tends to grow in a range of habitats on lime-poor soils; in the south it is usually in woods on lime-rich soils. It is the commonest of the five wintergreens that occur in Britain, the others being local or rare. Round-leaved Wintergreen (*Pyrola rotundifolia*), with a more dish-shaped flower than Common Wintergreen, and a conspicuously protruding stigma, occurs mainly in Scotland, in pine woodland and on mountain ledges. However, on coasts from North Devon to Cumbria, also at one site in County Wexford, it grows in the slacks of sand-dunes, locally in great crowds.

Another member of the wintergreen family, Yellow Bird's-nest, is a saprophyte, deriving nutrition from decaying leaf-litter. It is described under Bird's-nest Orchid (p.367), which is very similar in both appearance and ecology.

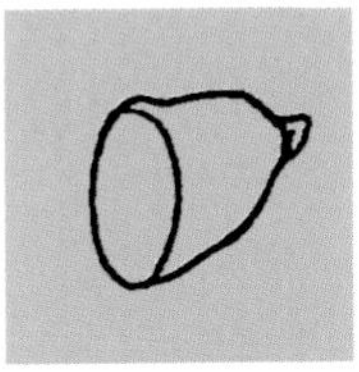

FLOWER TYPE

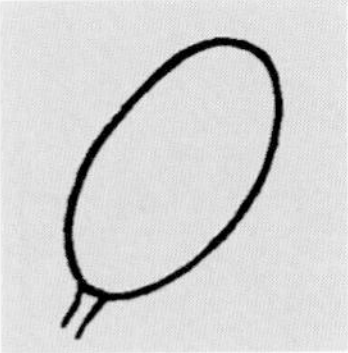

IDENTIFICATION

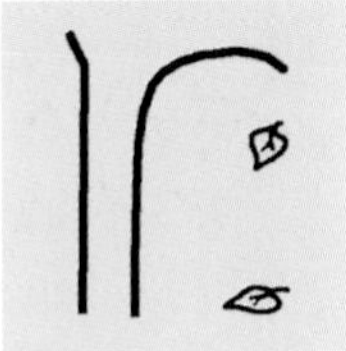

HABITAT

POPULATION

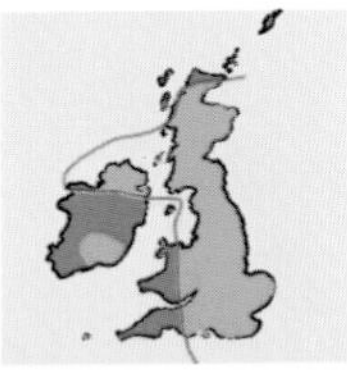

MAP

Top *Common Wintergreen* (Pyrola minor) *occurs on leaf-mould in woods in Scotland as well as moors and rocky ground.*

Bottom *Round-leaved wintergreen* (Pyrola rotundifolia) *has recently been found colonising worked-out gravel pits in south-east England, a long way from its traditional habitats in Scotland or the west country.*

Primrose

PRIMROSE FAMILY
(Primulaceae)

SPECIES INFORMATION	
COMMON NAME	Primrose
SCIENTIFIC NAME	Primula vulgaris
RELATED SPECIES	Cowslip, Oxslip
HEIGHT/SPREAD	5–20 cm tall
FLOWERING TIME	February–May
HABITAT	Woodland, hedgerows, old pastures

Note: The large, scented flowers, one to a stalk, are unmistakable.

FLOWER TYPE

IDENTIFICATION

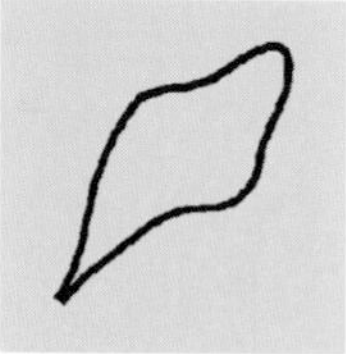

HABITAT

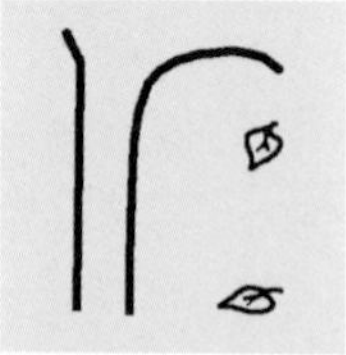

POPULATION

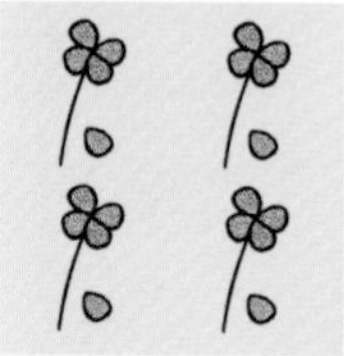

MAP

Size and appearance: A tufted perennial with rosettes of leaves and numerous solitary flowers on slender leafless stalks 5–20 cm (2–8 in) tall.
Leaves: Spoon-shaped, tapered into a winged stalk, wrinkled, downy beneath.
Flowers: 20–40 mm (¾–½ in) across, pale yellow with a darker centre, fragrant; sepals forming a bell-shaped, pleated tube.
Fruits: Egg-shaped capsule, enclosed within persistent calyx.
Related or similar plants: Cowslip (p.191) has smaller, deeper yellow flowers massed in a head; Oxlip (see Cowslip p.191) has 1-sided heads of primrose-like flowers.
Habitat and distribution: Common on well-drained soils in open woodland, scrub, old pastures and churchyards, on grassy banks, railway cuttings and embankments, sea-cliffs and sometimes sand-dunes; locally absent however, especially near conurbations, owing to pillage by gardeners (although this has been exaggerated).
Flowering time: February to May, but from October to November onwards in milder western areas.

PRIMROSES ARE ONE of the best-loved and most familiar of all our wild flowers, and equally popular in cottage-style or 'wild' gardens. The name derives from the Latin *prima rosa* (first rose).

Primroses often cross with Cowslips where the two grow together, producing progeny rather similar to garden polyanthus, but always with primrose-yellow flowers. Where wild Primroses cross with garden Primrose and polyanthus the progeny may display an array of form and colour. The occasional pink or red Primrose in the wild probably results from such a cross.

The flowers are either 'pin', with the pin-like female stigma visible at the mouth, or 'thrum', with a ring of male stamens visible. A visiting insect brushes against either male or female parts and thus transfers pollen between different flowers.

SPECIES INFORMATION	
COMMON NAME	Cowslip
SCIENTIFIC NAME	Primula veris
RELATED SPECIES	Primrose
HEIGHT/SPREAD	5–10 cm tall
FLOWERING TIME	April–May
HABITAT	Grassland and woodland margins

Note: A familiar and unmistakable spring flower.

Cowslip

PRIMROSE FAMILY

(Primulaceae)

FLOWER TYPE

IDENTIFICATION

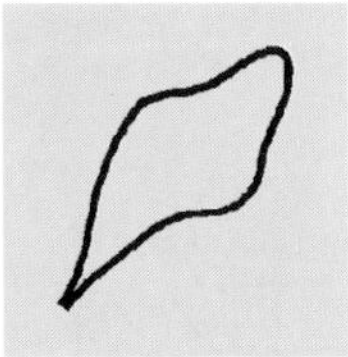

HABITAT

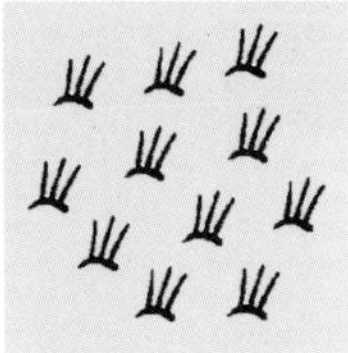

POPULATION

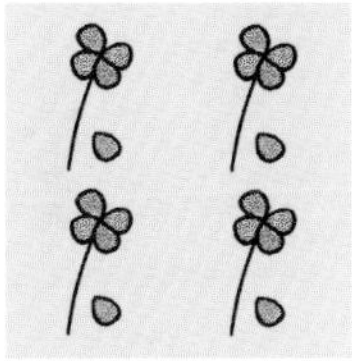

MAP

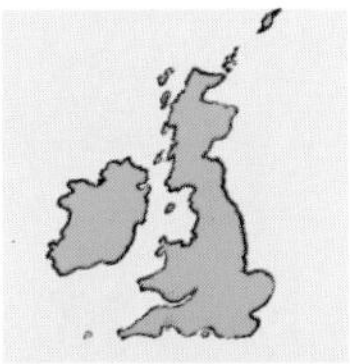

Size and appearance: Tufted, downy perennial with rosettes of leaves and flowers on leafless stalks 5–10 cm (2–4 in) tall.
Leaves: All basal, more or less oval, contracted abruptly into stalk, indistinctly toothed, wrinkled.
Flowers: 8–25 mm (1/5–1 in) across, golden-yellow with orange spot at the base of each petal lobe, in nodding 1-sided cluster; calyx bell-shaped, pleated, pale green.
Fruits: Capsules enclosed within persistent calyx-tube.
Related or similar plants: Primrose (p.190) has larger, always solitary flowers; hybrids with Primrose and Oxlip have larger, paler flowers.
Habitat and distribution: Widespread but rather local in old meadows and pastures, on railway cuttings and embankments, coastal cliffs and road-verges, usually on lime-rich or clayey soils.
Flowering time: April to May.

ONE OF OUR MOST familiar and best-loved wild flowers, although local in Scotland, sadly reduced by the destruction of grassland by modern agriculture, but now returning along motorway verges and other newly sown grassland. It sometimes crosses with Primrose to form a handsome, Polyanthus-like hybrid ('False Oxlip').

Top and bottom left *Cowslip* (Primula veris) *carpeting chalk downland is not often seen in this abundance now.*

Bottom right *Oxlip* (Primula elatior) *is a scarce plant of woods over boulder clay in East Anglia, flowering March–May. It tolerates wet soils and shade better than either Primrose or Cowslip. The pale yellow flowers, in a nodding 1-sided cluster, are 15–30 mm (1/16–1/8 in) across and the leaves are abruptly contracted into the stalk. Cowslip* (Primula Veris) *carpeting chalk downland is not often seen in this abundance now.*

Bird's-eye Primrose

PRIMROSE FAMILY
(Primulaceae)

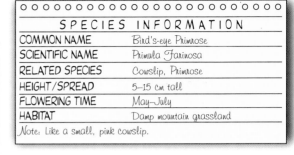

SPECIES INFORMATION	
COMMON NAME	Bird's-eye Primrose
SCIENTIFIC NAME	Primula farinosa
RELATED SPECIES	Cowslip, Primrose
HEIGHT/SPREAD	5–15 cm tall
FLOWERING TIME	May–July
HABITAT	Damp mountain grassland

Note: Like a small, pink cowslip.

FLOWER TYPE

IDENTIFICATION
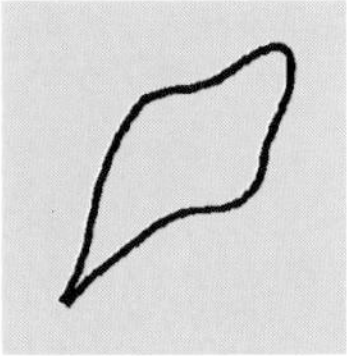

HABITAT

POPULATION

MAP
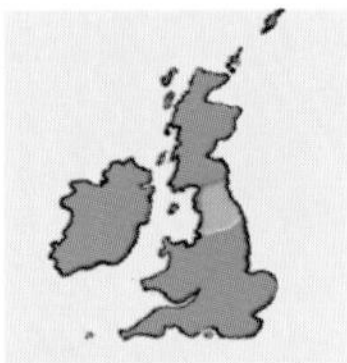

Size and appearance: Small, tufted perennial with rosettes of leaves and flowers on leafless, floury stalks 5–15 cm (2–6 in) tall.
Leaves: All basal, spoon-shaped, pale green on upper surface, floury and white beneath, the margin with blunt teeth.
Flowers: 8–16 mm (⅓–⅔ in) across, pink to lilac with a central yellow eye, in an upright cluster; calyx floury, often purplish.
Fruits: Capsules enclosed within persistent calyx-tube.
Related or similar plants: Cowslip (p.191) has yellow flowers; Primrose (p.191) has larger, always solitary flowers.
Habitat and distribution: Local in damp mountain grassland and by streams on limestone in northern England.
Flowering time: May to July.

ALTHOUGH LOCAL in distribution, this is a characteristic wild flower of early summer in parts of the Pennines, especially some of the Yorkshire Dales. It is a mountain plant with an interesting distribution, common in the Alps but not found either in Scandinavia or in the Scottish mountains. In Britain it extends from sea-level to over 500 m (1500 ft) of altitude.

It grows with other moisture-loving plants such as Grass-of-Parnassus (p.97) in damp pastures, around springs and along streams. It has decreased over the last 50 years, but locally survives in abundance, especially in steep-sided limestone valleys where the grassland has not been overgrazed or 'improved' with fertiliser.

Bird's-eye Primrose (Primula farinosa), *a charming small perennial with a rosette of pale green, blunt-toothed, narrow-lanceolate leaves which are white beneath. At the top of a leafless stalk, there is a cluster of lilac-pink flowers with a central yellow eye. Found near springs, streams and damp pastures.*

SPECIES INFORMATION	
COMMON NAME	Water Violet
SCIENTIFIC NAME	Hottonia palustris
RELATED SPECIES	Cowslip, Primrose
HEIGHT/SPREAD	30–80 cm tall
FLOWERING TIME	May–July
HABITAT	Shallow, still or slow moving water

Note: The flower-clusters are like whorls of small primroses.

Water Violet

PRIMROSE FAMILY (Primulaceae)

Size and appearance: Almost hairless, aquatic perennial with flowers in whorls on rather stout, erect, leafless stalks 30–80 cm (12–32 in) tall.
Leaves: All submerged or floating and finely divided into feathery, pale green segments.
Flowers: 20–25 mm (⅘–1 in) across, pale lilac with a central yellow eye, in tiered whorls; calyx with bristle-like teeth.
Fruits: Small spherical capsules.
Related or similar plants: No other native plants with primrose-like flowers are aquatic.
Habitat and distribution: Local in shallow, still or slow-moving waters in southern and eastern England, extending to North Wales and Lancashire; introduced to a few places in Ireland.
Flowering time: May to July.

AN UNCOMMON PLANT in many areas but sometimes present in quantity, especially in flooded ditches and small, quiet ponds.

FLOWER TYPE

IDENTIFICATION

HABITAT

POPULATION

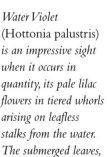

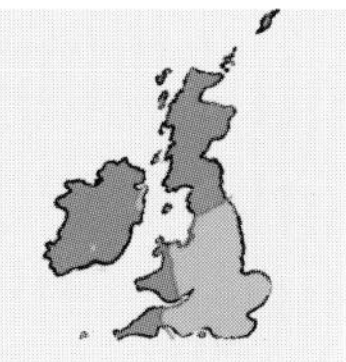
MAP

Water Violet (Hottonia palustris) *is an impressive sight when it occurs in quantity, its pale lilac flowers in tiered whorls arising on leafless stalks from the water. The submerged leaves, also in whorls, are finely divided into feathery segments.*

Yellow Pimpernel

PRIMROSE FAMILY

(Primulaceae)

SPECIES INFORMATION	
COMMON NAME	Yellow Pimpernel
SCIENTIFIC NAME	Lysimachia nemorum
RELATED SPECIES	Scarlet Pimpernel
HEIGHT/SPREAD	10–45cm
FLOWERING TIME	May–September
HABITAT	Damp woodland, shady places

Note: Like a perennial, yellow-flowered Scarlet Pimpernel.

FLOWER TYPE

IDENTIFICATION

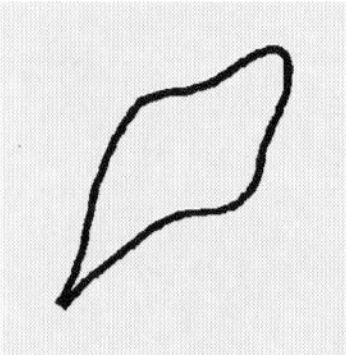

HABITAT

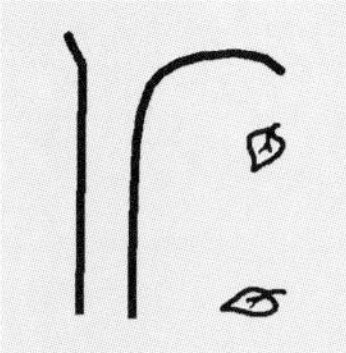

POPULATION

MAP

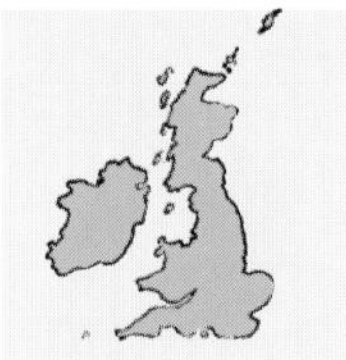

THIS VERY PRETTY little flower, despite a long flowering season, is frequently overlooked and is not nearly so well known as its famous cousin Scarlet Pimpernel (p.197). Nevertheless, Yellow Pimpernel is likely to be found in almost any damp woodland glade or ride where the soil does not contain too much lime. It ought to be more popular with gardeners in this country.

The first half of the scientific name of this and the related Yellow-flowered Loosestrifes may commemorate Lysimachos, a ruler of Thrace in the 4th century BC who had been a general in the army of Alexander the Great. This story goes back to the writing of Roman naturalist Pliny the Elder (23–79 AD). The name may also be a direct translation from the Greek lysimachos (loosestrife), referring to an ancient belief that certain plants had the power to calm agitated farm animals.

Size and appearance: A slender, creeping, rather leafy, hairless perennial, with stems 10–45 cm (4–18 in) long.
Leaves: In opposite pairs, oval to heart-shaped, pointed.
Flowers: In pairs, each on a slender stalk from a leaf-angle, dish-shaped, yellow, 6–8 mm (¼–⅓ in) across; calyx with 5 bristle-like lobes.
Fruits: Spherical capsules, splitting by 5 teeth, enclosed within the persistent calyx.
Related or similar plants: Scarlet Pimpernel (p.197) has scarlet flowers and grows in disturbed ground; Creeping Jenny (p.197) has larger, bell-shaped flowers.
Habitat and distribution: Common in woodland, mostly along wet rides, on banks and by streams, and other damp, shady places, throughout, but mainly on lime-poor soils.
Flowering time: May to September.

Yellow Pimpernel is a delicate, creeping perennial of damp, shady places and woods. It is common but often overlooked.

SPECIES INFORMATION	
COMMON NAME	Creeping Jenny
SCIENTIFIC NAME	Lysimachia nummularia
RELATED SPECIES	Yellow Pimpernel
HEIGHT/SPREAD	Stems 10–60 cm long
FLOWERING TIME	June–September
HABITAT	Damp, grassy places and gardens

Note: Creeping plant with conspicuous yellow flowers.

Creeping Jenny

PRIMROSE FAMILY
(Primulaceae)

Size and appearance: An elegant, leafy, creeping perennial, with prostrate stems 10–60 cm (4–24 in) long that root at each pair of leaves.
Leaves: In opposite pairs, oval, blunt.
Flowers: In pairs, each on a short, stout stalk from a leaf-angle, bell-shaped, yellow, 10–20 mm (⅖–⅘ in) across; calyx with 5 broad lobes.
Fruits: Spherical capsules c. 3 mm (⅛ in) across, but these have never been seen in Britain or Ireland.
Related or similar plants: Yellow Pimpernel (p.194) also creeps, but has smaller, dish-shaped flowers on slender stalks.

Habitat and distribution: Lake-shores, banks, ditches, wet grassy and shady places, churchyards and untended gardens north to central Scotland, but rare in Scotland and much of Ireland except Ulster. It is known to be introduced in Devon and Cornwall, and is often clearly a garden escape elsewhere.
Flowering time: June to September.

IN THE FACE of the evidence, Creeping Jenny does not look like a good native plant. It is known to be a garden escape over much of northern Europe, and it fails to set seed in Britain. It has a marked tendency to grow around villages or sites of former settlements. However, many such cottage garden plants have a history of collection from the wild, cultivation, escape and re-establishment in the wild.

The plant's failure to set seed may just be the result of some complex genetic factor. It compensates by ready vegetative reproduction from rooting stem fragments and can become a persistent, if inoffensive, garden weed.

FLOWER TYPE

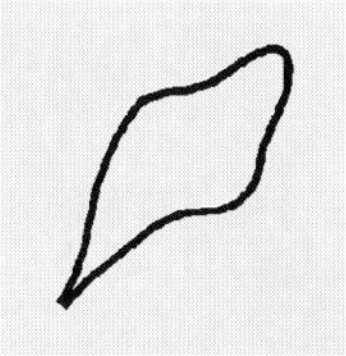

IDENTIFICATION

HABITAT

POPULATION

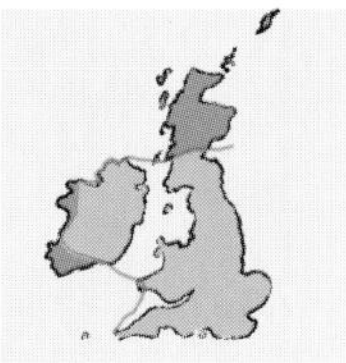

MAP

Creeping Jenny (Lysimachia nummularia) *is a favourite in cottage gardens and can often be found around the margins of village ponds. Compared to the Yellow Pimpernel, Creeping Jenny has more oval, blunt leaves set closer together and with large bell-shaped flowers on short, stout stalks.*

Yellow Loosestrife

PRIMROSE FAMILY

(Primulaceae)

SPECIES INFORMATION	
COMMON NAME	Yellow Loosestrife
SCIENTIFIC NAME	Lysimachia vulgaris
RELATED SPECIES	Dotted Loosestrife
HEIGHT/SPREAD	40–160 cm tall
FLOWERING TIME	July–September
HABITAT	Watersides and marshes

Note: Waterside plant with conspicuous yellow flowers.

FLOWER TYPE

IDENTIFICATION

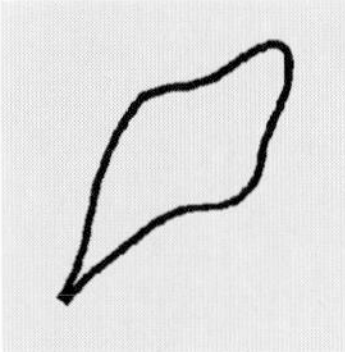

HABITAT

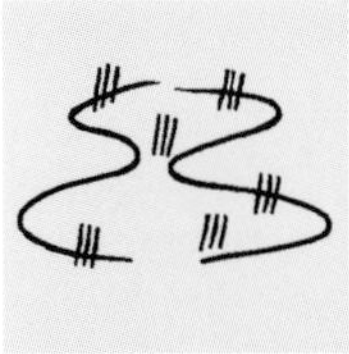

POPULATION

MAP

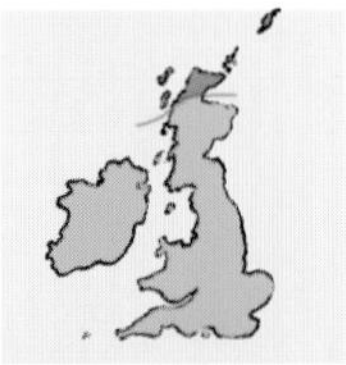

Related or similar plants: Dotted Loosestrife has larger flowers in long, dense clusters; Yellow Pimpernel (p.194) and Creeping Jenny (p.195) both creep along the ground.

Habitat and distribution: Widespread and common beside lakes, rivers and flooded gravel-pits, in alder carr, wet woodland rides, marshes and damp meadows throughout Britain and Ireland, except for northern and much of eastern Scotland.

Flowering time: July to September.

Size and appearance: An erect, downy perennial 40–160 cm (16–64 in), with far-creeping rhizomes forming clumps.

Leaves: In opposite pairs, 3s or 4s, up to 10 cm (4 in) long, short-stalked, oval to spear-shaped, marked with black dots.

Flowers: Cup-shaped, yellow, 15–20 mm (3/5–4/5 in) across, with 5 petals and sepals, clustered in loose, branched heads.

Fruits: Spherical capsules c. 5 mm (1/5 in) across.

THIS IS THE commonest of several native or introduced loosestrifes. The name seems to refer to an ancient belief that these and other plants had the power to calm agitated farm animals. Yellow Loosestrife is not related to Purple Loosestrife (p.161), which also occurs widely in wet and marshy habitats. The two species often grow together, especially on the banks of rivers.

Top left and bottom left *Yellow Loosestrife* (Lysimachia vulgaris) *flowers in conspicuous, leafy-branched terminal clusters.*

Bottom right *Dotted Loosestrife* (Lysimachia punctata), *similar but with long, dense clusters of larger yellow flowers 20–35 mm (4/5–1 2/5 in)across, is an aggressive garden escape that is spreading, especially in southern England.*

SPECIES INFORMATION	
COMMON NAME	Scarlet Pimpernel
SCIENTIFIC NAME	Anagallis arvensis
RELATED SPECIES	Bog Pimpernel, Yellow Pimpernel
HEIGHT/SPREAD	5–50 cm long
FLOWERING TIME	April–October
HABITAT	Cultivated ground, sand-dunes
Note: One of our very few scarlet-flowered annual weeds.	

Scarlet Pimpernel

PRIMROSE FAMILY

(Primulaceae)

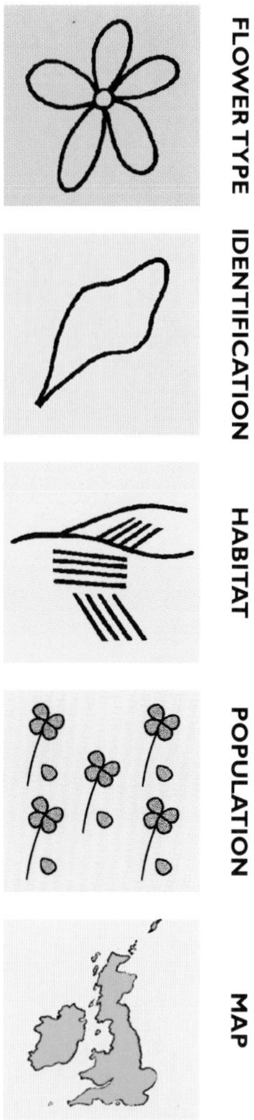

Size and appearance: A slender, hairless annual or sometimes biennial, with prostrate, sprawling or erect, 4-angled stems 5–50 cm (4–20 in) long.

Leaves: In opposite pairs, oval to heart-shaped, pointed, marked beneath with tiny black dots.

Flowers: In pairs, each on a slender stalk from a leaf-angle, dish-shaped, usually scarlet with a small purple eye, 3–8 mm (⅛–⅓ in) across; calyx with 5 spear-shaped lobes.

Fruits: Small spherical capsules on down-turned stalks, splitting around the middle so the 'lid' falls off to release the seeds.

THIS VERY PRETTY little flower is one of our best-known wild plants, at least by repute. Country folk long called it Poor man's Weather-glass or similar names on account of the flowers being fully open only in sunshine. They soon close in cloudy or damp weather. Note, however, that they usually close anyway by mid-afternoon!

The flowers show considerable variation in colour, but in most plants they are the familiar scarlet. Plants with pinkish or flesh-coloured flowers are locally frequent on or near the coasts of Ireland, south-west England and Wales. One may also be lucky enough to find plants with lilac, maroon or deep blue flowers as well. Always they have the purple eye in the centre. Plants from sand-dunes have rather fleshy leaves.

Related or similar plants: Yellow Pimpernel (p.194) has yellow flowers and grows in damp, shady places.

Habitat and distribution: A common weed of cultivated and waste land, and on sand-dunes, shingle beaches and open, damp or sandy places near the sea, through most of Britain and Ireland, but in Scotland rare and mostly on or near the coast.

Flowering time: April to October.

Scarlet Pimpernel (Anagallis arvensis) *usually has bright scarlet flowers but sometimes can be found with pink, maroon or even blue flowers. Occasionally both red and blue forms grow together.*

Bog Pimpernel

PRIMROSE FAMILY

(Primulaceae)

SPECIES INFORMATION	
COMMON NAME	Bog Pimpernel
SCIENTIFIC NAME	Anagallis tenella
RELATED SPECIES	Sea Milkwort
HEIGHT/SPREAD	5–15 cm long
FLOWERING TIME	June–August
HABITAT	Damp grassland, marshy ground

Note: Elegant, pink flower of boggy grassland.

FLOWER TYPE

IDENTIFICATION

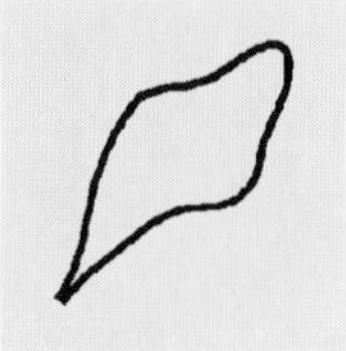

HABITAT

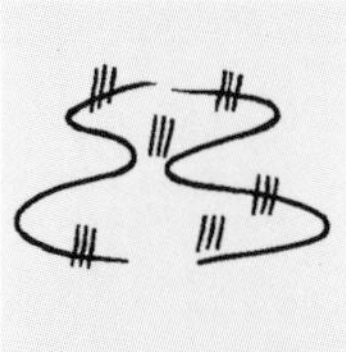

POPULATION

MAP

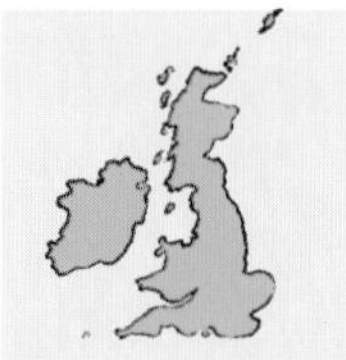

Size and appearance: A slender, creeping, hairless perennial, with stems 5–15 cm (2–6 in) long that root at each pair of leaves, forming a mat.
Leaves: In opposite pairs, short-stalked, oval, rounded at tip, less than 10 mm (⅖ in) long.
Flowers: In pairs, each on a slender stalk from a leaf-angle, bell-shaped, pink with darker veins, 6–10 mm (¼–⅖ in) long; calyx with 5 slender lobes.
Fruits: Spherical capsules, splitting into 5 teeth, enclosed within the persistent calyx.
Related or similar plants: Scarlet Pimpernel (p.197) has scarlet flowers and grows in disturbed ground.
Habitat and distribution: Common, but mainly in the west and north, in damp grassland, marshy and boggy ground, lake shores, usually on lime-poor soils and especially near the coast. The western half of Ireland is its headquarters in these islands; in the far west it grows on exposed banks and grassy walls.
Flowering time: June to August.

THE ELEGANT LITTLE FLOWERS of Bog Pimpernel, often borne in dense profusion, brighten damp or boggy places, for example in many coastal areas of western and north-western Ireland. In some areas it grows well in damp meadows that have not been ploughed or treated with fertiliser.

Bottom right *Sea Milkwort* (Glaux maritima)*, another pink- or whitish-flowered member of the Primrose family, has more erect stems and upper leaves in 4s. The stalkless flowers, each at the base of a leaf, are 3–6 mm (⅛–¼ in) across. Widespread in grassy salt-marshes and on coastal rocks.*

SPECIES INFORMATION	
COMMON NAME	Chickweed Wintergreen
SCIENTIFIC NAME	Trientalis europaea
RELATED SPECIES	Pimpernels
HEIGHT/SPREAD	5–30 cm tall
FLOWERING TIME	June–July
HABITAT	Coniferous woods and moors

Note: A solitary white flower and whorl of untoothed leaves

Chickweed Wintergreen

PRIMROSE FAMILY (Primulaceae)

Size and appearance: A dainty, hairless perennial, with slender, creeping rhizomes and erect stems 5–30 cm (4–12 in) tall.
Leaves: In a whorl at the top of the stem, stalkless, oval or spear-shaped, up to 9 cm (3½ in) long.
Flowers: Solitary on a slender stalk from the leaf-whorl, white or palest pink, shallow bowl-shaped, 10–18 mm (⅖–¾ in) across; petals 7 (or 5–9), the calyx with 5 very slender lobes.
Fruits: Spherical capsules, splitting into 5 teeth.
Related or similar plants: The superficially similar Wood Anemone (p.52) has separate petals, not fused at the base, and flowers in early spring.
Habitat and distribution: A plant of humus-rich and lime-poor soils of mossy woodland, especially coniferous woods, heaths and moors; common in the Highlands of Scotland (but not the Islands), and much more local south to Yorkshire and Derbyshire, also in east Suffolk; not in Ireland.
Flowering time: June to July.

CHICKWEED WINTERGREEN is a characteristic plant of the coniferous forest belt of northern Europe and thus represents an interesting geographical element in our native flora. It is most at home in the woodlands and moors of the Scottish Highlands, where it is an ancient relict species of the former extensive Caledonian native pine forests, which are only now being restored to health by conservationists.

It is not one of the true wintergreens, which also occur in northern woodlands and are somewhat similar, with white flowers. These are members of the heather family and only one of them, Common Wintergreen (p.189), which has flowers in clusters, is at all widespread.

Chickweed Wintergreen (Trientalis europaea) *is a delicate little perennial with a whorl of broad, lanceolate, pale green leaves set towards the top of the single unbranched stem. The flowers are solitary on slender stalks which arise from the whorl of leaves. It is locally common in pinewoods and moors in Scotland.*

FLOWER TYPE

IDENTIFICATION

HABITAT

POPULATION

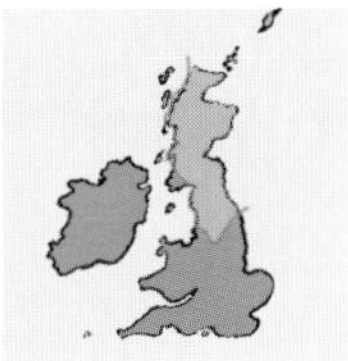
MAP

Thrift

THRIFT AND SEA-LAVENDER FAMILY
(Plumbaginaceae)

SPECIES INFORMATION	
COMMON NAME	Thrift, Sea Pink
SCIENTIFIC NAME	Armeria maritima
RELATED SPECIES	Common Sea-lavender
HEIGHT/SPREAD	Stems 5–20 cm tall
FLOWERING TIME	May–August
HABITAT	Coastal rocks and salt-marshes

Note: An unmistakable seaside plant.

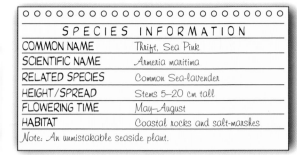

FLOWER TYPE

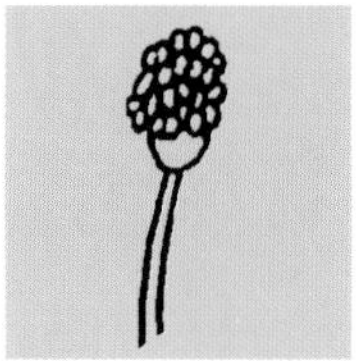

IDENTIFICATION

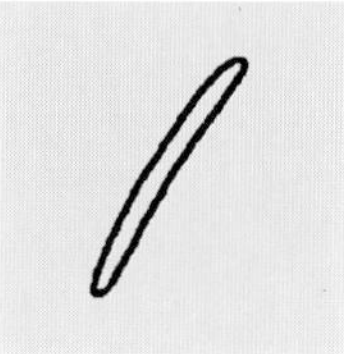

HABITAT

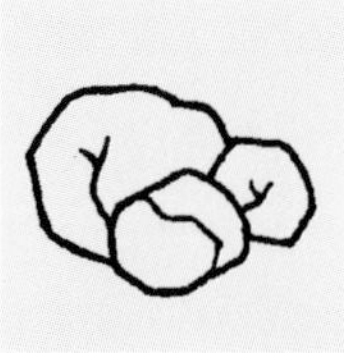

POPULATION

MAP

Size and appearance: A low-growing perennial, woody at the base, forming dense, springy mats; flowering stems erect, downy, 5–20 cm (2–8 in) tall, sometimes up to 35 cm (14 in).
Leaves: Numerous, all basal, dense, slender, pointed, grass-like, slightly fleshy.
Flowers: Small, pink, scented, in dense, rounded heads 1–3 cm (⅖–1⅕ in) across, with papery brown scales at the base; calyx funnel-shaped, papery, persistent in fruit.
Fruits: Small, 1-seeded, in a papery head.
Related or similar plants: Sea-lavenders (p.201) have bluish-lilac flowers in branched spikes.

Habitat and distribution: Abundant around most of the coasts, on rocks, cliffs and salt-marshes, on rocks and in grassland in the mountains, on the spoil-heaps of old copper and lead mines, and more rarely in dry grassy heaths; usually near coasts, but far inland in the northern Pennines and the Highlands of Scotland.
Flowering time: May to August, from April in warmer springs and producing a few flowers at other times.

THRIFT IS A FAMILIAR plant from seaside holidays, the rock garden and the reverse side of the pre-decimal, 12-sided 'threepenny bit' coin. Although largely a plant of seaside salt spray, it grows inland on mountains and where the soil is contaminated by metals such as copper, lead and zinc. In these habitats, for example on part of the shore of the Lower Lake at Killarney, County Kerry, it grows with another mostly seaside plant, Sea Campion (p.45).

An even more unusual habitat is the few remnants of grassy heathland in Lincolnshire. These plants are taller, with hairy-edged leaves and paler pink flowers, a variant of Thrift that is more widespread in Germany, Poland and elsewhere in northern-central Europe. Thrift is generally variable in height, leaf hairiness and shades of flower colour. Compact cultivars, often with darker flowers, are popular as rockery and (less so now) edging plants in gardens.

A tufted perennial with cushions of fleshy linear leaves from which the flowers arise in roundish heads above the papery calyx. Thrift can be very abundant, covering large areas of cliffs or the whole of small islands with a springy turf that flowers profusely in early summer.

SPECIES INFORMATION	
COMMON NAME	Marsh Marigold or Kingcup
SCIENTIFIC NAME	Limonium vulgare
RELATED SPECIES	Thrift
HEIGHT/SPREAD	20–40cm tall
FLOWERING TIME	July–August
HABITAT	Saltmarshes

Note: The plant that colours saltmarshes in summer.

Common Sea-lavender

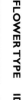

THRIFT AND SEA-LAVENDER FAMILY
(Plumbaginaceae)

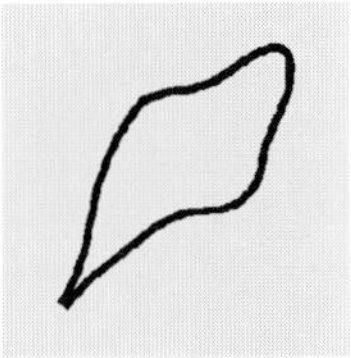

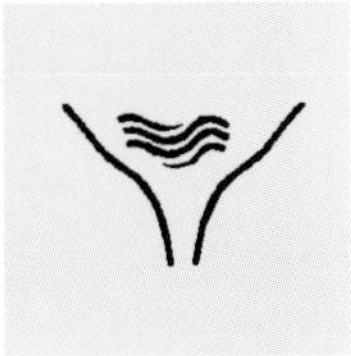

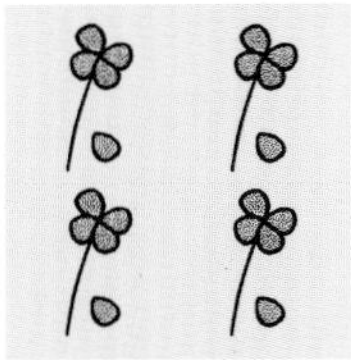

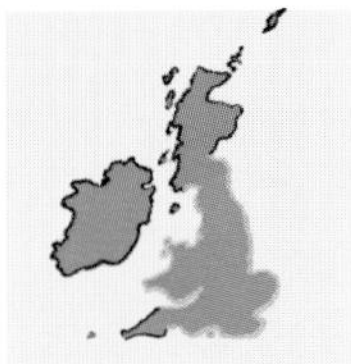

Size and appearance: A hairless perennial, rather woody at the base, forming dense stands; flowering stems erect, round in section, 20–40 cm (8–16 in) tall, sometimes up to 70 cm (28 in), branched above.

Leaves: All basal in a rosette, stalked, broadly spear-shaped or elliptical, pointed, fleshy.

Flowers: Small, bluish-violet, in dense, 1-sided, branched spikes forming flat-topped clusters; calyx funnel-shaped, papery, persistent in fruit.

Fruits: Small, 1-seeded, in a papery head.

Related or similar plants: Lax-flowered Sea-lavender has longer, looser flower-spikes; Rock Sea-lavender is smaller and has spoon-shaped leaves.

Habitat and distribution: Common around much of the coast, often in huge, dense stands in salt-marshes, and less frequently on cliffs, rocks and shingle beaches, north to the Firth of Forth; rarer in Scotland and absent from Ireland (but see note below on Lax-flowered Sea-lavender).

Flowering time: June to August, with a peak in July–August and a few flowers right through to October.

COMMON SEA-LAVENDER is not so well known as its cousin Thrift, but during July and August provides an equally spectacular floral display. The massed flowers colour whole salt-marshes with their unmistakable lavender-like tint.

Lax-flowered Sea-lavender (*Limonium humile*) is similar but never more than 40 cm (15 in) tall, with angled stems that branch low down, and longer, looser spikes of flowers. It has a similar range to Common Sea-lavender in Britain, although it is less widespread and abundant, and occurs all round the Irish coast. Both species are rather local, with populations concentrated in East Anglia and around the Solent. Of several other sea-lavenders, Rock Sea-lavender (*Limonium binervosum*), smaller and with spoon-shaped leaves, is widespread on rocks, shingle beaches and drier salt-marshes north to Galloway, and locally in Ireland. Dried, it is the 'lucky white heather' sold on the streets by gypsies.

Common Sea-lavender (Limonium vulgare) *can dominate certain parts of a salt-marsh, particularly the higher plateau between the creeks. In summer these lavender 'meadows' become a sheet of deep lilac.*

Centaury

GENTIAN FAMILY

(Gentianaceae)

SPECIES INFORMATION	
COMMON NAME	Centaury
SCIENTIFIC NAME	Centaurium erythraea
RELATED SPECIES	Yellow-wort
HEIGHT/SPREAD	Stems 10–30 cm tall
FLOWERING TIME	June–October
HABITAT	Dry grassland and sand-dunes

Note: Like a small pink gentian.

FLOWER TYPE

IDENTIFICATION

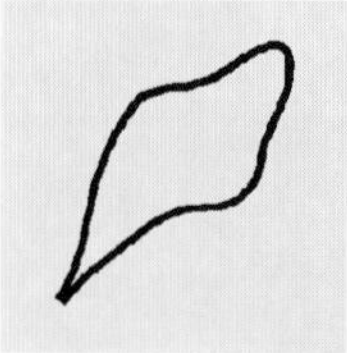

HABITAT

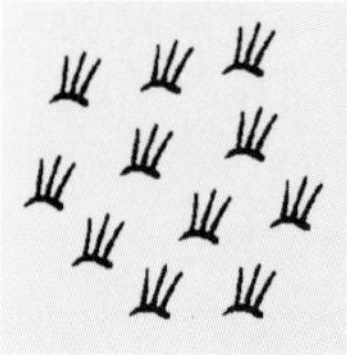

POPULATION

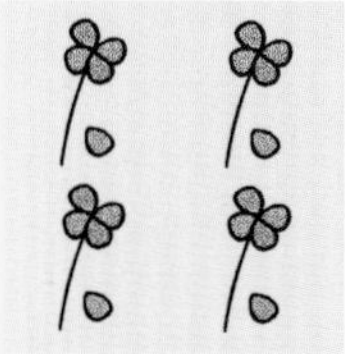

MAP

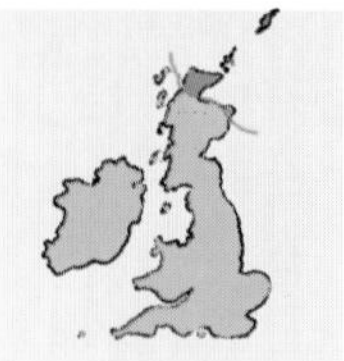

CENTAURY IS THE commonest native gentian. It is a variable species that has been much classified by botanists into subspecies and varieties. Dwarf and narrow-leaved variants are found locally on the coast, where rarer related species of centaury also occur. Centaury has healing properties and has long been used in herbal medicine as a rather bitter infusion to ease digestion.

Size and appearance: A slender, hairless, erect biennial or short-lived perennial, 10–30 cm (4–12 in) tall, sometimes up to 50 cm (20 in), usually with a single square stem that is branched above.

Leaves: Light green, oval or oblong, blunt, in a basal rosette and (smaller and more pointed) in opposite pairs up the stem.

Flowers: Pink, tubular, 5–8 mm (⅕–⅓ in) across, with 5 spreading lobes, in dense, rather flat-topped clusters; sepals tubular, with 5 narrow teeth.

Fruits: Cylindrical capsules with many small seeds.

Related or similar plants: Yellow-wort (p.203) has fused upper pairs of leaves and yellow flowers.

Habitat and distribution: Common in dry grassland, coastal heaths, cliffs and sand-dunes, especially on lime-rich soils; local and mainly coastal in Scotland.

Flowering time: June to October.

Centaury (Centaurium erythraea) *has a basal rosette of oval, prominently veined, blunt leaves, with small and pointed paired stem leaves. The pink flowers are tubular, with spreading lobes in dense flat-topped clusters. It is widespread but locally common in dry, grassy places and sand dunes.*

SPECIES INFORMATION	
COMMON NAME	Yellow-wort
SCIENTIFIC NAME	Blackstonia perfoliata
RELATED SPECIES	Yellow Centaury
HEIGHT/SPREAD	Stems 10–60 cm tall
FLOWERING TIME	July–September
HABITAT	Dry grassland and sand-dunes

Note: The fused pairs of bluish-green leaves are distinctive.

Yellow-wort

GENTIAN FAMILY (Gentianaceae)

Top *Yellow-wort* (Blackstonia perfoliata) *is distinctive with its waxy-grey appearance, paired leaves clasping the single stem and a flat-topped cluster of yellow flowers.*

YELLOW-WORT, one of our few widespread wild gentians, is a plant mainly of dry grasslands, but also the drier parts of fens. It is a characteristic species of chalk grassland, where it often grows with the related Centaury (p.202). Yellow-wort has expanded its range somewhat in recent years, especially in northern England, due to its inclusion in commercial wild flower seed mixtures on road-verges and other landscaped sites. On the Continent, Yellow-wort often occurs in damp or salt-rich habitats.

The first half of the scientific name commemorates John Blackstone (1712–53), English apothecary and botanist, and in 1736 the first scientist to record Fritillary (p.336) in Britain.

Bottom *A plant of chalk and limestone soils Yellow-wort can occur on road-verges, railway banks, grassy places and sand-dunes.*

Size and appearance: An erect, hairless, bluish-green perennial, 10–60 cm (4–24 in) tall.

Leaves: Stalkless, in a loose basal rosette and in opposite pairs up the stem, these usually fused into cup-like 'collars'.

Flowers: Yellow, 8–15 mm ($\frac{1}{3}$–$\frac{3}{5}$ in) across, with a short tube and 6–8 spreading lobes, in a loose, more or less flat-topped cluster; sepals with 6–12 narrow lobes.

Fruits: Cylindrical capsules with many small seeds.

Related or similar plants: Centaury (p.202) has pink flowers and unfused pairs of leaves.

Habitat and distribution: Widespread but local in grassland on chalk and limestone, road-verges, sand-dunes and fens, north to Yorkshire and County Sligo.

Flowering time: July to September.

FLOWER TYPE

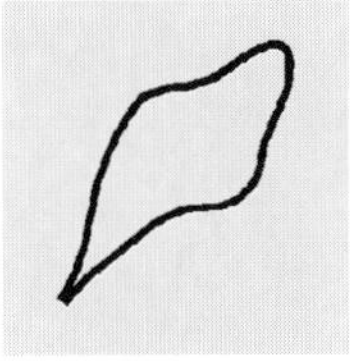

IDENTIFICATION

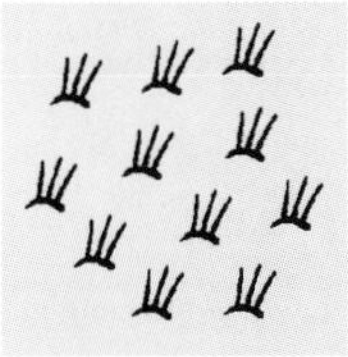

HABITAT

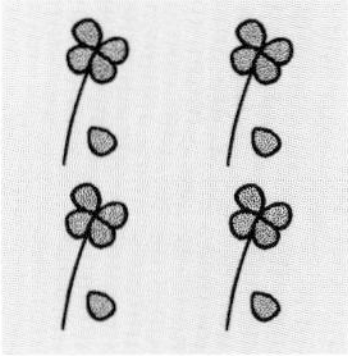

POPULATION

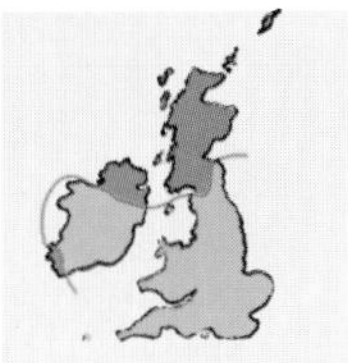

MAP

Felwort

GENTIAN FAMILY
(Gentianaceae)

SPECIES INFORMATION	
COMMON NAME	Felwort, Autumn Gentian
SCIENTIFIC NAME	Gentianella amarella
RELATED SPECIES	Other Gentians, Centaury
HEIGHT/SPREAD	Stems 5–10 cm tall
FLOWERING TIME	July–September
HABITAT	Dry grassland and sand-dunes

Note: The commonest autumn-flowering gentian, with 4–5 petals.

FLOWER TYPE

IDENTIFICATION

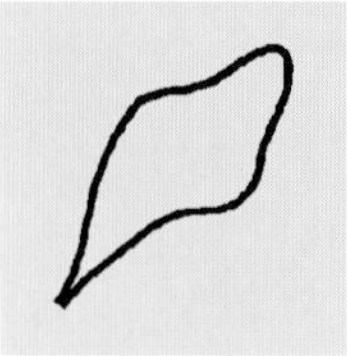

HABITAT

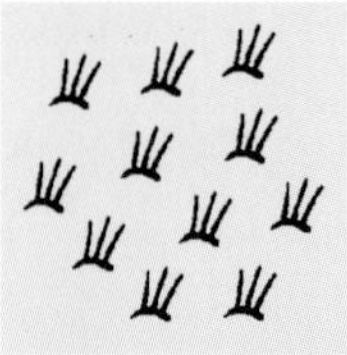

POPULATION

MAP

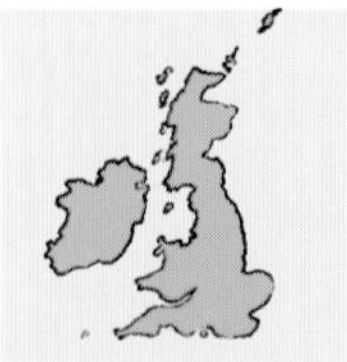

Related or similar plants: Other gentians are very similar but mostly rare; Centaury (p.202) has pink flowers.

Habitat and distribution: Widespread but local in grassland on chalk and limestone, and on sea-cliffs and sand-dunes.

Flowering time: July to September.

THIS ATTRACTIVE LITTLE gentian is sometimes abundant in chalk grassland at the end of the summer, when few other plants are coming into flower. Felwort belongs to a group (*Gentianella*) of six similar British gentians, all annuals or biennials. These differ from the perennial (sometimes annual), mostly blue-flowered, 'true' gentians (*Gentiana*) in small floral features, notably in having a conspicuous fringe of hairs around the throat of the petal-tube.

Of these gentians, only Felwort is at all common, although Field Gentian (*Gentianella campestris*) is more widespread in Scotland and north-western Ireland. This species has bluish-purple, 4-lobed petals and a 4-lobed calyx with 2 larger outer and 2 smaller inner lobes.

Size and appearance: An erect, often small, hairless annual or biennial, 10–30 cm (2–12 in) tall.

Leaves: In opposite pairs, broadly spear-shaped, pointed, purplish.

Flowers: Dull purple or pinkish-purple, bell-shaped, 12–20 mm (½–¾ in) across, with a long tube hairy at the throat, and 4–5 spreading lobes; calyx with 4–5 equal lobes.

Fruits: Cylindrical capsules with many small seeds.

Top and bottom left *Felwort* (Gentianella amarella) *has dull purple, bell-shaped flowers that have a long tube which is hairy at the throat.*

Bottom right *Field Gentian* (Gentianella campestris) *grows erect to 30 cm (12 in), and the flowers are bluish-purple to almost white, with narrowly oblong lobes. Locally frequent in grassland and dunes in the north.*

SPECIES INFORMATION	
COMMON NAME	Spring Gentian
SCIENTIFIC NAME	Gentiana verna
RELATED SPECIES	Marsh Gentian
HEIGHT/SPREAD	Stems 5–10 cm tall
FLOWERING TIME	April–June
HABITAT	Rocky grassland on limestone

Note: The true 'chocolate-box' gentian.

Spring Gentian

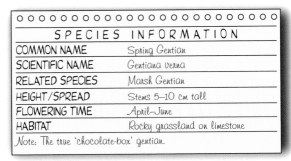

GENTIAN FAMILY (Gentianaceae)

Habitat and distribution: Rare, but locally abundant, in short, species-rich rocky grassland on limestone in a small area of the Pennines in Upper Teesdale, and especially in the Burren and adjacent parts of County Galway in western Ireland.

Flowering time: April to June.

SPRING GENTIANS ARE for many people most closely associated with the Burren of County Clare, one of the most remarkable places in these islands for wild flowers. In May the display of gentians there is quite astonishing, as good as any to be seen in the Alps. From coastal sand-dunes to mountain slopes, on limestone pavement, ancient green roads, even in ordinary cow-pastures, the grassland is splashed with blue. Primroses (p.190), Cowslips (p.191) and Early Purple Orchids (p.364) add to the colourful scene.

Spring Gentian is a plant of the Alps and adjacent regions, extending to Britain and Ireland but nowhere else in northern Europe. The British population in Teesdale, discovered in 1797, is more localised. Happily, these beautiful plants are now fully protected from picking or uprooting by the Wildlife and Countryside Act 1981.

Size and appearance: A striking, hairless perennial, 5–10 cm (2–4 in) tall, forming loose clumps of leaf-rosettes.

Leaves: Mostly in basal rosettes, a few in opposite pairs on the flowering stems, oval to spear-shaped, 1–2 cm ($\frac{2}{5}$–$\frac{4}{5}$ in) long.

Flowers: Deep blue, trumpet-shaped, 15–20 mm ($\frac{3}{5}$–$\frac{4}{5}$ in) across, with 5 wide-spreading petal-lobes; calyx winged.

Fruits: Cylindrical capsules with many small seeds.

Related or similar plants: Marsh Gentian has taller, leafy stems and grows on damp, lime-poor heaths.

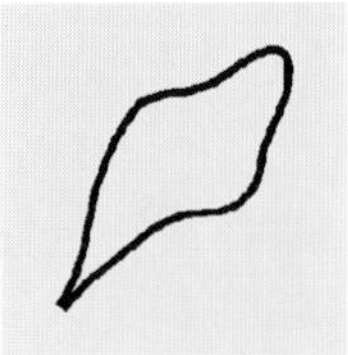

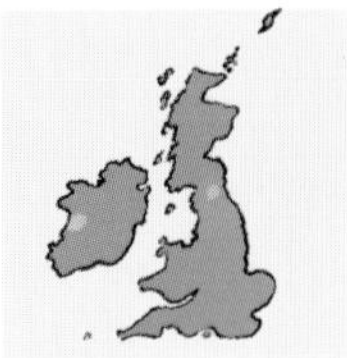

***Bottom left** Marsh Gentian* (Gentiana pneumonanthe) *is similar but leafier and taller, 40 cm (16 in) tall, the blue flowers streaked with green outside, solitary or in an elongate cluster of 2–6. It is scarce but occurs locally in quantity, on wet heaths in southern England, and in scattered sites north to Cumbria.*

Jacob's Ladder

JACOB'S LADDER FAMILY (Polemoniaceae)

SPECIES INFORMATION	
COMMON NAME	Jacob's Ladder
SCIENTIFIC NAME	Polemonium caeruleum
RELATED SPECIES	None
HEIGHT/SPREAD	30–80 cm tall
FLOWERING TIME	June–September
HABITAT	Limestone rocks and screes

Note: Somewhat similar to the often blue-flowered borage family.

FLOWER TYPE

IDENTIFICATION

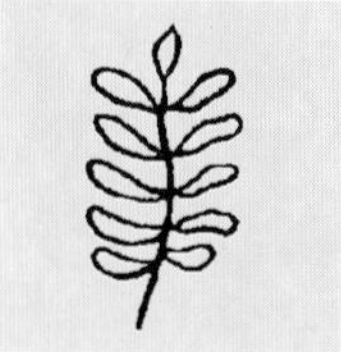

HABITAT

POPULATION

MAP

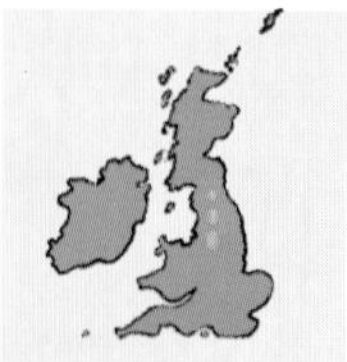

Size and appearance: Leafy perennial with erect stems 30–80 cm (12–64 in) tall.
Leaves: Compound, with 10–12 regular pairs of oval to spear-shaped leaflets and a terminal leaflet.
Flowers: Blue, shortly tubular, 8–15 mm ($\frac{1}{3}$–$\frac{3}{5}$ in) across, with 5 broad, overlapping, spreading lobes, in a compact branched cluster; calyx-lobes spear-shaped.
Fruits: Almost spherical capsules.
Related or similar plants: Members of the borage family (pp.220–226) have blue flowers but these are more markedly tubular, without spreading petal-lobes; they also have simple leaves.
Habitat and distribution: A rare native of rocks, screes and grassland in the limestone Pennines of northern England; also an escape from gardens in grassy places and woodland margins.
Flowering time: June to September.

JACOB'S LADDER IS widespread over much of northern Europe and the mountains of central Europe. Not only is its British distribution restricted, but also its habitat here is rocky grassland, cliffs and screes – whereas on the Continent it often grows in open woodland. We know from fossil evidence that it was more widely distributed here in the post-Glacial period, and its present British distribution is apparently a relict one. As dense woodland cover re-established itself after the Ice Age, subsequently to be cleared for farming, Jacob's Ladder and other plants retreated to the broken, rocky ground where they now survive.

The Jacob's Ladder family is mainly North American, with just two other (arctic) species in Europe. However, these plants are popular with gardeners. The blue wild variant of Jacob's Ladder is widely grown in cottage gardens and herbaceous borders, along with a striking cultivar with white petals. Jacob's Ladder has been familiar to British botanists since John Ray described it growing at Malham Cove, Yorkshire, in 1671. Discovered there five years before, it still grows at the same site.

Top *Jacob's Ladder* (Polemonium caeruleum) *has mauve flowers with five broad, overlapping lobes, which contrast with the yellow of the stamens.*

Bottom left and right *Very local in stoney places on limestone in the Pennines but more widespread in Europe, Jacob's ladder makes a swathe across an alpine meadow.*

SPECIES INFORMATION	
COMMON NAME	Bogbean, Buckbean
SCIENTIFIC NAME	Menyanthes trifoliata
RELATED SPECIES	Fringed Water-lily
HEIGHT/SPREAD	20–40 cm tall
FLOWERING TIME	May–July
HABITAT	Marshes and boggy pools

Note: Like a white- and hairy-flowered gentian of wet places.

Bogbean

BOGBEAN FAMILY (Menyanthaceae)

Top *Bogbean* (Menyanthes trifoliata) *is a distinctive, far-creeping aquatic perennial which often forms patches in shallow ponds in the New Forest. It is occasionally introduced into ornamental and village ponds.*

FLOWER TYPE

IDENTIFICATION

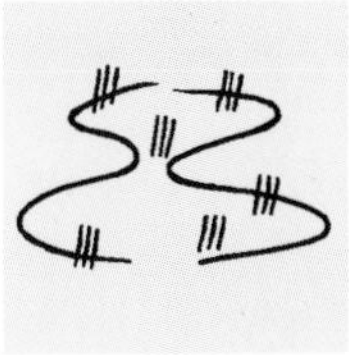
HABITAT

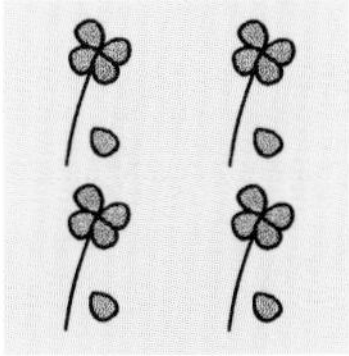
POPULATION

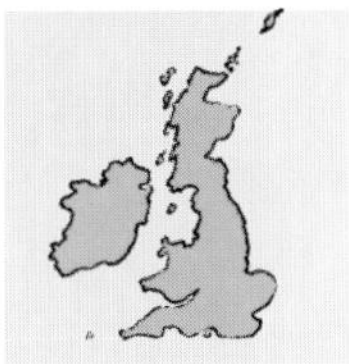
MAP

BOGBEAN IN FLOWER is one of the glorious floral displays of moorland and mountain. Beside a still tarn or loughan, the showy pink and white flowers contrast with and complement the green and brown slopes and bogs, the dark rocks and black peaty waters of highland Britain and Ireland. Nor is it merely ornamental. The leaves have a bitter taste and, like those of Ground-ivy (p.239) and other plants, were formerly employed to flavour beer. They were also used to treat rheumatism, while the seeds were regarded as a remedy for colds and coughs. The English name derives from the similarity of the trefoil leaves to those of broad beans.

Size and appearance: A far-creeping aquatic perennial, with a stout, creeping rhizome, forming patches, and erect flowering stems 20–40 cm (8–16 in) tall.

Leaves: Held above the water, all more or less basal, long-stalked with sheathing base, trifoliate with 3 blunt, oval, hairless leaflets, 1–2 cm (⅜–¾ in) long.

Flowers: White, pink outside, star-shaped, c. 15 mm (⅝ in) across, with 5 spreading lobes densely fringed with white hairs, in long, showy clusters; calyx-lobes oval.

Fruits: Egg-shaped capsules with many small seeds.

Related or similar plants: Fringed Water-lily (p.208) has floating leaves and yellow flowers; Water Violet (p.193), mainly in southern England, has feathery leaves and hairless petals.

Habitat and distribution: Widespread and often common in the shallow water of muddy or peaty lakes and pools, and wet places in bogs and marshes, especially in the north and west, although local over much of central and southern England.

Flowering time: April to July.

Bottom *The large, hairless trifoliate leaves are held above the water as are the conspicuous spikes of white flowers, which are pink outside and have petals fringed with white hairs.*

Fringed Water-lily

BOGBEAN FAMILY
(Menyanthaceae)

SPECIES INFORMATION	
COMMON NAME	Fringed Water-lily
SCIENTIFIC NAME	Nymphoides peltata
RELATED SPECIES	Bogbean
HEIGHT/SPREAD	Stems up to 160 cm long
FLOWERING TIME	June–September
HABITAT	Lakes, ponds and slow rivers

Note: Superficially like the unrelated Yellow Water-lily (p.53).

FLOWER TYPE

IDENTIFICATION

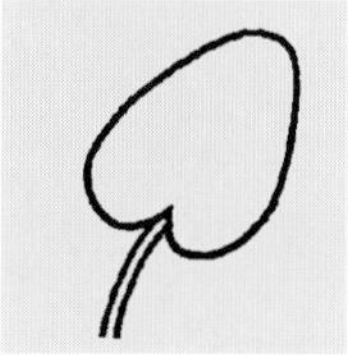

HABITAT

POPULATION

MAP

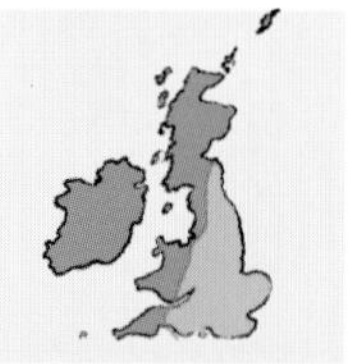

Bottom left *The five broad, spreading lobes are fringed with hairs.*

Size and appearance: Aquatic perennial with floating leaves and creeping and floating stems up to 160 cm (64 in) long, forming extensive patches.
Leaves: All floating, long-stalked with sheathing base, up to 10 cm (4 in) across, round to kidney-shaped at base, obscurely toothed.
Flowers: Yellow, 30–40 mm (1⅕–1⅗ in) across, with 5 broad, spreading lobes fringed with hairs, in clusters of 2–5; calyx-lobes bluntly spear-shaped.
Fruits: Egg-shaped capsules with many small seeds.
Related or similar plants: Bogbean (p.207) has trifoliate leaves and white and pink flowers; the unrelated Yellow Water-lily (p.49) has leaves up to 40 cm (16 in) across and hairless petals.
Habitat and distribution: Widespread and locally common in still or slow-moving waters; native in the Fens and parts of the Thames Valley, but widely introduced and spreading in England and Wales, although still rare in northern Britain.
Flowering time: June to September.

FRINGED WATER-LILY is an attractive plant that, although rare as a true native, is spreading as an escape from gardens and as a deliberate introduction. It is now a feature of many bodies of water across England south of a line from the Mersey to the Humber, especially lakes, gravel pits and large ponds that are managed for angling. It has been extensively introduced to provide cover and a food-rich habitat for fish. This is a happy success story for an aquatic plant, so many of which have declined over recent years.

Top and bottom right *Fringed Water-lily* (Nymphoides peltata) *has rounded, shallowly toothed leaves which are purplish underneath. Large areas of water in suitable ponds and slow-moving water are likely to be colonised by this plant.*

SPECIES INFORMATION	
COMMON NAME	Field Madder
SCIENTIFIC NAME	Sherardia arvensis
RELATED SPECIES	Bedstraws
HEIGHT/SPREAD	10–40 cm tall
FLOWERING TIME	May–September
HABITAT	Dry grassland, cultivated ground

Note: The only pink-flowered, annual bedstraw-like plant.

Field Madder

BEDSTRAW FAMILY

(Rubiaceae)

FLOWER TYPE

IDENTIFICATION

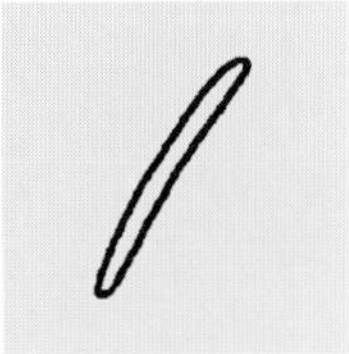

HABITAT

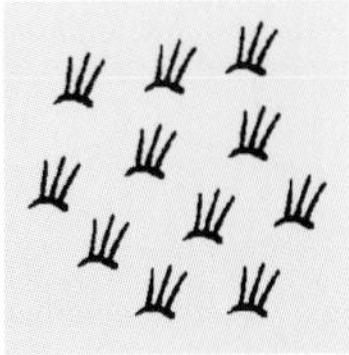

POPULATION

MAP

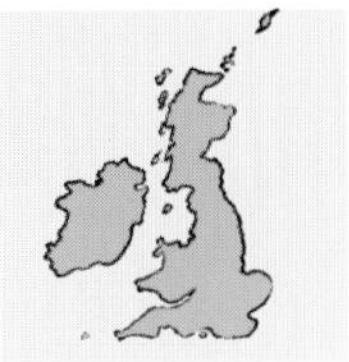

Size and appearance: Prostrate or sprawling annual 10–40 cm (4–16 in) tall, with 4-angled stems covered with minute, down-curved prickles.

Leaves: In whorls of 4–6, narrow, spear-shaped, stiff, pointed.

Flowers: Lilac to pink or whitish, funnel-shaped with 4 spreading petal-lobes, c. 2.5 mm (1/10 in) across, in a cluster surrounded by 8–10 leaf-like bracts.

Fruits: 2-lobed, bristly, crowned by the persistent, enlarged calyx-teeth.

Related or similar plants: Squinancywort (p.210) has pink flowers, but is perennial with whorls of 4 leaves, and lacks the bracts around the flowers.

Habitat and distribution: Widespread in dry grassland, banks and grassy walls, unmanicured lawns and cultivated ground, especially on lime-rich soils, across much of Britain; rare in northern Scotland and rather local in Ireland.

Flowering time: May to September.

PATCHES OF THIS attractive little plant, the pink flowers framed by a ruff of bracts, brighten dry, rather open places like disturbed ground on chalk or dry banks by the sea. It is not the true Madder (*Rubia tinctorum*, also in the bedstraw family), a more robust, perennial plant, the roots of which yield a red dye. It is also quite distinct from Wild Madder (see under Goosegrass, p.214). The first half of the scientific name commemorates William Sherard (1659–1728), a distinguished professor of botany at the University of Oxford.

Field Madder (Sherardia arvensis) *is a prostrate hairy annual with square stems and whorls of four to six small stiff leaves. The cluster of flowers are a delicate lilac surrounded by leaf-like bracts. It is widespread in field edges and cultivated ground, especially on chalk and limestone soils.*

Squinancywort

BEDSTRAW FAMILY

(Rubiaceae)

SPECIES INFORMATION	
COMMON NAME	Squinancywort
SCIENTIFIC NAME	*Asperula cynanchica*
RELATED SPECIES	Bedstraws
HEIGHT/SPREAD	Stems 10–40 cm long
FLOWERING TIME	June–September
HABITAT	Dry grassland, sand-dunes

Note: The only pink-flowered, perennial bedstraw-like plant.

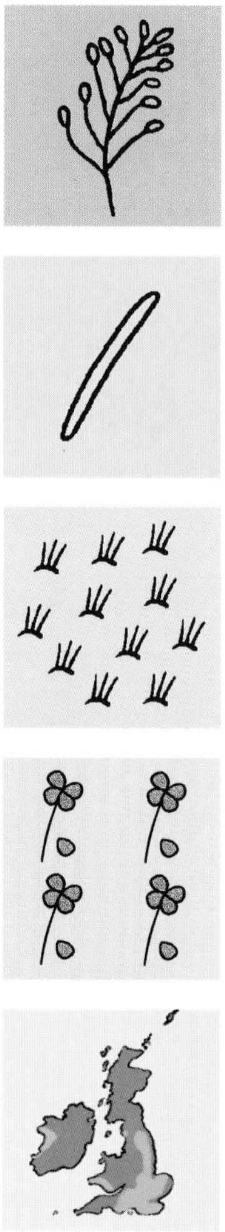

Size and appearance: Tufted perennial, with a woody rootstock and sprawling or prostrate, 4-angled stems 10–40 cm (4–16 in) long, and leafy, vegetative shoots.
Leaves: In whorls of 4, very narrow, fine-pointed.
Flowers: Lilac to pink or white, broadly funnel-shaped with 4 spreading petal-lobes, c. 4 mm (⅙ in) across, in much-branched clusters.
Fruits: Small, egg-shaped, 2-lobed, minutely warty.
Related or similar plants: Wild Madder has pink flowers, but is an annual with whorls of 4–6 leaves, and a whorl of leaf-like bracts around the flowers.
Habitat and distribution: A plant of dry grassland and sand-dunes, mainly on chalk and limestone, always on lime-rich soils, in southern England, south Wales and western Ireland, with a few sites north to Cumbria.
Flowering time: June to September.

SQUINANCYWORT IS QUITE common within the relatively restricted areas in which it occurs, often making patches of pink in short grassland. The curious English name refers to its use as a gargle in the treatment of quinsy, a severe or ulcerating sore throat. This plant has the distinction of being first observed in Britain, during the 16th century, at the renowned archeological site of Silbury Hill, Wiltshire. Here Thomas Johnson (1604–44), one of our first serious field botanists, and his fellow apothecary-botanists, saw it in 1634 during a journey from London to Bath.

Squinancywort (Asperula cynanchica) *is a low, prostrate, hairless slender bedstraw with whorls of four to six linear leaves which is locally frequent in open chalk and limestone turf. The pinkish-white flowers occur in terminal clusters.*

SPECIES INFORMATION	
COMMON NAME	Sweet Woodruff
SCIENTIFIC NAME	Galium odoratum
RELATED SPECIES	Bedstraws
HEIGHT/SPREAD	10–25 cm tall
FLOWERING TIME	May–Junee
HABITAT	Woods

Note: An upright woodland plant with neat whorls of leaves.

Sweet Woodruff

BEDSTRAW FAMILY

(Rubiaceae)

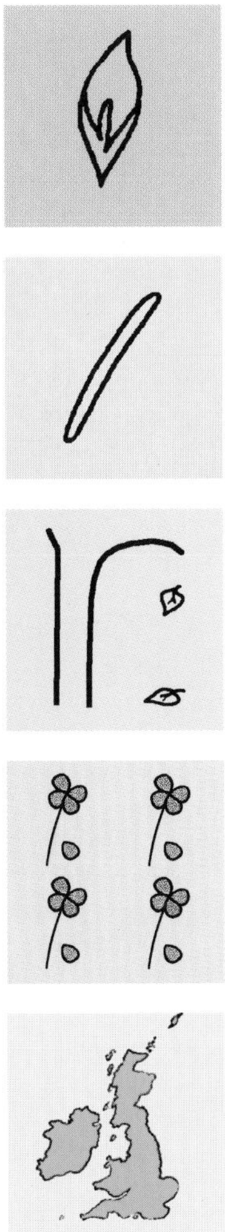

Size and appearance: A nearly hairless perennial with creeping underground stems and erect, unbranched, 4-angled, leafy stems 10–25 cm (4–10 in) tall.

Leaves: In whorls of 6–9, spear-shaped, shiny, up to 5 cm long.

Flowers: White, 4–6 mm (⅙–¼ in) across, funnel-shaped, with 4–5 spreading petal-lobes, in small, long-stalked domed clusters.

Fruits: Up to 3 mm (⅛ in) across, 2-lobed, covered with hooked hairs.

Related or similar plants: Other white-flowered plants in the bedstraw family have branched stems and longer or more branched flower clusters.

Habitat and distribution: Widespread in woods and shady places on damp but well-drained soils on chalk and limestone, especially where there is plenty of leaf-mould, but local in Ireland, East Anglia and northern Scotland.

Flowering time: May to June.

THE WHOLE PLANT smells of new-mown hay when dried, hence its former wide use for stuffing mattresses, scenting linen and strewing on floors to sweeten the air of churches and other buildings. Garlands of this plant are still hung in some churches on the feast of St Barnabus on 11 June. A tea made from Sweet Woodruff is a mild digestive and general tonic and the plant has been used to flavour alcoholic drinks. It is an ideal flower for the shadier garden and is readily available from nurseries specialising in cottage garden plants.

Sweet Woodruff (Galium odoratum) *has erect, shiny-leaved stems which gradually spread out and form carpets across the woodland floor. The small white flowers occur in loose heads on long stalks above the leaves.*

Lady's Bedstraw

BEDSTRAW FAMILY

(Rubiaceae)

SPECIES INFORMATION	
COMMON NAME	Lady's Bedstraw
SCIENTIFIC NAME	Galium verum
RELATED SPECIES	Hedge Bedstraw
HEIGHT/SPREAD	10–80 cm tall
FLOWERING TIME	May–September
HABITAT	Dry grassland, sand-dunes

Note: Our only yellow-flowered bedstraw.

FLOWER TYPE

IDENTIFICATION

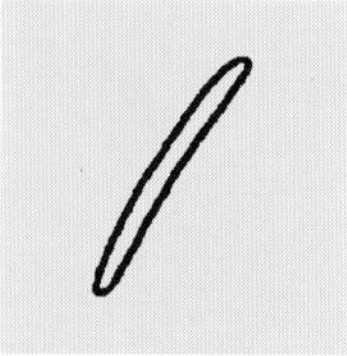

HABITAT

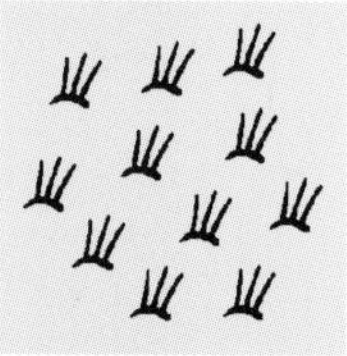

POPULATION

MAP

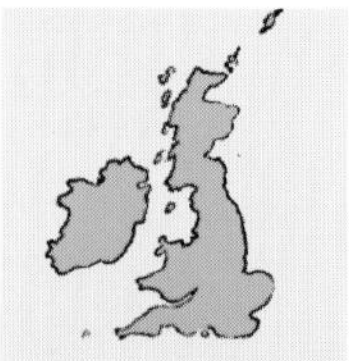

Size and appearance: A shortly hairy, erect or sprawling perennial, with creeping, underground shoots and leafy stems 10–80 cm (4–32 in) tall, sometimes up to 120 cm (48 in).

Leaves: In whorls of 8–12, very narrow, 1-veined, dark green, white-hairy beneath with inrolled margins, pointed.

Flowers: Yellow, honey-scented, 2–3 mm ($\frac{1}{12}$–$\frac{1}{8}$ in) across, funnel-shaped, with 4 spreading petal-lobes, in long, dense, often branched clusters.

Fruits: c. 2 mm ($\frac{1}{12}$ in) across, 2-lobed, black, smooth.

Related or similar plants: Hedge Bedstraw (p.213) has untidier, more sprawling stems, broader leaves and white flowers.

Habitat and distribution: Common in dry or well-drained grassland, on sunny banks, sand-dunes and shingle beaches, in churchyards and not infrequently on lawns, especially on lime-rich soils, throughout Britain and Ireland.

Flowering time: May to September.

Lady's Bedstraw (Galium verum) *is common in dry, well-drained grassland. In the Essex coastal grazing marshes, it occurs on large anthills where, when in flower, it gives the impression of the anthill wearing a yellow wig. It grows along with Sea Bindweed on sand-dunes and shingle beaches.*

HAY MADE FROM this useful and attractive wild plant was popular for stuffing mattresses. It is both sweet-scented and a natural deterrent to fleas and other vermin. The name Lady's Bedstraw is by association with the Virgin Mary, said to have lain on a bed of this plant during the birth of Christ. Thus, so legend tells, the plant won its yellow (golden) rather than white flowers like other bedstraws. Its traditional values other than for bedding material included use as a substitute for rennet to curdle cheese, and the extraction of a red dye from the underground stems.

Lady's Bedstraw has largely disappeared from extensive tracts of countryside with the ploughing of old grassland, but pockets survive well in churchyards, on roadside banks and unfertilised lawns. Plants from coastal cliffs, sand-dunes and shingle beaches are often dwarfed, with unbranched flower clusters.

SPECIES INFORMATION	
COMMON NAME	Hedge Bedstraw
SCIENTIFIC NAME	Galium mollugo
RELATED SPECIES	Lady's Bedstraw
HEIGHT/SPREAD	Stems 30–160 cm long
FLOWERING TIME	June–September
HABITAT	Hedge-banks and grassland

Note: The largest white-flowered bedstraw.

Hedge Bedstraw

BEDSTRAW FAMILY (Rubiaceae)

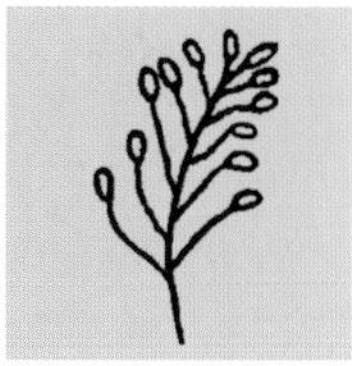

FLOWER TYPE

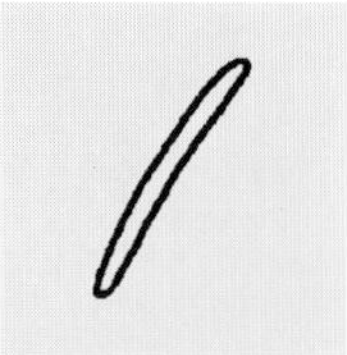

IDENTIFICATION

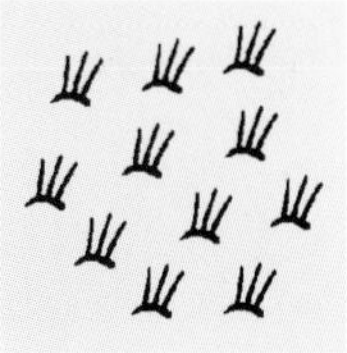

HABITAT

POPULATION

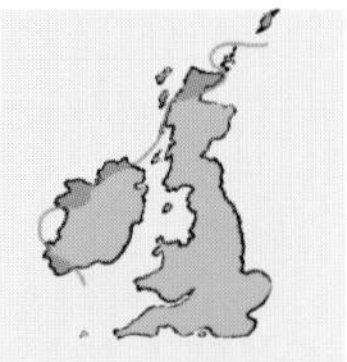

MAP

Size and appearance: A sprawling or less frequently erect perennial, with underground runners and square, hairy, leafy stems 30–160 cm (12–64 in) long.

Leaves: In whorls of 6–8, dark green, narrowly oblong, 1-veined pointed, with rough-prickly margins.

Flowers: White, 2–3 mm (1⁄12–1⁄8 in) across, funnel-shaped, with 4 spreading petal-lobes, in rather loose, much-branched clusters.

Fruits: c. 2 mm (1⁄12 in) across, 2-lobed, purplish or greyish, wrinkled.

Related or similar plants: Heath Bedstraw, of heaths and lime-poor pastures, has short, prostrate stems and leaves in whorls of 4–6; several other bedstraws have white flowers.

Habitat and distribution: Widespread in dry grassland, scrub and woodland clearings, and often abundant on hedge-banks and decayed retaining walls, less associated with lime-rich soils than Lady's Bedstraw (p.212); common over most of England but much more scattered in Wales, Scotland and Ireland.

Flowering time: June to September

HEDGE BEDSTRAW SOMETIMES crosses with Lady's Bedstraw (p.212), when the two occur together, giving rise to vigorous plants with pale yellow flowers.

The perennial bedstraws, all plants of grassland and marshes and, with the exception of Lady's Bedstraw (p.212), white-flowered, are not always easy to tell apart. Common Marsh-bedstraw (*Galium palustre*), has weak, minutely prickly, sprawling stems up to 100 cm (40 in) long, spear-shaped leaves with minutely-prickly margins, and flowers in very loose, spreading clusters. It occurs throughout in wet places.

Top and bottom right *Hedge Bedstraw* (Galium mollugo) *is floppy and scrambling and this bedstraw is often abundant on hedge-banks where its white flowers, in their loose, much-branched clusters, make a fine show in summer.*

Bottom left *Heath Bedstraw* (Galium saxatile) *is similar but has mostly prostrate stems not more than 30 cm (12 in) long, with leaves in whorls of 4–6; heaths and pastures on lime-poor soils.ngate cluster of 2–6. It is scarce but occurs locally in quantity, on wet heaths in southern England, and in scattered sites north to Cumbria.*

Goosegrass

BEDSTRAW FAMILY

(Rubiaceae)

SPECIES INFORMATION	
COMMON NAME	Goosegrass, Cleavers
SCIENTIFIC NAME	Galium aparine
RELATED SPECIES	Bedstraws
HEIGHT/SPREAD	Stems 50–200 cm long
FLOWERING TIME	May–September
HABITAT	Woodland margins, cultivated land

Note: A familiar straggling plant with 'velcro'-like stems.

FLOWER TYPE

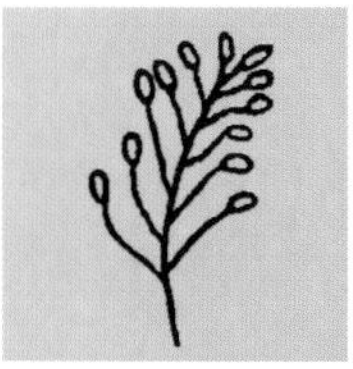

IDENTIFICATION

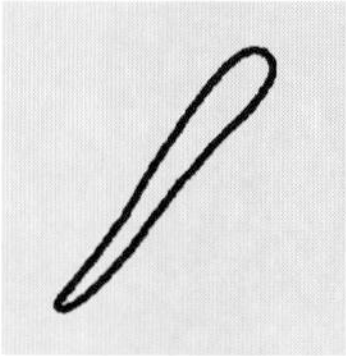

HABITAT

POPULATION

MAP

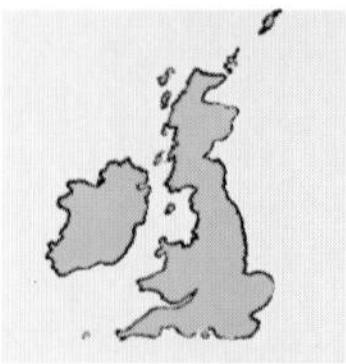

GOOSEGRASS IS, by its sheer numbers, a feature of the countryside. In autumn and late winter its seedlings are emerging in crowds; and by midsummer it has formed blankets of adhesive stems up hedges and over bushes and fences. In late summer the bristly fruits stick firmly to clothes and passing dogs and cats. It is almost impossible to take a walk without at least a few becoming tangled in one's socks or the dog's coat. This is one of the really successful modes of seed dispersal. It is a variable species, which seems to have much smaller fruits when growing as a weed of cultivation. A compact, prostrate variant occurs on shingle beaches.

Size and appearance: A scrambling or climbing annual, with 4-angled stems 50–200 cm (20–80 in) long, covered with minute, down-curved prickles.

Leaves: In whorls of 6–9, narrow, oblong, pointed, prickly-rough with hooked bristles.

Flowers: Greenish-white or white, c.2 mm (1/12 in) across, funnel-shaped with 4 spreading petal-lobes, in loose, few-flowered clusters.

Fruits: 2-lobed, densely covered with hooked bristles.

Related or similar plants: Hedge Bedstraw (p.213) is perennial with smooth rather than bristly stems, and large clusters of white flowers.

Habitat and distribution: Abundant almost everywhere, sometimes in huge numbers, in hedges, scrub and open woodland or along woodland margins, on waste ground and shingle beaches, and invading cultivated ground and crops.

Flowering time: May to September.

Goosegrass (Galium aparine) *is a far-straggling annual which readily clings to clothing by the tiny prickles which coat the stems, leaves and fruits. A successful weed has to flower early in life; plants barely two cm (4/5 in) high can already form a flower.*

SPECIES INFORMATION	
COMMON NAME	Crosswort
SCIENTIFIC NAME	Cruciata laevipes
RELATED SPECIES	Hedge Bedstraw
HEIGHT/SPREAD	12–60 cm tall
FLOWERING TIME	May–June
HABITAT	Dry grassland and scrub
Note: Like a yellow-flowered bedstraw.	

Crosswort

BEDSTRAW FAMILY (Rubiaceae)

Size and appearance: A softly-hairy perennial, with a creeping rootstock and semi-erect or sprawling, little-branched, leafy stems 12–60 cm (8–60 in) tall.
Leaves: In neat, regular whorls of 4, broadly spear-shaped or elliptical, 3-veined, dark green, white-hairy beneath with inrolled margins, pointed.
Flowers: Yellow, scented, 2–3 mm (1/12–1/8 in) across, funnel-shaped, with 4 spreading petal-lobes, in small dense clusters of 5–9 in the angle of yellowish leaves.
Fruits: 2–3 mm (1/12–1/8 in) across, nearly spherical, black, smooth.
Related or similar plants: Lady's Bedstraw (p.212) has narrower leaves in whorls of 8–12 and larger, denser flower clusters.
Habitat and distribution: Common in dry or well-drained, rough grassland and scrub, on sunny hedge-banks and roadsides, open woodland and woodland margins, especially on lime-rich soils, north to central Scotland, with scattered sites further north; absent from some areas like west Wales, and in Ireland introduced at Downpatrick in Ulster.
Flowering time: May to June.

CROSSWORT IS A GOOD indicator of lime-rich soils, and its presence on a roadside bank is often one the first signs of a change in geology. Many wild flowers are found only on chalk or limestone. In some cases, as with several of the orchids (pp.364–377), this is because these rocks give rise to well-drained soils that are warm and dry in summer. This mimics ecological conditions found further south in Europe.

Plants such as Crosswort, known by botanists as calcicoles, are unable to tolerate lime-poor soils, being chemically adapted to grow only in the presence of lime. If lime is absent, other minerals such as aluminium are more soluble and can poison the plant. Conversely, some plants such as heathers (pp.186–188), so-called calcifuges are unable to tolerate lime which prevents them from taking up minerals such as iron.

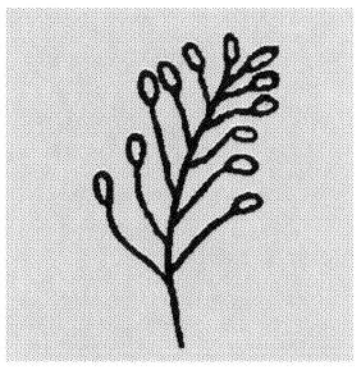
FLOWER TYPE

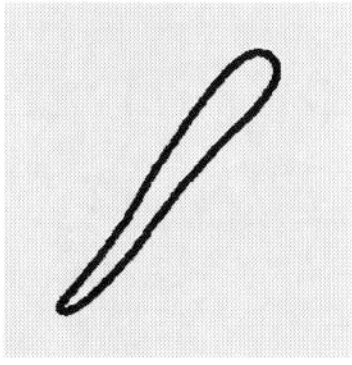
IDENTIFICATION

HABITAT

POPULATION

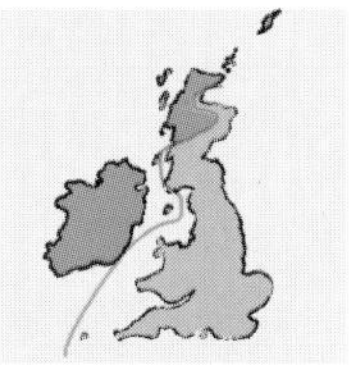
MAP

Crosswort (Cruciata laevipes) *is a tufted, softly hairy bedstraw with whorls of small yellow fragrant flowers at the base of the whorls of four elliptical, three-veined leaves. It is common on dry or well-drained grassy hedge-banks, especially on chalk and limestone soils.*

Field Bindweed

BINDWEED FAMILY

(Convolvulaceae)

SPECIES INFORMATION	
COMMON NAME	Field Bindweed
SCIENTIFIC NAME	Convolvulus arvensis
RELATED SPECIES	Hedge Bindweed
HEIGHT/SPREAD	Stems 50–200 cm long
FLOWERING TIME	May–September
HABITAT	Hedges, waysides and cultivated land

Note: A familiar climbing plant with large flowers.

FLOWER TYPE

IDENTIFICATION

HABITAT

POPULATION

MAP

Size and appearance: An often hairy perennial, with extensively branched, fleshy roots and numerous prostrate or (anti-clockwise) twining stems 50–200 cm (20–80 in) long, exuding a milky sap when cut.

Leaves: Oblong, triangular, spear- or arrow-shaped, rather blunt.

Flowers: Solitary or 2–3 together, white, or pink striped with white, funnel-shaped, 15–25 mm (⅗–1 in) across, slightly scented, without a pair of sepal-like bracts at the base (see Hedge Bindweed (p.217).

Fruits: Small, 2-celled, almost spherical capsules.

Related or similar plants: Hedge Bindweed (p.217) is much larger and has usually white flowers 30–60 mm (1⅕–2⅖ in) across.

Habitat and distribution: An all-too abundant plant of cultivated and waste ground, waysides and grassy places, either prostrate or climbing and trailing over other plants and man-made structures, but less common in northern Britain and Ireland.

Flowering time: May to September; the flowers close during dull or wet weather.

THIS IS A justifiably despised plant, one of the worst weeds of all, as even the smallest root-fragment will grow into a new plant. Nevertheless, it is one of the most attractive of all wild flowers, best seen in quantity brightening waste ground or elegantly disguising wire-netting fences. It is very variable in the shape and size of the leaves, flower colour and, of considerable significance for agriculture worldwide, in attributes like growth rate and weedkiller resistance.

Field Bindweed (Convolvulus arvensis) *comes in many colour forms, including white, a delicate pink, white with pink stripes reminiscent of Sea Bindweed and even white with red lines forming a circle around the inside of the funnel-shaped flower.*

SPECIES INFORMATION	
COMMON NAME	Hedge Bindweed, Bellbine
SCIENTIFIC NAME	Calystegia sylvestris
RELATED SPECIES	Field Bindweed
HEIGHT/SPREAD	Stems 1–3 m long
FLOWERING TIME	May–October
HABITAT	Hedges, waysides and cultivated land

Note: A familiar straggling or climbin plant.

Hedge Bindweed

BINDWEED FAMILY

(Convolvulaceae)

Size and appearance: A sparsely-hairy perennial with thick, fleshy roots and numerous tough, (anti-clockwise) twining stems 1–3 m (3–10 ft) long, exuding a milky sap when cut.
Leaves: Heart- or arrow-shaped, pointed.
Flowers: White, sometimes pink and white, funnel-shaped, 30–60 mm (1⅕–2⅖ in) across, unscented, with a pair of large, sepal-like bracts, sometimes much-inflated, at the base.
Fruits: Spherical, 1-celled capsules, enclosed by the large, persistent sepals.
Related or similar plants: Field Bindweed (p.216) is a smaller plant with white or pink flowers 15–25 mm (⅗–1 in) across; Sea Bindweed (p.218) has very short stems and round leaves, and occurs on sand-dunes.
Habitat and distribution: A common and familiar plant of woodland margins, scrub, hedgerows, tall riverside vegetation and marshes, waste ground, and as an unwelcome invader of gardens; in some districts the plants envelope hedges, roadsides and wire-netting with their vigorous climbing and trailing stems; throughout, but scarcer in Scotland.
Flowering time: May to October

LIKE FIELD BINDWEED (p.216), this plant is highly invasive but the flowers are terribly attractive. Hedge Bindweed is a variable species, divided by botanists into several distinct subspecies. American Bellbine, a large introduced subspecies, presumably once grown by gardeners with an eye for the picturesque but little grasp of reality, exhibits much more vigorous, leafier growth and larger white flowers, 60–75 mm (2⅜–3 in) across, with strongly inflated sepal-like bracts at the base. It is quite a landscape feature of some districts and seems particularly widespread in the south-east.

Near western coasts of Britain and Ireland, north to central Scotland, a native variant with slightly smaller, pink-striped flowers and downy stems and flower-stalks is an attractive plant of sheltered hedges and lanes.

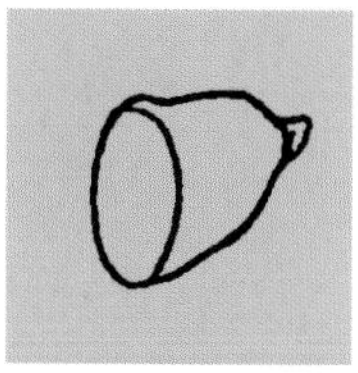

FLOWER TYPE

IDENTIFICATION

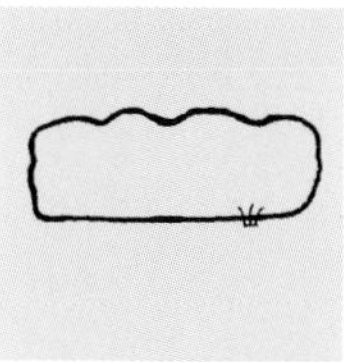

HABITAT

POPULATION

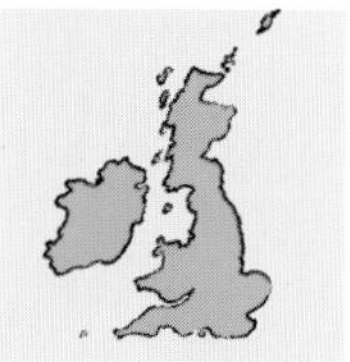

MAP

Hedge Bindweed (Calystegia sepium) *has pure white funnel-shaped flowers 30-60 mm (1 ⅕-2 ⅖ in) across. Close under the flower are two large, broad, pointed sepal-like bracts which enfold the narrower sepals. It is widespread and common in hedges and similar places but can also cover a wire fence, twining through each chain link as it makes its way to the top.*

Sea Bindweed

BINDWEED FAMILY

(Convolvulaceae)

SPECIES INFORMATION

COMMON NAME	Sea Bindweed
SCIENTIFIC NAME	Calystegia soldanella
RELATED SPECIES	Hedge Bindweed
HEIGHT/SPREAD	Stems 5–50 cm long
FLOWERING TIME	June–August
HABITAT	Sand-dunes

Note: A dwarf bindweed of coastal sands.

FLOWER TYPE

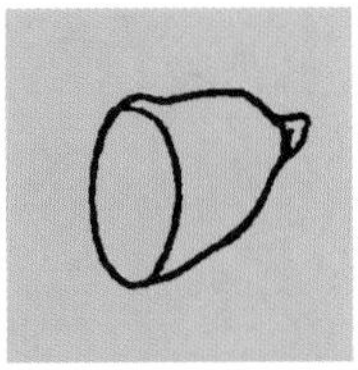

IDENTIFICATION

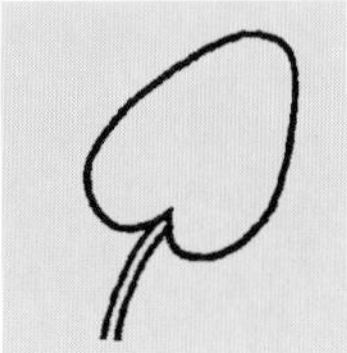

HABITAT

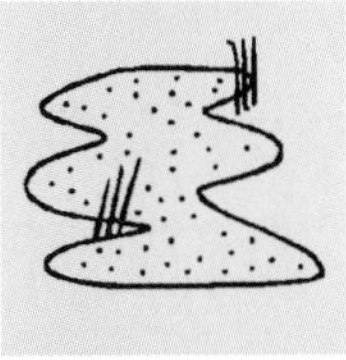

POPULATION

MAP

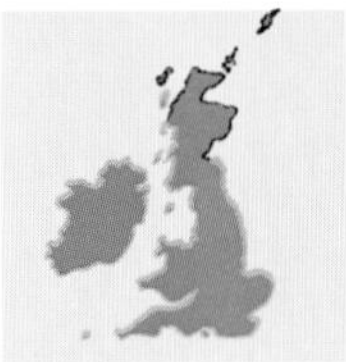

Size and appearance: A small, hairless perennial with stems 5–50 cm (2–20 in) long, creeping through sand rather than twining as in other bindweeds, exuding a milky sap when cut.

Leaves: Small, fleshy, dark green, kidney-shaped, blunt.

Flowers: Pink striped with white, funnel-shaped, 3–5 cm (1⅕–2 in) across, unscented, with a pair of small, sepal-like bracts at the base.

Fruits: Spherical, 1-celled capsules.

Related or similar plants: The other bindweeds (pp.216–219) have long, twining stems and usually heart- or arrow-shaped leaves.

Habitat and distribution: Locally common on sand-dunes and the upper parts of sandy beaches, and on fine shingle, all around the coasts of Britain and Ireland, but scarce over long stretches and almost totally absent from most of northern and eastern Scotland.

Flowering time: June to August.

THIS IS ONE of the choicest wild flowers of the seaside, the pink-and-white-striped flowers and neat, rounded leaves half buried in sand or nestling among the sparse vegetation. The stems of Sea Bindweed push through sand rather than climb, but in parts of western Ireland, plants sometimes twine slightly among grasses and other vegetation.

Sea Bindweed (Calystegia soldanella) *is a delightful member of this family, with its pink and white striped flowers and dark green kidney-shaped leaves creeping out from under grassy tussocks across the sand-dunes.*

SPECIES INFORMATION	
COMMON NAME	Dodder
SCIENTIFIC NAME	Cuscuta epithymum
RELATED SPECIES	Bindweeds
HEIGHT/SPREAD	Stems 5–50 cm long
FLOWERING TIME	July–September
HABITAT	Heaths and rough grassland

Note: Like masses of thin, purplish or reddish spaghetti.

Dodder

BINDWEED FAMILY
(Convolvulaceae)

Size and appearance: A rootless, hairless annual with weak, branched, purplish or reddish stems 5–50 cm (2–20 in) long, (anticlockwise) twining and spreading like a net over other plants.
Leaves: Inconspicuous, scale-like.
Flowers: Tiny, bell-shaped, waxy-white tinged pink, the calyx reddish, in dense, spherical clusters up to 10 mm (⅜ in) across.
Fruits: Clusters of small, 2-celled capsules, each enclosed in the persistent flower-parts.
Related or similar plants: The other bindweeds (pp.216–218) are leafy and green; compare, however, Lesser Broomrape and Bird's-nest Orchid (p.367).
Habitat and distribution: Sometimes frequent on heaths and in rough grassland, parasitic on a range of plants including heather, gorse and clovers, mostly south of a line between the rivers Severn and Humber, with a few sites in Wales and the Isle of Man and on Irish coasts.
Flowering time: July to September.

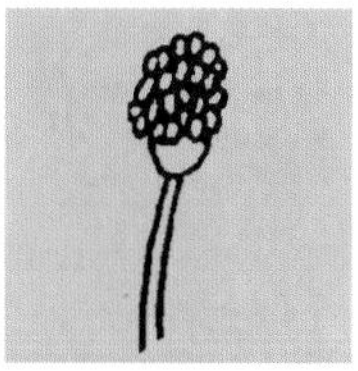
FLOWER TYPE

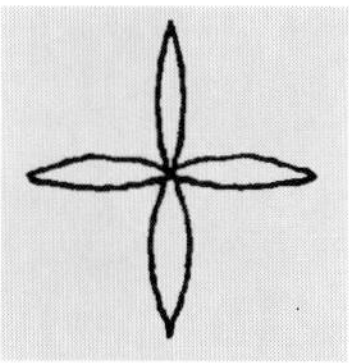
IDENTIFICATION

HABITAT

POPULATION

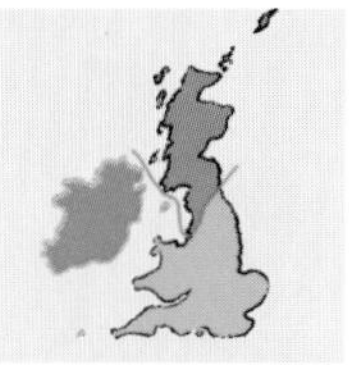
MAP

DODDER IS IN THE SAME FAMILY as the bindweeds but its ecology and life-history are quite different. The plant is a rootless parasite that, after the seed has germinated, attaches itself as a seedling to other plants, both shrubs and herbaceous perennials, even annuals, by means of root-like penetrating structures. It then grows by absorbing nutrients and water from the host. In the summer it produces flowers and seed just like any other plant. When Dodder is abundant, it forms conspicuous, rather sinister masses of stems among the plants that it parasitises.

Dodder (Cuscuta epithymum) *is a parasitic plant. From a distance it looks like masses of thin, purplish or reddish spaghetti adhering to other plants. Upon closer inspection, the tiny clusters of pinkish-white, bell-shaped flowers can be seen on the twining stems.*

Viper's Bugloss

COMFREY AND FORGET-ME-NOT FAMILY

(Boraginaceae)

SPECIES INFORMATION	
COMMON NAME	Viper's Bugloss
SCIENTIFIC NAME	Echium vulgare
RELATED SPECIES	Borage
HEIGHT/SPREAD	30–100 cm tall
FLOWERING TIME	June–August
HABITAT	Dry, open ground

Note: The most striking of our commoner blue flowers.

FLOWER TYPE

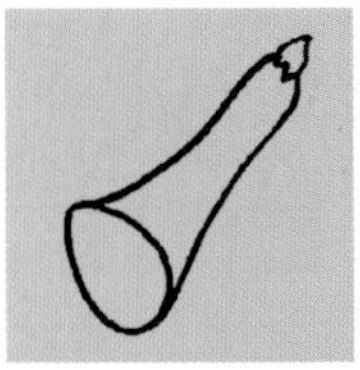

IDENTIFICATION

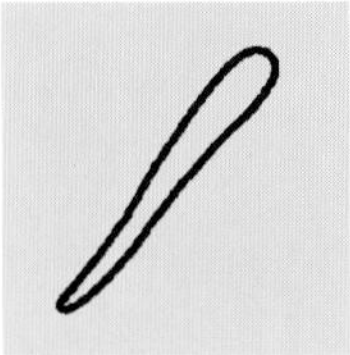

HABITAT

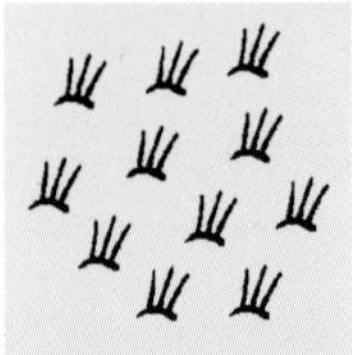

POPULATION

MAP

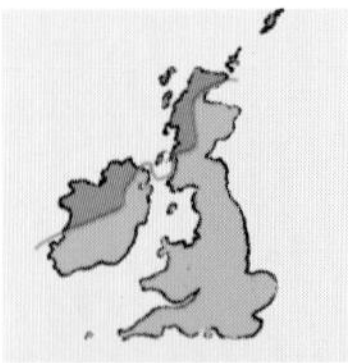

ESPECIALLY WHERE IT occurs in quantity, Viper's Bugloss is one of the most stately and handsome wild flowers. It dominates open, dry places such as a bare chalk slope, a disused railway siding or a coastal shingle beach. Elsewhere in the world, where it has been introduced, it is not so welcome: farmers in eastern North America call it Blue Thistle or Blue Devil. Purple Viper's Bugloss (*Echium plantagineum*), a related, mainly Mediterranean species with larger, purplish flowers, colours grazing land in Australia, where it is known as Paterson's Curse after its introducer. It is a rare Cornish native, hanging on in a few potato fields.

Size and appearance: A very bristly-hairy, erect biennial 30–100 cm (12–40 in) tall.
Leaves: Mostly in a basal rosette that withers by flowering, spear- or strap-shaped, blunt.
Flowers: Blue (the buds purplish-red), trumpet-shaped, 10–20 mm (⅖–⅘ in) long, with 4–5 protruding stamens, in a dense spike of curved, 1-sided clusters.
Fruits: A cluster of 4 nutlets.
Related or similar plants: Borage has larger flowers in loose, branched, leafy clusters.
Habitat and distribution: A widespread plant of dry, open and stony places such as dry grassland, waysides, waste ground, concrete rubble, sand-dunes and shingle beaches, usually on lime-rich soils, mainly in eastern and southern England, and rare over much of Scotland; in Ireland only on or near the east coast.
Flowering time: June to August.

Bottom left *Borage* (Borago officinalis)*, the only blue-flowered plant likely to be confused with Viper's Bugloss, is an annual with spear-shaped leaves and loose, branched, leafy clusters of flowers. These are 20–30 mm (1⅕–2 in)across and have 5 spreading lobes. An escape from gardens, Borage has become locally established, mainly by the sea.*

SPECIES INFORMATION	
COMMON NAME	Common Comfrey
SCIENTIFIC NAME	Symphytum officinale
RELATED SPECIES	Tuberous Comfrey
HEIGHT/SPREAD	50–120 cm tall
FLOWERING TIME	May–July
HABITAT	Damp grassy places and riverbanks

Note: With bristly leaves and usually white or purplish flowers.

Common Comfrey

COMFREY AND FORGET-ME-NOT FAMILY

(Boraginaceae)

Size and appearance: A robust, rough-hairy, leafy perennial with erect, branched, winged stems 50–120 cm (20–48 in) tall, forming large patches.
Leaves: Basal leaves stalked, broadly spear-shaped, pointed, the upper leaves stalkless and running down the stem as a wing.
Flowers: White, or violet-purple, pinkish or blue, tubular, 12–20 mm (½–⅘ in) long, with back-turned lobes, in curved, 1-sided clusters.
Fruits: A cluster of 4 smooth, black, shiny nutlets.
Related or similar plants: The most wide-spread of several similar comfreys, most of them garden escapes; the more distinctive Tuberous Comfrey has pale yellow flowers.

Habitat and distribution: Locally common and forming conspicuous clumps or dense stands in damp and grassy places, along hedgerows and ditches, and by streams and rivers; throughout, but local in northern Scotland and Ireland, where it is introduced.
Flowering time: May to July.

COMFREY IS A coarse-looking plant, yet one that has gained a massive reputation both as a compost and soil improver, and as a healing herb. It grows vigorously, and the leaves decay to release a large amount of absorbed plant nutrient. As a herb, Comfrey reduces inflammation and aids healing. It has been employed since ancient times to treat almost any type of wound, bruise, skin complaint or bone fracture. Some people cook and eat the nutritious leaves like spinach or fried in batter, but the plant may be harmful taken internally in large quantities.

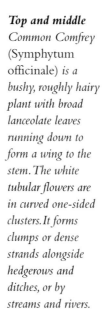

***Top and middle** Common Comfrey* (Symphytum officinale) *is a bushy, roughly hairy plant with broad lanceolate leaves running down to form a wing to the stem. The white tubular flowers are in curved one-sided clusters. It forms clumps or dense strands alongside hedgerows and ditches, or by streams and rivers.*

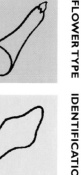

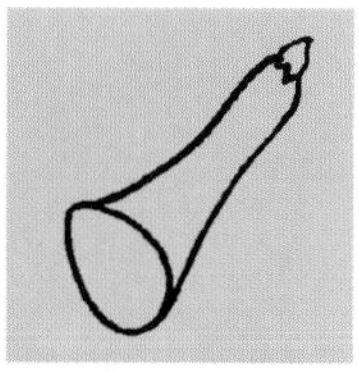

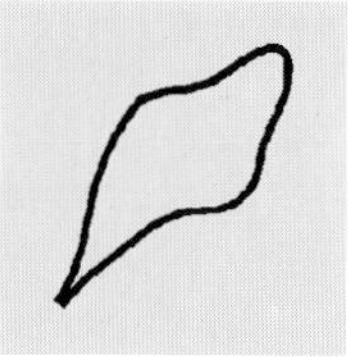

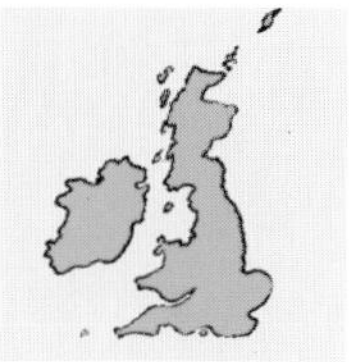

***Bottom** Tuberous Comfrey* (Symphytum tuberosum) *is a smaller plant, up to 50 cm (20 in) tall, with tuberous roots, basal leaves withered by flowering, only slightly winged stems, and pale yellow flowers. It occurs in woods mainly in Scotland but with scattered introductions elsewhere.*

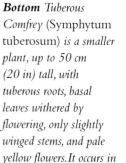

Hound's-tongue

COMFREY AND FORGET-ME-NOT FAMILY (Boraginaceae)

SPECIES INFORMATION	
COMMON NAME	Hound's-tongue
SCIENTIFIC NAME	Cynoglossum officinale
RELATED SPECIES	Common Comfrey
HEIGHT/SPREAD	30–60 cm tall
FLOWERING TIME	May–August
HABITAT	Dry, open habitats

Note: Softly greyish-hairy and smelling of mice when bruised.

FLOWER TYPE

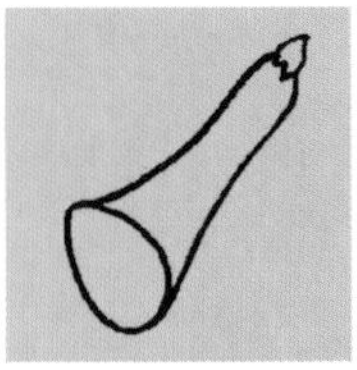

IDENTIFICATION

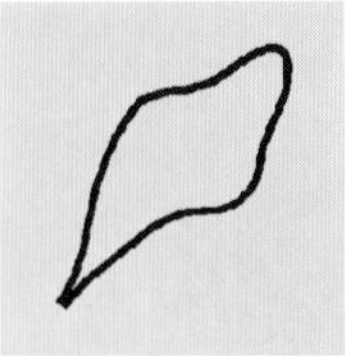

HABITAT

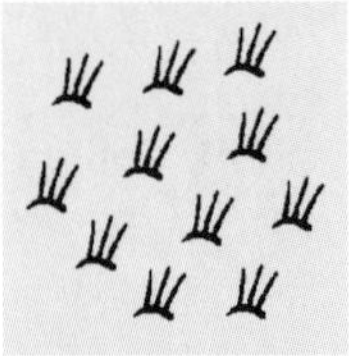

POPULATION

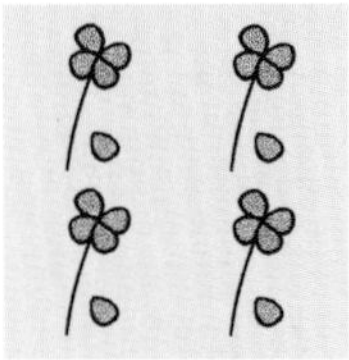

MAP

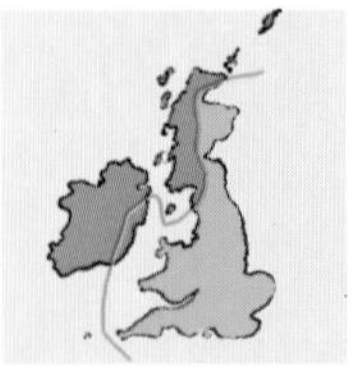

Size and appearance: A softly-hairy, leafy biennial 30–60 cm (12–24 in) tall, with erect, winged stems.

Leaves: Basal leaves stalked, oblong or spear-shaped, with dense, grey-silky hairs, pointed, the upper leaves narrower, stalkless.

Flowers: Purplish-red, funnel-shaped 5–6 mm (⅕–¼ in) across, with 5 scales closing the throat, in curved, 1-sided clusters.

Fruits: A cluster of 4 flattened, egg-shaped nutlets, with raised borders and covered with short, hooked spines.

Related or similar plants: Common Comfrey (p.221) has winged stems and spear-shaped leaves but is more robust and usually has white or purplish flowers.

Habitat and distribution: Widespread but local in dry, open, stony and grassy places and sand-dunes, especially on lime-rich or sandy soils, throughout England and Wales but local in the west, extending to the east coasts of Scotland and Ireland.

Flowering time: May to August.

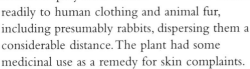

HOUND'S-TONGUE is a curious-looking plant, drab but for the deep-toned flowers, not unlike a tawny port in colour. The soft leaves smell unpleasantly of mice when bruised – the actual chemical is acetamide. Hound's-tongue is unpalatable to grazing animals, and plants survive in quantity about rabbit burrows. The rather attractive spiny fruits adhere readily to human clothing and animal fur, including presumably rabbits, dispersing them a considerable distance. The plant had some medicinal use as a remedy for skin complaints.

Hound's-tongue (Cynoglossum officinale) *is a softly downy, grey perennial with broad lance-olate leaves continuing up the stem and often wavy edged. The deep purplish-red flowers are in curved clusters which all face the same direction. Widespread but local in bare, dry, chalky or sandy soils, it is often found around rabbit burrows where the soil has been disturbed by their activities.*

SPECIES INFORMATION	
COMMON NAME	Oysterplant, Northern Shorewort
SCIENTIFIC NAME	Mertensia maritima
RELATED SPECIES	Common Comfrey
HEIGHT/SPREAD	Stems 20–60 cm long
FLOWERING TIME	June–August
HABITAT	Sand and shingle beaches
Note: A distinctive, blue-flowered plant of northern beaches.	

Oysterplant

COMFREY AND FORGET-ME-NOT FAMILY
(Boraginaceae)

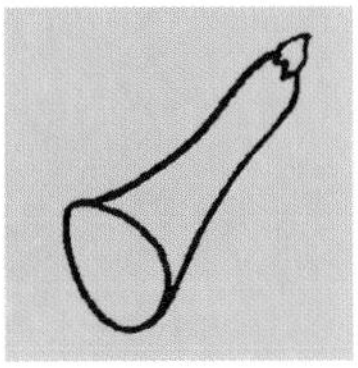

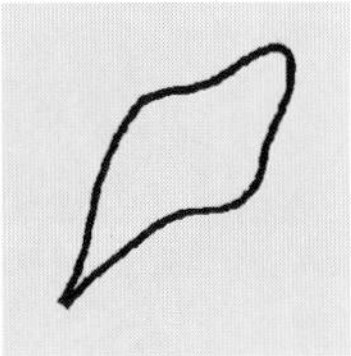

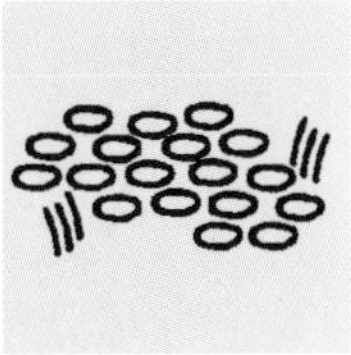

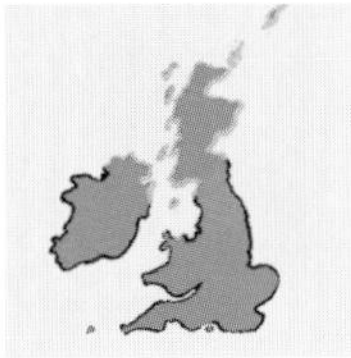

Size and appearance: A greyish-hairy perennial, with a rope-like taproot and prostrate or semi-erect stems 20–60 cm (8–24 in) long.

Leaves: Leaves fleshy, the basal long-stalked, oval to spoon-shaped, the upper similar but stalkless.

Flowers: Blue and purplish-pink (pink in bud), bell-shaped, 5–6 mm (⅕–¼ in) across, in branched, leafy clusters.

Fruits: A cluster of 4 fleshy nutlets.

Related or similar plants: Oysterplant is extremely distinct in appearance and habitat, and no other plant is likely to be confused with it.

Habitat and distribution: A generally scarce, northern plant that is restricted to sand and shingle beaches, fluctuating in numbers and often growing with few other species among the seaweed and flotsam of the strand-line; around the coasts of Scotland, but rarer in the east, extending south to north Wales, the Isle of Man and northern Ireland.

Flowering time: June to August.

OYSTERPLANT IS A mysterious and beautiful beach flower of the north, sporadic in appearance and slowly decreasing. It used to occur as far south as Norfolk and the Shannon estuary, However, its numbers are apparently stable in much of its Scottish range, especially in Orkney. Like many beach plants, it suffers from the trampling of beaches by visitors and the removal of shingle for building or coastal defence. Numbers of many beach plants do fluctuate, and the seeds of Oysterplant can remain dormant for several years. They are dispersed by seawater, so can travel some distance. The leaves are said to taste like oysters.

Oysterplant (Mertensia maritima) *is a plant of strand-lines of shingle beaches more common in Scotland where it can sometimes be found at the head of the sea. The purplish-blue flowers combined with the thick, oval, grey leaves on long prostrate stems fanning out from a central rosette make this plant quite distinctive.*

Purple Gromwell

COMFREY AND FORGET-ME-NOTFAMILY
(Boraginaceae)

SPECIES INFORMATION	
COMMON NAME	Purple Gromwell
SCIENTIFIC NAME	Lithospermum purpureocaeruleum
RELATED SPECIES	Viper's Bugloss
HEIGHT/SPREAD	20–60 cm tall
FLOWERING TIME	May–June
HABITAT	Cliffs and scrub

Note: The magnificent, rich blue flowers are like those of no other native.

FLOWER TYPE

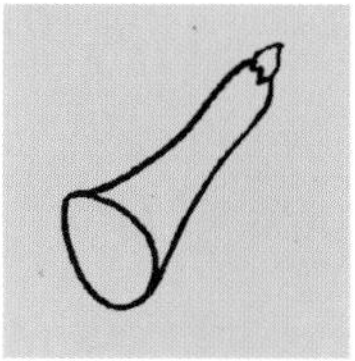

IDENTIFICATION

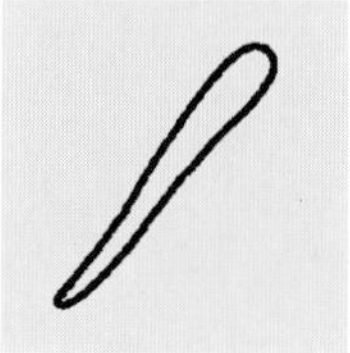

HABITAT

POPULATION

MAP

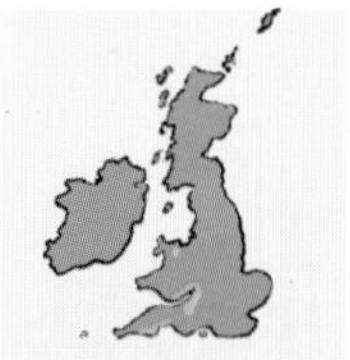

Size and appearance: A densely-downy perennial, with sprawling, rooting, vegetative shoots and erect flowering stems 20–60 cm (8–24 in) long.
Leaves: Leaves narrowly spear-shaped, dark green, pointed.
Flowers: Reddish-purple, becoming a rich blue, funnel-shaped, 12–15 mm (½–⅗ in) across, in 2–3 leafy clusters.
Fruits: A cluster of 4 smooth, white, spherical nutlets.
Related or similar plants: Viper's Bugloss (p.220) has bristly leaves and flowers in tall spikes.
Habitat and distribution: A rarity of scrub, cliffs and hedge-banks, always on limestone, in the West Country and Wales; an occasional garden escape elsewhere.
Flowering time: May to June.

THIS MAGNIFICENT, gentian-blue flower survives well in a few places, mainly near the coast. Fortunately many of its sites are remote or steep, and the flowers soon fade and wither if picked. Plants for gardens, where the plant can be rampant, are readily available via the nursery trade. Purple Gromwell is mostly a plant of south and south-eastern Europe, but extends north-west to reach the northern limit of its range in Wales.

The first half of the scientific name comes to us from ancient times, from the Greek *lithos* (stone) and *sperma* (seed), denoting the white, stone-like seeds. These persist conspicuously on withered stems through the autumn. The old herbalists recommended them to expel stones from body organs, but no basis for this exists other than that they look like stones (the 'doctrine of signatures').

Top and bottom right *Purple Gromwell* (Lithospermum purpureocaeruleum) *has flowers in terminal clusters, which are first a reddish-purple and then turn a deep blue.*

Bottom left *Corn Gromwell* (Lithospermum arvense)*, a smaller, relatively drab relation of Purple Gromwell, is a little-branched annual, with strap-shaped, blunt leaves, short clusters of white or bluish flowers 3–4 mm (⅛–⅙ in) across, and minutely warty nuts.*

SPECIES INFORMATION	
COMMON NAME	Field Forget-me-not
SCIENTIFIC NAME	Myosotis arvensis
RELATED SPECIES	Water Forget-me-not
HEIGHT/SPREAD	5–25 cm tall
FLOWERING TIME	May–September
HABITAT	Cultivated ground

Note: The common small forget-me-not of open ground.

Field Forget-me-not

COMFREY AND FORGET-ME-NOT FAMILY

(Boraginaceae)

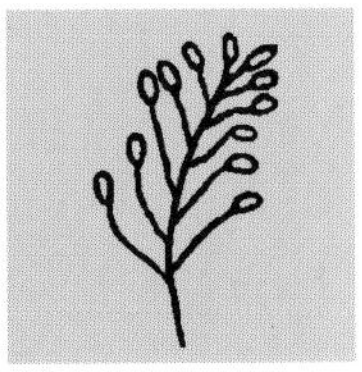

FLOWER TYPE

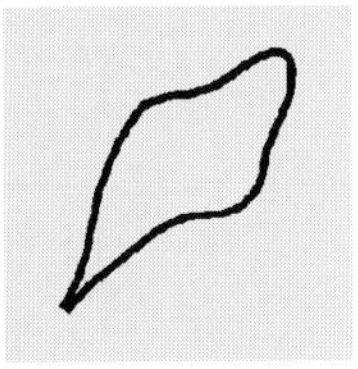

IDENTIFICATION

HABITAT

POPULATION

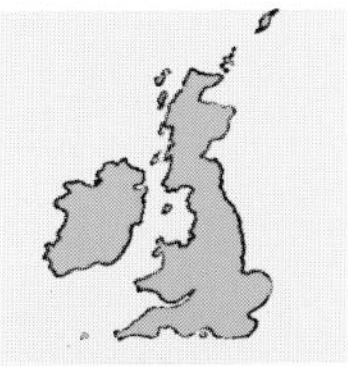

MAP

Size and appearance: An erect, greyish-hairy annual 5–25 cm (2–10 in) tall, sometimes up to 50 cm (20 in).
Leaves: Elliptical, the upper stalkless, spear-shaped.
Flowers: Pale blue, with a yellow central eye, dish-shaped, 3–5 mm ($\frac{1}{8}$–$\frac{1}{5}$ in) across, in 1-sided, rather flat-topped clusters that lengthen in fruit.
Fruits: Clusters of 4 blackish, shiny nutlets, enclosed within the persistent calyx.
Related or similar plants: Water Forget-me-not (p.226) has larger flowers and grows in wet places.
Habitat and distribution: Widespread and common on open and disturbed ground, especially arable fields on light soils.
Flowering time: May to September.

THE FLOWER CLUSTERS of all forget-me-nots are short and condensed in bud, but the main stalk then lengthens and curves as the individual flowers open. The resulting shape, characteristic of the whole family, somewhat resembles a scorpion's curled tail. Hence scorpion-grass, an earlier name for forget-me-not from both French and German. Forget-me-not as a name seems to have gained popularity during the Romantic art movement of the early 19th century.

Two other small annual forget-me-nots occur on open ground, both with smaller flowers only 2–3 mm ($\frac{1}{12}$–$\frac{1}{8}$ in) across. Early Forget-me-not (*Myosotis ramosissima*) has bright blue flowers. It grows on dry or sandy ground, especially on sand-dunes, and is mostly coastal in the west. Changing Forget-me-not (*Myosotis discolor*) has flowers that are yellow when they first open, changing colour to pinkish or blue. It is a widespread but local plant of dry banks, sandy fields and heaths.

Top *Field Forget-me-not* (Myosotis arvensis) *is the most widespread species common along field margins.*

Bottom right *Changing Forget-me-not* (Myosotis discolor) *can be identified by the flowers, which are yellow when they first open and then turning to the more familiar blue.*

Bottom left *Early Forget-me-not* (Myosotis ramosissima) *is confused with Changing Forget-me-not but its flowers are always blue with spoon-shaped lower leaves.*

Water Forget-me-not

COMFREY AND FORGET-ME-NOT FAMILY
(Boraginaceae)

SPECIES INFORMATION	
COMMON NAME	Water Forget-me-not
SCIENTIFIC NAME	Myosotis scorpioides
RELATED SPECIES	Field Forget-me-not
HEIGHT/SPREAD	10–50 cm tall
FLOWERING TIME	May–September
HABITAT	Wet places

Note: The commonest forget-me-not of wet places.

FLOWER TYPE

IDENTIFICATION

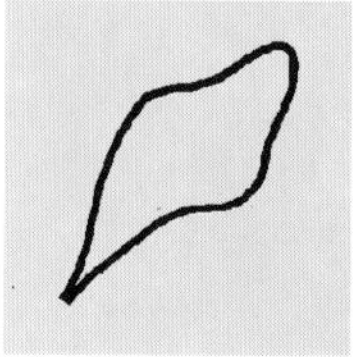

HABITAT

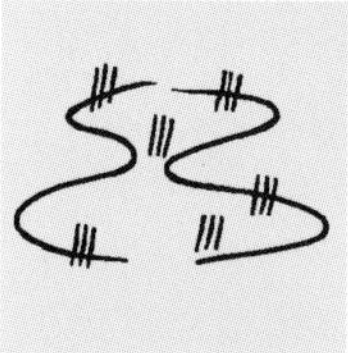

POPULATION

MAP

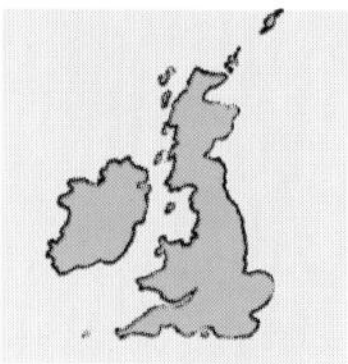

Size and appearance: A mostly erect, hairless or slightly hairy, pale green perennial with creeping runners and stems 10–50 cm (4–20 in) tall, sometimes sprawling up to 100 cm (40 in) long.

Leaves: Spear- or spoon-shaped, blunt, the upper smaller, stalkless.

Flowers: Pale blue, with a yellow eye, rarely pink or white, 8–10 mm (⅓–⅜ in) across, disc-shaped, in leafless, 1-sided, rather flat-topped leafless clusters that lengthen in fruit; calyx-teeth short, triangular.

Fruits: Clusters of 4 blackish, shiny nutlets, enclosed within the persistent calyx.

Related or similar plants: Water Forget-me-not differs from several forget-me-nots of wet places.

Habitat and distribution: Widespread and sometimes very abundant beside and in streams, and in marshes, rides and glades of wet woods, and damp meadows.

Flowering time: May to September.

THIS AND OTHER forget-me-nots provide an attractive floral display in wet places everywhere. Creeping Water Forget-me-not (*Myosotis secunda*), also with runners and pale blue flowers, is hairier and has flowers 6–8 mm (¼–⅓ in) across with long, pointed calyx-teeth, in leafier clusters. It is a plant of lime-poor marshes and bogs, more especially in the west and north of Britain and Ireland. Tufted Water Forget-me-not (*Myosotis laxa*) lacks runners and has bright blue flowers not more than 5 mm (⅕ in) across.

Garden forget-me-nots sometimes escape on to hedge-banks and open ground.

Water Forget-me-not (Myosotis scorpioides) *is a pale green creeping perennial with relatively large blue and yellow flowers at first coiled and then opening out into flat-topped clusters. It is common along the margins of streams and ponds.*

SPECIES INFORMATION	
COMMON NAME	Common Water-starwort
SCIENTIFIC NAME	Callitriche stagnalis
RELATED SPECIES	Other water-starworts
HEIGHT/SPREAD	Stems 10–100 cm long
FLOWERING TIME	April–October
HABITAT	Streams and ponds

Note: The commonest 'green water weed'.

Common Water-starwort

WATER-STARWORT FAMILY (Callitrichaceae)

FLOWER TYPE

IDENTIFICATION

HABITAT

POPULATION

MAP

Size and appearance: A hairless, pale green perennial, with slender, weak stems 10–100 cm (4–40 in) long, trailing in water or prostrate on bare mud.

Leaves: In opposite pairs, short-stalked, elliptical, blunt, the uppermost forming floating rosettes.

Flowers: Minute, 4-lobed, inconspicuous but for a single pale yellow stamen.

Fruits: Tiny, broadly winged, pale brown.

Related or similar plants: Other water-starworts differ in tiny details of leaf-shape and fruit; several are rare.

Habitat and distribution: Widespread and often common in slow streams, lakes, ponds, flooded ditches, wet roadside runnels, and ruts and hollows in wet woodland rides; sometimes on bare, wet mud as well as floating in the water.

Flowering time: April to October.

Top *Common Water-starwort* (Callitriche stagnalis) *produces minute inconspicuous flowers in the centre of a floating rosette of leaves which are often a bright apple green. The submerged leaves are usually narrower.*

COMMON WATER-STARWORT is one of those wild plants that many of us overlook, although actually ubiquitous and quite a feature of wet places. It is particularly noticeable, especially in late summer, rooting on the wet mud of drying streams and ponds. The flowers are so small that the plant might not be recognised as having them at all.

The only other common water-starwort, out of a total of seven very similar native species, is Various-leaved Water-starwort (*Callitriche platycarpa*), which has narrower, darker green leaves and narrowly winged fruits. It is widespread but local in lime-rich streams and pools.

Bottom *The commonest species of Water-starwort can be found in ponds, rivers, ditches and even water-logged cart-tracks in woods.*

Bugle

MINT FAMILY

(Labiatae or Lamiaceae)

SPECIES INFORMATION	
COMMON NAME	Bugle
SCIENTIFIC NAME	Ajuga reptans
RELATED SPECIES	Skullcap
HEIGHT/SPREAD	10–40 cm tall
FLOWERING TIME	April–July
HABITAT	Woodland

Note: The tall spikes of numerous blue flowers are distinctive.

FLOWER TYPE

IDENTIFICATION

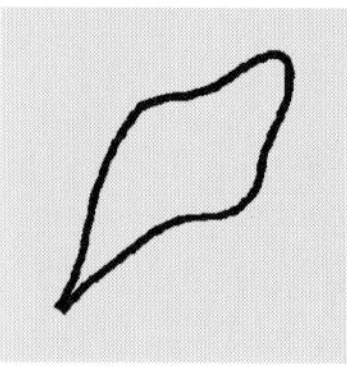

HABITAT

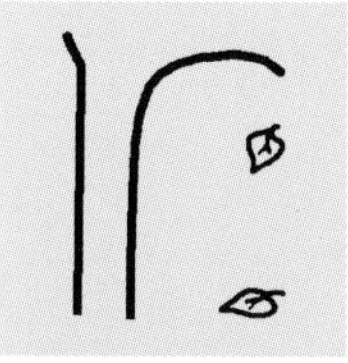

POPULATION

MAP

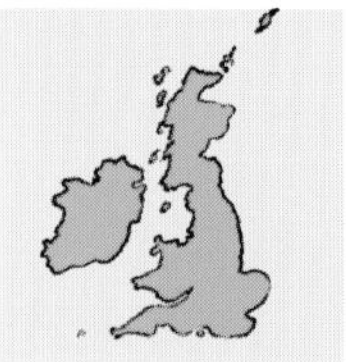

BUGLE IS A DISTINCTIVE and attractive flower of woodland in spring, and variants with bronze or multicoloured leaves are popular plants for cottage-style and wild gardens. It is a useful, if invasive, cover plant for placement rockeries and the edges of shady borders.

Like other members of this family, such as Selfheal (p.240), Bugle has long been prized as a medicinal herb that cures bruises and wounds. It was especially used to staunch bleeding, for example from nicks from tools and agricultural implements – hence one of its local names, Carpenter's Herb.

Bugle (Ajuga reptans) *has far-creeping runners which produce dense patches of erect, unbranched spikes of blue flowers. The flowers themselves have a very short upper lip and a three-lobed lower lip; the central lobe being the largest and slightly notched. Widespread and common along damp woodland rides.*

Size and appearance: A perennial with far-creeping runners and erect, square stems 10–40 cm (4–16 in) tall, hairy on opposite sides at each leaf insertion.

Leaves: In opposite pairs, stalked, oval, obscurely toothed, the upper ones smaller.

Flowers: Blue, rarely pink or white, 15–18 mm (⅗–¾ in) long, tubular with a lip, in whorls in a tall, leafy spike; upper stem and leaves tinged bluish or violet.

Fruits: Clusters of 4 nutlets, enclosed within the persistent calyx.

Related or similar plants: Skullcap (p.230) has blue flowers, but in pairs in a very loose, 1-sided spike; Selfheal (p.240) has bluish-purple flowers.

Habitat and distribution: Often common in woods, especially along rides and in glades, in hedges and damp meadows; almost throughout, except for parts of northern Scotland and western Ireland.

Flowering time: April to July.

SPECIES INFORMATION	
COMMON NAME	Wood Sage
SCIENTIFIC NAME	Teucrium scorodonia
RELATED SPECIES	Bugle
HEIGHT/SPREAD	20–50 cm tall
FLOWERING TIME	June–September
HABITAT	Heaths and rocky ground
Note: A shrubby mint-like plant.	

Wood Sage

MINT FAMILY
(Labiatae or Lamiaceae)

Size and appearance: A branched shrublet, woody below, with tough, erect or semi-erect, square stems 20–50 cm (8–20 in) tall.
Leaves: In opposite pairs, triangular to oval, with a heart-shaped base, rounded teeth and wrinkled surface.
Flowers: Greenish-yellow, sometimes white or marked with red, 8–10 mm (⅓–⅖ in) long, conspicuously lipped, in pairs in leafless, spike-like clusters; calyx bell-shaped, hairy.
Fruits: Clusters of 4 nutlets, enclosed within the persistent calyx.
Related or similar plants: The non-shrubby Yellow Archangel (p.235) has yellow flowers, but they are larger and come in spring.
Habitat and distribution: Widespread on heaths, in scrub and open woods, on dry, sandy or limestone banks and rocky ground, on both lime-rich and lime-poor soils throughout Britain, except parts of central England; also rare in central Ireland.
Flowering time: June to September.

FLOWER TYPE

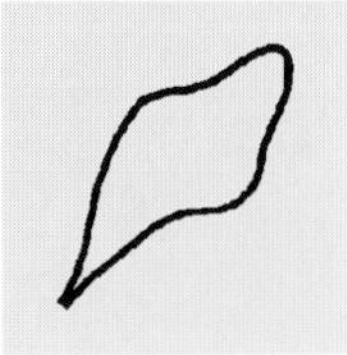

IDENTIFICATION

HABITAT

POPULATION

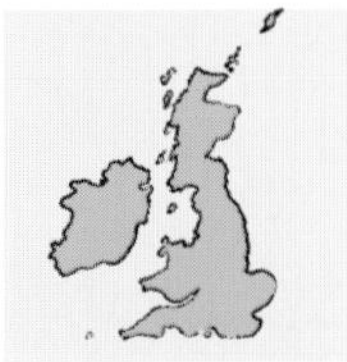

MAP

THE FLOWERS OF this rather dowdy-looking plant of dry, heathy places and woods are well worth a closer look. They are neat in structure, with a pronounced, 5-lobed lower lip that is often finely marked with red. The stamens too are red. Wood Sage, like Ground Ivy (p.239) in the same family, was formerly used to flavour and preserve beer. It is also an ancient medicinal herb with healing properties. It is not a true sage, and the leaves lack the strong scent and flavour of Garden Sage (*Salvia officinalis*), originally from southern Europe.

Botanists have found by garden and other experiments that the adaptation of plants of Wood Sage to either lime-rich or lime-poor soil type has a genetic basis.

Top *Wood Sage* (Teucrium scorodonia) *has greenish-yellow flowers with only one lip which is five-lobed; the four side lobes being short and the middle lobe large. Four maroon stamens poke out at the top, the two outer ones being the longer. The flowers are in pairs in branched one-sided leafless spikes.*

Bottom left and right
A perennial with creeping rootstock producing erect branched stems. The leaves are in opposite pairs, stalked with a heart-shaped base, bluntly toothed and with a wrinkled surface. It is a plant of well-drained conditions, whether it be on sandy heaths or in a limestone gryke.

Skullcap

MINT FAMILY

(Labiatae or Lamiaceae)

SPECIES INFORMATION	
COMMON NAME	Skullcap
SCIENTIFIC NAME	Scutellaria galericulata
RELATED SPECIES	Lesser Skullcap
HEIGHT/SPREAD	10–50 cm tall
FLOWERING TIME	June–September
HABITAT	Riversides and marshes

Note: A blue-flowered 'mint' of wet places.

FLOWER TYPE

IDENTIFICATION

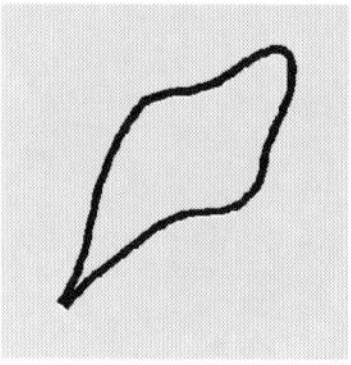

HABITAT

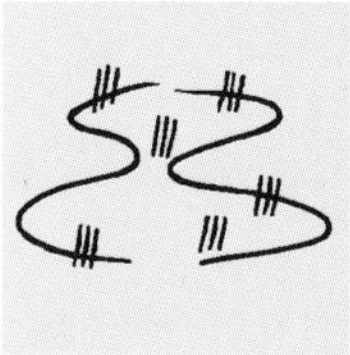

POPULATION

MAP

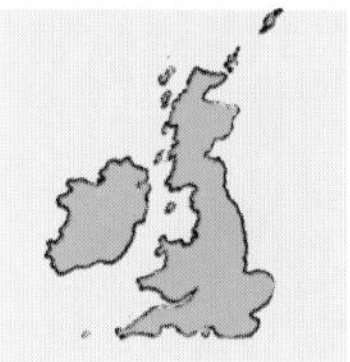

SKULLCAP IS AN elegant, rather elusive plant of riversides and marshy places. In western districts one may also come across the smaller Lesser Skullcap. Where the two species occur together they sometimes cross with one another. The scientific and English names refer to the pouch- or skullcap-like calyx. Both of the rather long Latin names indicate this (Latin: *scutella*, a bowl-shaped dish; *galericulata*, a little leather helmet, like that worn by a Roman soldier).

***Top** Skullcap* (Scutellaria galericulata) *has blue, white-spotted flowers in pairs up its leafy stem. On the top of the two-lipped calyx is a small, domed outgrowth from whence the plant derives its name. It is widespread and common in marshy places and along the banks of streams and rivers.*

Size and appearance: A downy perennial, with creeping, rooting runners and erect or semi-erect, square stems 10–50 cm (4–20 in) tall.

Leaves: in opposite pairs, ovate to broadly spear-shaped, heart-shaped at the base, pointed, with a few rounded teeth.

Flowers: blue, with a white-spotted lip, 10–20 mm ($\frac{3}{8}$–$\frac{3}{4}$ in) long, in pairs in a loose, 1-sided spike.

Fruits: clusters of 4 nutlets, enclosed within the persistent, pouch-like calyx.

Related or similar plants: Bugle (p.228) has blue flowers in whorls in a denser spike; Lesser Skullcap has lilac flowers.

Habitat and distribution: Widespread and sometimes common in marshy places, along the banks and margins of streams and rivers, in damp woods and meadows, but very local in eastern Scotland and in Ireland.

Flowering time: June to September.

***Bottom** Lesser Skullcap* (Skutellaria minor) *is a smaller plant than the Skullcap, with purple-spotted, lilac flowers, growing on damp heaths and moss in the west of England.*

SPECIES INFORMATION	
COMMON NAME	Common Hemp-nettle
SCIENTIFIC NAME	Galeopsis tetrahit
RELATED SPECIES	Red Dead-nettle
HEIGHT/SPREAD	10–50 cm tall
FLOWERING TIME	June–September
HABITAT	Cultivated and disturbed ground

Note: Like a robust, bristly dead-nettle.

Common Hemp-nettle

MINT FAMILY

(Labiatae or Lamiaceae)

Size and appearance: A bristly-hairy, erect, branched annual 10–50 cm (4–20 in) tall, the square stems with a swelling at each leaf insertion and hairs on opposite sides.

Leaves: In opposite pairs, oval or broadly spear-shaped, pointed, coarsely toothed.

Flowers: Pink or whitish, sometimes pale yellow, with darker markings, 15–20 mm (⅗—⅘ in) long, in dense whorls; calyx-teeth bristle-like.

Fruits: Clusters of 4 nutlets, enclosed within the persistent calyx.

Related or similar plants: Red Dead-nettle (p.234) is superficially similar but has purplish-pink flowers and calyx-teeth pointed but not bristle-like.

Habitat and distribution: Widespread but rather local along woodland margins and rides, in hedgerows and on cultivated land, especially on peaty soils; it is much less common than formerly as an arable weed.

Flowering time: June to September.

FLOWER TYPE

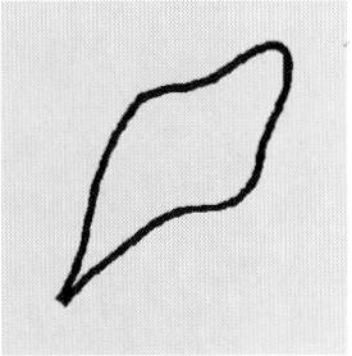

IDENTIFICATION

HABITAT

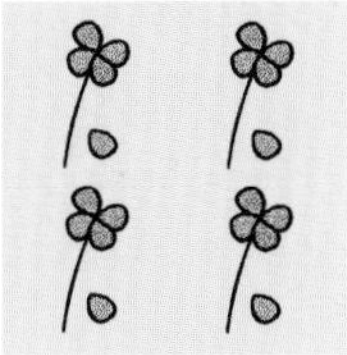

POPULATION

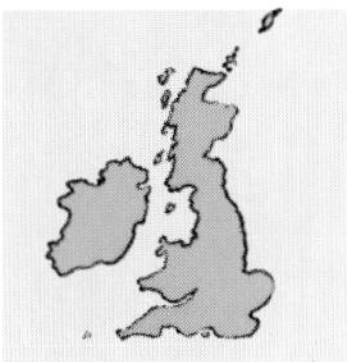

MAP

Top *Common Hemp-nettle* (Galeopsis tetrahit) *has broad, lanceolate, toothed-stalked leaves with prominent veins.*

THIS UNDISTINGUISHED, rather scruffy plant has a special place in the history of research into plant genetics and evolution. During the 1930s Swedish botanists, who suspected that the species derived from a cross between two other hemp-nettles, artificially crossed the putative parents. They then doubled up the genetic material of the progeny, eventually producing plants that were indistinguishable from Common Hemp-nettle. The project had for the first time recreated in the experimental garden the sort of complex process of species formation that we believe to occur naturally in the wild.

Bottom *Red or Narrow-leaved Hemp-nettle* (Galeopsis angustifolia) *is similar but has stems not more than 40 cm (16 in) tall, without swellings, narrower silky-hairy leaves and bright reddish-pink, yellow-marked flowers 15–25 mm (3/5–1 in) long. It is a rather scarce plant of arable fields and open, stony ground, appearing mainly in southern England, but extending to Yorkshire, central Wales and east-central Ireland.*

Large-flowered Hemp-nettle

MINT FAMILY

(Labiatae or Lamiaceae)

SPECIES INFORMATION	
COMMON NAME	Large-flowered Hemp-nettle
SCIENTIFIC NAME	Galeopsis speciosa
RELATED SPECIES	Common Hemp-nettle
HEIGHT/SPREAD	30–100 cm tall
FLOWERING TIME	July–September
HABITAT	Cultivated and disturbed ground

Note: A robust hemp-nettle with showy flowers.

FLOWER TYPE

IDENTIFICATION

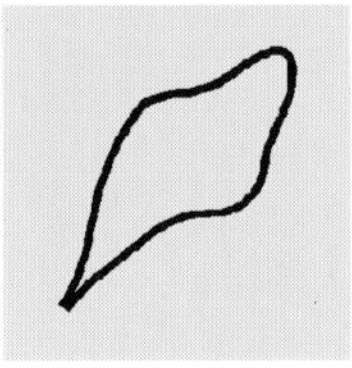

HABITAT

POPULATION

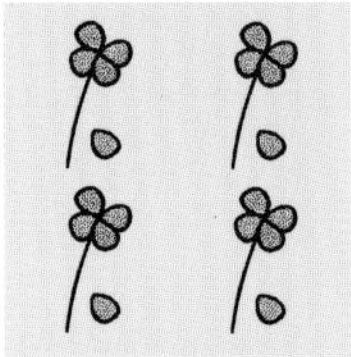

MAP

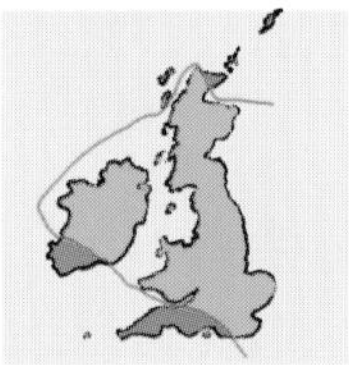

Size and appearance: A robust, hairy, erect, often much-branched annual 30–100 cm (12–40 in) tall, the square stems with a swelling at each leaf insertion and bristly-hairy.

Leaves: In opposite pairs, oval or broadly spear-shaped, pointed, coarsely toothed.

Flowers: Pale yellow, the lip boldly marked with darker yellow and purple, 25–35 mm (1–1⅜ in) long, in dense whorls; calyx-teeth bristle-like.

Fruits: Clusters of 4 nutlets, enclosed within the persistent calyx.

Related or similar plants: Yellow Archangel (p.235) has all-yellow flowers and is a perennial plant of woodland.

Habitat and distribution: Widespread and sometimes common on disturbed and cultivated ground, especially on lime-poor or light, peaty soils, mainly in northern Britain, but locally elsewhere as in the Fens; introduced in northern Ireland.

Flowering time: July to September.

LARGE-FLOWERED Hemp-nettle is one of the most handsome of all our weeds of cultivation, and one that persists in the face of modern agriculture. Indeed, it is an invasive plant that can severely infest fields of potatoes and other root-crops on peaty soils.

Top *Large-flowered Hemp-nettle* (Galeopsis speciosa) *is a robust, showy species with clusters of pale yellow flowers which have a violet lower lip. The tube of the flower is about twice as long as its calyx.*

Bottom left *When the flowers fall from the Large-flowered Hemp-nettle, they leave a ruff formed by the bristle-like teeth of the calyx.*

Bottom right *Bastard Balm* (Melittis melissophyllum) *is another native member of the mint family with showy, purple-splashed flowers. A perennial up to 70 cm (28 in) tall, it has clusters of 2–8 flowers 25–40 mm (1–1⅗ in) long, variously patterned with white, pink or purple. Flowering late April–July, it is scarce but locally a feature of hedge-banks and woodland margins, mostly in Devon and Cornwall.*

SPECIES INFORMATION	
COMMON NAME	White Dead-nettle
SCIENTIFIC NAME	Lamium album
RELATED SPECIES	Red Dead-nettle
HEIGHT/SPREAD	20–80 cm tall
FLOWERING TIME	March–November
HABITAT	Waysides and hedgerows

Note: The common white-flowered dead-nettle of waysides.

White Dead-nettle

MINT FAMILY

(Labiatae or Lamiaceae)

FLOWER TYPE

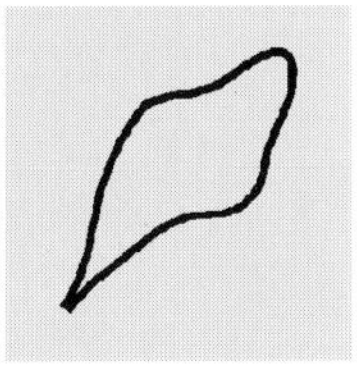

IDENTIFICATION

HABITAT

POPULATION

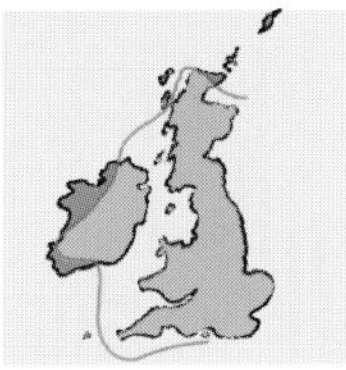

MAP

Size and appearance: A hairy perennial, with erect or semi-erect, square, brittle stems 20–80 cm (8–32 in) tall.

Leaves: In opposite pairs, triangular to oval, pointed, coarsely toothed.

Flowers: Creamy white, 18–25 mm (¾–1 in) long, in dense whorls; upper lip of corolla domed, the lower lip flap-like; calyx-teeth bristle-like.

Fruits: Clusters of 4 nutlets, enclosed within the persistent calyx.

Related or similar plants: Yellow Archangel (p.235) has yellow flowers.

Habitat and distribution: A common, familiar plant of roadsides, along paths and hedges, on grassy or shady waste ground and in untended gardens, but very local in northern and western Scotland; in Ireland, where it is probably introduced, mainly in the east. It rarely occurs away from settlements or roads.

Flowering time: March to November.

THE FLOWERS YIELD plentiful nectar, which one can extract in a drop from the base, as in Honeysuckle (p.273). The nectar makes them very attractive to bumblebees, hence one of the plant's commoner local names, Bee-nettle. A more whimsical Somerset name, Adam-and-Eve-in-the-Bower, describes the pair of blackish and yellow stamens lying side by side in the domed upper lip of the flower. The dead-nettles are so called because the shape and toothing of their leaves recall those of Stinging Nettle (p.13). They possess no stinging hairs

White Dead-nettle (Lamium album) *is a familiar plant of roadsides and hedge-banks as well as waste places. It is a hairy, creeping perennial with stout, square stems. The leaves are more or less heart-shaped, toothed and are reminiscent of Stinging Nettle but do not possess the stinging hairs. The flowers are in whorls of rather large white flowers with a wide open mouth. They are a source of plentiful nectar, which is particularly welcome to early flying insects in March.*

Red Dead-nettle

MINT FAMILY

(Labiatae or Lamiaceae)

SPECIES INFORMATION	
COMMON NAME	Red Dead-nettle, Annual Nettle
SCIENTIFIC NAME	Lamium purpureum
RELATED SPECIES	White Dead-nettle
HEIGHT/SPREAD	10–40 cm tall
FLOWERING TIME	February–November
HABITAT	Waysides and hedgerows

Note: The common red-flowered dead-nettle of waysides.

FLOWER TYPE

IDENTIFICATION

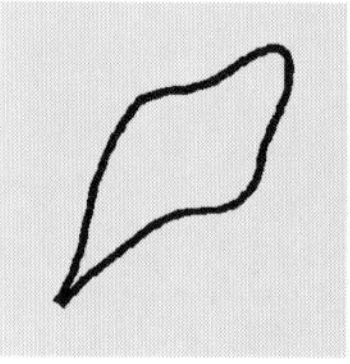

HABITAT

POPULATION

MAP

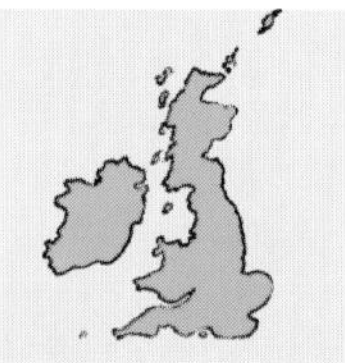

Size and appearance: A downy, purplish-tinged, erect or semi-erect annual 10–40 cm (4–16 in) tall, aromatic when bruised.

Flowers: Pinkish-purple, rarely pale pink or white, 10–18 mm long (⅖–¾ in), in conspicuous whorls; calyx-teeth pointed but not bristle-like.

Fruits: Clusters of 4 nutlets, enclosed within the persistent calyx.

Related or similar plants: Common Hemp-nettle (p.231) is a coarser plant with pink, whitish or yellowish flowers and bristle-like calyx-teeth.

Habitat and distribution: A ubiquitous and familiar weed of disturbed, waste and cultivated land, especially in gardens and amongst vegetable crops; throughout, but local in some upland districts and parts of western Ireland.

Flowering time: February to November, but all through mild winters; mostly in spring and early summer.

IF THIS WAS NOT such a persistent weed it would be regarded as one of the prettiest wild flowers. It is certainly a welcome sight on vegetable patch or waysides as one of the first plants to come into flower at winter's end, alongside Chickweed (p.35), Shepherd's Purse (p.72) and Groundsel (p.307). The flowers of Red Dead-nettle are never red as such, but usually pinkish-purple. They yield plentiful nectar and are attractive to bees and bumble-bees. The plant had some medicinal use as a healing herb, and was formerly a winter green for people and pigs.

Red Dead-nettle (Lamium purpureum) *is a ubiquitous and familiar weed which can be found in flower throughout the year in mild winters. It is a downy annual with square stems, which are often leafless below the leafy flower-spike. The stalked leaves have a heart-shaped base, are often pointed at the tip and blunt toothed with a rather wrinkled surface. The flowers are usually a dark pinkish-purple but lighter colours occur as do wholly white variants. As with white dead nettles it is a good nectar source for bumble-bees. Red Dead-nettle is a widespread and abundant weed of cultivated ground.*

SPECIES INFORMATION	
COMMON NAME	Yellow Archangel, Yellow Dead-nettle
SCIENTIFIC NAME	Lamiastrum galeobdolon
RELATED SPECIES	White Dead-nettle
HEIGHT/SPREAD	20–60 cm tall
FLOWERING TIME	March–November
HABITAT	Woods and hedgerows

Note: The yellow-flowered dead-nettle of woodland.

Yellow Archangel

MINT FAMILY
(Labiatae or Lamiaceae)

Size and appearance: A perennial with leafy runners, forming patches, and erect, square stems 20–60 cm (8–24 in) tall.

Leaves: In opposite pairs, oval to spear-shaped, heart-shaped at the base, stalked, pointed, toothed.

Flowers: Yellow, marked with reddish-brown, 15–25 mm (⅝–1 in) long, 6–10 in showy whorls; stamens hairy.

Fruits: Clusters of 4 nutlets, enclosed within the persistent calyx.

Related or similar plants: White Dead-nettle (p.233) has white flowers, with hairless stamens, and a much longer flowering time.

Habitat and distribution: Locally common in woods and coppices, on the shady banks of lanes and in old hedges, especially on better-drained, lime-rich soils, through most of England and Wales; very rare in Scotland, and in Ireland only near the east coast.

Flowering time: March to November.

YELLOW ARCHANGEL is one of the handsomest flowers of spring woodlands. The runners, a common means of vegetative reproduction in this family, enable the plant to build up extensive patches. The curious but appealing name Archangel was also widely applied in former times to the related White (p.233) and Red (p.234) Dead-nettles. It may reflect the fact that these superficially nettle-like plants do not sting. A vigorous garden variant with white-spotted leaves and far-creeping runners makes an effective ground-cover plant. However, it often escapes on to shady banks and lanesides where it can swamp native plants.

Yellow Archangel (Lamiastrum galeobdolon) *is a charming plant of shady woodlands. It has numerous leafy runners which are produced at or after the time of flowering. The yellow flowers are in dense whorls around the stem, the corolla is two-lipped, the upper being laterally compressed and helmet-shaped whilst the lower is three-lobed, with the middle lobe only slightly larger than the two side lobes. The lower lip has brownish markings, more so on the central lobe.*

FLOWER TYPE

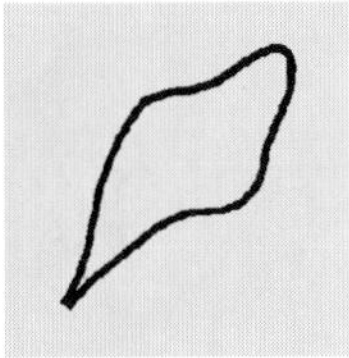
IDENTIFICATION

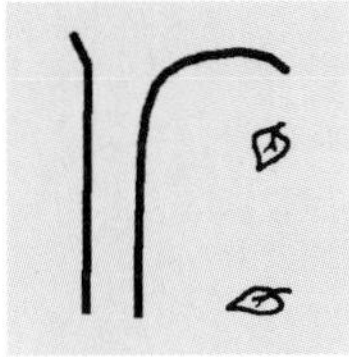
HABITAT

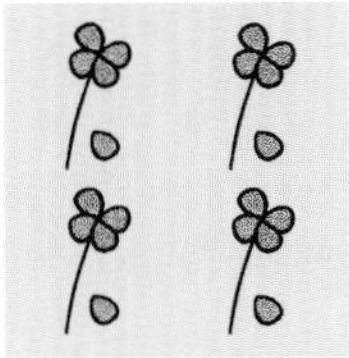
POPULATION

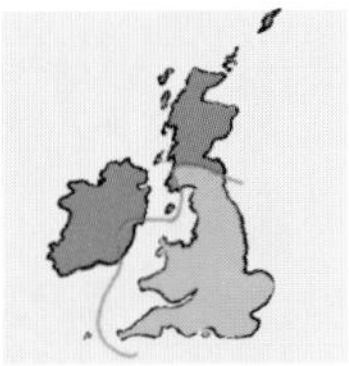
MAP

Betony

MINT FAMILY

(Labiatae or Lamiaceae)

SPECIES INFORMATION	
COMMON NAME	Betony
SCIENTIFIC NAME	Stachys officinalis
RELATED SPECIES	Woundworts
HEIGHT/SPREAD	10–100 cm tall
FLOWERING TIME	June–September
HABITAT	Woods and hedgerows

Note: The neat basal leaves are most characteristic.

FLOWER TYPE

IDENTIFICATION

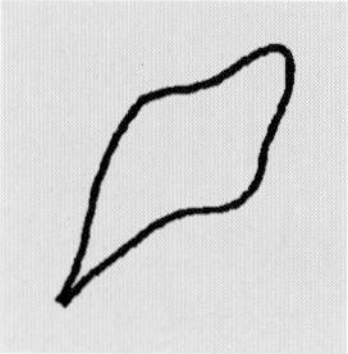

HABITAT

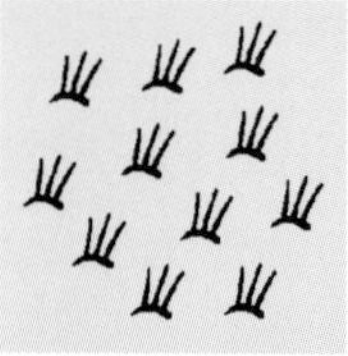

POPULATION

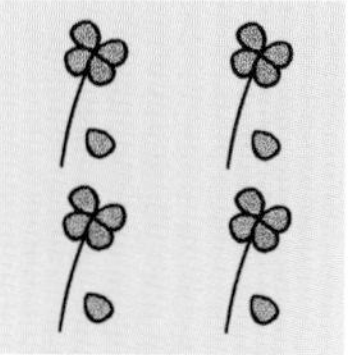

MAP

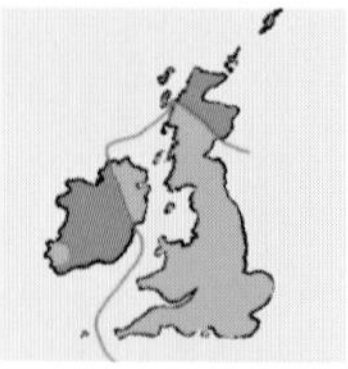

Size and appearance: A perennial with hairy, erect, unbranched, square stems 10–100 cm (4–40 in) tall.

Leaves: Mostly in a basal rosette, those on the stem in opposite pairs, stalked, oblong or narrowly oval, heart-shaped at the base, the margins elegantly scalloped.

Flowers: Reddish-purple, rarely pink or white, 12–18 mm (½–¾ in) long, numerous in whorls in a cylindrical spike.

Fruits: Clusters of 4 nutlets, enclosed within the persistent calyx.

Related or similar plants: Marsh Woundwort (p.237) has unstalked leaves; Hedge Woundwort (p.238) has a strong smell when bruised.

Habitat and distribution: Widespread but rather local in open woods, scrub, roadside banks and dry meadows, on rocky ground and coastal cliffs in England and Wales, but rare and scattered in Scotland and Ireland.

Flowering time: June to September.

BETONY NOT ONLY is a most attractive summer flower, but also has a long history of use as a medicinal herb, noted for its healing properties. An infusion of the leaves makes a bitter tonic and mildly sedative drink, and has also been used to bathe cuts and bruises. It is a plant that usually indicates plant-rich habitats such as pockets of unimproved grassland. Some populations of plants from exposed coastal cliffs in south-western England and elsewhere are compact and dwarf in stature. Similar plants, also variants with pink or white flowers, are cultivated, although the typical wild plant deserves to be more popular with gardeners.

Betony (Stachys officinalis) *has flowers in whorls around the stem with a pair of leafy bracts below each whorl forming a terminal spike. The flowers are a rich magenta with a slightly concave upper lip and a lower lip with well-developed lateral lobes. The stalked leaves have elegantly scalloped edges and are mostly basal. Betony is a plant of open woods, hedgebanks and grassy places, usually on the lighter soils.*

SPECIES INFORMATION	
COMMON NAME	Marsh Woundwort
SCIENTIFIC NAME	Stachys palustris
RELATED SPECIES	Hedge Woundwort
HEIGHT/SPREAD	20–100 cm tall
FLOWERING TIME	July–September
HABITAT	Damp ground

Note: The stalkless leaves distinguish this from related species.

Marsh Woundwort

MINT FAMILY

(Labiatae or Lamiaceae)

Size and appearance: A perennial with creeping, tuberous rhizomes and square, hollow, leafy stems 20–100 cm (8–40 in) tall.

Leaves: In opposite pairs, spear-shaped, short-stalked or stalkless, coarsely toothed, with a faint smell when bruised.

Flowers: Dull pinkish-purple, 12–15 mm (½–⅗ in) long, in whorls in a dense, pyramidal spike.

Fruits: Clusters of 4 nutlets, enclosed within the persistent calyx.

Related or similar plants: Hedge Woundwort (p.238) has solid stems, stalked leaves and darker red flowers.

Habitat and distribution: Widespread and often common in marshes, the margins of lakes, ponds and rivers, damp ditches and poorly drained fields throughout Britain and Ireland; in western districts less restricted to damp ground and so often a weed of disturbed and cultivated land.

Flowering time: July to September.

Marsh Woundwort (Stachys palustris) *is a stout, hairy creeping perennial with square, hollow stems. The toothed lanceolate leaves are in opposite pairs and sometimes on short stalks. Flowers are a pale rose-purple in about six-flowered whorls forming a dense spike above but interrupted below. It is widespread and common by fresh water, streams, ditches and in marshes, but can also occur as a weed of poorly-drained arable fields.*

FLOWER TYPE

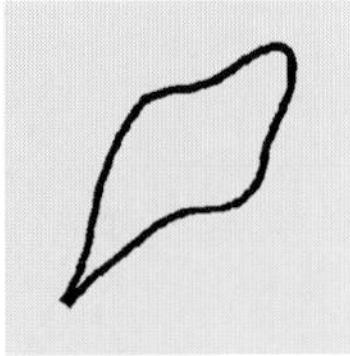

IDENTIFICATION

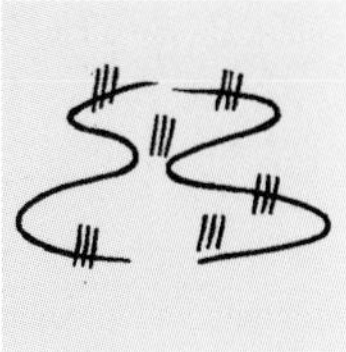

HABITAT

POPULATION

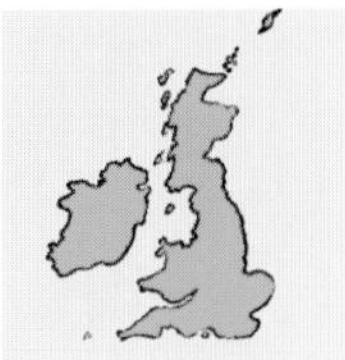

MAP

AS THE NAME suggests, Marsh Woundwort has been used, like several other plants in this family, to staunch bleeding and heal wounds. John Gerard, author of the famous 1597 *Herball*, thought very highly indeed of this plant, regarding it almost as a miracle cure! The leaves give off some smell when they are bruised, but it is much less strong and unpleasant than the distinctive smell of Hedge Woundwort (p.238). Where the two species grow together they can cross with one another, producing vigorous, leafy plants intermediate between them in form.

Hedge Woundwort

MINT FAMILY

(Labiatae or Lamiaceae)

SPECIES INFORMATION	
COMMON NAME	Hedge Woundwort
SCIENTIFIC NAME	Stachys sylvatica
RELATED SPECIES	Marsh Woundwort
HEIGHT/SPREAD	50–120 cm tall
FLOWERING TIME	July–September
HABITAT	Woods and hedgerows

Note: The unpleasant smell of the leaves is itself diagnostic.

FLOWER TYPE

IDENTIFICATION

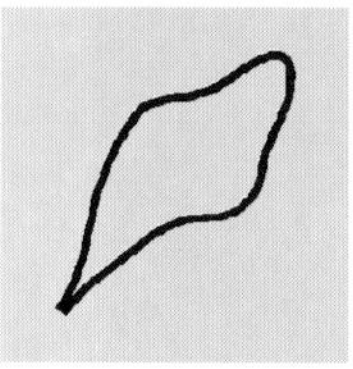

HABITAT

POPULATION

MAP

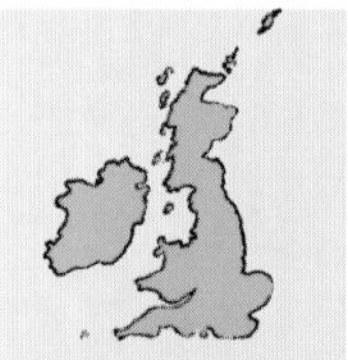

Size and appearance: A rough-hairy perennial, with creeping rhizomes and square, solid stems 50–120 cm (20–48 in) tall.
Leaves: in opposite pairs, oval, stalked, pointed, coarsely toothed, with an unpleasant smell when bruised.
Flowers: dark reddish-purple with whitish blotches, rarely pink or white, 13–18 mm (½–¾ in) long, in whorls in a dense, pyramidal spike.
Fruits: clusters of 4 nutlets, enclosed within the persistent calyx.
Related or similar plants: Marsh Woundwort (p.237) has solid stems, unstalked leaves and pinkish-purple flowers.
Habitat and distribution: A common and characteristic plant of woods, hedges, shady places, abandoned cultivated land and overgrown gardens across most parts of Britain and Ireland.
Flowering time: July to September

THE RED WINE-COLOURED flowers are quite attractive, but the plant gives off a strong, unpleasant smell when bruised or cut. Nevertheless, like several other plants in this family, Hedge Woundwort is an old medicinal herb, once widely used to staunch bleeding and to heal wounds, but with much less of a reputation than Marsh Woundwort (p.237). The first half of the scientific name of the woundworts derives from the Greek *stachys* (an ear of corn), alluding to their usually dense spikes of flowers. Ancient Greek herbalists knew Downy Woundwort (*Stachys germanica*) by this name. Mainly a plant of southern and central Europe, it is also a rare native of the Cotswolds.

Hedge Woundwort (Stachys sylvatica) *is very similar to Marsh Woundwort but the leaves are broader with heart-shaped bases and they have an unpleasant smell. The flowers are a dark reddish-purple with whitish blotches. It is a plant of hedgerows, woods and copses although where these are close to streams and marshy areas hybridisation with Marsh Woundwort can occur.*

SPECIES INFORMATION	
COMMON NAME	Ground Ivy
SCIENTIFIC NAME	Glechoma hederacea
RELATED SPECIES	Self heal, Woundworts
HEIGHT/SPREAD	10–50 cm tall
FLOWERING TIME	March–June
HABITAT	Woods and hedge-banks

Note: A distinctive, often purplish plant of spring woodlands.

Ground Ivy

MINT FAMILY

(Labiatae or Lamiaceae)

Size and appearance: A rather slender, soft-hairy, often purple-tinged perennial, with stems either far-creeping and rooting or semi-erect and flowering 10–50 cm (4–20 in) tall.
Leaves: In opposite pairs, stalked, heart- or kidney-shaped, with scalloped margins.
Flowers: Pale or deep violet, with darker purplish spots, rarely pink or white, 15–25 mm ($\frac{3}{5}$–1 in) long, in whorls of 3–6 in a loose, rather 1-sided spike.
Fruits: Clusters of 4 nutlets, enclosed within the persistent calyx.
Related or similar plants: Selfheal (p.240) has more bluish-purple flowers later in the year.
Habitat and distribution: Common and frequently abundant in woods and hedges, on shady banks and lanesides, and in churchyards, untended gardens and shadier grassy places throughout Britain and Ireland.
Flowering time: March to June, from February in mild winters.

GROUND IVY IS one of the earliest of spring wild flowers, but also a link with early summer, as it continues to give a good show all through May. To our ancestors it was less a decorative plant than a valuable and useful one, its bitter taste being employed to flavour and preserve beer. This gave the plant its old name Alehoof, which persisted until recently as a wide-spread local name. Like the closely related wound-worts, it was also a healing herb. So useful was it that it went with early colonists to the United States, where it is still nat-uralised in New England.

Some plants have female as well as hermaphrodite flowers, a device that probably encourages cross-pollination. This floral adaptation turns up elsewhere in the mint family.

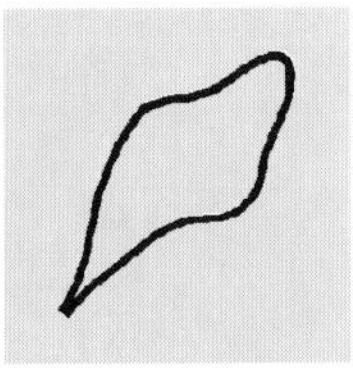

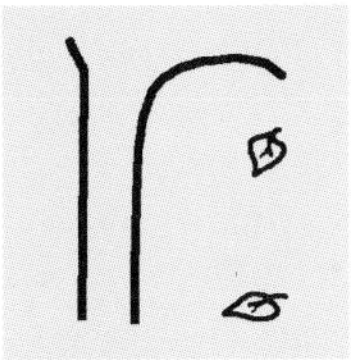

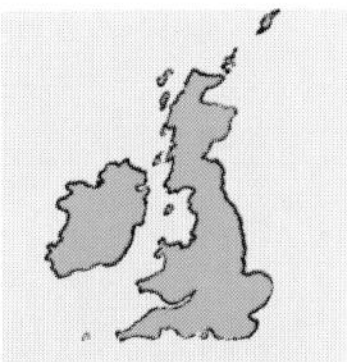

Top *The plant sends out long rooting runners which mean that Ground Ivy can form carpets in suitable habitats, such as along hedgebanks.*

Bottom left and right *Ground Ivy* (Glechoma hederacea) *can be found flowering from as early as February through to June, but is at its best in late April and early May. The conspicuous blue-violet flowers are in loose whorls at the base of the leaves. The leaves are softly hairy, long-stalked and kidney-shaped with scalloped margins. They are often purple tinged.*

Selfheal

MINT FAMILY

(Labiatae or Lamiaceae)

SPECIES INFORMATION	
COMMON NAME	Selfheal
SCIENTIFIC NAME	Prunella vulgaris
RELATED SPECIES	Ground Ivy, Woundworts
HEIGHT/SPREAD	5–50 cm tall
FLOWERING TIME	June–September
HABITAT	Grassland and woodland clearings

Note: The flower-heads look rather cone-like in fruit.

FLOWER TYPE

IDENTIFICATION

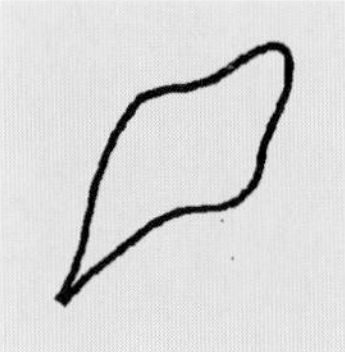

HABITAT

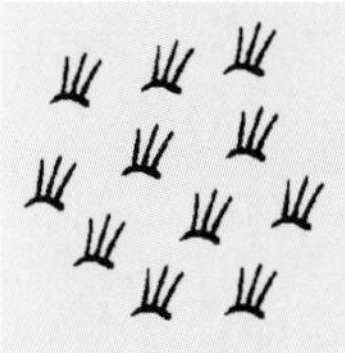

POPULATION

MAP

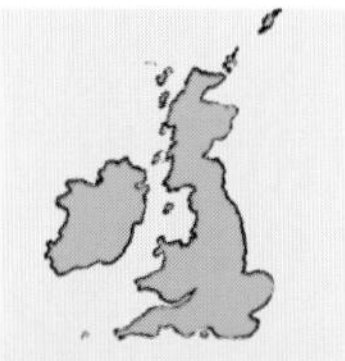

Size and appearance: A hairy, tufted, prostrate, sprawling or semi-erect annual, biennial or short-lived perennial 5–50 cm (2–20 in) tall.

Leaves: In opposite pairs, stalked, oval, blunt, untoothed or with a few teeth.

Flowers: Rich, bluish-purple, occasionally violet, pink or white, 12–15 mm long (½–⅗ in), in a compact, cylindrical head, with broad, purplish, hairy leaf-like bracts.

Fruits: Clusters of 4 nutlets, enclosed within the persistent calyx and bracts.

Related or similar plants: Ground Ivy (p.239) has violet flowers earlier in the year; Bugle (p.228) has blue flowers and long runners.

Habitat and distribution: Widespread and often common in the clearings and rides of woods, in damp or dry grassland and grassy waste places, on waysides, damper parts of sand-dunes and unmanicured lawns throughout Britain and Ireland.

Flowering time: June to September.

SELFHEAL IS A common plant, but one that also favours 'good' habitats like unploughed grassland and seaside turf. Its wide habitat tolerance partly reflects great variation in form, especially in height, habit and life-history. Cultivation experiments have shown this variation to have a genetic basis. For example, dwarf, prostrate plants from lawns keep their features when grown in good garden soil alongside larger plants from lush grassland. The common name reflects the long use of the plant as a medicinal herb to staunch and heal wounds.

The cone-like, persistent flower-spikes are distinctive even when the flowers have fallen, and separate Selfheal from other 'mints'.

Top *Selfheal* (Prunella vulgaris) *is often regarded as a short prostrate plant because of its occurrence in churchyard turf and unmanicured lawns, where it will keep a low profile underneath the cutting blades. However, it can reach up to 50 cm (20 in) in suitable conditions such as woodland rides.*

Bottom left and right *The bluish-purple flowers and the large purplish bracts are set in terminal heads which are rather oblong or squarish.*

SPECIES INFORMATION	
COMMON NAME	Black Horehound
SCIENTIFIC NAME	Ballota nigra
RELATED SPECIES	Woundworts
HEIGHT/SPREAD	30–80 cm tall
FLOWERING TIME	June–September
HABITAT	Waysides and waste ground

Note: The dense but widely spaced whorls of flowers.

Black Horehound

MINT FAMILY
(Labiatae or Lamiaceae)

Size and appearance: An untidy, hairy perennial, with erect or semi-erect stems 30–80 cm (12–32 in) tall.
Leaves: In opposite pairs, oval or heart-shaped, stalked, coarsely toothed.
Flowers: Dull purple, 12–18 mm (½–¾ in) long, in dense whorls at intervals in a long spike; calyx funnel-shaped, with triangular teeth.
Fruits: Clusters of 4 nutlets, enclosed within the persistent calyx and bracts.
Related or similar plants: Ground Ivy (p.239) has violet flowers earlier in the year; Bugle (p.228) has blue flowers and long runners.
Habitat and distribution: A widespread plant of waste places and disturbed ground, along hedges and by paths and roadsides, often in partial shade, over much of England and Wales, but rare and probably not native in Scotland and Ireland.
Flowering time: June to September.

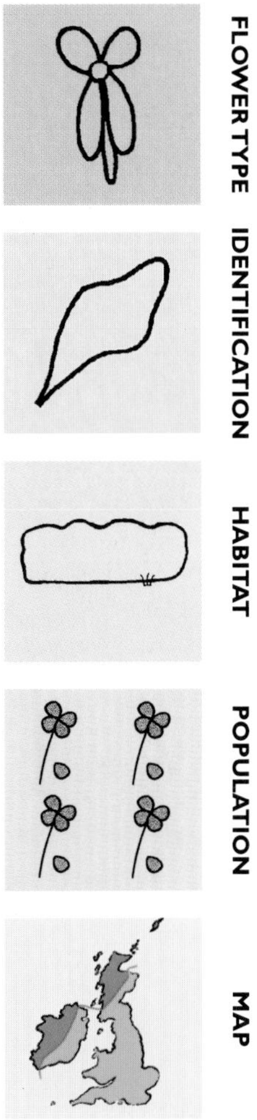

BLACK HOREHOUND IS a dowdy, bushy and rather characteristic plant of waysides and waste places. Despite its extremely unpleasant smell, it has an ancient history of medicinal use. Pedanios Dioscorides, a Greek doctor serving in the 1st century Roman army who wrote perhaps the most famous of all herbals, knew this plant as *Balloti.* He regarded it as a remedy for the worst of infected wounds. It is one of those plants that is not an invasive weed, but nevertheless persists about human settlement and was probably widely introduced in the past as a medicinal plant.

***Top** Black Horehound* (Ballota nigra) *is readily identifiable by the stink of its leaves when crushed. It is a bushy plant frequently found on roadsides, in hedgerows and in waste places.*

***Bottom** The purplish-pink flowers are in dense whorls up the leafy stem with the calyx being funnel-shaped with triangular teeth. The leaves occur in opposite pairs and are stalked and oval with coarse toothing around their margins.*

Marjoram

MINT FAMILY

(Labiatae or Lamiaceae)

SPECIES INFORMATION	
COMMON NAME	Marjoram
SCIENTIFIC NAME	Origanum vulgare
RELATED SPECIES	Wild Basil
HEIGHT/SPREAD	20–80 cm tall
FLOWERING TIME	June–September
HABITAT	Chalk and limestone grassland

Note: The strong smell of marjoram or oregano.

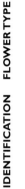

FLOWER TYPE

IDENTIFICATION

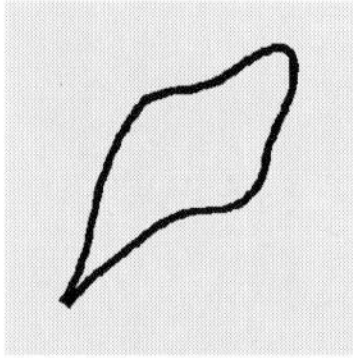

HABITAT

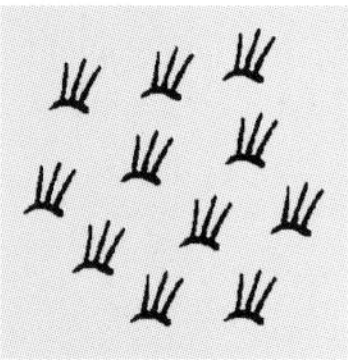

POPULATION

MAP

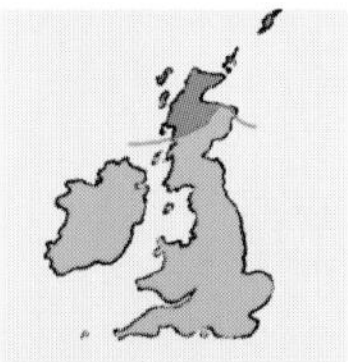

Size and appearance: A downy perennial with stiff, erect stems 20–80 cm (8–32 in) tall, branched above.

Leaves: In opposite pairs, oval, untoothed or with a few teeth, strongly and pleasantly aromatic when bruised.

Flowers: Purplish-violet or dark pink, 4–8 mm (1/6–1/3 in) long, with small, oval, purplish leaf-like bracts, in several loose heads arranged in a flat-topped cluster.

Fruits: Clusters of 4 nutlets, enclosed within the persistent calyx and bracts.

Related or similar plants: Wild Basil has fewer flowers up to 20 mm (4/5 in) long.

Habitat and distribution: Common in grassland and scrub, on woodland margins and along hedges and roadside banks on chalk and limestone, and in other lime-rich or coastal habitats, north to the Moray Firth, and over much of Ireland.

Flowering time: June to September.

Top and bottom left *Marjoram* (Origanum vulgare) *is a pleasant-smelling herb found in sunny situations on chalk and limestone soils.*

MARJORAM IS A well-known wild flower and a popular garden plant. It is both an ornamental and a culinary herb, and an infusion which was used to alleviate a number of illnesses. In late summer, the flowers attract numerous butterflies in search of nectar. Mediterranean variants of the plant ('Origane') have a more pungent smell and flavour. *Origanon*, from which the first half of the scientific name derives, was the ancient Greek name for the plant.

Bottom right *Wild Basil* (Clinopodium vulgare)*, a related plant of similar habitats on chalk and limestone, is hairier, has little smell, and has fewer, bright purplish-pink flowers 15–20 mm* (3/5–4/5 in)

SPECIES INFORMATION	
COMMON NAME	Wild Thyme
SCIENTIFIC NAME	Thymus praecox
RELATED SPECIES	Marjoram
HEIGHT/SPREAD	5–10 cm tall
FLOWERING TIME	June–September
HABITAT	Rocky places and dry grassland

Note: The strong smell of thyme is instantly recognisable.

Wild Thyme

MINT FAMILY

(Labiatae or Lamiaceae)

Size and appearance: A rather hairy, mat-forming perennial, woody at the base, with a mass of creeping, rooting runners and sprawling flowering stems 5–10 cm (2–4 in) tall, hairy on two opposite sides.

Leaves: In opposite pairs, 4–8 mm (⅙–⅓ in) long, short-stalked, elliptical or spear-shaped, strongly and pleasantly aromatic when bruised.

Flowers: Reddish-purple or shades of pink, 3–4 mm (⅛–⅙ in) long, with a 3-lobed lip, in tight, almost spherical heads; calyx bell-shaped, purplish.

Fruits: Clusters of 4 nutlets, enclosed within the persistent calyx and bracts.

Related or similar plants: Marjoram (p.242) and Wild Basil are more robust plants with much larger leaves.

Habitat and distribution: Widespread in dry or rocky grassland, on heaths, sunny banks, mountain rocks and cliffs, sand-dunes, old walls and sometimes lawns, especially on lime-rich soils and by the sea; throughout, but particularly widespread on the chalk and in highland Britain.

Flowering time: June to September

LIKE MARJORAM (p.242), Wild Thyme is as much an ornamental garden plant as a wild flower. These two richly aromatic plants scent chalk and limestone grassland in the summer. As with so many members of the mint family, the plant has soothing and healing properties. In the Highlands of Scotland, Wild Thyme was formerly a popular herbal tea. The plant of the herb garden is the bushier Garden Thyme (*Thymus vulgaris*), originally from south-west Europe.

Top and bottom left *Wild Thyme* (Thymus polytrichus) *can make a wonderful splash of colour among the short cropped turf whether on a chalk downland or coastal cliffs. It spreads out through the turf using thin woody runners which root as it extends. An aromatic plant, its presence can often be detected when not in flower by the smell as its leaves are bruised when trodden on.*

Bottom right *The bright reddish-purple flowers are in almost spherical heads with a two-lipped flower, the lower having three lobes.*

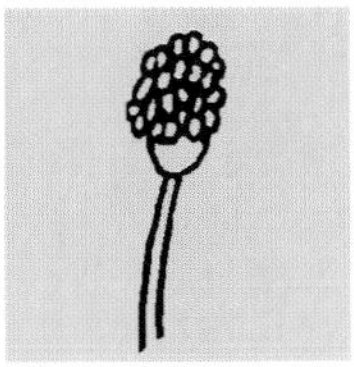

FLOWER TYPE

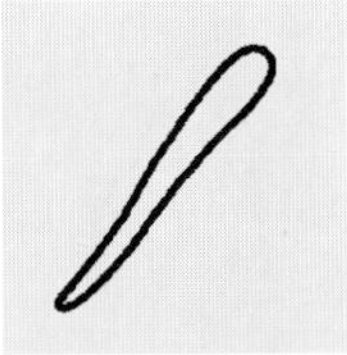

IDENTIFICATION

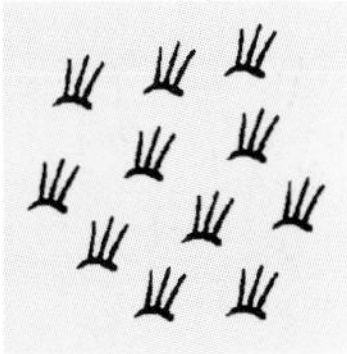

HABITAT

POPULATION

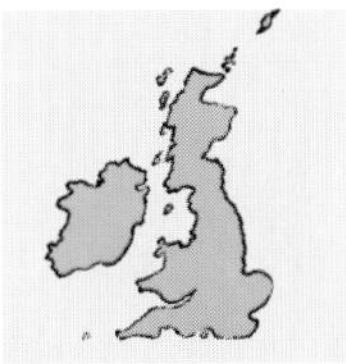

MAP

Gypsywort

MINT FAMILY

(Labiatae or Lamiaceae)

SPECIES INFORMATION	
COMMON NAME	Gypsywort
SCIENTIFIC NAME	Lycopus europaeus
RELATED SPECIES	Water Mint
HEIGHT/SPREAD	30–100 cm tall
FLOWERING TIME	June–October
HABITAT	Watersides and marshes

Note: The neat ranks of leaves are distinctive.

A CHARACTERISTIC PLANT of watersides, conspicuous by its neatly ranked pairs of jagged-toothed leaves. The plant yields a black dye. This gave rise to an old defamatory rumour that gypsies used it to darken their skin and hair, thus emphasising their exotic origin. It is unfortunate that this lamentable piece of racial prejudice was passed down from generation to generation as a credible story by compilers of herbals and botanical books, who should have known better.

FLOWER TYPE

IDENTIFICATION

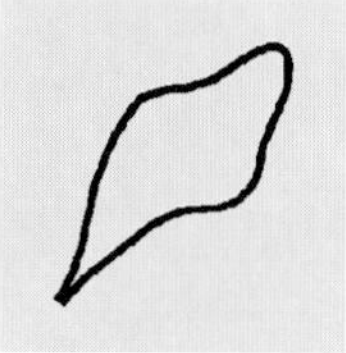

HABITAT

POPULATION

MAP

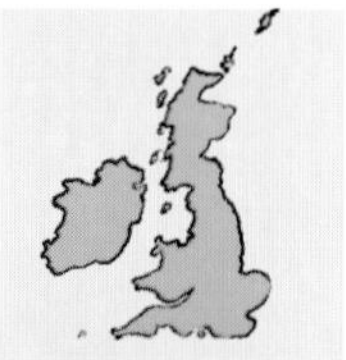

Gypsywort (Lycopus europaeus) *has dense whorls of flowers at the base of the leaves all up the stem. The flowers themselves are small, bell-shaped and white with a few small purple dots on the lower lip. The plant is widespread and common by fresh water along the margins of ponds and streams and also in wet woodland rides and marshy places.*

Size and appearance: A hairy, mint-like perennial, with creeping rhizome and runners, forming patches, and erect stems 30–100 cm (12–40 in) tall.

Leaves: In regular ranks of opposite pairs, spear-shaped, short-stalked, with jagged teeth, scentless when bruised.

Flowers: whitish with purple dots, bell-shaped, 3–4 mm (1/8–1/6 in) long, in dense, wide-spaced whorls; long, hairy calyx; stamens protruding.

Fruits: clusters of 4 nutlets, enclosed within the persistent calyx and bracts.

Related or similar plants: Water Mint and Corn Mint (p.245) have larger, lilac flowers and strongly aromatic leaves.

Habitat and distribution: Widespread and often common along the margins of ponds, streams, rivers and canals, and in wet woodland rides, marshes and ditches; almost throughout, but local in the north, except near western coasts, and in Ireland.

Flowering time: June to October.

SPECIES INFORMATION	
COMMON NAME	Water Mint
SCIENTIFIC NAME	Mentha aquatica
RELATED SPECIES	Corn Mint
HEIGHT/SPREAD	20–60 cm tall
FLOWERING TIME	July–October
HABITAT	Watersides and marshes

Note: Other mints have flowers in spaced whorls.

Water Mint

MINT FAMILY

(Labiatae or Lamiaceae)

Size and appearance: A hairy perennial with erect or semi-erect stems 20–60 cm (8–24 in) tall.
Leaves: In opposite pairs, stalked, oval, toothed, green but occasionally bronze-coloured, richly aromatic when bruised.
Flowers: Pale mauve or deep lilac, 3–4 mm (⅛–⅙ in) long, most in a dense head, with more widely spaced whorls lower down the stem; calyx hairy and stamens protruding.
Fruits: Clusters of 4 nutlets, enclosed within the persistent calyx and bracts.
Related or similar plants: Corn Mint has paler lilac flowers in separate whorls up the stem.
Habitat and distribution: Abundant in marshy ground, along the margins of ponds, streams, rivers and canals, and in wet woodland rides, damp pastures and ditches throughout Britain and Ireland.
Flowering time: July to October.

FLOWER TYPE

IDENTIFICATION

HABITAT

POPULATION

MAP

THE MOST OBVIOUS feature of the mints is their aromatic leaves. Water Mint, the commonest mint of wet places and watersides, imparts a characteristic rich odour to marsh vegetation when crushed underfoot in summer and autumn. Another feature of mints is that they easily cross with each other. Water Mint frequently crosses with Corn Mint to produce a confusing range of intermediate plants.

A dozen or so other mints have escaped from gardens to become naturalised in damp or waste places. Of these, Spearmint (*Mentha spicata*), mostly hairless and with flowers in narrow spikes, is probably the commonest, and the one most used to make mint sauce. Crossed with Water Mint it gave rise to another familiar plant, Peppermint (*Mentha piperita*).

Top right *Water Mint* (Mentha aquatica) *has pale mauve flowers in a terminal head, often with more in whorls lower down the stem.*

Bottom left *The large-leaved Apple Mint is one of many different varieties of mint.*

Bottom right *Corn Mint* (Mentha arvensis) *is very similar but has a coarser scent and pale lilac flowers in distinct whorls up the stem.*

Deadly Nightshade

NIGHTSHADE AND POTATO FAMILY
(Solanaceae)

SPECIES INFORMATION	
COMMON NAME	Deadly Nightshade
SCIENTIFIC NAME	Atropa belladonn
RELATED SPECIES	Henbane
HEIGHT/SPREAD	50–150 cm tall
FLOWERING TIME	June–September
HABITAT	Woodland clearings and scrub

Note: An unmistakable, rather sinister-looking plant.

FLOWER TYPE
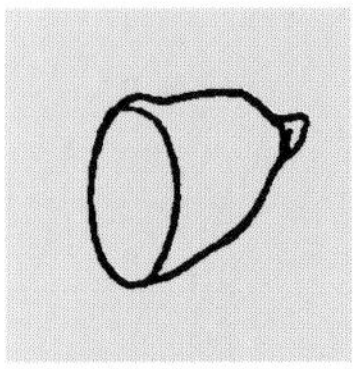
IDENTIFICATION
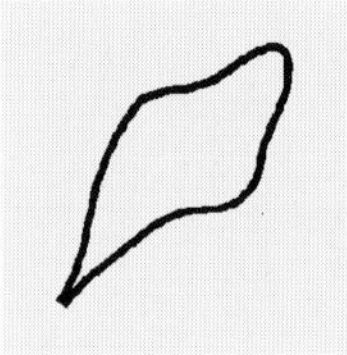
HABITAT
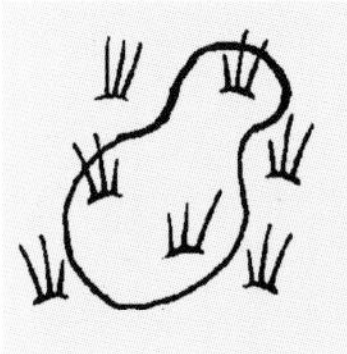
POPULATION

MAP
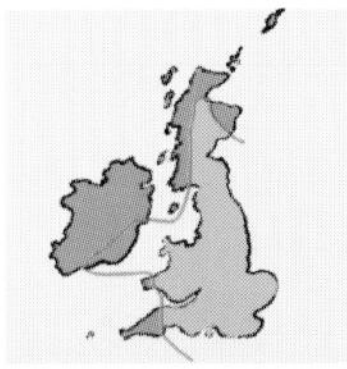

Size and appearance: A robust, often hairless perennial, with erect, arched, stout, leafy stems 50–150 cm (20–60 in) tall.
Leaves: Stalked, 10–20 cm (4–8 in) long, oval, pointed, untoothed, the upper in opposite pairs.
Flowers: Solitary or in pairs, bell-shaped, 5-lobed, 25–30 mm (1–1⅕ in) long, brownish-purple, yellowish with violet veins inside.
Fruits: Black, shiny, spherical berries up to 20 mm (⅘ in) across, framed by the persistent calyx.
Related or similar plants: Henbane (p.247) is sticky-hairy, with clusters of yellowish flowers; Woody Nightshade (p.249) is a scrambling plant with smaller flowers and scarlet berries.
Habitat and distribution: A local plant of woodland clearings, scrub, old quarries and tracksides on chalk and limestone, but quite common in some districts, mainly in south-eastern and central England but with a few sites elsewhere; sometimes associated with old ruins.
Flowering time: June to September.

DEADLY NIGHTSHADE IS a famous plant with a bad reputation. The whole plant, especially the berry, is extremely poisonous and should not be handled. The shiny berries are almost too alluring, but Deadly Nightshade has a sinister feel about it that ought to banish any thought of eating them.

However, the plant has a long and honourable role in medicine, used in medicines (like those for 'traveller's tummy') that calm the stomach, and by ophthalmologists to dilate the pupil of the eye.

Deadly nightshade often grows in and around woods, but is really a plant of disturbed and semi-open ground, for example where a tree has fallen or a new track or road has been cut.

Top and bottom left *Deadly Nightshade* (Atropa belladonna) *has stalked, oval, pointed leaves, at the base of which occur the often solitary flowers. These are shaped as rather tubular bells, have five-lobes and are an unusual browinish-purple.*

Bottom right *Apple-of-Peru* (Nicandra physalodes) *is another poisonous plant of the same family, that increasingly turns up on rubbish tips, waste ground and flower beds. An alien from Peru, it has coarsely toothed, oval leaves, solitary violet flowers 2–4 cm (4/5–1⅗ in) across, and brown berries enclosed in the enlarged, papery, persistent calyx.*

SPECIES INFORMATION	
COMMON NAME	Henbane
SCIENTIFIC NAME	Hyoscyamus niger
RELATED SPECIES	Deadly Nightshade
HEIGHT/SPREAD	30–80 cm tall
FLOWERING TIME	June–October
HABITAT	Sandy and manured ground

Note: An other unmistakable, rather sinister-looking plant.

Henbane

NIGHTSHADE AND POTATO FAMILY
(Solanaceae)

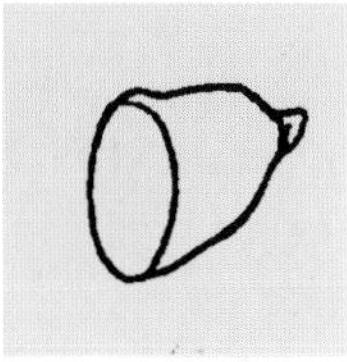

FLOWER TYPE

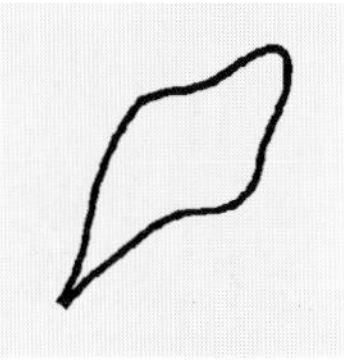

IDENTIFICATION

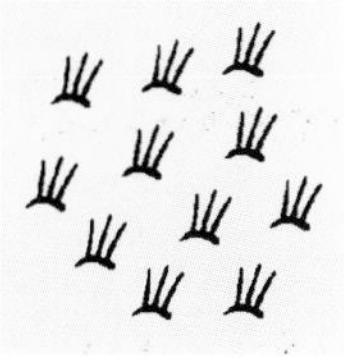

HABITAT

POPULATION

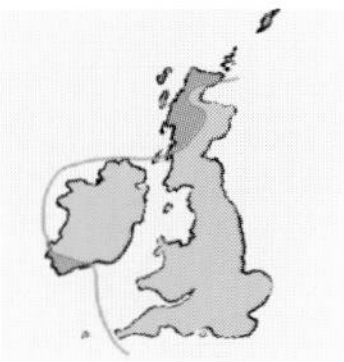

MAP

Size and appearance: A robust, sticky-hairy, leafy annual or biennial 30–80 cm (12–32 in) tall.
Leaves: The lower stalked, 10–20 cm (4–8 in) long, oval or oblong, deeply toothed or lobed, greyish-green, with a strong smell when bruised.
Flowers: In 2-rowed clusters, funnel-shaped, 5-lobed, 20–30 mm (⅘–1⅕ in) across, dull yellowish with prominent violet-purple veins.
Fruits: Spherical capsules up to 20 mm (⅘ in) across, enclosed within the persistent calyx.
Related or similar plants: Deadly Nightshade (p.246) is a perennial with bell-shaped flowers and black berries.
Habitat and distribution: Local in open, sandy or manure-rich ground and waysides, especially near the sea and around rabbit warrens, north to the Moray Firth, but rare in northern Britain and in Ireland; frequently associated with old ruins.
Flowering time: June to October

HENBANE LOOKS, and smells, even more sinister than Deadly Nightshade, and similarly the whole plant is extremely poisonous and should not be handled. It is an ancient medicinal plant, formerly employed as an anaesthetic and sedative. It can induce hallucinations and eventually death – and was the poison that Dr Crippen used to murder his wife in 1913, in one of the century's most celebrated criminal cases. Henbane survives around rabbit warrens because of its toxicity, while thriving on the high nutrient levels, a curious ecological niche.

Top and bottom right *Henbane* (Hyoscyamus niger) *has rather sinister looking flowers with violet-purple veins and dark centres.*

Bottom left *Thorn-apple* (Datura stramonium) *is another poisonous plant with deeply toothed or lobed oval leaves, but has solitary, white, trumpet-shaped flowers 5–8 cm (1/5–1/3 in) long and spiny, egg-shaped capsules 2.5–5 cm (1–2 in) long. An American alien it can turn up almost anywhere, especially in hot summers in south-eastern England.*

Black Nightshade

NIGHTSHADE AND POTATO FAMILY

(Solanaceae)

SPECIES INFORMATION	
COMMON NAME	Black Nightshade
SCIENTIFIC NAME	Solanum nigrum
RELATED SPECIES	Woody Nightshade
HEIGHT/SPREAD	10–60 cm tall
FLOWERING TIME	July–October
HABITAT	Cultivated land

Note: The only annual weed with black berries.

FLOWER TYPE

IDENTIFICATION

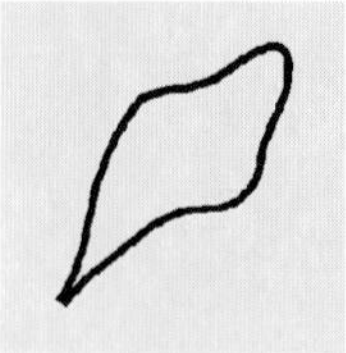

HABITAT

POPULATION

MAP

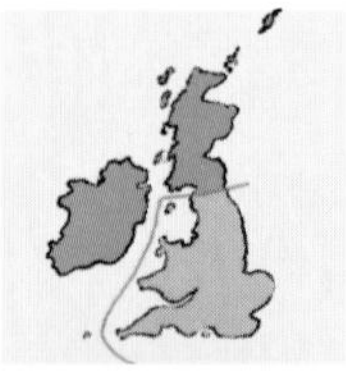

Size and appearance: An erect or semi-erect, much-branched, hairless or downy annual 10–60 cm (4–24 in) tall.

Leaves: Stalked, 3–6 cm (1⅕–2⅖ in) long, more or less oval or diamond-shaped, pointed, irregularly toothed.

Flowers: White, 6–10 mm (¼–⅖ in) across, with petals becoming down-curved and stamens forming a yellow cone, in small, clusters.

Fruits: A loose cluster of spherical, black, shiny berries c. 8 mm (⅓ in) across.

Related or similar plants: Woody Nightshade (p.249) has similar flowers but is a much larger perennial with red berries.

Habitat and distribution: A locally common weed of vegetable crops and gardens on light, rich soils north to Yorkshire and the Isle of Man; here and there in Ireland, mainly in the east.

Flowering time: July to October.

NOTE THAT THE berries, ripening from green to black in late summer to early autumn, are poisonous, like those of its cultivated relative, the potato, with which it so often grows. The leaves, too, contain variable amounts of poisonous substances, but in southern Europe they can be seen being sold, cooked and eaten as a green vegetable similar to spinach.

Other annual nightshades, mostly introduced from South America and all poisonous, with black, red or green berries, turn up from time to time as weeds of cultivated or waste ground. The most widespread of them is Leafy-fruited Nightshade (*Solanum sarrachoides*), which has green or black berries partially covered by a swollen, persistent calyx.

Black Nightshade (Solanum nigrum) *has white flowers with yellow stamens, similar to those of its close relative, the Potato. It is a weed of cultivated ground and is often locally common in allotments and other similar places where it can grow from 10-60 cm (4-24 in) tall with just a few oval or diamond-shaped leaves to quite a bushy leafy plant.*

SPECIES INFORMATION	
COMMON NAME	Woody Nightshade, Bittersweet
SCIENTIFIC NAME	Solanum dulcamara
RELATED SPECIES	Black Nightshade
HEIGHT/SPREAD	50–200 cm tall
FLOWERING TIME	May–October
HABITAT	Shady places and wet woods

Note: The purplish flower and red berries are distinctive.

Woody Nightshade

NIGHTSHADE AND POTATO FAMILY
(Solanaceae)

Size and appearance: A rather woody, downy perennial, with climbing or straggling stems 50–200 cm (20–80 in) tall, sometimes up to 400 cm (13 ft).
Leaves: Stalked, 5–8 cm (2–3⅕ in) long, the lower 3-lobed, the upper spear-shaped, with an unpleasant smell when bruised.
Flowers: Violet-purple, c.15 mm (⅗ in) across, with back-swept petals and stamens forming a yellow cone, in loose clusters; each petal with 2 green nectary patches at the base.
Fruits: A loose cluster of egg-shaped, scarlet, shiny, translucent berries c.10 mm (⅖ in) long.
Related or similar plants: Deadly Nightshade (p.246) is an erect plant with larger, bell-shaped flowers and black berries.
Habitat and distribution: Widespread and common in shady places, in wet woodland, by streams and rivers, in hedgerow ditches and neglected gardens, and on coastal shingle beaches through most of England and Wales; more local in Scotland, where it tends to be coastal and along rivers, and in Ireland.
Flowering time: May to October.

FLOWER TYPE

IDENTIFICATION

HABITAT

POPULATION

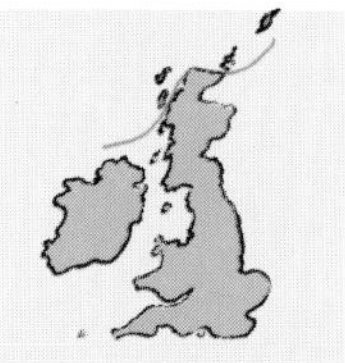

MAP

WOODY NIGHTSHADE GROWS in a variety of shady and damp habitats. It is a particularly characteristic species of swamp woodland, a rare habitat today after millennia of woodland clearance. In areas such as the Norfolk Broads, Woody Nightshade can grow to a huge size scrambling through flooded woods. By contrast, it is also a typical plant of shingle beaches, where the plants are compact, prostrate, and have fleshy leaves.

Woody Nightshade is a fine-looking plant, but note that, as with other nightshades, the most attractive berries are poisonous. Some people call it Deadly Nightshade, but that is a quite different plant (see p.246)

Top and bottom right *Woody Nightshade* (Solanum dulcamara) *is a conspicuous plant with clusters of scarlet berries, often adorning pondsides where it straggles or climbs over the other vegetation. It can also occur in other situations, such as alongside a roadside crash barrier.*

Bottom left *In flower, it is a showy species, with violet-purple petals contrasting with the cone of yellow stamens.*

Monkey Flower

FIGWORT AND FOXGLOVE FAMILY

(Scrophulariaceae)

SPECIES INFORMATION	
COMMON NAME	Monkey Flower
SCIENTIFIC NAME	Mimulus guttatus
RELATED SPECIES	Blood-drop Emlets
HEIGHT/SPREAD	10–50 cm tall
FLOWERING TIME	June–September
HABITAT	Streamsides
Note: A conspicuous, superficially snapdragon-like flower.	

FLOWER TYPE

IDENTIFICATION

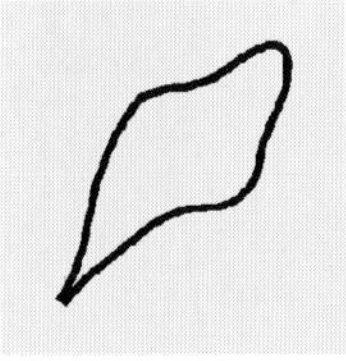

HABITAT

POPULATION

MAP

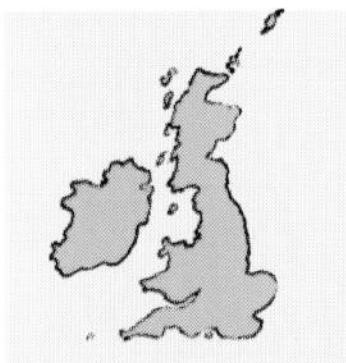

CONTROVERSY RAGES ABOUT the dangers of introduced plants, but here is a most welcome invader. Great sheets of this lovely flower now carpet streamsides in northern England and elsewhere. It came in as a garden plant during the early 19th century, it is said from Alaska, and spread along the expanding canal system. Originally spreading rapidly in southern England, it clearly found the northern climate more like that of its native range.

Size and appearance: A perennial, sticky-downy in the upper part, with erect, hollow stems 10–50 cm (8–20 in) tall.

Leaves: In opposite pairs, oval, irregularly toothed, the upper stalkless, clasping the stem.

Flowers: Bright yellow, 25–40 mm (1–1⅗ in) across, 2-lipped, the almost closed throat usually with small red spots, in loose, leafy clusters.

Fruits: Oblong capsules containing numerous seeds.

Related or similar plants: Blood-drop Emlets is hairless and the flowers have large red blotches.

Habitat and distribution: A native of western North America that is widely established, often in great abundance, on watersides and in other damp places, especially by streams in upland parts of northern Britain; scarce in East Anglia, and in Ireland found mainly in the north.

Flowering time: June to September.

Top and bottom left *Monkey Flower* (Mimulus guttatus) *is a very attractive wild flower from north-west America, which has colonised watersides and can form extensive colonies along the banks. As a garden escape there are several varieties and hybrids that can be found.*

Bottom right *Blood-drop Emlets* (Mimulus luteus) *is very similar but is hairless, with narrower leaves, and the open-throated flower is blotched boldly with red. Another garden escape, originally from Chile, it is locally naturalised by streams in northern Britain and Wales.*

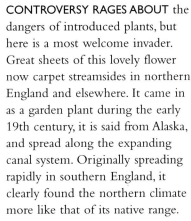

SPECIES INFORMATION	
COMMON NAME	Great Mullein, Aaron's Rod
SCIENTIFIC NAME	Verbascum thapsus
RELATED SPECIES	Other Mulleins
HEIGHT/SPREAD	80–200 cm tall
FLOWERING TIME	June–September
HABITAT	Open and waste ground

Note: The flower-spires are locally a landscape feature.

Great Mullein

FIGWORT AND FOXGLOVE FAMILY (Scrophulariaceae)

Size and appearance: A robust, erect, white-felted, biennial 80–200 cm (32–80 in) tall.

Leaves: The basal in a rosette, broadly oval, up to 30 cm (12 in) long; stem leaves stalkless but running down the stem, broadly spear-shaped, pointed.

Flowers: Pale yellow, 20–35 mm ($\frac{4}{5}$–1$\frac{2}{5}$ in) across, 5-lobed, with a very short tube, in small clusters in the angle of small, leaf-like bracts, numerous in dense, usually unbranched spikes; stamens yellowish-hairy.

Fruits: Egg-shaped capsules containing numerous tiny seeds.

Related or similar plants: Several other species of mullein occur in similar habitats in southern Britain.

Habitat and distribution: Widespread and locally a feature of dry sunny banks and roadsides, waste ground, scrub and woodland margins, but rare in northern and western Scotland; scattered in Ireland, where it tends to be associated with settlements or ruins.

Flowering time: June to September.

GREAT MULLEIN, like other mulleins, can produce many thousands of very tiny seeds. It is a typical biennial that develops a cabbage-like rosette of leaves at the end of its first summer. The great flower-spike appears in the early summer of the second year and the plant usually dies in the autumn, after setting seed.

Great Mullein is the commonest mullein. Six other native or naturalised species occur in Britain, mainly in the south. They occur in similar dry, open or grassy habitats. The most widespread of these others is Dark Mullein (*Verbascum nigrum*), which has leaves that are dark green above, and flowers 12–20 mm ($\frac{1}{2}$–$\frac{4}{5}$ in) across, with purple-hairy stamens.

Top Great Mullein (Verbascum thapsus) *is the commonest species with its robust spike of yellow flowers and great, felty grey leaves.*

Middle Dark Mullein (Verbascum nigrum) *is a smaller plant which usually has several spikes of flowers with mauve spots at the base of their deeper yellow petals and the stalks to the anthers clothed in purple hairs.*

Bottom White Mullein (Verbascum lychnitis) *has, as its name suggests, white flowers.*

FLOWER TYPE

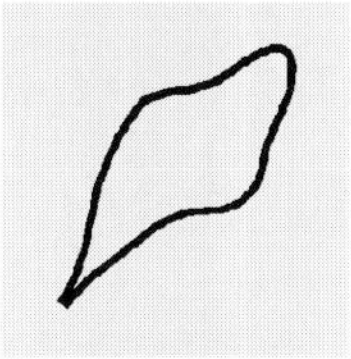
IDENTIFICATION

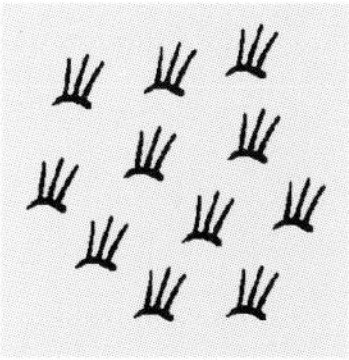
HABITAT

POPULATION

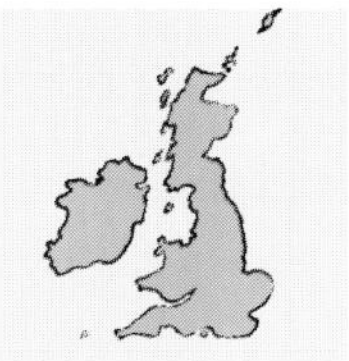
MAP

Common Figwort

FIGWORT AND FOXGLOVE FAMILY
(Scrophulariaceae)

SPECIES INFORMATION	
COMMON NAME	Common Figwort
SCIENTIFIC NAME	Scrophularia nodosa
RELATED SPECIES	Water Figwort
HEIGHT/SPREAD	40–100 cm tall
FLOWERING TIME	June–September
HABITAT	Woods and damp shady places

Note: Likely to be confused only with Water Figwort.

FLOWER TYPE

IDENTIFICATION

HABITAT

POPULATION

MAP

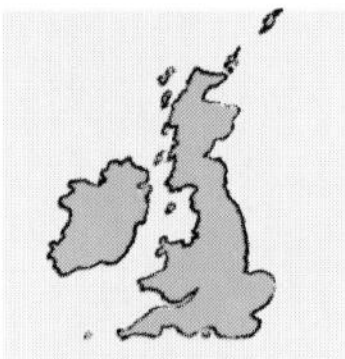

Size and appearance: A hairless perennial, with thick, knobbly rhizomes and erect, square stems 40–100 cm (16–40 in) tall.
Leaves: In opposite pairs, oval, short-stalked with a cut-off or heart-shaped base, pointed, double-toothed, unpleasant-smelling when bruised.
Flowers: Green with a purplish-brown upper lip, c. 10 mm (⅜ in) long, helmet-like, in loose, leafy clusters.
Fruits: Egg-shaped, pointed capsules.
Related or similar plants: Water Figwort, with winged stems and blunt leaves, grows in wet places.
Habitat and distribution: Widespread and common in woods and damp, shady places, on hedge-banks and beside rivers through most of Britain and Ireland, although rare in northern Scotland.
Flowering time: June to September

COMMON FIGWORT (together with Water Figwort) has a long history of medicinal use, especially in the healing of skin complaints, bruises and wounds. Indeed, in Ireland country people regarded it as the 'queen of herbs', imbued with magic. It is not at all a pretty plant, being both dowdy and smelly, but gardeners sometimes grow a variant with white-variegated leaves. Unusually, the flowers, like those of several species of figwort, are pollinated largely by wasps.

Top right and left *Common Figwort* (Scrophularia nodosa) *has oval leaves which are short-stalked and have a cut-off or heart-shaped base. It is a plant widespread and common in woodlands, particularly at the edge of rides.*

Bottom *Water figwort* (Scrophularia aquatica)*, similar but often taller, with broadly winged stems, blunt leaves and spherical seed-capsules, is generally common in wet places, although almost absent from Scotland.*

SPECIES INFORMATION	
COMMON NAME	Common Toadflax
SCIENTIFIC NAME	Linaria vulgaris
RELATED SPECIES	Ivy-leaved Toadflax
HEIGHT/SPREAD	30–80 cm tall
FLOWERING TIME	July–October
HABITAT	Open and waste ground

Note: Like a miniature yellow snapdragon.

Common Toadflax

FIGWORT AND FOXGLOVE FAMILY

(Scrophulariaceae)

Size and appearance: A greyish-hairy perennial, with slender, creeping rhizomes and erect, leafy stems 30–80 cm (12–32 in) tall, branched above.

Leaves: Numerous, crowded, very narrow, spear-shaped, pointed.

Flowers: Snapdragon-like, pale yellow, 20–30 mm (⅘–1⅕ in) long, with a pale orange central patch, and a long, slender spur, in dense pyramidal clusters.

Fruits: Egg-shaped capsules.

Related or similar plants: Ivy-leaved Toadflax (p.254) is a trailing plant of walls with lilac flowers; other rarer toadflaxes, mostly garden escapes, usually have purple or red flowers.

Habitat and distribution: Common in grassland, on hedge-banks, roadsides and waste land through most of Britain, but rare in northern and western Scotland; local in Ireland, mainly in the east.

Flowering time: July to October, often into November.

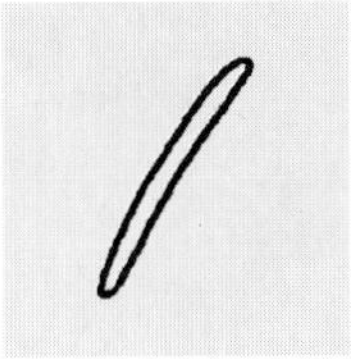

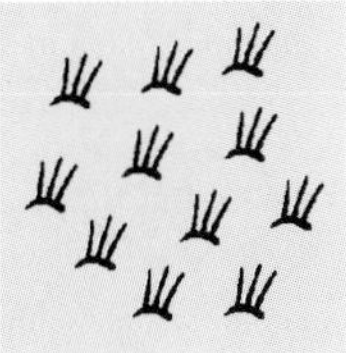

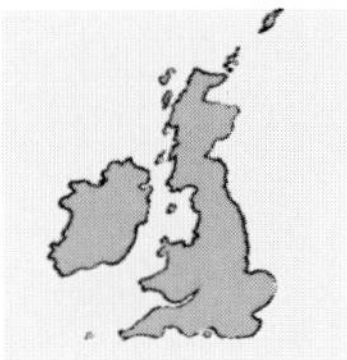

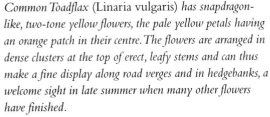

Common Toadflax (Linaria vulgaris) *has snapdragon-like, two-tone yellow flowers, the pale yellow petals having an orange patch in their centre. The flowers are arranged in dense clusters at the top of erect, leafy stems and can thus make a fine display along road verges and in hedgebanks, a welcome sight in late summer when many other flowers have finished.*

COMMON TOADFLAX IS one of our most elegant wild flowers and frequently a feature of the late summer countryside. The flowers are pollinated by bees and bumble-bees, attracted by the nectar in the long spurs. Sometimes they steal the nectar directly by biting through the spur, thus failing to pollinate the flower. The first half of the scientific name denotes the similarity of the leaves to those of flax (Latin: *linum*, flax).

The very similar Purple Toadflax (*Linaria purpurea*), with long, narrow spikes of smaller purplish or pink flowers, frequently escapes from gardens on to waste ground, walls and dry banks.

Ivy-leaved Toadflax

FIGWORT AND FOXGLOVE FAMILY

(Scrophulariaceae)

SPECIES INFORMATION	
COMMON NAME	Ivy-leaved Toadflax
SCIENTIFIC NAME	Cymbalaria muralis
RELATED SPECIES	Common Toadflax
HEIGHT/SPREAD	Stems 10–60 cm long
FLOWERING TIME	April–October
HABITAT	Walls

Note: Like a miniature creeping snapdragon on walls.

FLOWER TYPE

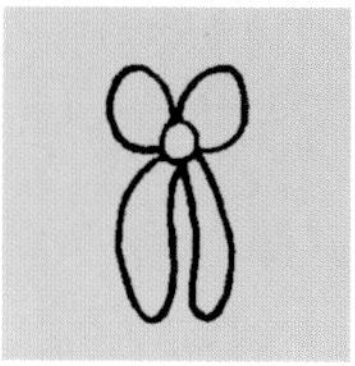

IDENTIFICATION

HABITAT

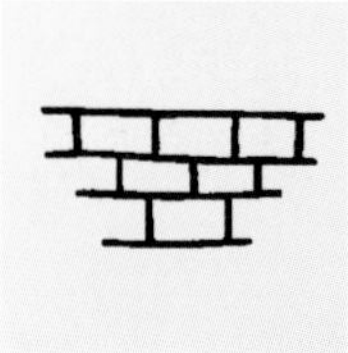

POPULATION

MAP

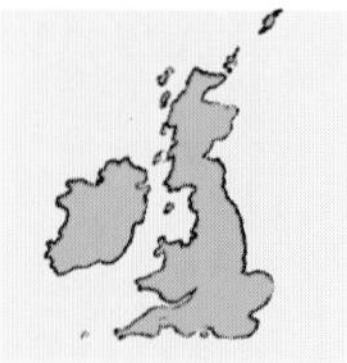

Size and appearance: A hairless, often purplish-tinged perennial, with weak, trailing stems 10–60 cm (4–24 in) long.

Leaves: Long-stalked, like minature ivy leaves, rounded or kidney-shaped with 5–9 shallow lobes, slightly fleshy.

Flowers: Solitary on long stalks, snapdragon-like, lilac or sometimes white, with a yellow and white central patch, 10–15 mm (⅖–⅗ in) long.

Fruits: Small, spherical capsules, on stiff, curved stalks.

Related or similar plants: A distinctive plant unlikely to be confused with other toadflaxes, or any other plant.

Habitat and distribution: A common plant of walls and other masonry, even at quite isolated sites like old bridges, and occasionally on rocks and cliffs, limestone pavement and coastal shingle beaches; throughout, except for much of the Scottish Highlands.

Flowering time: April to October.

THIS WIDESPREAD AND familiar plant has been known in Britain only since 1640. Once it had a rather restricted native range in Italy and adjacent parts of the Alps, but now has spread from gardens across western Europe. The plant is well adapted to its rocky or stony habitat. The stalks of the seed capsules grow away from the light, curving downwards as the seeds ripen to push the fruits into chinks and crannies of the wall. Here they can germinate safely, and the young plants can establish and grow on to maturity.

Top left and right *Ivy-leaved Toadflax* (Cymbalaria muralis) *is now a widespread and familiar plant of walls, albeit that it originally came from Italy. The lilac flowers have either a white or central yellow patch and they contrast with the rather shiny miniature ivy-like leaves.*

Bottom *Once established in its crevice, this plant sends out long trailing stems which often take on a purplish hue.*

SPECIES INFORMATION	
COMMON NAME	Sharp-leaved Fluellen
SCIENTIFIC NAME	Kickxia elatine
RELATED SPECIES	Round-leaved Fluellen
HEIGHT/SPREAD	Stems 10–50 cm long
FLOWERING TIME	July–October
HABITAT	Open and cultivated ground
Note: Like a tiny snapdragon with shield-shaped leaves.	

Sharp-leaved Fluellen

FIGWORT AND FOXGLOVE FAMILY (Scrophulariaceae)

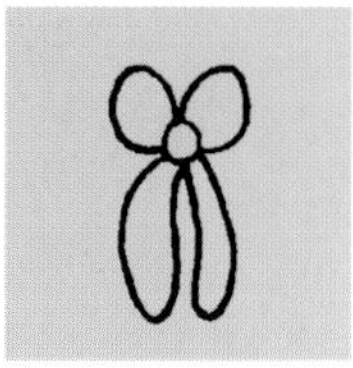

FLOWER TYPE

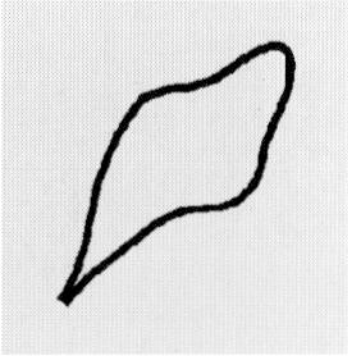

IDENTIFICATION

HABITAT

POPULATION

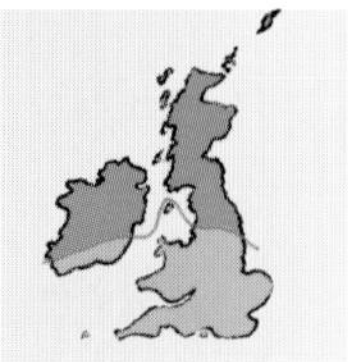

MAP

Size and appearance: A hairy, prostrate or weakly erect, leafy annual with stems 10–50 cm (4–20 in) long, branched from the base.
Leaves: Stalked, halberd-shaped, with a pair of basal lobes.
Flowers: Solitary on long stalks, snapdragon-like, yellow, the upper lip purplish, 6–8 mm (¼–⅓ in) long, with a straight spur.
Fruits: Small, almost spherical capsules.
Related or similar plants: Round-leaved Fluellen has broadly oval leaves and larger flowers.
Habitat and distribution: A local plant of cultivated land and open or disturbed ground, mainly on light or lime-rich soils, south-east of a line between the Severn estuary and the Wash, and extending here and there north to Humberside; also in Wales and southern Ireland, but rare and mainly coastal.
Flowering time: July to October.

SHARP-LEAVED FLUELLEN and Round-leaved Fluellen are not that common, but are often overlooked and it is always worth looking out for them. Both of these attractive little species have declined, like many other arable weeds, in the face of modern intensive agriculture and the use of selective weedkillers. They are summer annuals, germinating in May to June and most prominent in late summer. Sometimes chalky arable land in autumn may be covered by quite large, prostrate, flowering plants of either or both species.

Top *Sharp-leaved Fluellen* (Kickxia elatine) *has trailing stems with stalked, arrow-shaped, hairy leaves. The charming yellow and purple flowers are on long slender stalks and can be found along the stem, but each is solitary.*

Bottom *Round-leaved Fluellen* (Kickxia elatine) *has broadly oval to heart-shaped leaves, and flowers 10–15 mm (⅖–⅗ in) long, with a deep purple upper lip and a curved spur.*

Foxglove

FIGWORT AND FOXGLOVE FAMILY

(Scrophulariaceae)

SPECIES INFORMATION	
COMMON NAME	Foxglove
SCIENTIFIC NAME	Digitalis purpurea
RELATED SPECIES	Toadflaxes
HEIGHT/SPREAD	50–180 cm tall
FLOWERING TIME	June–September
HABITAT	Woodland clearings, banks

Note: A familiar and unmistakable flower.

FLOWER TYPE

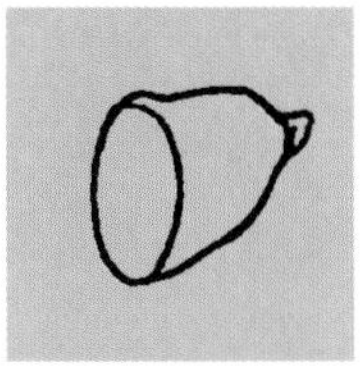

IDENTIFICATION

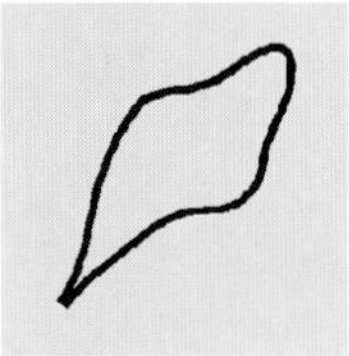

HABITAT

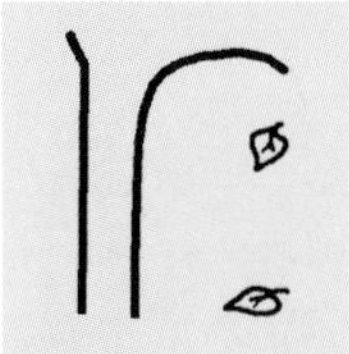

POPULATION

MAP

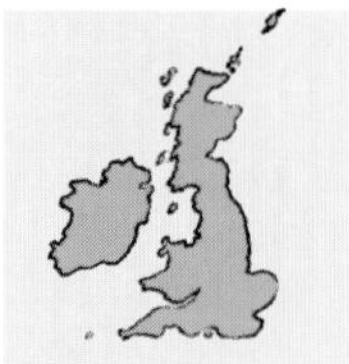

Size and appearance: An erect, unbranched, greyish-downy biennial or short-lived perennial 50–180 cm (20–72 in) tall.

Leaves: The basal in a rosette, stalked, broadly spear-shaped, wrinkled, softly hairy; upper leaves stalkless.

Flowers: Pinkish-purple to purplish-red, paler, red-spotted and hairy inside, 35–50 mm (1⅖–2 in) long, flared tubular, in a long, dense, rather 1-sided spike.

Fruits: Egg-shaped capsules containing numerous seeds.

Related or similar plants: No other wild foxgloves or similar plants occur in Britain or Ireland.

Habitat and distribution: Widespread and often abundant in open woods and scrub, on heaths and banks, always on lime-poor soils, especially where ground has been cleared or burned throughout Britain and Ireland, but more plentiful in the west and local in some areas such as the Irish midlands and south-central areas of England.

Flowering time: June to September.

FOXGLOVE IS ONE of the most conspicuous, magnificent and large-scale displays of any wild flower, frequently colouring the landscape, as on some new road-verges in Wales and elsewhere. The whole plant is very poisonous, and is still the source of the drug digitoxin, used to slow the pace of the heart-beat. The plant was an ancient herbal remedy — albeit a hazardous one! A study of the effects of Foxglove by the physician William Withering in 1785 was the first scientific examination of a herbal medicine. In Ireland the plant is surrounded by myth and magic, and country people called it 'king of herbs'. Similar beliefs exist in Scotland and Wales, where the flower was celebrated in poetry.

Foxglove (Digitalis purpurea) *is a stately plant which is familiar to many. It is often visited by bumble-bees; they start at the bottom of the spike, crawling a little way up the long tubular flower to reach the nectar with their long tongues. Backing out, they visit the next flower higher up the stem and continue until the upper flowers are not producing sufficient nectar; then they start at the bottom of another spike.*

SPECIES INFORMATION	
COMMON NAME	Brooklime
SCIENTIFIC NAME	Veronica beccabunga
RELATED SPECIES	Speedwells
HEIGHT/SPREAD	Stems 20–50 cm long
FLOWERING TIME	May–September
HABITAT	Streams and wet ground

Note: The blue speedwell that blocks streams and runnels.

Brooklime

FIGWORT AND FOXGLOVE FAMILY

(Scrophulariaceae)

BROOKLIME IS ONE of a group of four perennial speedwells of wet places. All have the characteristic disc-shaped (usually blue) flowers, with 2 stamens of this genus of plants (*Veronica*). The other common species in this group, Blue Water-speedwell, is described below. The leaves of Brooklime have a sharp taste and have been used as a salad, like Watercress (p.83) with which it often grows. They were formerly regarded as a preventative against scurvy and a general tonic for the health.

FLOWER TYPE

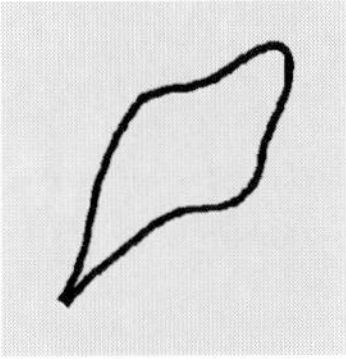

IDENTIFICATION

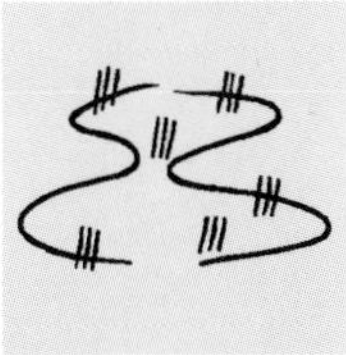

HABITAT

POPULATION

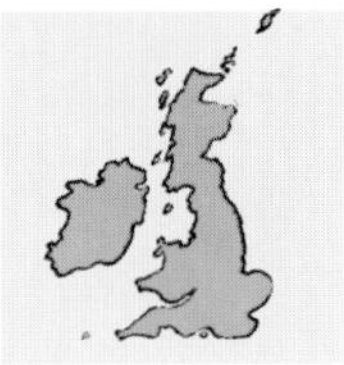

MAP

Size and appearance: A slightly fleshy, hairless perennial, with far-creeping, rooting, sprawling or semi-erect, hollow stems 20–50 cm (8–20 in) long.

Leaves: In opposite pairs, short-stalked, oval to oblong, blunt, shallowly toothed, shiny.

Flowers: Bright blue, rarely pink, 5–8 mm (1/5–1/3 in) across, disc-shaped, 4-lobed, with 2 stamens, in paired, pyramidal spikes arising from a pair of leaves.

Fruits: Flattened, rounded capsules, splitting into 4 segments.

Related or similar plants: Blue Water-speedwell has broadly spear-shaped, pointed leaves and paler blue flowers.

Habitat and distribution: Widespread and common in streams, ditches and other wet places, throughout most of Britain and Ireland, although much more local in north-western Scotland.

Flowering time: May to September.

Top and bottom *Brooklime* (Veronica beccabunga) *has startling blue flowers in paired pyramidal spikes. They arise from the leaf bases which are also paired; the leaves rather thick and fleshy, appearing shiny, oval or oblong with blunt tips.*

Middle *Blue Water-speedwell* (Veronica anagallis-aquatica) *is more erect, with stalkless, spear-shaped, pointed leaves and paler blue flowers 5–6 mm (1/5–1/4 in) across. Flowering June–August, it is locally common, except in the higher mountains.*

Germander Speedwell

FIGWORT AND FOXGLOVE FAMILY
(Scrophulariaceae)

SPECIES INFORMATION	
COMMON NAME	Germander Speedwell, Bird's Eye
SCIENTIFIC NAME	Veronica chamaedrys
RELATED SPECIES	Other speedwells
HEIGHT/SPREAD	10–30 cm tall
FLOWERING TIME	April–July
HABITAT	Woodland rides and grassy places

Note: The common lowland speedwell with the largest flowers.

FLOWER TYPE

IDENTIFICATION

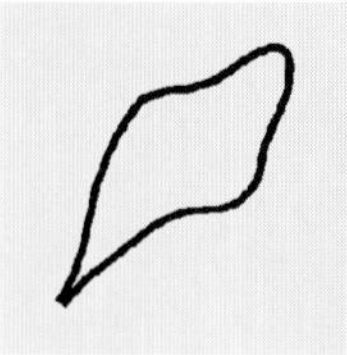

HABITAT

POPULATION

MAP

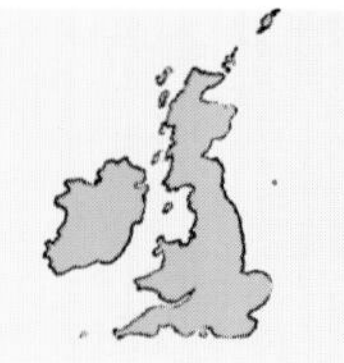

Size and appearance: A hairy perennial, with far-creeping, rooting, semi-erect stems 10–30 cm (4–12 in) tall, marked with 2 opposite lines of white hairs.
Leaves: In opposite pairs, very short-stalked, oval-triangular, toothed.
Flowers: Deep blue with a white eye, c. 10 mm (⅜ in) across, disc-shaped, 4-lobed, with 2 stamens, in loose pyramidal clusters of 10–20, each one from a pair of leaves.
Fruits: Heart-shaped, hairy capsules, splitting into 2 segments.
Related or similar plants: Heath Speedwell (p.259) has stems hairy all round and dense clusters of bluish-lilac flowers.
Habitat and distribution: Common on the margins and in rides and clearings of woods, hedge-banks and grassy places throughout Britain and Ireland, and is rare only in the Outer Hebrides and Shetland.
Flowering time: April to July, but often in flower in March.

THE EXQUISITE BLUE flowers of Germander Speedwell are a welcome sign of spring. The individual flowers are very delicate and fall easily, which is perhaps the best reason for not picking them! There is too a widespread superstition that harm will come to the eyes of anyone who picks the flowers, or to his or her mother. In Ireland, the plant was regarded as a good luck charm for the traveller. It is certainly a plant that brightens waysides.

Germander Speedwell (Veronica chamaedrys) *has deep blue flowers with a white eye from which comes two stamens. They are displayed in loose pyramidal clusters of 10-20, flowers making a splash of colour on the hedgebank or in the grassland. The two lines of white hairs running up on opposite sides of the stem are quite easily seen.*

SPECIES INFORMATION	
COMMON NAME	Heath or Common Speedwell
SCIENTIFIC NAME	Veronica officinalis
RELATED SPECIES	Other speedwells
HEIGHT/SPREAD	Stems 10–30 cm long
FLOWERING TIME	June–August
HABITAT	Heaths and dry grassy places

Note: The common lowland speedwell of dry grassland.

Heath Speedwell

FIGWORT AND FOXGLOVE FAMILY

(Scrophulariaceae)

Size and appearance: A hairy, mat-forming perennial, with creeping, rooting, more or less prostrate stems 10–30 cm (4–12 in) long, hairy all round.

Leaves: In opposite pairs, very short-stalked, oval or oblong, shallowly toothed.

Flowers: Pale blue or lilac-blue with dark veins, 6–8 mm (¼–⅓ in) across, disc-shaped, 4-lobed, with 2 stamens, in paired, dense cylindrical or pyramidal clusters, arising from a pair of leaves.

Fruits: Heart-shaped, hairy capsules, splitting into 2 segments.

Related or similar plants: Germander Speedwell (p.258) has stems with 2 opposite lines of white hairs and deep blue flowers c.10 mm (2/5 in) across.

Habitat and distribution: A widespead plant of heaths, dry grassland, sunny banks, rocky places and open woods, especially of beech, mostly on more lime-poor soils, through most of Britain and Ireland.

Flowering time: June to August.

HEATH SPEEDWELL HAS a considerable reputation on the Continent as a valuable healing plant. It has been used widely to treat coughs, as a tonic to aid digestion and as a diuretic. Plants that have *officinalis* (Latin: kept at the druggist's shop or *officina*) as the second half of their scientific name are usually those of real of supposed medicinal value. Many of these epithets pre-date the achievement of the great Swedish botanist Carl Linnaeus in tidying up Latin names in the mid-18th century.

Top and bottom right *Heath Speedwell* (Veronica officinalis) *has creeping prostrate stems and, with its dense cylindrical spikes of pale lilac flowers, forms pretty patches on the floor of woodland glades in mid-summer.*

Bottom left *Another mostly prostrate speedwell, with similar-sized flowers, Thyme-leaved Speedwell* (Veronica serpyllifolia) *is hairless and has oval leaves 10–20 mm (⅖–⅘ in) long, and spikes of pale blue or white flowers on semi-erect, leafy, flowering stems. Flowering March–October, it is widespread in damp, open or grassy places, and is often a weed of gardens.*

FLOWER TYPE

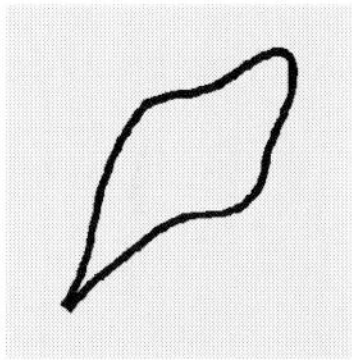

IDENTIFICATION

HABITAT

POPULATION

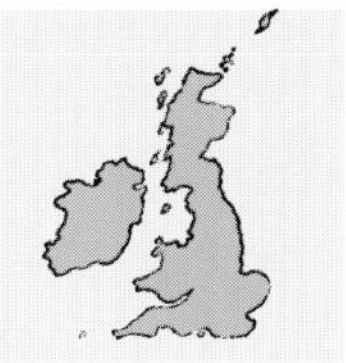

MAP

Common Field-speedwell

FIGWORT AND FOXGLOVE FAMILY (Scrophulariaceae)

SPECIES INFORMATION	
COMMON NAME	Common Field-speedwell
SCIENTIFIC NAME	Veronica persica
RELATED SPECIES	Other speedwells
HEIGHT/SPREAD	Stems 10–50 cm long
FLOWERING TIME	February–November
HABITAT	Cultivated ground

Note: The common speedwell of cultivated land.

FLOWER TYPE

IDENTIFICATION

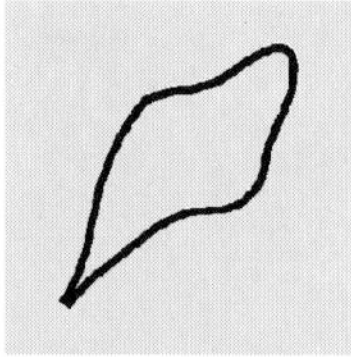

HABITAT

POPULATION

MAP

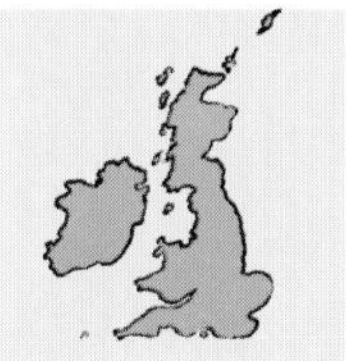

Size and appearance: A hairy, prostrate or sprawling annual, branched from the base, with wiry stems 10–50 cm (4–20 in) long.
Leaves: In opposite pairs, short-stalked, oval or triangular, very coarsely toothed.
Flowers: Solitary on slender stalks, blue, with darker bluish-violet veins, white eye and white markings, 8–12 mm (⅓–½ in) across, disc-shaped, 4-lobed, with 2 stamens.
Fruits: Hairy capsules with two widely spreading lobes.
Related or similar plants: Other annual field-speedwells.
Habitat and distribution: A ubiquitous weed of disturbed gound, especially rich, light, cultivated soil, throughout Britain and Ireland, although less abundant in the west. Having arrived in Britain from south-west Asia in the early 19th century, it is now our commonest speedwell of cultivated land.
Flowering time: February to November, but all through mild winters.

Common Field-speedwell (Veronica persica) *has solitary flowers on slender stalks arising at the leaf bases. The blue flowers are marked with blue-violet veins and have a white eye in their centre. It is a plant of field margins and cultivated land.*

COMMON FIELD-SPEEDWELL is one of a group of eight annual speedwells, several of which are now rare or decreasing as a result of modern intensive agriculture. Common Field-speedwell, almost alone, has emerged as one of the most successful of agricultural weeds that can severely infest vegetable crops, allotments and gardens.

Another widespread and sometimes persistent weed, Ivy-leaved Speedwell (*Veronica hederifolia*), with neat, slightly fleshy, 3- to 5-lobed leaves, smaller lilac or blue flowers and stout, rounded fruits, occurs in gardens and also disturbed ground in woodland.

SPECIES INFORMATION	
COMMON NAME	Slender Speedwell
SCIENTIFIC NAME	Veronica filiformis
RELATED SPECIES	Other speedwells
HEIGHT/SPREAD	Stems 5–20 cm long
FLOWERING TIME	April–June
HABITAT	Lawns and damp grasslands

Note: The speedwell that colours lawns and other grassland.

Slender Speedwell

FIGWORT AND FOXGLOVE FAMILY

(Scrophulariaceae)

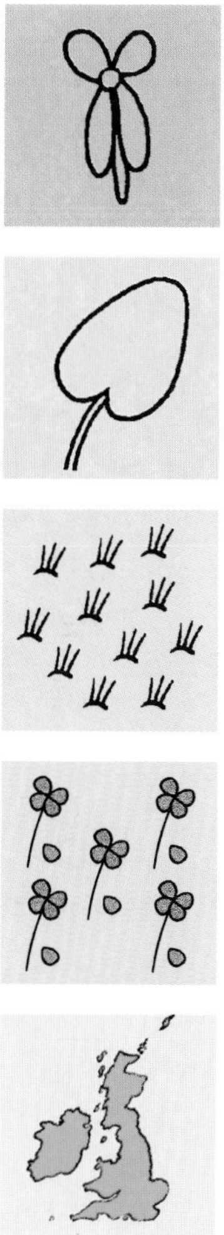

FLOWER TYPE

IDENTIFICATION

HABITAT

POPULATION

MAP

Size and appearance: A slender, mat-forming perennial, with creeping stems that root at the nodes, and sprawling flowering stems 5–20 cm (2–8 in) long.

Leaves: In opposite pairs, kidney-shaped, blunt, round-toothed,

Flowers: Solitary on long, slender stalks, pale blue, with a white eye and lilac veins, 10–15 mm (⅜–⅝ in) across, disc-shaped, 4-lobed, with 2 stamens.

Fruits: Capsules rarely known to form.

Related or similar plants: Common Field-speedwell (p.260) has solitary blue flowers but is an annual of cultivated ground.

Habitat and distribution: Locally common and still spreading in damp grassland, along river banks, in churchyards, amenity grassland and lawns, anywhere where there is short, fairly damp grass, throughout Britain and Ireland, although less abundant in the west.

Flowering time: April to June.

SLENDER SPEEDWELL HAS spread in a spectacular fashion in recent decades, and now turns up almost anywhere in Britain or Ireland. A native of the Caucasus and eastern Turkey, it was introduced to Britain in 1808 as a garden plant, but soon escaped into the wild. It has never been known to set seed in Britain and Ireland, but mowing and other disturbance readily disperses numerous rooting fragments of stem. Slender Speedwell is one of the most elegant of all wild flowers and a worthy addition to our flora. In April to May, grassy places and lawns shimmer with its massed, pale blue flowers.

Slender Speedwell (Veronica filiformis) *has solitary flowers on long, slender stalks, and they are a pale blue with lilac veins. It has creeping stems which spread through the turf and can form great swathes of colour.*

Red Bartsia

FIGWORT AND FOXGLOVE FAMILY
(Scrophulariaceae)

SPECIES INFORMATION	
COMMON NAME	Red Bartsia
SCIENTIFIC NAME	Odontites verna
RELATED SPECIES	Common Cow-wheats
HEIGHT/SPREAD	20–50 cm tall
FLOWERING TIME	June–September
HABITAT	Grassland and disturbed ground

Note: Branched and purple-tinged, with 1-sided flower-spikes.

FLOWER TYPE

IDENTIFICATION

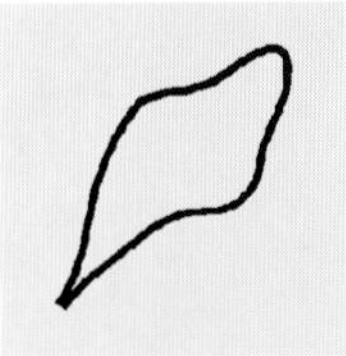

HABITAT

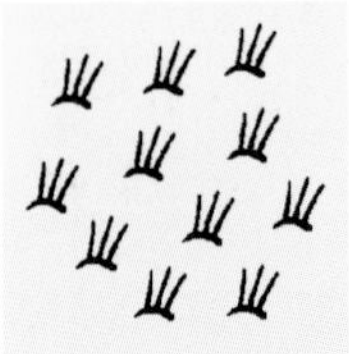

POPULATION

MAP

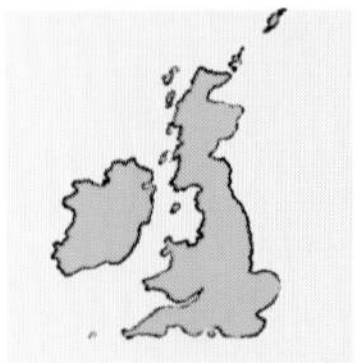

Size and appearance: A downy, usually purplish perennial, with tough, much-branched, erect stems 20–50 cm (8–20 in).
Leaves: In opposite pairs, spear-shaped, tapering or rounded at the base, toothed or not.
Flowers: Reddish-pink, 8–10 mm (⅓–⅜ in) long, 2-lipped, in long, loose, 1-sided spikes, with reddish, leaf-like bracts.
Fruits: Oblong, downy capsules.
Related or similar plants: Yellow Rattle (p.264) has toothed leaves and yellowish-green leaf-like bracts.
Habitat and distribution: Widespread in rough grassland and on tracksides, road-verges and waste or disturbed ground throughout Britain and Ireland.
Flowering time: June to September.

RED BARTSIA IS a scruffy little plant that one might pass by without noticing that it is there. Yet it is a rather characteristic plant of waysides and rough pastures in late summer, especially in the west. Writer Geoffrey Grigson, in his book *The Englishman's Flora*, described it unkindly as a 'red, dullish, disregarded annual … a weed which has not even incurred the hatred of farmers'! However, it does have an interesting ecology. Like Common Cow-wheat (p.263), Yellow Rattle (p.264) and several other members of this family, Red Bartsia is a so-called hemiparasite. It produces its own food by photosynthesis, but is able to extract water and minerals from the roots of other plants.

Red Bartsia (Odontites verna) *produces leafy spikes 20-50 cm (8-20 in) tall with reddish-pink flowers in loose one-sided spikes. It occurs throughout the British Isles in rough grassland, tracksides and road-verges, flowering from June to September.*

SPECIES INFORMATION	
COMMON NAME	Common Cow-wheat
SCIENTIFIC NAME	Melampyrum pratense
RELATED SPECIES	Yellow Rattle
HEIGHT/SPREAD	20–60 cm tall
FLOWERING TIME	May–September
HABITAT	Heaths and open woods

Note: The flowers are very variable in colour.

Common Cow-wheat

FIGWORT AND FOXGLOVE FAMILY
(Scrophulariaceae)

COMMON COW-WHEAT is a very variable species. Plants growing on moors sometimes have pinkish-purple flowers; another striking variant has bright golden-yellow flowers. The plant is, like Red Bartsia (p.262) and Yellow Rattle (p.264) a hemiparasite, taking water and minerals from the roots of various trees, shrubs and heathers.

The first half of the scientific name comes from the supposed resemblance of the seeds to black grains of wheat (Greek *melas*, black; *puros*, wheat). The ancient Greeks knew a plant that grew in wheat fields by this name, perhaps a species of Cow-wheat, some of which do parasitise cereal crops. In southern England, Field Cow-wheat (*Melampyrum arvense*), a handsome plant with showy spikes of yellow and pink flowers, with reddish-purple bracts, was once a widespread weed. Now it is restricted to half a dozen small sites.

Size and appearance: A mostly hairless, slender, branched annual 20–60 cm (8–24 in) tall.

Leaves: In opposite pairs, very short-stalked, narrowly oval or spear-shaped, pointed, untoothed.

Flowers: Golden-yellow or pale yellow to whitish, sometimes purple-tinged, 10–18 mm (⅖–¾ in) long, in pairs in a very loose, 1-sided cluster, with leaf-like bracts.

Fruits: 4-seeded capsules.

Related or similar plants: Yellow Rattle (p.264) has toothed leaves and yellowish-green leaf-like bracts.

Habitat and distribution: A widespread and variable plant of dry, open woods, scrub, moors, heaths, hedgerows and grassland on a range of soils, but mostly those poor in lime; throughout, but local in eastern England and much of Ireland.

Flowering time: May to September.

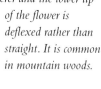

Bottom right *Small Cow-wheat* (Melampyrum sylvaticum) *can be mistaken for a deep yellow variety of Common Cow-wheat but it is slenderer and the lower lip of the flower is deflexed rather than straight. It is common in mountain woods.*

Bottom left *Field Cow-wheat* (Melampyrum arvense) *– the showiest cow-wheat.*

Top *Common Cow-wheat* (Melampyrum pratense) *has pairs of pale to golden-yellow flowers.*

FLOWER TYPE

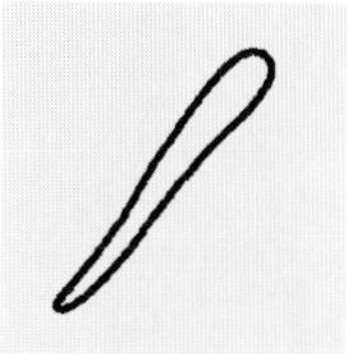
IDENTIFICATION

HABITAT

POPULATION

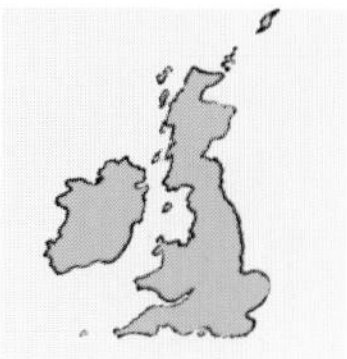
MAP

Yellow Rattle

FIGWORT AND FOXGLOVE FAMILY
(Scrophulariaceae)

SPECIES INFORMATION

COMMON NAME	Yellow Rattle, Hay Rattle
SCIENTIFIC NAME	Rhinanthus minor
RELATED SPECIES	Common Cow-wheat
HEIGHT/SPREAD	10–50 cm tall
FLOWERING TIME	May–July
HABITAT	Grassland

Note: The papery seed-pods rattle when they are ripe.

FLOWER TYPE

IDENTIFICATION
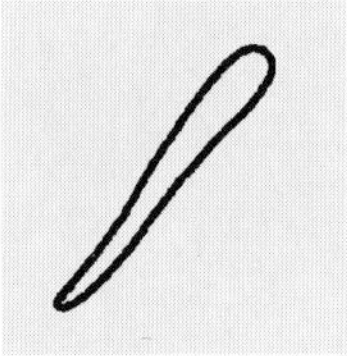

HABITAT
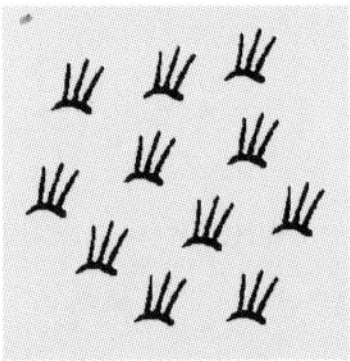

POPULATION
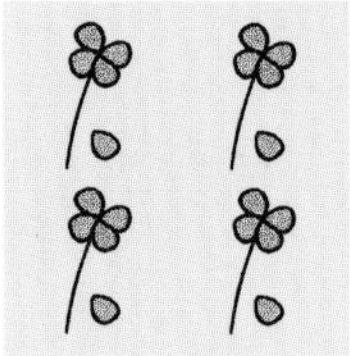

MAP
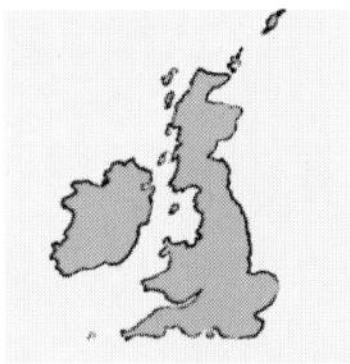

YELLOW RATTLE IS one of the most typical wild flowers of old, species-rich meadows, now greatly reduced in extent by modern farming methods, which favour temporary rye-grass leys. Like several other members of the family, Yellow Rattle is a hemiparasite, taking water and minerals from the roots of other plants. For this reason, conservationists are carrying out experiments to use it as a management tool for the control of vigorous grassy swards. The English name derives from the rattling of the ripe seeds within the seed-capsules.

Top left and right *Yellow Rattle* (Rhinanthus minor) *has bright yellow flowers with two short, violet teeth. The calyx is yellowish-green and inflated. The flowers are in loose spikes.*

Size and appearance: A more or less hairless, erect, rather stiff, usually little-branched annual 10–50 cm (4–20 in) tall.
Leaves: In opposite pairs, stalkless, narrowly oblong or spear-shaped, pointed, toothed.
Flowers: Yellow, with 2 short, violet teeth, 12–15 mm (½–⅗ in) long, the calyx yellowish-green and inflated, in loose spikes, with triangular, leaf-like bracts.
Fruits: Capsules enclosed within the persistent, inflated calyx; seeds flat, winged.
Related or similar plants: Common Cow-wheat (p.263) has untoothed leaves and green, leaf-like bracts.
Habitat and distribution: Widespread and sometimes locally common in grassland, often on more lime-rich soils, and especially in damper places and in the west and north, but much decreased in many areas from the loss of old meadows, due to intensive agriculture.
Flowering time: May to July.

Bottom *Yellow Bartsia* (Parentucellia viscosa) *is similar but sticky-hairy, with larger flowers 15–25 mm (⅗–1 in) long, that have a prominent 3-lobed lip. Flowering June–September, it is a local plant of damp, grassy and sandy places, mainly in the mainly in the West Country and south-western Ireland.*

SPECIES INFORMATION	
COMMON NAME	Eyebright
SCIENTIFIC NAME	Euphrasia nemorosa
RELATED SPECIES	Other eyebrights
HEIGHT/SPREAD	5–35 cm tall
FLOWERING TIME	June–October
HABITAT	Grassland

Note: Plants are often bushy and dark green or bronze-green.

Eyebright

FIGWORT AND FOXGLOVE FAMILY
(Scrophulariaceae)

EYEBRIGHT BELONGS WITHIN a very variable group of some 20 closely related 'microspecies'. This is a widespread, attractive and variable group, which has evolved a range of differences in growth habit, leaf-shape and flower size and colour. The plants regularly self-fertilise, which means that distinctive local characters can become fixed. Rare crossing between ecologically or geographically separated populations encourages this evolution. Several of these native microspecies are widespread, but some have very narrow distributions, especially on northern coasts and mountains.

Like Yellow Rattle (p.264) and several other members of the family, Eyebright is a hemiparasite, taking water and minerals from the roots of other plants. The plant has a long history as a herbal treatment for inflammation of the eyes, although it is not clear whether this was effective.

Size and appearance: A hairy or sticky-hairy, often much-branched annual 5–35 cm (2–14 in) tall.
Leaves: In opposite pairs, stalkless, oval or triangular, rounded at the base, with jagged teeth, dark green or bronze-green.
Flowers: White, with a yellow spot and flushed or streaked with lilac and purple, 5–12 mm ($\frac{1}{5}$–$\frac{1}{2}$ in) long, with a 3-lobed lip, in very loose, leafy clusters.
Fruits: Small oblong, blunt capsules containing many small seeds.
Related or similar plants: Several closely related species of eyebright occur in Britain and Ireland.
Habitat and distribution: Common in grassland, on heaths, sand-dunes, rocky ground and mountain ledges, on a range of soils, throughout Britain and Ireland.
Flowering time: June to October.

Top *Eyebright* (Euphrasia nemorosa) *is an attractive plant of grassland with its leafy spikes of white flowers. Its lower three-lobed lip is marked with a yellow spot and delicately painted purple lines.*

Bottom *Due to its many microspecies, Eyebright is rather variable and can range from very short to medium height, branched or unbranched, leaves which are dark green to a purplish bronze-green, as well as variations in flower size and colour.*

FLOWER TYPE

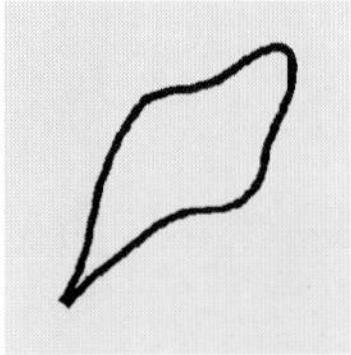
IDENTIFICATION

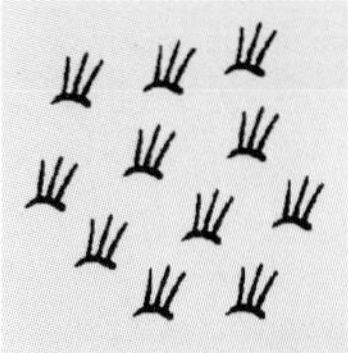
HABITAT

POPULATION

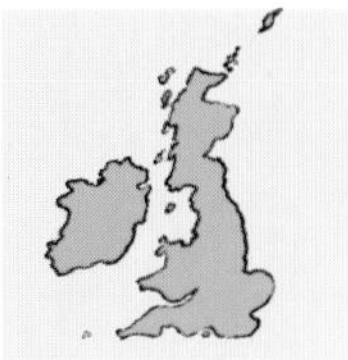
MAP

Lousewort

FIGWORT AND FOXGLOVE FAMILY
(Scrophulariaceae)

SPECIES INFORMATION	
COMMON NAME	Lousewort
SCIENTIFIC NAME	Pedicularis sylvatica
RELATED SPECIES	Red Rattle
HEIGHT/SPREAD	Stems 15–20 cm long
FLOWERING TIME	May–August
HABITAT	Damp heaths and moors

Note: A conspicuous plant of damp, lime-poor places.

FLOWER TYPE

IDENTIFICATION

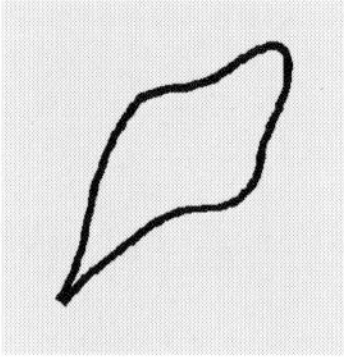

HABITAT

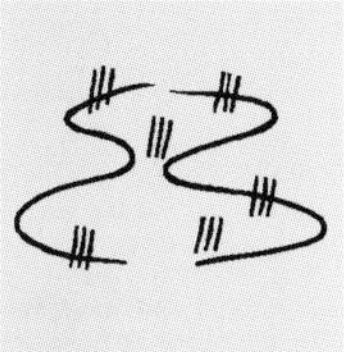

POPULATION

MAP

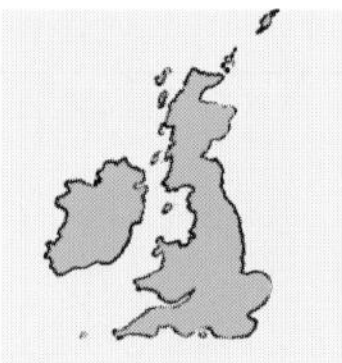

Size and appearance: A tufted perennial, branched at the base, with sprawling or semi-erect stems 5–20 cm (2–8 in) long.
Leaves: Oblong in outline but deeply cut and toothed, dark green or purplish, hairless.
Flowers: Reddish- or purplish-pink, 15–25 mm (⅗–1 in) long, with 2-toothed upper lip, 3-lobed lower lip and a usually hairless calyx that has 4 small, leafy lobes, in short, loose clusters.
Fruits: Flattened, curved capsules, enclosed within the persistent, inflated calyx.
Related or similar plants: Red Rattle is up to 50 cm (20 in) tall with a single, branched stem.
Habitat and distribution: A widespread and locally common plant of moors, heaths, open woods, bogs and lime-poor grassland, especially in the west where it even grows on damp lawns; throughout, but scarce in some lowland areas, especially central England and East Anglia.
Flowering time: May to August.

LIKE EYEBRIGHT (p.265) and several other members of the family, Lousewort is a hemiparasite, taking water and minerals from the roots of other plants. The English name and the first half of the scientific name (Latin: *pediculus*, louse) refer to the 'lice' or liver-flukes, that can infest animals grazing in the wet pastures in which the plant often grows.

Most plants in Ireland, and in a few places in western Wales, have a hairy calyx, which can cause confusion with Red Rattle.

Top and bottom left
Lousewort (Pedicularis sylvatica) *has flowers in leafy spikes, bright pink, two-lipped; the upper lip is longer with two teeth and the lower lip has three lobes.*

Bottom right *Red Rattle or Marsh Lousewort* (Pedicularis palustris) *is similar but an annual up to 50 cm (20 in) tall.*

SPECIES INFORMATION	
COMMON NAME	Common Broomrape
SCIENTIFIC NAME	Orobanche minor
RELATED SPECIES	Ivy Broomrape
HEIGHT/SPREAD	10–50 cm tall
FLOWERING TIME	May–July
HABITAT	Grassland

Note: A strange, fleshy flower, without green leaves.

Common Broomrape

BROOMRAPE FAMILY

(Orobanchaceae)

THIS ODD-LOOKING plant produces no green chlorophyll at all, and is a parasite on the roots of several different plants, especially members of the clover and daisy families, including garden plants. It is thought to have been spread more widely with clover seed. From its hosts the plant extracts water, sugars and minerals to sustain its own growth and flowering. Most of the 12 native broomrapes are rare and they can be very difficult to tell apart. In other countries, broomrapes are serious weeds that can devastate clover and bean crops, especially during hot weather when the water they extract is in short supply.

Top right and left *Common Broomrape* (Orobanche minor) *is parasitic, producing no green chlorophyll and the whole plant is therefore shades of brown suffused with pink. Often only producing a single erect spike, there can sometimes be clusters of several.*

Size and appearance: An erect, fleshy, hairy, yellow, brownish, pink or purplish perennial 10–50 cm (8–20 in) tall, superficially resembling an orchid.
Leaves: Small, scale-like (never green).
Flowers: Yellowish, tinged and streaked with violet, pink or purple, 10–15 mm (⅖–⅗ in) long, tubular, slightly curved, 5-lobed, with a purplish or reddish stigma, in a compact, pyramidal spike.
Fruits: Cylindrical capsules, containing numerous dust-like seeds.
Related or similar plants: Common Broomrape is the commonest of twelve native species of broomrape, some of them very rare; Ivy Broomrape is locally common.
Habitat and distribution: Local and often erratic in appearance, a plant of dry grassland, less often in parks or gardens; widespread in the south and south-east, extending to a few sites in northern England, to the coasts of Wales and the southern half of Ireland.
Flowering time: May to July.

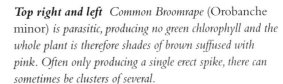

FLOWER TYPE

IDENTIFICATION

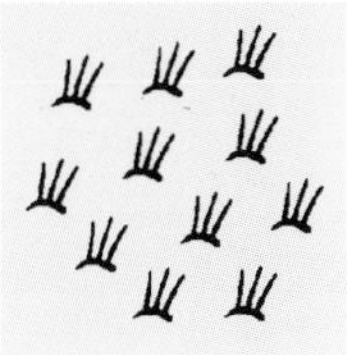

HABITAT

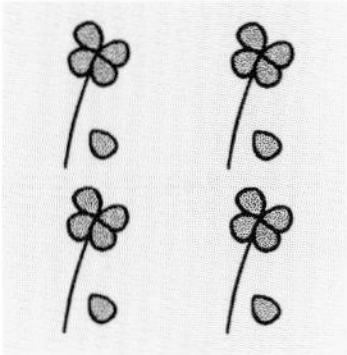

POPULATION

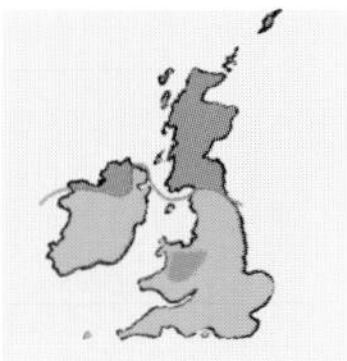

MAP

Bottom *Ivy Broomrape* (Orobanche hederae) *is similar but reddish-purple or yellowish, the slightly larger flowers cream tinged purple, with a yellowish or white stigma. Flowering May–July, it is a locally conspicuous parasite of Ivy, mainly near the coasts of south-west England, Wales and southern Ireland.*

Toothwort

BROOMRAPE FAMILY

(Orobanchaceae)

SPECIES INFORMATION	
COMMON NAME	Toothwort
SCIENTIFIC NAME	Lathraea squamaria
RELATED SPECIES	None
HEIGHT/SPREAD	10–30 cm tall
FLOWERING TIME	April–May
HABITAT	Woodland

Note: A distinctive, fleshy, white or cream spring flower.

FLOWER TYPE

IDENTIFICATION

HABITAT

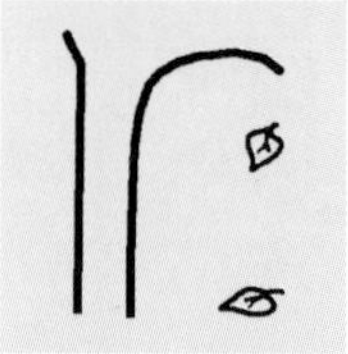

POPULATION

MAP

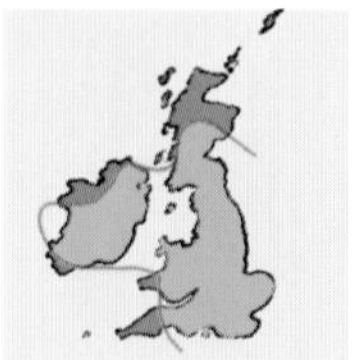

Size and appearance: A white or cream, sticky-hairy, fleshy perennial, with stout, erect stems 10–30 cm (4–12 in) tall.

Leaves: Crowded below, small, scale-like (never green), clasping the stem.

Flowers: Pale pink, 15–18 mm (⅝–¾ in) long, tubular, 2-lipped with a protruding stigma, hanging slightly, in a dense, 1-sided spike.

Fruits: Almost spherical capsules, containing numerous seeds.

Related or similar plants: Superficially similar to Common Broomrape (p.267) and Bird's-nest Orchid (p.367), which flower later in the year.

Habitat and distribution: A very local but, where it occurs, conspicuous plant of woods and hedges on more lime-rich soils, especially where there is hazel and elm, north to central Scotland; rarer in Ireland.

Flowering time: April to May.

LIKE COMMON BROOMRAPE (p.267), this is an unusual-looking plant that few would pass by without comment. It produces no green chlorophyll at all, and is a parasite on the roots of trees such as hazel, elm and elder, extracting water, sugars and minerals for its own growth and flowering. In Yorkshire, where it is sometimes common in woods on limestone, it was known as Corpse-flower, a sinister but perhaps appropriate name for such a curious plant.

Toothwort (Lathraea squamaria) *is another wholly parasitic plant which is predominantly white or cream but can sometimes be tinged with pink. With a branched and creeping rootstock, Toothwort can produce large numbers of its one-sided flower spikes where conditions are favourable.*

SPECIES INFORMATION	
COMMON NAME	Common Butterwort
SCIENTIFIC NAME	Pinguicula vulgaris
RELATED SPECIES	Other butterworts
HEIGHT/SPREAD	5–10 cm tall
FLOWERING TIME	May–July
HABITAT	Grassland

Note: The rosettes of pale, sticky leaves are diagnostic.

Common Butterwort

BUTTERWORT AND BLADDERWORT FAMILY

(Lentibulariaceae)

Size and appearance: An elegant, tufted perennial, with leafless flowering stems 5–10 cm (2–4 in) tall, sometimes up to 20 cm (8 in).

Leaves: All in a neat basal rosette, oval or oblong, pale or yellowish-green, glutinously sticky above.

Flowers: Solitary on slender stems, violet, usually with a white throat, 10–15 mm (⅖–⅗ in) long, with a straight spur 4–6 mm (⅙–¼ in) long.

Fruits: Egg-shaped capsules, containing numerous small seeds.

Related or similar plants: Other butterworts; Greater Bladderwort (p.270) also traps insects, but is an aquatic with yellow flowers.

Habitat and distribution: Common in bogs, on wet moors and heaths, also wet mountain rocks and damp, lime-poor grassland, including old meadows, throughout Britain and Ireland, but rare in southern and eastern England.

Flowering time: May to July.

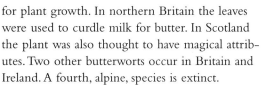

COMMON BUTTERWORT shares with the unrelated Round-leaved Sundew (p.86) the remarkable ability to trap and digest small insects in order to supplement its nutrition. The boggy places in which it grows are poor in the minerals needed for plant growth. In northern Britain the leaves were used to curdle milk for butter. In Scotland the plant was also thought to have magical attributes. Two other butterworts occur in Britain and Ireland. A fourth, alpine, species is extinct.

Large-flowered Butterwort or Kerry Violet (*Pinguicula grandiflora*), with purple flowers 25–35 mm (1–1⅖ in) long that have a spur c. 10 mm (⅖ in) long, flowering April to June, is a feature of the mountains of County Kerry and a few other sites in Ireland.

Pale Butterwort (*Pinguicula lusitanica*), with smaller, lilac flowers that have a down-curved spur 2–4 mm (1/12–⅙ in) long, is locally common in western Britain and western Ireland.

Top right *Pale Butterwort* (Pinguicula lusitanica) *flowers later than the Common Butterwort, and has smaller, pale lilac flowers with a pale yellow throat.*

Top left *Common Butterwort* (Pinguicula vulgaris) *has a basal rosette of broad yellow-green leaves from which arises the flower stem holding the mauve flower which has a broad white patch.*

Bottom *Large-flowered Butterwort* (Pinguicula grandiflora) *is altogether a much larger plant than the other Butterworts with larger purple flowers.*

FLOWER TYPE

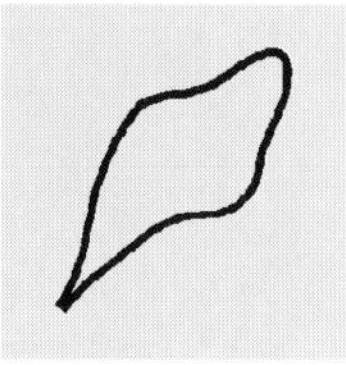

IDENTIFICATION

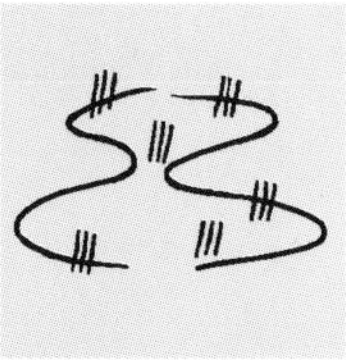

HABITAT

POPULATION

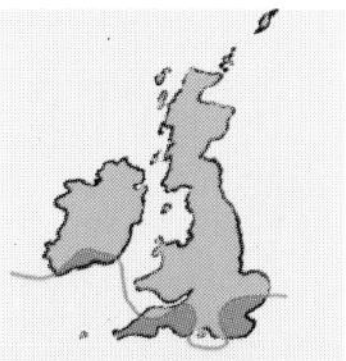

MAP

Greater Bladderwort

BUTTERWORT AND BLADDERWORT FAMILY
(Lentibulariaceae)

SPECIES INFORMATION	
COMMON NAME	Greater Bladderwort
SCIENTIFIC NAME	Utricularia vulgaris
RELATED SPECIES	Common Butterwort
HEIGHT/SPREAD	Flowering stems 10–30 cm tall
FLOWERING TIME	July–August
HABITAT	Boggy pools
Note: Numerous little bladders on the submerged stems.	

FLOWER TYPE

IDENTIFICATION

HABITAT

POPULATION

MAP
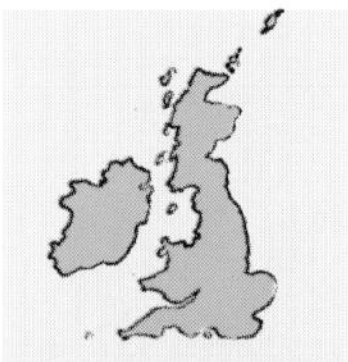

Size and appearance: An aquatic perennial with submerged stems up to 100 cm (40 in) or more long, also erect, leafless flowering stems 10–30 cm (4–12 in) tall, sometimes up to 20 cm (8 in).
Leaves: Submerged, finely divided, equipped with tiny bladders for trapping insects.
Flowers: Slightly snapdragon-like, deep yellow, 12–18 mm (½–¾ in) long, with a conical spur, in a cluster of 4–10.
Fruits: Egg-shaped capsules, containing numerous small seeds.
Related or similar plants: Common Butterwort (p.269) also traps insects, but grows on land and has violet flowers.
Habitat and distribution: Local in still waters, usually lime-poor, especially ponds and boggy pools, scattered through most of Britain and Ireland.
Flowering time: July to August.

BLADDERWORT IS PERHAPS the most unusual of all the plants that trap animals. The leaves and stems (which are undifferentiated, nor does the plant have roots) bear great numbers of tiny bladders. When a small water animal touches sensitive hairs, the bladder opens suddenly and the animal is carried in by the mini-torrent of water. The bladder then secretes chemicals that digest its prey, later absorbing the remains to supplement the plant's nutrition. Three other species of bladderwort occur in Britain and Ireland, mainly in the north and west, but they are difficult to tell apart.

Top and bottom left Greater Bladderwort (Utricularia vulgaris) *is a floating, rootless aquatic which is usually only seen when it sends up its leafless spikes of flowers which are a rich yellow, two-lipped with a blunt spur.*

Bottom right Lesser Bladderwort (Utricularia minor) *is more slender than the Greater Bladderwort with pale yellow flowers and found around boggy pools and fens.*

SPECIES INFORMATION	
COMMON NAME	Greater Plantain
SCIENTIFIC NAME	Plantago major
RELATED SPECIES	Hoary Plantain
HEIGHT/SPREAD	5–40 cm tall
FLOWERING TIME	April–November
HABITAT	Grassy places and lawns

Note: The broad-leaved plantain of lawns.

Greater Plantain

PLANTAIN FAMILY

(Plantaginaceae)

Size and appearance: A tufted perennial with rosettes of leaves and numerous, semi-erect, leafless flowering stems 5–40 cm (2–16 in) tall, sometimes up to 60 cm (24 in).

Leaves: In a crowded basal rosette, sometimes very large, stalked, oval or elliptical, usually with 5–9 parallel veins, irregularly toothed, tough and hairless.

Flowers: Small, greenish, massed in a dense, cylindrical spike; stamens lilac, soon fading to yellowish or brown.

Fruits: Egg-shaped capsules, opening by a lid, usually containing 8–12 seeds.

Related or similar plants: Hoary Plantain (p.272) has hairy leaves, whitish flowers and lilac stamens.

Habitat and distribution: Ubiquitous and abundant in grassland, grassy waste places, and on waysides and all trampled ground, especially by or near paths and gates; also (see below) as a weed of cultivated land and open habitats such as lake-shores and the upper part of salt-marshes.

Flowering time: April to November.

Bottom left *An untrampled specimen of Greater Plantain* (Plantago major)*, at the edge of a path.*

FLOWER TYPE

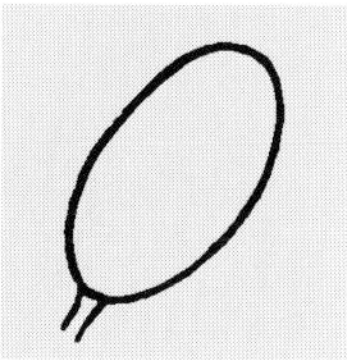

IDENTIFICATION

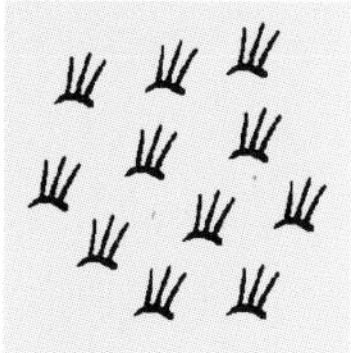

HABITAT

POPULATION

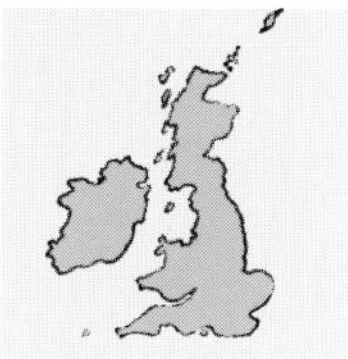

MAP

GREATER PLANTAIN IS one of the commonest and most successful grassland weeds. Its compact growth habit, leathery leaves and tough stems adapt it to being able to withstand heavy trampling. In fact it gains from trampling, as this discourages other plants with which it might be competing. It is a camp-follower of people, so much so that the native American Indians are said to have called it 'White Man's Foot'. It is also a useful plant. The tough leaves were once used extensively to dress wounds and the plant has healing and soothing properties.

It is a very variable species. One variant specially, regarded by botanists as a distinct sub-species, occurs widely in cultivated and disturbed ground, and along lake shores. Plants are annual or biennial, are more erect and have pale green, hairy leaves with 3–5 veins; the seed-capsules each contain 13–30 seeds. This most interesting variant is generally overlooked but seems to be quite common in garden flower-beds, often growing near to typical plants in the lawn.

Top and bottom right *The stalked, often wavy, broad, oval leaves with prominent unbranched veins are in a crowded basal rosette. From the centre of this arises the dense spike of small greenish flowers which go on to form egg-shaped capsules as shown in the photograph to the right.*

Hoary Plantain

PLANTAIN FAMILY
(Plantaginaceae)

SPECIES INFORMATION	
COMMON NAME	Hoary Plantain
SCIENTIFIC NAME	Plantago media
RELATED SPECIES	Greater Plantain
HEIGHT/SPREAD	10–40 cm tall
FLOWERING TIME	May–August
HABITAT	Grassland

Note: The most attractive plantain, with lilac stamens.

FLOWER TYPE

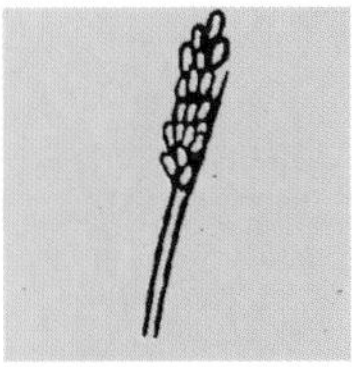

IDENTIFICATION

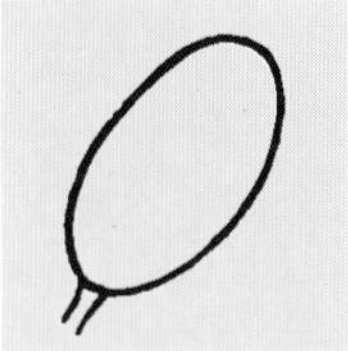

HABITAT

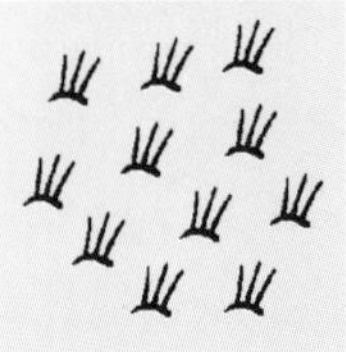

POPULATION

MAP

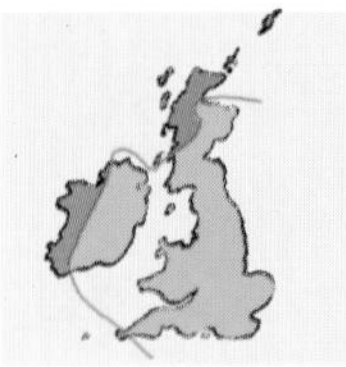

Size and appearance: A tufted perennial with rosettes of leaves and erect, leafless flowering stems 10–40 cm (4–16 in) tall.
Leaves: In a flat basal rosette, short-stalked, elliptical, with parallel veins, greyish-hairy.
Flowers: Small, whitish, massed in a long, dense, cylindrical spike; stamens lilac.
Fruits: Egg-shaped capsules, opening by a lid.
Related or similar plants: Ribwort Plantain has narrower, less hairy leaves and egg-shaped flower-spikes; Greater Plantain (p.271) has usually hairless leaves and greenish flowers.
Habitat and distribution: Widespread but rather local in short, dry grassland, including country churchyards and untended lawns, especially on lime-rich soils; over most of England and Wales, but rare in Scotland and Ireland.
Flowering time: May to August.

HOARY PLANTAIN IS much the handsomest of a mostly drab group of plants. Its elegant, hairy leaf rosettes and long, slightly scented, silvery-lilac spikes of flowers make it a welcome feature of churchyards, for which it seems to have a special preference. It is not so resilient to trampling, weedkillers and excessive fertiliser as Greater Plantain (p.271) or Ribwort Plantain. Although the plantains are traditionally regarded as wind-pollinated, with their massed, small green flowers, Hoary Plantain especially attracts foraging insects.

Top and bottom left *Hoary Plantain* (Plantago media) *is the prettiest of our plantains, with its dense cylindrical spike of flowers appearing a delicate lilac, which originates from the colour of its stamens.*

Bottom right *Ribwort Plantain* (Plantago lanceolata) *has narrower, stalkless, spear-shaped, less hairy and slightly toothed leaves, elongate egg-shaped flower-spikes and cream stamens, fading to yellow. Flowering April–October, it is an abundant plant of grassy and waste places.*

SPECIES INFORMATION	
COMMON NAME	Honeysuckle, Woodbine
SCIENTIFIC NAME	Lonicera periclymenum
RELATED SPECIES	Shrubs such as elder
HEIGHT/SPREAD	Stems 2–6 m long
FLOWERING TIME	May–August
HABITAT	Hedges and woods

Note: The familiar garden and hedgerow flower.

Honeysuckle

HONEYSUCKLE FAMILY (caprifoliaceae)

Size and appearance: A woody climber, with tough stems 2–6 m (6–18 ft) long, scrambling and (clockwise) twining over other plants.
Leaves: In opposite pairs, very short-stalked, oval, downy, slightly paler beneath.
Flowers: Yellowish-cream tinged with lilac or red, fading to orange, 3–5 cm (1⅕–2 in) long, tubular, 2-lipped, richly scented, in whorled clusters of c. 12.
Fruits: A cluster of shiny, red berries.
Related or similar plants: Other honeysuckles sometimes escape from gardens.
Habitat and distribution: Widespread and still common in woods and hedges, climbing up among the branches of trees and shrubs, or trailing on or near the ground; in coastal heathland in the west.
Flowering time: May to August.

ONE OF OUR most familiar and best-loved flowers, Honeysuckle is a conspicuous feature of hedgerows when in bloom. In late winter, the new green leaves are one of the first signs of coming spring in woodland. The rich scent of the flowers is best developed at night, when the flowers are visited by long-tongued moths. One can readily extract a large drop of nectar from the base of the flower. Honeysuckle is the foodplant for the caterpillars of the White Admiral butterfly.

Note that the the berries are poisonous. and should not be confused with any of the edible berries of the hedgerow.

FLOWER TYPE

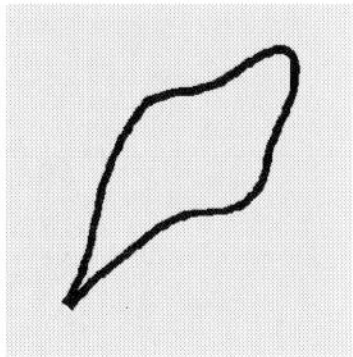
IDENTIFICATION

HABITAT

POPULATION

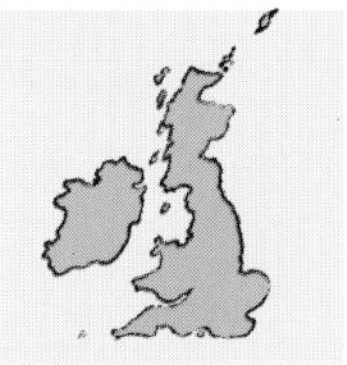
MAP

Top and bottom left *Honeysuckle* (Lonicera periclymenum) *has two-lipped flowers with a long slender tube from which five stamens and one style protrudes. Initially cream, they deepen to orange-buff after pollination.*

Bottom right *A deciduous woody climber honeysuckle can scramble up and through hedges or cover an old wall.*

Townhall Clock

MOSCHATEL FAMILY
(Adoxaceae)

SPECIES INFORMATION	
COMMON NAME	Townhall Clock, Moschatel
SCIENTIFIC NAME	Adoxa moschatellina
RELATED SPECIES	None
HEIGHT/SPREAD	5–15 cm tall
FLOWERING TIME	March–May
HABITAT	Woods

Note: The flowers are like a miniature clock-tower.

FLOWER TYPE

IDENTIFICATION

HABITAT

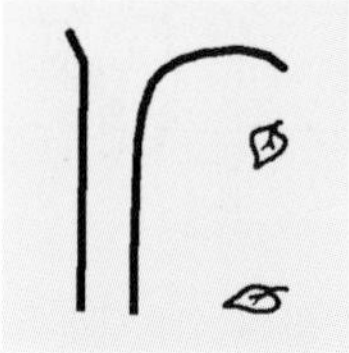

POPULATION

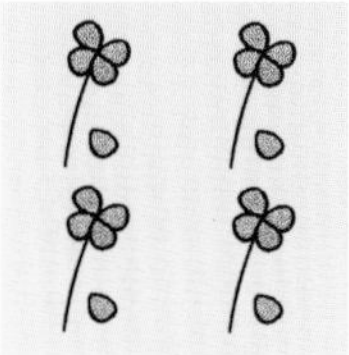

MAP

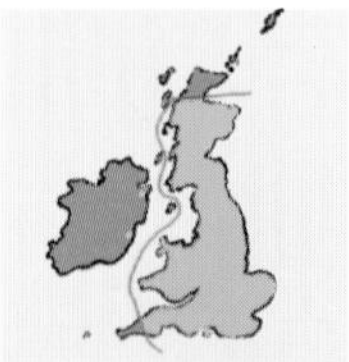

Size and appearance: A pale green, hairless perennial 5–15 cm (2–6 in) tall, forming patches up to several metres across.

Leaves: Mostly basal, long-stalked, somewhat fleshy, 3-lobed, the lobes further divided into rounded segments.

Flowers: Small, yellowish-green, 5 in a compact head 6–8 mm (¼–⅓ in) across, each flower with 5 petals and 10 pale yellow stamens, except the uppermost with 4 and 8 only.

Fruits: Small, green, 1-seeded dry drupes.

Related or similar plants: The young leaves are easily confused with those of Wood Anemone (p.52) but have less feathery segments.

Habitat and distribution: Locally common in woods, hedges and damp, shady places throughout Britain, except the Fens and the far north of Scotland; probably introduced at its only two Irish sites near Dublin and Belfast.

Flowering time: March to May.

Bottom left *Townhall Clock* (Adoxa moschatellina) *has cube-shaped heads with a flower on each of its four sides and one on top.*

MOSCHATEL IS ONE of the most delicate and unobtrusive of all spring flowers, but one of the most perfect. The neatly cut leaves and the tiny clock-tower of flowers, the uppermost built from a different number of parts from the others, makes it a natural curiosity of the countryside. When the plant is wet it smells faintly of musk. Perhaps oddest of all, the seeds are said to be dispersed by snails.

Moschatel is famous among botanists as the only species in its family, but one distributed all around the northern hemisphere. It apparently looks pretty similar from China to Colorado. The arrangement of the flowers clearly gives the plant the English name Townhall Clock. They also have Christian symbolism – as they look out in all directions to observe the second coming of Christ.

Top and bottom right *This is a charming plant, forming extensive patches in damp shady places and woodlands where its three-lobed, divided leaves appear very early in the year; once flowering is finished they soon disappear.*

SPECIES INFORMATION	
COMMON NAME	Common Cornsalad
SCIENTIFIC NAME	Valerianella locusta
RELATED SPECIES	Common Valerian
HEIGHT/SPREAD	5–20 cm tall
FLOWERING TIME	March–May
HABITAT	Cultivated ground and walls

Note: Regularly branched with heads of tiny flowers.

Common Cornsalad

VALERIAN FAMILY (Valerianaceae)

Size and appearance: A slender, erect, branched annual 5–20 cm (2–8 in) tall, sometimes up to 40 cm (16 in).
Leaves: In opposite pairs, spoon-shaped, the upper more oblong and slightly toothed.
Flowers: Pale lilac, tiny, funnel-shaped, grouped in pairs of dense, rather flat-topped clusters 10–20 mm (⅖–⅘ in) across.
Fruits: 2–3 mm long (1/12–⅛ in), yellowish, 1-seeded, swollen but flattened.
Related or similar plants: Four other native cornsalads are difficult to distinguish .
Habitat and distribution: A plant of cultivated land, dry banks, walls, rock outcrops and sand-dunes; throughout, but local in Scotland and Ireland, tending to be coastal.
Flowering time: March to May.

Top Common Cornsalad (Valerianella locusta) *is a low, much-forked annual plant with unstalked, opposite, oblong leaves.*

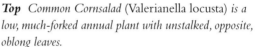

Middle *This plant is often only noticed when several plants are growing together and their delicately pale lilac flowers take on a bluish-white look from a distance.*

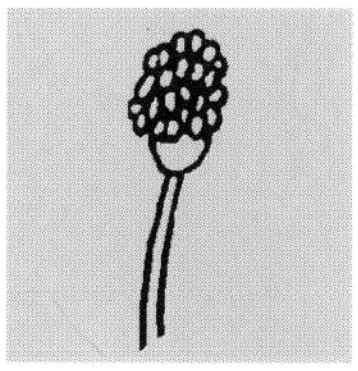

FLOWER TYPE

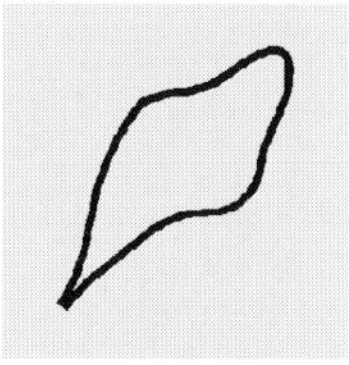

IDENTIFICATION

HABITAT

POPULATION

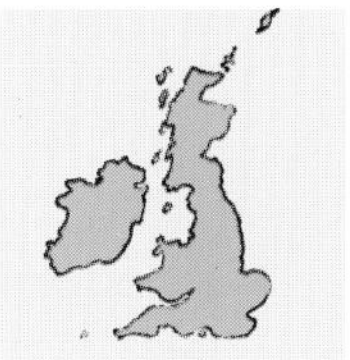

MAP

A VARIABLE SPECIES, especially on the coast, where a range of compact, dwarf plants occurs on sand-dunes and banks by the sea. A particularly robust variant (Lamb's Lettuce or Mache) is an increasingly popular, commercial salad crop, especially on the Continent, and also turns up in gardens. These plants, and the wild ones too, are not very flavoursome but make a welcome addition to late winter salads. Common Cornsalad is by far the commonest of our five native species of cornsalad, all plants of similar open and disturbed habitats. The others have declined drastically as a result of modern intensive agriculture and liberal use of weedkillers.

Bottom *Hairy-fruited Cornsalad* (Valerianella eriocarpa) *is an introduced species occurring on banks, walls and rough ground. It is very scattered in southern England and is probably decreasing in number.*

Common Valerian

VALERIAN FAMILY
(Valerianaceae)

SPECIES INFORMATION	
COMMON NAME	Common Valerian
SCIENTIFIC NAME	Valeriana officinalis
RELATED SPECIES	Marsh Valerian
HEIGHT/SPREAD	50–150 cm tall
FLOWERING TIME	June–August
HABITAT	Grassland, woods and riverbanks

Note: One of the tallest wild flowers of grassland.

FLOWER TYPE

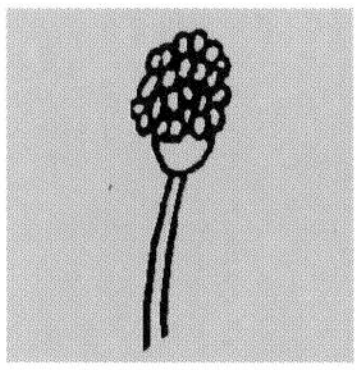

IDENTIFICATION

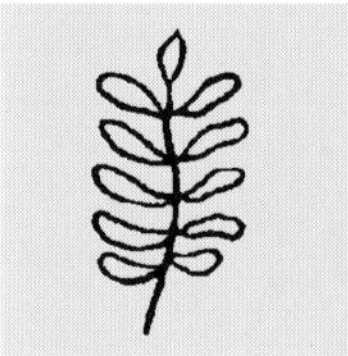

HABITAT

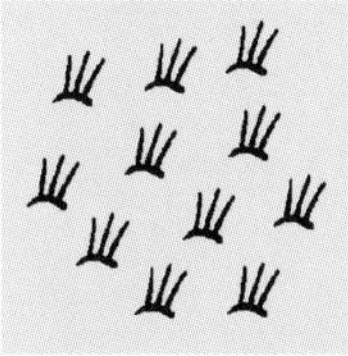

POPULATION

MAP

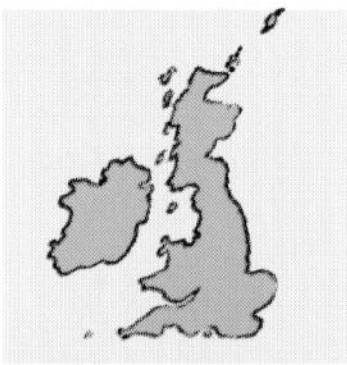

Size and appearance: A rather hairy, robust perennial, with often solitary, erect stems 50–150 cm (20–60 in) tall.
Leaves: In opposite pairs, stalked, compound or deeply lobed, the leaflets narrowly spear-shaped, toothed.
Flowers: Pale pink or white, 5 mm ($\frac{1}{5}$ in) across, tubular with a pouch-like spur, vanilla-scented, densely grouped in a flat head.
Fruits: 1-seeded, 2–5 mm ($\frac{1}{12}$–$\frac{1}{5}$ in) long, with a crown of hairs derived from the persistent calyx.
Related or similar plants: Marsh Valerian is a smaller plant with less divided leaves, growing in marshes.
Habitat and distribution: Widespread and common in damp or dry grassland, scrub, clearings and glades of woods, and on riverbanks throughout Britain and Ireland.
Flowering time: June to August.

COMMON VALERIAN AND related species have an unpleasant but very characteristic smell when bruised, and cats are said to find the root irresistible. An extract from this plant has been used since ancient times as a sedative. This is reflected in the first half of the scientific name (Latin: *valere*, to heal). The second half of the name denotes that it is a recognised a medicinal plant (see comments under *Veronica officinalis*, p.259). The sleeping draught known as valerian drops often appears in crime novels, where it is frequently abused by the characters as a convenient way to knock out witnesses or intended victims.

Top and bottom left *Common Valerian* (Valeriana officinalis) *is a plant which is widespread and frequent in woods and rough grassy places, usually where it is damp – it is often found alongside streams and in marshy areas. It usually grows in clumps, its tall erect stems reaching above the surrounding vegetation. The leaves are arranged in opposite pairs up the stem, each leaf being divided into pairs of leaflets, usually between four and six. From June to August, it produces heads of pale-pink flowers which give off a sweet fragrance and attract insect pollinators, who come for the nectar, which is held in a pouch at the base of the corolla.*

Bottom right *Marsh Valerian* (Valeriana dioica) *is similar but a smaller plant not more than 50 cm (20 in) tall, with creeping runners and less divided lower leaves.*

SPECIES INFORMATION	
COMMON NAME	Red Valerian, Spur Valerian
SCIENTIFIC NAME	Centranthus ruber
RELATED SPECIES	Common Valerian
HEIGHT/SPREAD	30–80 cm tall
FLOWERING TIME	May–September
HABITAT	Walls and rocky banks
Note: A feature of old walls, especially near the sea.	

Red or Spur Valerian

VALERIAN FAMILY

(Valerianaceae)

Size and appearance: A hairless, tufted perennial, rather woody at the base with semi-erect or erect stems 30–80 cm (12–32 in) tall.

Leaves: In opposite pairs, broadly spear-shaped, pointed, mostly untoothed, greyish-green.

Flowers: Red, but also pink or white, c. 5 mm (1/5 in) across, tubular with a slender spur, scented, in branched clusters in a pyramidal head.

Fruits: 1-seeded, crowned with a feathery plume derived from the persistent calyx.

Related or similar plants: Common Valerian (p.276) has green leaves and pink or white flowers, with a short, pouch-like spur.

Habitat and distribution: A native of southern Europe that has established itself widely on walls, old buildings, rocks, cliffs, road and railway cuttings, and in waste places and untended gardens, especially on the coast, through Britain north to central Scotland and in much of eastern and southern Ireland.

Flowering time: May to September.

RED VALERIAN HAS invaded walls and rocky places even more successfully than the long-established Wallflower (p.75). Escaping from gardens, it has been naturalised on cliffs and rocks in the West Country since the 18th century, and the area remains one of its strongholds. It has spread widely during the present century, for example as a planting to enhance the cuttings of new roads, and is still spreading. It is still absent from large areas of northern Britain and the midlands and west of Ireland. It makes a showy garden plant, especially if one can combine the red, pink and white variants, but it is invasive and seedlings need to be controlled. The young leaves can be eaten as a salad.

Top left and right *Red Valerian (Centranthus ruber) has flowers borne in branched clusters from June to August. The typical colour is red, but white forms do occur.*

Bottom *Originally from the Mediterranean, it has colonised old walls, cliffs and quarries. It can often be found on medieval ruins in the lime-rich mortar and cracks and crevices, usually on south-facing aspects.*

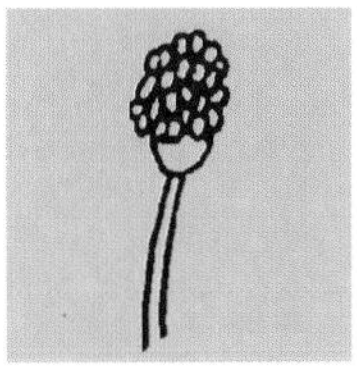

FLOWER TYPE

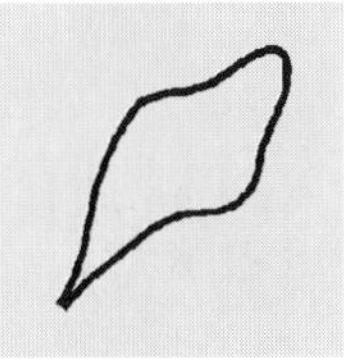

IDENTIFICATION

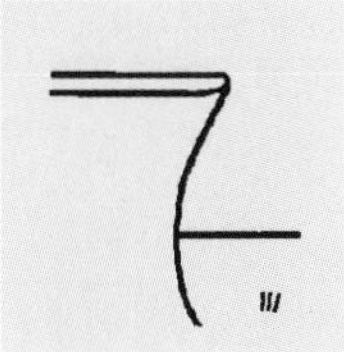

HABITAT

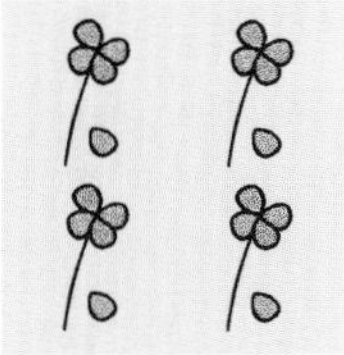

POPULATION

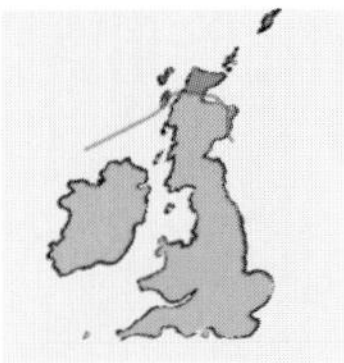

MAP

Teasel

SCABIOUS FAMILY
(Dipsacaceae)

SPECIES INFORMATION	
COMMON NAME	Teasel
SCIENTIFIC NAME	Dipsacus fullonum
RELATED SPECIES	Devil's-bit Scabious
HEIGHT/SPREAD	50–200 cm tall
FLOWERING TIME	July–September
HABITAT	Damp places and waste grounds

Note: Huge thistle-like plant of waysides and river-banks.

FLOWER TYPE

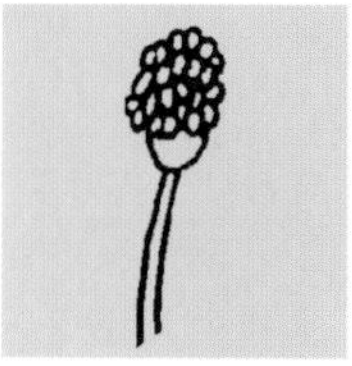

IDENTIFICATION

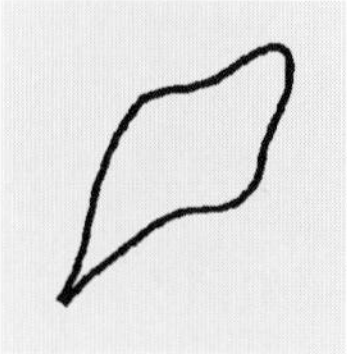

HABITAT

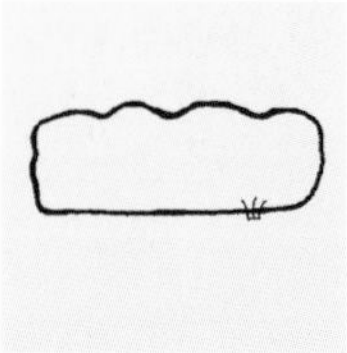

POPULATION

MAP

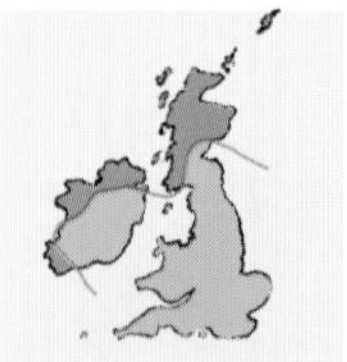

Size and appearance: A robust, hairless, erect biennial 50–200 cm (20–80 in) tall, sometimes up to 300 cm (9 ft), the stems with prickly angles.
Leaves: In opposite fused pairs, spear-shaped, pointed, untoothed, prickly beneath.
Flowers: Pale purple, each with a scale-like floral bract, massed in an egg-shaped head 5–9 cm (2–$3\frac{3}{5}$ in) long surrounded by a whorl of 8–12 narrow, upcurved, spiny, leaf-like bracts as long as itself.
Fruits: 1-seeded, massed in persistent, egg-shaped heads.
Related or similar plants: A distinctive plant unlikely to be confused with any other.
Habitat and distribution: An often common and conspicuous plant of streamsides, damp and grassy places, waysides and waste ground in southern Britain, extending north to Fife; rare in the north and in Wales, and scattered in Ireland.
Flowering time: July to September.

TEASEL IS ONE of the most stately and ornamental of all our wild plants and deserves a place in (larger) gardens. The cups formed by the broad bases of the fused pairs of leaves fill with rain and dew, drowning many insects and even the odd frog. On one occasion this gave rise to press reports of 'monster plants'.

The dried seed-heads of Fuller's Teasel, a variant with curled-back floral bracts, regarded by some botanists as a distinct species, have long been used to raise the nap or pile of woollen cloth. The plant is still raised as a crop near Taunton in Somerset for this purpose. It is also the origin of the English name, referring to the 'teasing' of the cloth.

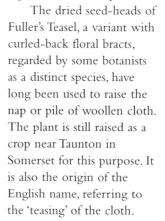

Teasel (Dipsacus fullonum) *has an unusual flowering pattern with a ring of those in the middle of the head blooming first. These are followed by those above and below them.*

The top image is of a freshly flowering specimen and shows how the ring of flowers has not yet separated into two, one at the top and the other at the bottom of the flower.

SPECIES INFORMATION	
COMMON NAME	Devil's-bit Scabious
SCIENTIFIC NAME	Succisa pratensis
RELATED SPECIES	Teasel
HEIGHT/SPREAD	20–100 cm tall
FLOWERING TIME	July–September
HABITAT	Damp grassland and marshes

Note: The only bluish-purple wild scabious.

Devil's-bit Scabious

SCABIOUS FAMILY

(Dipsacaceae)

THE NAME DERIVES from the short thick rhizome that has an abruptly cut-off end, said to have been bitten off by Old Nick himself. It is a character as distinctive as the rich bluish-purple of the flowers. The name Scabious derives from the former use of this and related plants as a herbal cure for scabies and other unpleasant skin complaints.

Devil's-bit Scabious is sometimes extremely abundant in grassland, as in western Ireland and elsewhere in the west and north of these islands. For students recording vegetation in sample plots or quadrats it is one of those plants that, like certain grasses, turns up every time. The plant is one of the main food sources for the caterpillar of the scarce and declining Marsh Fritillary butterfly.

Devil's-bit Scabious (Succisa pratensis) *has rounded heads of massed dark bluish-purple flowers with purple anthers at the end of the stamens. Flowering sometimes right through into the autumn, it is a favourite of late-flying insects looking for a nectar source.*

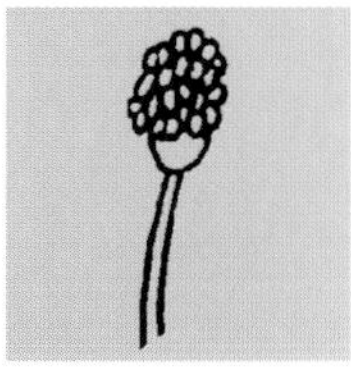

FLOWER TYPE

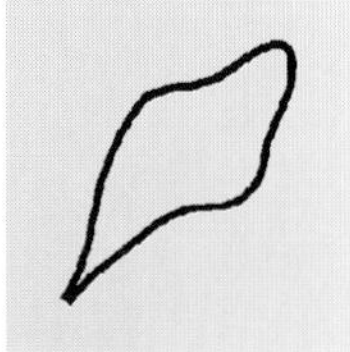

IDENTIFICATION

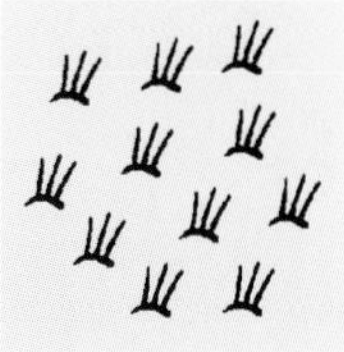

HABITAT

POPULATION

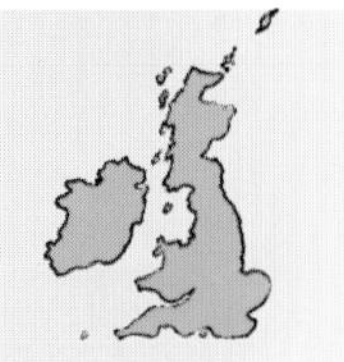

MAP

Size and appearance: An erect perennial, with a short, thick, blunt rhizome and stems 20–100 cm (8–40 in) tall.

Leaves: The basal in a rosette, the stem leaves in opposite pairs, elliptical, the upper narrower.

Flowers: Dark bluish-purple, rarely pink or white, the petal-tube 4-lobed, the outer florets larger than the inner, in a long-stalked, domed head 18–25 mm (¾–1 in) across.

Fruits: 1-seeded, c. 5 mm (1/5 in) long.

Related or similar plants: Field Scabious and Small Scabious (p.280) have lilac flowers in heads more than 25 mm (1 in) across.

Habitat and distribution: A common, frequently abundant plant of damp grassland and marshes, especially on lime-poor soils, throughout Britain and Ireland.

Flowering time: July to September.

Field Scabious

SCABIOUS FAMILY

(Dipsacaceae)

SPECIES INFORMATION	
COMMON NAME	Field Scabious
SCIENTIFIC NAME	Knautia arvensis
RELATED SPECIES	Small Scabious
HEIGHT/SPREAD	30–100 cm tall
FLOWERING TIME	July–October
HABITAT	Grassland, scrub and roadsides

Note: The common bluish-lilac wild scabious.

FLOWER TYPE

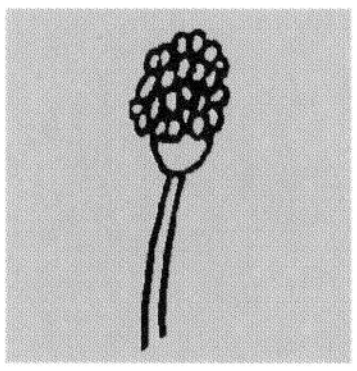

IDENTIFICATION

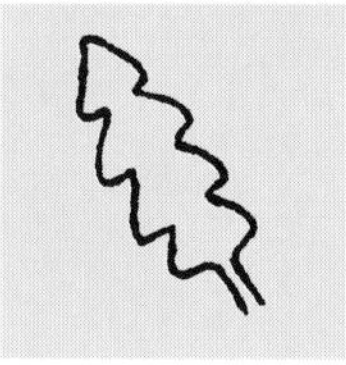

HABITAT

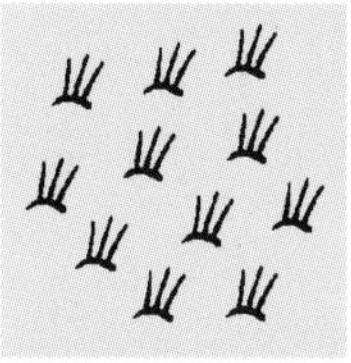

POPULATION

MAP

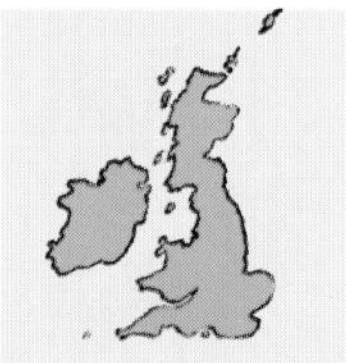

THIS AND OTHER scabious were old herbal remedies for scabies and other skin complaints, but are now prized more for ornament. All our native scabious species are important food plants for the caterpillars of the Chalkhill Blue butterfly.

Top and bottom left *Field scabious* (Knautia arvensis) *has flattish, domed heads, rather reminiscent of an old-fashioned pincushion. The blue-lilac flowers have four unequal sized corolla lobes, which are particularly noticeable on the larger outer flowers. Generally a plant of grassy open hedgebanks, it can occasionally form quite large stands across a meadow.*

Bottom right *Small Scabious* (Scabiosa columbaria) *is similar but usually shorter, with flower-heads 20–30 mm (⅘–1⅕ in) across, 5-lobed florets and calyx-teeth ending in purple bristles. Flowering July–October, it is locally frequent in grassland on lime-rich soils north to southern Scotland; but not in Ireland.*

Size and appearance: An erect, hairy biennial or short-lived perennial 30–100 cm (12–40 in) tall.

Leaves: In opposite pairs, the lower spoon-shaped, entire or shallowly lobed, the upper deeply lobed, with a large, broadly spear-shaped end leaflet.

Flowers: Lilac or bluish-lilac, rarely white, the petal-tube 4-lobed, the outer florets larger than the inner, in a long-stalked, flat head 25–40 mm (1–1⅗ in) across.

Fruits: 1-seeded, 5–6 mm (⅕–¼ in) long.

Related or similar plants: Small Scabious has smaller flower-heads and 5-lobed florets; Devil's-bit Scabious (p.279) has smaller, bluish-purple flowers.

Habitat and distribution: Widespread in grassland, scrub and open woods, on dry hedge-banks and road-verges; formerly on cultivated land; almost throughout, but rare in northern and western Scotland and in western Ireland.

Flowering time: July to October.

SPECIES INFORMATION	
COMMON NAME	Giant Bellflower
SCIENTIFIC NAME	Campanula latifolia
RELATED SPECIES	Creeping Bellflower
HEIGHT/SPREAD	50–150 cm tall
FLOWERING TIME	July–September
HABITAT	Woods and shady places

Note: The largest wild bellflower.

Giant Bellflower

BELLFLOWER FAMILY

(Campanulaceae)

GIANT BELLFLOWEr is a stately, striking and very characteristic wild plant of some areas of northern Britain such as the limestone dales in Derbyshire and the West Riding of Yorkshire. Gardeners cultivate it for ornament, including white and paler-flowered variants, but few today bother to harvest the young shoots, which can be cooked and eaten like spinach.

The first half of the scientific name is a straight translation from the Latin (*campanula*, little bell). Bellflowers are an easy group to recognise at a glance, and usually have flowers in some shade of blue or violet. They also exude a white sap when cut. About a dozen species are now native or naturalised in Britain, and many more are grown in gardens.

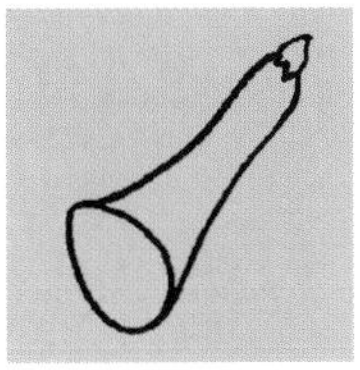
FLOWER TYPE

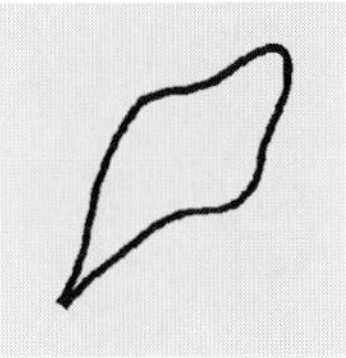
IDENTIFICATION

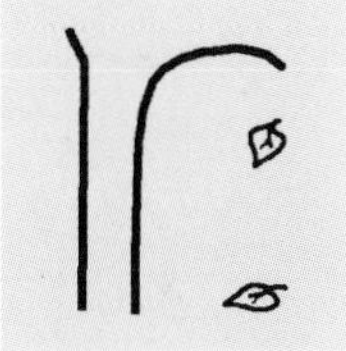
HABITAT

POPULATION

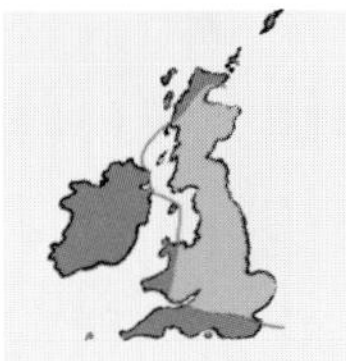
MAP

Size and appearance: A robust, hairless or downy perennial with erect, unbranched, leafy stems 50–150 cm (20–60 in) tall.
Leaves: Basal leaves up to 20 cm (8 in) long, stalked, oval, irregularly toothed, the upper narrower, stalkless.
Flowers: Blue or violet-blue, 40–55 mm ($1\frac{3}{5}$–$2\frac{1}{5}$ in) long, bell-shaped, with narrowly triangular calyx-teeth up to 25 mm (1 in) long, numerous in a long, leafy spike.
Fruits: Dome-shaped capsules, containing numerous tiny seeds.
Related or similar plants: This biggest of the bellflowers is not easily confused with any of the other species.
Habitat and distribution: Locally common in woods, hedges and shady places, and on river-banks and streamsides in northern Britain, but absent from southern England, and in Ireland only locally naturalised in the north.
Flowering time: July to September.

Giant Bellflower (Campanula latifolia) *is a handsome plant, tall and erect with leafy stems. Its large bell-shaped flowers are set singly in a long spike and can vary in colour from a rich violet-blue to a delicate blue-tinged white.*

Creeping Bellflower

BELLFLOWER FAMILY

(Campanulaceae)

SPECIES INFORMATION	
COMMON NAME	Creeping Bellflower
SCIENTIFIC NAME	Campanula rapunculoides
RELATED SPECIES	Other bellflowers
HEIGHT/SPREAD	40–100 cm tall
FLOWERING TIME	July–September
HABITAT	Hedges and grassy places

Note: The numerous, 1-sided spikes of flowers are distinctive.

FLOWER TYPE

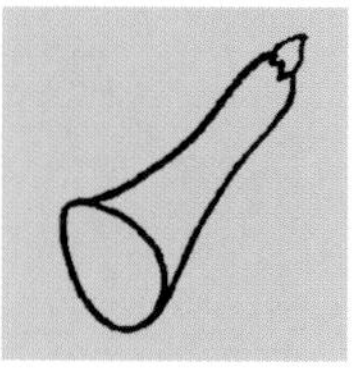

IDENTIFICATION

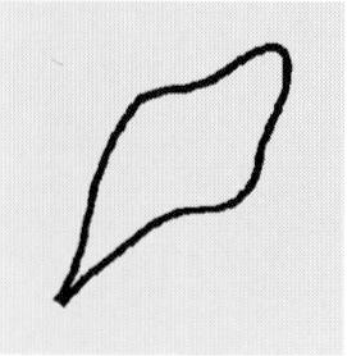

HABITAT

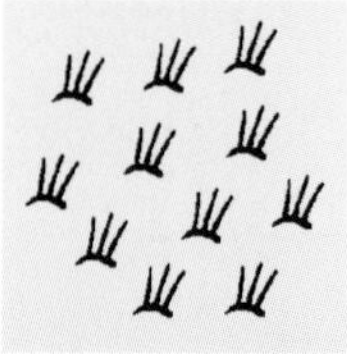

POPULATION

MAP

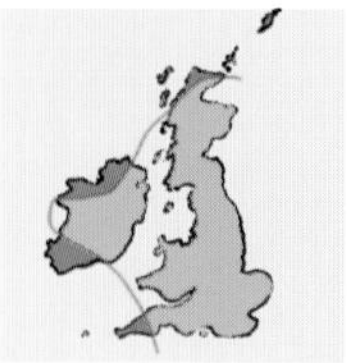

Size and appearance: A downy or hairless perennial, with thick roots and far-creeping underground runners that give rise to clumps, and erect stems 40–100 cm (16–40 in) tall.

Leaves: Basal leaves up to 7.5 cm (3 in) long, stalked, oval, heart-shaped at the base, toothed, the upper narrower, stalkless.

Flowers: Violet-blue, 20–30 mm (⅘–1⅕ in) long, bell-shaped, with narrowly triangular calyx-teeth bent back at flowering, numerous in a long, 1-sided spike.

Fruits: Dome-shaped capsules, containing numerous tiny seeds.

Related or similar plants: Giant Bellflower (p.281) and Nettle-leaved Bellflower have larger flowers and the flower-spikes are not 1-sided.

Habitat and distribution: Widespread but scattered in hedges, scrub and grassland, and on road verges, and as a garden weed through much of Britain except northern Scotland and south-western England; in Ireland, mostly near the east coast.

Flowering time: July to September.

CREEPING BELLFLOWER IS not native to Britain or Ireland, although it is present as an indigenous wild plant over most of Europe. It was formerly grown here in gardens, as both vegetable and ornamental, but few now tolerate its invasive abilities. The edible, whitish, tuberous roots are an adaptation for rapid spread. The plant has escaped, or has been cast out in disgust, to become widely naturalised.

Top and bottom left *Creeping Bellflower* (Campanula rapunculoides) *has a long tapering spike of violet-blue drooping flowers which open mostly from the bottom. Widely naturalised in hedgerows and waste places it is usually found near habitation.*

Bottom right *Nettle-leaved Bellflower* (Campanula trachelium) *is taller, bristly-hairy, and has triangular, coarsely toothed nettle-like leaves and dark violet-blue flowers 30–40 mm (1⅕–1⅗ in) long. It occurs in woods and hedges, mostly in southern and eastern England, and a few sites in south-eastern Ireland.*

SPECIES INFORMATION	
COMMON NAME	Clustered Bellflower
SCIENTIFIC NAME	Campanula glomerata
RELATED SPECIES	Other bellflowers
HEIGHT/SPREAD	15–50 cm tall
FLOWERING TIME	June–October
HABITAT	Chalk and limestone grassland

Note: The only bellflower with flowers in a tight head.

Clustered Bellflower

BELLFLOWER FAMILY
(Campanulaceae)

CLUSTERED BELLFLOWER IS one of the most reliable plants that indicate the presence of lime in the soil. It is also one of several wild flowers of chalk grassland that have an extended or late flowering season. This autumn floral display is one of many features that make this plant-rich habitat so pleasurable for the botanist or naturalist. It is rarely difficult to find a few flowers of Clustered Bellflower well into October.

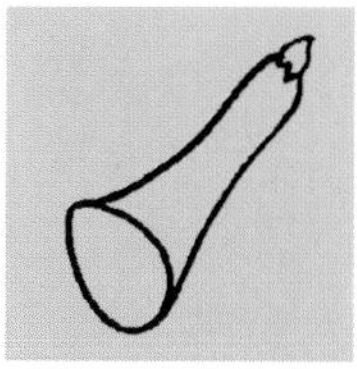
FLOWER TYPE

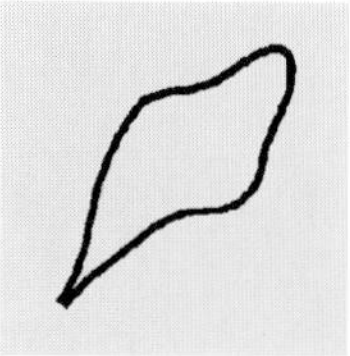
IDENTIFICATION

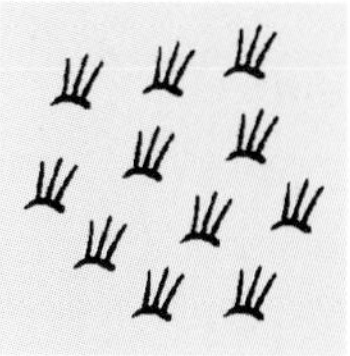
HABITAT

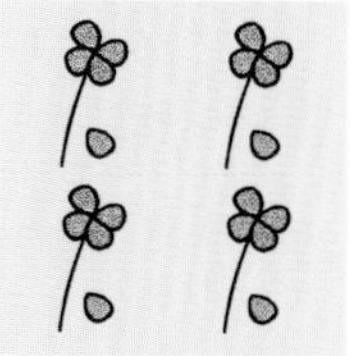
POPULATION

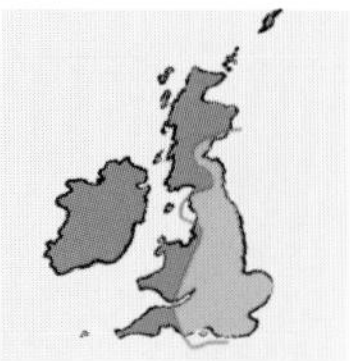
MAP

Size and appearance: A hairy perennial, with erect, reddish stems 15–50 cm (6–20 in) tall.

Leaves: Lower leaves oval to spear-shaped, long-stalked, rounded at the base, with blunt teeth, the upper narrower, stalkless.

Flowers: Violet-blue, 20–25 mm (⅘–1 in) long, narrowly bell-shaped, with spear-shaped calyx-teeth, numerous in a tight head, a few others down stem.

Fruits: Dome-shaped capsules, containing numerous tiny seeds.

Related or similar plants: Giant Bellflower (p.281) and Creeping Bellflower (p.282) have larger flowers and flowers in spikes.

Habitat and distribution: Locally common in dry grassland and scrub over chalk and limestone and on other lime-rich soils in England, especially the chalk of central-southern England, extending to south Wales and as far north as the coast of eastern Scotland; absent from Ireland.

Flowering time: June to October.

Clustered Bellflower (Campanula glomerata) *is found in chalk and limestone grassland. It is a rather stiff, hairy perennial with oval- to spear-shaped leaves rounded at the base; those higher up the stem are stalkless. The heads are tightly-packed violet-blue, narrow bell-shaped flowers.*

Harebell

BELLFLOWER FAMILY

(Campanulaceae)

SPECIES INFORMATION	
COMMON NAME	Harebell
SCIENTIFIC NAME	Campanula rotundifolia
RELATED SPECIES	Other bellflowers
HEIGHT/SPREAD	10–50 cm tall
FLOWERING TIME	June–September
HABITAT	Heaths and grassland

Note: The most dainty of the bellflowers.

FLOWER TYPE

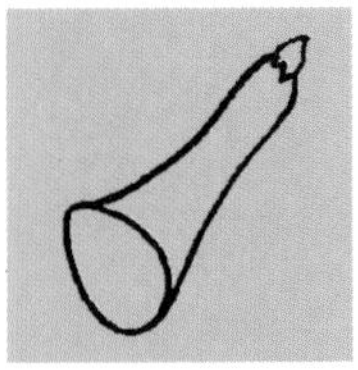

IDENTIFICATION

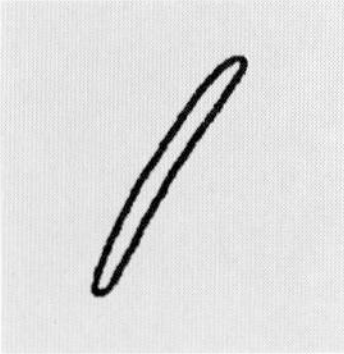

HABITAT

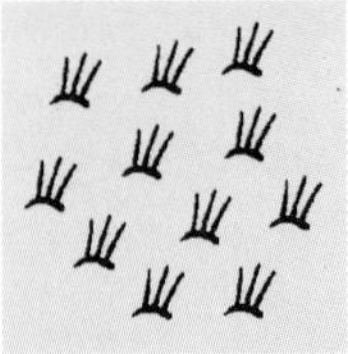

POPULATION

MAP

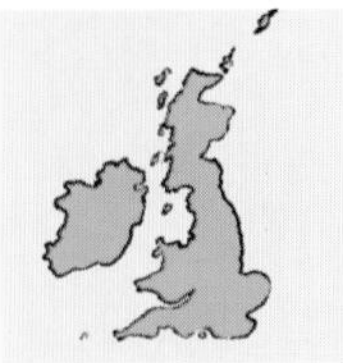

Size and appearance: A slender, hairless, creeping perennial, with erect or semi-erect, little-branched stems 10–50 cm (4–20 in) tall.
Leaves: The lower stalked, heart-shaped, almost circular, toothed, the upper spear-shaped, only slightly toothed.
Flowers: Violet-blue, 12–20 mm (½–¾ in) long, bell-shaped, with very narrow, pointed calyx-teeth, nodding, in open, loose, branched clusters.
Fruits: Broadly conical capsules that nod when ripe, containing numerous tiny seeds.
Related or similar plants: Other bellflowers are more robust, with larger flowers.
Habitat and distribution: Common and locally abundant in dry grassland, on hedge-banks, heaths, rocky ground and sand-dunes, from sea-level to high in the mountains, always on well-drained soils; throughout, but absent from most of the West Country and the greater part of southern and eastern Ireland.
Flowering time: June to September.

HAREBELL IS A universally popular wild flower and one of our finest. It is still remarkably common, despite so much destruction of good habitats in recent years. The second half of the name is a puzzle at first (Latin: *rotundifolia*, round-leaved), but a search at ground level soon reveals the circular basal leaves. Harebell is a very variable species that needs study, especially the nature of the handsome plants that occur on and near western coasts. These have fewer, slightly larger flowers, and some botanists regard them as a separate species. In Europe, Harebell has been divided up into numerous small and often local species, several of them of perhaps doubtful validity.

Minor controversy has raged for some time in botanical circles about if this is the true Bluebell of Scotland – Scottish people referring to Bluebell (p.338) as Wild Hyacinth. The evidence suggests that Bluebell has been a local name for Harebell in England as well.

Harebell (Campanula rotundifolia) *has a slender flower stalk and from a distance, it can look as though the violet-blue flowers, in their loose, nodding, open clusters, are magically suspended above the ground.*

SPECIES INFORMATION	
COMMON NAME	Sheep's-bit
SCIENTIFIC NAME	Jasione montana
RELATED SPECIES	Bellflowers
HEIGHT/SPREAD	10–50 cm tall
FLOWERING TIME	June–September
HABITAT	Heaths and rocky ground

Note: Like a small, blue-flowered scabious.

Sheep's-bit

BELLFLOWER FAMILY

(Campanulaceae)

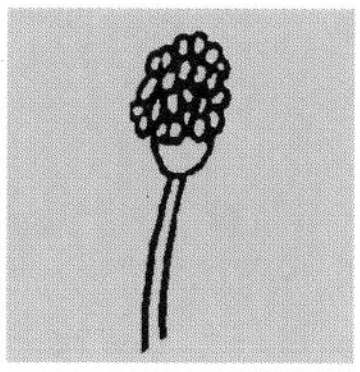

FLOWER TYPE

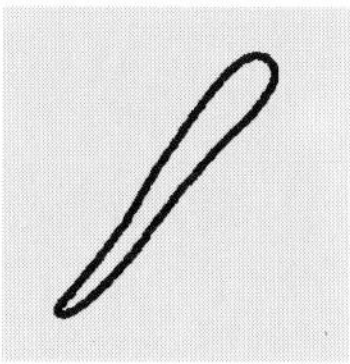

IDENTIFICATION

HABITAT

POPULATION

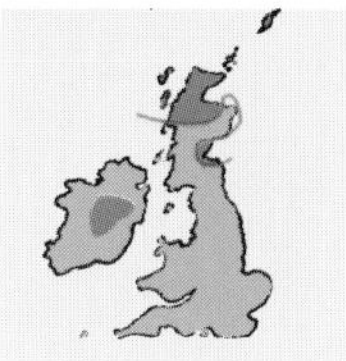

MAP

Size and appearance: A hairy annual, biennial or short-lived perennial, with erect, semi-erect or prostrate stems 10–50 cm (4–20 in) tall.
Leaves: Narrowly oblong or spear-shaped, blunt, with untoothed or slightly toothed, wavy margins.
Flowers: Blue, c. 5 mm (⅕ in) long, tubular, 5-lobed, in long-stalked, hemispherical heads 10–25 mm (⅖–1 in) across surrounded by oval or triangular, leaf-like bracts.
Fruits: Egg-shaped capsules.
Related or similar plants: The unrelated Field Scabious and Small Scabious (p.280) have lilac flowers in flat heads; Devil's-bit Scabious (p.279) is more robust, with bluish-purple flowers.
Habitat and distribution: Widespread and locally common on heaths, dry banks, rocks, cliffs and mountain ledges, mostly on lime-poor, sandy or stony, well-drained soils, especially by the sea; mainly in western Britain north to central Scotland and in the west and south of Ireland, also in Shetland.
Flowering time: June to September.

SHEEP'S-BIT IS a variable species. Plants from cliffs and walls near the sea on western coasts are more robust, with showy flower-heads 20–35 mm (⅘–1⅖ in) across. This scabious-like plant is often called Sheep's-bit Scabious, but is of course closer to the bellflowers rather than the true scabious. Scabious species (pp. 279–280) have stamens protruding from the mouths of the flowers. The stamens of Sheep's-bit never protrude.

Sheep's-bit is an example of a plant that was once found on open spaces close to London, but has disappeared in recent decades. This is due partly to habitat destruction, but also to the encroachment of scrub and trees on to former open, grassy heathland.

Sheep's-bit (Jasione montana) *looks initially rather like a member of the scabious family with its domed, pin-cushion-shaped blue flowerheads. It is widespread on dry banks and rocky outcrops.*

Hemp Agrimony

DAISY AND DANDELION FAMILY

(Compositae or Asteraceae)

SPECIES INFORMATION	
COMMON NAME	Hemp Agrimony
SCIENTIFIC NAME	Eupatorium cannabinum
RELATED SPECIES	Golden-rod
HEIGHT/SPREAD	30–180 cm tall
FLOWERING TIME	July–September
HABITAT	Marshy places

Note: Conspicuous, pink-flowered clumps in wet places.

FLOWER TYPE

IDENTIFICATION

HABITAT

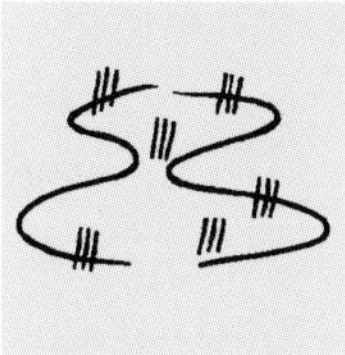

POPULATION

MAP

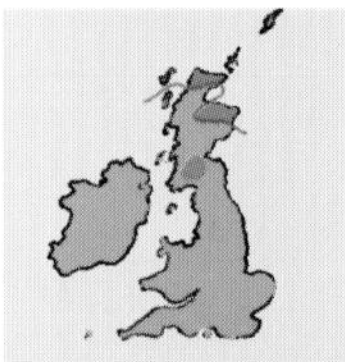

IN MANY DISTRICTS Hemp Agrimony is one the larger, conspicuous plants of late summer, wherever there is damp ground. In the west especially it is less restricted to wet places, and in the Burren of County Clare a dwarf variant occurs in crevices or grykes of the limestone. The plant has been used in the past as a medicinal herb to treat a number of complaints.

The English name and the second half of the scientific name describe the elegant compound leaves, rather similar to those of Hemp (see under Hop (p.12)).

Size and appearance: A robust, downy perennial with erect, leafy, reddish stems 30–180 cm (12–72 in) tall.

Leaves: In opposite pairs, 3- to 5-lobed, the lobes spreading, spear-shaped and toothed.

Flowers: Pink or reddish-lilac, without outer ray florets, in groups of 5–6, in heads 3–5 mm (⅛–⅕ in) across, in branched, flat-topped clusters.

Fruits: heads of 1-seeded fruits, each with a 'parachute' of white hairs.

Related or similar plants: Unrelated to Agrimony (p.101); some superficial resemblance to Common Valerian (p.276), which has compound or deeply lobed leaves.

Habitat and distribution: Widespread in wet woods, marshes, hedgerows, damp grassy places and scrub, sometimes in drier places such as shingle beaches or among limestone rocks, or a street weed; throughout, but but mostly coastal in Scotland.

Flowering time: July to September.

Top and bottom left *The small, whitish-pink flowers in large, dense, terminal clusters look somewhat fluffy from a distance. On closer inspection it will be seen that there are no ray florets, the flowers being composed only of disk florets.*

Bottom right *Hemp Agrimony* (Eupatoria cannabinum) *is a robust, downy plant with large three- to five- lobed leaves reminiscent of those of Hemp. It is widespread in marshes, by streamsides and in damp shady situations in woods.*

SPECIES INFORMATION	
COMMON NAME	Goldenrod
SCIENTIFIC NAME	Solidago virgaurea
RELATED SPECIES	Canadian Golden-rod
HEIGHT/SPREAD	30–180 cm tall
FLOWERING TIME	July–September
HABITAT	Heaths and rocky ground

Note: A tall yellow flower of heathy places in late summer.

Goldenrod

DAISY AND DANDELION FAMILY

(Compositae or Asteraceae)

Size and appearance: A somewhat downy perennial, with erect, stiff, leafy stems 30–180 cm (12–72 in) tall.

Leaves: Dark green, somewhat leathery, the lower spoon-shaped, slightly toothed, in a loose rosette, those along the stems spear-shaped, narrower.

Flowers: Yellow, with outer ray florets, in heads 5–10 mm (⅕–⅖ in) across, numerous in long, leafy, often branched spikes.

Fruits: Heads of 1-seeded fruits, each with a crown of brownish hairs.

Related or similar plants: Canadian Goldenrod, taller, with many tiny heads of flowers in dense, 1-sided clusters, often escapes.

Habitat and distribution: Common in dry, open woods, on heaths, hedge-banks and rocky ground, especially on well-drained, lime-poor soils, but local or rare in much of central England and East Anglia, and in the Irish midlands.

Flowering time: July to September, but from June in some coastal habitats.

Top and bottom left Goldenrod (Solidago virgaurea) *has small, bright-yellow, shortly rayed flowers. It can thrive on a rocky outcrop beside a stream.*

FLOWER TYPE

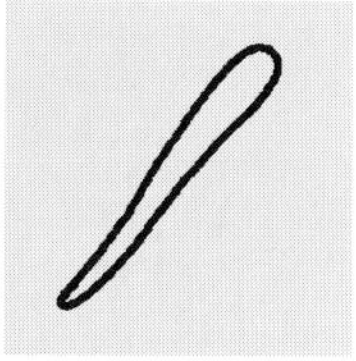
IDENTIFICATION

HABITAT

POPULATION

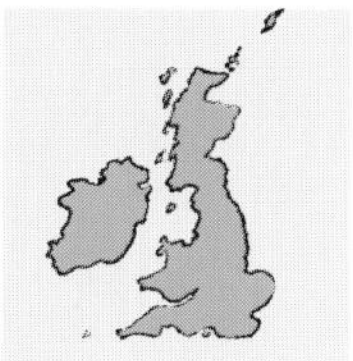
MAP

THIS UNOBTRUSIVE FLOWER of the tail end of summer is much less familiar to many people than the cultivated plant that brightens gardens and urban waste ground at the same time. Yet it is often a feature of heathy and rocky ground. Goldenrod is a very variable species. Particularly interesting are dwarf plants from some coastal sites, flowering June to July, especially in the Burren of County Clare. Many populations of the plant do not flower until August. An infusion of this plant was regarded in the past as a valuable medicinal herb for treating a number of complaints.

Bottom right
Canadian Goldenrod (Solidago canadensis) *is similar but taller, with many tiny flower-heads in more showy, dense, 1-sided clusters. Flowering August–October, this popular garden plant from North America often escapes on to waste ground, especially in towns.*

Daisy

DAISY AND DANDELION FAMILY
(Compositae or Asteraceae)

SPECIES INFORMATION	
COMMON NAME	Daisy
SCIENTIFIC NAME	Bellis perennis
RELATED SPECIES	Sea Aster
HEIGHT/SPREAD	5–20 cm tall
FLOWERING TIME	February–December
HABITAT	Grassland and lawns

Note: The familiar flower of lawns.

FLOWER TYPE

IDENTIFICATION

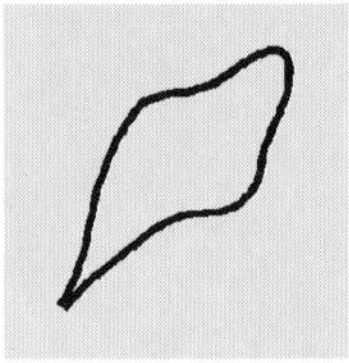

HABITAT

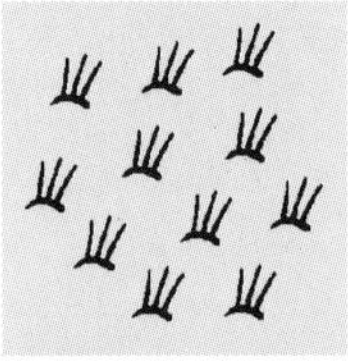

POPULATION

MAP

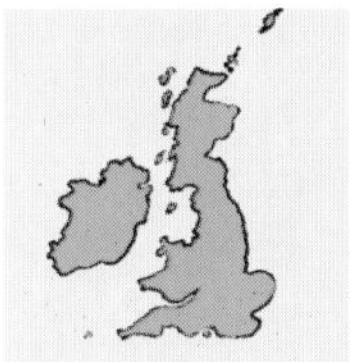

Size and appearance: A tufted, downy perennial, with numerous, erect, leafless flowering stems 5–20 cm (2–8 in) tall.

Leaves: Crowded in a basal rosette, spoon-shaped, stalked, bluntly toothed, slightly fleshy and leathery.

Flowers: Tightly packed in solitary heads 10–30 mm ($\frac{3}{8}$–$1\frac{1}{5}$ in) across, the central disc florets yellow, the outer ray florets white, reddish or purplish below.

Fruits: Heads of 1-seeded fruits, without attached hairs.

Related or similar plants: Ox-eye Daisy (p.302) is a much larger and robust plant.

Habitat and distribution: Very common everywhere in all grassy places, including the grassland of mountains, coastal cliff-tops and sand-dunes, on hedge-banks and, especially, lawns and other amenity grassland.

Flowering time: February to December, with a peak in late spring, but all through mild winters. The flowers close in the evening and on dull or wet days.

DAISY IS PERHAPS the most familiar of all wild flowers, known even to hardened non-botanists. It is a first sign of real spring, and poets and writers from Geoffrey Chaucer to Thomas Hardy and to the present day have celebrated its cheery charm. Ironically, this ubiquitous wild flower is mostly associated with closely mown grass, especially lawns, even where they are tiny pockets in a town or city. Gardeners grow double and large-flowered variants, which sometimes escape. The plant's native habitat of unimproved pastures is now sadly reduced, apart from places like seaside banks and churchyards. Apart from ornament, the Daisy plant was formerly regarded as a valued herb for healing wounds.

Daisy (Bellis perennis) *is such a familiar plant of lawns that people often forget that this is a native wild flower occurring in all sorts of grassy places. However, it is not often seen in such abundance as in the photograph below. It survives quite happily in garden lawns as its leaves lie in a flat, basal rosette, with the mower passing over the top. However, it may not flower if cutting occurs too frequently.*

SPECIES INFORMATION	
COMMON NAME	Sea Aster
SCIENTIFIC NAME	Aster tripolium
RELATED SPECIES	Michaelmas Daisy
HEIGHT/SPREAD	20–80 cm tall
FLOWERING TIME	July–October
HABITAT	Saltmarshes
Note: A Michaelmas Daisy-like plant of saltmarshes.	

Sea Aster

DAISY AND DANDELION FAMILY
(Compositae or Asteraceae)

Size and appearance: A fleshy annual, biennial or short-lived perennial 20–80 cm (8–32 in) tall, sometimes up to 150 cm (60 in).
Leaves: Very fleshy, spear-shaped, untoothed or slightly toothed, the upper narrower, stalkless.
Flowers: In heads 10–25 mm (⅜–1 in) across, the inner disc florets yellow, the 10–30 outer ray florets mauve or lilac, or sometimes absent, in loose clusters.
Fruits: Heads of 1-seeded fruits, each with a parachute of whitish hairs.
Related or similar plants: Michaelmas Daisy, a frequent garden escape, is taller and does not have fleshy leaves.
Habitat and distribution: Often abundant in salt-marshes, from the lower marsh to the uppermost strand-line, on sea-cliffs and coastal rocks, and along the banks of tidal rivers to some distance inland, all around the coasts of Britain and Ireland; also, in the West Midlands, in a few inland salt-marshes.
Flowering time: July to October.

Sea Aster was grown in gardens long before Michaelmas Daisy was introduced from North America in the 17th century. Both provide colour as autumn approaches.

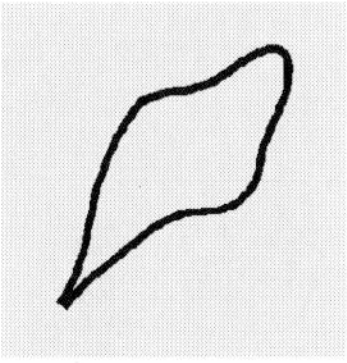

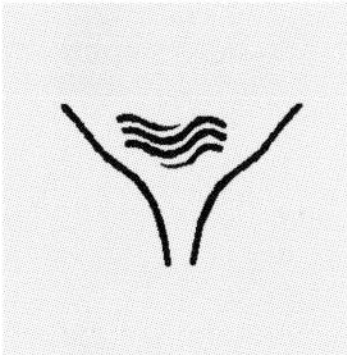

SEA ASTER IS a common and very variable plant, not only in form but also in life-history and flowering time. These differences relate to both geography and to the part of the salt-marsh in which the plants are growing. In some parts of England, notably in East Anglia and about the Thames Estuary, the flowers often lack the outer ray florets. They look more like the yellow button-flowers of Tansy (p.300).

Top *Sea Aster* (Aster tripolium) *with mauve outer florets. In some locations, it is more frequently found without these and just has the central yellow disc florets.*

Bottom left *An abundant plant of salt marshes, where it grows on the bare mud at the edges to the creeks or all across the marsh as if in a meadow.*

Bottom right *Michaelmas Daisy* (Aster novi-belgii) *is similar but taller and not fleshy, with more numerous and showy flowers; vigorous rhizomes give to extensive clumps. Flowering September–October, it frequently escapes or is discarded from gardens to embellish waste ground and railway embankments.*

Ploughman's Spikenard

DAISY AND DANDELION FAMILY

(Compositae or Asteraceae)

SPECIES INFORMATION	
COMMON NAME	Ploughman's Spikenard
SCIENTIFIC NAME	Inula conyza
RELATED SPECIES	Fleabanes
HEIGHT/SPREAD	30–100 cm tall
FLOWERING TIME	July–September
HABITAT	Scrub and grassland

Note: Most other members of this family have conspicuous rays.

FLOWER TYPE

IDENTIFICATION

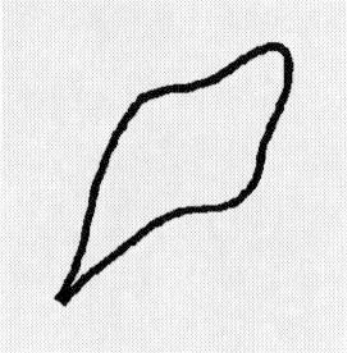

HABITAT

POPULATION

MAP

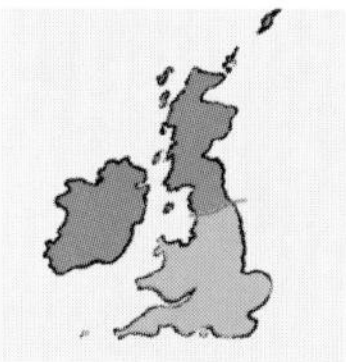

Size and appearance: A downy biennial or short-lived perennial, with erect, tough, reddish stems 30–100 cm (12–40 in) tall.

Leaves: The lower oval or oblong, narrowed into a stalk, finely toothed, the upper narrower, stalkless.

Flowers: In yellowish, egg-shaped heads c. 10 mm (⅖ in) across, with inconspicuous ray florets, numerous in loose, flat-topped clusters.

Fruits: Heads of 1-seeded fruits, each with a parachute of whitish hairs.

Related or similar plants: Trifid Bur-marigold (p.294) and Tansy (p.300) also lack ray florets, but are both plants of damper habitats.

Habitat and distribution: Locally common in grassland, scrub and open woodland on chalk and limestone, especially on banks or broken ground, in England, north to County Durham, and Wales.

Flowering time: July to September.

THE UNUSUAL NAME of this plant alludes to its aromatic root. Country people would hang roots up in their cottages to freshen the air – spikenard is an expensive perfume that would have been unavailable to them. The leaves of Ploughman's Spikenard are a little like those of a mullein or Foxglove (p.256). It is an unfamiliar, undistinguished-looking plant that many people pass by or ignore. It is a good indicator of lime-rich soil.

Ploughman's Spikenard (Inula conyza) *is an erect, downy plant, generally only branched towards the top. The upper leaves are narrow and unstalked, the yellow flower heads rather small but numerous, in a flat-topped cluster.*

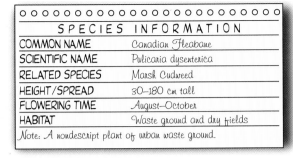

SPECIES INFORMATION	
COMMON NAME	Canadian Fleabane
SCIENTIFIC NAME	Pulicaria dysenterica
RELATED SPECIES	Marsh Cudweed
HEIGHT/SPREAD	30–180 cm tall
FLOWERING TIME	August–October
HABITAT	Waste ground and dry fields

Note: A nondescript plant of urban waste ground.

Canadian Fleabane

DAISY AND DANDELION FAMILY
(Compositae or Asteraceae)

Size and appearance: An erect, hairy, branched, leafy annual 30–180 cm (12–72 cm) tall.
Leaves: Numerous, narrow, spear-shaped, untoothed or finely toothed, pale green.
Flowers: In heads 3–5 mm (1/8–1/5 in) across, with yellowish inner disc florets and white or pinkish outer ray florets, numerous in long, branched loose clusters.
Fruits: Heads of 1-seeded fruits, each with a parachute of white hairs.
Related or similar plants: Marsh Cudweed (p.293) is somewhat similar but smaller and white-woolly, with flowers in flat-topped clusters.
Habitat and distribution: An increasingly common plant of dry waste places, derelict industrial and railway land, fallow fields and sand-dunes, and as a weed of gardens, mainly in southern and eastern England but spreading rapidly elsewhere.
Flowering time: August to October.

CANADIAN FLEABANE WAS one of our first weed invaders from North America, arriving in the 17th century. According to legend it came in as seed inside a stuffed bird. Today it is especially common in southern and eastern England, and has long been a feature of waste ground and scruffy pavements in and around London. From now on it is likely that it will turn up on urban waste land almost anywhere. Since 1983 it has begun to become established in Ireland, in and around Dublin. It is regarded by botanists as one of the weeds most likely to spread on to farmland set aside under EU rules.

It is a major weed in parts of eastern Europe, which has a drier climate than ours, suggesting that it may expand its range further should we indeed be entering a period of climate change and global warming.

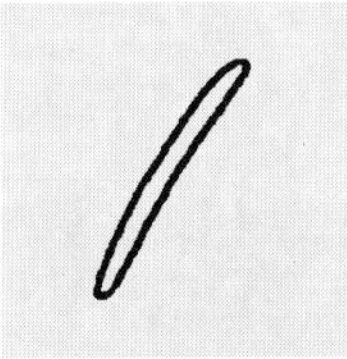

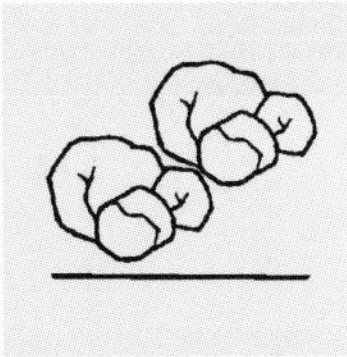

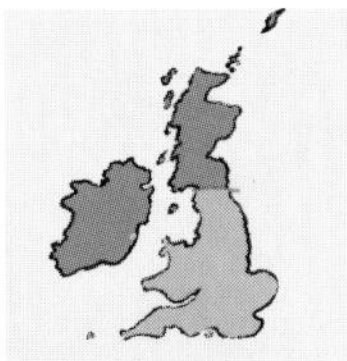

Top and bottom left *Canadian Fleabane* (Conyza canadensis) *can grow to a good-sized plant but it is equally capable of flowering at a height of a few inches from a crack in the pavement at the base of a wall.*

Bottom right *Blue Fleabane* (Erigeron acer) *is a smaller native plant not more than 40 cm (16 in) tall, with few to numerous flower-heads 6–12 mm (1/4–1/2 in) across of yellow disc florets and pale purple ray florets. Flowering June–August, it is widespread in dry, open or grassy places, mainly in England and Wales.*

Common Fleabane

DAISY AND DANDELION FAMILY

(Compositae or Asteraceae)

SPECIES INFORMATION	
COMMON NAME	Common Fleabane
SCIENTIFIC NAME	Pulicaria dysenterica
RELATED SPECIES	Blue Fleabane
HEIGHT/SPREAD	20–60 cm tall
FLOWERING TIME	July–October
HABITAT	Damp ground

Note: Forming huge patches in damp places in late summer.

FLOWER TYPE

IDENTIFICATION

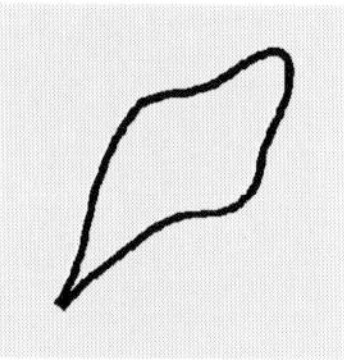

HABITAT

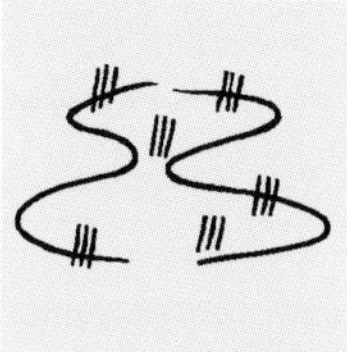

POPULATION

MAP

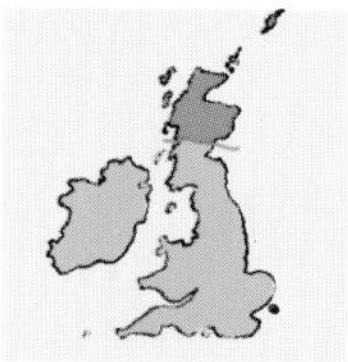

Size and appearance: A hairy perennial with far-creeping runners, forming large patches, and sprawling to erect, often woolly, stems 20–60 cm (8–24 in) tall.

Leaves: Oblong or spear-shaped, wrinkled, remotely toothed, the upper clasping the stem.

Flowers: In heads 15–30 mm (⅗–1⅕ in) across, the inner disc and outer ray florets golden-yellow, numerous in loose, flat-topped clusters.

Fruits: Heads of 1-seeded fruits, only the innermost with a parachute of white hairs.

Related or similar plants: Corn Marigold (p.299) is a hairless annual of cultivated and disturbed ground.

Habitat and distribution: Common in marshes, ditches and wet hollows, on damp road-verges and in over-grazed or disturbed, wet pastures, especially on clay soils, north to Cumbria and Yorkshire; widespread in most of Ireland, but only in southern Scotland, usually near the sea.

Flowering time: July to October.

COMMON FLEABANE IS one of the best shows of colour in late summer, especially in damp, rushy places. The rather strongly scented leaves were dried and used to repel fleas, the origin of both the English name and the first half of the scientific name (Latin: *pulices*, fleas). Several plants are credited with the quality of discouraging fleas and other small vermin, which must have been a major problem before modern public health.

Elecampane (*Inula helenium*) is somewhat similar in general form but a very much more robust plant up to 100 cm (40 in) tall, with huge flowerheads 50–75 mm (2–3 in) across. It an ancient medicinal herb found occasionally near houses and ruins, especially on western coasts.

Top *Common Fleabane* (Pulicaria dysenterica) *has large, daisy-type flowers with yellow rays and a deeper, golden centre.*

Bottom left *The wrinkling of the leaves of the Common Fleabane is conspicuous.*

Bottom right *A plant associated with damp grassy situations, including marshes, wet hollows and pastures.*

SPECIES INFORMATION	
COMMON NAME	Marsh Cudweed
SCIENTIFIC NAME	Gnaphalium uliginosum
RELATED SPECIES	Fleabanes
HEIGHT/SPREAD	5–20 cm tall
FLOWERING TIME	July–October
HABITAT	Damp ground

Note: Forming grey patches in damp places.

Marsh Cudweed

DAISY AND DANDELION FAMILY

(Compositae or Asteraceae)

THIS IS THE commonest of several native cudweeds, all plants of open ground with small flowers and narrow, often greyish leaves. They form a group of 'botanist's plants', hard to distinguish from one another, and on the basis of tiny, complex characters. One of the most widespread, Heath Cudweed (*Omalotheca sylvatica*), has the general look of Marsh Cudweed, but is a perennial with erect, unbranched stems 10–60 cm (4–24 in) tall, leaves green on the upper surface, and pale yellow flower-heads 5–6 mm ($\frac{1}{5}$–$\frac{1}{4}$ in) long, surrounded by brownish scale-like bracts. It is a plant of heaths and dry grassland, mainly in eastern Britain.

Marsh Cudweed has obviously attracted some attention in its time. John Gerard observed whimsically in his 1597 *Herball*, while explaining why it was known in Scotland as 'Son-afore-the-father': 'bicause the yonger, or those flowers that spring up later, are higher, and over top those that come first, as many wicked children do unto their parents'.

FLOWER TYPE

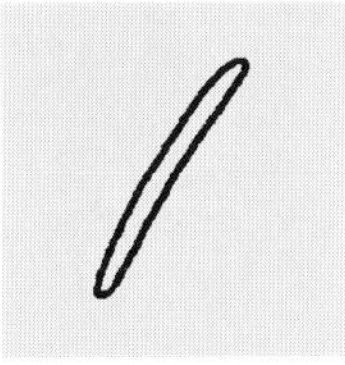
IDENTIFICATION

HABITAT

POPULATION

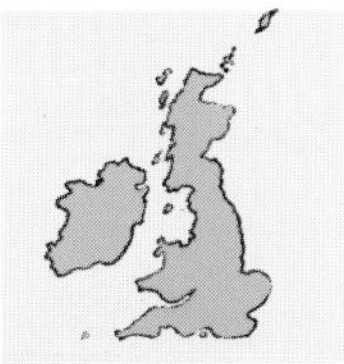
MAP

Size and appearance: A low, tufted, much-branched, pale grey-woolly annual 5–20 cm (2–8 in) tall.
Leaves: Narrow, oblong or spoon-shaped, untoothed or sometimes slightly toothed, densely woolly-hairy.
Flowers: In heads 3–4 mm ($\frac{1}{8}$–$\frac{1}{6}$ in) across, surrounded by pale brown, scale-like bracts, the inner disc and outer ray florets yellowish-brown, 3–10 in dense clusters surrounded by leaf-like bracts.
Fruits: Heads of 1-seeded fruits, each with a tiny parachute of hairs.
Related or similar plants: One of a group of similar cudweeds; Canadian Fleabane (p.291) is a taller, pale-green plant with loose clusters of flower-heads.
Habitat and distribution: A widespread and common plant of open, damp ground, marshes and heaths, especially on disturbed ground, grassy paths and damp, rutted tracks, throughout Britain and Ireland.
Flowering time: July to October.

Marsh Cudweed (Gnaphalium uliginosum) *is a low, often-bushily tufted plant appearing rather grey-green due to its cottony covering of down. The unstalked flowers heads are in crowded clusters of small yellowish-brown flowers which are surrounded by scale-like bracts.*

Trifid Bur-marigold

DAISY AND DANDELION FAMILY

(Compositae or Asteraceae)

SPECIES INFORMATION	
COMMON NAME	Trifid Bur-marigold
SCIENTIFIC NAME	Bidens tripartita
RELATED SPECIES	Nodding Bur-marigold
HEIGHT/SPREAD	20–60 cm tall
FLOWERING TIME	July–October
HABITAT	Watersides and damp waste ground

Note: Forming patches on drying mud in late summer.

FLOWER TYPE

IDENTIFICATION

HABITAT

POPULATION

MAP

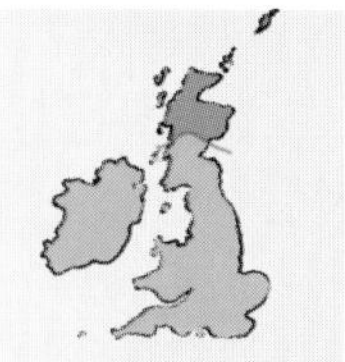

Size and appearance: An erect, branched, often hairy annual 20–60 cm (8–24 in) tall, with purplish, winged stems.

Leaves: In opposite pairs, 3-lobed or sometimes 5-lobed, the lobes spear-shaped and coarsely toothed.

Flowers: In heads 10–25 mm (⅖–1 in) across, the disc florets yellow, the outer ray florets almost always absent, in branched clusters with 5–8 leaf-like bracts just below.

Fruits: Heads of flattened, wedge-shaped, 1-seeded fruits, each with 3–4 barbed bristles.

Related or similar plants: Nodding Bur-marigold has spear-shaped leaves and nodding flower-heads.

Habitat and distribution: Widespread and locally common on the margins or drying mud of lakes, ponds and rivers, also in ditches, wet fields and damp waste places, north to central Scotland; much more local in northern Britain and in Ireland.

Flowering time: July to October.

TRIFID BUR-MARIGOLD can be a conspicuous feature of drying mud in late summer, often forming great, dense crowds. The bristly fruits are superbly adapted to dispersal by animals, having both barbed bristles and stiff, down-turned hairs on the margins, which stick firmly on to clothing and animal fur. They are very difficult to remove from woolly socks.

Top and bottom left *Trifid Bur-marigold* (Bidens tripartita) *has stout round-topped heads of yellow disc-florets; the outer ray-florets are nearly always absent. Immediately below are five to eight leaf-like bracts. An erect, branched plant with an often purplish stem, leaves in opposite pairs, mostly with three spear-shaped lobes, with the central lobe being the longest.*

Bottom right *Nodding Bur-marigold* (Bidens cernua) *is similar but has pairs of spear-shaped leaves and nodding flower-heads, sometimes with short ray-florets. It has a similar ecology and distribution, but is rather less common.*

SPECIES INFORMATION	
COMMON NAME	Gallant Soldier
SCIENTIFIC NAME	Galinsoga parviflora
RELATED SPECIES	Shaggy Soldier
HEIGHT/SPREAD	10–80 cm tall
FLOWERING TIME	May–November
HABITAT	Cultivated land

Note: A scruffy weed of gardens.

Gallant Soldier

DAISY AND DANDELION FAMILY (Compositae or Asteraceae)

GALLANT SOLDIER WAS introduced to England from the Andes, escaping from The Royal Botanic Gardens at Kew during the 1860s. Since then it has spread across much of Britain, although it is still most abundant around London and in the south. Tiny bristles on the fruit adhere to clothing or fur or help the small seed to catch the wind. The English name, a fascinating corruption of the first half of the scientific name, is clearly of recent derivation. Local names include a variation on this, Soldiers of-the-Queen, and Kew Weed, the last perhaps invented by a frustrated gardener who knew just who was to blame for the new weed infestation.

FLOWER TYPE

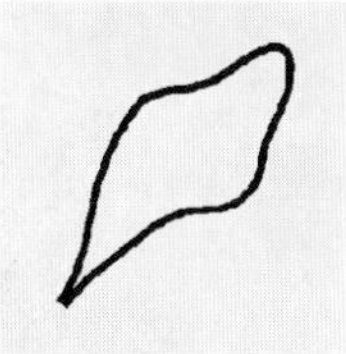
IDENTIFICATION

HABITAT

POPULATION

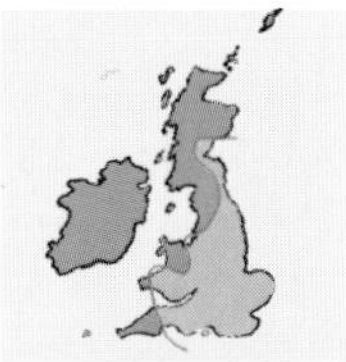
MAP

Size and appearance: An almost hairless (except for flower-stalks), erect, branched annual 10–80 cm (4–32 in) tall.
Leaves: In opposite pairs, oval, pointed, with a few large teeth.
Flowers: In heads 3–5 mm (⅛–⅕ in) across, the inner disc florets yellow, the 5 small, outer ray florets white, in loose, branched clusters.
Fruits: Heads of flattened, oval, 1-seeded fruits, each with a tuft of scales.
Related or similar plants: Shaggy Soldier has hairy stems.
Habitat and distribution: A locally common and increasing weed of cultivated land that can be abundant in gardens, allotments, nursery beds and vegetable crops, especially in south-eastern England; not in Ireland.
Flowering time: May to November.

Top *Gallant Soldier* (Galinsoga parviflora) *has leaves which are oval and pointed, in opposite pairs up the stem. The flowers are small, with white outer ray florets and yellow inner disc florets.*

Bottom *Shaggy Soldier* (Galinsoga quadriradiata) *is very similar but the upper stems especially are white-hairy, the leaves are slightly more toothed, and the flower-heads have 4–5 ray florets. It is less widespread, being found mainly in south-east England, but it is also in Ireland, around Dublin and Belfast.*

Scentless Mayweed

DAISY AND DANDELION FAMILY

(Compositae or Asteraceae)

SPECIES INFORMATION	
COMMON NAME	Scentless Mayweed
SCIENTIFIC NAME	Matricaria perforata
RELATED SPECIES	Pineapple Weed
HEIGHT/SPREAD	10–80 cm tall
FLOWERING TIME	April–November
HABITAT	Cultivated and disturbed ground

Note: The common mayweed of cultivated land.

FLOWER TYPE

IDENTIFICATION

HABITAT

POPULATION

MAP

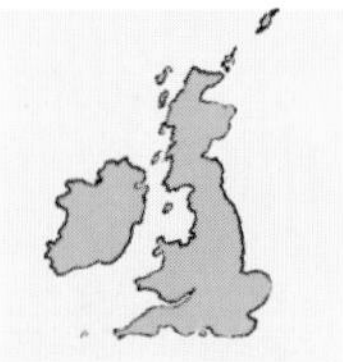

Size and appearance: An erect, semi-erect or sprawling, much-branched annual 10–80 cm (4–32 in) tall, with tough stems.

Leaves: Compound, 2- to 3-times divided into numerous narrow, feathery segments.

Flowers: Daisy-like, in flat heads 25–45 mm (1–1⅘ in) across, the inner disc florets yellow, the outer ray florets white, solitary or in very loose clusters.

Fruits: conical heads of 1-seeded, minutely ribbed fruits, without hairs.

Related or similar plants: Pineapple Weed has no ray florets; other mayweeds and related chamomiles, several of them rare, are difficult to distinguish.

Habitat and distribution: Widespread and often abundant on cultivated land, field borders, roadsides and waste ground throughout Britain and Ireland. Similar plants on seashores are regarded as a separate species.

Flowering time: April to November.

BOTANISTS NOW USUALLY distinguish similar but more perennial plants from seashores and shingle beaches, with fleshy leaves and slightly larger flowers, as a separate species, Sea Mayweed (*Matricaria maritima*). The two are very similar and one probably evolved from the other. Although Scentless Mayweed is a common and successful weed, several other mayweeds and closely related chamomiles have decreased markedly since 1945 owing to modern intensive farming methods, especially the use of weedkillers.

The various other mayweeds and chamomiles are difficult to distinguish. Chamomile (*Chamaemelum nobile*), a popular cottage-garden plant but also a decreasing plant of grazed commons and coastal heaths, is similar in general form to Scentless Mayweed but smaller and less coarse. It is a mat-forming, aromatic perennial with flower-heads 18–25 mm (¾–1 in) across.

Scentless Mayweed (Tripleurospermum inodorum) *can range from being an erect to a sprawling plant, common in cultivated fields and waste places. It has bushy leaves, which are finely divided into hair-like segments. The daisy-like flowers are flat at first, but form a solid cone in fruit.*

SPECIES INFORMATION	
COMMON NAME	Pineapple Weed
SCIENTIFIC NAME	Matricaria discoidea
RELATED SPECIES	Scentless Mayweed
HEIGHT/SPREAD	5–40 cm tall
FLOWERING TIME	June–October
HABITAT	Trampled places

Note: The flower-heads look like conical buttons.

Pineapple Weed

DAISY AND DANDELION FAMILY

(Compositae or Asteraceae)

PINEAPPLE WEED IS as widespread as any plant in these islands, yet it is not a native and it has been here for less than a century and a half. The first record for Britain, in North Wales, was in 1871, and for Ireland in 1894. Since then it has spread right across both islands, even into remote or mountainous areas. So widely is this most successful weed now distributed worldwide that its origin, probably somewhere in north-east Asia or western North America, is unknown. Always it occurs wherever there is at least a degree of trampling. Like Greater Plantain (p.271) its tolerance of trampling enables it to survive in an ecological niche that most other plants, perhaps more competitive, cannot tolerate.

Pineapple Weed (Matricaria discoidea) *is a weed of footpaths and other trampled places. It is a dark-green, bushy plant which does indeed smell of pineapple when the leaves are crushed. It has unrayed, yellowish-green, conical flowers heads which are hollow in the centre.*

FLOWER TYPE

IDENTIFICATION

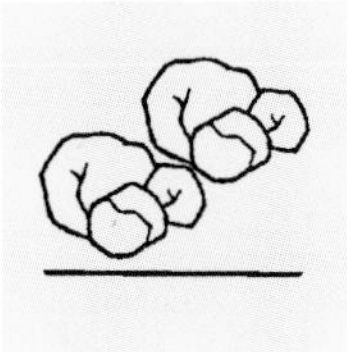

HABITAT

POPULATION

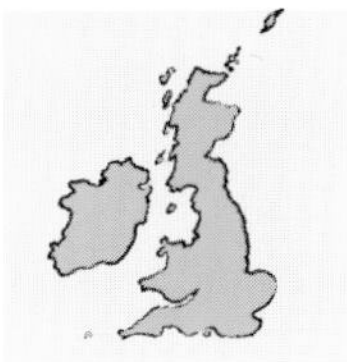

MAP

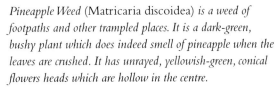

Size and appearance: An erect, stiffly branched, rather bushy annual 5–40 cm (2–16 in) tall.

Leaves: Compound, 2- to 3-times divided into numerous narrow, feathery segments, smelling strongly of pineapple when bruised.

Flowers: In domed or conical heads of greenish-yellow florets, 5–10 mm (⅕–⅖ in) across, without outer ray florets, solitary or in very loose clusters.

Fruits: Conical heads of 1-seeded fruits, without hairs.

Related or similar plants: Scentless Mayweed (p.296) has conspicuous white ray florets.

Habitat and distribution: A common plant of waysides, pathsides, beside field gates and in other trampled places, waste ground and sometimes field borders and cultivated land throughout Britain and Ireland.

Flowering time: June to October

Yarrow

DAISY AND DANDELION FAMILY
(Compositae or Asteraceae)

SPECIES INFORMATION	
COMMON NAME	Yarrow
SCIENTIFIC NAME	Achillea millefolium
RELATED SPECIES	Sneezewort
HEIGHT/SPREAD	10–100 cm tall
FLOWERING TIME	June–November
HABITAT	Dry grassland
Note: The common cut-leaved plant of dry grassland.	

FLOWER TYPE

IDENTIFICATION

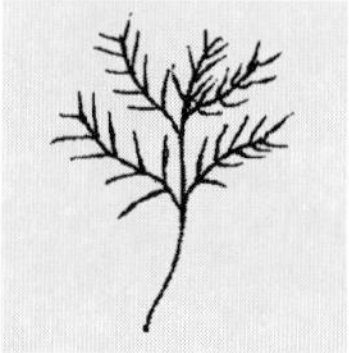

HABITAT

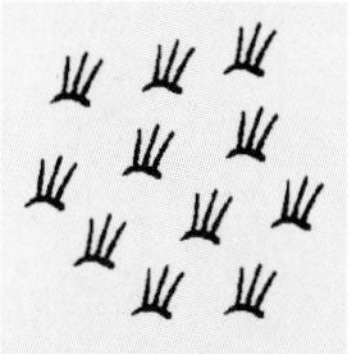

POPULATION

MAP

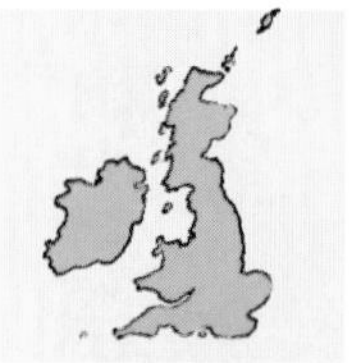

Size and appearance: A hairy perennial, with creeping runners, forming clumps and patches, and erect, tough stems 10–100 cm (4–40 in) tall.
Leaves: Most in basal rosettes, stalked, compound, 2- to 3-times divided into numerous narrow, feathery segments, aromatic when bruised, the upper stalkless.
Flowers: In heads 3–6 mm (⅛–¼ in) across, the inner disc florets white or cream, the 5 ray florets white, pink or purple, in dense, flat-topped clusters.
Fruits: Heads of 1-seeded fruits, without hairs.
Related or similar plants: Scentless Mayweed (p.296) has conspicuous white ray florets.
Habitat and distribution: Common in dry grassland, scrub, hedgerows and waste places, and on grassy roadsides, village greens and lawns, throughout Britain and Ireland.
Flowering time: June to November.

YARROW IS ONE of the commonest wild flowers of dry grassland and readily persists in even well-kept lawns. It is drought-tolerant, and during dry spells can be spotted as green patches, frequently in flower, on brown lawns and roadsides. It is a very variable species in height and flower colour, with pink-flowered plants fairly frequent in the wild. More exotic colour variants, fom apricot to purple, make good garden plants, with the added advantage that they will survive the driest summers. The plant has a long history as a healing, and magical, herb. Yarrow tea is said to alleviate colds and rheumatism.

Top right *Yarrow* (Achillea millefolium) *is a downy, little-branched, aromatic, dark-green plant. The flower heads are small but numerous, in a flattish terminal cluster. Although mainly white, some plants produce flowers suffused with varying degrees of pink.*

Bottom left *Yarrow is widespread and common in hedgerows and dry grassy places, including lawns, where it never has a chance to flower.*

Bottom right *Sneezewort* (Achillea ptarmica) *is similar but has undivided, saw-toothed leaves and looser clusters of flower-heads 12–18 mm (½–¾ in) across, with greenish disc and white ray florets. Flowering July–August, it is widespread on damp heaths and in marshes on lime-poor soils, although local in southern Ireland and much of south-eastern England.*

SPECIES INFORMATION	
COMMON NAME	Corn Marigold
SCIENTIFIC NAME	Chrysanthemum segetum
RELATED SPECIES	Yarrow, Tansy
HEIGHT/SPREAD	15–60 cm tall
FLOWERING TIME	May–September
HABITAT	Cultivated and disturbed ground

Note: The big, yellow 'daisy' of cultivated land.

Corn Marigold

DAISY AND DANDELION FAMILY (Compositae or Asteraceae)

CORN MARIGOLD IN quantity is a magnificent sight, a sheet of gold (Gold was one of its old names), but it was once a major problem to arable farmers. It has decreased considerably, like so many arable weeds, since 1945, but is having a small come-back due to its popularity in wild flower seed-mixtures. It makes an ideal hardy annual for the garden and looks good in flower arrangements.

Corn Marigold is a native of south-west Asia and the Mediterranean region, where it is also now in decline. It probably arrived in Britain and Ireland with ancient farmers; the earliest fossil evidence is from human settlements.

Corn Marigold (Chrysanthemum segetum) *was once a common weed of cornfields but is now rarely seen in profusion. An attractive plant, it is popular as a component of wild flower seed mixes. Its flowers are solitary on stalks which are thickened towards the top, with both types of florets being a golden yellow.*

FLOWER TYPE

IDENTIFICATION

HABITAT

POPULATION

MAP

Size and appearance: A hairless, bluish-green, erect or semi-erect, often branched annual 15–60 cm (6–24 in) tall.

Leaves: Oblong or wedge-shaped, jagged-toothed, rather fleshy, the upper almost toothless, clasping the stem.

Flowers: In solitary, golden-yellow heads 35–60 mm (1⅜–2⅜ in) across, with prominent outer ray florets.

Fruits: Heads of 1-seeded fruits, without hairs, the outer ones flattened.

Related or similar plants: Ox-eye Daisy (p.302) has white ray florets.

Habitat and distribution: Widespread but local and decreasing on cultivated land, waysides and waste ground, especially on lime-poor, light or sandy soils, throughout Britain and Ireland.

Flowering time: May to September.

Tansy

DAISY AND DANDELION FAMILY
(Compositae or Asteraceae)

SPECIES INFORMATION	
COMMON NAME	Tansy
SCIENTIFIC NAME	Tanacetum vulgare
RELATED SPECIES	Feverfew
HEIGHT/SPREAD	50–150 cm tall
FLOWERING TIME	July–September
HABITAT	River-banks and waste ground

Note: The massed yellow buttons of the flower-heads are unique.

TANSY IS A useful plant that is probably native but has been much spread by people and their migrations. Like other aromatic members of the daisy and dandelion family, the fresh leaves or an infusion of them can be used to keep away flies and other insects, including greenfly. They have also been employed to discourage mice. The plant has a strong, rather bitter taste, but is the essential ingredient in tansy cakes and puddings, once widely eaten at Easter, and of drisheen, an esteemed, spicy black pudding from south-western Ireland.

FLOWER TYPE

IDENTIFICATION

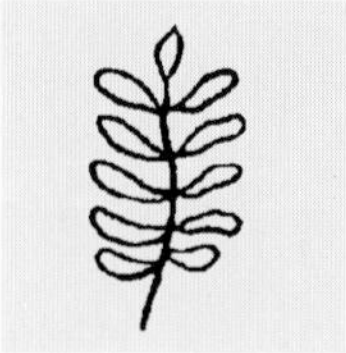

HABITAT

POPULATION

MAP

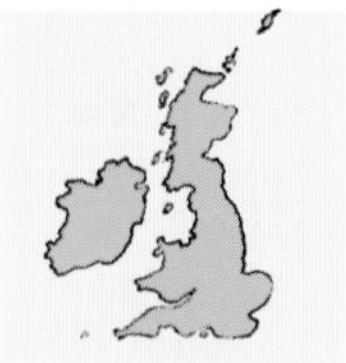

Tansy (Tanacetum vulgare) *is a robust, stiff, aromatic plant, popular in the cottage garden. It is often found on hedgebanks close by habitation and roadsides, but is equally at home on alongside streams. The golden-yellow, button-like heads are massed in flat-topped clusters standing out starkly from the dark-green foliage. The compound leaves have numerous narrow and deeply toothed leaflets which are rather fern-like or feathery.*

Size and appearance: A robust perennial, with creeping rhizomes, forming clumps, and erect, leafy stems 50–150 cm (20–60 in) tall, branched above.

Leaves: Compound, oblong, cut into deeply lobed, toothed, fern-like segments, dark green, sweetly aromatic when bruised.

Flowers: In golden-yellow, button-heads 8–12 mm (⅓–½ in) across, without outer ray florets, massed in flat-topped clusters.

Fruits: Heads of ribbed, 1-seeded fruits, without hairs.

Related or similar plants: Feverfew (p.301) is smaller, with yellowish-green leaves and flower-heads with white ray florets.

Habitat and distribution: Widespread in waste places, on roadsides, in hedgerows and along the banks of streams and rivers, often near settlements or ruined buildings; throughout Britain, but more local in Ireland.

Flowering time: July to September.

SPECIES INFORMATION	
COMMON NAME	Feverfew, Bachelor's Buttons
SCIENTIFIC NAME	Tanacetum parthenium
RELATED SPECIES	Tansy
HEIGHT/SPREAD	30–80 cm tall
FLOWERING TIME	July–September
HABITAT	Waste places and gardenss

Note: The yellowish-green, strongly aromatic leaves

Feverfew

DAISY AND DANDELION FAMILY
(Compositae or Asteraceae)

Size and appearance: A biennial or short-lived perennial with erect, ridged, leafy stems 30–80 cm (12–32 in) tall.

Leaves: Compound, oblong, cut into broad, often lobed, blunt segments, yellowish-green, strongly aromatic when bruised.

Flowers: In daisy-like heads 12–20 mm (½–⅘ in) across, the inner disc florets yellow, the outer ray florets white, in flat-topped clusters.

Fruits: Heads of ribbed, 1-seeded fruits, without hairs.

Related or similar plants: Tansy (p.300) is taller, with dark green leaves and flower-heads without ray florets.

Habitat and distribution: A plant of gardens, but also of waste places, waysides, hedgerows and churchyards, mostly near settlements; throughout, but local in western Scotland and in Ireland.

Flowering time: July to September.

FEVERFEW IS a classic plant of the old-fashioned cottage garden, where it provided, and still provides, colour and texture, scent and medicine. Originally from scrub and rocky ground in the mountains of the Balkans and south-west Asia, it now occurs in gardens or as an established escape through much of Europe. Like those of Tansy (p.300), the leaves can be used to discourage flies, but it has been more important as medicine. They were used in the treatment of fevers and headaches and also for calming the stomach.

For a while in the 1970s, Feverfew was touted as a wonder drug for severe headaches, but the results were inconclusive and few can cope with the bitter taste! Its best place is in the garden, where it is hardy and persistent. Some gardeners grow a double-flowered variant, with extra ray florets.

Another plant popular in the cottage garden because of its medicinal properties, Feverfew is now widespread along waysides and hedgerows usually near habitation, it is frequent in churchyards. Its yellowish foliage, topped by the white and yellow daisy-like flowers, makes a pleasing sight in any herbaceous border.

FLOWER TYPE

IDENTIFICATION

HABITAT

POPULATION

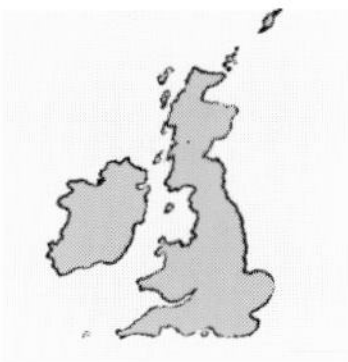
MAP

Ox-eye Daisy

DAISY AND DANDELION FAMILY

(Compositae or Asteraceae)

SPECIES INFORMATION	
COMMON NAME	Ox-eye Daisy, Moon Daisy
SCIENTIFIC NAME	Leucanthemum vulgare
RELATED SPECIES	Tansy, Feverfew
HEIGHT/SPREAD	20–100 cm tall
FLOWERING TIME	May–October
HABITAT	Waste places and gardens
Note: The big daisy of grassland and churchyards.	

FLOWER TYPE

IDENTIFICATION

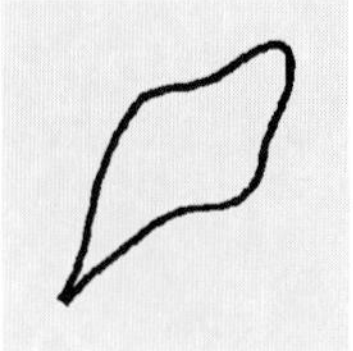

HABITAT

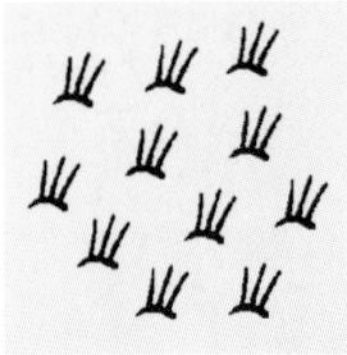

POPULATION

MAP

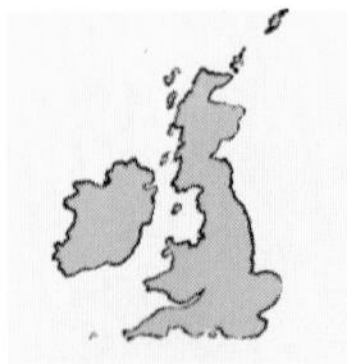

Size and appearance: A short-lived perennial with erect, usually little-branched stems 20–100 cm (8–40 in) .

Leaves: Oblong, oval or spoon-shaped, toothed, dark green, the upper narrower, stalkless, clasping the stem.

Flowers: In solitary, daisy-like heads 25–50 mm (1–2 in) across, the disc florets yellow, the ray florets white, the scale-like surrounding bracts with brownish margins.

Fruits: Heads of 1-seeded, ribbed fruits, without hairs.

Related or similar plants: Daisy (p.288) also has solitary flower-heads, but is smaller and has leafless flowering stems.

Habitat and distribution: Widespread and locally common in grassland, including old, traditionally managed meadows and pastures, churchyards, roadside banks and verges, sand-dunes and other coastal grassland.

Flowering time: May to October.

OX-EYE DAISY IS, like Yellow Rattle (p.264) and others, a classic wild flower of old meadows. Today, however, the larger stands of this plant are more likely to derive from wild flower seed-mixtures, especially on new road-verges. Unfortunately, much of the seed appears to be of garden origin, and the plants are more robust than the native ones. Many botanists are concerned about the possible loss of native variation in wild flowers through competition and crossing with introduced variants. Some of the best native populations probably survive in country churchyards, often fragments of ancient meadows.

Ox-eye Daisy is certainly variable, with several distinctive variants such as the attractive, dwarf plants that grow on sea-cliffs and coastal heaths in western Britain.

The plant was formerly used to treat wounds and a variety of ailments. This may have had less to do with its healing potential than with the fact that the herbalists thought they recognised it from the writings of ancient Greek physicians.

Ox-eye Daisy (Leucanthemum vulgare) *is a plant that always brings a smile to the on-looker. Its daisy-like flowers are usually solitary at the top of slender stalk and wave in the breeze. It is a plant of grassland and can be found in churchyards when, as in the photograph to the left, it can put on a fine show if the grass is not cut during the summer months. It is equally at home on cliff tops.*

SPECIES INFORMATION	
COMMON NAME	Mugwort
SCIENTIFIC NAME	Artemisia vulgaris
RELATED SPECIES	Wormwood
HEIGHT/SPREAD	50–180 cm tall
FLOWERING TIME	July-September
HABITAT	Dry waste places

Note: An untidy, greyish plant of dry, urban waste-ground.

Mugwort

DAISY AND DANDELION FAMILY

(Compositae or Asteraceae)

Size and appearance: A scruffy perennial with erect, tough, reddish stems 50–180 cm (20–72 in) tall.

Leaves: Compound, deeply lobed, the spear-shaped lobes further dissected, green above, white-woolly beneath

Flowers: In reddish-brown, egg-shaped heads 2–3 mm (1/12–1/8 in) across, without ray florets, in large, loose, branched clusters.

Fruits: Heads of nut-like, 1-seeded fruits, without hairs.

Related or similar plants: Wormwood is aromatic and has silky-hairy, silvery leaves.

Habitat and distribution: A common and characteristic plant of dry waysides, waste ground, demolition sites, neglected pavements and old concrete runways, almost always near buildings or roads; throughout but more local in rural Scotland and Ireland.

Flowering time: July to September, but prominent in fruit through autumn.

MUGWORT IS NOT handsome, but is part of the urban and suburban landscape. It is perhaps the most typical plant of dry, dusty waste or derelict land. It is a plant surrounded by magic that, like St John's Wort (p.152), was part of the ritual to ward off evil spirits during pagan festivities around St John the Baptist's Day on 24 June. In the Isle of Man, people wear sprigs of Mugwort on 4 July for the open-air session of the Tynwald or Manx parliament.

Although the plant is not particularly aromatic, the leaves have long been smoked as a herbal tobacco. The more aromatic Wormwood is the basis of a notorious alcoholic drink, which is currently enjoying a revival.

Top right and bottom left *Mugwort* (Artemisia vulgaris) *is a common plant of road verges, waysides and waste places. The flower heads are small and egg-shaped, with reddish-brown disc-florets, and is numerous in dense much-branched spikes.*

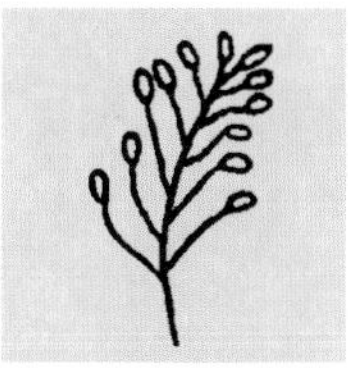

FLOWER TYPE

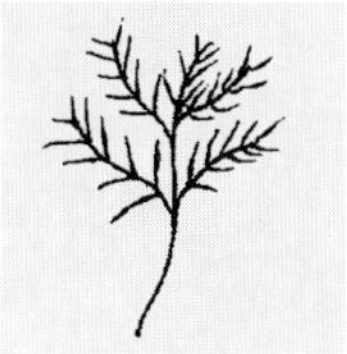

IDENTIFICATION

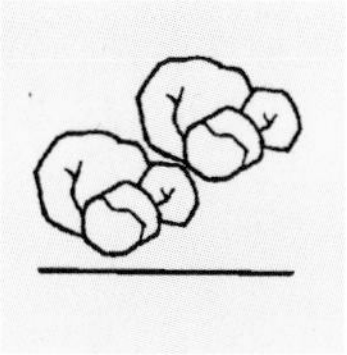

HABITAT

POPULATION

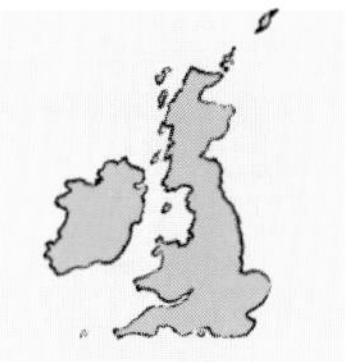

MAP

Bottom right *Wormwood* (Artemisia absinthium) *is similar but rarely more than 80 cm (32 in) tall, with sweetly aromatic, 2- to 3-times cut, silky-hairy, silvery leaves, and yellowish flower-heads 3–4 mm (1/8–1/6 in) across, flowering in July to August.*

Coltsfoot

DAISY AND DANDELION FAMILY

(Compositae or Asteraceae)

SPECIES INFORMATION	
COMMON NAME	Coltsfoot
SCIENTIFIC NAME	Tussilago farfara
RELATED SPECIES	Butterbur
HEIGHT/SPREAD	10–30 cm tall
FLOWERING TIME	February–April
HABITAT	Bare ground and river-banks

Note: A dandelion-like plant of very early spring.

FLOWER TYPE

IDENTIFICATION

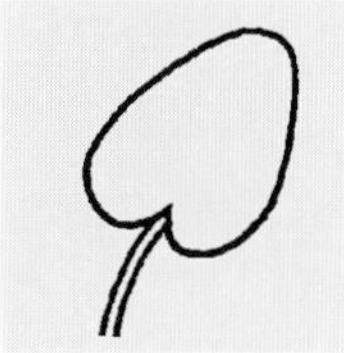

HABITAT

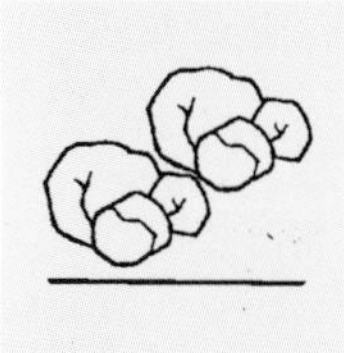

POPULATION

MAP

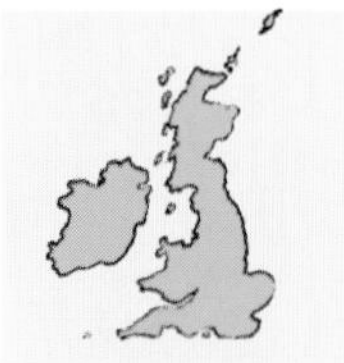

Size and appearance: A perennial with thick, creeping rhizomes, forming large patches, and clusters of stout, erect, scaly, pink stems 10–30 cm (4–12 in) tall.

Leaves: Appearing after the flowers, all basal, triangular to heart-shaped, up to 25 cm (10 in) across, shallowly toothed, cobwebby beneath.

Flowers: In solitary, yellow heads 20–35 mm ($\frac{4}{5}$–1$\frac{2}{5}$ in) across, the outer ray florets orange beneath.

Fruits: Heads of 1-seeded fruits, each with a parachute of long hairs.

Related or similar plants: Dandelion (p.320) has hollow, leafless flowering stems at the same time as leaves.

Habitat and distribution: Widespread and sometimes locally abundant on bare waste ground, road-verges, the banks of rivers and streams, and low sea-cliffs, often on clay soils, especially eroding clay banks of rivers and by the sea, throughout Britain and Ireland.

Flowering time: February to April.

COLTSFOOT IS ONE of the most welcome signs of coming spring, sometimes appearing in great crowds on roadsides or river-banks. It is a colonist of open ground on a range of soils, and is indeed one of the first plants to invade ground left bare by retreating Alpine glaciers. Coltsfoot has been used to treat coughs and chest illness since ancient times (*tussis*, as in Tussilago, is Latin for cough). It has also been smoked as a herbal tobacco – either to cure or start a cough. The hairy parachutes from the seeds, in fact the modified calyx, were dried and used in tinder-boxes for lighting fires and pipes.

Coltsfoot (Tussilago farfara) *blooms as early as February, sending up its golden-yellow flowers on stems covered with purplish scales. When the flowers start to die down, the triangular- to heart-shaped leaves appear. Covered at first with a whitish down, they soon become green above but retain the cobwebby effect underneath.*

SPECIES INFORMATION	
COMMON NAME	Butterbur
SCIENTIFIC NAME	Petasites hybridus
RELATED SPECIES	Winter Heliotrope, Coltsfoot
HEIGHT/SPREAD	20–30 cm tall
FLOWERING TIME	February–April
HABITAT	Roadsides and river-banks
Note: The massive flower-spikes are distinctive.	

Butterbur

DAISY AND DANDELION FAMILY (Compositae or Asteraceae)

BUTTERBUR IS ONE of our most handsome wild flowers of early spring, and quite a surprise for anybody who has not seen it before. The stout flower-spikes are impressive enough, but the massive, rhubarb-like leaves, forming great thickets in summer, are even more remarkable. They were once used to wrap butter, hence the English name of the plant. The first half of the scientific name also refers to the leaves, coming from the ancient Greek word for a broad-brimmed hat (*petasos*).

The common plant is the male. The female plant, with more numerous flower-heads in a spike that elongates up to 60 cm (24 in) in fruit, is restricted mainly to parts of northern England.

FLOWER TYPE

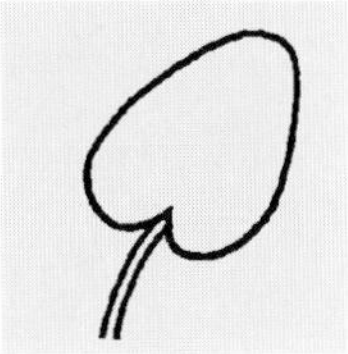

IDENTIFICATION

HABITAT

POPULATION

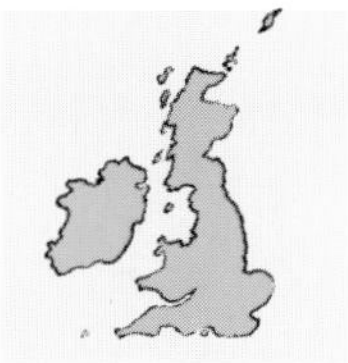

MAP

Butterbur (Petasites hybridus) *is another plant which flowers early in the year before the leaves. In the photograph at top left, there is a spike of the young male plant just emerging; at top right the spikes are further advanced and have expanded. In the photograph below, some of the enormous leaves are just beginning to appear.*

Size and appearance: A robust perennial, with large, creeping rhizomes, forming large, conspicuous patches, and stout flower-spikes 20–30 cm (8–12 in) tall in spring.

Leaves: Appearing after the flowers, all basal, rhubarb-like, up to 100 cm (3 ft) across, toothed, cobwebby beneath.

Flowers: Male and female flowers on separate plants; almost scentless, in lilac-pink heads, without ray florets, 50 or more in stout, conical spikes 10–30 cm (4–12 in) tall, the stem with huge, pinkish scale-leaves.

Fruits: Heads of 1-seeded fruits, each with a parachute of hairs.

Related or similar plants: Winter Heliotrope (p.306) has richly scented flowers in looser clusters at the same time as the leaves.

Habitat and distribution: Widespread but local on the banks of streams and rivers, in damp woods and on road-verges, especially on sandy or well-drained soils; throughout, but rare in northern Scotland.

Flowering time: February to April.

Winter Heliotrope

DAISY AND DANDELION FAMILY

(Compositae or Asteraceae)

SPECIES INFORMATION	
COMMON NAME	Winter Heliotrope
SCIENTIFIC NAME	Petasites fragrans
RELATED SPECIES	Butterbur, Coltsfoot
HEIGHT/SPREAD	15–25 cm tall
FLOWERING TIME	November–March
HABITAT	Roadsides and streamsides

Note: The fragrant winter flowers are unmistakable.

FLOWER TYPE

IDENTIFICATION

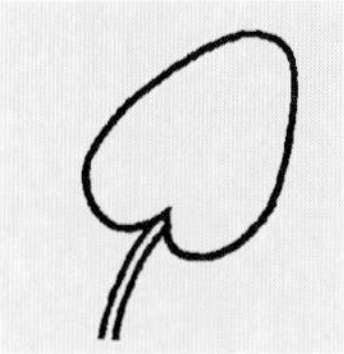

HABITAT

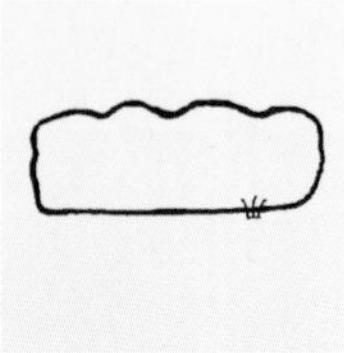

POPULATION

MAP

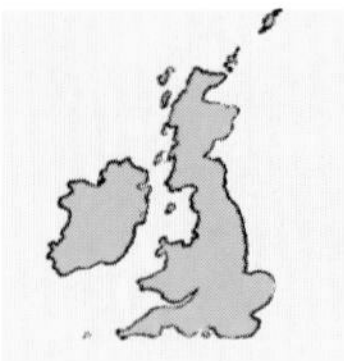

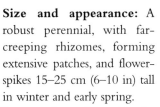

Size and appearance: A robust perennial, with far-creeping rhizomes, forming extensive patches, and flower-spikes 15–25 cm (6–10 in) tall in winter and early spring.

Leaves: Appearing with the flowers, all basal, heart-shaped, blunt, up to 20 cm (8 in) across, regularly toothed, green beneath.

Flowers: Richly scented, in lilac heads, with a few short outer ray florets, 50 or more in short, loose spike 3–6 cm (1⅕–2⅖ in) tall, the stem with narrow scale-leaves.

Fruits: Heads of 1-seeded fruits, each with a parachute of hairs.

Related or similar plants: Butterbur (p.305) has almost scentless flowers in larger, denser clusters, before the leaves.

Habitat and distribution: A widespread escape from gardens established on roadsides, in grassy waste places and beside rivers and streams throughout Britain and Ireland, but infrequent and mainly coastal in Scotland.

Flowering time: November to March, sometimes from October, but mostly in late winter.

Winter Heliotrope (Petasites fragrans) *is a creeping perennial which can carpet great swathes of ground. Unlike the previous two species, this produces its leaves and flowers are the same time, the latter being lilac in a loose head.*

WINTER HELIOTROPE, originally from the central Mediterranean region, including Sardinia and North Africa, was much planted in the 19th century in larger gardens. The exquisitely fragrant flowers, the scent reminiscent of cherry pie, during the cold winter months make it a very desirable plant. Unfortunately it has vigorous rhizomes and is a rampant garden weed. As a naturalised plant it tends to dominate native vegetation.

In Scotland especially, the related White Butterbur (*Petasites albus*) is sometimes naturalised on road-verges and elsewhere. It has fragrant white flowers in March–April, followed by leaves that are white-hairy beneath.

SPECIES INFORMATION	
COMMON NAME	Groundsel
SCIENTIFIC NAME	Senecio vulgaris
RELATED SPECIES	Ragwort, Oxford Ragwort
HEIGHT/SPREAD	5–40 cm tall
FLOWERING TIME	February–December
HABITAT	Open and cultivated ground
Note: A familiar weed with flower-heads like tiny shaving brush.	

Groundsel

DAISY AND DANDELION FAMILY
(Compositae or Asteraceae)

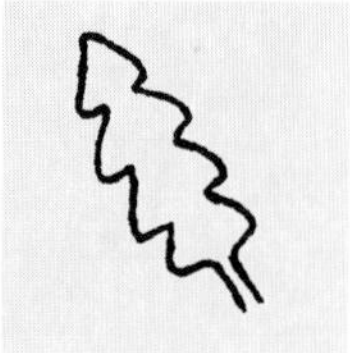

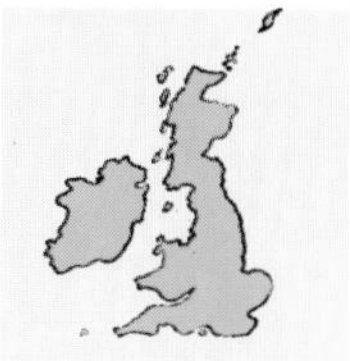

Size and appearance: An erect, branched, rather hairy annual 5–40 cm (2–16 in) tall.

Leaves: Coarsely and bluntly but usually shallowly lobed and irregularly toothed, hairy beneath.

Flowers: In yellow, shaving brush-like heads 4–5 mm ($\frac{1}{6}$–$\frac{1}{5}$ in) across, usually without ray florets, in loose, branched clusters.

Fruits: Heads of downy, 1-seeded fruits, each with a parachute of white hairs.

Related or similar plants: Ragwort (p.308) and Oxford Ragwort (p.309) have larger flower-heads and conspicuous ray florets.

Habitat and distribution: A ubiquitous weed of open and waste places, wall-tops, paths and pavements, gardens and other cultivated ground, rocky places, sand-dunes and shingle beaches.

Flowering time: February to December, but all through mild winters.

The first half of the scientific name of this plant and the ragworts refers to the white fruit-heads (Latin: *senex*, old man).

Groundsel (Senecio vulgaris) *is a ubiquitous weed of any bare, disturbed ground, from flower beds and allotments to scuffed waysides. It spreads its seeds by means of a feathery parachute and the assistance of the wind. The flowers heads are small, yellow and look like shaving brushes on short stalks in terminal clusters. As with all weeds of this kind, it can flower and set seed when only a couple of inches in height, but in ideal conditions can grow considerably taller.*

GROUNDSEL IS AN everyday weed, but still welcome as one of the first flowers of late winter and early spring, together with Chickweed (p.35), Shepherd's Purse (p.72) and Red Dead-nettle (p.234). Both Groundsel and Chickweed are fed as greenstuff to caged birds. Groundsel has a very short life-cycle, going from germination to shedding seed in just a few weeks. This, combined with the effective seed dispersal by the wind, makes it a most successful colonist and weed. Occasional populations of plants with short ray florets may derive from infrequent crossing and subsequent back-crossing with Oxford Ragwort (p.309). Similar plants occur here and there on coastal shingle beaches.

Ragwort

DAISY AND DANDELION FAMILY
(Compositae or Asteraceae)

SPECIES INFORMATION	
COMMON NAME	Ragwort
SCIENTIFIC NAME	Senecio jacobaea
RELATED SPECIES	Oxford Ragwort
HEIGHT/SPREAD	30–150 cm tall
FLOWERING TIME	April–November
HABITAT	Grassland and sand-dunes

Note: An abundant yellow weed of pastures in summer.

FLOWER TYPE

IDENTIFICATION

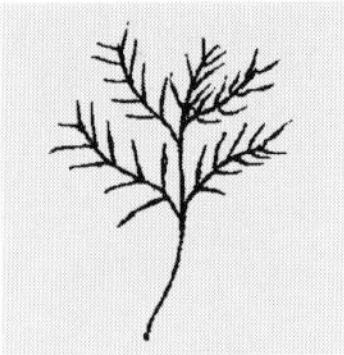

HABITAT

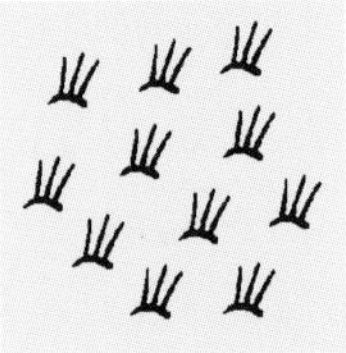

POPULATION

MAP

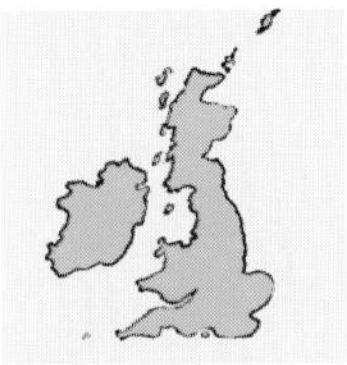

Size and appearance: A rather hairy biennial or short-lived perennial with usually a single erect, leafy stem 30–150 cm (12–60 in) tall.
Leaves: Deeply lobed, with a larger end lobe, irregularly toothed, usually hairy beneath, the upper clasping the stem.
Flowers: In yellow heads 15–25 mm (⅗–1 in) across, with 12–15 conspicuous ray florets (sometimes absent in coastal plants), in branched, often dense, flat-topped clusters.
Fruits: Heads of 1-seeded fruits, each with a parachute of white hairs.
Related or similar plants: Oxford Ragwort (p.309) has lobed, toothed leaves and loose clusters of flower-heads.
Habitat and distribution: Widespread and common in pastures, also on waysides, waste ground, sand-dunes and shingle beaches.
Flowering time: April to November.

The yellow- and black-striped caterpillars of the Cinnabar Moth feed on Ragwort, accumulating its poisonous chemicals to protect themselves against predatory birds – hence their warning colours. In years when they are plentiful they can strip Ragwort plants completely of their leaves.

RAGWORT IS A very poisonous plant, which accounts for its abundance in pastures, since animals mostly avoid it when it is alive. However, it remains poisonous when dried, when it can be an even bigger menace should it find its way into hay, especially to horses. In July to August it can flower in great crowds, a magnificent sight if one is not a farmer or owner of horses. The leaves give off an unpleasant smell when bruised, hence one of its local names, 'Stinking Willie' or variations on that theme.

Ragwort (Senecio jacobaea) *can spread across a field quite quickly if left unchecked, making a welcome source of food for insects, including the caterpillars of the Cinnabar Moth. The golden-yellow, daisy-like flowers are in large, dense, flat-topped terminal clusters above deeply lobed leaves, which usually have a larger end lobe.*

SPECIES INFORMATION	
COMMON NAME	Oxford Ragwort
SCIENTIFIC NAME	Senecio squalidus
RELATED SPECIES	Oxford Ragwort
HEIGHT/SPREAD	20–60 cm tall
FLOWERING TIME	April–November
HABITAT	Walls, wasteground and railways

Note: A yellow 'daisy' of waste ground.

Oxford Ragwort

DAISY AND DANDELION FAMILY

(Compositae or Asteraceae)

OXFORD RAGWORT HAS one of the most interesting stories of any introduced plant. Originally a relatively scarce species from the mountains of southern Europe, the plant escaped from the Oxford Botanic Garden on to walls in the city, where it was first spotted in 1794. During the 19th century it moved along an expanding railway network to other parts of the country. It reached London along the Great Western Railway. Bombing during the Second World War and subsequent redevelopment, not to mention more recent urban decay, gave the plant a new lease of life. It was in Ireland, around Cork City, by the early 19th century, but has spread further only in recent years. Oxford Ragwort is continuing to spread today.

FLOWER TYPE

IDENTIFICATION

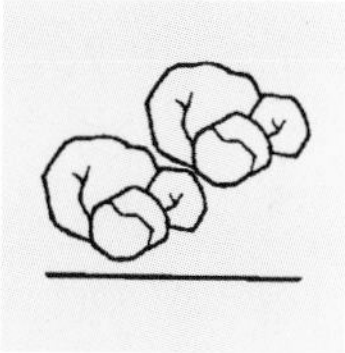

HABITAT

POPULATION

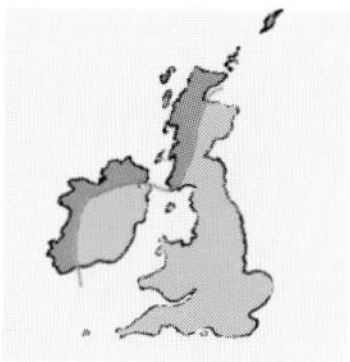

MAP

Size and appearance: An erect or semi-erect, branched annual, biennial or perennial 20–60 cm (8–24 in) tall.

Leaves: Compound, deeply lobed into narrow, pointed, irregularly toothed segments, the upper clasping the stem.

Flowers: In bright yellow heads 15–25 mm (⅝–1 in) across, always with ray florets, in loose, branched, flat-topped clusters.

Fruits: Heads of 1-seeded fruits, each with a parachute of white hairs.

Related or similar plants: Ragwort (p.308) has more deeply toothed leaves and denser, flat-topped clusters of flower-heads.

Habitat and distribution: Widespread but local in mainly urban habitats, on walls, waste ground, paths and road-verges, and derelict buildings, even as a garden weed, but especially on railway ballast, through most of Britain; in Ireland, mainly in and around Belfast, Cork and Dublin.

Flowering time: April to November.

Oxford Ragwort (Senecio squalidus) *has the golden-yellow, daisy-like heads of the previous species, but it is a much smaller, branched and straggling plant. It is virtually hairless and its leaves are rather glossy, deeply lobed into narrow, pointed, irregularly toothed segments. A plant of waste places, paths, derelict sites, walls and railway lines, the photograph below shows it growing in the latter habitat.*

Carline Thistle

DAISY AND DANDELION FAMILY
(Compositae or Asteraceae)

SPECIES INFORMATION	
COMMON NAME	Carline Thistle
SCIENTIFIC NAME	Carlina vulgaris
RELATED SPECIES	Other thistles
HEIGHT/SPREAD	15–60 cm tall
FLOWERING TIME	July–October
HABITAT	Dry grassland

Note: One of our few native 'everlasting flowers'.

FLOWER TYPE

IDENTIFICATION

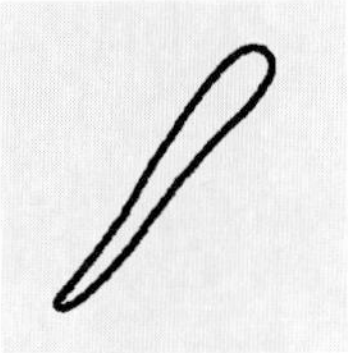

HABITAT

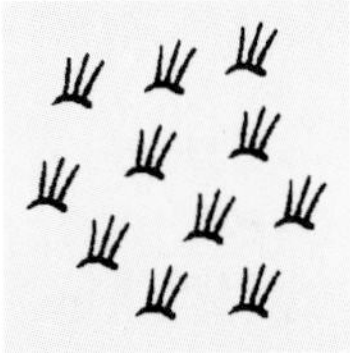

POPULATION

MAP

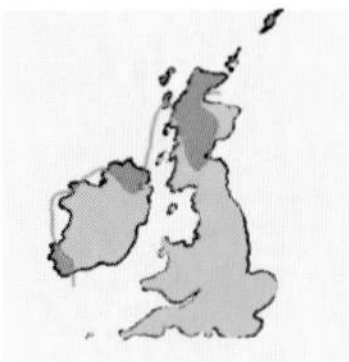

Size and appearance: An erect, often cottony-downy, spiny, branched biennial 15–60 cm (6–24 in) tall.

Leaves: Oblong to narrowly oval, lobed and with wavy, spiny margins, the lower short-stalked, the upper clasping the stem.

Flowers: Solitary or 2–3 together, yellowish-brown, in heads 15–35 mm (⅝–1⅜ in) across, surrounded by long, straw-coloured, papery, petal-like bracts and an outer layer of green, spiny bracts.

Fruits: Heads of hairy, 1-seeded fruits, each with a parachute of hairs.

Related or similar plants: None of the other thistles has the straw-coloured, papery 'flower' of bracts.

Habitat and distribution: A local plant of dry grassland, rocky ground, sand-dunes, shingle beaches and waysides, mostly on chalk and limestone or on lime-rich soils; almost throughout, but mostly coastal in many areas, especially in Scotland.

Flowering time: July to October.

This is our only species of carline thistle. It is said that a larger-flowered species, Stemless Thistle (*Carlina acaulis*), which is a distinctive plant of pastures in the Alps and other European mountains, gave rise to the name of these plants. Towards the end of the 9th century, the Emperor Charlemagne of France, crossing mountains with an undernourished army, was able to use the stout flower-buds as a source of greens to prevent scurvy and other diseases among his troops. His Latinised name has since been applied to this group of unusual thistles.

CARLINE THISTLE IS quite a feature of the dry, lime-rich, grassy habitats in which it grows. The dead plants persist through the winter as 'everlasting flowers'. The long, papery, petal-like bracts spread open during dry weather and close up again when it is wet or misty.

Carline Thistle (Carlina vulgaris) *is a distinctive plant which is not likely to be confused with other members of the thistle family. Its terminal heads, either singly or in small groups, are yellow-brown and unrayed with long, straw-coloured, papery bracts and an outer layer of green, spiny bracts.*

SPECIES INFORMATION	
COMMON NAME	Lesser Burdock
SCIENTIFIC NAME	Arctium minus
RELATED SPECIES	Greater Burdock
HEIGHT/SPREAD	50–150 cm tall
FLOWERING TIME	June–September
HABITAT	Woods, hedgerows and waste places

Note: A large-leaved feature of woods.

Lesser Burdock

DAISY AND DANDELION FAMILY
(Compositae or Asteraceae)

Size and appearance: A robust, downy biennial, with numerous leafy, branched stems 50–150 cm (20–60 in) tall
Leaves: Oval, with a heart-shaped base, up to 50 cm long, cottony beneath, with a long, hollow stalk, the upper smaller and narrower.
Flowers: Purple, in spherical heads 15–20 mm (3/5–4/5 in) across, surrounded by dense, narrow, scale-like, hooked bracts, in long, loose clusters.
Fruits: Egg-shaped heads or burs, enclosed by stiff, hooked scales derived from the bracts.
Related or similar plants: Greater Burdock has solid leaf-stalks and larger flower-heads and burs.
Habitat and distribution: Widespread and common in dry woods, scrub and hedgerows, on waysides and in waste places, throughout Britain and Ireland.
Flowering time: June to September.

THE HOOKED BURS, each shed as a single unit, adhere readily to clothing or fur, efficiently dispersing the 1-seeded fruits enclosed within. This ability to stick fast has made the fruits irresistible to generations of children. Consequently, the latest in Lesser Burdock's long line of numerous local names is Velcro-plant. The young shoots and the roots are edible, and the plant is an essential ingredient in that traditional northern beverage, Dandelion and Burdock.

At an annual fair on the second Friday in August, the Burry Man, his flannel costume densely studded with these burs, parades silently around South Queensferry in West Lothian. The plant is such a feature of woods and waysides that it often appeared as a detail in the work of John Constable, George Stubbs and other English artists.

Top *Lesser Burdock has smaller flower heads than the species below; the purple florets are longer than the purple-tipped, hooked bracts.*

Bottom *Greater Burdock* (Arctium lappa) *is similar but has broader basal leaves with solid stalks, and flower-heads 30–40 mm (1 1/5–1 3/5 in) across. Widespread in southern Britain, north to south Yorkshire, and can also be found at a few sites in Ireland.*

FLOWER TYPE

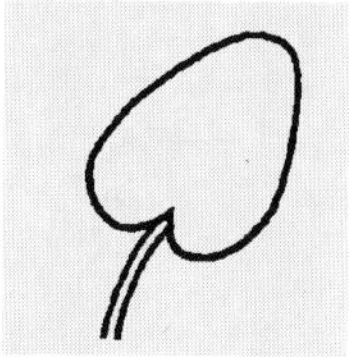

IDENTIFICATION

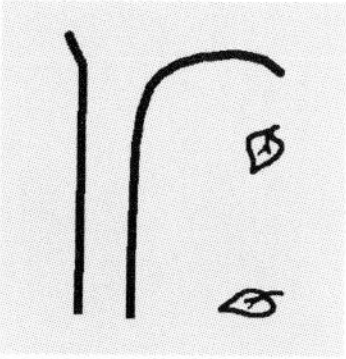

HABITAT

POPULATION

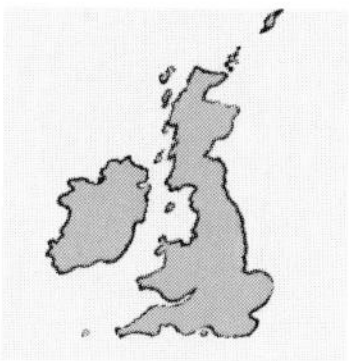

MAP

Common Thistle

DAISY AND DANDELION FAMILY

(Compositae or Asteraceae)

SPECIES INFORMATION	
COMMON NAME	Common Thistle, Spear Thistle
SCIENTIFIC NAME	Cirsium vulgare
RELATED SPECIES	Creeping Thistle
HEIGHT/SPREAD	30–180 cm tall
FLOWERING TIME	July–October
HABITAT	Grassland and waste places

Note: The common, spiny, large-headed thistle.

FLOWER TYPE

IDENTIFICATION

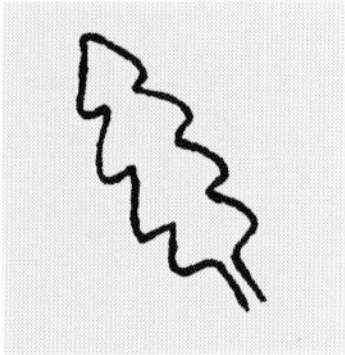

HABITAT

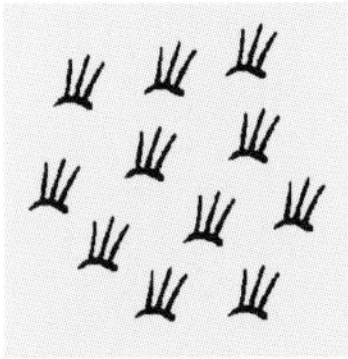

POPULATION

MAP

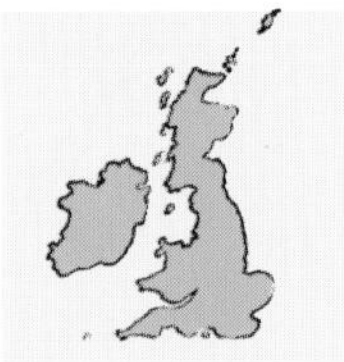

Size and appearance: An erect, leafy, fiercely spiny, hairy annual or biennial 30–180 cm (12–72 in) tall, the stem cottony, with spiny wings.
Leaves: Spear-shaped, deeply lobed and toothed, each tooth with a sharp spine, with a long, narrow end lobe.
Flowers: Purple, scented, in egg-shaped heads 30–50 mm (1⅕–2 in) across, surrounded by spine-tipped, green scale-like bracts, solitary or in small, loose clusters.
Fruits: Heads of 1-seeded fruits, each with a parachute of soft, feathery (thistle-down) hairs.
Related or similar plants: Stemless Thistle is stemless or nearly so, with very wavy, spiny leaves; Creeping Thistle (p.313), is a perennial with non-spiny, mauve flower-heads 15–20 mm (⅗–⅘ in) across.
Habitat and distribution: Ubiquitous in pastures, hedgerows, waste places and neglected gardens, on waysides, disturbed ground and shingle beaches.
Flowering time: July to October.

THIS IS PERHAPS the commonest thistle, but also one of the most attractive. It is the main source of the thistle-down that blows about in late summer. It is a good plant for the wild garden, because it supports so much wildlife. Like other thistles, the flowers are very attractive to bumble-bees, butterflies and other insects. The fruits are often eaten by beetle larvae, and the large flower-heads become home to a whole community of other 'mini-beasts' as the fruits ripen. Goldfinches eat the ripe fruits.

Stemless or Dwarf Thistle (*Cirsium acaule*) has similar but slightly smaller flowers but is a stemless (or nearly so) perennial, with numerous rosettes of deeply cut, wavy, spine-edged leaves. Flowering July–September, it is locally common in chalk and limestone grassland in southern and eastern England and South Wales.

Common Thistle (Cirsium vulgare) *has a large head with spine-tipped, green, scale-like bracts topped by a head of purple disc-florets. These are much in demand by visiting insects as a valuable nectar source.*

SPECIES INFORMATION	
COMMON NAME	Creeping Thistle
SCIENTIFIC NAME	Cirsium arvense
RELATED SPECIES	Other thistles
HEIGHT/SPREAD	50–150 cm tall
FLOWERING TIME	June–September
HABITAT	Waste places and waysides

Note: The only thistle with far-creeping roots, forming patches.

Creeping Thistle

DAISY AND DANDELION FAMILY

(Compositae or Asteraceae)

Size and appearance: A vigorous perennial, with extensive, far-creeping rhizomes and erect, unwinged, little-branched, leafy stems 50–150 cm (20–60 in) tall.
Leaves: Spear-shaped or oblong, often with triangular, spiny lobes, variably hairy.
Flowers: Mauve, in egg-shaped heads 10–15 mm (2/5–3/5 in) across, surrounded by purplish, scale-like bracts, solitary or in clusters of 2–5.
Fruits: Heads of 1-seeded fruits, each with a parachute of soft, feathery hairs.
Related or similar plants: Spear Thistle is annual and has larger, purple flower-heads.
Habitat and distribution: Common, often forming large patches in grassland and woodland clearings, on road-verges, waysides and waste ground, and as a weed of arable fields and gardens.
Flowering time: June to September.

Creeping Thistle (Cirsium arvense) *spreads successfully as it initially has a slender tap-root, from which arises far-creeping, whitish lateral roots bearing numerous non-flowering and flowering shoots. Its leaves are spear-shaped or oblong in outline but have triangular, spiny lobes. The upper leaves are stalkless, often half-clasping the stem. Male and female flowers are on separate heads, the male heads being round and the female oval-oblong in shape; both have pale-lilac flowers. The surrounding bracts are purplish and closely pressed to the flower head.*

FLOWER TYPE

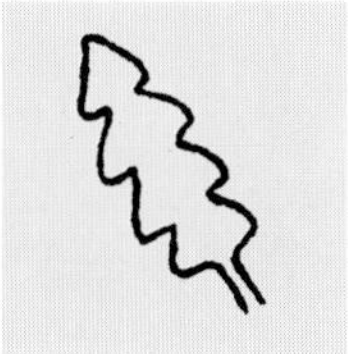

IDENTIFICATION

HABITAT

POPULATION

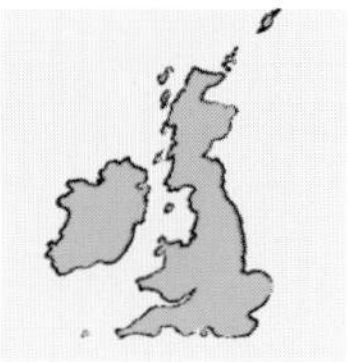

MAP

CREEPING THISTLE IS an invasive and persistent weed that can be very difficult to control. Even the smallest fragments of the brittle rhizomes will regenerate in a few weeks to produce new growth. The plant is very variable, for example in the amount of lobing and hairiness of the leaves and in flower colour, suggesting that it has evolutionary flexibility. Some populations have even developed resistance to particular weedkillers. It is a very successful weed, listed under the Weeds Control Order 1959, whereby a landowner is obliged by law to remove it from his or her land. It sets little good seed, as each clump or group of clumps, derived from a single individual, is unable to self-fertilise.

Marsh Thistle

DAISY AND DANDELION FAMILY

(Compositae or Asteraceae)

SPECIES INFORMATION	
COMMON NAME	Marsh Thistle
SCIENTIFIC NAME	Cirsium palustre
RELATED SPECIES	Other thistles
HEIGHT/SPREAD	50–180 cm tall
FLOWERING TIME	July–September
HABITAT	Marshes and damp grassland

Note: The whole plant is often purplish-tinged.

FLOWER TYPE

IDENTIFICATION

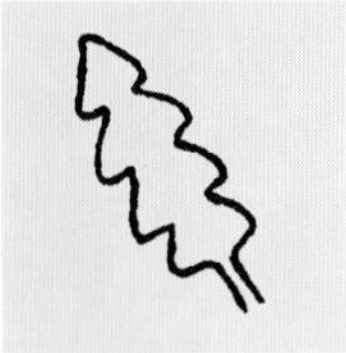

HABITAT

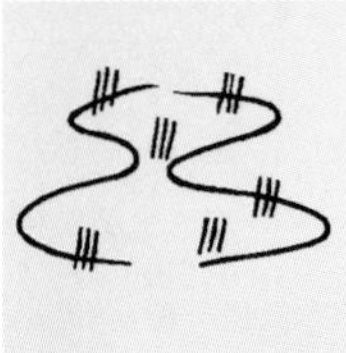

POPULATION

MAP

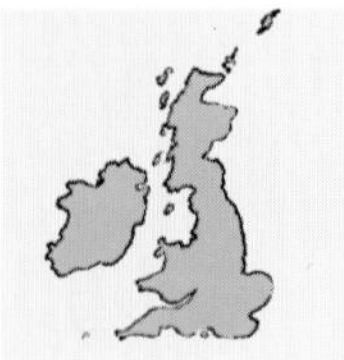

Size and appearance: An erect, hairy, dark green or purplish biennial, with usually a single winged, spiny, little-branched stem 50–180 cm (20–72 in) tall.

Leaves: Narrowly spear-shaped, deeply lobed, with densely spiny margins.

Flowers: Purple or white, in egg-shaped heads 15–20 mm (⅗–⅘ in) across, surrounded by weakly spine-tipped, purplish or green, scale-like bracts, in crowded, leafy clusters.

Fruits: Heads of 1-seeded fruits, each with a parachute of soft, feathery hairs.

Related or similar plants: Creeping Thistle (p.313) is perennial and the mauve flower-heads are in looser clusters.

Habitat and distribution: Widespread and often common, especially in the north and west, in marshes, damp woods and wet, grassy places, and on sea-cliffs in the west, especially on more lime-poor soils throughout Britain and Ireland.

Flowering time: July to September.

THIS ATTRACTIVE AND rather stately thistle is a feature of marshy ground, especially in damp grassland in the north and west. Here the great, purplish leaf-rosettes and the tall flowering stems are often a characteristic feature of the landscape. The flowers attract large numbers of bumblebees and other insects.

Marsh Thistle (Cirsium palustre) *has a hairy and cottony stem with spiny wings all the way up to the flower head. These are short-stalked in crowded leafy clusters; the flowers are usually purple, but sometimes white-flowered plants are found. The flowers are surrounded by weakly spiny-tipped, purplish or green, scale-like bracts. Where the terminal bud is damaged, the plant may produce side branches, which also have spiny wings and end in clusters of flowers.*

SPECIES INFORMATION	
COMMON NAME	Nodding Thistle, Musk Thistle
SCIENTIFIC NAME	Carduus nutans
RELATED SPECIES	Other thistles
HEIGHT/SPREAD	50–120 cm tall
FLOWERING TIME	May–August
HABITAT	Open ground and dry grasslands

Note: The large, nodding, purple flower-heads are characteristic.

Nodding Thistle

DAISY AND DANDELION FAMILY (Compositae or Asteraceae)

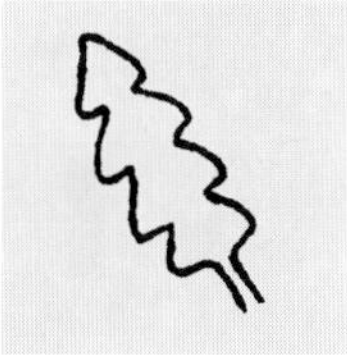

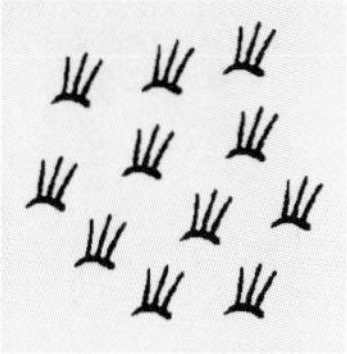

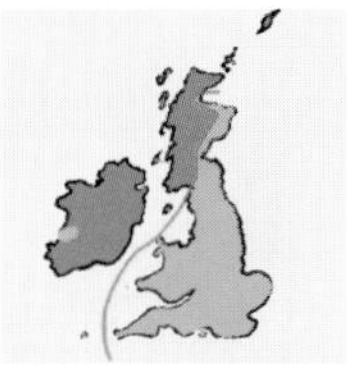

Size and appearance: A biennial with erect, spiny-winged, branched, leafy stems 50–120 cm (20–48 in) tall.

Leaves: The basal elliptical, with wavy margins, the stem leaves deeply lobed, the lobes spine-tipped.

Flowers: Reddish-purple, in egg-shaped heads c. 5 cm (2 in) across, surrounded by purplish, cottony-hairy, turned-back, sharp-tipped, scale-like bracts, solitary on long spineless stalks, nodding, scented.

Fruits: Heads of 1-seeded fruits, each with a parachute of soft, feathery hairs.

Related or similar plants: Woolly Thistle has similar large, but densely cobwebby-hairy flower-heads.

Habitat and distribution: Widespread and locally common, often forming patches in dry grassland, on disturbed ground and field margins, sand-dunes and waysides, on lime-rich soils, especially on chalk and limestone, throughout England and Wales; rare in Scotland and in Ireland only around Galway Bay.

Flowering time: May to August.

Bottom right *Woolly Thistle* (Cirsium eriophorum)*, another thistle with large, purple flowers that grows on lime-rich soils, has huge basal leaves, white-cottony beneath, always with two rows of upward-pointing spiny-lobes, unwinged cottony stems, and almost spherical, cobwebby-hairy flower-heads 5–7.5 cm. (2–3 in) across. It is very local in dry grassland in southern Britain, north to County Durham.*

THIS VERY HANDSOME thistle is easily recognised by the large, nodding heads. It makes a good garden plant, but it is seen at its best dotting dry grassland, or in a crowd on a bare chalky wayside. The scented flowers attract large numbers of bumble-bees and other insects.

Bottom left *The photograph clearly shows the sharp-tipped, scale-like bracts of the Nodding Thistle.*

Top *Nodding Thistle* (Carduus nutans) *is widespread on disturbed ground with well-drained soils, particularly on chalk and limestone.*

Saw-wort

DAISY AND DANDELION FAMILY

(Compositae or Asteraceae)

SPECIES INFORMATION	
COMMON NAME	Saw-wort
SCIENTIFIC NAME	Serratula tinctoria
RELATED SPECIES	Knapweed
HEIGHT/SPREAD	10–100 cm tall
FLOWERING TIME	July–September
HABITAT	Heaths and woods

Note: Like a knapweed, but with smaller flower-heads.

FLOWER TYPE

IDENTIFICATION

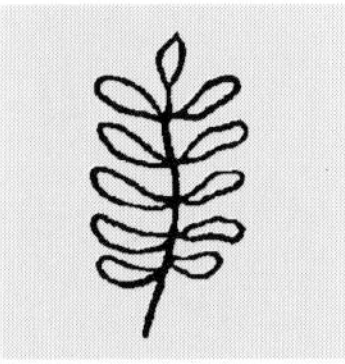

HABITAT

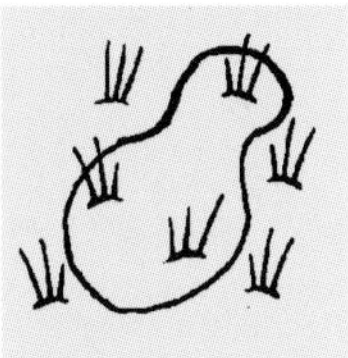

POPULATION

MAP

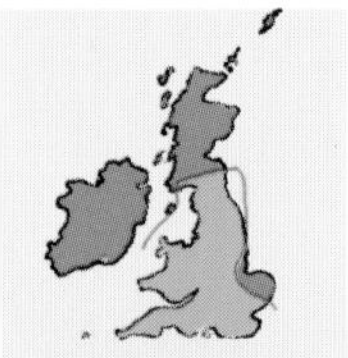

Size and appearance: A hairless perennial, with erect, tough, leafy stems 10–100 cm (4–40 in) tall.

Leaves: Stalked, oval to spear-shaped or deeply lobed, finely toothed, the upper stalkless, clasping.

Flowers: Purple, in narrowly egg-shaped heads 15–20 mm ($\frac{3}{5}$–$\frac{4}{5}$ in) long, surrounded by scale-like purplish bracts, usually in a loose cluster.

Fruits: Heads of 1-seeded fruits, each with a plume of hairs, enclosed by the persistent bracts.

Related or similar plants: Greater Knapweed (p.317) and Common Knapweed (p.318) have larger, solitary flower-heads.

Habitat and distribution: Widespread but very local in rough or damp grassland, heaths and open woods, on lime-rich or somewhat lime-poor soils, throughout England and Wales, except for most of East Anglia; in Scotland, only in Galloway.

Flowering time: July to September.

SAW-WORT IS a very variable species, especially in growth habit and leaf dissection. Much of the variation relates to the range of soils and habitats in which it grows. For example, compact plants not more than 15 cm tall occur in coastal heaths in south-west England, whereas plants from woodland can be up to 100 cm (40 in) tall and bushy in habit.

The leaves yield a greenish-yellow dye similar to that obtained from Weld (p.84). The second half of the scientific name denotes that Saw-wort is a dye-plant (Latin: *tinctorius*, used in dyeing).

Saw-wort (Serratula tinctoria) *disperses its seeds, as do many thistles, by the use of a pappus, a collection of hairs which is borne away on the wind, carrying the seeds with it. In this case, the hairs are stiff and simple with some other thistles they are soft and simple and yet in others, soft and feathery.*

SPECIES INFORMATION	
COMMON NAME	Greater Knapweed
SCIENTIFIC NAME	Centaurea scabiosa
RELATED SPECIES	Common Knapweed
HEIGHT/SPREAD	50–180 cm tall
FLOWERING TIME	June–August
HABITAT	Dry grassland

Note: The knapweed with deeply lobed leaves.

Greater Knapweed

DAISY AND DANDELION FAMILY

(Compositae or Asteraceae)

Size and appearance: A hairy perennial, with erect, branched stems 50–180 cm (20–72 in) tall.

Leaves: Stalked, deeply lobed, the margins of the lobes toothed, the stem leaves stalkless.

Flowers: Reddish-purple, in solitary head 30–50 mm (1⅕–2 in) across, with long-stalked outer ray florets and surrounded by scale-like green bracts, with brown, toothed margins.

Fruits: Heads of 1-seeded fruits, each with a crwon of bristly hairs, enclosed by the persistent bracts.

Related or similar plants: Common Knapweed (p.318) has unlobed or only slightly lobed leaves, although the flower-heads sometimes have long, stalked ray florets.

Habitat and distribution: Widespread in dry grassland and scrub, on hedge-banks, road-verges, sand-dunes and sea-cliffs, especially on lime-rich soils. through much of England and Wales; rare and mostly eastern in Scotland, and local in Ireland.

Flowering time: June to August.

FLOWER TYPE

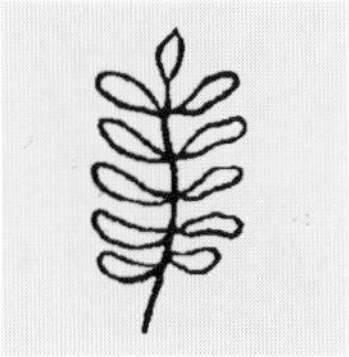
IDENTIFICATION

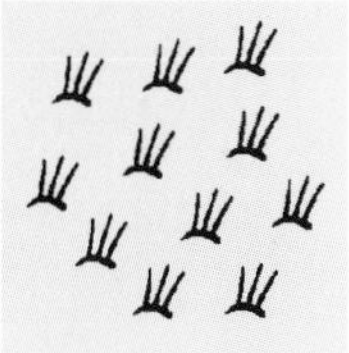
HABITAT

POPULATION

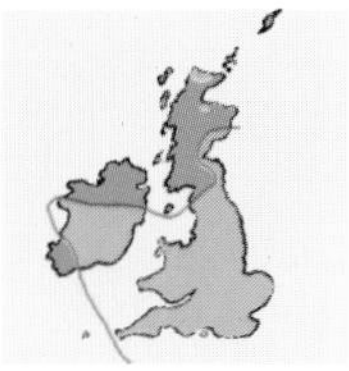
MAP

GREATER KNAPWEED IS a conspicuous plant that is, in inland districts at least, a good indicator plant for chalk or limestone. The flowers attract large numbers of bumble-bees and butterflies. The large, stalked ray florets are sterile, but serve to make the flower-head more conspicuous to foraging insects.

We have few native knapweeds in Britain, but they comprise a large group of over 220 species across Europe. Also, our knapweeds have purplish flowers, whereas in southern Europe the different species exhibit various shades of red, purple, lilac, pink, white or yellow.

Top *Greater Knapweed* (Centaurea scabiosa) *has a stunning flower with its long, rayed, outer florets. It is a tall and branched plant topped by solitary flowers on long stalks.*

Common Knapweed

DAISY AND DANDELION FAMILY
(Compositae or Asteraceae)

SPECIES INFORMATION	
COMMON NAME	Common Knapweed, Hardheads
SCIENTIFIC NAME	Centaurea nigra
RELATED SPECIES	Greater Knapweed
HEIGHT/SPREAD	30–180 cm tall
FLOWERING TIME	June–September
HABITAT	Grassland
Note: The knapweed with unlobed or scarcely lobed leaves.	

FLOWER TYPE

IDENTIFICATION

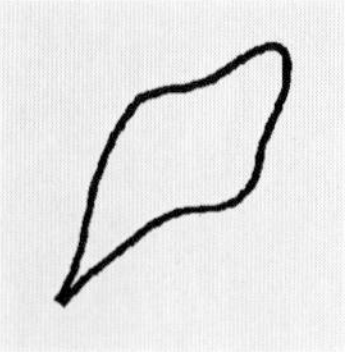

HABITAT

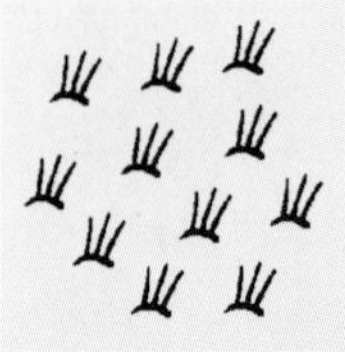

POPULATION

MAP

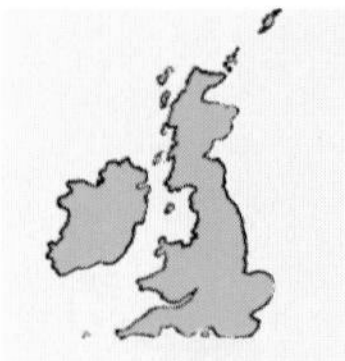

Size and appearance: A downy perennial, with erect, tough, usually branched stems 30–180 cm (12–72 in) tall.

Leaves: Oval or spear-shaped, the upper much narrower.

Flowers: Reddish- or pinkish-purple, in solitary heads 20–40 mm ($\frac{4}{5}$–$1\frac{3}{5}$ in) across, rarely with long-stalked ray florets; surrounded by scale-like brown, fringed bracts.

Fruits: Heads of 1-seeded fruits, each with a crown of bristly hairs, enclosed by the persistent bracts.

Related or similar plants: Greater Knapweed (p.317) has deeply lobed leaves and flower-heads up to 50 mm (2 in) across.

Habitat and distribution: Widespread and common in dry and damp grasslands, on waysides and on sea-cliffs and sand-dunes; throughout, but not nearly so common as it once was over much of lowland England owing to the loss of old meadows.

Flowering time: June to September.

MANY COMMON KNAPWEED plants from the few surviving old lowland meadows flower earlier in the year than plants of the same species from other habitats. The flower-heads frequently have long-stalked ray florets similar to those of Greater Knapweed (p.317). The hard, knobbly flower-heads give Common Knapweed its other English name. Common Knapweed is an example of a plant that, although common, we ought to have more of in the countryside. We often forget how much of an older landscape has been lost since 1945, including at least 95 per cent of the old meadows in which so many colourful flowers once grew.

Common Knapweed (Centaurea nigra) *has reddish or pinkish-purple flowers in a solitary head. Occasionally a plant will be found with long-stalked ray florets as in the photograph top left. The flowers are surrounded by numerous, overlapping flat bracts, their top part broader, dull brown or blackish and feathered with long, fine teeth.*

SPECIES INFORMATION	
COMMON NAME	Chicory
SCIENTIFIC NAME	Cichorium intybus
RELATED SPECIES	Dandelion
HEIGHT/SPREAD	30–120 cm tall
FLOWERING TIME	July–October
HABITAT	Waste places and field margins

Note: The only pale blue-flowered 'dandelion'.

Chicory

DAISY AND DANDELION FAMILY
(Compositae or Asteraceae)

CHICORY IS PROBABLY NOT native, although it has been cultivated in England since at least the 16th century and has been established here for a long time as an escape. It is still widely cultivated, especially in gardens, where many prize it as a productive winter salad. It also has medicinal value as a diuretic and laxative. The roasted roots, which have a bitter taste, are used as a substitute for coffee, especially in central Europe. The flowers look their best in the morning, fading after midday.

Top *Chicory* (Cichorium intybus) *has pale-blue flowers set at the base of the leaves up the stem. They are 30-50 mm (1-2 in) across, sometimes solitary, but can be in clusters of up to three. There are no disc florets, the whole flower being composed of ray florets only.*

Bottom *A widespread but local plant of waysides, field margins and waste places, especially on chalk and limestone soils, it is often a rather untidy plant with its stiffly branched, zigzag stems.*

FLOWER TYPE

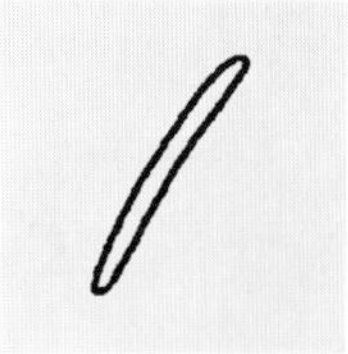

IDENTIFICATION

HABITAT

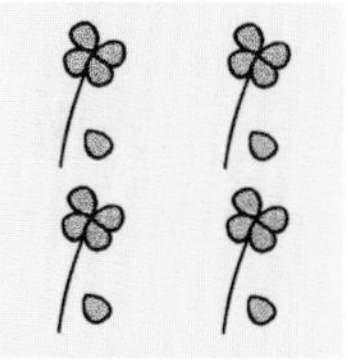

POPULATION

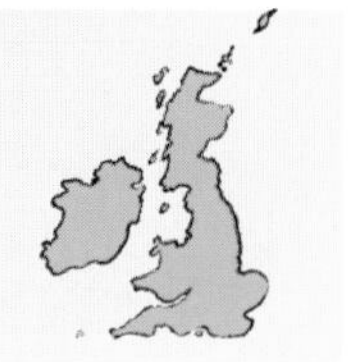

MAP

Size and appearance: An untidy perennial, with tough, erect, stiffly branched, zigzag stems 30–120 cm (12–48 in) tall.
Leaves: Basal rosettes, deeply and coarsely lobed, the upper spear-shaped, pointed.
Flowers: Pale blue, in heads 30–50 mm (1⅕–2 in) across, 1–3, in the angles of the upper leaves.
Fruits: Heads of nut-like, 1-seeded fruits, without hairs.
Related or similar plants: Chicory looks like no other plant.
Habitat and distribution: Widespread and locally common in dry waste places, waysides, field margins and sometimes grassland, especially on lime-rich soils; throughout, but commonest in the south and east, scattered in Scotland and rare in Ireland.
Flowering time: July to October, the flowers fading after midday.

Dandelion

DAISY AND DANDELION FAMILY

(Compositae or Asteraceae)

SPECIES INFORMATION	
COMMON NAME	Dandelion
SCIENTIFIC NAME	Taraxacum officinale
RELATED SPECIES	Chicory
HEIGHT/SPREAD	5–40 cm tall
FLOWERING TIME	March–October
HABITAT	Grassy and open places

Note: The weak, hollow flowering stem is diagnostic.

FLOWER TYPE

IDENTIFICATION

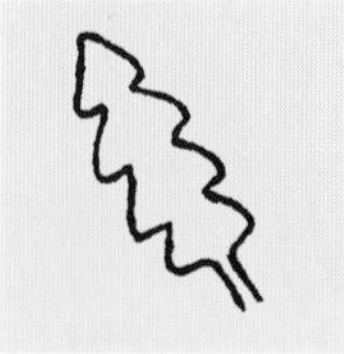

HABITAT

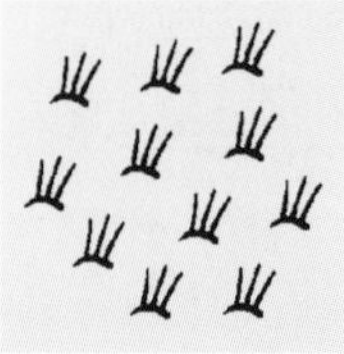

POPULATION

MAP

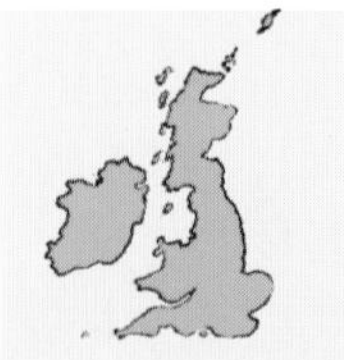

DANDELION IS ONE of those wild flowers that everybody thinks they know, but it can easily be confused with one of the other plants in the family with yellow 'dandelion' flowers. The solitary flower atop a weak, hollow, often reddish stalk is quite diagnostic, however, for the true Dandelion. Dandelion grows anywhere that is open or grassy. Since the plant is somewhat salt-tolerant, over recent decades it has colonised road-verges on a huge scale. The floral display in April can be spectacular.

Botanists divide the humble Dandelion into over 200 'microspecies', each based on arcane attributes such as variation in leaf-shape.

Dandelion is also a useful plant. The leaves make a bitter salad, which has become fashionable, with a distinct diuretic effect; the flowers are the basis of a country wine; and the roots make an acceptable substitute for coffee, particularly popular in central and eastern Europe. During the Second World War, latex (the milky sap) from dandelions provided the former Soviet Union with the rubber the country needed for its war effort.

Size and appearance: A hairless perennial, with a deep taproot, a rosette of basal leaves, and weak, hollow, erect, unbranched, often reddish flowering stems 5–40 cm (2–16 in) tall.

Leaves: All in a basal rosette, deeply and coarsely lobed and toothed, sometimes with dark spots.

Flowers: In a solitary, yellow head 25–40 mm (1–1⅗ in) across, the outer ray florets often greenish, brownish or reddish beneath, surrounded by green, scale-like bracts, the outer back-turned.

Fruits: Heads of 1-seeded fruits, each with a parachute of feathery hairs.

Related or similar plants: Dandelion can be separated readily from similar members of the family with yellow 'dandelion' flowers.

Habitat and distribution: A ubiquitous plant of open and grassy places, sand-dunes, wet places, rocky and stony ground, road-verges, waysides, pavements and paths, and as a weed of allotments, flower-beds and lawns.

Flowering time: March to October, but all through mild winters, with a peak in spring.

Top *The familiar golden yellow flower of the Dandelion* (Taraxacum officinale) *composed of ray florets by the side of a head in fruit with its parachutes of feathery hairs ready to float the seeds away at the first puff of wind.*

Bottom right *A mass of Dandelions in full bloom.*

SPECIES INFORMATION	
COMMON NAME	Common Cat's-ear
SCIENTIFIC NAME	Hypochoeris radicata
RELATED SPECIES	Hawkbits
HEIGHT/SPREAD	10–60 cm tall
FLOWERING TIME	June–September
HABITAT	Grassland
Note: Branched flowering stem and hairy leaves.	

Common Cat's-ear

DAISY AND DANDELION FAMILY
(Compositae or Asteraceae)

FLOWER TYPE

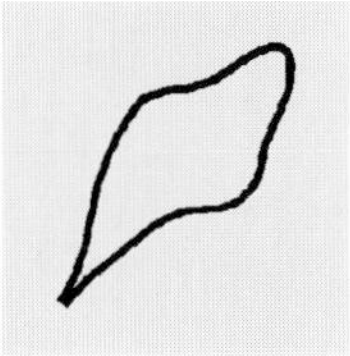

IDENTIFICATION

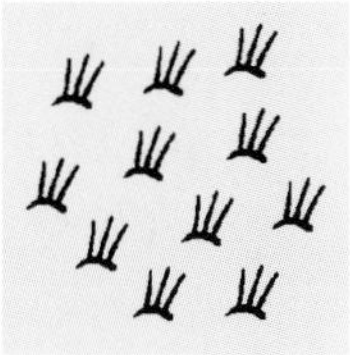

HABITAT

POPULATION

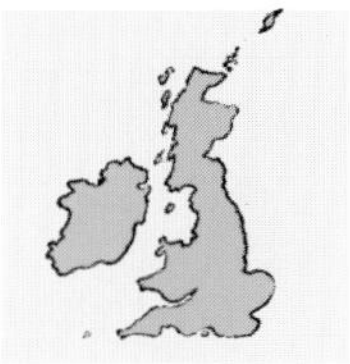

MAP

Size and appearance: A tufted, usually branched perennial 10–60 cm (4–24 in) tall.

Leaves: All in a basal rosette, deeply lobed and toothed, covered with rough hairs.

Flowers: In a solitary, yellow head 25–40 mm (1–1⅗ in) across, erect in bud, the outer ray florets greenish or greyish beneath, surrounded by green, scale-like bracts.

Fruits: Heads of 1-seeded fruits, each with a parachute of feathery hairs.

Related or similar plants: Lesser Hawkbit (p.322), has unbranched stems, and flowerheads 12–20 mm (½–⅘ in) across.

Habitat and distribution: Common in all types of shorter grassland, and on grassy heaths, as well as road-verges, sand-dunes and lawns, on a range of well-drained soils, but tending to avoid those that are more lime-rich, throughout Britain and Ireland.

Flowering time: June to September.

COMMON CAT'S-EAR is the most abundant of several widespread yellow, dandelion-like flowers. It is also the one most likely to occur on garden lawns or in parks and other anemity grasslands, where it forms prominent green patches in dry spells. The common name derives, rather obscurely, from the shape of a few tiny, leaf-like bracts on the flowering stems. The leaves have been eaten as a salad, but are not very interesting as food.

Common Cat's-ear (Hypochaeris radicata) *is a common and widespread plant coping as well with waste places, as in the photograph above, as it does with sand dunes (left) and grassy meadows (right). The dandelion-like flowers are set on sparingly branched stems, up which are scattered a few scale-like bracts. Further bracts surround the flower, the outer florets of which are greenish or greyish in colour.*

Lesser Hawkbit

DAISY AND DANDELION FAMILY

(Compositae or Asteraceae)

SPECIES INFORMATION	
COMMON NAME	Lesser Hawkbit
SCIENTIFIC NAME	Leontodon taraxacoides
RELATED SPECIES	Rough Hawkbit
HEIGHT/SPREAD	10–25 cm tall
FLOWERING TIME	June–September
HABITAT	Dry grassland

Note: The drooping buds and grey backs to the ray florets.

FLOWER TYPE

IDENTIFICATION

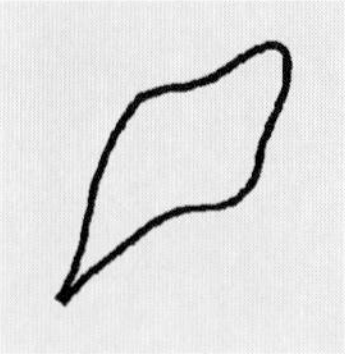

HABITAT

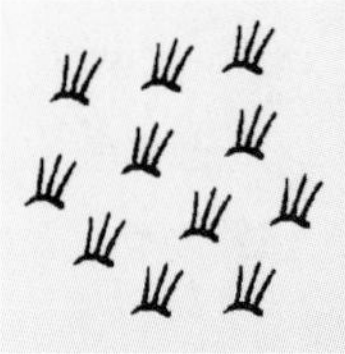

POPULATION

MAP

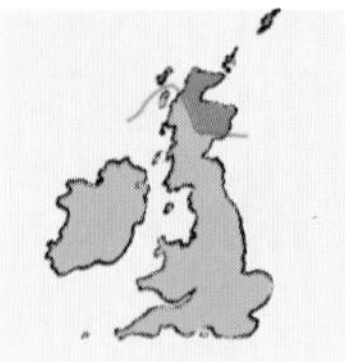

Top *Lesser Hawkbit* (Leontodon saxatilis) *has a basal rosette of leaves with solitary, dandelion-like, yellow flowers, greyish below.*

Bottom *Rough Hawkbit* (Leontodon hispidus) *is similar but hairier and taller, up to 40 cm (16 in), with flower-heads 25–40 mm (1–1 ⅗ in) across, the outer ray florets reddish or orange beneath. Its main distribution extends further north, to central Scotland, with a stronger preference for lime-rich soils.*

Size and appearance: A variably hairy, tufted perennial, with leafless flowering stems 10–25 cm (4–10 in) tall.
Leaves: All in a basal rosette, oblong to spear-shaped, wavy-toothed or lobed, sparsely hairy.
Flowers: In solitary, yellow heads 20–25 mm (⅘–1 in) across, drooping in bud, the outer ray florets greyish beneath, surrounded by green, scale-like bracts.
Fruits: Heads of 1-seeded fruits, each with a parachute of feathery hairs.
Related or similar plants: Rough Hawkbit has flower-heads 25–40 mm (1–1 ⅗ in) across.
Habitat and distribution: Common in dry grassland, especially heaths and sand-dunes; throughout, but rare in Scotland and northern Ireland.
Flowering time: June to September.

THIS IS ONE of the most widespread of a group of yellow, dandelion-like flowers of grassland.

SPECIES INFORMATION	
COMMON NAME	Autumn Hawkbit
SCIENTIFIC NAME	Leontodon autumnalis
RELATED SPECIES	Lesser Hawkbit
HEIGHT/SPREAD	10–60 cm tall
FLOWERING TIME	June–October
HABITAT	Grassy and open places

Note: Numerous, very deeply cut basal leaves.

Autumn Hawkbit

DAISY AND DANDELION FAMILY

(Compositae or Asteraceae)

AUTUMN HAWKBIT, as its name suggests, has a peak of flowering in late summer and continues flowering well into autumn. It is certainly the most conspicuous of the yellow dandelion-like wild flowers of late summer and early autumn. To identify the full range of the hawkbits and their other dandelion-like relatives, which are very difficult to tell apart, requires careful examination, with a lens, of leaf-hairs and other small features.

FLOWER TYPE

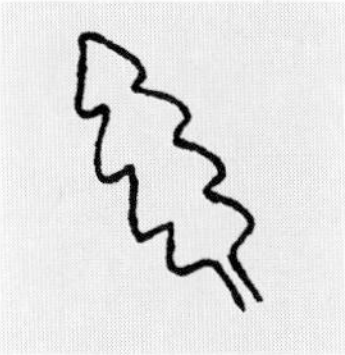

IDENTIFICATION

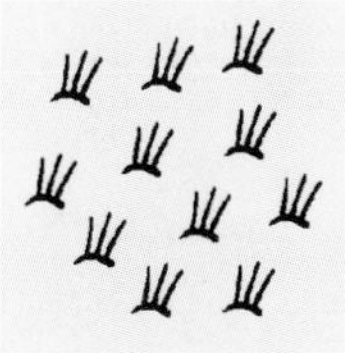

HABITAT

POPULATION

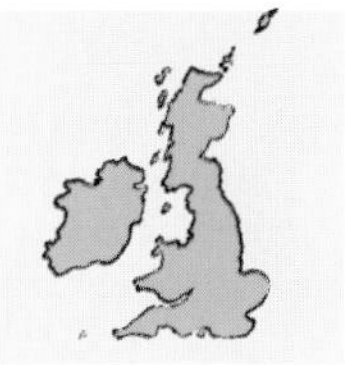

MAP

Size and appearance: An erect, slightly branched, sparsely hairy perennial 10–60 cm (4–24 in) tall.

Leaves: All in a basal rosette, very deeply lobed, shiny, more or less hairless.

Flowers: In a solitary, yellow head 12–35 mm (½–1⅜in) across, erect in bud, the outer ray florets often reddish-streaked beneath, surrounded by green, scale-like bracts.

Fruits: Heads of 1-seeded fruits, each with a parachute of feathery hairs.

Related or similar plants: Lesser Hawkbit (p.322), has unbranched stems and flower-heads 12–20 mm (½–⅘ in) across.

Habitat and distribution: Common in a range of dry and damp grassland, including lawns, on waysides and open stony ground such as lake-shores, especially on more lime-poor soils, throughout Britain and Ireland.

Flowering time: June to September, often into October.

Autumn Hawkbit (Leontodon autumnalis) *is another of the dandelion look-alikes. All its leaves are in a basal rosette, they are very deeply lobed, shiny and hairy to varying degrees, often just along the midrib on the underside. The flowers are solitary on branched stems. In profile, the base of the flowers widen gradually from the stem to the underneath of the outer ray-florets, which are often streaked with red beneath.*

Bristly Oxtongue

DAISY AND DANDELION FAMILY
(Compositae or Asteraceae)

SPECIES INFORMATION	
COMMON NAME	Bristly Oxtongue
SCIENTIFIC NAME	Picris echioides
RELATED SPECIES	Hawkweed Oxtongue
HEIGHT/SPREAD	30–100 cm tall
FLOWERING TIME	June–October
HABITAT	Grassland and disturbed ground

Note: The bristly leaves identify this as an oxtongue.

FLOWER TYPE

IDENTIFICATION

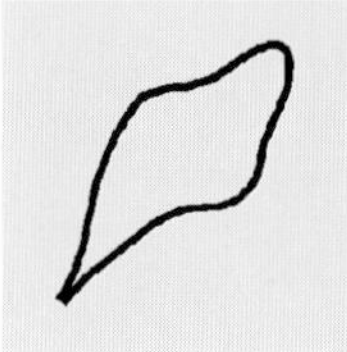

HABITAT

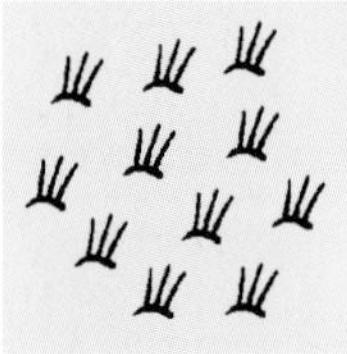

POPULATION

MAP

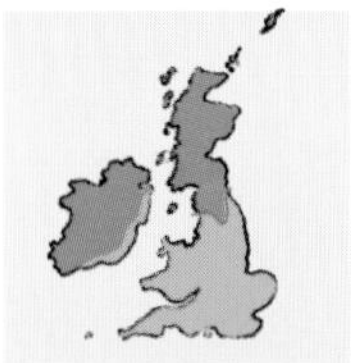

Size and appearance: A scruffy, semi-erect or weakly erect, bristly annual, biennial or short-lived perennial, with stiff, branched stems 30–100 cm (12–40 in) tall.

Leaves: Oblong, often coarsely toothed, covered with swollen-based prickly bristles, the upper smaller, heart-shaped, clasping the stem.

Flowers: In a pale yellow head 20–25 mm (⅘–1 in) across, with 5 large, triangular, pointed outer leaf-like bracts, in branched clusters.

Fruits: Heads of 1-seeded, long-beaked fruits, each with a 'parachute' of stiff, feathery hairs.

Related or similar plants: Hawkweed Oxtongue has spear-shaped lower leaves and narrow outer bracts.

Habitat and distribution: Local but sometimes frequent in rough grassland and disturbed ground, along field margins and road-verges, and on waste land, especially on lime-rich, clayey soils; north to Yorkshire, but mostly coastal in the West Country and Wales; in Ireland, only near the east coast.

Flowering time: June to October.

THE PLANT PRODUCES two different types of fruits. At the margin of each head, 3–5 of the fruits are larger, with a smaller parachute of hairs, and are shed close to the parent plant. This sort of seed variation within a single plant is a widespread phenomenon in flowering plants, giving some flexibility of adaptation to the habitat.

Top and bottom left *Bristly Oxtongue* (Picris echioides) *has yellow dandelion-like flowers, but the leaves have distinctive 'blisters' from the pale swollen-based bristles.*

Bottom right *Hawkweed Oxtongue* (Picris hieracioides) *has spear-shaped, somewhat lobed lower leaves, narrow outer bracts, and seeds without a long beak. It has a similar distribution to Bristly Oxtongue but is less common and is only a rare introduction to Ireland.*

SPECIES INFORMATION	
COMMON NAME	Goat's Beard
SCIENTIFIC NAME	Tragopogon pratensis
RELATED SPECIES	None
HEIGHT/SPREAD	30–80 cm tall
FLOWERING TIME	May–August
HABITAT	Grassy places and waysides

Note: The grass-like leaves are distinctive.

Goat's Beard

DAISY AND DANDELION FAMILY
(Compositae or Asteraceae)

Size and appearance: An erect annual, biennial or short-lived perennial 30–80 cm (12–32 in) tall, with a deep taproot.
Leaves: Oblong, often coarsely toothed, covered with swollen-based prickly bristles, the upper smaller, heart-shaped, clasping the stem.
Flowers: Yellow, in solitary, long-stalked heads 30–50 mm (1⅕–2 in) across, surrounded by 8 slender, pointed bracts up to 30 mm (1⅕ in) long.
Fruits: Large, conspicuous heads of 1-seeded fruits, each with a parachute of stiff, feathery hairs.
Related or similar plants: This plant is very distinctive and unlikely to be confused with other dandelion-like flowers.
Habitat and distribution: A widespread and locally common plant of dry grassland, hedge-banks, road-verges and waste ground; almost throughout, but absent from much of Scotland and very local in Ireland.
Flowering time: May to August; the flowers close after midday.

GOAT'S BEARD IS a rather distinguished-looking plant with its long bracts, and large fruiting 'clock'. Because the flowers close round about midday, and on dull days, the plant has earned the local name Jack (or John)-go-to-bed-at-noon. Gardeners sometimes cultivate the closely related purple-flowered Salsify as a root vegetable, and it even turns up in the wild from time to time as an escape or throw-out. The large fruits of Goat's Beard demonstrate clearly the features of the 'dandelion-type' seed-fruit unit and its dispersal mechanism.

Top *Goat's Beard* (Tragopogon pratensis) *has yellow dandelion-like flowers with narrow, fleshy, grass-like leaves sheathing around the stem, which is very slightly swollen under the flower heads.*

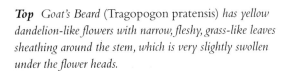

Bottom *Each fruit has a parachute of stiff, feathery hairs which form large, conspicuous heads in the grass before being dispersed by the wind.*

FLOWER TYPE

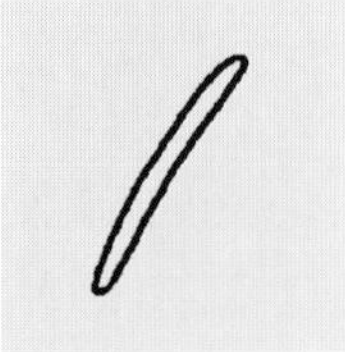

IDENTIFICATION

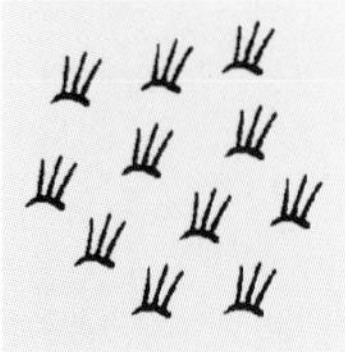

HABITAT

POPULATION

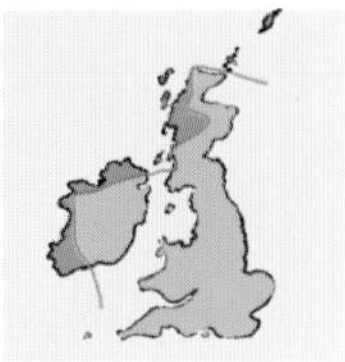

MAP

Perennial Sowthistle

DAISY AND DANDELION FAMILY

(Compositae or Asteraceae)

SPECIES INFORMATION	
COMMON NAME	Perennial or Corn Sowthistle
SCIENTIFIC NAME	Sonchus arvensis
RELATED SPECIES	Smooth Sowthistle
HEIGHT/SPREAD	50–150 cm tall
FLOWERING TIME	July–October
HABITAT	Cultivated land and waste ground

Note: The tallest and most conspicuous dandelion-like flower.

FLOWER TYPE

IDENTIFICATION

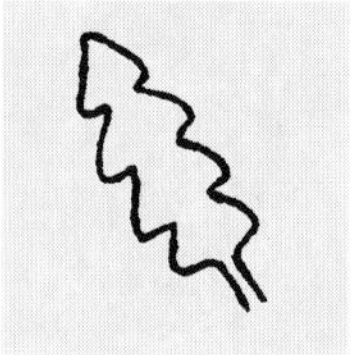

HABITAT

POPULATION

MAP

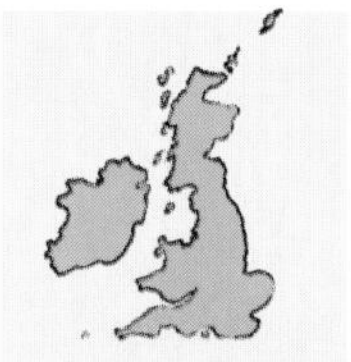

Size and appearance: A robust perennial, with a network of far-creeping rhizomes, producing large patches, and erect, leafy stems 50–150 cm (20–60 in) tall.

Leaves: Oblong to spear-shaped, deeply lobed and spiny-toothed, the upper smaller, clasping the stem.

Flowers: In solitary, yellow heads 30–50 mm (1⅕–2 in) across, slightly scented, surrounded by green, scale-like bracts, on long stalks covered with large, yellowish hairs.

Fruits: Heads of 1-seeded fruits, each with a parachute of hairs.

Related or similar plants: Smooth Sowthistle and Prickly Sowthistle (p.327) are annuals, with paler yellow flower-heads 20–25 mm (⅘–1 in) across.

Habitat and distribution: A common weed of cultivated land, field margins and waste ground, also on the banks of streams and rivers, on sand-dunes and shingle beaches; almost throughout but absent from some highland areas.

Flowering time: July to October.

PERENNIAL SOWTHISTLE IS one of the most handsome and striking wild flowers of late summer and autumn. However, it is also a pestilential weed. By means of vigorous rhizomes, it can produce quite extensive patches of growth even within a single season. The smallest fragments of chopped-up root are able to grow into new plants, making this a very serious weed if it is not controlled early enough. The large flowers are attractive to many insects, including bees and bumble-bees.

Perennial Sowthistle (Sonchus arvensis) *is a robust, showy plant with leafy stems and large, golden-yellow flowers, each set singly in a branched head. It flowers from mid-summer through to autumn. It is often called Corn Sowthistle as it occurs at the edges of fields of wheat and other cereals, but it is equally at home beside streams and in marshy fens. When it grows in reedbeds, it is over-topped by the reeds but, because of its showy yellow flowers, it is still possible to determine its presence.*

SPECIES INFORMATION	
COMMON NAME	Smooth Sowthistle
SCIENTIFIC NAME	Sonchus oleraceus
RELATED SPECIES	Perennial Sowthistle
HEIGHT/SPREAD	30–120 cm tall
FLOWERING TIME	June–October
HABITAT	Cultivated ground
Note: Pale-yellow, dandelion-like flowers.	

Smooth Sowthistle

DAISY AND DANDELION FAMILY

(Compositae or Asteraceae)

Size and appearance: Erect, branched, often red- or purple-tinged annual 30–120 cm (20–48 in) tall.

Leaves: Deeply and variably lobed, with a large end lobe and a pair of pointed flanges at the base, spiny-toothed, the upper clasping the stem.

Flowers: In pale-yellow heads 20–25 mm (⅘–1 in) across, the ray florets purplish beneath, surrounded by green, scale-like bracts, numerous in loose, branched clusters.

Fruits: Heads of 1-seeded fruits, each with a parachute of hairs.

Related or similar plants: Prickly Sowthistle is less branched, with more clustered flower-heads.

Habitat and distribution: A common weed of cultivated land, where it can be a troublesome weed, especially in vegetable crops and as a persistent weed of gardens, although it will grow in any open habitat, including all sorts of waste ground.

Flowering time: June to October.

THE FIRST HALF of the scientific name derives from *Sonchos*, the ancient Greek name for this plant. In Greece it is still on sale in markets for winter salad. The French feed this plant to edible snails to fatten them for the kitchen.

Bottom left and top right *Smooth Sowthistle* (Sonchus oleraceus) *is a hairless annual which varies a great deal in height. The leaves are deeply and variably lobed with the end lobe being much the largest; they are rather dull on top and paler beneath. The heads of yellow flowers are loosely clustered*

Bottom right *Prickly Sowthistle* (Sonchus asper) *is similar but less branched, with rather glossy green leaves that have rounded flanges at the base, and more clustered, darker yellow flower-heads. It is as widespread as Smooth Sowthislte, but more likely to be found away from human habitation and influence.*

Nipplewort

DAISY AND DANDELION FAMILY
(Compositae or Asteraceae)

SPECIES INFORMATION	
COMMON NAME	Nipplewort
SCIENTIFIC NAME	Lapsana communis
RELATED SPECIES	Wall Lettuce
HEIGHT/SPREAD	30–120 cm tall
FLOWERING TIME	June–October
HABITAT	Shady places and hedgerows

Note: Large numbers of small, pale yellow heads.

FLOWER TYPE

IDENTIFICATION

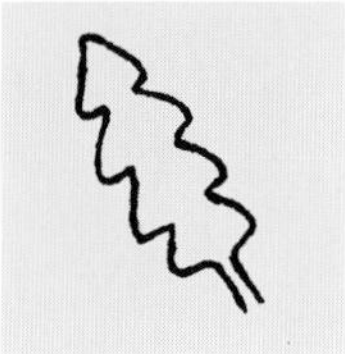

HABITAT

POPULATION

MAP

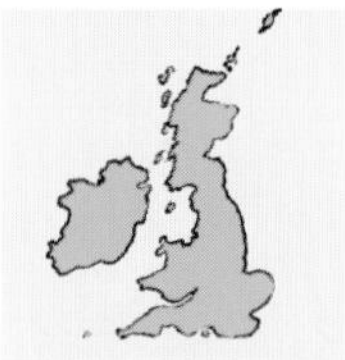

Size and appearance: A somewhat hairy, erect, branched, leafy annual or biennial 30–120 cm (12–48 in) tall.

Leaves: Oval, deeply lobed, with a large end lobe, toothed, the upper stalkless, spear-shaped, untoothed.

Flowers: In numerous pale-yellow heads 15–20 mm (3/5–4/5 in) across, in loose, branched clusters.

Fruits: Narrowly egg-shaped heads of nut-like, 1-seeded fruits, without hairs, partly enclosed by the persistent bracts.

Related or similar plants: Wall Lettuce (p.329) is somewhat similar but has hairless leaves with winged stalks.

Habitat and distribution: Widespread and common on waysides, in hedgerows and wood margins, shady gardens and sometimes on cultivated land, where it can sometimes be a troublesome weed, especially on clay soils.

Flowering time: June to October.

Top right *Nipplewort* (Lapsana communis) *flowers, in profile, expand out abruptly from the stem and then nip in to form a tight waist beneath the pale-yellow, dandelion-like heads, which are set in loose, branched clusters.*

Bottom left *A plant of waysides, waste places and disturbed ground, it often grows by the side of a fence or wall where it has managed to find a few inches of ground in which to grow.*

Bottom right *An annual or biennial of varying height from 10-130 cm (12-48 in) tall. It has stiff, leafy stems which are branched many times, often giving Nipplewort an untidy appearance, particularly if it has been knocked about by the wind.*

THE YOUNG LEAVES of Nipplewort are edible, and were once used as a salad. Slightly larger, longer-lived plants are found here and there, and may be relics of former cultivation. The common name derives less from any healing properties than from a reference to the shape of the buds. Nipplewort is an example of a herbal 'remedy' being based merely on the 'doctrine of signatures', whereby people looked for a similarity between the plant and the organ they wanted to treat. Fortunately, many other ancient herbal cures had a much more logical, scientific base.

SPECIES INFORMATION	
COMMON NAME	Wall Lettuce
SCIENTIFIC NAME	Mycelis muralis
RELATED SPECIES	Nipplewort
HEIGHT/SPREAD	30–100 cm tall
FLOWERING TIME	July–September
HABITAT	Rocks and walls

Note: A distinctive plant that does often grow on walls.

Wall Lettuce

DAISY AND DANDELION FAMILY

(Compositae or Asteraceae)

Size and appearance: A hairless, often reddish or purplish perennial, with erect, branched stems 30–100 cm (12–40 in) tall.

Leaves: The lower cut into deep lobes, the end lobe much larger and often 3-lobed, with winged stalks; the upper narrower, stalkless and clasping the stem.

Flowers: Flowers pale yellow in cylindrical heads 8–10 mm (⅓–⅜ in) across, with 5 ray florets, surrounded by green, scale-like, narrow bracts, numerous in a flat-topped cluster, with spreading branches.

Fruits: Heads of 1-seeded, blackish fruits, each with a parachute of hairs.

Related or similar plants: This plant is distinctive compared with other dandelion-like plants.

Habitat and distribution: A widespread and locally common plant of open and rocky woods, heaths, banks and roadsides, and cliffs, rocks and walls, especially on lime-rich soils, throughout England, but rare in Scotland and Ireland.

Flowering time: July to September.

FLOWER TYPE

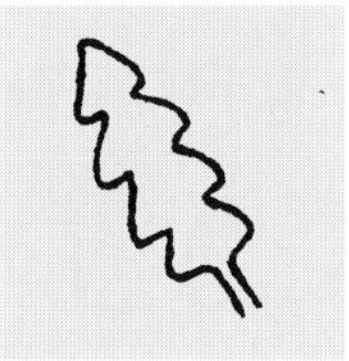

IDENTIFICATION

HABITAT

POPULATION

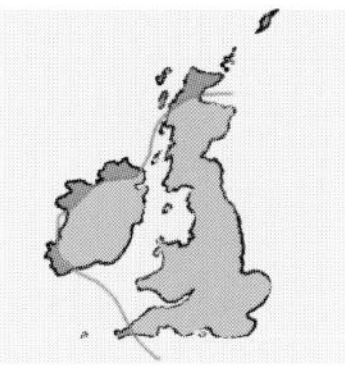

MAP

WALL LETTUCE IS very much a plant of walls, but it does occur in more natural habitats on rocks and cliffs, and on slopes and banks in woods. However, it may not always be native. It is common in among the limestone rocks of the Burren of County Clare, looking as if it is in its pure native habitat. Alas, it was not recorded there until 1939, so appears to be an incomer. Native status is always one of the most difficult but most interesting problems in plant geography.

We also have three native species of true wild lettuce.

Wall Lettuce (Mycelis muralis) *is a slender and often graceful plant, with its flower heads set on spreading branches in candelabra-like clusters. The pale-yellow flowers contrast to the often purplish colouration of their stalks and branches. It is a plant of shady, rocky banks and woodland margins as well as walls.*

Leafy Hawkweed

DAISY AND DANDELION FAMILY

(Compositae or Asteraceae)

SPECIES INFORMATION	
COMMON NAME	Leafy Hawkweed
SCIENTIFIC NAME	Hieracium umbellatum
RELATED SPECIES	Mouse-ear Hawkweed
HEIGHT/SPREAD	30–80 cm tall
FLOWERING TIME	June–October
HABITAT	Dry banks and heaths

Note: A tall, leafy 'dandelion'.

FLOWER TYPE

IDENTIFICATION

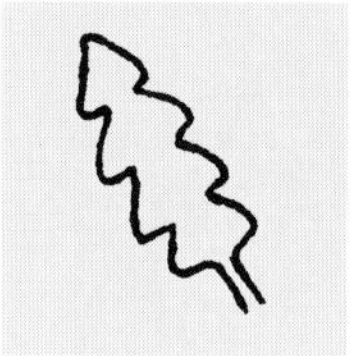

HABITAT

POPULATION

MAP

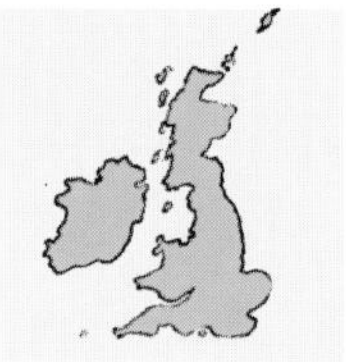

Size and appearance: A hairy perennial, with erect, very leafy flowering stems 30–80 cm (12–32 in) tall.

Leaves: All on the stems, narrowly spear-shaped, slightly toothed or not, hairy beneath.

Flowers: In yellow heads 30–40 mm (1⅕–1⅗ in) across, surrounded by green, scale-like bracts with curved-back tips, numerous in a flat-topped cluster.

Fruits: Heads of 1-seeded fruits, each with a parachute of hairs.

Related or similar plants: The numerous, narrow stem leaves distinguish this plant from other hawkweeds and dandelion-like plants.

Habitat and distribution: Widespread and common in open woods, on heaths, banks and roadsides, on dry or well-drained soils, throughout Britain and Ireland.

Flowering time: June to October.

LEAFY HAWKWEED is one the most distinct species in a very difficult group of closely related plants.

Top *Leafy Hawkweed* (Hieracium umbellatum) *has loosely branched, flat-topped clusters of yellow dandelion-like flowers set on an erect, leafy stem. In this species the leaves are narrow and spear-shaped.*

Bottom *Fox and Cubs* (Pilosella aurantiaca) *has tawny-orange flowers. It is a garden escape and is now naturalised in waste places and along railway banks.*

SPECIES INFORMATION	
COMMON NAME	Mouse-ear Hawkweed
SCIENTIFIC NAME	Hieracium pilosell
RELATED SPECIES	Leafy Hawkweed
HEIGHT/SPREAD	5–20 cm tall
FLOWERING TIME	June–October
HABITAT	Dry banks and heaths

Note: Pale yellow flower-heads and leafy runners.

Mouse-ear Hawkweed

DAISY AND DANDELION FAMILY

(Compositae or Asteraceae)

Size and appearance: An erect, hairy perennial, with far-creeping, leafy runners, forming patches, and erect, leafless flowering stems 5–20 cm (2–8 in) tall, sometimes up to 35 cm (14 in).

Leaves: Elliptical to spear-shaped, blunt, with long, pale hairs.

Flowers: In pale yellow heads 18–25 mm (¾–1 in) across, the florets red-striped beneath, solitary on long, leafless stems.

Fruits: Heads of 1-seeded fruits, each with a parachute of hairs.

Related or similar plants: The only dandelion-like plant with leafy runners.

Habitat and distribution: Widespread and common in the short turf of dry pastures, on heaths and open, rocky ground, dry banks, walls and un-manicured lawns.

Flowering time: June to October.

MOUSE-EAR HAWKWEED is one of the most characteristic plants of dry, sunny places like road and railway cuttings, banks on old lawns and earth-filled stone walls, especially on sandy soils or near the sea. Although the hawkweeds are divided by botanists into many 'microspecies', this plant is readily identified by the combination of pale yellow flowers and long runners. It is, however, a variable species and several subspecies can probably be recognised within it.

Mouse-ear Hawkweed (Pilosella officinarum) *is a very variable, hairy and sometimes shaggy, perennial. It is usually quite low-growing, although some varieties can reach 20 cm (8 in). The leaves are untoothed, elliptical- to spear-shaped and, on their upper surface, pale-green in colour with long white hairs. Underneath they are quite white from the covering of hairs, the lemon yellow heads are solitary on long, usually leafless stalks.*

FLOWER TYPE

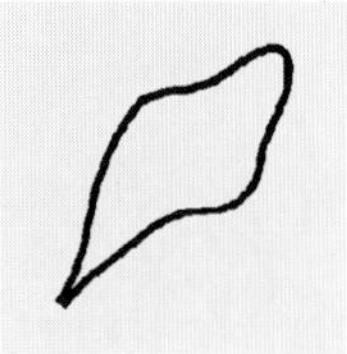

IDENTIFICATION

HABITAT

POPULATION

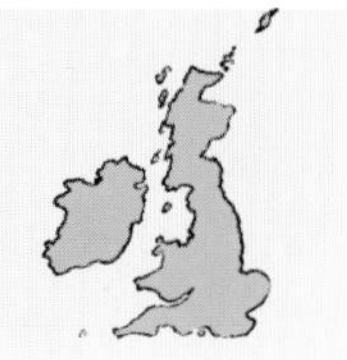

MAP

Water-plantain

WATER-PLANTAIN FAMILY
(Alismataceae)

SPECIES INFORMATION	
COMMON NAME	Water-plantain
SCIENTIFIC NAME	Alisma plantago-aquatica
RELATED SPECIES	Arrowhead
HEIGHT/SPREAD	30–100 cm tall
FLOWERING TIME	June–August
HABITAT	Edges of lakes, ponds and streams

Note: The rosettes of spear-shaped basal leaves are distinctive.

FLOWER TYPE

IDENTIFICATION

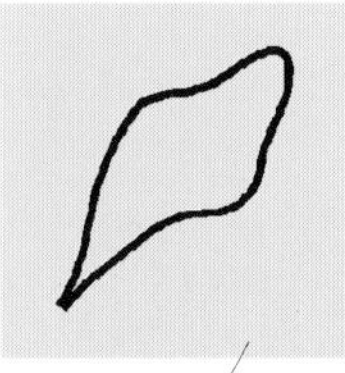

HABITAT

POPULATION

MAP

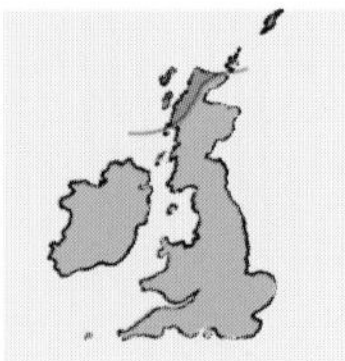

THIS IS THE commonest of the five native species of water-plantain. Unlike many water plants, it can persist and thrive in disturbed habitats and can be seen even in sordid, muddy, suburban streams alongside garbage and discarded supermarket trolleys.

The flowers of water-plantains closely resemble those of buttercups and water-crowfoots (pp.28–31 & 50–63), in having numerous stamens and 1-seeded fruits. However, the water-plantains have 3 petals and sepals rather than 6. Botanists have argued that this, and related families, may have evolved many millions of years ago directly from the buttercups, which are regarded as a relatively primitive group of flowering plants.

Size and appearance: A hairless, aquatic or semi-aquatic perennial with erect flowering stems 30–100 cm (12–40 in) tall.
Leaves: All basal in a large rosette, oval or spear-shaped, with a rounded or heart-shaped base.
Flowers: White or pale lilac with a yellow centre, c. 10 mm (⅜ in) across, with 3 petals and 3 green sepals, widely spaced in a loose, domed or pyramidal cluster with long branches in whorls.
Fruits: 1-seeded in a flattish whorl.
Related or similar plants: Arrowhead (p.333) has arrow-shaped leaves and larger, usually purple-blotched flowers, and grows in deeper water.
Habitat and distribution: Common on marshy or muddy ground and on the margins of lakes, ponds, canals and streams; throughout, but rare in northern Scotland.
Flowering time: June to August; the flowers open after midday.

Top left *Narrow-leaved Water-plantain* (Alisma lanceolatum) *is small, with narrow, pointed spear-shaped leaves tapering into the stalk.*

Top right and bottom *Water-plantain* (Alisma plantago-aquatica) *often grows on bare mud, but it is more usually found at the edges of shallow ponds and streams or in marshy places, as below.*

SPECIES INFORMATION	
COMMON NAME	Arrowhead
SCIENTIFIC NAME	Sagittaria sagittifolia
RELATED SPECIES	Water-plantain
HEIGHT/SPREAD	50–100 cm tall
FLOWERING TIME	July–August
HABITAT	Streams and small rivers

Note: Our only aquatic plant with arrow-shaped leaves.

Arrowhead

WATER-PLANTAIN FAMILY

(Alismataceae)

Size and appearance: A hairless, erect, aquatic perennial, with runners and small tubers, and flowering stems 50–100 cm (20–40 in) tall.

Leaves: All basal, long-stalked, the blade up to 25 cm (10 in) long, arrow-shaped, pointed, held above the water; in faster-flowing water some leaves are submerged and narrow, others float and are oval or spear-shaped.

Flowers: Either male or female, 20-25 mm (⅘–1 in) across, with 3 white petals usually with a large purple blotch, 3 green sepals and numerous purple stamens, in a whorled cluster.

Fruits: 1-seeded, 4–6 mm (⅙–¼ in) long, in a spherical head.

Related or similar plants: Water-plantain (p.332) has spear-shaped leaves and much smaller flowers, and grows in shallow water or on mud.

Habitat and distribution: Widespread but local in slow-moving streams and small rivers with muddy bottoms in England and Wales; absent from Scotland and Cornwall, and much of Wales and Ireland.

Flowering time: July to August.

ALL MEMBERS OF the water-plantain family are restricted to wet or marshy habitats. Arrowhead, which is able to produce a range of submerged, floating or aerial leaves, is well adapted to survive in deeper, usually slow-flowing waters. Noting the shape of the leaves, both halves of the scientific name come straight from the Latin (*sagitta*, an arrow).

Arrowhead makes a handsome garden plant, with both the wild plant and a double-flowered cultivar being grown. The species is widespread in Eurasia, and in tropical Asia the tubers are eaten by both people and pigs. A related North American plant, Duck-potato (*Sagittaria latifolia*), that occasionally escapes from gardens here, was much prized for this reason by Native Americans.

Arrowhead (Sagittaria sagittifolia) *is a striking aquatic perennial. Its flowers, in whorled spikes, are set on leafless stems; they have three white petals with a purple patch at their base. The fruiting heads are globular. The arrow-shaped leaves on their long-stalks, rising 15 cm (6 in) or more above the water, are quite conspicuous. A plant of shallow, slow-moving streams and small rivers, in faster water, it also produces long, narrow submerged leaves.*

FLOWER TYPE

IDENTIFICATION

HABITAT

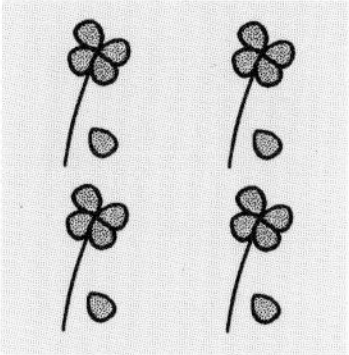
POPULATION

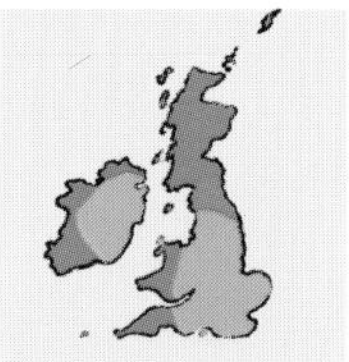
MAP

Flowering Rush

FLOWERING RUSH FAMILY

(Butomaceae)

SPECIES INFORMATION	
COMMON NAME	Flowering Rush
SCIENTIFIC NAME	Butomus umbellatus
RELATED SPECIES	None, but see Water-plantain
HEIGHT/SPREAD	50–150 cm tall
FLOWERING TIME	June–September
HABITAT	Watersides and flooded ditches

Note: A distinctive and distinguished water plant.

FLOWER TYPE

IDENTIFICATION

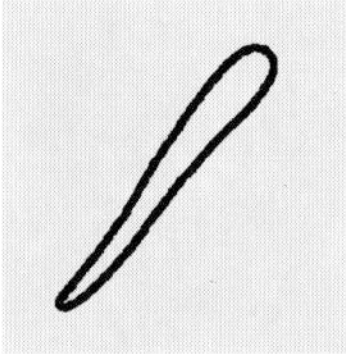

HABITAT

POPULATION

MAP

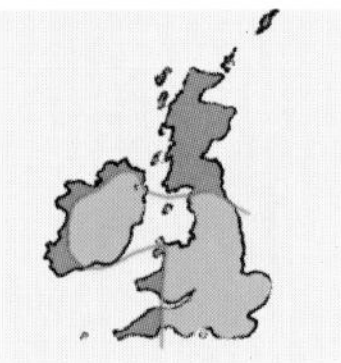

Size and appearance: A hairless, aquatic perennial with a stout, creeping rhizome and erect flowering stems 50–150 cm (20–60 in) tall.

Leaves: All basal, grass-like, 3-angled near the base, somewhat twisted.

Flowers: Long-stalked, pink with darker veins, 25–30 mm (1–1⅕ in) across, numerous in a loose, domed cluster; each with 3 petals, 3 sepals (greenish beneath), and 9 reddish-purple stamens.

Fruits: A whorl of 6 several-seeded, egg-shaped, reddish-purple pods, fused at the base.

Related or similar plants: Arrowhead (p.333) and Water-plantain (p.332) have broader leaves and 1-seeded fruits.

Habitat and distribution: Widespread but local in slow streams, canals, rivers, and flooded ditches in England, but very local in Wales and Ireland, and absent from Scotland.

Flowering time: June to September.

THIS HANDSOME WATER PLANT remains remarkably widespread, especially in parts of eastern and southern England. Poet and botanist Geoffrey Grigson, in his book *The Englishman's Flora*, makes a plea for the plant's rather unprepossessing English name to be replaced with 'Pride of the Thames', a name that commemorates the river on which it was first recorded in 1570. John Gerard, author of the famous 16th century *Herball* also knew it there. It survives on some of the   tributaries.

The plant is in a family all of its own and occurs throughout temperate Asia and north-west Africa. The flowers are similar to those of the water-plantain family (pp.332–333), but have 3 rather than 6 petals and sepals, and 9 rather than 6 stamens. Another difference is that the fruits of Flowering Rush contain several seeds.

Flowering Rush (Butomus umbellatus) *is another striking aquatic. Unless it is in flower, its long thin leaves, triangular in cross section, go unnoticed. The flowers consist of three rosy-pink petals which are marked with darker veins, three sepals of similar colour, although greenish beneath, and nine reddish-purple stamens. These are set in a large umbel at the top of a tall leafless stalk, and the plant makes a fine sight along watersides. Flowering Rush is a fine sight along watersides.*

SPECIES INFORMATION	
COMMON NAME	Bog Asphodel
SCIENTIFIC NAME	Narthecium ossifragum
RELATED SPECIES	Blue-eyed Grass
HEIGHT/SPREAD	10–30 cm tall
FLOWERING TIME	July–August
HABITAT	Bogs and wet heaths

Note: A characteristic yellow flower of boglands.

Bog Asphodel

LILY FAMILY

(Liliaceae)

Size and appearance: A hairless, creeping perennial with erect flowering stems 10–30 cm (4–12 in) long.

Leaves: All basal, in 2 ranks, narrow, sword-shaped, flat, like those of a miniature iris.

Flowers: Up to 20 in a compact spike, starry, with 6 bright yellow petals, greenish beneath, and orange stamens.

Fruits: Stiff spikes of reddish-orange, narrowly egg-shaped, tapered capsules, splitting into 3 segments.

Related or similar plants: The basal leaves of Blue-eyed Grass (p.353) are similar but the flowers are blue.

Habitat and distribution: Widespread and often abundant in bogs and on wet heaths and moors, mostly in the north and west and over most of Ireland; local in southern England and absent from most of East Anglia and the Midlands.

Flowering time: July to August, but still conspicuous in fruit during autumn.

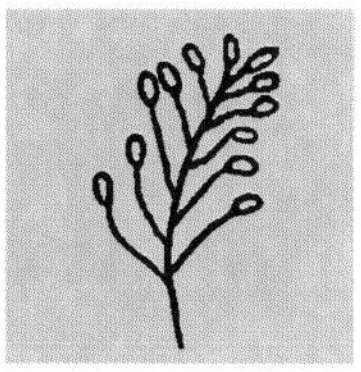

FLOWER TYPE

IDENTIFICATION

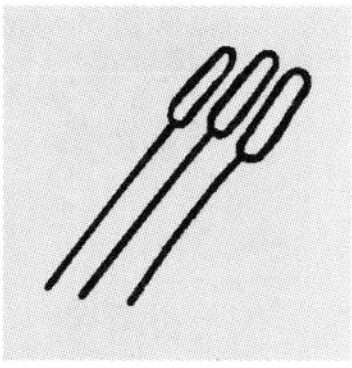

HABITAT

POPULATION

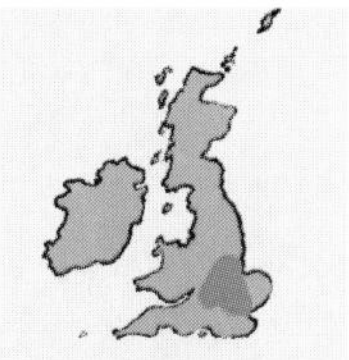

MAP

BOG ASPHODEL IS a characteristic plant of peat-bogs, and a fine sight in flower during summer. It was formerly a source of an orange dye used to colour cloth and tint women's hair. It is poisonous to sheep, and has a reputation for weakening the bones of cattle, hence the *ossifragum* (Latin, 'bone-breaking') of the scientific name.

The plant was once more widespread in England, but has decreased with the draining and reclamation of wet heaths and small bogs. The true Asphodels do not occur in Britain or Ireland. They are larger plants, with long spikes of white or yellow flowers, of dry and overgrazed habitats in southern Europe and the Mediterranean region.

Top right *Bog Asphodel* (Narthecium ossifragum) *has pyramidal spikes of bright-yellow petals with orange stamens.*

Bottom left *Bog Asphodel can colour the bogland landscape in summer.*

Bottom right *With basal tufts of small, flattened, sword-shaped leaves which are often a rather orange-green, and the spikes of bright-yellow, star-like flowers, Bog Asphodel is a distinctive species.*

Fritillary

LILY FAMILY
(Liliaceae)

SPECIES INFORMATION	
COMMON NAME	Fritillary, Snake's Head
SCIENTIFIC NAME	Fritillaria meleagris
RELATED SPECIES	Garden lilies and tulips
HEIGHT/SPREAD	10–40 cm tall
FLOWERING TIME	Apri–May
HABITAT	Damp, lime-rich meadows

Note: The bell-like, pink or white flowers are unmistakable.

FLOWER TYPE

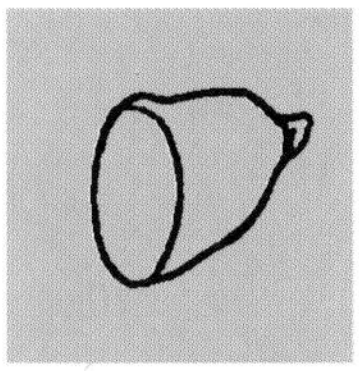

IDENTIFICATION

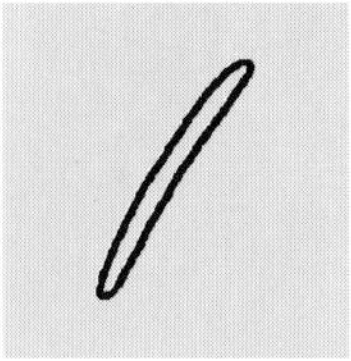

HABITAT

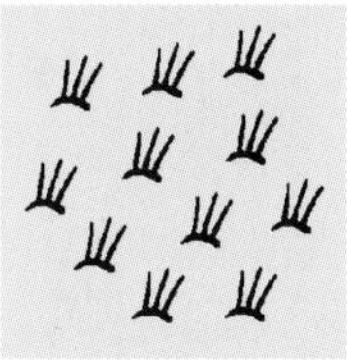

POPULATION

MAP

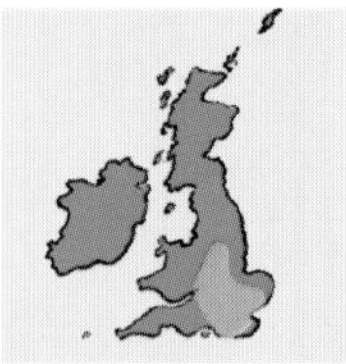

Size and appearance: A bulbous perennial with a single erect flowering stem 10–40 cm tall.
Flowers: Solitary, tulip-like but nodding, 3–4.5 cm long, pinkish-purple chequered purplish-brown, or white with pink or green veins.
Leaves: Few, narrow, U-shaped in section, greyish-green.
Fruits: Almost spherical, angled capsules, splitting into 3 segments.
Related or similar plants: Garden lilies have flowers in clusters, and tulips have solitary but erect flowers.
Habitat and distribution: Rare, but can be seen in huge numbers in a few damp meadows across southern and central England, especially in the upper Thames Valley.
Flowering time: April to May.

LIKE MANY OF our wild lilies, this is an ornamental plant that has long been grown in gardens. However, it is apparently native in damp meadows, especially those that were formerly managed as water-meadows deliberately flooded in late winter to early spring. The flowers appeared after floodwaters had subsided and before the cattle were put out to graze on the meadow in early summer.

Sadly, Fritillary has declined considerably since the 1930s – more than almost any other wild British plant.

Top *Colours can range from pure white to the more usual dull purple, which is chequered with darker blotches.*

Bottom right *A Fritillary meadow in the Thames Valley during spring.*

Bottom left *Fritillary (Fritillaria meleagris) is one of our most distinctive and attractive wild flowers, which is now very rare and can only be seen at a few protected sites. In these meadows, however, it is quite abundant.*

SPECIES INFORMATION

COMMON NAME	Meadow Saffron, Naked Ladies
SCIENTIFIC NAME	Colchicum autumnale
RELATED SPECIES	Garden lilies and tulips
HEIGHT/SPREAD	10–30 cm tall
FLOWERING TIME	August–October
HABITAT	Damp woods and meadows

Note: The flowers, like those of a crocus, have 3 stamens.

Meadow Saffron

LILY FAMILY

(Liliaceae)

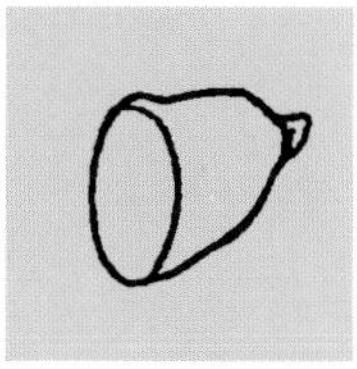

FLOWER TYPE

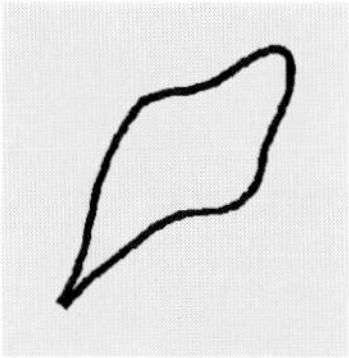

IDENTIFICATION

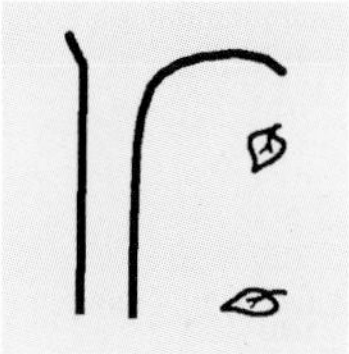

HABITAT

POPULATION

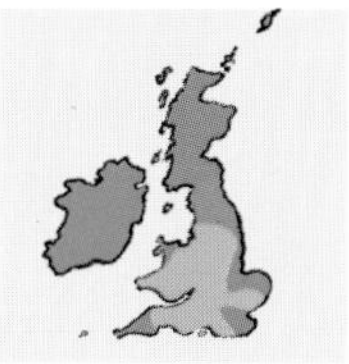

MAP

Size and appearance: A hairless perennial, rising from a large corm, with several flowers 10–30 cm (4–12 in) tall, appearing directly from the ground, without leaves.

Flowers: Solitary, crocus-like, 6-lobed, pale purplish-pink; the unbranched stigma and 6 stamens are orange; the long stalk is actually an extended floral tube.

Leaves: Produced after the flowers, up to 40 cm long, spear-shaped, pointed, shiny.

Fruits: Stalked, egg-shaped capsules up to 5 cm (2 in) long, produced in spring.

Related or similar plants: Crocuses (Iris family), several species of which are naturalised from gardens, have 3 stamens.

Habitat and distribution: Rather scarce, but locally numerous in damp woods and meadows, from the south-west Midlands to mid-Wales and Somerset, and sometimes elsewhere, often on limestone, north to Cumbria; also a few places in the river-valleys of southern Ireland.

Flowering time: August-October.

ONE OF THE MOST attractive of our small number of true autumn flowers, Meadow Saffron is an indicator of both ancient woodland and old meadows, although it also has a long history of cultivation for use in medicine. The drug colchicine, extracted from this plant, is an old and tried remedy for gout that remains in common use, and fully accepted by a medical establishment that is not always friendly to plant-based drugs.

This is one of the most poisonous wild plants and needs to be treated with respect.

Top right *Looking down into the crocus-like flowers you can clearly see the orange stamens, the petals still hold droplets of water from a recent shower.*

Bottom left *Meadow Saffron* (Colchicum autumnale) *grow in a hay meadow in the Dolomite mountains in Europe.*

Bottom right *Autumn Crocus* (Crocus nudiflorus), *a member of the Iris family introduced from SW Europe, is similar but has purplish-violet flowers, 3 stamens and a much-branched stigma; the leaves, produced later, are narrow with a white stripe. Also flowering August-October it grows in a few grassy places in Southern England.*

Bluebell

LILY FAMILY

(Liliaceae)

SPECIES INFORMATION	
COMMON NAME	Bluebell, Wild Hyacinth
SCIENTIFIC NAME	Hyacinthoides non-scripta
RELATED SPECIES	Star-of-Bethlehem, Wild Garlics
HEIGHT/SPREAD	10–40 cm tall
FLOWERING TIME	April–June
HABITAT	Woodland, pastures, coastal cliffs
Note: The massed, richly scented flowers are unmistakable.	

FLOWER TYPE

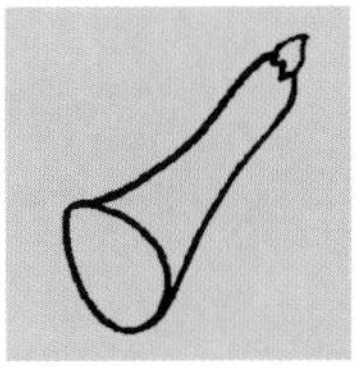

IDENTIFICATION

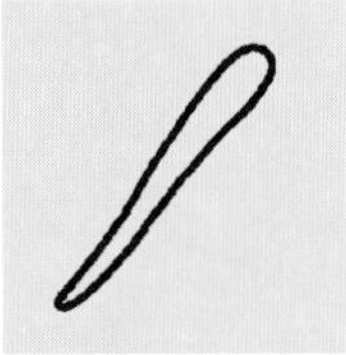

HABITAT

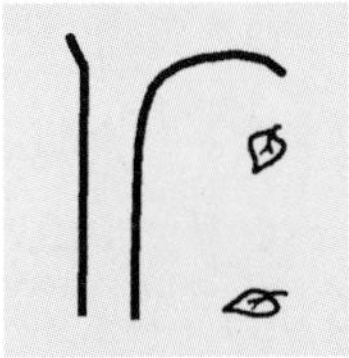

POPULATION

MAP

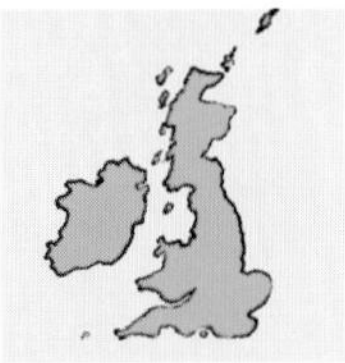

Size and appearance: A tufted, bulbous perennial with a rosette of leaves and an erect flowering stem 10–40 cm (4–16 in) long.
Leaves: Narrow, slightly fleshy, V-shaped in cross-section.
Flowers: In a loose, 1-sided cluster, drooping at the tip, dark violet-blue (sometimes white or purplish-pink), richly scented.
Fruits: Almost spherical, angled capsule, splitting into 3 segments.
Related or similar plants: Triquetrous Garlic looks like a white-flowered Bluebell but has fewer flowers in a more compact cluster, and the leaves smell of garlic.
Habitat and distribution: Still abundant on well-drained soils in woods, scrub and old pastures, on hedge-banks, heaths and sea-cliffs.
Flowering time: April to June, with a peak in early to mid-May.

BLUEBELLS SURVIVE THE drought of summer by means of their bulbs. These are large, fleshy buds that store food in the form of sugar and starch. By late winter they are putting out leafy shoots, and the leaves are fully grown by flowering, after which they gradually die down.

Bluebells are one of the best-known of all our wild flowers, and a glory of the late spring. They grow in great crowds, colouring the woodland floor and scenting the air. Britain and Ireland are the centre of distribution of this plant, restricted to western and north-western Europe, from Portugal to the Netherlands. Few floral displays on Earth compare with an English Bluebell wood in May.

Spanish or Garden Bluebell (*Hyacinthoides hispanica*), with wider leaves and more erect spikes of larger, paler flowers, frequently escapes from gardens. It also crosses with wild Bluebells.

Top left and right *Bluebell* (Hyacinthoides non-scripta), *with its long green glossy leaves and clusters of blue flowers, is an attractive flower on its own, but when massed across a woodland floor it is unforgettable.*

Bottom *A magnificent English Bluebell wood in May.*

SPECIES INFORMATION	
COMMON NAME	Spring Squill
SCIENTIFIC NAME	Scilla verna
RELATED SPECIES	Bluebell, Autumn Squill
HEIGHT/SPREAD	5–20 cm tall
FLOWERING TIME	March–May
HABITAT	Short turf of coastal cliffs

Note: Like a miniature, pale-flowered Bluebell, always coastal.

Spring Squill

LILY FAMILY
(Liliaceae)

Size and appearance: A tufted, bulbous perennial with a rosette of leaves and an erect flowering stem 5–20 cm tall.
Flowers: Starry, 2–12, in a loose, domed cluster, bluish-violet, each with a conspicuous, bluish leaf-like bract.
Leaves: Very narrow, grass-like, curly.
Fruits: Almost spherical, angled capsules, splitting into 3 segments.
Related or similar plants: Bluebell (p.338) is much larger, with more numerous, darker flowers; Autumn Squill flowers in autumn, before the leaves emerge.

Habitat and distribution: Scattered but locally common in short grass on sea-cliffs in south-west England and along both sides of the Irish Sea; also in north-east England and from the Hebrides to Shetland.
Flowering time: March to May.

SPRING SQUILL LOOKS at first sight like a small Blubell. Where it does occur it may be present in large numbers, colouring the short turf.

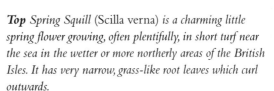

Top *Spring Squill* (Scilla verna) *is a charming little spring flower growing, often plentifully, in short turf near the sea in the wetter or more northerly areas of the British Isles. It has very narrow, grass-like root leaves which curl outwards.*

Middle *The leafless stalks bear short spikes of star-like bluish-violet flowers, each of which has a bluish leaf-like bract. Flowering as early as March in the south west of England, this becomes later further northwards, so that in the Shetland Islands it is possible to find it in full flower as late as the end of June.*

Bottom *Autumn Squill* (Scilla autumnalis) *produces a longer spike of purplish flowers in late summer and autumn, before the leaves emerge. It occurs here and there in dry grassland on the coasts of southern England.*

FLOWER TYPE

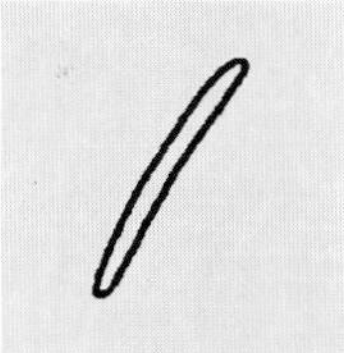

IDENTIFICATION

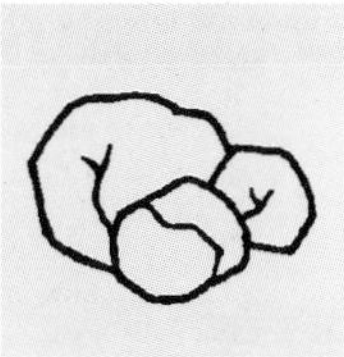

HABITAT

POPULATION

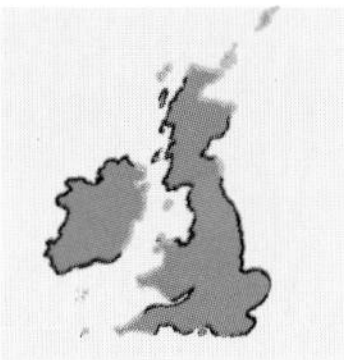

MAP

Ramsons

LILY FAMILY
(Liliaceae)

SPECIES INFORMATION	
COMMON NAME	Ramsons, Wild Garlicp
SCIENTIFIC NAME	Allium ursinum
RELATED SPECIES	Crow Garlic
HEIGHT/SPREAD	15–50 cm tall
FLOWERING TIME	April–June
HABITAT	Damp woodland

Note: The oval leaves smelling strongly of garlic are diagnostic.

FLOWER TYPE

IDENTIFICATION

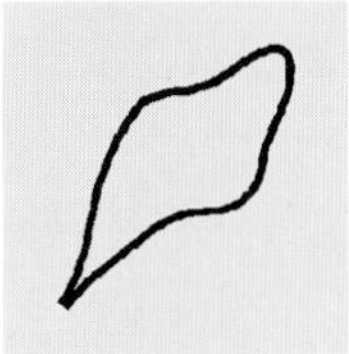

HABITAT

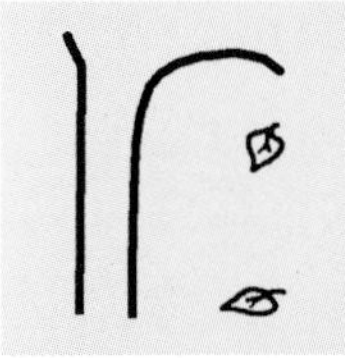

POPULATION

MAP

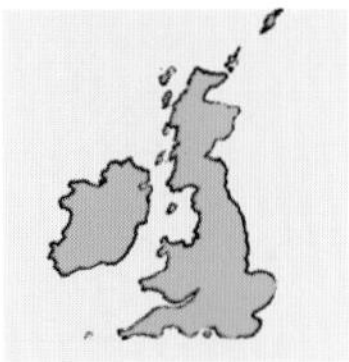

Size and appearance: A hairless perennial with an erect flowering stem 15–50 cm (6–20 in) tall, emerging from a bulb and forming large patches.
Leaves: All basal, elliptical, flat with a keeled midvein, up to 25 cm (10 in) long, smelling strongly of garlic when bruised.
Flowers: White, starry, nodding slightly, 6–20 in a domed head.
Fruits: Cylindrical, 3-lobed capsules.
Related similar plants: Triquetrous Garlic has narrow leaves and 3-angled stems; the similar leaves of Lily-of-the-Valley (p.346) do not smell of garlic.
Habitat and distribution: Widespread and often abundant in damp woods, hedge-banks and shady streamsides, especially on lime-rich soils, throughout Britain; local in north-eastern Scotland, and very scattered in Ireland.
Flowering time: April to June.

RAMSONS SOMETIMES carpets damp woods, and any step taken releases an overpowering smell of garlic. The young leaves are edible and make a tasty, if pungent, addition to a green salad or peanut butter sandwich. The name is ancient, from the Old English name *Hramsa*, and appears as a prefix in the name of several towns and villages, for example Ramsey in Essex, Huntingdonshire and the Isle of Man.

Onion or garlic smells are rare in the plant kingdom and, certainly in Britain, usually indicate a member of the genus *Allium*. The sulphur-containing chemicals that create the smell originally evolved as a defence against insects and other predators. Note that the quite different and unrelated Hedge Mustard (p.71) also smells of garlic when bruised.

Several wild leeks, onions and garlics grow in Britain and Ireland, all of them narrow-leaved plants of open, rocky or sandy ground.

Top left *Ramsons* (Allium ursinum) *has large, elliptical leaves from which arise the pom-pom clusters of white, starry flowers.*

Top right *A large patch of Ramsons in a woodland clearing in summer.*

Bottom *Triquetrous Garlic* (Allium triquetrum) *is similar but has narrow, strap-shaped leaves, 3-angled and slightly winged flowering stems, and a head of bell-shaped, drooping flowers. A garden escape, it is spreading rapidly, mostly on or near western and south-western coasts of England and Wales and in Ireland.*

SPECIES INFORMATION	
COMMON NAME	Crow Garlic, Wild Onion
SCIENTIFIC NAME	*Allium vineale*
RELATED SPECIES	Ramsons
HEIGHT/SPREAD	15–60 cm tall
FLOWERING TIME	April–August
HABITAT	Dry grassland and fields

Note: The commonest narrow-leaved wild garlic or onion.

Crow Garlic

LILY FAMILY (Liliaceae)

CROW GARLIC IS particularly characteristic of some areas such as grassy sea-walls and banks around the estuaries of large rivers like the Severn and Shannon. The flowers are usually replaced by little bulbs, and a common variant of the plant has no flowers at all. The heads of bulbs shatter in late summer and each bulb can then grow into a new plant. Crow Garlic used to be a serious weed of crops, and the garlic smell can taint the milk of grazing animals.

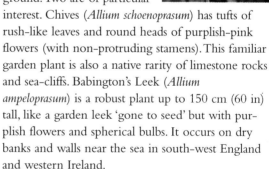

A dozen or so wild leeks, onions and garlics grow wild in Britain and Ireland, most of them native but at the north-western edge of their range. They are all narrow-leaved plants of open, rocky or sandy ground. Two are of particular interest. Chives (*Allium schoenoprasum*) has tufts of rush-like leaves and round heads of purplish-pink flowers (with non-protruding stamens). This familiar garden plant is also a native rarity of limestone rocks and sea-cliffs. Babington's Leek (*Allium ampeloprasum*) is a robust plant up to 150 cm (60 in) tall, like a garden leek 'gone to seed' but with purplish flowers and spherical bulbs. It occurs on dry banks and walls near the sea in south-west England and western Ireland.

Size and appearance: A hairless, bulbous perennial with an erect flowering stem 15–60 cm (6–24 in) tall, sometimes up to 100 cm (40 in).

Leaves: Few, sheathing the lower stem, narrow, more or less tubular, smelling strongly of garlic when bruised.

Flowers: Usually few, long-stalked, greenish-white, pinkish or purplish, or mostly replaced by small, egg-shaped, pointed bulbs, in a spherical head; stamens protruding.

Fruits: Most fruits are replaced by bulbs.

Related similar plants: Ramsons and Triquetrous Garlic have flat leaves and white flowers; also other wild garlics.

Habitat and distribution: Widespread and locally common in dry grassland, on field borders, hedge-banks, rocky or sandy ground and crumbling walls, road-verges and river-banks; rarer and mostly near the coast in Scotland and Ireland.

Flowering time: April to August.

FLOWER TYPE

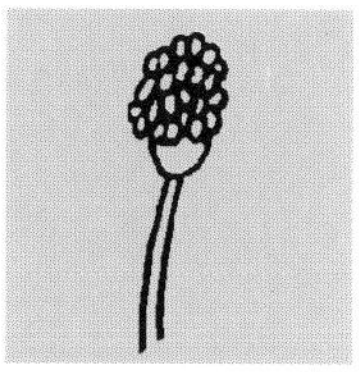

IDENTIFICATION

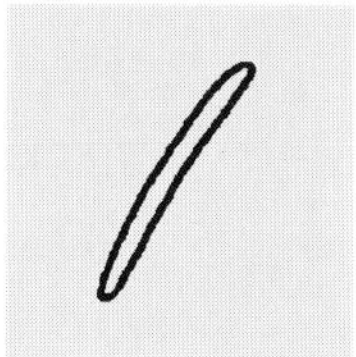

HABITAT

POPULATION

MAP

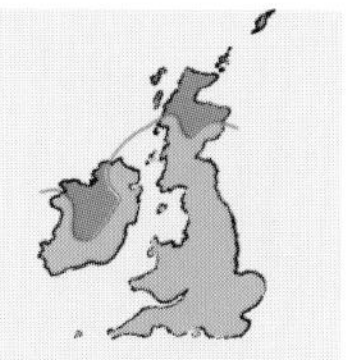

Top left *Rosy Garlic* (Allium roseum) *has attractive, long-stalked pink flowers. These are often mixed with bulbils, that are a dark-burgundy-red.*

Top right *Crow Garlic* (Allium vineale) *showing a head of bulbils that are beginning to sprout.*

Bottom right *Sand Leek* (Allium scorodoprasum) *is a tall perennial to 80 cm (33 1/3 in) tall with round stems and flat leaves, 7-20 mm (3/10-8/10 in) wide, which are slightly keeled. The flower head is a mixture of bulbils and flowers which are a deep pink to reddish-purple, and it is found in dry grassland and scrub in northern Britain.*

Butcher's Broom

LILY FAMILY
(Liliaceae)

SPECIES INFORMATION	
COMMON NAME	Butcher's Broom
SCIENTIFIC NAME	Ruscus aculeatus
RELATED SPECIES	Other 'lilies'
HEIGHT/SPREAD	30–100 cm tall
FLOWERING TIME	February–April
HABITAT	Woods and scrub

Note: Flowers and red fruits appear from the middle of leaf.

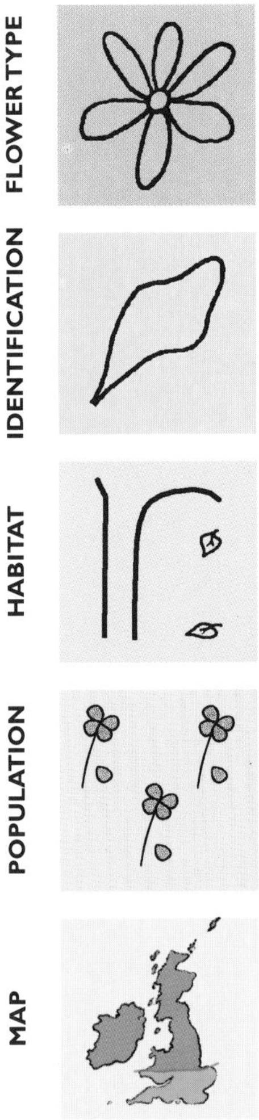

Size and appearance: An evergreen shrub 30–100 cm (12–40 in)tall, with a creeping rhizome and stiff, erect stems; branches covered with leaf-like, sharp-pointed flattened stems.

Leaves: Reduced to tiny papery scales on the stems and 'leaves'.

Flowers: Either male or female, tiny, greenish, on the upper surface of a 'leaf'.

Fruits: Bright red, spherical berries about 1 cm (⅜ in) across.

Related or similar plants: No other members of the lily family in Britain are woody.

Habitat and distribution: Local in dry woods and scrub-covered sea-cliffs in southern England and south-west Wales.

Flowering time: January to April, but most conspicuous when the fruits are ripe in winter.

BUTCHER'S BROOM IS an exotic-looking member of our flora. Like several other members of the lily family, it is at the edge of its range – it is more at home further south, in the woods and scrublands of the Mediterranean region.

It is unusual in the family in being a shrub rather than a herbaceous perennial. Much more strange, however, are its 'leaves', each in fact a flattened stem, known to botanists as a cladode. That is why the flowers and cherry-like fruits appear to emerge from the middle of a leaf.

The dried stems were formerly harvested and tied in bundles to make small brooms, hence the English name.

Butcher's Broom (Ruscus aculeatus) *has tiny, greenish flowers growing from the centre of the upper surface of the leaf in late winter. The fruit is a scarlet berry which looks conspicuous against the dark-evergreen foliage. While these look like sharp-pointed leaves, they are actually flattened stems. It is local in dry woods in the south of England.*

SPECIES INFORMATION.	
COMMON NAME	Yellow Star-of-Bethlehem
SCIENTIFIC NAME	Gagea lutea
RELATED SPECIES	Early Star-of-Bethlehem
HEIGHT/SPREAD	5–25 cm tall
FLOWERING TIME	March–May
HABITAT	Woods on limestone

Note: Scarce yellow lily of spring woods.

Yellow Star-of-Bethlehem

LILY FAMILY

(Liliaceae)

FLOWER TYPE

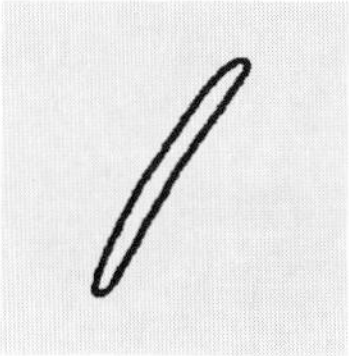

IDENTIFICATION

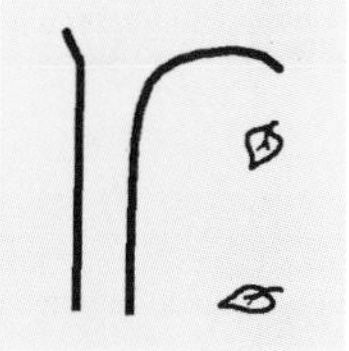

HABITAT

POPULATION

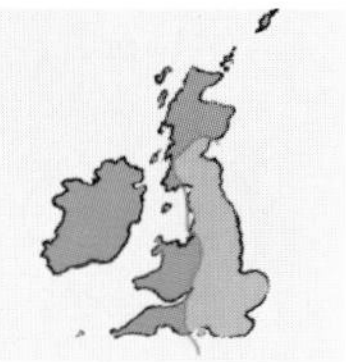

MAP

Size and appearance: A bulbous perennial with flowering stems 5–25 cm (2–10 in) tall.
Leaves: Numerous, grass-like, grooved; flowering stems with 1 basal leaf and 2 broader upper leaves.
Flowers: In a cluster of 2–7, star-like, yellow but petals greenish on the outside.
Fruits: Almost spherical, angled capsules, splitting into 3 segments.
Related or similar plants: Early Star-of-Bethlehem, with yellow flowers, and Snowdon Lily, with white flowers, both very rare plants of upland Wales.
Habitat and distribution: Local in damp woods over limestone or chalk, sometimes in old pastures, here and there from Dorset to southern Scotland; not in Ireland.
Flowering time: March to May.

WHERE IT DOES occur, this attractive little plant is sometimes present in enormous numbers, but it is often very shy to flower. The leaves are inconspicuous and, as is the case with so many bulbous plants, a good deal more plentiful than the attractive yellow flowers.

A similar plant, Early Star-of-Bethlehem (*Gagea bohemica*) has been known for 30 years on rocks at one site on the Welsh border. No more than 5 cm tall, with very narrow, curly leaves, stems with 2 basal leaves and 2-4 broader upper leaves, and 1-3 flowers, it flowers from January to early March.

Top *Yellow Star-of-Bethlehem* (Gagea lutea) *is a charming spring flower with an umbel-like cluster of greenish-yellow flowers. Its leaves are similar to the Bluebell, but have a yellower-green and are narrowed into a hooded tip. It has between three and five ribs on the underside.*

Bottom *Early Star-of-Bethlehem* (Gagea bohemica) *has two basal leaves, which are very narrow, and curly leaves; they can be seen trailing on the ground in the above photograph. Further up the stem are a pair of pointed leaves. The flowers are a bright yellow.*

Common Star-of-Bethlehem

LILY FAMILY

(Liliaceae)

SPECIES INFORMATION	
COMMON NAME	Common Star-of-Bethlehem
SCIENTIFIC NAME	Ornithogalum umbellatum
RELATED SPECIES	Spiked Star-of-Bethlehem
HEIGHT/SPREAD	1–30 cm tall
FLOWERING TIME	April–June
HABITAT	Dry grassland and road-verges

Note: The bold white stripes on the leaves distinguish this plant.

FLOWER TYPE

IDENTIFICATION

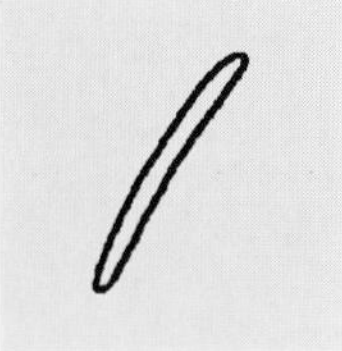

HABITAT

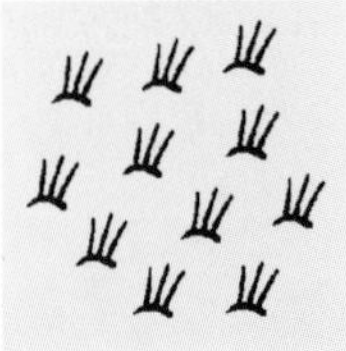

POPULATION

MAP

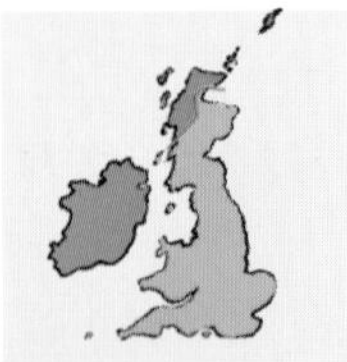

Size and appearance: A bulbous perennial with flowering stems 10–30 cm (4–12 in) tall.
Leaves: Numerous, narrow, grooved, with a prominent, central white stripe.
Flowers: In a spreading, flat-topped cluster, starry, white, the petals each with a green stripe on the outside.
Fruits: Cylindrical capsule, splitting into 3 segments.
Related or similar plants: Spiked Star-of-Bethlehem is taller, with greyish-green leaves and spikes of pale greenish-yellow flowers.
Habitat and distribution: Grassland and road-verges in East Anglia, but widespread elsewhere in grassy places as a garden escape.
Flowering time: April to early June, the flowers opening after mid-morning and only on sunny days.

Top right and bottom left Common Star-of-Bethlehem (Ornithogalum angustifolium) *has flowers in a flat-topped cluster.*

THIS IS ONE of those plants that many botanists have suspected of being introduced. However, in the dry grassland of the Breckland of East Anglia, it gives every appearance of being native. Like many plants at the northern edge of its range it favours dry, open habitats similar to those it occupies in southern Europe.

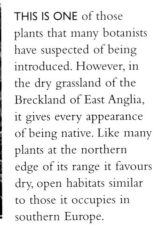

Bottom right
Spiked Star-of-Bethlehem (Ornithogalum pyrenaicum) *is similar but up to 100 cm (40 in) tall, with greyish-green leaves withered by flowering, and tall spikes of pale greenish-yellow flowers. It is locally common in open woodland, flowering in June and July.*

SPECIES INFORMATION	
COMMON NAME	Common Solomon's-seal
SCIENTIFIC NAME	Polygonatum multiflorum
RELATED SPECIES	Lily-of-the-Valley
HEIGHT/SPREAD	30–80 cm tall
FLOWERING TIME	May–June
HABITAT	Woodland and scrub

Note: The arching flower-stems are distinctive.

Common Solomon's-seal

LILY FAMILY (Liliaceae)

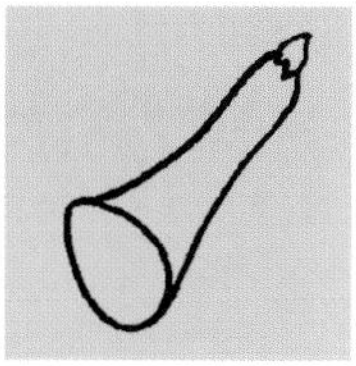

FLOWER TYPE

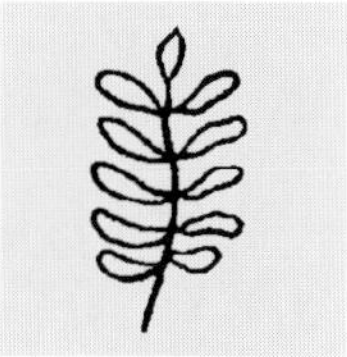

IDENTIFICATION

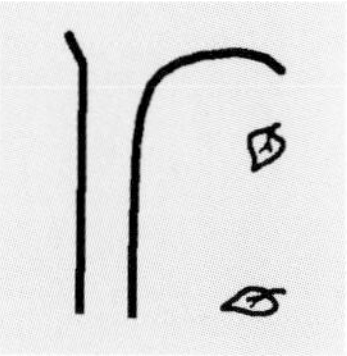

HABITAT

POPULATION

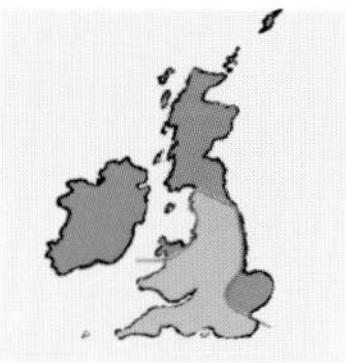

MAP

Size and appearance: A hairless perennial with a creeping rhizome, forming small patches, and arching flowering stems 30–80 cm (12–32 in) tall.
Leaves: Alternate along the stem in 2 loose ranks, 5–12 cm (2–4½ in) long, almost stalkless, oval to spear-shaped, greyish-green.
Flowers: In stalked, hanging clusters of 2-5, narrowly bell-shaped, slightly pinched in middle, greenish-white, without scent.
Fruits: Almost spherical, bluish-black berries.
Related similar plants: Angular Solomon's-seal has solitary or paired, scented flowers; Lily-of-the-Valley (p.346) has scented flowers in a leafless cluster.
Habitat and distribution: Woodland and scrub on chalk and limestone in southern England and South Wales, with scattered sites northwards to Cumbria.
Flowering time: May to June.

THIS ELEGANT PLANT, along with two other native Solomon's-seals, is one of several rhizomatous or bulbous plants that are indicators of ancient woodland.

The English name may refer to the fleshy, white rhizome, which is covered with round scars from the stems of previous years. It also alludes to the legendary wisdom of Solomon, in all matters including medicine, for it was long prized as a healing herb for broken bones and other ailments. This was probably how it was first brought into gardens, although the usual garden plant is in fact a hybrid between Common and Angular Solomon's-seal.

Angular Solomon's-seal (*Polygonatum odoratum*), which is shorter, up to 60 cm (24 in) tall, with angular stems and solitary or paired, scented flowers, is restricted to woods on limestone from the Cotswolds to Cumbria, and a few sites in Wales.

Common Solomon's-seal (Polygonatum multiflorum) *has round, arching stems from which dangle clusters of between one and three greenish-white flowers. It is a plant of ancient woodlands on lime-rich soils.*

Lily-of-the-Valley

LILY FAMILY

(Liliaceae)

SPECIES INFORMATION	
COMMON NAME	Lily-of-the-Valley
SCIENTIFIC NAME	Convallaria majalis
RELATED SPECIES	Solomon's-seals
HEIGHT/SPREAD	15–30 cm tall
FLOWERING TIME	May–July
HABITAT	Drywoods and well-drained soils
Note: The 2-3 large basal leaves are distinctive.	

FLOWER TYPE

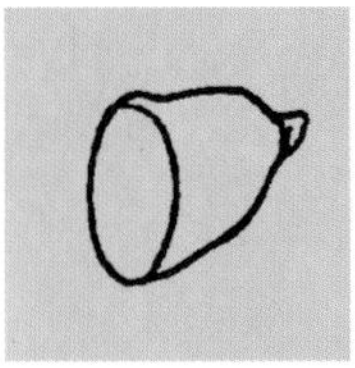

IDENTIFICATION

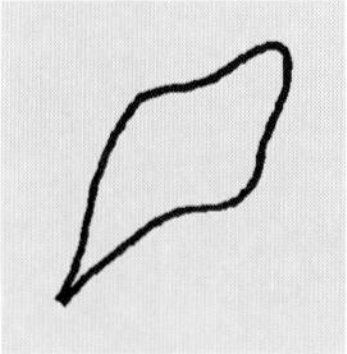

HABITAT

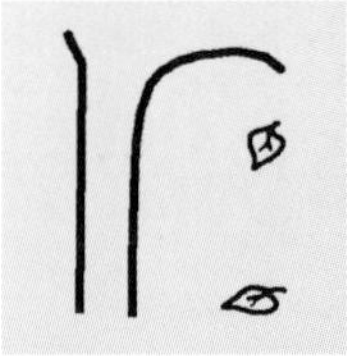

POPULATION

MAP

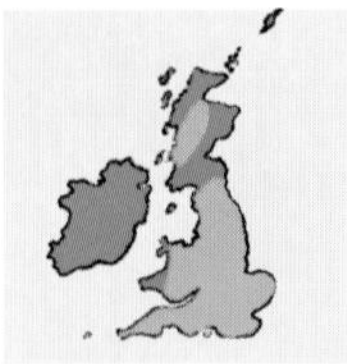

Size and appearance: A hairless perennial with a far-creeping rhizome, forming extensive patches, and erect flowering stems 15–30 cm (6–12 in) tall.

Leaves: In basal pairs or 3s, almost stalkless, oval to spear-shaped, up to 20 cm (8 in) long.

Flowers: Nodding on a slender stalk, each bulbously bell-shaped, creamy-white, richly scented, in a 1-sided cluster.

Fruits: A loose cluster of spherical, red berries just under 10 mm (⅜ in) in diameter.

Related similar plants: Solomon's-seals (p.345) have numerous leaves along the upper stem; the rare May Lily is smaller and has heart-shaped leaves.

Habitat and distribution: Dry woods, scrub, rocky ground and limestone pavements on well-drained soils, where it sometimes carpets the woodland floor; in scattered localities north to the Moray Firth.

Flowering time: May to July.

A POPULAR GARDEN plant that is rather uncommon in the wild, but can be locally abundant, as in limestone woods in parts of the north of England, and in woods over sand in the south-east, even near London. Where the plant is native, it is, like Common Solomon's-seal, an indicator of ancient woodland.

The plant is poisonous, and has medicinal properties similar to those of Foxglove (p.256). It is a symbol of purity and of the Virgin Mary's tears at the Crucifixion, and in France it is a traditional love-gift (*Muguet de Mai*) on 1 May. This charming custom alludes to a passage in the biblical Song of Solomon: 'I am the Rose of Sharon, and the lily of the valleys'.

A somewhat similar but much rarer plant, May Lily (*Maianthemum bifolium*), has two shiny, heart-shaped leaves and a spike of small, white flowers with strongly protruding stamens. Widespread in northern Europe and the Alps, in England it is restricted to a handful of woods in the north and east.

Top left and right *Lily-of-the-Valley* (Convallaria majalis) *has a pair of erect, broad, elliptical basal leaves from the centre of which arises the flower spike. The graceful spray of white, bell-shaped flowers is richly fragrant.*

Bottom *Lily-of-the-Valley sometimes can be found carpeting woodland floors.*

Grape-hyacinth

LILY FAMILY

(Liliaceae)

SPECIES INFORMATION	
COMMON NAME	Grape-hyacinth
SCIENTIFIC NAME	Muscari neglectum
RELATED SPECIES	Bluebell, Spring Squill
HEIGHT/SPREAD	10–30 cm tall
FLOWERING TIME	April–May
HABITAT	Grassland and hedge-banks

Note: The true wild plant has darker flowers than garden plants.

Size and appearance: A tufted, bulbous perennial with a rosette of numerous leaves and an erect flowering stem 10–30 cm (4–12 in) tall.
Leaves: Grass-like, deeply grooved, up to 30 cm (12 in) long.
Flowers: 3–5 mm (⅛–⅕ in) long, dark violet-blue, smelling of cheap soap, in a dense, egg-shaped spike; uppermost flowers smaller, paler.
Fruits: Almost spherical, 3-angled capsule, splitting into 3 segments.
Related similar plants: Garden Grape-hyacinth has uniformly paler blue, less scented flowers; Bluebell (p.338) has larger flowers in a loose, 1-sided spike.
Habitat and distribution: A scarce plant of dry grassland, road-verges and hedge-banks in East Anglia and central England.
Flowering time: April to May

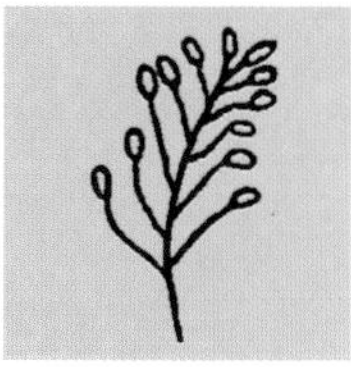

FLOWER TYPE

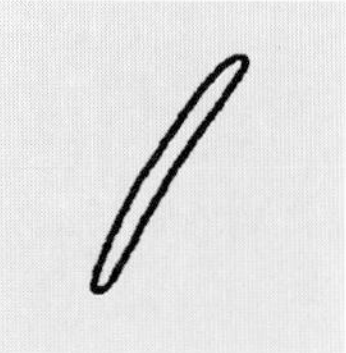

IDENTIFICATION

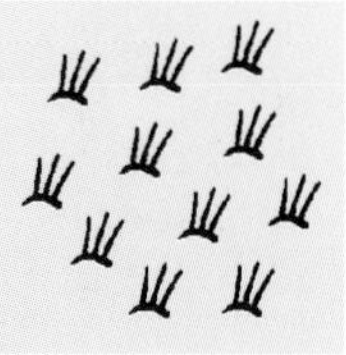

HABITAT

POPULATION

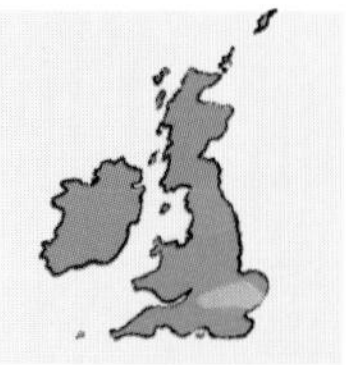

MAP

THIS STRIKING PLANT is one of a group of handsome but rare or shy-flowering members of the lily family. Seemingly exotic plants, almost all of them natives, they are one of the most colourful elements of spring and early summer flora.

Garden Grape-hyacinth (*Muscari armeniacum*) is more robust, with uniformly paler blue, much less scented flowers. It often escapes into grassy and waste places, especially where garden rubbish has been dumped. It has been suggested that the wild Grape-hyacinth is not native either, but came into England as an introduced weed in fields of cultivated Saffron Crocus.

Grape-hyacinth (Muscari neglectum) *sends up egg-shaped flower spikes. Only some of the flowers are fertile, and these are a deep blue with white lobes; those that are sterile are smaller and a paler blue. The long narrow leaves are deeply grooved and semi-cylindrical lying in a limp heap at the base of the erect flower stalks. Grape-hyacinths are rare in the wild, but in a few places in East Anglia can sometimes be seen in large numbers.*

Field Wood-rush

RUSH AND WOOD-RUSH FAMILY (Juncaceae)

SPECIES INFORMATION	
COMMON NAME	Field Wood-rush, Good Friday Grass
SCIENTIFIC NAME	Luzula campestris
RELATED SPECIES	Rushes
HEIGHT/SPREAD	5–30 cm tall
FLOWERING TIME	April–June
HABITAT	Grassland and lawns

Note: The earliest grass-like plant to flower in spring.

FLOWER TYPE

IDENTIFICATION

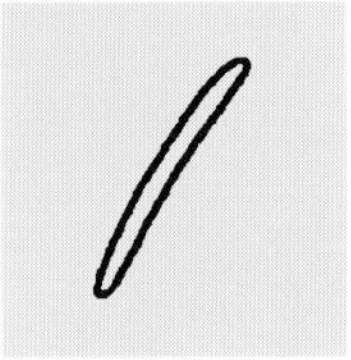

HABITAT

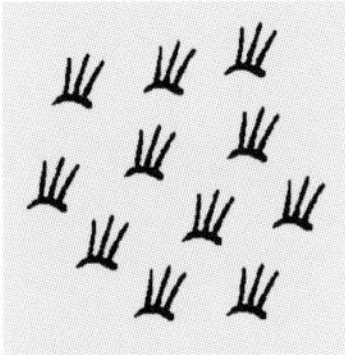

POPULATION

MAP

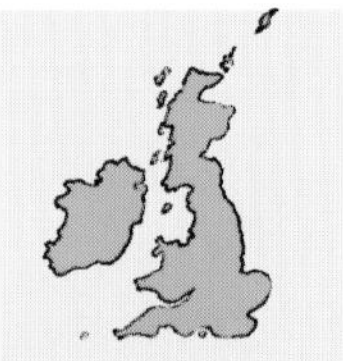

Size and appearance: A small, tufted perennial 5–30 cm (2–12 in) tall, with loose rosettes of leaves.

Leaves: Mostly basal, grass-like, pale green, with scattered long, white hairs.

Flowers: 3–4 mm (⅛–⅙ in) long, pale brown or reddish-brown, rather shiny, with 6 conspicuous pale yellow stamens, in a cluster of stalked heads.

Fruits: Egg-shaped, brown capsules, each with 3 seeds.

Related or similar plants: The rushes (not included in this book) have long, hairless, usually cylindrical leaves, and stems that contain white pith.

Habitat and distribution: A common plant of short, damp, for the most part lime-poor grassland, lawns and woodland clearings.

Flowering time: April to June.

FIELD WOOD-RUSH IS a characteristic plant of grassy places on poor soil, not least neglected lawns. The early flowering season - most grasses and grass-like plants flower in summer - gives it the popular name Good Friday Grass. It is the commonest of 10 species of wood-rush native to Britain and Ireland. This and Great Wood-rush, which is a feature of woods in the north and west, are relatively easy to distinguish, but the others are in general hard to identify and several are rare.

Rush flowers have parts in 6s and are similar to those of the lily family, but the petals are small and brown rather than conspicuous and coloured.

Top *Field Wood-rush* (Luzula campestris) *is a short, creeping plant which sends up dark clusters of nut-brown flowers in a drooping cluster of close, short-stalked heads. The yellow anthers are conspicuous and much longer than their stalks.*

Bottom left *The limp, flat, grass-like leaves are shiny and fringed with long, white, cottony hairs.*

Bottom right *Great Wood-rush* (Luzula sylvatica) *is a robust plant up to 80 cm (32 in) tall and with darker green, hairier leaves 5–25 mm (⅕–1 in) wide. Sometimes forming a leafy carpet and widespread in damp and rocky woodlands, especially on lime-poor soils in the north and west.*

SPECIES INFORMATION	
COMMON NAME	Wild Daffodil, Lent Lily
SCIENTIFIC NAME	Narcissus pseudonarcissus
RELATED SPECIES	Snowdrop
HEIGHT/SPREAD	15–40 cm tall
FLOWERING TIME	February–April
HABITAT	Woodland, pastures, churchyards

Note: A smaller plant than escaped garden daffodils.

Wild Daffodil

DAFFODIL FAMILY

(Amaryllidaceae)

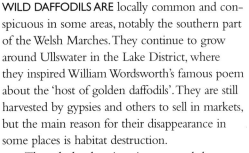

WILD DAFFODILS ARE locally common and conspicuous in some areas, notably the southern part of the Welsh Marches. They continue to grow around Ullswater in the Lake District, where they inspired William Wordsworth's famous poem about the 'host of golden daffodils'. They are still harvested by gypsies and others to sell in markets, but the main reason for their disappearance in some places is habitat destruction.

The whole plant is poisonous and the sap causes skin and other allergies in some people. Animals, even pigs, avoid eating the plants when they grow in pastures. The Latin name *Narcissus* comes via Greek probably from an even more ancient language, and is thus one of the oldest words in use. Daffodil too is an ancient name, a corruption of the medieval Latin *Affodilus*, itself derived from the ancient Greek *Asphodelus*, Asphodel (actually another plant, in the Lily family).

Wild Daffodil (Narcissus pseudonarcissus) *is a much slenderer plant than the garden varieties. Its nodding flowers are also smaller. The trumpet-like tube of the inner petals is as long as the outer petals, but is of a darker yellow. The leaves are long, narrower than most garden species, and a rather greyish green. For many the first sign of spring is the sight of a mass of daffodils colouring the woodland floor.*

FLOWER TYPE

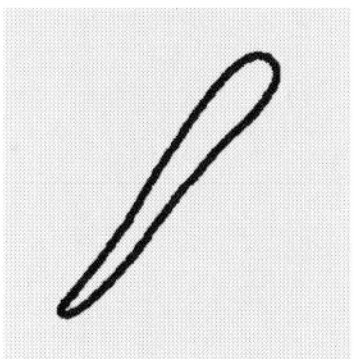

IDENTIFICATION

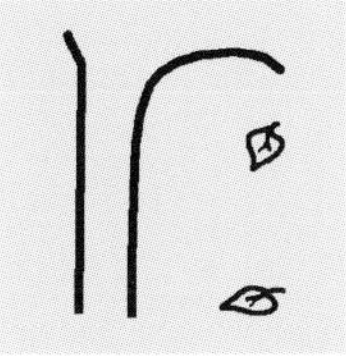

HABITAT

POPULATION

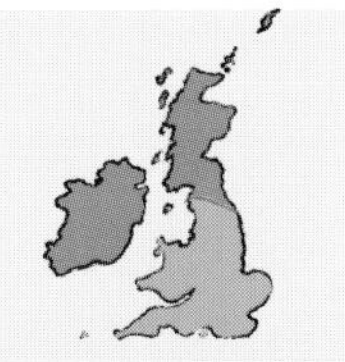

MAP

Size and appearance: An erect, hairless, bulbous perennial 15–40 cm (6–16 in) tall, forming clumps and patches.

Leaves: All basal, narrow, strap-shaped, greyish-green.

Flowers: Solitary, 35–60 mm (1⅖–2⅖ in) across, nodding, slightly scented, pale yellow, the central trumpet deeper in colour; buds in a papery sheath.

Fruits: Stalked, egg-shaped capsules 10–25 mm (⅖–1 in) long.

Related or similar plants: Escaped or wild-planted garden daffodils are usually more robust and uniformly golden-yellow in colour.

Habitat and distribution: Widespread but local in England, where it is commonest in the west, and parts of Wales; on damp but well-drained, humus-rich soils in open and coppiced woods, scrub, old pastures and churchyards; introduced in Scotland and Ireland.

Flowering time: February to April.

Snowdrop

DAFFODIL FAMILY

(Amaryllidaceae)

SPECIES INFORMATION	
COMMON NAME	Snowdrop
SCIENTIFIC NAME	Galanthus nivalis
RELATED SPECIES	Wild Daffodil
HEIGHT/SPREAD	10–25 cm tall
FLOWERING TIME	January–March
HABITAT	Woodland, pastures, churchyards

Note: A familiar winter wild flower, and like no other.

FLOWER TYPE

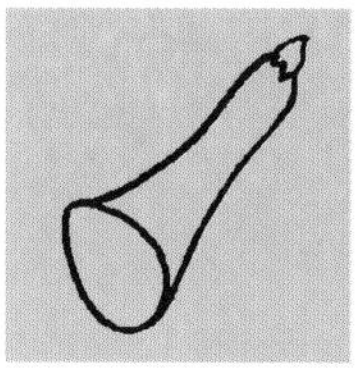

IDENTIFICATION

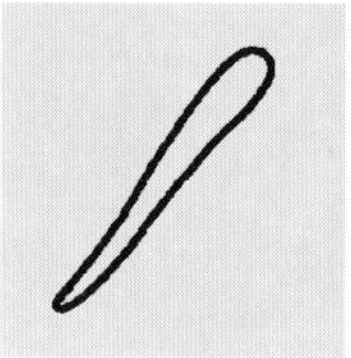

HABITAT

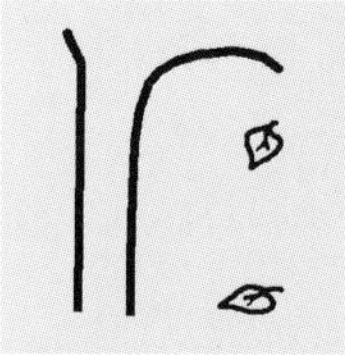

POPULATION

MAP

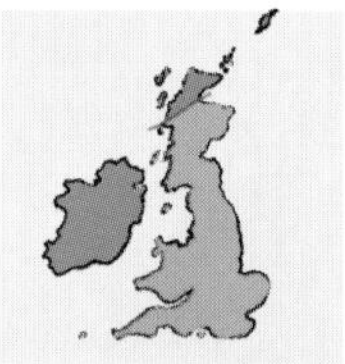

SNOWDROPS BRIGHTEN THE countryside even when it is still in the grip of winter. This plant is often assumed to be introduced, but some botanists, especially those of a romantic disposition, remain undecided about its native status. The evidence does largely point to human introduction, as the plants are often associated with settlements past or present. Certainly it is often found around churches and earlier pagan sites of worship. This favourite flower of late winter is particularly associated with Candlemas on 2 February, the feast of the Purification of the Virgin Mary. However, it might be native in a few river-valleys in the uplands of south-west England.

The related Summer Snowflake or Loddon Lily (*Leucojum aestivum*) is a true native but rarer. It is larger, 30–60 cm (12–24 in) tall, with wider, green leaves and flowers in clusters of 3-5. It is a feature of swamp woodland and riversides in the Thames Valley, especially along the River Loddon in Berkshire, and in a few other places in southern England and in southern Ireland.

Size and appearance: An erect, hairless, bulbous perennial 10–25 cm (4–10 in) tall, forming clumps and patches.

Leaves: All basal, narrow, strap-shaped, greyish-green.

Flowers: Solitary, nodding, scented, white, the 3 inner petals with green-patterned, notched tips; buds in a membranous sheath.

Fruits: Egg-shaped capsules 8–15 mm (⅓–⅗ in) long, on slender nodding stalks.

Related or similar plants: Summer Snowflake is taller with flowers in clusters of 3-5.

Habitat and distribution: Widespread and locally abundant on damp but well-drained, usually humus-rich soils in open woods, scrub, hedges, streamsides and churchyards; local in Scotland and almost absent from Ireland.

Flowering time: January to March, but from Christmas onwards in mild winters.

Snowdrops (Galanthus nivalis) *make a charming picture carpeting a woodland floor in late winter. Their grey-green leaves surround the nodding heads of white flowers with their neat, green markings. They are well known for brightening up a winter churchyard.*

SPECIES INFORMATION	
COMMON NAME	Black Bryony
SCIENTIFIC NAME	Tamus communis
RELATED SPECIES	None
HEIGHT/SPREAD	Stems 1–4 m tall
FLOWERING TIME	May–August
HABITAT	Hedges, scrub and woodland

Note: The only native climber with glossy heart-shaped leaves.

Black Bryony

YAM FAMILY
(Dioscoreaceae)

Size and appearance: A hairless, climbing perennial, twining clockwise, with stems 1–4 m (3–12 ft) tall, rising from a large tuber.
Leaves: Elongate heart-shaped, long-stalked, pointed, dark green, shiny, up to 15 cm long.
Flowers: Either male or female on separate plants, 3–6 mm (⅛–¼) across, with 6 greenish-yellow petals, in long, loose spikes from the leaf-angles.
Fruits: Loose clusters of shiny scarlet berries c. 10 mm (⅜ in) across.
Related or similar plants: The bindweeds (p.214–216) have glossy, less pointed leaves; the unrelated White Bryony (p.160) has lobed leaves and spring-like tendrils.
Habitat and distribution: A widespread plant of hedgerows, woods and scrub, from northern England southwards; in Ireland only around Lough Gill, County Sligo.
Flowering time: May-August, but conspicuous in fruit during autumn.

FLOWER TYPE

IDENTIFICATION

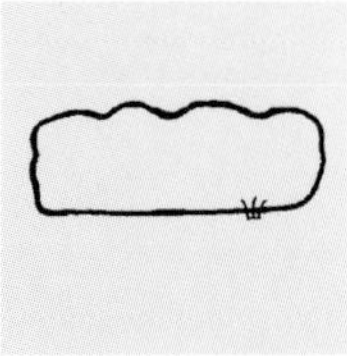

HABITAT

POPULATION

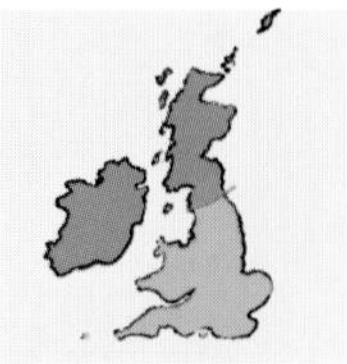

MAP

BLACK BRYONY IS the only representative of the important tropical yam family in our flora. The blackish, lobed tuber is an indication of its affinities. Note that both the tuber and the berries are poisonous. However, the youngest spring shoots used to be cooked and eaten like asparagus, and are still sold as such in markets throughout southern Europe.

This is one of four wild yams in Europe, and by far the most widespread of these, extending from western Europe and the Mediterranean region to the Caucasus. Two others occur in the Pyrenees, another in the Balkans.

Hedges are Black Bryony's (Tamus communis) *characteristic habitat, climbing over and through the shrubs. The leaves are an elegant heart-shape, dark green and shiny while the flowers form loose spikes with tiny greenish-yellow petals. These give rise to loose clusters of shiny and scarlet poisonous berries*

Yellow Flag

IRIS AND CROCUS FAMILY
(Iridaceae)

SPECIES INFORMATION	
COMMON NAME	Yellow Flag, Yellow Iris
SCIENTIFIC NAME	Iris pseudacorus
RELATED SPECIES	Stinking Iris
HEIGHT/SPREAD	50–150 cm tall
FLOWERING TIME	May–July
HABITAT	Watersides, marshes, wet fields

Note: Our only wild yellow iris; always in wet places.

FLOWER TYPE

IDENTIFICATION

HABITAT

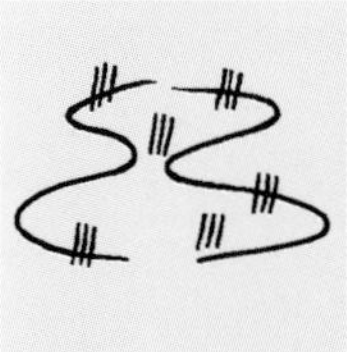

POPULATION

MAP

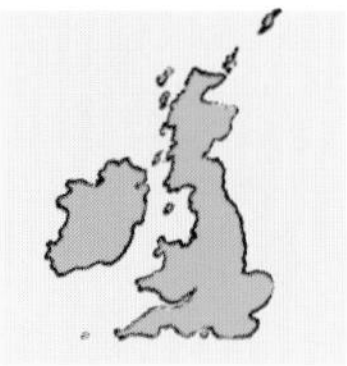

THIS IS ONE of our most handsome and distinctive wild flowers, a feature of wet places and watersides. So many other wetland plants have decreased or even disappeared, but Yellow Flag persists in a range of marshy, often man-made, habitats. The seeds float and are dispersed by water. The rhizome, which is adapted to survive in airless, waterlogged soils, is the source of a black dye.

Top left and right *Yellow Flag* (Iris pseudacorus) *has stiff broad leaves that have a raised midrib. The conspicuous stout flower stems have up to a dozen flowers, only a few of which are open at any one time. These are of a bright yellow with some purple veins in the centre. This is much the commonest Iris, being widespread and frequent in marshes, streamsides and wet pastures.*

Bottom *Stinking Iris or Roast-Beef Plant* (Iris foetidissima) *is a smaller plant, up to 60 cm (24 in) tall, with narrow leaves and greyish-violet or sometimes pale yellow flowers, and conspicuous scarlet seeds. It is a local plant of woods, hedges, coastal scrub and sand-dunes, mainly in south-western England.*

Size and appearance: A robust, erect perennial with stout, fleshy rhizomes, forming large clumps and stems 50–150 cm (20–60 in) tall.
Leaves: Evergreen, sword-shaped, flat, sharp-edged, pointed.
Flowers: Bright yellow, in a cluster of 4-12 but only 1-3 open at once, each emerging from a green sheath or bract; 3 outer petals nodding, purple-veined in the centre.
Fruits: Cylindrical capsules, splitting into 3 segments; seeds brown.
Related or similar plants: Stinking Iris has narrow leaves and greyish-violet flowers, and grows in dry places.
Habitat and distribution: Common and sometimes abundant in marshes, ditches and wet fields, and along the sides of rivers, canals, lakes, muddy streams, ponds and flooded gravel-pits throughout Britain and Ireland.
Flowering time: May to July.

SPECIES INFORMATION	
COMMON NAME	Blue-eyed Grass
SCIENTIFIC NAME	Sisyrinchium bermudiana
RELATED SPECIES	Irises
HEIGHT/SPREAD	15–25 cm tall
FLOWERING TIME	July–August
HABITAT	Damp grassy places, lake-shores

Note: Superficially like a miniature, blue-flowered iris.

Blue-eyed Grass

IRIS AND CROCUS FAMILY (Iridaceae)

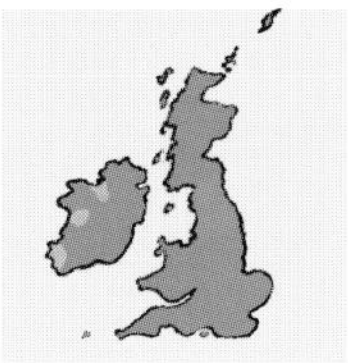

Size and appearance: A hairless, tufted perennial with a short rhizome and erect, winged flowering stems up to 15–25 cm (6–10 in) tall.

Leaves: Very narrow, up to 15 cm (6 in) long, spear-shaped, flat, pointed, pale green.

Flowers: Dish-shaped, rather lily-like, 15–20 mm (⅗–⅘ in) across, light blue with 6 petals and yellow stamens, in 2-3 small clusters.

Fruits: Almost spherical capsules c. 5 mm (½ in) long, stalked and nodding when ripe.

Related or similar plants: Yellow-eyed Grass has yellow flowers and is much rarer; other species are grown in gardens.

Habitat and distribution: Damp grassy places and open vegetation on stony lake-shores in western and north-western Ireland, especially County Kerry; not in Britain.

Flowering time: July to August, the flowers opening only in sunshine.

BLUE-EYED GRASS has the distinction, like Pipewort, of being one of the few wild flowers that these islands share with North America. It is also one of 15 native Irish plants that do not occur in Britain. The American Blue-eyed Grass is slightly different and some botanists treat it as a separate species. It is grown in gardens in Britain (as are several species and cultivars of these attractive plants) and occasionally escapes into the wild.

Another garden escape, Yellow-eyed Grass (*Sisyrinchium californicum*), from western USA, with yellow flowers and larger fruits, is established in one or two places in Ireland.

Blue-eyed Grass (Sisyrinchim bermudiana) *has a tuft of linear leaves. The terminal clusters of flowers are on a stiff, winged, leaf-like stem which makes them look as though they are growing out of the top of the leaves. The flowers themselves are blue with six pointed petals and yellow stamens. They open in sunshine, closing in the afternoon or dull weather. This is a plant of damp grassy places in western Ireland.*

Montbretia

IRIS AND CROCUS FAMILY
(Iridaceae)

SPECIES INFORMATION	
COMMON NAME	Montbretia
SCIENTIFIC NAME	Tritonia crocosmiflora
RELATED SPECIES	Irises
HEIGHT/SPREAD	50–110 cm tall
FLOWERING TIME	July–September
HABITAT	Hedges, banks and stream-banks

Note: The 1-sided sprays of orange flowers are distinctive.

FLOWER TYPE

IDENTIFICATION

HABITAT

POPULATION

MAP

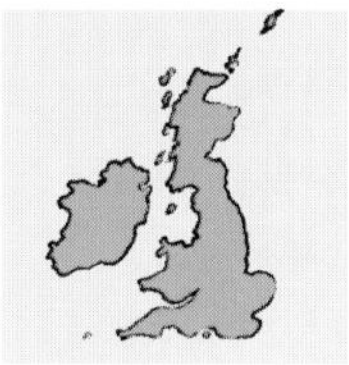

Size and appearance: A hairless, handsome but rather untidy perennial with stems up to 100 cm (3 ft) tall, rising from corms and far-creeping runners or stolons, forming extensive patches.

Leaves: Narrowly spear-shaped, up to 40 cm long, flat, pointed, pale green.

Flowers: Lily-like, bright orange with yellow stamens, in loose, branched, 10- to 20-flowered, 1-sided clusters.

Fruits: Small, broadly egg-shaped capsules, splitting into 3 segments.

Related or similar plants: Yellow Flag and Stinking Iris (p.352) have larger 'iris' flowers.

Habitat and distribution: A naturalised escape from gardens that is locally abundant on hedge-banks, rocky slopes, streamsides, waysides and waste ground, especially near the sea and in the west.

Flowering time: July to September.

THIS COLOURFUL GARDEN escape adds an exotic feel to hedges, banks and gullies, especially in coastal areas of southern and western Britain and Ireland. It is a vigorous garden hybrid derived from a cross between two South African species.

Montbretia (Crocosmia x crocosmiiflora) *is a colourful garden escape which can occur in large quantities on seaside banks as well as streamsides and hedge-banks. It has the flat leaves typical of the Iris family, but the flowers are rather lily-like, with orange petals and yellow stamens held in a one-sided spike.*

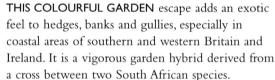

SPECIES INFORMATION	
COMMON NAME	Lords-and-Ladies, Cuckoo-pint
SCIENTIFIC NAME	Arum maculatum
RELATED SPECIES	Italian Arum
HEIGHT/SPREAD	20–40 cm tall
FLOWERING TIME	April–May
HABITAT	Woods and hedges

Note: The cowl-like flowers are unlike any other.

Lords-and-Ladies

ARUM FAMILY
(Araceae)

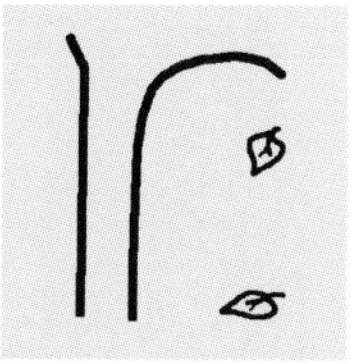

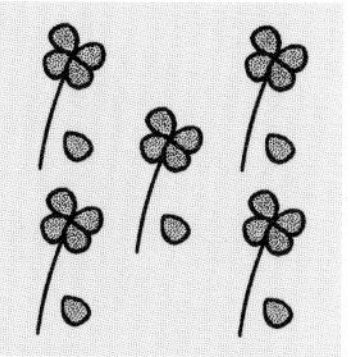

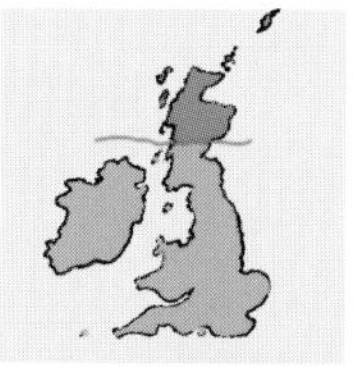

Size and appearance: A hairless perennial 20–40 cm (8–16 in) tall, rising from a tuberous rhizome and forming clumps and patches.

Leaves: All basal, arrow-shaped, long-stalked, shiny, often spotted with blackish-purple.

Flowers: Small but massed in a columnar cluster topped by a cream or purple club-shaped spadix; flowers enveloped by a conspicuous pale yellowish-green or purplish, cowl-like spathe up to 25 cm (10 in) long.

Fruits: Stout, cylindrical spike, 4–8 cm ($1\frac{3}{5}$–$3\frac{1}{5}$ in) long, of scarlet berries.

Related or similar plants: Italian Arum is very similar but much rarer.

Habitat and distribution: Common in woods, hedgerows and untended gardens north to Fife; widespread but more local in Ireland.

Flowering time: April to May, sometimes into early June; also conspicuous in fruit in autumn.

THE POLLINATION MECHANISM of this and related plants is remarkable and involves the trapping of midges at the base of the flower-cluster. Attracted by a carrion smell given off by the spadix, they enter by crawling past an upper ring of hairs, but are unable to push back out again. The stamens are not yet mature, but the midges may brush pollen from another plant on to the female flowers below them. After a day the stamens mature and shed pollen on to the midges. The hairs wither and the midges escape, dispersing the pollen of the male flowers to another plant.

Starch stored in the rhizome was formerly used as a thickening agent in the manner of arrowroot, and as a laundry starch, stiffening the elaborate ruffs of the Elizabethan Age. The handsome fruits are poisonous, hence the country name of Adder's Meat. This curious and distinctive plant has attracted almost more names than any other, some lewd, almost all humorous. Best of all is Kitty-come-down-the-lane-jump-up-and-kiss-me.

Italian Arum (*Arum italicum*) is similar but has unspotted leaves, that emerge in autumn. Flowering in May–June, with a stout yellow spadix and drooping spathe, it is scattered along or near the south coast of England and in the Isles of Scilly.

Lords-and-Ladies (Arum maculatum) *has an unusual flower which appears in spring. The photograph to the right shows a close-up of the purple spadix surrounded by the cowl-like spathe.*

Common Duckweed

DUCKWEED FAMILY

(Lemnaceae)

SPECIES INFORMATION	
COMMON NAME	Common Duckweed
SCIENTIFIC NAME	Lemna minor
RELATED SPECIES	Other duckweeds
HEIGHT/SPREAD	2–5 mm across, in dense masses
FLOWERING TIME	June–July
HABITAT	Still waters
Note: Green 'pond-scum', barely recognisable as a wild flower.	

FLOWER TYPE

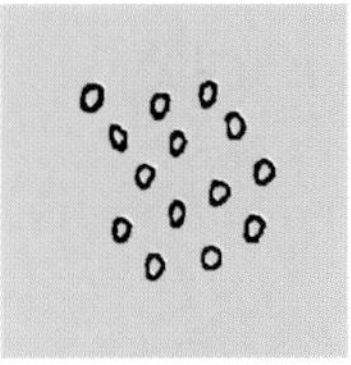

IDENTIFICATION

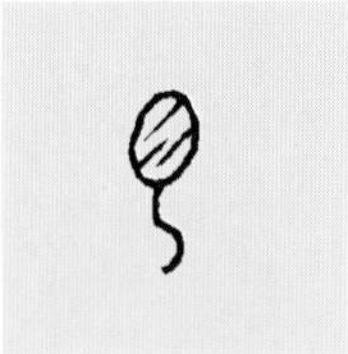

HABITAT

POPULATION

MAP

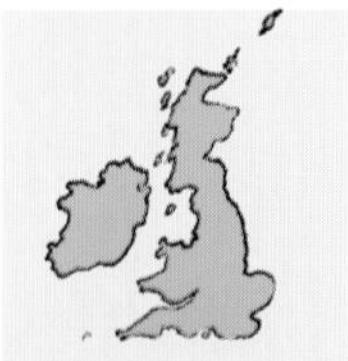

Size and appearance: A minute, floating, aquatic perennial with rounded fronds that replace stems and leaves; a single root hangs beneath.
Leaves: Green shoots reduced to a flat, 3-veined frond or floating plate.
Flowers: Minute, inconspicuous, enclosed in a sheath; 1 stamen only.
Fruits: Minute and rarely formed in Britain.
Related or similar plants: Other duckweeds; Azolla, a small, floating, usually reddish or purplish fern, is the only similar plant.
Habitat and distribution: Commonly forming a green mat on the surface of quiet or stagnant lakes and ponds, slow-flowing streams and flooded ditches, even in water-butts, or the puddles and ruts of tracks and roadsides, throughout Britain and Ireland.
Flowering time: June to July.

Top *Common Duckweed* (Lemna minor) *is a small aquatic which floats around on the water's surface being taken wherever the wind and water-flow dictate; as a consequence they are commonest on still or slow-flowing water.*

THIS IS THE commonest duckweed, of which five others are native and one is introduced. Of these, Least Duckweed (*Lemna minuscula*), very similar to Common Duckweed but with narrower, 1-veined fronds, is spreading rapidly along rivers and canals. Introduced from the Americas, it was first recorded in Britain only in 1977. Greater Duckweed (*Spirodela polyrhiza*), up to 10 mm (3/8 in) across, often purplish beneath and bearing several roots, is found mostly in southern and eastern England. All are much eaten by wildfowl.

Bottom left *Great Duckweed* (Spirodela polyrhiza) *is, by comparison, a much larger plant, but it is not as common, requiring better quality water than Common Duckweed.*

Bottom right *The photograph below shows three Duckweeds: the Great Duckweed, the Common Duckweed and the Rootless Duckweed which has tiny fronds approximately 1.2–1.5 mm (1/20–1/16 in) across and which is swollen on both sides. It is native in ponds and ditches, but very local in southern England and parts of Wales.*

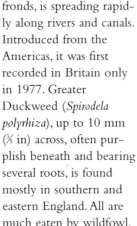

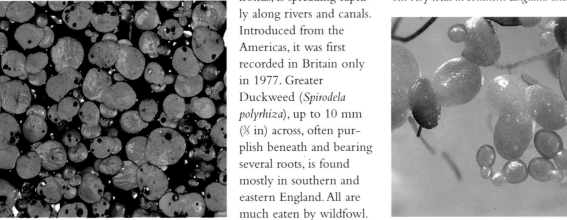

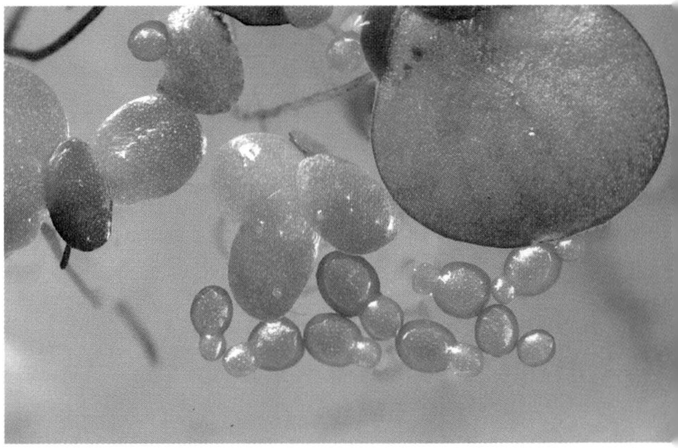

SPECIES INFORMATION	
COMMON NAME	Branched Bur-reed
SCIENTIFIC NAME	Sparganium erectum
RELATED SPECIES	Unbranched Bur-reed
HEIGHT/SPREAD	30–150 cm tall
FLOWERING TIME	June–August
HABITAT	Marshes and shallow water

Note: The spherical clusters of flowers are characteristic.

Branched Bur-reed

BUR-REED FAMILY
(Sparganiaceae)

Size and appearance: A robust, hairless perennial with a short rhizome and erect, zigzag stems 30–150 cm (12–60 in) tall.
Leaves: Grass-like, triangular in section, stiff, erect or sometimes floating in water.
Flowers: Tiny, massed in spherical clusters on 3-8 branches.
Fruits: 1-seeded, in spherical, spiky clusters 6–10 mm (¼–⅜ in) across.
Related or similar plants: Unbranched Bur-reed has unbranched stems.
Habitat and distribution: A widespread plant of marshes and the watersides, shallow water or exposed mud of rivers and streams, disused canals, ponds and marshy fields; throughout Britain and Ireland.
Flowering time: June to August, but conspicuous in fruit during late summer.

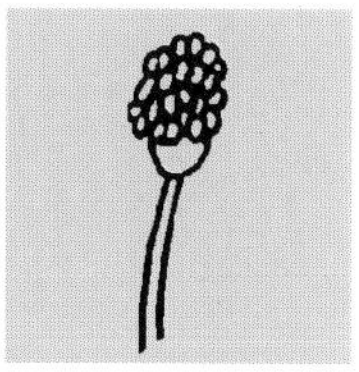

FLOWER TYPE

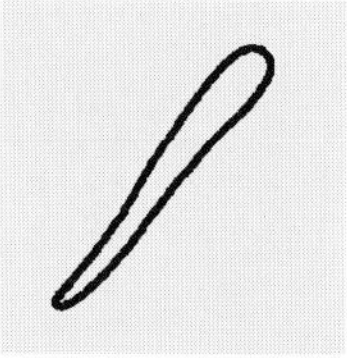

IDENTIFICATION

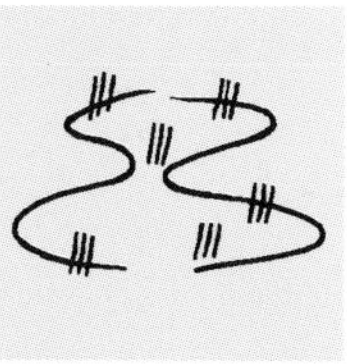

HABITAT

POPULATION

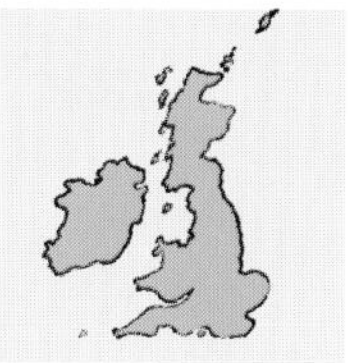

MAP

A VARIABLE SPECIES, especially in the form of the fruits, and the commonest of four native bur-reeds. Of these others, only Unbranched Bur-reed is at all common, whereas the other two are scarce plants mostly found in peaty pools and lakes in western Scotland and western Ireland.

Top *Branched Bur-reed* (Sparganium erectum) *has long, erect leaves which are three-sided especially lower down, where they sheath into the base. The male and female flowers are separate; the smaller males are at the top of the flower stalk, where their yellow anthers soon fade, and the larger females are lower down on the stalk — these swell into the bur-like heads.*

Bottom *Unbranched Bur-reed* (Sparganium emersum)*, similar but smaller and unbranched, often with floating leaves, is also widespread in wet places but is more scattered in distribution*

Common Reedmace

REEDMACE FAMILY

(Typhaceae)

SPECIES INFORMATION	
COMMON NAME	Common Reedmace, Bulrush
SCIENTIFIC NAME	Typha latifolia
RELATED SPECIES	Lesser Reedmace
HEIGHT/SPREAD	1–2.5 m tall, in large patches
FLOWERING TIME	June–August
HABITAT	Rivers, lakes and ponds

Note: The sausage-like flower-spikes are distinctive.

FLOWER TYPE

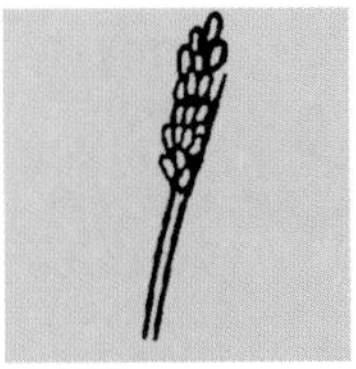

IDENTIFICATION

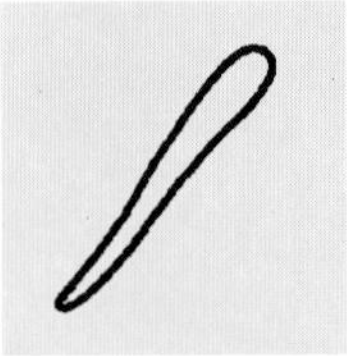

HABITAT

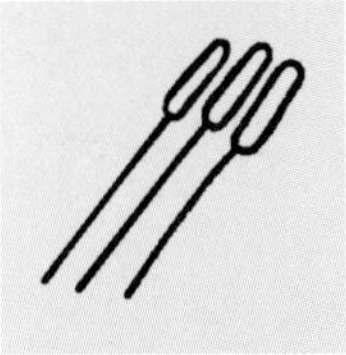

POPULATION

MAP

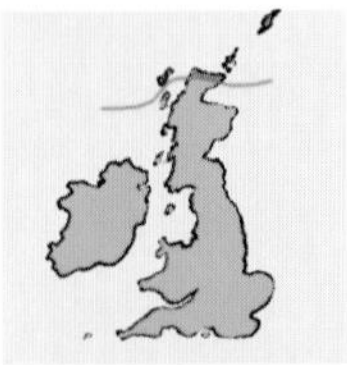

REEDMACES ARE A well-known feature of wet places, often forming tall, dense stands. The more familiar name Bulrush is often applied by botanists to Common Club-rush, a large member of the sedge family. The sausage-like fruit masses explode when they are ripe, releasing huge numbers of seeds and hairs into the wind.

The reedmace or cat-tail family comprises a single genus of a dozen species worldwide. They are widely used in other countries to make thatch, mats, ropes, paper and even clothing, and the flower-spikes are eaten as a vegetable.

Size and appearance: A robust, grass- or reed-like perennial 1–2.5 m (3–7½ ft) tall, with a stout, far-creeping rhizome giving rise to extensive patches.

Leaves: Mostly basal, in two opposite rows, sword-like, rather greyish-green.

Flowers: Minute female flowers massed in brown, sausage-like spikes 10-15 x c. 2.5 cm (4–5 x 1 in) long, topped by a narrow, yellowish spike of male flowers.

Fruits: Tiny, packed among soft hairs derived from the reduced flower-parts, within the persistent female flower-spike.

Related or similar plants: Lesser Reedmace has narrower leaves; grasses and reeds lack the sausage-like flower-spike.

Habitat and distribution: A common waterside plant of slow rivers and streams, lakes, ponds and ditches throughout Britain and Ireland, but local in Scotland.

Flowering time: June to August, but most conspicuous in fruit from late summer through autumn and winter.

Common Reedmace (Typha latifolia) *is a tall, aquatic plant familiar at the sides of ponds and rivers and quite capable of surviving being snowed-in in winter. It has long, stiff, greyish-green leaves but it is the flower-heads which most people notice. At first there are both male and female flowers, but the smaller yellowish males soon wither leaving the more obvious deep-brown female flowers massed into sausage-shaped spikes. As winter progresses, they release their fluffy seeds, often aided by tits and finches.*

SPECIES INFORMATION	
COMMON NAME	Pipewort
SCIENTIFIC NAME	Eriocaulon aquaticum
RELATED SPECIES	None
HEIGHT/SPREAD	20–40 cm tall
FLOWERING TIME	July–September
HABITAT	Shallow peaty lakes

Note: A strange plant found in W & NW Atlantic fringes.

Pipewort

PIPEWORT FAMILY
(Eriocaulaceae)

PIPEWORT IS ONE of a select group of plants, found especially in western Ireland, that we share with North America. It is the only native species in Europe of a largely tropical family, although an Asian species is naturalised in rice-fields in Italy.

Pipewort (Eriocaulon aquaticum) *is an aquatic which occurs in shallow peaty lakes in western Ireland. It has a dense basal tuft of short, narrow, translucent leaves which taper to a point from which the flower stem arises with terminal button-like clusters.*

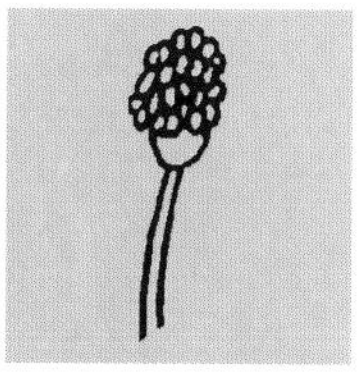
FLOWER TYPE

IDENTIFICATION

HABITAT

POPULATION

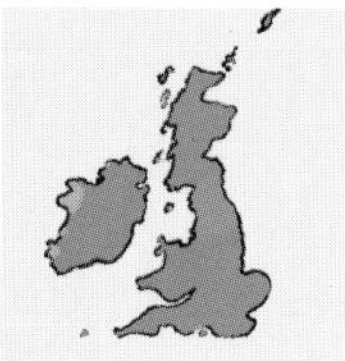
MAP

Size and appearance: An unusual hairless perennial with white, worm-like roots and far-creeping stolons that give rise to clumps and mats, and fragile, erect flowering stems 20–60 cm (8–24 in) tall.

Leaves: All basal in a rosette, up to 10 cm (4 in) long, narrow, tapering to a point, translucent.

Flowers: Male and female, small, massed in a greyish, button-like cluster 10–20 mm ($\frac{2}{5}$–$\frac{4}{5}$ in) across, at the top of the stem.

Fruits: Numerous small capsules.

Related or similar plants: None, as this species is our only representative of a largely tropical family.

Habitat and distribution: Restricted in distribution, but locally common in shallow peaty pools and margins of lakes in western Ireland, especially Connemara, and the Inner Hebrides (where it is rare).

Flowering time: July to September.

Broad-leaved Pondweed

PONDWEED FAMILY

(Potamogetonaceae)

SPECIES INFORMATION	
COMMON NAME	Broad-leaved Pondweed
SCIENTIFIC NAME	Potamogeton natans
RELATED SPECIES	Bog Pondweed
HEIGHT/SPREAD	Stems 1–3 m long
FLOWERING TIME	May–September
HABITAT	Still and flowing water

Note: The commonest pondweed with large floating leaves.

FLOWER TYPE

IDENTIFICATION

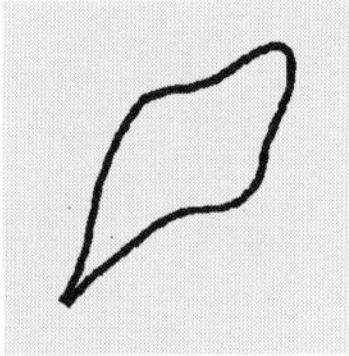

HABITAT

POPULATION

MAP

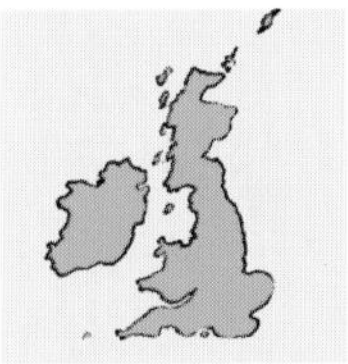

'PONDWEED' IS A loose term applied to many aquatic plants, but also has a precise botanical meaning. Broad-leaved Pondweed is the commonest of a group of some 20 native pondweeds, species of Potamogeton. This name comes from the Greek word for river (*potamos*), the same root as the derivation of another habitual river-dweller, the hippopotamus. Broad-leaved Pondweed has a very wide habitat tolerance. However, in northern and western areas it tends to be replaced by Bog Pondweed.

Size and appearance: An aquatic perennial with little-branched stems 1–3 m (3–9 ft) long, sheath-like stipules, and both submerged and floating leaves.

Leaves: Submerged, narrow and sheathing, or floating, long-stalked, with a flexible join between the stalk and the oval-to-oblong, green blade.

Flowers: Numerous, small, green, in dense spikes 2–6 cm (4/5–2 2/5 in) long, emerging from the water on a stout stalk.

Fruits: Long clusters of greenish, 1-seeded nutlets 3–4 mm (1/8–1/6 in) long.

Related or similar plants: Bog Pondweed has more broader submerged leaves and smaller nutlets.

Habitat and distribution: Widespread in fairly shallow, still or flowing water of ponds, lakes, streams, canals and rivers, both slow- and fast-flowing, throughout Britain and Ireland, but commonest in the lowlands.

Flowering time: May to September.

Top and bottom left *Broad-leaved Pondweed* (Potamogeton natans) *has submerged leaves, but it is the floating, oval leaves which are noticeable. Basically green, they are often tinged with brown, taking on a rather bronzey hue. The flowers are small and numerous in dense spikes which poke out above the leaves.*

Bottom right *Bog Pondweed* (Potamogeton polygonifolius) *is similar but the submerged leaves are broader, the brownish floating leaves lack the flexible stalk-blade joint, and the nutlets are small and reddish-brown.*

SPECIES INFORMATION	
COMMON NAME	Perfoliate Pondweed
SCIENTIFIC NAME	Potamogeton perfoliatus
RELATED SPECIES	Curled Pondweed
HEIGHT/SPREAD	Stems 1–3 m long
FLOWERING TIME	May–September
HABITAT	Still and flowing water

Note: The heart-shaped leaf-bases clasp the stem.

Perfoliate Pondweed

PONDWEED FAMILY (Potamogetonaceae)

PERFOLIATE PONDWEED NEEDS deeper water, but it has a wide habitat tolerance and is variable in form. Plants from lakes in northern Britain often have longer, narrower leaves. The typical, broad-leaved plant is one of the easiest pondweeds to recognise. It remains frequent in lowland England, where many aquatic plants have disappeared through pollution and drainage.

The 20 or so native pondweeds differ greatly in the shape of their leaves. In several species with totally submerged leaves, they are finely dissected. They occupy a range of wet habitats, but some have very precise ecological needs, such as brackish marshes and lime-rich or lime-poor water.

Top left and right *Perfoliate Pondweed* (Potamogeton perfoliatus) *is often found in still, clear water. It forms numerous, small green flowers in dense cylindrical spikes.*

Bottom *Curled Pondweed* (Potamogeton crispus) *has spear-shaped, blunt, finely toothed, often reddish-tinged, submerged leaves with very wavy margins and long-beaked nutlets. Flowering May-October, the plant is widespread in nutrient-rich, still or flowing waters.*

Size and appearance: An aquatic perennial with branched stems 1–3 m (3–9 ft) or more long, sheath-like stipules (soon falling) and submerged leaves.

Leaves: All submerged, stalkless, green, translucent, oval to broadly spear-shaped, the heart-shaped base clasping the stem.

Flowers: Numerous, small, green, in dense, cylindrical spikes 15–25 mm (⅗–1 in) long, emerging from the water on a stout stalk.

Fruits: Clusters of greenish, 1-seeded nutlets 3–4 mm (⅛–⅙ in) long.

Related or similar plants: Curled Pondweed has narrower, wavy leaves and larger nutlets.

Habitat and distribution: Widespread in deep, still or slow-flowing water of ponds, lakes, gravel-pits, streams, canals and rivers throughout Britain and Ireland, although locally absent as in Cornwall and much of West Wales.

Flowering time: May to September.

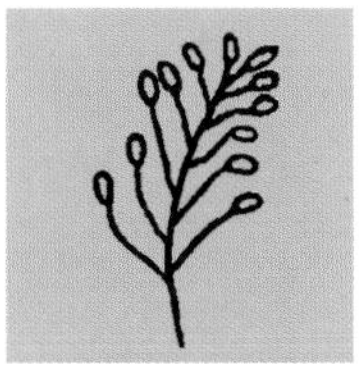
FLOWER TYPE

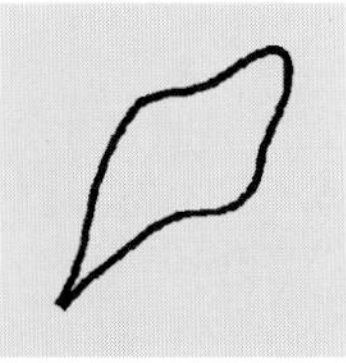
IDENTIFICATION

HABITAT

POPULATION

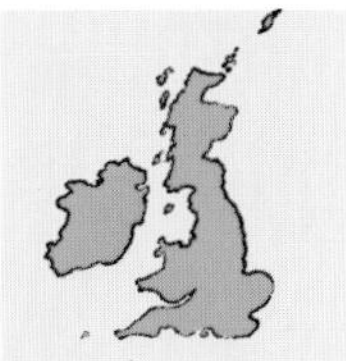
MAP

Beaked Tasselweed

PONDWEED FAMILY
(Potamogetonaceae)

SPECIES INFORMATION	
COMMON NAME	Beaked Tasselweed
SCIENTIFIC NAME	Ruppia maritima
RELATED SPECIES	Horned Pondweed
HEIGHT/SPREAD	Stems 20–40 cm long
FLOWERING TIME	July–September
HABITAT	Brackish ditches and pools

Note: Submerged, grass-like plant of seaside ditches.

FLOWER TYPE

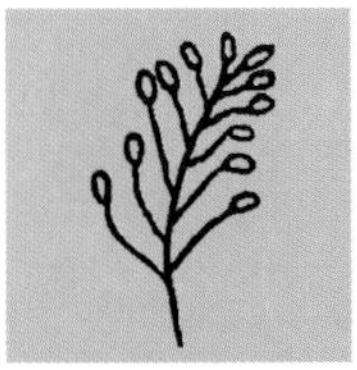

IDENTIFICATION

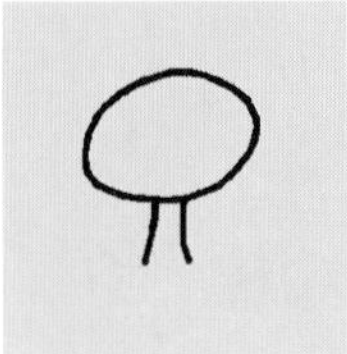

HABITAT

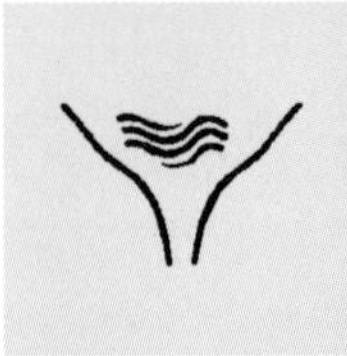

POPULATION

MAP

Size and appearance: An aquatic perennial with slender, branched stems 20–40 cm (8–16 in) long, and submerged leaves.

Leaves: All submerged, up to 10 cm (4 in) long, bright green, very narrow, grass-like, just the tips very finely toothed.

Flowers: Small, without petals or sepals, green, in small clusters.

Fruits: Clusters of stalked, greenish, 1-seeded, pear-shaped nutlets 2–3 mm (1/12–1/8 in) long.

Related or similar plants: Horned Pondweed has whorls of shorter leaves, and longer nutlets.

Habitat and distribution: Local in brackish lakes, pools, ditches, creeks and quiet estuaries around most of the coasts of Britain and Ireland, also in pools of inland salt-marshes in the west Midlands.

Flowering time: July to September.

BEAKED TASSELWEED IS mostly a plant of rather scruffy brackish pools and ditches, usually on its own but sometimes with Horned Pondweed. It is scattered in distribution but quite common, for example, on the coasts about the Thames Estuary. It can be distinguished from narrow-leaved pondweeds by the fine teeth at the tips of the leaves. It is not a plant that merits attention on its looks, but it has a most interesting, specialised ecological niche.

Top left and right
Beaked Tasselweed (Ruppia maritima) *is often found in dykes at the foot of taller vegetation.*

Bottom right
*Horned Pondweed (*Zannichellia palustris*), in its own but related family, is similar in general appearance but has leaves in opposite pairs, and whorls of 2-6 stalkless nutlets 4–5 mm (1/6–1/5 in) in long, with curved beaks. Flowering May–August, it is widespread in fresh or brackish waters, especially in England and eastern Ireland.*

SPECIES INFORMATION	
COMMON NAME	Eel-grass
SCIENTIFIC NAME	Zostera marina
RELATED SPECIES	Beaked Tasselweed
HEIGHT/SPREAD	Stems 50–150 cm long
FLOWERING TIME	June–September
HABITAT	Mud or sand flats

Note: Submerged, grass-like plant of seashores.

Eel-grass

PONDWEED FAMILY

(Potamogetonaceae)

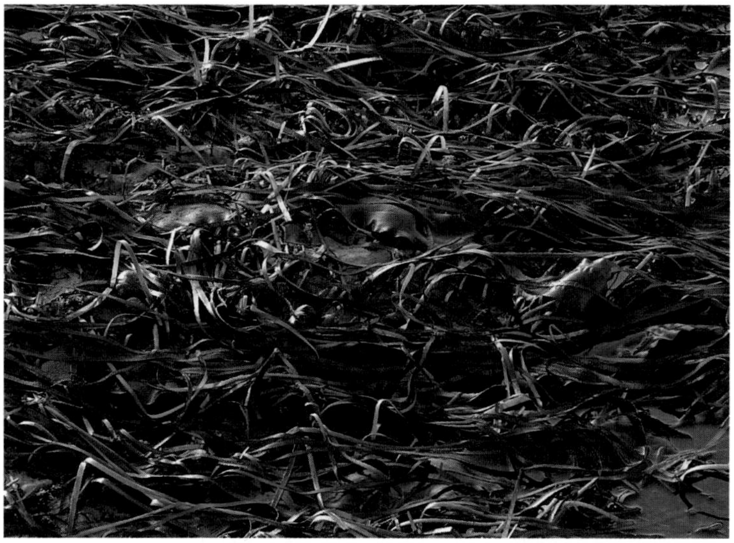

FLOWER TYPE

IDENTIFICATION

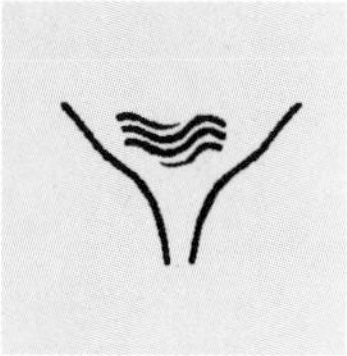

HABITAT

POPULATION

MAP

Size and appearance: An aquatic perennial with branched rhizomes, numerous tufts of leaves and leafy flowering stems 50–150 cm (20–60 in) long.

Leaves: All submerged, up to 120 cm (48 in) long, dark green, very narrow, ribbon-like, blunt.

Flowers: Small, without petals or sepals, green, in clusters within protecting leafy sheaths.

Fruits: Clusters of greenish, 1-seeded, egg-shaped nutlets 2–4 mm (1/12–1/6 in) long.

Related or similar plants: Beaked Tasselweed and Horned Pondweed (p.362) are smaller plants of brackish water.

Habitat and distribution: Locally abundant on submerged sand and muddy flats of shallow and sheltered coasts, all around Britain and Ireland, but commoner in the west and south.

Flowering time: June to September.

EEL-GRASS IS ONE of our most unusual native plants, not least because we see it only at the lowest tides. It is one of a specialised family of mostly tropical flowering plants that have taken on the form and habitat of the seaweeds. The plants are anchored by strong rhizomes, and the ribbon-like leaves float free, forming great beds at the bottom of the sea. Even pollination takes place in seawater. The plant is important because it helps to anchor sand and mud, and Eel-grass beds are home to numerous sea-creatures and fish.

It was even more common up until the 1930s, being gathered, dried and used to pack china and glass. It then fell prey to a fungal disease, but has come back in recent decades. The cast-up leaves, sometimes the fruits, are a feature of some seashores.

A smaller plant, Dwarf Eel-grass (*Zostera noltii*), with thread-like leaves not more than 20 cm (8 in) long, is locally common on mud flats of creeks and estuaries around the coasts of Britain and eastern Ireland.

Eel-grass (Zostera marina) *is only seen at low tide; in the photograph above it is growing with seaweeds. Below is Narrow-leaved Eel-grass (Zostera angustifolia), which has leaves only 1-2 mm (4/10-8/10 in) wide but up to 30 cm (12 in) long, with between three and five veins and notched at the tip. It occurs between the half-tide to the low-tide mark in estuaries and on coasts scattered around the British Isles.*

Early Purple Orchid

ORCHID FAMILY

(Orchidaceae)

SPECIES INFORMATION	
COMMON NAME	Early Purple Orchid
SCIENTIFIC NAME	Orchis mascula
RELATED SPECIES	Other orchids
HEIGHT/SPREAD	10–40 cm tall
FLOWERING TIME	April–June
HABITAT	Woods and coastal cliffs

Note: The earliest orchid to flower in spring.

FLOWER TYPE

IDENTIFICATION

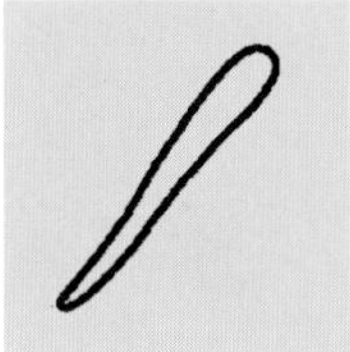

HABITAT

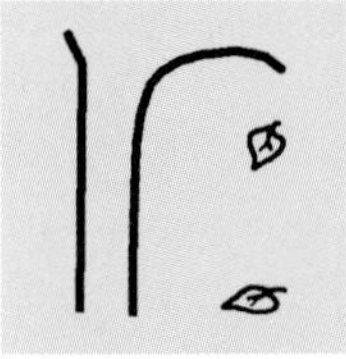

POPULATION

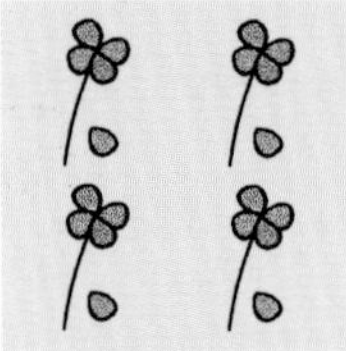

MAP

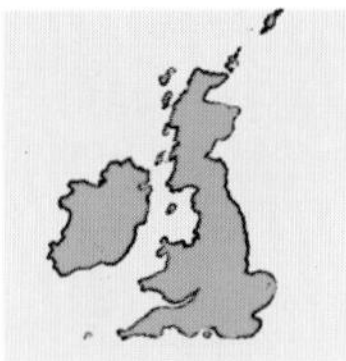

Size and appearance: An erect perennial 10–40 cm (4–16 in) tall, rising from two egg-shaped tubers.

Leaves: Oblong, mostly near the base of the stem, pale green with small purple spots.

Flowers: Purple, sometimes pink or white, with a 3-lobed lip 8–12 mm (⅓–½ in) long, in a rather loose cylindrical spike.

Fruits: Twisted, cylindrical capsules containing numerous dust-like seeds.

Related or similar plants: The spotted orchids (p.365) have paler, spotted flowers in dense spikes, from late May onwards.

Habitat and distribution: A widespread but rather local plant of woods, hedge-banks, pastures and low coastal cliffs; especially common on lime-rich or clayey soils, and in some western areas such as Cornwall and the Burren of County Clare.

Flowering time: April to June.

THIS IS PROBABLY the plant that William Shakespeare called 'long purples', an old country name, in his description in *Hamlet* of the garland worn by drowned Ophelia. The plant, presumably because of the tubers (*orchis* is Greek for testicle), formerly had a reputation as an aphrodisiac. In Shakespeare's day, and until the 19th century, the tubers were gathered, dried and made into a milky drink similar to the *salep* that is still popular in Turkey and elsewhere. It has medicinal use as a drink for invalids, being gentle on the stomach and full of minerals. However, its use has moved from being a cottage industry to being a major export, putting orchids at risk. In Britain it is illegal to dig up orchids (or other plants) without the consent of the landowner.

Early Purple Orchid (Orchis mascula) *has long, oblong leaves concentrated at the base of the stem, where they are broader and usually have purplish-black spots and blotches. The flowers can sometimes be white or pink but the most frequent colour is purple with a few dark mauve markings towards the centre. In some areas such as the Burren in County Clare, western Ireland, Early Purple Orchids are very abundant in spring.*

Common Spotted-orchid

ORCHID FAMILY

(Orchidaceae)

SPECIES INFORMATION	
COMMON NAME	Common Spotted-orchid
SCIENTIFIC NAME	Dactylorhiza fuchsii
RELATED SPECIES	Southern Marsh-orchid
HEIGHT/SPREAD	10–60 cm tall
FLOWERING TIME	June–July
HABITAT	Grassland and scrub

Note: The commonest orchid in many areas.

Size and appearance: An erect, short-lived perennial 10–60 cm (4–24 in) tall, rising from two tubers with finger-like lobes.

Leaves: Spear-shaped or oblong, pointed, becoming smaller and narrower up the stem, dark-spotted.

Flowers: Pink, lilac or pinkish-purple, sometimes white, with a deeply 3-lobed lip 8–12 mm (⅓–½ in) long, the middle lobe the longest, marked with crimson dots and streaks, in a dense cylindrical spike.

Fruits: Twisted, cylindrical capsules containing numerous dust-like seeds.

Related or similar plants: Early Purple Orchid (p.364) has purple flowers in loose spikes a few weeks earlier.

Habitat and distribution: Widespread and locally abundant in open woods, scrub and dry or damp grassland, on hedge-banks, road and railway cuttings and embankments, sand-dunes, unmanicured lawns and derelict industrial land, especially on lime-rich soils, throughout Britain and Ireland.

Flowering time: June to July, but from late May after warm springs, and extending into August in the hills.

COMMON SPOTTED-ORCHID is our commonest native orchid, and one of the few that one can still see in any quantity. It sometimes grows in great crowds in chalk or limestone grassland, on road cuttings or even on derelict urban or waste land. It is a variable species that often crosses with Southern Marsh-orchid (p.366) and other related plants. In the Burren of County Clare, almost white-flowered plants occur in quantity and are regarded by some botanists as a distinct subspecies. However, orchids are popular and do tend to be over-classified.

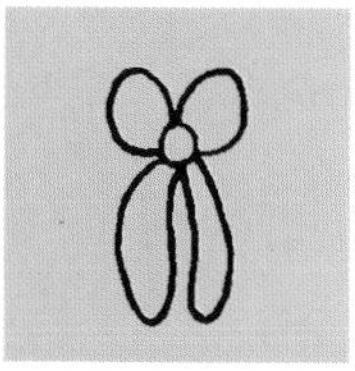

FLOWER TYPE

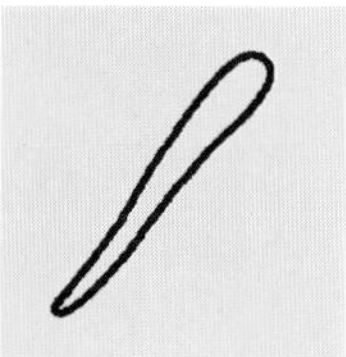

IDENTIFICATION

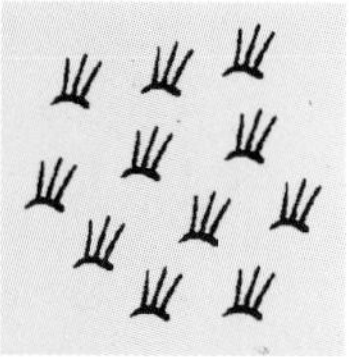

HABITAT

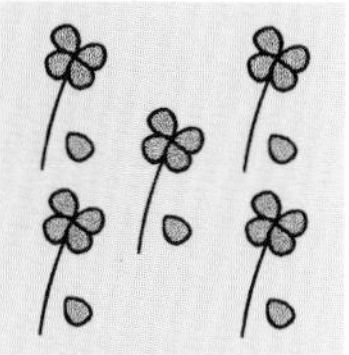

POPULATION

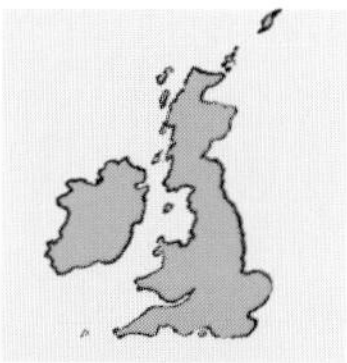

MAP

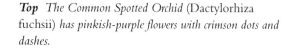

Top *The Common Spotted Orchid* (Dactylorhiza fuchsii) *has pinkish-purple flowers with crimson dots and dashes.*

Middle *A swathe of Common Spotted Orchids in grassland.*

Bottom
Heath Spotted Orchid (Dactylorhiza maculata) *is similar but the lip of the flower has shallower, more rounded lobes, with smallmiddle lobe; the flower-spikes are more conical and often shorter. Flowering June–August, it is widespread on moors and wet heaths, and in damp, lime-poor grassland.*

Southern Marsh-orchid

ORCHID FAMILY
(Orchidaceae)

SPECIES INFORMATION	
COMMON NAME	Southern Marsh-orchid
SCIENTIFIC NAME	Dactylorhiza praetermissa
RELATED SPECIES	Common Spotted-orchid
HEIGHT/SPREAD	20–80 cm tall
FLOWERING TIME	June–July
HABITAT	Marshes and damp grassland
Note: The common orchid of marshes in the south.	

FLOWER TYPE

IDENTIFICATION
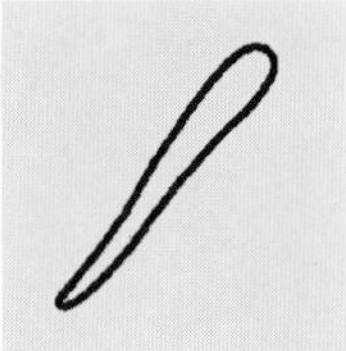

HABITAT
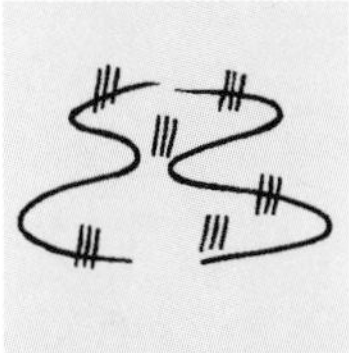

POPULATION

MAP
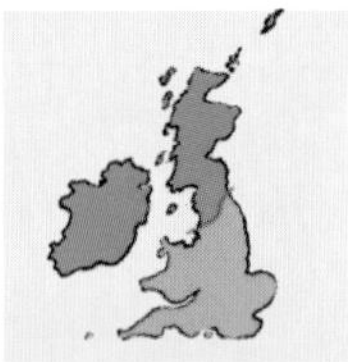

Size and appearance: An erect, short-lived perennial 20–80 cm (8–32 in) tall, rising from two tubers with finger-like lobes.

Leaves: Spear-shaped, pointed, becoming smaller and narrower up the stem, usually unspotted.

Flowers: Pink- to reddish-purple, with a shallowly 3-lobed lip 10–15 mm (⅜–⅝ in) long, marked with crimson dots and streaks, in a dense cylindrical spike.

Fruits: Twisted, cylindrical capsules containing numerous dust-like seeds.

Related or similar plants: Early Purple Orchid (p.364) has purple flowers in loose spikes a few weeks earlier.

Habitat and distribution: Widespread in marshes and damp fields in England and Wales, north to Lancashire and north Yorkshire, and in Ireland.

Flowering time: June to July, but from late May after warm springs, and extending into August in the hills.

SOUTHERN MARSH-ORCHID, like Common Spotted-orchid, is still common in many districts, and can form great crowds in marshy fields or the damp slacks of sand-dunes. It is a variable species: a widespread variant, so-called Leopard Marsh-orchid, has ring-spotted leaves. The marsh-orchids are a confusing group, difficult to distinguish satisfactorily from each other, and different books list them under a range of names.

In northern Britain, Southern Marsh-orchid is replaced by Northern Marsh-orchid (*Dactylorhiza purpurella*), a smaller plant not usually more than 30 cm (12 in) tall, with deep reddish-purple flowers. The lip of the flower is not more than 10 mm (⅜ in) long, almost unlobed and streaked with crimson. Flowering June–August, it is widespread in marshes and damp grassland north from West Wales, and in Ireland.

In much of western Ireland and the Outer Hebrides, both of the above are largely replaced by Western Marsh-orchid (*Dactylorhiza occidentalis*), which is 10–25 cm (4–10 in) tall and has violet-purple flowers in May–June.

Bottom left *The reddish-purple flowers have a shallowly three-lobed lip, which is patterned with crimson markings.*

Top *Southern Marsh-orchid* (Dactylorhiza praetermissa) *has leaves that are mostly basal and flowers in a dense cylindrical spike.*

Bottom right *Northern Marsh-orchid* (Dactylorhiza purpurella) *is generally shorter and stockier than its southern cousin with deeper purple flowers and usually only a very small central tooth to its lower lip.*

SPECIES INFORMATION	
COMMON NAME	Bird's-nest Orchid
SCIENTIFIC NAME	Neottia nidus-avis
RELATED SPECIES	Other orchids
HEIGHT/SPREAD	10–40 cm tall
FLOWERING TIME	May–June
HABITAT	Woodland

Note: Wholly brownish or yellow and growing in woodland.

Bird's-nest Orchid

ORCHID FAMILY (Orchidaceae)

THIS IS ONE of our few wild flowers that is a saprophyte, one that derives nutrition from decaying vegetable material. The root, a lobed, fleshy structure that indeed resembles a tiny bird's-nest, is heavily infested with a fungus. Fungus and orchid have a close nutritional relationship, the fungus facilitating the uptake of nutrients from the leaf-mould in which both grow.

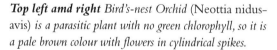

***Top left amd right** Bird's-nest Orchid* (Neottia nidus-avis) *is a parasitic plant with no green chlorophyll, so it is a pale brown colour with flowers in cylindrical spikes.*

FLOWER TYPE

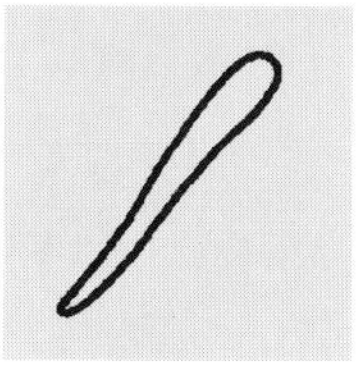

IDENTIFICATION

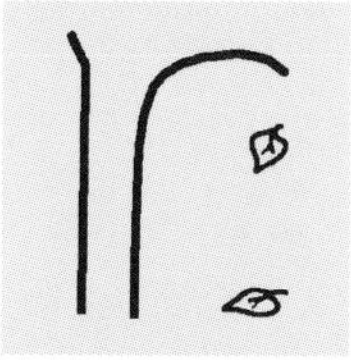

HABITAT

POPULATION

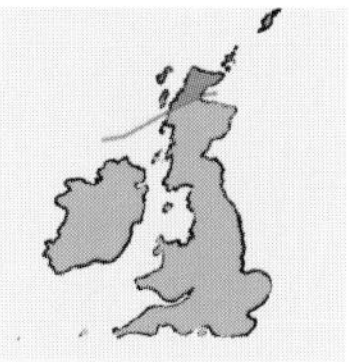

MAP

Size and appearance: An erect perennial 10–40 cm (4–16 in) tall, brownish and without any green colour.

Leaves: reduced to small, brown, sheathing scales.

Flowers: Pale brown, with a hood of upper sepals and petals and a 2-lobed lip 8–12 mm (⅓–½ in) long, in a rather loose cylindrical spike.

Fruits: Twisted, cylindrical capsules containing numerous dust-like seeds.

Related or similar plants: Other orchids have white, pink, purple, yellowish or greenish flowers; Yellow Bird's-nest is superficially similar but is a member of the wintergreen family.

Habitat and distribution: A widespread but local plant of shady woodland with deep leaf-litter, especially beechwoods, on lime-rich soils; north to the Moray Firth, but commonest in southern and central England.

Flowering time: May to June.

***Bottom right** Yellow Bird's-nest (*Monotropa hypopitys*), a quite unrelated saprophytic plant in the wintergreen family, is similar but yellowish or cream in colour, later becoming brownish, the bell-shaped flowers in a short, drooping cluster. Flowering June–September, it occurs in beechwoods.*

Burnt-tip Orchid

ORCHID FAMILY
(Orchidaceae)

SPECIES INFORMATION	
COMMON NAME	Burnt-tip Orchid, Dwarf Orchid
SCIENTIFIC NAME	Orchis ustulata
RELATED SPECIES	Green-winged Orchid
HEIGHT/SPREAD	10–25 cm tall
FLOWERING TIME	May–June
HABITAT	Unploughed limestone grassland

Note: The smallest orchid of grasslands.

FLOWER TYPE

IDENTIFICATION

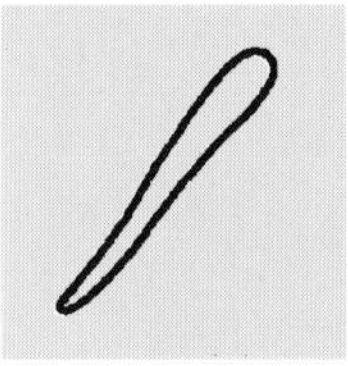

HABITAT

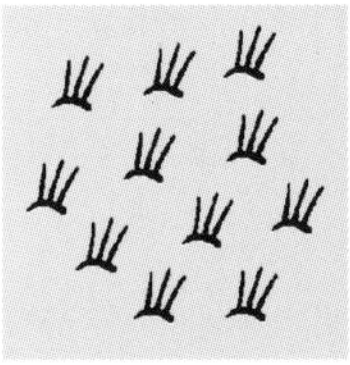

POPULATION

MAP

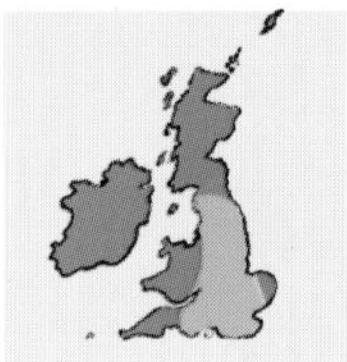

BURNT-TIP ORCHID IS one of the most special of our native wild flowers, a tiny orchid of great beauty and scarcity. Although it is rare, it is sometimes present in great numbers; in Wiltshire especially one can see thousands of plants at some of its better sites. It is a plant that, like Pasque Flower (p.60), cannot tolerate disturbance and therefore grows only in old, unploughed grassland. Like all orchids, the seed needs a fungal partner for it to germinate and grow. However, in Burnt-tip Orchid, it can take more than a decade for the young plant to flower, or even come into leaf.

Size and appearance: An erect perennial 10–25 cm (4–10 in) tall, taking many years to grow from seed.
Leaves: Few, mainly at the base of the stem, oblong, pointed, unspotted.
Flowers: Whitish, red-spotted, with a hood of darker sepals and petals and a 3-lobed lip 4–8 mm (⅙–⅓ in) long, scented, in a dense, cylindrical spike; brownish-purple flower-buds give the spike its 'burnt tip'.
Fruits: Twisted, cylindrical capsules containing numerous dust-like seeds.
Related or similar plants: The smallest of the grassland orchids, which are usually pink, purple or greenish-yellow, with a distinctive look to the flowers.
Habitat and distribution: A widespread but rare or very local plant of short, dry grassland or sometimes damp meadows on lime-rich soils in England, especially on chalk in Wiltshire and a few other places in the south, and sometimes present in large numbers.
Flowering time: May to June.

Burnt-tip Orchid (Orchis ustulata) *is a tiny orchid which only survives on very ancient, undisturbed grassland. The flowers are whitish but are marked with red spots, and the hoods are a dark maroon colour, which at first gives the 'burnt tip' effect.*

SPECIES INFORMATION	
COMMON NAME	Green-winged Orchid
SCIENTIFIC NAME	Orchis morio
RELATED SPECIES	Burnt-tip Orchid
HEIGHT/SPREAD	10–40 cm tall
FLOWERING TIME	April–May
HABITAT	Grassland

Note: A small purple orchid with unspotted leaves.

Green-winged Orchid

ORCHID FAMILY

(Orchidaceae)

Size and appearance: An erect perennial 10–40 cm (4–16 in) tall, dying after flowering.

Leaves: Mainly in a basal rosette, but also crowding the stem, spear-shaped, pointed, unspotted.

Flowers: Reddish-purple, pink or whitish, purplish-spotted, with a hood of sepals and petals, the sepals prominently green-veined, a 3-lobed, strongly folded lip and a cylindrical, blunt spur, in a short, loose cluster.

Fruits: Twisted, cylindrical capsules containing numerous dust-like seeds.

Related or similar plants: Early Purple Orchid (p.364), which flowers at the same time, is taller, with spotted leaves, and sepals without prominent green veins.

Habitat and distribution: A widespread but scattered and declining plant of open woodland, rocky ground, dry or damp meadows, old pastures, ancient village greens and sand-dunes, often on lime-rich soils, north to Galloway and County Sligo.

Flowering time: April to May.

GREEN-WINGED ORCHID is one of many plants especially characteristic of old grassland that has declined or locally quite disappeared owing to modern farming methods. It was once a familiar spring sight, often growing with Cowslips (p.191) in pastures. Flower books written before the 1960s treat it as one of the commoner orchids. Sadly, that is no longer true.

Where it does occur, it may be present in huge crowds, a magnificent sight that we must protect for future generations. Many good orchid meadows of this type have been purchased by County Naturalists' Trusts. It also persists here and there on the coast, too early to be disturbed by visitors, in places that are not suitable for farming, like rocky heathland.

It is very much a plant of ancient commons and village greens, such as those that survive in parts of East Anglia. On one occasion it achieved national fame by flowering on a village cricket pitch, protected by both players and spectators. Fortunately, it is able to persist without flowering if mowing and other factors are unfavourable.

FLOWER TYPE

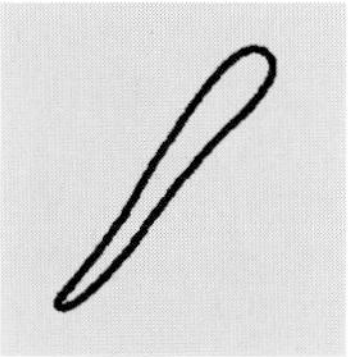
IDENTIFICATION

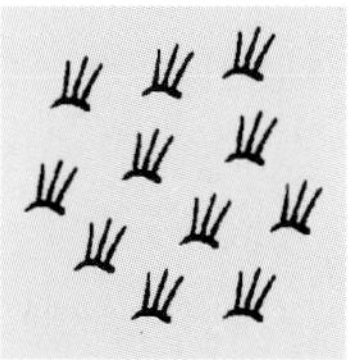
HABITAT

POPULATION

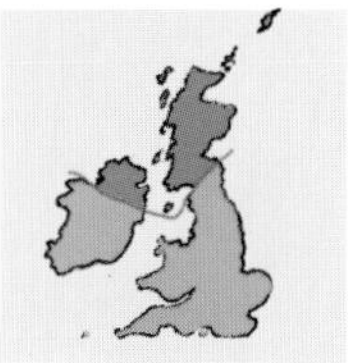
MAP

The green-winged Orchid (Orchis morio) *has a short, loose cluster of usually reddish-purple flowers with some spotting on the lower lip. The sepals of the hood are marked by green-veins. A plant of ancient pastures, it can form quite large colonies in the undisturbed turf.*

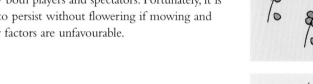

Pyramidal Orchid

ORCHID FAMILY
(Orchidaceae)

SPECIES INFORMATION	
COMMON NAME	Pyramidal Orchid
SCIENTIFIC NAME	Anacamptis pyramidalis
RELATED SPECIES	Fragrant Orchid
HEIGHT/SPREAD	10–40 cm tall
FLOWERING TIME	June–August
HABITAT	Grassland

Note: The dense, pyramidal spike is characteristic.

FLOWER TYPE

IDENTIFICATION

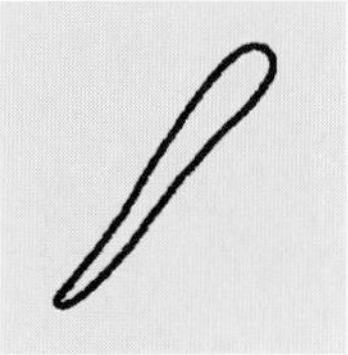

HABITAT

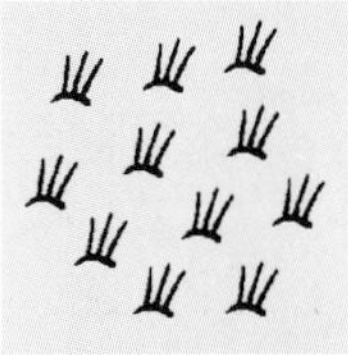

POPULATION

MAP

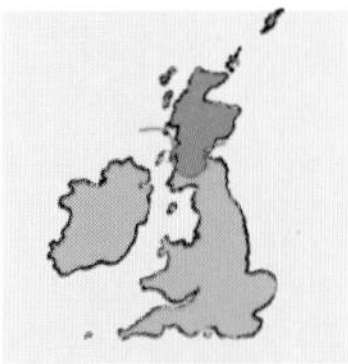

Size and appearance: An erect perennial 10–40 cm (4–16 in) tall, arising from two spherical tubers.

Leaves: Mainly near the base of the stem, the uppermost very narrow, spear-shaped, pointed, unspotted.

Flowers: Crimson or rich purplish-pink, with a hood of petals and sepals, a wedge-shaped, deeply 3-lobed lip 6–8 mm (¼–⅓ in) long, and a long, slender, tapered spur, in a dense, conical or domed cluster.

Fruits: Twisted, cylindrical capsules containing numerous dust-like seeds.

Related or similar plants: Fragrant Orchid (p.371), which flowers at the same time, has a longer, cylindrical spike of pink-to-lilac flowers.

Habitat and distribution: Widespread and sometimes common in open scrub and grassland, and on dry banks, glacial mounds and sand-dunes on lime-rich soils, in Britain north to Fife and the Outer Hebrides, and throughout Ireland.

Flowering time: June to August.

PYRAMIDAL ORCHID IS rather local in occurrence, but sometimes appears in great numbers, for example in chalk grassland in southern England or in pastures and banks on dry, glacial mounds and mature sand-dune grassland in Ireland. The Irish plants are said to have more intensely coloured flowers. Across Europe, Pyramidal Orchid shows some variation in flower colour, this often being pale pink or nearly white in the Mediterranean region. The nectar in the long spurs attracts the butterflies and moths that pollinate the flowers.

Pyramidal Orchid (Anacamptis pyramidalis) *has a few narrow, unspotted leaves, mainly near the base. The flower spike is a dense pyramidal- or dome-shaped cluster of crimson or rich purplish-pink flowers with hooding sepals and a deeply three-lobed lip with all lobes of equal proportion. It is a plant of grassland and dry banks, usually on chalk and limestone soils or on sand-dunes with a high shell content.*

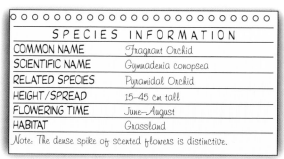

SPECIES INFORMATION	
COMMON NAME	Fragrant Orchid
SCIENTIFIC NAME	Gymnadenia conopsea
RELATED SPECIES	Pyramidal Orchid
HEIGHT/SPREAD	15–45 cm tall
FLOWERING TIME	June–August
HABITAT	Grassland

Note: The dense spike of scented flowers is distinctive.

Fragrant Orchid

ORCHID FAMILY

(Orchidaceae)

FRAGRANT ORCHID IS one of the commoner orchids that still appears in good numbers in many places. The fragrant scent is described as anything from carnation to orange-blossom, but all agree that it is strong, especially in the evening. Fragrant Orchid is a variable species and botanists have described several varieties and subspecies. The commonest significant variant is a dense-flowered plant, often with taller stems, and reputedly clove-scented flowers, of fens and damp, grassy places. Small plants are known from hill pastures and islands in north Britain.

Fragrant Orchid (Gymnadenia conopsea) *is widespread in grassy places, particularly on chalk and limestone soils where it can occur plentifully. It has long leaves, mainly near the base of the stem, which are rather narrow and shiny, unspotted and keeled. The pink or lilac flowers have a long slender spur and are in a dense cylindrical spike.*

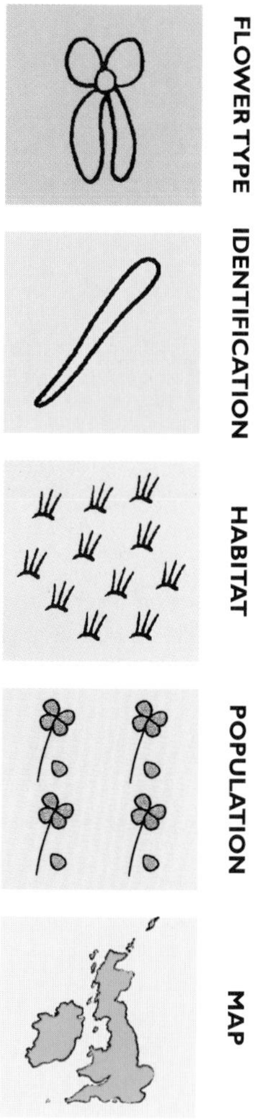

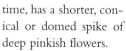

Size and appearance: An erect perennial 15–45 cm (6–18 in) tall, rising from two lobed tubers.
Leaves: Mainly near the base of the stem, narrowly spear-shaped, keeled, pointed, unspotted, rather shiny, the uppermost very narrow.
Flowers: Pink, lilac or purplish-pink, sometimes white, with a loose hood of petals and sepals, a 3-lobed lip, and a long, slender spur, richly scented, in a dense, cylindrical spike.
Fruits: Twisted, cylindrical capsules containing numerous dust-like seeds.
Related or similar plants: Pyramidal Orchid (p.370), which flowers at the same time, has a shorter, conical or domed spike of deep pinkish flowers.
Habitat and distribution: A widespread and locally common plant of open woods, scrub and damp or dry grassland, mostly on lime-rich soils, throughout Britain and Ireland.
Flowering time: June to August.

Man Orchid

ORCHID FAMILY

(Orchidaceae)

SPECIES INFORMATION	
COMMON NAME	Man Orchid
SCIENTIFIC NAME	Aceras anthropophorum
RELATED SPECIES	Fragrant Orchid
HEIGHT/SPREAD	15–30 cm tall
FLOWERING TIME	May–June
HABITAT	Chalk grassland and scrub

Note: The flowers are like little yellow human figures.

FLOWER TYPE

IDENTIFICATION

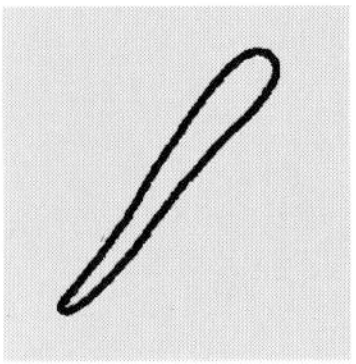

HABITAT

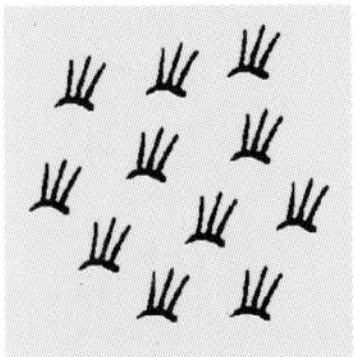

POPULATION

MAP

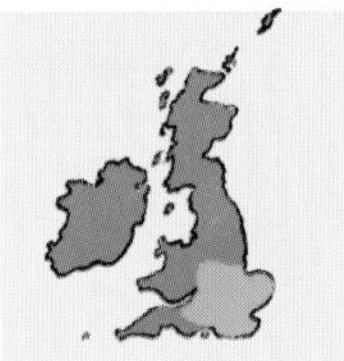

Size and appearance: An erect perennial 15–30 cm (6–12 in) tall.

Leaves: Mainly near the base of the stem, narrowly spear-shaped or oblong, pointed, unspotted, shiny, the uppermost very narrow.

Flowers: Yellowish or greenish, edged and flushed with vinous red, with a domed, greenish but often red-veined hood of petals and sepals, and a 4-lobed, greenish-yellow lip 12–15 mm (½–⅝ in) long, in a narrow, rather loose, cylindrical spike.

Fruits: Twisted, cylindrical capsules containing numerous dust-like seeds.

Related or similar plants: A very distinctive plant, unlikely to be confused with any other native orchid.

Habitat and distribution: A rare plant, with a few large populations surviving, of woodland margins, scrub and grassland, also old quarries, on chalk in southern and south-eastern England.

Flowering time: May to June.

MAN ORCHID IS one of the rarer of our 50 or so native wild orchids, but one which is holding its own in several places in the south. It has, however, all but disappeared from some former haunts, such as the chalk of East Anglia. It rarely returns after grassland has been ploughed. It often grows in company with other orchids. Like some other scarce orchids, it is a more typically Mediterranean plant that just reaches Britain at the furthest north-western corner of its range. Its habitat on the dry, warm soil of the chalk, especially the North Downs from Surrey to east Kent, mimics the sort of climatic conditions that this species would enjoy in southern Europe.

The main enemy of the Man Orchid, and our other rare orchids, is habitat destruction, although unscrupulous collectors do still exist. Nevertheless, the knowledge that it is wrong to pick or dig up orchids is now widespread and firmly rooted. The name Man Orchid is typical of the fanciful ideas that the intricate and beautiful flowers of orchids suggest to the onlooker.

Man Orchid (Aceras anthropophorum) *has individual flowers, which are shaped rather like a matchstick-man wearing a very large helmet. They are a mixture of shades of yellow, green and brown often tinged or veined with red. Now a rare plant, there are still some East Anglian chalk grasslands where this orchid occurs in large numbers.*

SPECIES INFORMATION	
COMMON NAME	Lesser Butterfly-orchid
SCIENTIFIC NAME	Platanthera bifolia
RELATED SPECIES	Greater Butterfly-orchid
HEIGHT/SPREAD	20–45 cm tall
FLOWERING TIME	May–June
HABITAT	Open woods and grassland

Note: The large, white flowers have very long spurs.

Lesser Butterfly-orchid

ORCHID FAMILY

(Orchidaceae)

LESSER BUTTERFLY-ORCHID is commoner in northern Britain, especially in certain areas like western Scotland. It is one of our most handsome wild flowers, the long flower-spurs and rich scent recalling some tropical orchids. In southern Britain one is more likely to see Greater Butterfly-orchid, especially in chalk landscapes.

Top left and right *Lesser Butterfly Orchid* (Platanthera bifolia) *is an orchid of moors and heaths. The close-up of an individual flower, shows the parallel pollen masses.*

Bottom *Greater Butterfly-orchid* (Platanthera chlorantha) *is similar but generally slightly taller and more robust, with larger flowers in a bigger spike; flowers more greenish, with a shorter, broader lip and shorter spur 18–25 mm (¾–1 in) long. It is widespread but local in woods, scrub and grassland, mostly on lime-rich soils.*

Size and appearance: An erect perennial 20–45 cm (8–18 in) tall.
Leaves: Oval, in an almost opposite pair at the base of the stem, with stem leaves narrow, almost scale-like.
Flowers: White, with a loose hood of petals and sepals, and a strap-shaped, greenish-white lip 6–10 mm (¼–⅜ in) long, and a spur 25–30 mm (1–1⅕ in) long, fragrant, especially at night, in a rather loose, cylindrical spike.
Fruits: Twisted, cylindrical capsules containing numerous dust-like seeds.
Related or similar plants: Greater Butterfly-orchid is a larger plant, but the flowers have shorter spurs.
Habitat and distribution: Widespread but local on moors and heaths, in open woods, scrub and grassland, on a wide range of soils; throughout, but rarer in eastern England and much more common in the north.
Flowering time: May to June.

FLOWER TYPE

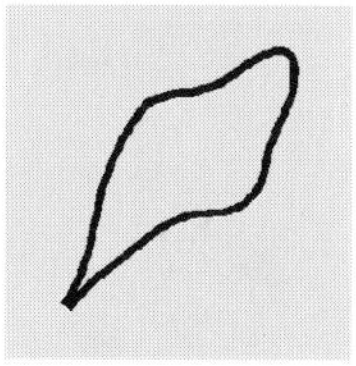

IDENTIFICATION

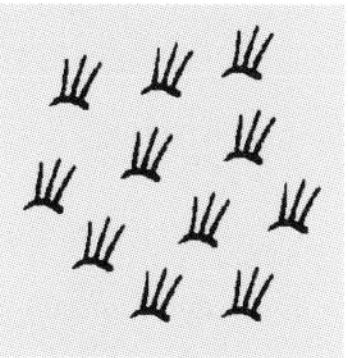

HABITAT

POPULATION

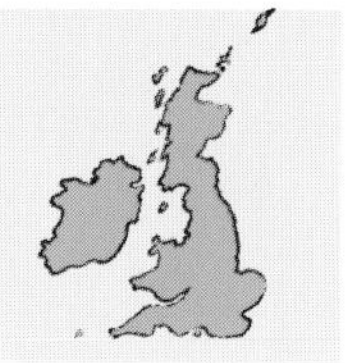

MAP

Common Twayblade

ORCHID FAMILY

(Orchidaceae)

SPECIES INFORMATION	
COMMON NAME	Common Twayblade
SCIENTIFIC NAME	Listera ovata
RELATED SPECIES	Lesser Twayblade
HEIGHT/SPREAD	30–60 cm tall
FLOWERING TIME	May–July
HABITAT	Open woods and grassland

Note: The paired basal leaves are a feature.

FLOWER TYPE

IDENTIFICATION

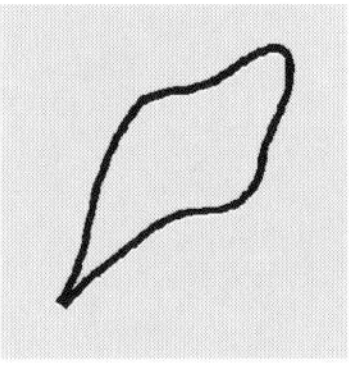

HABITAT

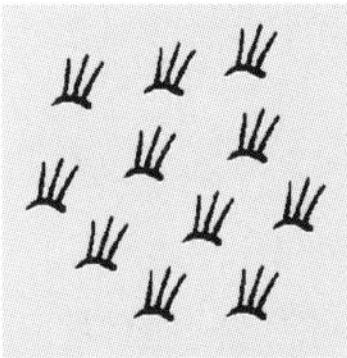

POPULATION

MAP

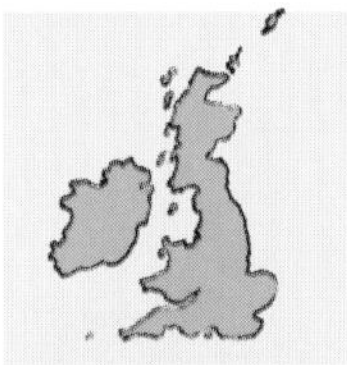

Size and appearance: An erect perennial 30–60 cm (12–24 in) tall.

Leaves: In a single opposite pair at the base of the stem, broadly oval, blunt, rather dull green.

Flowers: Yellowish-green, with a loose hood of petals and sepals, and a strap-shaped, deeply notched lip 10–15 mm (⅖–⅗ in) long, in a rather loose, cylindrical spike.

Fruits: Twisted, cylindrical capsules containing numerous dust-like seeds.

Related or similar plants: Lesser Twayblade is a smaller plant of heather moors and open woods, mainly in the north.

Habitat and distribution: Widespread and rather common in open woods, scrub and grassland, on a range of soils but especially characteristic of more lime-rich sites, throughout most of Britain and Ireland.

Flowering time: May to July.

Common Twayblade (Listera ovata) *is an orchid easily recognised by the single pair of opposite, broad, oval, unstalked and rather dull green leaves at the base of the flower stalk. The two photographs below show close-ups of the individual greenish flowers, which have a loose hood and a deeply notched lower lip.*

TWAYBLADE SEEMS RATHER drab to be an orchid, but has the typical orchid flower. The English name is in fact more lowland Scots – 'Twa Blades', describing the paired basal leaves. The first half of the scientific name commemorates Martin Lister (1638–1712), naturalist and physician to Queen Anne.

Lesser Twayblade (*Listera cordata*) is a much smaller plant, not more than 20 cm (8 in) tall, with shiny basal leaves and a short spike of 4-12 smaller, reddish flowers. Flowering June to September, it is a cryptic plant of moors and open pine woodland, often totally hidden under heather tussocks; mainly in Scotland, but extending locally to Ireland, North Wales and Exmoor.

SPECIES INFORMATION	
COMMON NAME	White Helleborine
SCIENTIFIC NAME	Cephalanthera damasonium
RELATED SPECIES	Other helleborines
HEIGHT/SPREAD	20–60 cm tall
FLOWERING TIME	May–July
HABITAT	Beechwoods

Note: A conspicuous, white-flowered orchid of beechwoods.

White Helleborine

ORCHID FAMILY
(Orchidaceae)

Size and appearance: An erect perennial 20-60 cm (8–24 in) tall.
Leaves: All along the stem, oval to spear-shaped or oval, pointed.
Flowers: Creamy white, egg-shaped, c. 2 cm (⅘ in) long, the pointed petals and sepals barely opening, the lip with a hidden orange blotch, up to 12, in a loose, cylindrical spike.
Fruits: Cylindrical capsules containing numerous dust-like seeds.
Related or similar plants: Some other, mostly rarer, helleborines occur in similar habitats.
Habitat and distribution: Local but sometimes common in beechwoods over chalk and limestone, occasionally in other woodland, scrub or more open places, in southern England west to Dorset.
Flowering time: May to July.

White Helleborine (Cephalanthera damasonium) *has egg-shaped, creamy-white flowers which rarely open fully, so it is not easy to see the orange-yellow spot on the inside of the lower lip. Beneath each flower is a leaf-like bract. It is a leafy orchid with broad lanceolate leaves at the base, which become narrower towards the top. It is an orchid of beechwoods on the chalk soils of southern England.*

WHITE HELLEBORINE is a typical member of the flora of shady beechwoods on chalk. It is one of a group of a dozen orchids known as helleborines that share features such as leafy stems (without basal leaves), flowers in almost 1-sided spikes, a 2-segmented lip and a straight rather than twisted seed-capsule. Some grow in woodland, including the beechwoods favoured by White Helleborine; others are plants of marshes, sand-dunes and rocky slopes.

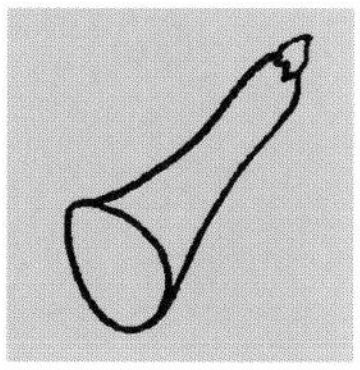
FLOWER TYPE

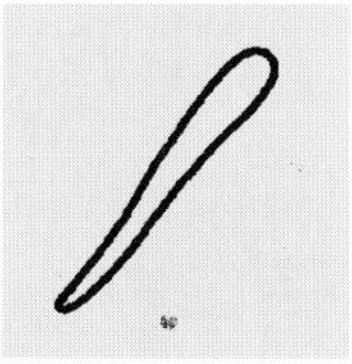
IDENTIFICATION

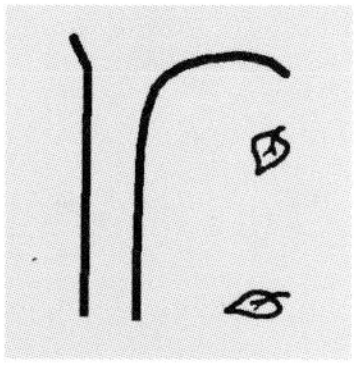
HABITAT

POPULATION

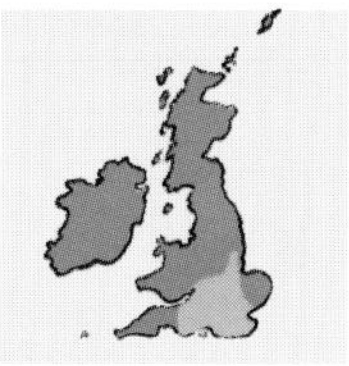
MAP

Autumn Lady's-tresses

ORCHID FAMILY (Orchidaceae)

SPECIES INFORMATION	
COMMON NAME	Autumn Lady's-tresses
SCIENTIFIC NAME	Spiranthes spirali
RELATED SPECIES	Creeping Lady's-tresses
HEIGHT/SPREAD	5–20 cm tall
FLOWERING TIME	August–September
HABITAT	Grassland, especially on the coast

Note: A very late-flowering orchid with a twisted flower-spike.

FLOWER TYPE

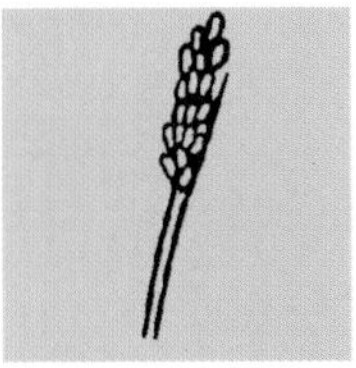

IDENTIFICATION

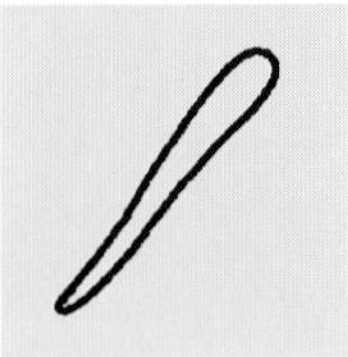

HABITAT

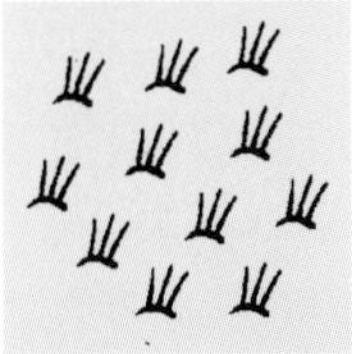

POPULATION

MAP

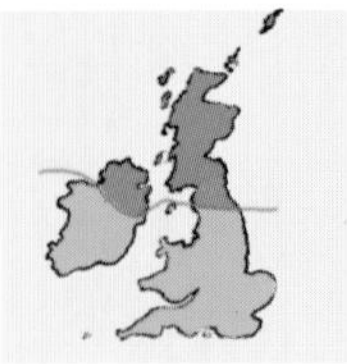

Size and appearance: A small, bluish-green, erect perennial 5–20 cm (2–8 in) tall.
Leaves: Mostly in a rosette, oval, withered by flowering, with a few very narrow, scale-like leaves along the stem.
Flowers: White, c. 6 mm (¼ in) long, with a down-curved, green-tinged lip, fragrant, up to 25, in a tight, spiral spike.
Fruits: Twisted, egg-shaped capsules containing numerous dust-like seeds.
Related or similar plants: Creeping Lady's-tresses, a larger plant of pine woods, creeping to form patches.
Habitat and distribution: Widespread but local in short grassland, sometimes on lawns, usually on lime-rich soils or on sand-dunes and turf-covered rocks or walls by the sea; mainly in the south of Britain and Ireland, but extending north to Cumbria, the Isle of Man and County Sligo.
Flowering time: August to September.

AUTUMN LADY'S-TRESSES is a neat and rather lovely orchid that is particularly exciting to find in that it flowers so late in the year. Where it does occur, and it is not always easy to spot, it can be abundant. Young plants bud off at the roots and loose patches develop over several years. Numbers fluctuate, and this orchid can postpone flowering if conditions are unfavourable. During the Second World War, when lawns were neglected, it turned up unexpectedly in several places where mowing was reduced or had ceased.

Autumn Lady's Tresses (Spiranthes spiralis) *is a small orchid which has white flowers which twist and spiral up the stem. The flower spike itself is grey-downy and has a few meagre scale leaves, and the basal leaves wither by flowering time. It is local in short grassland and can sometimes be found in the turf of old lawns, where it continues unnoticed for years until the lawn is not mown during the critical flowering period, when a plethora or dainty spikes appear.*

SPECIES INFORMATION	
COMMON NAME	Bee Orchid
SCIENTIFIC NAME	Ophrys apifera
RELATED SPECIES	Fly Orchid
HEIGHT/SPREAD	10–30 cm tall
FLOWERING TIME	June–July
HABITAT	Grassland and sand-dunes

Note: The flowers are like brown, furry bees.

Bee Orchid

ORCHID FAMILY

(Orchidaceae)

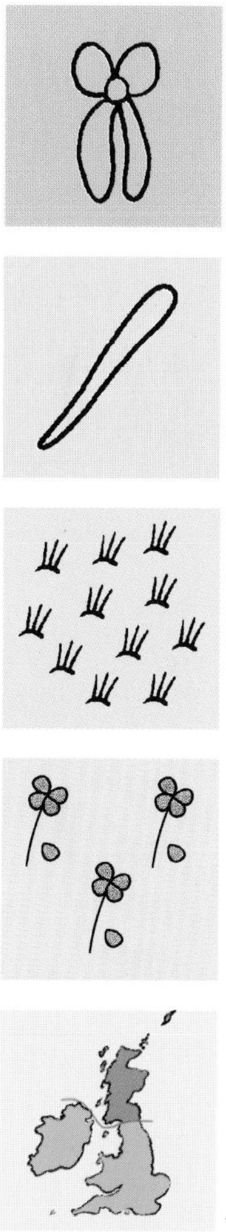

Size and appearance: An erect perennial 10–30 cm (4–12 in) tall.
Leaves: Narrowly oval, pointed, pale green.
Flowers: Few, each with 3 erect pink sepals, 2 small green petals and a fat lip like a small, velvet bumble-bee, reddish-brown patterned with greenish-yellow.
Fruits: Twisted, cylindrical capsules containing numerous dust-like seeds.
Related or similar plants: Fly Orchid is more a plant of woodland margins; the flower has a 4-lobed, dark brown lip with a bluish patch.
Habitat and distribution: A widespread but rather local orchid of open scrub, grassland, dry banks and sand-dunes, always on lime-rich soils, and in western areas such as Cornwall and the Burren of County Clare.
Flowering time: June to July.

BEE ORCHID IS one of the most exciting of our native wild flowers. It is not particularly rare, but is unpredictable in its appearance, often varying hugely in numbers from year to year. It does not occur in ranker grassland, needing quite open vegetation in which to thrive. One of its best habitats is new roadside embankments, which it can colonise within a year or two of their construction.

Bee Orchid and its relatives comprise a group of species characteristic of the open, rocky scrublands of the Mediterranean region. All have evolved flowers that mimic insects. Male insects mistake the flower for a female of their own species, try to mate and so pollinate the flower. In Britain the Bee Orchid is too far north for its pollinator, so pollinates itself, the pollen-masses falling forward on to the stigma. As well as Fly Orchid, we have in Britain two species of spider orchid, both of which are extremely rare.

Top right and bottom left *Bee Orchid* (Ophrys apifera) *is a stunning orchid with its pink sepals and velvetty brown beautifully marked fat lower lip.*

Bottom right *Fly Orchid* (Ophrys insectifera) *is similar but up to 60 cm (24 in) tall with up to 14 flowers; the sepals are green, the slightly conves lip 4-lobed, dark brown with a bluish patch. Flowering May–June, it occurs in open woods, scrub and sometimes grassland, or, in the fens, on lime-rich soils; local, mainly in southern and eastern England, not in Scotland.*

Useful Addresses

The following organisations are dedicated to the study and conservation of the wild flowers of Britain and Ireland. Membership of one or more of them is a helpful way to make contact with other enthusiasts and to learn more from experts, especially out in the field. Your local County Naturalist's Trust or Wildlife Trust is a good start.

Plantlife – The Wild Plant Conservation Charity
21 Elizabeth Street, London SW1W 9RP
(Tel 0171-808-0100, or e-mail enquiries@plantlife.org.uk)
A charity that promotes wider public interest in the wild flowers of Britain. Plantlife campaigns for their protection, including the purchase of nature reserves, and publishes an illustrated magazine.

The Botanical Society of the British Isles
c/o Natural History Museum,
Cromwell Road, London SW7 5BD
For amateur and professional botanists, who record and research the wild plants of Britain and Ireland. The society publishes a scientific journal and a newsletter, and holds field meetings.

The Wild Flower Society
68 Outwoods Road, Loughborough,
Leicestershire LE1 1 3LY
Encourages an appreciation of the wild flowers of Britain and Ireland, especially among younger people. It encourages plant hunting by means of recording diaries, and publishes a newsletter.

The Irish Biogeographical Society
c/o Natural History Museum, Kildare Street,
Dublin 2, Ireland
For amateur and professional botanists and biologists, who record and research the wild plants and animals of Ireland. It publishes a scientific journal.

The Royal Society for Nature Conservation
The Green, Witham Park,
Lincoln LN5 7JR
Co-ordinates the network of County Naturalists and Wildlife Trusts throughout Britain and Northern Ireland. It publishes an illustrated magazine, Natural World. *Most counties and regions, including Greater London, have an RSNC Trust which organizes a variety of activities and lectures.*

Numerous natural history societies and field clubs nationwide hold programmes of field meetings and lectures to study wild flowers and animals.

Selected Bibliography & Further Reading

Fitter, Richard, Fitter, Alistair & Blamey, Marjorie (1985), *The Wild Flowers of Britain and Northern Europe*, 4th ed. HarperCollins.

Garrard, Ian & Streeter, David (1998), *The Wild Flowers of the British Isles*, 2nd ed. Midsummer Books.

Gibbons, Bob & Brough, Peter (1992), *The Hamlyn Photographic Guide to the Wild Flowers of Britain and Northern Europe*. Hamlyn.

Grigson, Geoffrey (1955, reprinted), *The Englishman's Flora*. Phoenix House.

Keble Martin, W. (1965, many reprints), *The Concise British Flora in Colour*. Michael Joseph.

Mabey, Richard (1996) *Flora Britannica*. Sinclair Stevenson.

McClintock, David & Fitter, R.S.R. (1956, out of print but available second hand), *The Pocket Guide to Wild Flowers*. Collins.

Rackham, Oliver (1986), *The History of the Countryside*. J.M. Dent & Sons.

Rose, Francis (1981), *The Wild Flower Key*. Frederick Warne.

Stace, C.A. (1997), *New Flora of the British Isles*, 2nd ed. Cambridge University Press.

Vickery, Roy (1995), *A Dictionary of Plant Lore*. Oxford University Press.

Webb, D.A. , Parnell, J. & Doogue, D. (1996), *An Irish Flora*, 7th ed. Dundalgen Press, Dundalk.

Glossary

Aliens: These are plants that have been introduced from other countries planned or accidentally. They may or may not be established or naturalised.

Annuals: Plants that complete their life history within a year.

Berries: These are many-seeded fleshy fruits.

Biennials: Plants that complete their life history over two years.

Bracts: Leaf- or scale-like structures associated with flowers. They can be difficult to distinguish from leaves.

Bulbs: Specialised, fleshy, underground buds that serve for storage and reproduction.

Calyx: A collective term for the fused or unfused whorl of sepals – usually green but sometimes petal-like structures that enclosed the flower bud.

Calyx-teeth: The teeth or bristles that sometimes protrude from around the mouth of a calyx of fused sepals.

Capsules: Many-seeded, dry fruits that split or develop pores to release the seeds.

Carpels: Undeveloped fruits, containing one or more unfertilized ovules that will develop into seeds after fertilization.

Cladodes: Flattened stems that resemble leaves.

Corms: Specialised, fleshy, stem-bases that serve for storage and reproduction.

Cultivar: A variant of a species that has been selected by gardeners. Cultivars are often loosely termed 'varieties'.

Drupes: 1-seeded, usually fleshy, fruits.

Family: This is a principal unit of classification with all its members closely related and sharing major attributes. Thus the Buttercup family *(Ranunculaceae)* includes the buttercups and almost indistinguishable crowfoots and spearworts, as well as the similar Marsh Marigold and Wood Anemone.

Flowers: The reproductive structures of the flowering plants, the most dominant and successful group in the plant kingdom. They are usually showy and brightly coloured in order to attract the insects that pollinate them and thus fertilize the seeds.

Fruits: The structures that contain the ripe seeds. They are variable in shape, size and fleshiness.

Hybrids: Crosses between two species.

Invasive plants: The same as aliens, but the term is usually used to describe those that are a nuisance or are injurious to other plants, animals or people.

Naturalised plants: These come originally from other countries (they are 'aliens') but are now firmly established here as introductions, often after having escaped from gardens.

Nuts: 1-seeded, dry fruits.

Nutlets: Small, 1-seeded, dry fruits, often in clusters of four.

Ovules: The female reproductive parts of a flower which grow in to seeds after they have been fertilised by pollen.

Perennials: Grow and flower over several years.

Petals: Usually colourful, but sometimes green, structures that are the most conspicuous part of the flower.

Phylloclades: Flattened leaf-stalks that resemble leaves.

Pollen: Dust-like and often yellow or orange in colour, contains the male reproductive cells of the flower and fertilizes the female ovules to produce the seeds.

Pollination: The transfer or pollen, mostly by insects or wind, between the male and the female parts of the flower.

Rhizomes: Fleshy, usually horizontal, creeping roots that serve for storage and reproduction.

Seeds: The specialised reproductive structures of the flowering plants. Each is surrounded by a hard protective coat and contains a tiny plantlet or embryo and a food store.

Sepals: The usually green but sometimes petal-like structures that enclose the flower bud. They sometimes persist or even become enlarged in fruit.

Species: The basic building blocks of classification, sometimes loosely and incorrectly termed 'varieties'. Species are well-defined, although often variable, units of variation that breed among themselves.

Stigmas: Feathery structures that trap the pollen that will fertilize the ovules.

Subspecies: Variants or races of species that are distinctive in appearance. They occur within a particular habitat or have a distinct geographical distribution.

Stamens: The male reproductive parts of the flower. Each has a head of paired sac-like anthers, which contain pollen, at the end of the stalk or the filament.

Stipules: Small, paired, leaf- or scale-like structures that occur at the base of the leaves of some families of plants.

Weeds: Specialised, opportunist plants that colonise habitats disturbed by people and their activities. They are usually a nuisance.

Picture Credits & Acknowledgements

Flower illustrations by **Amanda Patton**: 8 (tl), 8 (tr), 8 (bl), 8 (br), 9 (tl), 9 (tr), 9 (bl), 9 (br), 10 (b), 63 (tr), 351 (t). **General illustrations** by Jennifer Kenna.

Natural Image: Bob Gibbons; 6 (tl), 6 (b), 7 (tl), 7 (tr), 7 (br), 8 (t), 10 (t), 11 (t), 11 (b), 12 (t), 12 (b), 13 (t), 13 (b), 14 (t), 14 (b), 15 (tl), 14 (tr), 14 (b), 16, 17 (t), 17 (b), 18 (t), 18 (b), 19 (b), 19 (t), 20 (t), 20 (b), 21 (b), 21 (tr), 23 (t), 24 (t), 24 (b), 25, 27 (t), 28 (t), 28 (b), 29 (bl), 29 (br), 30 (t), 31 (bl), 31 (t), 31 (br), 32 (t), 33 (t), 33 (b), 34 (bl), 34 (t), 34 (br), 35 (b), 35 (t), 36 (t), 36 (bl), 36 (br), 37 (t), 37 (b), 38, 39 (t), 39 (bl), 39 (br), 40 9t), 40 (b), 41 (t), 41 (b), 42 (t), 42 (b), 43 (t), 43 (b), 44 (t), 44 (bl), 44 (br), 45 (t), 45 (b), 46 (t), 46 (b), 47 (t), 47 (b),48 (t), 48 (b), 49 (t), 49 (b), 40 (t), 50 (bl), 50 (br), 51 (t), 51 (b), 52 (t), 52 (b), 53 (t), 53 (b), 54 (t), 54 (bl), 54 (br), 55 (t), 55 (b), 56 (t), 56 (b), 57 (t), 57 (b), 58 (t), 58 (b), 59 (t), 59 (b), 60 (t), 60 (b), 61 (t), 61 (br), 61 (bl), 62, 63 (t), 63 (b), 64 (t), 64 (b), 65 (t), 65 (t), 65 (bl), 65 (br), 66 (b), 67 (t), 67 (b), 68 (t), 68 (b), 69 (t), 69 (b), 70 (t), 70 (b), 71 (t), 71 (b), 71 (tl), 72 (tr), 73 (br), 74 (t), 74 (bl), 74 (br), 75 (t), 75 (b), 76 (tl), 76 (tr), 76 (b), 77 (t), 78 (t), 78 (b), 79 (t), 79 (b), 80 (t), 80 (b), 81 (t), 81 (bl), 81 (br), 82 (t), 82 (b), 83 (t), 83 (b), 84, 85 (t), 85 (b), 86 (t), 86 (b), 87 (t), 87 (b), 88 (t), 88 (b), 89 (t), 89 (b), 90 (t), 90 (b), 91 (t), 91 (b), 92 (t), 92 (b), 93 (l), 93 (r), 94 (t), 94 (b), 95 (t), 95 (b), 96 (t), 96 (b), 97 (t), 97 (b), 98 (b), 99 (t), 99 (bl), 99 (br), 100 (t), 100 (bl), 100 (br), 101 (t), 101 (b), 102 (t), 102 (b), 103, 104 (t), 104 (br), 105 (t), 105 (b), 106 (t), 106 (b), 107 (t), 107 (b), 108 (t), 108 (b), 109 (b), 110 (t), 110 (b), 111 (t), 111 (bl), 111 (br), 112 (t), 112 (b), 113 (t), 113 (b), 114 (t), 114 (bl), 114 (br), 115 (t), 115 (b), 116 (tl), 116 (tr), 116 (b), 117 (l), 117 (r), 118 (t), 118 (bl), 118 (br), 119 (t), 119 (b), 120 (t), 120 (b), 121, 122 (t), 122 (bl), 122 (br), 123, 124 (t), 124 (b), 125, 126 (bl), 126 (br), 127 (t), 127 (b), 129 (t), 129 (b), 130 (t), 130 (b), 130 (t), 130 (b), 132 (tr), 132 (tl), 132 (b), 133 (t), 133 (bl), 133 (br), 134 (t), 134 (b), 135 (tl), 135 (tr), 135 (b), 136 (t), 136 (b), 137 (t), 137 (bl), 137 (br), 138 (t), 138 (b), 139 (t), 139 (b), 140 (t), 140 (b), 141 (t), 141 (b), 142 (t), 142 (b), 143 (l), 144 (t), 144 (bl), 144 (br), 145 (t), 145 (bl), 145 (br), 146 (t), 146 (bl), 146 (br), 147 (t), 147 (bl), 147 (br), 148 (t), 148 (br), 148 (bl), 149 (t), 149 (b), 150 (b), 151 (r), 151 (l), 152 (tl), 152 (tr), 152 (b), 153 (t), 153 (b), 154 (t), 154 (b), 155 (t), 155 (b), 156 (t), 156 (bl), 156 (br), 157 (t), 157 (b), 158 (t), 158 (b), 159 (t), 159 (b), 160 (t), 160 (bl), 160 (br), 161 (t), 161 (b), 162 (r), 162 (l), 164 (tr), 164 (tl), 164 (b), 165 (b), 166 (t), 166 (b), 167 (tl), 167 (tr), 167 (b), 168 (t), 168 (b), 169 (t), 169 (bl), 169 (br), 170 (t), 170 (b), 171 (t), 171 (b), 172 (t), 172 (bl), 172 (br), 173 (t), 173 (br), 173 (bl), 174 (l), 175 (t), 175 (b), 177 (t), 177 (b), 178 (t), 178 (b), 179 (t), 179 (b), 180 (t), 180 (bl), 180 (br), 181 (t), 181 (br), 181 (bl), 182 (t), 182 (b), 183 (t), 183 (b), 184 (t), 184 (bl), 186 (t), 186 (b), 187 (t), 187 (b), 188 (tl), 188 (tr), 188 (b), 189 (t), 189 (b), 190, 191 (t), 191 (bl), 191 (br), 192 (tl), 192 (tr), 192 (b), 193 (t), 194 (t), 194 (b), 195 (t), 195 (bl), 195 (br), 196 (t), 196 (bl), 196 (br), 197 (tl), 197 (b), 198 (t), 198 (bl), 198 (br), 199 (t), 199(b), 200 (t), 200 (b), 201 (t), 201 (b), 202 (t), 202 (bl), 203 (b), 204 (br), 204 (bl), 205 (t), 205 (bl), 205 (br), 206 (t), 206 (bl), 206 (br), 207 (t), 207 (b), 208 (t), 208 (bl), 209 (t), 209 (b), 210 (t), 210 (bl), 210 (br), 211 (t), 211 (bl), 212 (bl), 212 (br), 213 (t), 213 (br), 213 (bl), 214 (t), 214 (b), 215 (t), 215 (b), 216 (t), 216 (b), 217 (t), 217 (b), 218 (t), 218 (bl), 218 (br), 219 (t), 219 (bl), 219 (br), 220 (t), 220 (bl), 220 (br), 221 (tl), 221 (tr), 221 (b), 222 (t), 222 (b), 223 (t), 223 (b), 226 (t), 226 (bl), 226 (br), 227 (t), 227 (b), 228 (t), 228 (br), 228 (bl), 229 (t), 229 (bl), 229 (br), 230 (t), 230 (b), 231 (t), 231 (bl), 231 (br), 232 (t), 232 (bl), 232 (br), 233 (t), 233 (b), 235 (tl), 235 (tr), 235 (b), 238 (t), 238 (bl), 238 (br), 239 (t), 239 (bl), 239 (br), 240 (t), 240 (br), 241 (l), 242 (t), 242 (bl), 242 (br), 243 (bl), 243 (br), 244 (t), 244 (bl), 244 (br), 245 (t), 245 (br), 245 (bl), 246 (t), 246 (bl), 246 (br), 247 (t), 247 (br), 247 (bl), 248 (t), 248 (bl), 249 (t), 249 (bl), 249 (br), 250 (t), 250 (bl), 250 (br), 251 (t), 251 (bl), 251 (br), 252 (tr), 252 (tl), 252 (b), 253 (t), 253 (bl), 253 (br), 254 (tl), 254 (tr), 254 (b), 255 (b), 256 (t), 256 (bl),), 284 (t), 284 (b), 285 (t), 285 (b), 286 (t), 286 (bl), 287 (bl), 287 (br), 288 (t), 288 (b), 289 (t), 289 (bl), 289 (br), 290 (t), 290 (bl), 290 (br), 291 (t), 291 (bl), 291 (br), 256 (br), 257 (t), 257 (bl), 257 (br), 258 (tl), 258 (tr), 258 (b), 259 (t), 259 (bl), 259 (br), 260 (t), 260 (b), 261 (t), 261 (b), 262 (tr), 262 (b), 263 (t), 263 (bl), 263 (br), 264 (tl), 264 (tr), 264 (b), 265 (t), 265 (b), 266 (t), 266 (bl), 266 (br), 267 (tl), 267 (tr), 267 (b), 268 (tl), 268 (tr), 268 (b), 269 (tr), 269 (tl), 269 (b), 270 (t), 270 (bl), 270 (br), 271 (t), 271 (bl), 271 (br), 272 (t), 272 (bl), 272 (br), 273 (bl), 273 (br), 274 (t), 274 (bl), 274 (br), 275 (tl), 275 (tr), 275 (b), 276 (t), 276 (bl), 276 (br), 277 (tl), 277 (tr), 277 (b), 278 (t), 278 (bl), 278 (br), 279 (t), 279 (b), 280 (t), 280 (br), 282 (t), 282 (bl), 282 (br), 292 (t), 292 (bl), 292 (br), 293 (t), 293 (b), 294 (t), 294 (bl), 294 (br), 295 (b), 296 (t), 296 (bl), 296 (br), 297 (t), 297 (b), 298 (t), 298 (bl), 298 (br), 299 (t), 299 (bl), 299 (br), 300 (t), 300 (bl), 300 (br), 301 (tl), 301 (tr), 301 (b), 302 (t), 302 (bl), 302 (br), 303 (t), 303 (bl), 303 (br), 304 (t), 304 (bl), 304 (br), 305 (tl), 305 (tr), 305 (b), 306 (t), 306 (bl), 306 (br), 307 (t), 307 (bl), 307 (br), 308 (t), 308 (bl), 308 (br), 309 (t), 309 (bl), 309 (br), 310 (t), 310 (bl), 310 (br), 311 (b), 312 (t), 312 (b), 313 (t), 313 (bl), 313 (br), 314 (t), 314 (b), 315 (t), 315 (bl), 315 (br), 316 (t), 316 (bl), 316 (br), 317 (t), 318 (t), 318 (b), 319 (t), 319 (b), 320 (t), 320 (bl), 320 (br), 321 (t), 321 (bl), 321 (br), 322 (b), 323 (t), 323 (b), 324 (t), 324 (bl), 324 (br), 325 (t), 325 (b), 326 (t), 326 (br), 327 (t), 327 (bl), 327 (br), 328 (t), 328 (bl), 328 (br), 329 (b), 330 (t), 330 (b), 331, 332 (tr), 332 (tl), 332 (b), 333 (tl), 333 (tr), 333 (b), 334 (tl), 334 (tr), 334 (b), 335 (t), 335 (bl), 335 (br), 336 (t), 336 (bl), 336 (br), 337 (t), 337 (bl), 337 (br), 338 (tl), 338 (b), 339 (tl), 339 (tr), 339 (b), 340 (tr), 340 (b), 341 (tl), 341 (tr), 341 (b), 342 (tl), 342 (tr), 342 (b), 343 (t), 344 (t), 344 (bl), 344 (br), 345 (t), 345 (b), 346 (tl), 346 (tr), 346 (b), 347 (bl), 348 (t), 348 (bl), 348 (br), 349 (t), 349 (bl), 349 (br), 350 (t), 350 (bl), 350 (br), 351 (bl), 351 (br), 352 (tr), 352 (b), 352 (tl), 353 (t), 353 (b), 355 (t), 355 (b), 356 (t), 356 (bl), 356 (br), 357 (t), 357 (b), 358 (t), 358 (bl), 358 (br), 359 (tr), 359 (tl), 359 (b), 360 (t), 360 (bl), 360 (br), 361 (b), 362 (b), 363 (t), 363 (b), 364 (tl), 364 (tr), 365 (b), 366 (tl), 366 (tr), 366 (b), 366 (t), 366 (bl), 366 (br), 367 (tl), 367 (tr), 367 (b), 368 (t), 368 (c), 368 (b), 369 (t), 372 (tl), 372 (tr), 372 (b), 373 (tl), 373 (tr), 373 (b), 374 (t), 374 (bl), 374 (br), 375 (t), 375 (bl), 375 (br), 376 (t), 376 (b), 377 (t), 377 (bl), 377 (br), 384, John Roberts; 21 (tl), 22 (b), 24 (tl), 73 (bl), 73 (t), 128 (t), 176 (tr), 234 (bl), 241 (r), **Andrew N. Gagg;** 22 (t), 26 (t), 26 (b), 27 (b), 29 (t), 77 (b), 126 (t), 128 (b), 174 (r), 176 (tl), 184 (br), 234 (br), 255 (t), 287 (t), 295 (t), 317 (b), 322 (t), 329 (t), 343 (b), 361 (tl), 361 (tr), 362 (tr), 362 (tl), **Peter Wilson;** 23 (b), 30 (b), 32 (bl), 32 (br), 66 (t), 72 (b), 98 (t), 104 (bl), 109 (t), 143 (r), 150 (t), 163, 165 (t), 185 (b), 185 (t), 193 (b), 197 (tr), 202 (br), 203 (t), 204 (t), 208 (br), 211 (br), 212 (t), 234 (tl), 240 (bl), 243 (t), 248 (br), 262 (tl), 273 (t), 280 (bl), 281 (t), 281 (b), 283 (t), 283 (b), 286 (br), 311 (t), 326 (bl), 338 (tr), 340 (tl), 347 (t), 347 (br), 369 (b), **Peter Brough;** 176 (bl).

Every effort has been made tocontact the copright holders and we apologise in advance for any ommissions. We will be pleased to insert appropriate acknowledgements in subsequent editions of the publication.

Index of Flower Names